THE CAMBRIDGE HANDBOOK OF JUDICIAL CONTROL OF ARBITRAL AWARDS

A unique collaboration between academic scholars, legal practitioners, and arbitrators, this handbook focuses on the intersection of arbitration – as an alternative to litigation – and the court systems to which arbitration is ultimately beholden. The first three parts analyze issues relating to the interpretation of the scope of arbitration agreements, arbitrator bias and conflict of interest, arbitrator misconduct during the proceedings, enforceability of arbitral awards, and the grounds for vacating awards. The next section features fifteen country-specific reviews, which demonstrate that, despite the commonality of principles at the international level, there are a significant number of differences in the application of those principles at the national level. This work should be read by anyone interested in the general rules and principles of the enforceability of foreign arbitral awards and the grounds for courts to vacate or annul such awards.

LARRY A. DIMATTEO is Huber Hurst Professor of Contract Law, Warrington College of Business and Levin College of Law at the University of Florida. He is the former Editor-in-Chief of the *American Business Law Journal*, a 2012 Fulbright Professor, and author of thirteen books, including *The Cambridge Handbook of Smart Contracts, Blockchain Technology and Digital Platforms* (with M. Cannarsa and C. Poncibò, Cambridge University Press, 2020).

MARTA INFANTINO is Associate Professor of Comparative Law, IUSLIT Department, University of Trieste. She has held visiting professorships in Canada, Colombia, and France. She has authored or co-authored eight books and more than sixty articles in Italian, French, and English. Her work has been translated into Greek, Chinese, and Spanish.

NATHALIE M-P POTIN is Academic Director of all Masters programmes at the Faculty of Law at Lyon Catholic University. She has practiced in several international commercial law firms and worked at the Secretariat of the International Court of Arbitration of the International Chamber of Commerce. She holds visiting professorships in Europe, the Middle East, and the United States.

The Cambridge Handbook of Judicial Control of Arbitral Awards

Edited by

LARRY A. DIMATTEO

University of Florida

MARTA INFANTINO

University of Trieste

NATHALIE M-P POTIN

Lyon Catholic University

CAMBRIDGE
UNIVERSITY PRESS

Shaftesbury Road, Cambridge CB2 8EA, United Kingdom

One Liberty Plaza, 20th Floor, New York, NY 10006, USA

477 Williamstown Road, Port Melbourne, VIC 3207, Australia

314–321, 3rd Floor, Plot 3, Splendor Forum, Jasola District Centre, New Delhi – 110025, India

103 Penang Road, #05–06/07, Visioncrest Commercial, Singapore 238467

Cambridge University Press is part of Cambridge University Press & Assessment, a department of the University of Cambridge.

We share the University's mission to contribute to society through the pursuit of education, learning and research at the highest international levels of excellence.

www.cambridge.org
Information on this title: www.cambridge.org/9781009293174

DOI: 10.1017/9781316998250

© Cambridge University Press & Assessment 2021

This publication is in copyright. Subject to statutory exception and to the provisions of relevant collective licensing agreements, no reproduction of any part may take place without the written permission of Cambridge University Press & Assessment.

First published 2021
First paperback edition 2023

A catalogue record for this publication is available from the British Library

Library of Congress Cataloging-in-Publication data
NAMES: Judicial Control over Arbitral Awards (Conference) (2019 : Université catholique de Lyon) | DiMatteo, Larry A, editor. | Infantino, Marta, editor. | Potin, Nathalie Marie-Pierre, 1967– editor. | Université catholique de Lyon, host institution.
TITLE: The Cambridge handbook of judicial control of arbitral awards / edited by Larry A. DiMatteo, University of Florida; Marta Infantino, University of Trieste; Nathalie M-P Potin, Lyon Catholic University.
DESCRIPTION: Cambridge, United Kingdom ; New York, NY, USA : Cambridge University Press, 2020. | Series: Cambridge law handbooks | Includes papers presented at the symposium "Judicial Control over Arbitral Awards: Scope, Vacation and Public Policy" held at the Université catholique de Lyon, April 26-29, 2019. | Includes bibliographical references.
IDENTIFIERS: LCCN 2020009257 (print) | LCCN 2020009258 (ebook) | ISBN 9781108488617 (hardback) | ISBN 9781316998250 (epub)
SUBJECTS: LCSH: Arbitration and award–Congresses. | Judicial review–Congresses.
CLASSIFICATION: LCC K2400.A6 J83 2020 (print) | LCC K2400.A6 (ebook) | DDC 347/.09–dc23
LC record available at https://lccn.loc.gov/2020009257
LC ebook record available at https://lccn.loc.gov/2020009258

ISBN 978-1-108-48861-7 Hardback
ISBN 978-1-009-29317-4 Paperback

Cambridge University Press & Assessment has no responsibility for the persistence or accuracy of URLs for external or third-party internet websites referred to in this publication and does not guarantee that any content on such websites is, or will remain, accurate or appropriate.

To my son, Ian Griffith DiMatteo, the pride and joy of my life.

LAD

To don Calogero Fausto Infantino, whose generosity is second only to his wisdom.

MI

À mes proches pour leur soutien indéfectible.

NP

Concise Contents

List of Contributors		*page* xxiii
Preface		xxvii

PART I VACATING COMMERCIAL ARBITRATION AWARDS

1. **Introduction: Intersection of Courts and Arbitration** — 3
   Larry A. DiMatteo, Marta Infantino, and Nathalie M-P Potin

2. **Independence and Impartiality of Arbitrators** — 12
   Carlos A. Matheus López

3. **Exploring the Parameters of Conflicts of Interest** — 29
   Nathalie M-P Potin and Tunde Ogunseitan

4. **Procedural Irregularities and Arbitrator Misconduct during Proceedings** — 54
   Alexander J. Bělohlávek

PART II ENFORCING COMMERCIAL ARBITRATION AWARDS

5. **Arbitrator Independence in Three Dimensions: Inter-arbitration Association Conflict** — 71
   Richard Happ

6. **Requirements for the Enforceability of Arbitral Awards: A Comparative Overview** — 84
   Dário Moura Vicente

PART III SCOPE AND INTERPRETATION OF ARBITRATION CLAUSES

7. **Judicial Interpretation of Standard Clauses** — 99
   Rocío Digón, Kamil Mehiz, and Tony Cole

8. **Industry-Specific Clauses and Their Interpretation** — 119
   Alexandra-Luiza Ionescu (Mareş)

9	Drafting, Interpretation, and Enforcement of Commercial Arbitration Clauses: A Practitioner's Perspective Philippe Cavalieros	130

PART IV JUDICIAL CONTROL OF ARBITRAL AWARDS: COUNTRY REPORTS

10	Judicial Control of Arbitral Awards in Argentina Maria Beatriz Burghetto	151
11	Judicial Control of Arbitral Awards in Australia Nobumichi Teramura, Luke Nottage, and James Morrison	175
12	Judicial Control of Arbitral Awards in Bulgaria Oleg Temnikov	198
13	Judicial Control of Arbitral Awards in Mainland China Chen Lei and Wang Hao	210
14	Certain Aspects of Judicial Control of Arbitral Awards in France Denis Bensaude	226
15	Commercial Arbitration in Germany Joseph Schwartz	243
16	Judicial Control of Arbitral Awards in Italy Marta Infantino	257
17	Judicial Control of Arbitral Awards in Nigeria Tunde Ogunseitan and Nathalie M-P Potin	275
18	Judicial Control of Arbitral Awards in Poland Jerzy Pisuliński and Piotr Tereszkiewicz	292
19	Judicial Control of Arbitral Awards in Russia Dmitry Dozhdev	306
20	Judicial Control of Arbitral Awards in Spain Teresa Rodríguez de las Heras Ballell	320
21	Judicial Control of Arbitral Awards in Switzerland Phillip Landolt	336
22	Judicial Control of Arbitral Awards in Ukraine Galyna Mykhailiuk and Nina Mykhailiuk	352
23	Judicial Control of Arbitral Awards in the United Kingdom Andrew Tetley	373
24	Judicial Control of Arbitral Awards in the United States Larry A. DiMatteo	397

PART V SUMMARY AND FINDINGS

25 Divergence, Themes, and Trends in National Arbitration Laws 417
   Larry A. DiMatteo, Marta Infantino, and Nathalie M-P Potin

26 The Shared Control of Arbitral Awards 443
   Friedrich Rosenfeld

Contents

List of Contributors   *page* xxiii

Preface   xxvii

PART I VACATING COMMERCIAL ARBITRATION AWARDS

1 **Introduction: Intersection of Courts and Arbitration**   3
Larry A. DiMatteo, Marta Infantino, and Nathalie M-P Potin
  1 Jurisdiction of Arbitral Panels and Judicial Intervention   4
    1.1 Standard of Review   4
    1.2 Principle of Separability and Kompetenz–Kompetenz   5
    1.3 Judicial Intervention   5
  2 Scope of the Book   6
    2.1 Roles of Courts and Governments   6
    2.2 Arbitrator Bias   6
    2.3 Misconduct during Arbitral Proceedings   6
    2.4 Role of Public Policy: Due Process   7
    2.5 Scope of Arbitration   7
    2.6 Enforcement of Arbitral Awards   7
    2.7 Industry-Specific Arbitration   7
    2.8 Drafting and Interpretation of Arbitration Clauses   7
    2.9 Comparative Analysis: Country Reports   7
  3 Structure of the Book   8

2 **Independence and Impartiality of Arbitrators**   12
Carlos A. Matheus López
  1 Background   12
  2 Independence and Impartiality   13
    2.1 Conceptual Analysis   13
    2.2 Summary   16
    2.3 Reflections from Legal Theory   17
  3 National Arbitration Laws and Rules   18
    3.1 National Arbitration Laws   18

	3.2 ICSID Convention and Rules	19
	3.3 UNCITRAL Arbitration Rules	20
	3.4 Institutional Rules	20
4	Standards for Assessing Independence and Impartiality	21
5	Complementary Element: Duty of Disclosure	22
6	Efforts to Systematize Regulations	23
7	Need to Set Limits	24
	7.1 Scope of Possible Relationships	25
	7.2 Model Proposal	27
8	Criteria to Challenge an Arbitrator	28

3 Exploring the Parameters of Conflicts of Interest 29
Nathalie M-P Potin and Tunde Ogunseitan

1 Introduction 29
  1.1 Definition 29
  1.2 Soft Law to Regulate Independence and Impartiality 30
  1.3 Disclosures under the IBA Guidelines and Consequences of Breach of Duty to Disclose 32
2 English Courts' Perspective 35
3 French Courts' Perspective 45
4 Duty of Disclosure for Third-Party Funding 49
5 Conclusion 52

4 Procedural Irregularities and Arbitrator Misconduct during Proceedings 54
Alexander J. Bělohlávek

1 Introduction 54
2 Procedural Irregularities and Arbitrator Misconduct: Remedies 54
  2.1 During Proceedings 54
  2.2 ICC and LCIA Challenges against Arbitrators during the Proceedings 56
    2.2.1 Bias 57
    2.2.2 Prejudgment 58
    2.2.3 Ex-Parte Communication 59
    2.2.4 Language of Animosity 59
    2.2.5 Case Study 60
3 Setting Aside and Preventing Enforcement 60
  3.1 Contracting Out of Challenging an Arbitral Award? 60
  3.2 Grounds for Setting Aside Awards and Resisting Enforcement under the New York Convention 61
  3.3 General Observations 62
  3.4 Are the Differences in Grounds Important? 62
4 Violation of Due Process 63
  4.1 Departure from Rule of Procedure 64
  4.2 Exceeding Powers 65
  4.3 Lesotho Case 66
  4.4 Occidental Case: Partial Annulment 66
5 Conclusion 67

PART II ENFORCING COMMERCIAL ARBITRATION AWARDS

5 **Arbitrator Independence in Three Dimensions: Inter-arbitration Association Conflict** 71
  Richard Happ
  1 Introduction 71
  2 Classical Two-Dimensional Framework for Conflicts of Interest 71
    2.1 Vertical Dimension 72
    2.2 Horizontal Dimension 73
  3 Commodity Arbitration 76
    3.1 History 76
    3.2 Major Commodity Trading Associations 77
    3.3 Commodity Arbitrations Are Similar but Different 78
      3.3.1 Procedural Peculiarities 78
      3.3.2 Requirements for Arbitrators 80
  4 Conflicts between Rules 81
  5 Analysis 81
  6 Interdimensional Conflicts 83

6 **Requirements for the Enforceability of Arbitral Awards: A Comparative Overview** 84
  Dário Moura Vicente
  1 The Problem Defined 84
    1.1 The Rationale for the Enforceability of Arbitral Awards and the Legal Challenges It Faces 84
    1.2 Relevant Legal Sources and Their Interaction 85
    1.3 Scope and the Outline of the Chapter 86
  2 Fundamental Approaches Underlying National Rules on Enforceability of Arbitral Awards 86
    2.1 Lex Facit Arbitrum 86
    2.2 Arbitral Awards as Expressions of an Autonomous Legal Order 87
    2.3 A Third Way 89
  3 Requirements for the Enforceability of Arbitral Awards in the Light of the Various Approaches to the Problem: Selected Aspects 90
    3.1 Need for Exequatur versus Direct Enforcement 90
    3.2 Enforceability versus Non-enforceability of Foreign Annulled Awards 92
    3.3 Domestic versus International or Transnational Public Policy 93
  4 Conclusion: A Perennial Problem? 94

PART III SCOPE AND INTERPRETATION OF ARBITRATION CLAUSES

7 **Judicial Interpretation of Standard Clauses** 99
  Rocío Digón, Kamil Mehiz, and Tony Cole
  1 Introduction 99
  2 Overview of Standard Clauses 101
  3 Interpreting Standard Clauses 104
  4 Comparative Analysis of Court Interpretations of Standard Clauses 105
    4.1 Interpretation of Standard Arbitration Clauses in France 105

		4.2 Interpretation of Standard Arbitration Clauses in the United States	107
		4.3 Interpretation of Standard Arbitration Clauses in Hong Kong, SAR and China	110
		4.3.1 Hong Kong	111
		4.3.2 Mainland China	112
		4.3.3 Interpretation of Standard Arbitration Clauses in Argentina	116
	5	Conclusion	117
8	**Industry-Specific Clauses and Their Interpretation**		119
	Alexandra-Luiza Ionescu (Mareş)		
	1	Introduction	119
		1.1 Dispute Resolution in the Energy Sector	119
		1.2 Governing Law and Dispute Resolution Clauses	120
		1.2.1 Governing Law Clause	120
		1.2.2 Dispute Resolution Clause	121
	2	Arbitration in the Energy Sector: Overview	122
		2.1 Choice of Law	122
		2.2 Type of Arbitration: Ad Hoc versus Institutional	122
		2.3 Drafting a Suitable Arbitration Agreement	123
		2.3.1 Scope of Express Agreement to Arbitrate	123
		2.3.2 Seat of Arbitration	124
		2.3.3 Language of the Arbitration	124
		2.3.4 Composition of Arbitration	124
	3	Pathological Clauses	125
		3.1 How Pathological Can an Arbitration Clause Be?	125
		3.2 SIAC's *Insigma* v. *Alstom*	125
	4	Mediation Clauses in Energy Contracts	127
	5	Conclusion	129
9	**Drafting, Interpretation, and Enforcement of Commercial Arbitration Clauses: A Practitioner's Perspective**		130
	Philippe Cavalieros		
	1	Introduction	130
	2	Drafting an Arbitration Agreement	131
		2.1 Negotiation	131
		2.2 Formal Requirements	131
		2.2.1 New York Convention	131
		2.2.2 Article II(1) of the New York Convention	132
		2.2.2.1 Agreement in Writing	132
		2.2.2.2 Existing or Future Disputes	133
		2.2.2.3 Defined Legal Relationship	133
		2.2.2.4 Subject Matter Capable of Settlement by Arbitration	133
		2.2.3 Article V(1)(a) of the New York Convention	134
		2.2.3.1 Parties' Legal Capacity	134
		2.2.3.2 Validity of the Arbitration Agreement	134

2.3 Practical Requirements — 135
  2.3.1 Essential Elements — 135
    2.3.1.1 Express Reference to Arbitration — 135
    2.3.1.2 Seat of Arbitration — 135
  2.3.2 Recommended Elements — 136
    2.3.2.1 Number of Arbitrators — 136
    2.3.2.2 Institutional versus Ad Hoc Arbitration — 136
    2.3.2.3 Choice of Law — 137
    2.3.2.4 Language — 138
    2.3.2.5 Exclusion of a Court Remedy — 138
  2.3.3 Optional Elements — 138
    2.3.3.1 Appointment of Arbitrators — 138
    2.3.3.2 Confidentiality — 139
  2.3.4 Templates — 139
3 Interpreting an Arbitration Agreement — 139
  3.1 Existence, Validity and Scope of the Arbitration Agreement — 139
  3.2 The Role of the Arbitrator — 141
    3.2.1 Exclusivity of Arbitration Agreements — 141
    3.2.2 Competence–Competence — 141
    3.2.3 Examples — 143
4 Enforcement of an Arbitration Agreement — 143
  4.1 Separability — 143
  4.2 Arbitrability — 144
  4.3 Nonsignatories — 145
  4.4 Judicial Review — 146
5 Conclusion — 147

PART IV JUDICIAL CONTROL OF ARBITRAL AWARDS: COUNTRY REPORTS

10 Judicial Control of Arbitral Awards in Argentina — 151
Maria Beatriz Burghetto

1 Introduction — 151
2 Background on Argentinean Arbitration Law — 152
  2.1 Evolution of Argentinean Law of Arbitration — 152
  2.2 Judicial and Governmental Attitudes towards Arbitration — 153
  2.3 Arbitration-Related International Treaties Ratified by Argentina — 154
  2.4 Recent Reforms to Argentinean Arbitration Law — 154
3 Impact of Recent Reforms — 154
  3.1 2015 Reform: Modernisation of the Rules of Arbitration — 154
  3.2 2018 Reform: New Federal Law on International Arbitration — 155
    3.2.1 General Aspects — 155
    3.2.2 ALIA and Judicial Control of Arbitration — 156
    3.2.3 Principles of Courts' Minimal Intervention under ALIA — 157
4 Judicial Control of Arbitration Agreement and Arbitral Proceedings — 157
  4.1 Interpretation of Arbitration Agreements — 158
  4.2 Arbitrator Disqualification: Conflict of Interest — 160
  4.3 Anti-arbitration Injunctions — 161

		4.3.1 Court's Order to Stay the Arbitral Proceedings while the Court Deals with the Terms of Reference	162
		4.3.2 Court's Order to Stay the Arbitral Proceedings while the Court Deals with the Challenge of an Arbitrator	163
	5	Judicial Control of Arbitral Awards	163
		5.1 Annulment of Arbitral Awards Rendered in Argentina	164
		5.1.1 General Grounds for Annulment	164
		5.1.2 Arbitrability	165
		5.1.3 Public Policy Violation	165
		5.1.3.1 Definition of Public Policy	165
		5.1.3.2 Assimilation of the Doctrine of Arbitrary Judgment	166
		5.1.3.3 The *Cartellone* Case	167
		5.1.3.4 Case Law Inspired by the *Cartellone* Case	168
		5.1.3.5 Supreme Court's Restrictive View of the Grounds for Annulment of Awards	169
		5.1.3.6 Future of the Doctrine of Arbitrary Judgments in International Cases	171
		5.2 Enforcement of Foreign Arbitral Awards	172
	6	Attractiveness of a Country as Arbitration Venue	173
	7	Conclusion	174
11	**Judicial Control of Arbitral Awards in Australia**	175
	Nobumichi Teramura, Luke Nottage, and James Morrison	
	1	Introduction	175
	2	Arbitrator Bias	178
	3	Conflict of Interest	180
	4	Procedural Irregularities and Arbitrator Misconduct during Proceedings	180
		4.1 Evidence and Hearings	181
		4.2 Exceeding Power	182
		4.3 Other Matters	183
	5	Objective Arbitrability	183
		5.1 Competition Law Issues	184
		5.2 Consumer Transactions	185
		5.2.1 Misleading and Deceptive Conduct	186
		5.2.2 Consumer Guarantees	188
		5.2.3 Unfair Contract Terms	188
		5.3 Other Arbitrability Issues	189
		5.4 Statutory Limitations on Objective Arbitrability	190
	6	Subjective Arbitrability: Judicial Interpretation of Arbitration Clauses	190
	7	Requirements for Enforcing Awards: Public Policy as a Ground for Refusal	193
	8	Conclusion	197
12	**Judicial Control of Arbitral Awards in Bulgaria**	198
	Oleg Temnikov	
	1	Introduction	198
		1.1 National Legislation	199
		1.2 International Conventions Concluded by Bulgaria	199

	1.3 ICAA Scope and Structure	200
	1.4 Arbitrability under Bulgarian Law	200
	1.5 Arbitration Agreement	201
	1.6 Mandatory Principles Applicable to the Arbitral Proceedings	202
	1.7 Intervention by State Courts	203
	1.8 Local Arbitration Institutions	203
	1.9 Trends or Statistics Relating to Arbitration	204
	2 Developments with Respect to the Scope of Arbitration in Bulgaria	204
	2.1 Non-arbitrability of Consumer Disputes	205
	2.2 Adaptation of Contracts	206
	3 Public Policy and Set Aside of Awards	207
	4 Other Recent Amendments in Relation to Arbitration	208
	4.1 Control of Arbitral Institutions	208
	4.2 Conditions and Qualifications for Arbitrators	208
	4.3 Obligation to Ensure Online Access to the Case File	209
	5 Conclusion	209
13	**Judicial Control of Arbitral Awards in Mainland China**	210
	Chen Lei and Wang Hao	
	1 Introduction	210
	2 Statutory Framework of Chinese Arbitration	210
	2.1 Dual-Track System and Its Legal Basis	210
	2.2 Institutional and Ad Hoc Arbitration	211
	2.3 Prior Reporting System	211
	3 Empirical Study on Enforcement of Foreign Arbitral Awards	212
	3.1 Legal Basis	212
	3.2 Empirical Studies	213
	3.3 Empirical Survey	214
	4 Case Analysis of Nonenforcement in Chinese Judicial Practice	217
	4.1 Validity of Arbitral Agreement	217
	4.2 Denial of Opportunity to Present Case	219
	4.3 Excess of Authority	220
	4.4 Defects in the Composition or Authority of Arbitral Tribunal	221
	4.5 Defects on the Binding Force of Arbitral Award	222
	4.6 Arbitrability	222
	4.7 Public Policy Exception	223
	5 Conclusion	225
14	**Certain Aspects of Judicial Control of Arbitral Awards in France**	226
	Denis Bensaude	
	1 History and French Arbitration Law	226
	2 Arbitration Agreements	228
	3 Arbitral Tribunal	231
	4 Award	235
	4.1 Enforcement of Award	236
	4.2 Setting Aside Awards	238

	4.3 Grounds for Setting Aside Awards	239
	4.3.1 Arbitral Tribunal Was Improperly Constituted	240
	4.3.2 Arbitral Tribunal Ruling Did Not Comply with Conferred Mission	240
	4.3.3 Violation of Principle of Due Process	241
	4.3.4 Enforcement of Award Contrary to International Public Policy	241
	5 Conclusion	242
15	**Commercial Arbitration in Germany**	243
	Joseph Schwartz	
	1 Introduction	243
	2 Arbitrator's Independence and Impartiality	244
	2.1 General Considerations	244
	2.1.1 Legal Basis	244
	2.1.2 Purpose	245
	2.1.3 General Requirements	245
	2.1.3.1 Disclosure Duty	245
	2.1.3.2 Objective Threshold for Challenges	246
	2.1.3.3 IBA Rules on Conflicts of Interest	246
	2.1.4 2018 DIS Arbitration Rules: Impartiality and Independence	246
	2.2 Application of Standards to Determine Arbitrator's Bias	246
	2.2.1 Challenges Due to Prior Statements or Opinions	247
	2.2.2 Arbitrator's Conduct in Promotion of Settlements and Preliminary Assessments	248
	2.3 Consequences of a Lack of Impartiality or Independence	249
	3 Arbitrability and Enforceability	251
	3.1 Scope and Judicial Interpretation of Arbitration Agreements	251
	3.2 Arbitrability and Enforceability	253
	4 Conclusion	255
16	**Judicial Control of Arbitral Awards in Italy**	257
	Marta Infantino	
	1 Introduction	257
	2 Narratives and Numbers	257
	3 Special Regimes	261
	4 The Scope of Arbitration	263
	5 Vacating Arbitral Awards	265
	6 Enforcement of Arbitral Awards	271
	7 Conclusion	274
17	**Judicial Control of Arbitral Awards in Nigeria**	275
	Tunde Ogunseitan and Nathalie M-P Potin	
	1 Introduction	275
	2 Role of Court before Commencement of Arbitration	277
	2.1 Arbitration Agreement	277
	2.1.1 Doctrine of Separability	277
	2.1.2 Arbitrability and Public Policy	278
	2.2 Stay of Proceedings	278

3 Role of Judiciary during Arbitration 280
    3.1 Procedural Irregularities and Arbitrator Misconduct during the
        Proceedings 280
    3.2 Determining Arbitrator Bias and Parameters of Conflict of Interest 281
  4 Role of Court after Arbitration: Recognition of Awards and Requirements for
    Enforceability 282
    4.1 Grounds for Refusal to Enforce 283
    4.2 Enforcement of Domestic Arbitral Awards 284
    4.3 Enforcement of International Awards 285
        4.3.1 Setting Aside of Award 285
        4.3.2 Procedure 286
        4.3.3 Grounds to Set Aside Award 286
        4.3.4 Setting Aside an International Arbitral Award 288
        4.3.5 Public Policy Ground 288
    4.4 How Far Can the Court Intervene? 289
    4.5 Delay to Decide Annulment 291
  5 Conclusion 291

18 **Judicial Control of Arbitral Awards in Poland** 292
   Jerzy Pisuliński and Piotr Tereszkiewicz
   1 Introduction 292
   2 Arbitrability of Disputes 292
     2.1 Equality of the Parties to an Arbitration Agreement 293
     2.2 Law Applicable to an Arbitration Agreement 294
   3 Nature and Formal Requirements of an Arbitration Agreement 294
     3.1 Legal Nature of the Arbitration Agreement 294
     3.2 Content of Arbitration Agreement 295
     3.3 Arbitration Agreement and Third Parties 296
     3.4 Legal Effects of an Arbitration Agreement 296
   4 Arbitral Proceedings 297
     4.1 Substantive Law Governing the Merits of the Dispute 297
     4.2 Selection of Arbitrators and the Composition of the Arbitral Tribunal 298
     4.3 Impartiality of Arbitrators 298
     4.4 Proceedings before the Arbitral Tribunal 299
     4.5 Arbitral Award 300
     4.6 Requirements of Enforceability of Arbitral Awards 301
   5 Setting Aside an Arbitral Award 301
     5.1 Limits of Judicial Review of Arbitral Awards 303
     5.2 Substantive Violations of Public Policy 304
     5.3 Procedural Violations of Public Policy 305
   6 Conclusion 305

19 **Judicial Control of Arbitral Awards in Russia** 306
   Dmitry Dozhdev
   1 Introduction: Structure of Arbitration Law in Russia 306
   2 State Courts and Arbitration: Issues of Assistance and Control 307
     2.1 Interim Measures 308

	2.2 Competence–Competence Principle	308
	2.3 Courts' Referring Parties to Arbitration	309
3	Scope of Arbitration	310
4	Vacating Arbitral Awards Issued in Russia	312
	4.1 Refusal from Challenging the Award	313
	4.2 Grounds for Vacation of Arbitral Awards	313
5	Recognition and Enforcement of Foreign Arbitral Awards	314
	5.1 Recognition and Enforcement of Foreign Arbitral Awards and Grounds for Refusal	314
	5.2 Public Policy Exception	315
6	Conclusion	319

20 Judicial Control of Arbitral Awards in Spain — 320
Teresa Rodríguez de las Heras Ballell

1 Spanish Arbitration Act in Context — 320
  1.1 Evolution and Main Features — 320
  1.2 Numbers and Statistics: Arbitration in Spain — 322
  1.3 Essence of Arbitration: Constitutionality and Sphere of Arbitrability — 323
2 Annulment of Arbitral Awards: Perimeter and Grounds — 324
  2.1 Grounds for Setting Aside Arbitral Awards — 325
  2.2 Interpretation and Application by Courts — 326
    2.2.1 Arbitration Agreement — 326
      2.2.1.1 Existence of a Clear, Unequivocal, and Observable Consent — 326
      2.2.1.2 Validity of Hybrid Clauses — 327
      2.2.1.3 Rules of Interpretation and the Scope of the Arbitration Agreement — 327
    2.2.2 Impartiality and Independence of Arbitrators — 329
    2.2.3 Procedural Irregularities — 329
  2.3 Waiver of the Action for Setting Aside the Arbitral Award — 330
3 Public Policy as Grounds for Setting Aside: Use and Abuse — 331
  3.1 Concept and Scope of Public Policy: Exception in Arbitration — 331
  3.2 Notion of "Economic Public Policy" as an Inflexion Point: Extent, Relevance, and Prospects — 332
4 Recognition and Enforcement of Foreign Arbitral Awards — 333
5 Assessment and Expectations — 334

21 Judicial Control of Arbitral Awards in Switzerland — 336
Phillip Landolt

1 General Comments on International Arbitration Law in Switzerland — 336
2 Judicial Interpretation of Scope of Arbitration Clauses — 337
3 Requirements for Enforceability of Awards — 341
4 Bias of Arbitrators — 343
5 Procedural Irregularities and Arbitrators' Misconduct during Proceedings — 345
6 Anti-arbitration Law and Public Policy — 348
7 Conclusion — 351

22	**Judicial Control of Arbitral Awards in Ukraine**	352
	Galyna Mykhailiuk and Nina Mykhailiuk	
	1 Introduction	352
	2 Grounds for Vacating Arbitral Awards Due to Arbitrator Bias	354
	3 Impartiality and Conflict of Interest	356
	4 Procedural Irregularities and Misconduct during Proceedings	357
	5 Anti-arbitration Law and Public Policy	361
	6 Requirements for Enforcing Foreign Arbitral Awards	364
	7 Interpretation of Arbitration Clauses by Courts	369
	8 Conclusion	371
23	**Judicial Control of Arbitral Awards in the United Kingdom**	373
	Andrew Tetley	
	1 Introduction	373
	2 Vacating Commercial Arbitration Awards	373
	2.1 Independence and Impartiality of International Arbitrators	373
	2.2 Parameters of Conflict of Interest	374
	2.3 Procedural Irregularity and Misconduct of Arbitrators during Proceedings	376
	2.3.1 Appeal on a Point of Law	376
	2.3.2 Substantive Jurisdiction	377
	2.3.3 Serious Irregularity	378
	3 Enforcing Commercial Arbitration Awards	381
	3.1 Anti-arbitration Law and Public Policy	381
	3.2 Public Policy	385
	3.3 Statistics	386
	3.4 Requirements for Enforceability of Awards	387
	4 Judicial Interpretation of Commercial Arbitration Clauses	394
24	**Judicial Control of Arbitral Awards in the United States**	397
	Larry A. DiMatteo	
	1 Introduction	397
	2 Principles of Separability and Kompetenz–Kompetenz in American Law	398
	3 Structure of Arbitration Law in the United States	400
	3.1 Federal Arbitration Act	400
	3.2 Grounds for Vacating Arbitral Awards: A Comparative Analysis	401
	3.3 Grounds for Judicial Modification of Arbitral Awards	403
	4 Recent Narrowing in Standing in Arbitration	403
	4.1 Class Action Arbitration	404
	5 Scope of Arbitration's Jurisdiction	405
	6 Enforcement and Vacation of Arbitral Awards	406
	6.1 Enforceability of Arbitral Awards	407
	6.2 Nonstatutory Grounds for Vacation of Awards: "Manifest Disregard Doctrine"	408
	6.3 Public Policy Exception	410
	7 Arbitrator Disqualification	411
	7.1 Impartiality and Conflict of Interest	411

	7.2 Fair Hearing Requirement	412
	7.3 Claims against Arbitral Institutions	412
	8 Conclusion	413

PART V SUMMARY AND FINDINGS

25 **Divergence, Themes, and Trends in National Arbitration Laws** 417
   Larry A. DiMatteo, Marta Infantino, and Nathalie M-P Potin
   1 Introduction 417
   2 Setting Aside and Enforceability of Arbitral Awards 418
     2.1 General Features 419
     2.2 Setting Aside of Domestic and International Awards 422
     2.3 Enforcement and Recognition of Foreign Arbitral Awards 425
   3 Arbitrator Bias and Conflict of Interest 427
     3.1 Arbitrator Bias 427
     3.2 Conflict of Interest 429
   4 Arbitrator Misconduct 431
   5 Arbitration Clauses: Interpretation and Scope 434
   6 Anti-arbitration Policy 437
   7 Conclusion 441

26 **The Shared Control of Arbitral Awards** 443
   Friedrich Rosenfeld
   1 Introduction 443
   2 Parties 443
     2.1 Limitations of Post-award Review 443
     2.2 Expansions of Post-award Review 446
   3 Arbitral Tribunal 446
     3.1 No Deference to Arbitral Determinations 447
     3.2 Deference to Arbitral Determinations 448
     3.3 Intermediary Positions 448
   4 Arbitral Institutions 449
     4.1 Deference to Determinations Made by Arbitral Institutions 449
     4.2 No Deference to Determinations Made by Arbitral Institutions 450
   5 Courts at the Seat 451
     5.1 Deference to Negative Decisions of Courts at the Seat 451
     5.2 Deference to Positive Decisions of Courts at the Seat 453
     5.3 Deference and the Need to Initiate Set-Aside Proceedings at the Seat 454
   6 Courts at the Place of Enforcement 455
   7 Conclusion 456

Contributors

Alexander J. Bělohlávek is Professor at the Faculty of Economics, VSB Technical University Ostrava (Czech Republic) and at the Faculty of Law, West Bohemia University (Czech Republic); Chair of the Institute of International Law, Faculty of Law and Public Administration, Collegium Humanum University, Warsaw, Poland; Attorney-at-Law, Arbitrator, past President of the WJA – The World Jurist Association, Washington D.C., United States-Czech Republic

Denis Bensaude is an international arbitrator, based in Paris, and a member of the New York and Paris Bars, France

Maria Beatriz Burghetto, LLM, is a qualified lawyer in Argentina and France, and a member of the Chartered Institute of Arbitrators, France

Philippe Cavalieros advises and represents companies, states, and state-owned entities in commercial and investment treaty arbitrations and regularly acts as arbitrator and expert, France

Lei Chen is Chair in Chinese Law, Durham Law School, Durham University, UK; Wenlan Visiting Professor of Zhongnan University of Economics and Law; Oriental Scholar Visiting Professor of East China University of Political Science and Law, People's Republic of China

Tony Cole is an arbitrator at JAMS and 33 Bedford Row and Reader in Arbitration and Investment Law at Leicester Law School, University of Leicester, United Kingdom

Rocío Digón is a research associate, University of Leicester and legal consultant, White & Case LLP, United Kingdom

Larry A. DiMatteo is Huber Hurst Professor of Contract Law, Warrington College of Business; Affiliate Professor at the Levin College of Law and Affiliate Professor at the Center for European Studies, University of Florida, United States

Dmitry Dozhdev is Professor, Dean of the Faculty of Law of the Moscow School of Social and Economic Sciences (MSSES), arbitrator at the Russian Arbitration Center (RAC), Russia

Richard Happ is Partner at the lawfirm Luther, Hamburg, Germany

Marta Infantino is Associate Professor of Comparative Law at the University of Trieste, Italy

Alexandra-Luiza Ionescu (Mareş) is a PhD student at the Faculty of Law of the University of Bucharest and an attorney at law in Bucharest, Romania

Phillip Landolt is a partner at Landolt & Koch and a senior lecturer at the Law Faculty of the University of Geneva, Switzerland

Carlos A. Matheus López is Professor of the School of Law at the Universidad César Vallejo, Chimbote (Peru); Associate Professor of the Academic Department of Law at the Pontificia Universidad Católica del Perú PUCP and Professor of Arbitration Law at the National University of San Marcos and the Peruvian Judicial School. Full Time Arbitrator, Peru

Kamil Mehiz is an associate at Jones Day in Dubai, United Arab Emirates

James Morrison is counsel and Acting Secretary-General, Australian Centre for International Commercial Arbitration (ACICA), Australia

Dário Moura Vicente is Full Professor at the Faculty of Law of Universidade de Lisboa, Portugal

Galyna Mykhailiuk, Dr. Habil., PhD, is Associate Professor at the National University of Kyiv-Mohyla Academy and lead scientific adviser at the Industrial Property Department of the Scientific Research Institute of Intellectual Property in the National Academy of Law Sciences of Ukraine, Ukraine

Nina Mykhailiuk, PhD, is Associate Professor at the International Humanitarian University, Ukraine

Luke Nottage is Professor of Comparative and Transnational Business Law, University of Sydney Law School, Australia

Tunde Ogunseitan is Solicitor of England and Wales (n.p.) and Barrister at Law Nigeria LLM, BL FCIArb, Nigeria and United Kingdom

Jerzy Pisuliński is Full Professor and Dean of the Faculty of Law and Administration of the Jagiellonian University in Cracow, Poland

Nathalie M-P Potin is Academic Director and Lecturer at the Faculty of Law, Lyon Catholic University; Solicitor of England and Wales (n.p.); and admitted to the French Bar, PhD, FCIArb, France

Teresa Rodríguez de las Heras Ballell is Associate Professor of Commercial Law, University Carlos III of Madrid; an arbitrator at the Madrid Court of Arbitration; and has acted as a sole arbitrator in arbitration proceedings administered by the Spanish Court of Arbitration, Spain

Friedrich Rosenfeld is Partner at the arbitration boutique Hanefeld Rechtsanwälte in Hamburg, Germany. He is also Global Adjunct Professor at NYU Law in Paris, Visiting Professor at the International Hellenic University in Thessaloniki and Lecturer at Bucerius Law School in Hamburg, Germany

Joseph Schwartz is a German attorney and partner of the firm Wagner Arbitration in Berlin and regularly acts as party counsel and arbitrator in commercial arbitration cases, Germany

Oleg Temnikov is Attorney-at-Law, Wolf Theiss Law Firm in Sofia, Bulgaria

Nobumichi Teramura is Associate at the Centre for Asian and Pacific Law at the University of Sydney (CAPLUS), Australia, and Legal Consultant at Bun & Associates (Cambodia)

Piotr Tereszkiewicz is Professor of Private Law at the Jagiellonian University in Cracow, Poland

Andrew Tetley is a French avocat, English solicitor and New Zealand barrister and solicitor with broad experience in commercial litigation and international arbitration and project work, partner Reed Smith LLP, New Zealand and United Kingdom

Hao Wang is a JSD candidate, School of Law, City University of Hong Kong; Deputy Chief Judge of the Hainan First International Civil and Commercial Court, People's Republic of China

Preface

This book comprises the collected and revised papers presented at a conference on the relationship between arbitration and the courts, held at Lyon Catholic University in April 2019. The topics selected for the conference and hence for the chapters of this book range from the theoretical to the analysis of rules and to arbitration practice. The analysis can be divided between the macro and the micro. The generic issues related to courts and arbitration are presented in the first three parts of the book and include arbitrator misconduct, bias, and conflict of interest; association-specific rules, drafting of arbitration clauses; the enforceability of arbitral awards; and the scope and interpretation of arbitration clauses. The book then shifts focus to view these issues on a country-to-country basis. The "country reports" act as case studies to show the commonalities and divergences among national arbitration laws. The counties selected for review are geographically diverse and include countries from six continents: Africa (Nigeria), Asia (China), Australia, Europe (Bulgaria, France, Germany, Italy, Poland, Russia, Spain, Switzerland, Ukraine, the United Kingdom), North America (the United States), and South America (Argentina).

As editors of this book, it has been a pleasure to work with a fine group of scholars and practitioners. We are in debt to all the contributors to this book. We are also indebted to the Lyon Catholic University, the University of Trieste, and the University of Florida for their financial support, especially the Law School at the Lyon Catholic University for hosting the conference. Special thanks to the Dean of Lyon Catholic University, Michael Cannarsa, for his encouragement and support. Finally, we were ably assisted by the editorial and production staff at Cambridge University Press, who had faith in the value of this book and who have been on hand to help us as it progressed from idea to finished work. In particular, we are grateful to Matt Gallaway, our editor.

PART I

Vacating Commercial Arbitration Awards

1

Introduction

Intersection of Courts and Arbitration

Larry A. DiMatteo, Marta Infantino, and Nathalie M-P Potin

This chapter broadly reviews the relationship between the arbitration and judicial systems as well as substantive national laws that restrict the use of the arbitration process. The relationship is inherently in tension because two core principles are in conflict: independence of commercial arbitration and judicial intervention to ensure the fairness of the arbitration process. This chapter reviews and suggests how best to balance these two competing interests. This will include an analysis of the principle of separability (contract arbitration clauses are independent of the contract) and kompetenz–kompetenz (whether the arbitration panel or the courts are empowered to determine the jurisdiction of the arbitration panel and the scope of the arbitration clause). The chapter concludes by describing the structure and content of the chapters to follow and providing some final remarks. The editors would like to note that the scholarly contributors include some of the very best minds in legal scholarship. The list of contributors includes a diverse mix of scholars and practitioners from fifteen countries.

Alternative dispute resolution in the form of arbitration is the most common means of dispute resolution in international commercial transactions. The word *alternative* is generally acknowledged as an alternative to litigation and recourse to national court systems. But alternative does not mean independence from national court systems. Disputants and arbitrators can never fully escape the reach of the courts. At a basic level the courts are a necessary component of international commercial arbitration if nothing more than to provide an enforcement mechanism for implementing arbitration awards. Generally, arbitration tribunals have little ability to enforce their awards.[1] Fortunately, the New York Convention[2] has provided a secure and expedited process for the enforcement of arbitral awards by national courts. In the 164 countries[3] that to date have acceded to the convention, the national courts are required to enforce foreign arbitration awards.

The enforceability of arbitration awards is only the most obvious example of judicial intervention into arbitration. As the essays collected in this book show, relationships between international commercial arbitration and the court systems are multiple and multifarious. The volume provides a comprehensive review of the broad assortment of issues dealing with the interaction of courts and the law with arbitration proceedings. Contributions offer both generalized and specific

---

[1] It is possible to conceive of a private enforcement mechanism, such as the escrowing of funds or the provision for letters of credit to guarantee payment on any forthcoming awards.
[2] Convention on the Recognition and Enforcement of Foreign Arbitral Awards (New York Convention) (June 10, 1958) at https://uncitral.un.org/sites/uncitral.un.org/files/media-documents/uncitral/en/new-york-convention-e.pdf.
[3] *See* https://uncitral.un.org/en/texts/arbitration/conventions/foreign_arbitral_awards/status2.

analyses of core issues related to the numerous areas of involving judicial intervention into the arbitration process and flesh out variations through a comparative analysis of a representative set of countries. The book demonstrates that, while there is general agreement internationally on the relationship between courts and arbitration, this general agreement on the independence of arbitration proceedings masks major differences in application of the principle of independence under national laws and by national court systems.

The analyses presented in the book relate to three broad topical areas: vacating commercial arbitration awards, enforcing commercial arbitration awards, and scope and interpretation of arbitration clauses.[4] Embedded in these broad categories are more specific issues, including (1) What are the standards or criteria for determining arbitrator bias? (2) What types of actions or omissions during the proceedings are considered to be grounds of arbitrator misconduct? (3) What facts constitute cases of conflict of interest involving arbitrators? (4) What types of procedural irregularities are grounds for vacating an arbitration award? (5) What are the requirements for judicial enforcement of arbitration awards? (6) How do arbitrators and judges deal with the scenario when arbitration agreements refer to industry-specific arbitration rules as well as model or generic institutional rules when the rules conflict on given issues? (7) What types of anti-arbitration laws and policies exist at the national level that prohibit the use of arbitration in certain areas of law? (8) What are the different approaches that courts use in interpreting standard arbitration clauses? (9) How does one draft an enforceable and comprehensive arbitration clause or agreement (practitioner's perspective)?

1 JURISDICTION OF ARBITRAL PANELS AND JUDICIAL INTERVENTION

This book aims to fully investigate the intersection between the courts and international commercial arbitration. Two common scenarios of this intersection are judicial intervention before arbitrators have had the opportunity to decide on their own jurisdiction and those cases that seek to challenge an already existing arbitral decision on jurisdictional or procedural grounds in the context of an action for vacation of an arbitral award. The questions presented in these scenarios include (1) Who determines the jurisdiction of arbitral tribunals – arbitrators or judges? (2) When is it appropriate for courts to intervene in arbitral proceedings in determining the scope of the arbitration (interpretation of arbitration agreement or clause) and the jurisdiction of the arbitral tribunal? (3) Assuming the general principle of deference – courts deferring to arbitration panels to answer questions of jurisdiction – what is the standard of review when a court needs to determine the validity of the arbitration agreement, when litigation has started and one party objects to the court's jurisdiction due to the existence of an arbitration agreement and also when a party seeks interim measures?

1.1 *Standard of Review*

One of the purposes of this book is to review the differences in national laws relating to these and other issues. For example, countries differ as to the standard of review in determining jurisdictional issues. In 2017, the Spanish Supreme Court adopted a pro-court standard of review providing that courts have the right to conduct a de novo review to determine the validity, enforceability, and scope of an arbitration clause when the court's jurisdiction is questioned.[5]

---

[4] The terms *arbitration clause* and *arbitration agreement* are used interchangeably in this chapter.
[5] *See* Chapter 20 (Spain).

Under this standard, courts have the power to resolve these issues before the arbitration panel comes into existence. France, on the other hand, has adopted an arbitrator-friendly approach by prohibiting lower courts from reviewing these issues once an arbitration panel is established. If the arbitration has yet to be constituted, the courts will refer the parties to arbitration if there is a prima facie argument of the existence of an arbitration agreement. On issues of the scope of an arbitration clause, French courts will always defer to the arbitrators to interpret a clause in determining its scope.[6] Under the English Arbitration Act, courts reject the prima facie approach in favor of an arbitrator-unfriendly approach of *beyond a reasonable doubt*. If the English court cannot determine the application or scope of an arbitration provision then the court will require a trial on jurisdictional issues before ordering a stay in the litigation.[7]

1.2 *Principle of Separability and Kompetenz–Kompetenz*

The concepts of separability and kompetenz–kompetenz are among the most significant principles in the field of international arbitration. The reason for their importance is that they provide the norms on which the basis of jurisdiction of arbitrators is defined. The core principle of separability promotes the autonomy of the arbitration agreement (clause) from the main contract. This is based on the fiction that the parties intended for an arbitration clause in a contract be treated independently of that contract. The accepted rationale for this autonomy is that the arbitration clause is procedural in nature, which is independent of the substantive rights and obligations provided elsewhere in the contract. Kompetenz–kompetenz recognizes the competence of arbitral panels to determine their own jurisdiction, such as deciding the scope of an arbitration clause. This does not prevent a party from challenging the arbitral panel's determination of jurisdiction by seeking judicial intervention. Thus the overarching principle of separability can be stated as follows: an arbitral panel determines its own jurisdiction (over the parties and the issues to be disputed) until a court says otherwise! Thus courts have the ultimate say as to the validity or enforceability of an arbitration agreement and its scope. The problem is that national court systems differ as to under which circumstances is it appropriate to for courts to intervene.[8]

1.3 *Judicial Intervention*

Despite the existence of the New York Convention, international arbitration awards need to be enforced at the national law. As such, the requirements of enforceability may vary from country to country. Also, disputing parties often seek judicial intervention in the interpretation of arbitration clauses, to challenge the qualification or independence of given arbitrators and to vacate arbitral awards due to arbitrator misconduct. National arbitration laws vary as to when and on what grounds it is appropriate for courts to intervene in arbitration proceedings or to deny enforcement of arbitral awards.[9]

The dominate role of commercial arbitration as the preferred means of dispute resolution[10] in international business transactions has not resulted in a seamless system due to competing

---

[6] *See* Chapter 14 (France).
[7] *See* Chapter 23 (United Kingdom).
[8] *See* Chapter 25, Section 2.1.
[9] *See* Id. at Section 2.3.
[10] Between 80 and 90 percent of international contracts concluded by multinationals and small- and medium-size enterprises (SMEs) are said to include arbitration clauses.

arbitration rules, anti-arbitration government policies and laws, and various types of judicial interventions in the arbitration process. This book focuses on the intersection between governmental and judicial control of arbitration with a focus on the vacation of arbitration awards due to arbitrator misconduct, public policy that limits the coverage of arbitration, interpretation of the scope of arbitration clauses, and requirements related to the enforcement of arbitration awards. So far the legal literature has failed to fully analyze the important role that government policy and judicial intervention play in the recognition and enforcement of arbitral awards. The book will fill this gap by investigating the differences and conflicts between arbitration rules – this often occurs when industry-specific rules conflict with more generic or institutional arbitration rules. National arbitration laws also prohibit the arbitration of certain types of claims. Anti-arbitration law and public policy also vary across countries.[11]

2 SCOPE OF THE BOOK

This book presents an opportunity for an in-depth analysis of the intersection of courts and arbitration tribunals. The volume brings together some of the top arbitration scholars and practitioners from the civil and common law systems, so that the topical areas are covered by a balanced mix of academics and lawyer–arbitrators. The core question to be discussed is whether the international arbitration system is as independent as perceived from national and judicial authorities. This core question leads to many other questions yet to be resolved involving the role governments, courts, and arbitration associations play in the management of the arbitration process and the enforceability of arbitral awards. A sampling of the questions that are discussed in the book includes the following categories.

2.1 *Roles of Courts and Governments*

Are there clearly defined roles for courts, government policy, and arbitration associations in the management and processing of disputes through the process of arbitration? Are there certain areas that these roles are blurred or fluid in nature?

2.2 *Arbitrator Bias*

What are the factors that arbitration association rules and courts use in determining arbitrator bias? What factors do courts use in determining conflicts of interest and whether such conflicts can be resolved?

2.3 *Misconduct during Arbitral Proceedings*

What types of actions during the arbitral proceedings are grounds for a court to vacate an arbitration award? What types of actions taken by arbitrators are considered irregular in nature? What factors do courts use to determine if an arbitral panel has exceeded its powers? What type of actions or omissions do courts consider to be representative of arbitrator misconduct?

---

[11] *See supra* note 8, at Section 6.

2.4 Role of Public Policy: Due Process

How do national rules of evidence interrelate to the admission or failure to admit evidence in arbitration? What necessary factors are recognized by courts to ensure a fair hearing? Do national or constitutional principles of due process affect courts view of arbitral due process?

2.5 Scope of Arbitration

How do countries vary in determining if certain subject matters are outside of the scope of arbitration? Can victims of violations of fundamental or human rights be forced to arbitrate (broad arbitration clause)? How do national legal systems vary as to the recognition of class action arbitration claims?

2.6 Enforcement of Arbitral Awards

Do national arbitration laws vary as to the requirements needed for the enforcement of arbitration awards? What are the grounds for courts to invalidate or vacate an arbitration award? Do the types of grounds for vacation vary from country to country? How have courts interpreted generic arbitration clauses? How have courts determined the scope of standard language, such as "any and all claims related"?

2.7 Industry-Specific Arbitration

How have industry-specific arbitration clauses and industry-specific arbitration rules been interpreted by courts? How have courts ferreted out conflicts between general versus industry-specific arbitration rules where both sets of rules are applied in a dispute?

2.8 Drafting and Interpretation of Arbitration Clauses

What factors and issues should a lawyer consider in drafting an enforceable arbitration clause? How does a lawyer provide guidance for future judicial interpretation of arbitration clauses?

2.9 Comparative Analysis: Country Reports

How do specific countries (Argentina, Australia, Bulgaria, China, France, Germany, Italy, Nigeria, Poland, Russia, Spain, Switzerland, Ukraine, the United Kingdom, and the United States) compare as to the stated issues? What are the areas of divergence?

The effectiveness of arbitration as an independent, self-enforcing dispute resolution system is not as clear or simple as has been largely accepted in the legal and practitioner-focused scholarship. Despite the power of the freedom of contract principle, arbitration cannot fully escape the formal court system or government policies. For example, in some countries an employee cannot be required to pursue arbitration when the subject of the claim relates to a fundamental or human right, while others allow it.[12]

In light of such divergences, the country reports analyze how the procedural and substantive issues presented in Parts I–III of the book are dealt with in given countries. Each chapter

---

[12] See Id.

explores a given country's approach to the independence of the arbitration system, examining in particular how domestic law allocates the determination of jurisdiction and scope of arbitration between the arbitral panel and the courts, and what types of grounds are recognized for vacating arbitration awards. In the area of arbitrability, the national chapters discuss nuances of government law and policies that are anti-arbitration in nature. More specifically, in the area of vacation, the reports analyze factors and/or criteria used by national courts to vacate arbitration awards in the widely accepted areas of arbitrator misconduct, conflict of interest, and procedural irregularities. They also examine the differences among countries in the interpretation of standard and industry-specific arbitration clauses. The national reports allow for an academic-theoretical discussion of key issues to be tested by their resolution in a representative sampling of countries.

3 STRUCTURE OF THE BOOK

The book is partitioned into five parts consisting of a total of twenty-six chapters.

Part I discusses the scenarios and factors used in the vacating of arbitral awards. The chapters examine the grounds for vacating arbitration awards, with a focus on arbitrators and their actions. The areas of arbitrator malfeasance include arbitrator bias, conflict of interest, and arbitrator misconduct during the proceedings (such as, admission or lack thereof of probative evidence, procedural irregularities, and not conducting a fair hearing). In particular, Chapter 2 provides a summary of some available precedents in international arbitrations about arbitrators' independence and impartiality and examines how the question is treated by reference to a sample of institutional rules, model laws, professional guidelines, and several national arbitration laws. Chapter 3 continues the discussion of arbitrator bias by focusing on the specific issue of conflict of interest. It reviews factors that are used to disqualify an arbitrator due to conflicts of interest or the appearance of impropriety. It examines the different views on which potential conflicts are considered sufficient to disqualify an arbitrator. Finally, it shows how certain conflicts may be overcome by full disclosure. Finally, Chapter 4 focuses on the arbitrators' discretion in how to conduct arbitration proceedings. This discretion varies depending on the applicable arbitration rules. However, there are core principles as to the basic conduct of arbitration that arbitrators have to respect. The chapter examines cases where arbitration proceedings have been considered to be flawed, leading to the vacation of the award. The areas of malfeasance covered by the chapter include lack of fair notice and inability to provide a fair hearing, evidentiary issues (especially for the arbitrators' failure to admit or consider probative evidence), and excess of powers.

Part II then investigates the issues relating to the enforcement of arbitral awards. Chapter 5 analyzes the relationship between different arbitral institutions and the possible enforceability problems that may arise from the overlapping competences of a plurality of arbitral organizations and rules. Chapter 6 examines the requirements for the enforceability of arbitral awards – that is, the generic requirements for enforceability under the New York Convention and in most national laws. The chapter investigates different national approaches to the issue of enforceability of foreign arbitral awards, and offers a conceptual systematization for understanding different countries' attitudes to the issue.

Part III reviews issues relating to the scope and interpretation of arbitral clauses. A vague, overly broad arbitration clause is often the grist for disputes within the arbitration process and reason for judicial intervention. Chapter 7 examines generic arbitration clauses and the ubiquitous phrase of scope: "any and all claims related to the contract." Does this arbitration clause capture ex contractu causes and claims, such as those based on tort (or delict) and competition law, employer–employee relationships, sexual harassment, and other claims based on public and private law? The chapter examines the different approaches that might be used in interpreting such standard arbitration clauses. Chapter 8 looks at issues relating to industry-specific arbitration clauses, including their divergence from generic or institutional clauses and their interpretation. Industry-specific arbitration clauses often incorporate industry-specific arbitration rules. Such industry-specific arbitration rules may raise interpretative doubts requiring arbitration panels, and eventually courts, to resolve such conflicts. The chapter delves into the problem raised by industry-specific arbitration clauses and also provides a case study involving clauses and rules found in the energy sector. Chapter 9 then views arbitration clauses from the practitioner's perspective relating to the drafting of arbitration clauses. The chapter reviews cases where arbitration agreements and awards are held not to be legally enforceable. While the New York Convention provides that foreign arbitration awards are to be fully enforced in all member states, arbitration awards may be held to be unenforceable in national courts if they are the outcome of a proceeding that failed to meet due process standards of appropriate notice and fair hearing. This chapter examines what factors the courts analyze in making their determinations on due process and reviews the other types of claims that can be brought against the enforceability of arbitration awards. It also assesses the issues that most often give rise to disputes and judicial challenges, and offers some suggestions on how to write a clause that minimizes the risk of multiple interpretations.

Part IV surveys a number of countries and their legal systems to determine the extent that courts exert jurisdiction or control over arbitration proceedings and the enforcement of awards. This survey allows for an analysis of the variety of divergences between national arbitration laws despite the universal recognition of arbitration as a preferred means of dispute resolution, especially in international business transactions. The countries chosen to review were based on geographical location and on the importance of the countries as seats of arbitration.

The European countries surveyed are Bulgaria, France, Germany, Italy, Poland, Russia, Spain, Switzerland, Ukraine, and the United Kingdom. Starting from eastern Europe, Bulgaria provides a case study on the evolution of an arbitration system in a former Soviet republic. Chapter 12 reviews the recent developments of Bulgarian arbitration law and practice on the issues covered in the book. Chapter 18, on Poland, also acts as a case study of a former Soviet satellite that has advanced from a developing to a developed country. The chapter examines this shift from the perspective of arbitration law and practice, highlighting the major developments that have taken place in recent years. Post-socialism is also the historical framework of Chapters 19 and 22, on Russia and Ukraine, respectively. Chapter 19 investigates Russian arbitration rules, as well as rules and regulations of the International Commercial Arbitration Court at the Chamber of Commerce and Industry of the Russian Federation (ICAC), an independent permanent arbitration institution located in Moscow that is also the leading arbitration institution in Russia and in eastern Europe. Chapter 22 delves into Ukraine's recent arbitration reform and improved rules of judicial control over arbitration. In particular, the chapter scrutinizes Ukraine's new procedural rules on courts and their power of vacating arbitration awards, issues about the scope of arbitration clauses and public policy against arbitration, and recognition and enforcement of domestic and international arbitral awards.

Moving to western Europe, Chapter 14 shows how, in the last decades, France moved from a restrictive arbitration regime to a more arbitration-friendly one. The chapter focuses in particular on French arbitration law and practice after the major arbitration reform undertaken in 2011. Chapter 15 provides insights into German arbitration rules as well as the rules of the German

Arbitration Institute (*Deutsche Institution für Schiedsgerichtsbarkeit*; DIS), showing that German is an arbitration-friendly country, and German arbitrators are highly regarded and appointed in international commercial arbitration. In contrast, Chapter 16 on Italy demonstrates that, despite the fact that current Italian rules on arbitration are largely in line with those of other jurisdictions, as well as with international legal standards, Italy is generally perceived as a nonfriendly arbitration country. The chapter investigates the factors underlying the Italian view on arbitration and, in particular, the attitude of Italian courts toward arbitral proceedings and awards. Chapter 20 analyzes the current Spanish Arbitration Act (Act 60/2003 of December 23, 2003) and its amendments. The Act is based on the UN Commission on International Trade Law (UNCITRAL) Model Law, is aligned with international principles, and has largely succeeded in setting up a modern legal framework for arbitration that has enabled a very positive evolution and sound consolidation of arbitration in Spain for more than a decade. Nonetheless, the chapter also underlines that, in recent years, the escalation of disputes related to interest rate swap agreements settled by arbitration triggered a succession of rulings setting aside arbitral awards on the grounds of breach of "economic public policy." Chapter 21 deals with Switzerland, a very important country for international arbitration, given its highly developed arbitration system and the popularity of Swiss law as the applicable law to international transactions. The chapter examines the main features and the reasons underlying the global success of the Swiss arbitration system. Finally, Chapter 23 shows that the United Kingdom's arbitration law, found in the English Arbitration Act (EAA), is less friendly to the independence of the arbitration system than one might expect it to be. The chapter explores the features of the United Kingdom's arbitration system and shows how it provides for a greater role of courts in the interpretation and enforcement of arbitration clauses and agreements.

The Asian-Pacific venues studied are Australia and China. Chapter 11 analyzes Australian arbitration laws as a hybrid system influenced by English common law's restrictive view of arbitration and the explosion of cases in Asian arbitration venues, such as Singapore, Shanghai, and Hong Kong. The chapter explains the most recent developments in Australian arbitration law in the context of the country's hope to capture a larger portion of the ever-growing arbitration industry in Southeast Asia. Chapter 13, on mainland China, presents the specificities of Chinese arbitration law, including its unique "prior reporting system" to ensure uniformity in the judicial review of arbitral awards. The chapter also provides an original quantitative study of annulment and enforcement procedures carried out in China.

In the Americas, the South and North American countries examined are, respectively, Argentina and the United States. Chapter 10 on Argentina investigates a vibrant international arbitration system. Yet the chapter also provides an overview of the specificity and the struggles that Argentinian arbitration law and practice have faced in recent years. Chapter 24 on the United States focuses on the US Federal Arbitration Act, which sets federal policy in favor of arbitration as the country's preferred means of dispute resolution. The chapter examines how courts at the federal level have expanded the areas for which arbitration is allowed, while more recently the US Supreme Court placed obstacles for arbitrating certain types of actions, such as class arbitration claims.

The sole African country explored is Nigeria. Chapter 17 shows how the Nigerian arbitration system lies between the well-advanced arbitration systems of Egypt and South Africa and those of lesser-developed African countries. The chapter highlights the features and specificities of Nigerian arbitration law and practice. As noted, the country reports provide the means to perform a comparative analysis to determine how generally accepted are the principles of arbitral independence and the enforceability of arbitral awards. This is done in Part V, which provides a meta-analysis of the countries surveyed.

Chapter 25 focuses on the commonalities and divergences across national laws. It ferrets out trends and provides a greater understanding of the nuances of national arbitration laws, dealing in particular with setting aside and enforceability of awards, arbitrator bias, conflict of interest and misconduct, interpretation and scope of arbitration clauses and the effect of anti-arbitration policy. Chapter 26, written by the recognized German arbitration practitioner and scholar Friedrich Rosenfeld, reconceptualizes the shared governance exerted by arbitration panels and courts in the operation of the arbitration system. The chapter starts from the premise that arbitration has a dual foundation in party autonomy on the one hand and the applicable arbitration framework on the other and that the ultimate guardians tasked to examine whether an arbitral award produces legal effects are state courts. However, the chapter also emphasizes that the arbitration framework does not always reflect a strict binary allocation of responsibility among private and public actors. The responsibility to control arbitration proceedings is shared among multiple actors, including arbitral tribunals, the parties, arbitral institutions, state courts at the place of arbitration and state courts at the place of recognition and enforcement. The chapter provides a taxonomy of the different layers of judicial control and, in particular, examines whether and, if so, to what extent determinations made at an earlier level of control (e.g., determinations by the parties, arbitral tribunals, arbitral institutions, courts at the place of arbitration) have effects upon the assessment at a later level of control (e.g., determinations by a court at the place of recognition and enforcement).

2

Independence and Impartiality of Arbitrators

Carlos A. Matheus López

1 BACKGROUND

The maxim *nemo iudex sua causa* (no one may judge his own case) applies to the arbitral process as much as it does in the judicial process.[1] Human rights instruments recognize the independence and impartiality of tribunals as fundamental human rights. For example, the following conventions state:

> *Article 10 of the Universal Declaration of Human Rights*
> Everyone is entitled in full equality to a fair and public hearing by an *independent and impartial* tribunal, in the determination of his rights and obligations and of any criminal charge against him.
>
> *Article 6.1 of the European Convention on Human Rights*
> In the determination of his civil rights and obligations or of any criminal charge against him, everyone is entitled to a fair and public hearing within a reasonable time by an *independent and impartial* tribunal established by law.
>
> *Article 8.1 of the American Convention on Human Rights*
> Every person has the right to a hearing, with due guarantees and within a reasonable time, by a competent, *independent, and impartial* tribunal, previously established by law.

Independence and impartiality of tribunals are important principles of due process.[2] The parties in an arbitration are free to determine, according to the principle of party autonomy, the characteristics of the proceedings, subject to minimum safeguards of due process.[3] Fundamental

---

[1] See Fabién Gelinas, *The Independence of International Arbitrators and Judges: Tampered with or Well Tempered?*, 24 INTERNATIONAL LAW REVIEW 1–48, 10 (2011). *See also* Koorosh H. Amelie, *Impartiality and Independence of International Arbitrators*, 27–28 REVUE DE RECHERCHE JURIDIQUE 89–109, 93 (1999), states that: "The requirement of impartiality and independence of arbitrators emanates from a fundamental principle of natural justice recognized in almost every legal system that one may not be a judge of his own cause (nemo iudex in sua causa)."

[2] In this sense, William W. Park, *Arbitrator Bias*, 1 TRANSNATIONAL DISPUTE MANAGEMENT 1–83, 3 (2015), states that: "A relative measure of distance from troubling connections to litigants, along with a willingness to listen carefully to both sides of a dispute, constitutes essential elements of basic due process."

[3] *See* MARTIN F. GUSY, JAMES M. HOSKING, & FRANZ T. SCHWARZ, A GUIDE TO THE ICDR INTERNATIONAL ARBITRATION RULES 84 (2011). *See also* SIMON GREENBERG, CHRISTOPHER KEE, & J. ROMESH WEERAMANTRY 306–307 INTERNATIONAL COMMERCIAL ARBITRATION. AN ASIA PACIFIC PERSPECTIVE (2011), states that: "The consensus in virtually all systems of law is that these principles are essential requirements akin to basic human rights that cannot be overridden by private agreement. An award might be set aside or be unenforceable if tainted by transgressions of such due process requirements."

elements of due process include notice of claimant, an opportunity to present its case in an evidentiary hearing, an opportunity to confront adverse witnesses, assistance of counsel, and a decision rendered by an independent and impartial arbitrator. Due process requires "equal treatment" of the parties during a dispute.[4] The essential function of the impartiality and the independence requirement is to ensure that the arbitrator is unbiased and fair minded. It is this neutral state of mind that gives parties confidence that arbitrators render a decision based on the relevant facts in light of the applicable law.[5]

Nevertheless, it is impracticable to expect absolute independence and impartiality. Human beings by nature establish relationships at different levels with people, places, things, and ideas, and because of this, biases are inevitable. Conflicts of interest are a changing reality because economic, social, professional, and human relationships are mutable – that is, they are permanently changing.[6] The independence and impartiality of arbitrators are issues linked to the intensity of relationships and other types of nuances.[7] As the poet Antonio Machado stated, "The best among the good ones is that one who knows that everything in life is a matter of measure: a little bit more, something less."[8]

2 INDEPENDENCE AND IMPARTIALITY

2.1 *Conceptual Analysis*

The main rules of arbitration (national law, international conventions, and in the regulations of the most important arbitration institutions) contain some variations in rules relating to the fundamental standards for the ethical conduct of arbitrators – that is, independence and impartiality.[9]

Traditionally, independence is an objective element that involves the assessment of factual links, while impartiality is subjective and assessed in terms of intellectual predispositions.[10]

---

[4] Similarly, Fabricio Fortese & Lotta Hemmi, *Procedural Fairness and Efficiency in International Arbitration*, 3 GRONINGEN JOURNAL OF INTERNATIONAL LAW 110, 112 (2015) ("The core guarantees of procedural due process comprise the arbitrator's duty to treat the parties equally, fairly and impartially, and to ensure that each party has an opportunity to present its case and deal with that of its opponent. It also comprises the arbitral tribunal's duty to deal with all of the issues that are put to it. Therefore, access to arbitration is not enough; the procedure itself must also be fair."). *See also*, MARIA NICOLE CLEIS, THE INDEPENDENCE AND IMPARTIALITY OF ICSID ARBITRATORS: CURRENT CASE LAW, ALTERNATIVE APPROACHES, AND IMPROVEMENT SUGGESTIONS 22 (2017), states that: "At their core, independence and impartiality aim to ensure parties' equality of arms, fair trial and procedural justice."
[5] *See* Melanie Van Leeuwen, *Pride and Prejudice in the Debate on Arbitrator Independence*, in 12–13 NEW DEVELOPMENTS IN INTERNATIONAL COMMERCIAL ARBITRATION (Christoph Müller & Antonio Rigozzi eds., 2013).
[6] In this sense, William W. Park, *Arbitrator Integrity: The Transient and the Permanent*, 46 SAN DIEGO LAW REVIEW 629–703, 630–631 (2009), states that: "New patterns of misbehavior create new types of ethical challenges. Few criteria for evaluating arbitrator independence and impartiality will likely stay foolproof for long, given how ingenious fools often prove themselves to be ... Conflict-of-interest principles will remain useful only if implemented with sensitivity to new trouble spots."
[7] *See* Park, *supra* note 2, at 1, states that: "From the command post of bland generalities, the job of evaluating independence or impartiality may seem simple. In light of specific challenges, however, the task becomes one of nuance and complexity, often implicating subtle wrinkles to the comportment of otherwise honourable and experienced individuals."
[8] *Id.* at 3, states that: "Notwithstanding the elusiveness of perfect objectivity, a reasonable measure of arbitrator integrity remains both desirable and attainable. Although few people are free of predispositions in an absolute sense, some will prove relatively more detached than others with respect to any given dispute."
[9] *See* Doak Bishop & Lucy Reed, *Practical Guidelines for Interviewing, Selecting and Challenging Party-Appointed Arbitrators in International Commercial Arbitration*, 4 ARBITRATION INTERNATIONAL 395, 397–398 (1998).
[10] *See* Thomas Clay, *L'indépendance et L'impartialité de L'arbitre et les Règles du Procès Équitable*, in 213–214 L'IMPARTIALITÉ DU JUGE ET DE L'ARBITRE (Jacques Van Compernolle & Giuseppe Tarzia eds., 2006). In this sense,

Independence focuses on the position or situation of the arbitrator, while impartiality refers to an attitude of intellectual or psychological order.[11] Independence objectively determines if a situation of nondependence exists between an arbitrator and a party. Impartiality subjectively suggests that an arbitrator possesses preconceived opinions (bias) that will interfere with making a decision solely based on the merits of the case.[12]

An impartial arbitrator is one who is not predisposed in favor or biased against, a particular party or its case. An independent arbitrator is one who has no close relationship – financial, professional, personal, or otherwise – with any of the parties or their counsels.[13] Arbitrator independence is questionable where there are preexisting relationships between the arbitrator and the parties, while impartiality concerns the relationships between the arbitrator and the subject matter of the dispute.[14] Professional relationships include cases where the arbitrator or the arbitrator's partner

---

Nora Ciancio, *The Implications of Recent ICSID Arbitrator Disqualifications for Latin America*, 6 YEARBOOK ON ARBITRATION AND MEDIATION 440, 447 (2014), states that: "The former contemplates improper connections an arbitrator may have to the dispute. (...) Arbitrator impartiality contemplates arbitrators' preconceived notions that could threaten the neutrality of the arbitral process."

[11] See Pierre Lalive, *Sur L'impartialité de L'arbitre International en Suisse*, 112 LA SEMAINE JUDICIAIRE 362–371, 364 (1990). In this sense, Martin Svatoš, *Independence and Impartiality of Arbitrators and Mediators – The Castor and Pollux of the ADR World?*, in CZECH (& CENTRAL EUROPEAN) YEARBOOK OF ARBITRATION (Alexander J. Bělohlávek, Naděžda Rozehnalová, & Filip Černý eds., 2014), states that: "It is a state of mind of not being interested regarding the outcome of the procedure. In other words, the presence of bias causes absence of impartiality and vice versa: the absence of bias means impartiality."

[12] Similarly, Marc Henry, *Les Obligations d'Indépendance et d'Information de L'arbitre à la Lumière de la Jurisprudence Récente*, 1 REVUE DE L'ARBITRAGE 193, 195 (1991). *See, e.g.*, Van Leeuwen, *supra* note 5, at 12, states that:

> the impartiality requirement is a subjective standard, while the independence requirement is an objective standard. That is, impartiality is a subjective standard that goes to the state of mind of the arbitrator and which requires him/her to hear and judge the case in a neutral, unbiased, fair-minded manner, without prejudice with respect to any of the issues in dispute and without predisposition towards any of the parties involved in the arbitration. Independence, however, is an objective standard that is aimed at ensuring the absence of unacceptable external relations or connections between an arbitrator on the one hand and one or more of the parties or counsel involved in an arbitration on the other.

On the other hand, Antonio Crivellaro, *Does the Arbitrators' Failure to Disclose Conflicts of Interest Fatally Lead to Annulment of the Award? The Approach of the European State Courts*, 1 ARBITRATION BRIEF 121, 121–122 (2014), states that:

> (i) independence is an objective "state of profession", so that where the arbitrator's remuneration is originated, directly or through his law firm, by professional services performed for one of the parties (or its affiliates) appearing in the arbitration, his financial relationship with the party is established and he ceases to be independent; and (ii) impartiality is a subjective "state of mind", implying absence of bias or predisposition towards the outcome of the case, caused by the arbitrator's publications, or public statements, or positions manifested as arbitrator or counsel in previous cases, that might be seen as impairing his impartial judgment on the merits.

See also, Mary Jude V. Cantorias, *Party-Appointed Arbitrator Ethics and Ethos – Cross-Cultural Differences and How They Affect Arbitrator Behaviour in Rendering Arbitral Awards*, 1 ARELLANO LAW AND POLICY REVIEW 53, 56 (2014), states that:

> impartiality may be considered as having a more "subjective status", seen in light of party perception, ... impartiality is a product of purposeful behavior characterized by bad faith or malicious intent or gross negligence. On the other hand, arbitrator independence is almost always seen in light of the circumstances surrounding the behavior that shows or reflects independence. In ordinary terms, independence relates to lack of "improper connections" by the arbitrator, while impartiality speaks to a "prejudgment" of the dispute before all facts and evidence are on hand.

[13] *See, e.g.*, Bishop & Reed, *supra* note 9, at 398. *See also* Michael Hwang & Kevin Lim, *Issue Conflict in ICSID Arbitrations*, in 478–479 SELECTED ESSAYS ON INTERNATIONAL ARBITRATION (Michael Hwang, Eunice Chan, & Elain Lim eds., 2013), states that: "Independence is thus concerned with a decision maker's relationships with parties, which affect his or her views or attitudes on the merits of the dispute submitted for consideration. In contrast, when a decision maker is said to lack impartiality, his or her state of mind is directly put in issue."

[14] Similarly, *e.g.*, Henry, *supra* note 12, at 195.

has acted as a counselor, employee, or consultant on behalf of a party to the dispute. An arbitrator (or a partner) holding an executive or nonexecutive position in a company or who is a party to a business transaction (ownership or shares) involving one of the parties should be excluded. Personal relationships range from a friendship between the arbitrator and a party (improper) to simply sharing for a short period an office with the counsel of a party (permissible). Independence depends on the degree of closeness or distance in time and place of relationships.[15]

Impartiality relates to a state of mind, evidenced by behavior that demonstrates some degree of partiality. An arbitrator is partial when the arbitrator shows preference for one party or against another or when a reasonable third party perceives such bias. The factors used to determine a likelihood of partiality or bias include (1) a professional, business, or personal relationship that gives rise to a reasonable belief that the arbitrator is biased and (2) the arbitrator's behavior in the absence of such a relationship demonstrates bias, such as a statement derogatory to one of the parties.[16] Leon Trakman postulated that the obligations of independence and impartially have different time durations – independence exists throughout the arbitration and a reasonable period after, while impartiality exists at the time the arbitration award is rendered.[17] As noted earlier, the words *independence* and *impartiality* are distinguishable, with independence focusing on the parties and impartiality relating to the subject matter; however, this is not always the case.[18] For example, French and Swiss law view them as part of the same element. French and Swiss courts use the concept of "independence of spirit,"[19] which relates both to the parties and to their controversy.[20]

---

[15] See CARLOS A. MATHEUS LÓPEZ, LA INDEPENDENCIA E IMPARCIALIDAD DEL ÁRBITRO EN EL ARBITRAJE DOMÉSTICO E INTERNACIONAL 180–181 (2016).

[16] See Leon Trakman, *The Impartiality and Independence of Arbitrators Reconsidered*, 4 INTERNATIONAL ARBITRATION LAW REVIEW 124–135, 127–128 (2007). See also Ronán Feehily, *Neutrality, Independence and Impartiality in International Commercial Arbitration, a Fine Balance in the Quest for Arbitral Justice*, 1 PENN STATE JOURNAL OF LAW & INTERNATIONAL AFFAIRS 89–114, 94–95 (2019), states that:

> Impartiality requires that an arbitrator is free from bias due to preconceived notions regarding the dispute, or any other reason that may result in favouring one party over the other. As noted above, impartiality relates to the arbitrator's state of mind and actual bias. Proving actual bias requires a factual, subjective approach. In light of its abstract nature, measuring impartiality is quite difficult. Courts consequently review the facts and circumstances in which the arbitrator exercised his or her functions before inferring whether there was bias, and the courts have consequently relied upon a finding of apparent bias rather than actual bias in determining arbitrator impartiality. Hence, while impartiality relates to the state of mind of the arbitrator that is demonstrated through conduct, partiality is displayed through showing preference to one of the parties usually leading to the detriment of the other. Albeit a subjective concept, impartiality must be demonstrated through some external behaviour that establishes the arbitrator's state or frame of mind, such as a professional or personal relationship with one of the parties that may reasonably lead to a conclusion that an arbitrator was partial. Where no such relationship exists, partiality may be demonstrated through the arbitrator's conduct.

[17] For a better understanding of the issue. See SAM LUTTRELL, BIAS CHALLENGES IN INTERNATIONAL COMMERCIAL ARBITRATION. THE NEED FOR A 'REAL DANGER' TEST 21–22 (2009).

[18] Similarly, *e.g.*, Feehily, *supra* note 16, at 90, affirms that: "Impartiality and independence are often used synonymously to reflect the unbiased quality that arbitrators are expected to possess. While often used interchangeably, they are conceptually different albeit linked."

[19] See, *e.g.*, Clay, *supra* note 10, at 214, states that: in France, "To regulate the issue, French jurisprudence adopted for the arbitrator a standard that stands halfway between independence and impartiality since it refers to the 'independence of spirit' of the arbitrator. The courts thus made an amalgamation of the objective and subjective components of independence and impartiality, and that makes the distinction of the two terms definitely dangerous, if not useless, for the arbitrator." *Cf.*, Lalive, *supra* note 11, at 60, who states: in Switzerland, "We could think that independence is an objective notion, and refers to the situation, the position of the arbitrator; while impartiality, would be subjective and would rather refer to an intellectual attitude; but the statement, at first sight seductive, is somewhat questioned by the frequency of references, in practice, to the 'independence of spirit' of the arbitrators."

[20] See V. V. Veeder, *L'indépendance et L'impartialité de L'arbitre dans L'arbitrage International*, in 228 MÉDIATION ET ARBITRAGE. ALTERNATIVE DISPUTE RESOLUTION. JUSTICE ALTERNATIVE OU ALTERNATIVE À LA JUSTICE? PERSPECTIVES COMPARATIVES (Loïc Cadiet, Emmanuel Jeuland, & Thomas Clay eds., 2005).

These are very similar concepts. Although the terminology is different, the words have similar legal meanings.[21] These terms are analyzed together[22] since they are viewed as a single requirement without a definitive distinction between them.[23] What has led some national laws to treat independence and impartiality synonymously, using them interchangeably?[24] The answer is that words have become a pleonasm or express a hybrid concept and not two different and dissociable requirements,[25] or act as a joint technical expression.[26] Likewise, the distinction between the two terms, from a teleological point of view, are independent of the arbitral award because awards are presumed to be impartial.[27] Various national laws and institutional arbitration rules either use (1) both terms (following the UNCITRAL Model Law), (2) only one of the terms, or (3) an equivalent or broader expression. A single term can serve as a generic notion that encompasses the ideas of independence, impartiality, and neutrality or objectivity.[28]

2.2 Summary

Independence refers to the arbitrator's position or situation in relationship to the parties and their counsels. Impartiality refers to an arbitrator's attitude or intellectual or psychological nature (state of mind).[29] If we try to visualize this graphically we would see two circles that appear to be completely separate from one another. If you look at the circles in the graph in more detail, independence has only an objective component: it indicates the absence of unacceptable relationships between an arbitrator and a party or an individual linked to it – for example, familial, financial, professional, or personal relationships.

Impartiality has both a subjective and an objective component: whether the arbitrator is actually predisposed to be partial would be the subjective component. Arbitrators are presumed to be biased when there is a familial, financial, professional, or personal relationship with a party or an individual linked to the party; this is the objective component of the bias test.[30] To sum up, independence and impartiality are complex notions of a unitary nature. If we try to visualize this, we would see two circles that overlap. They are redundant, or in other words, they express a

---

[21] *Id.* at 224.
[22] *See, e.g.,* Trakman, *supra* note 16, at 128.
[23] *See, e.g.,* Lalive, *supra* note 11, at 60.
[24] *Id.* at 59, states that: since "the confusing and persistent ambiguity that surrounds basic concepts such as the 'impartiality' and 'independence' of the arbitrators, [it is possible to confirm that they are] two apparently different terms but often used as practically interchangeable in the texts (conventional or legislative), jurisprudence, or doctrine."
[25] In this sense, *e.g.,* Veeder, *supra* note 20, at 229–230.
[26] *See* ALAN REDFERN, MARTIN HUNTER, NIGEL BLACKABY, & CONSTANTINE PARTASIDES 305 TEORÍA Y PRÁCTICA DEL ARBITRAJE COMERCIAL INTERNACIONAL (2006).
[27] *See, e.g.,* Clay, *supra* note 10, at 214.
[28] *Id.* at 215.
[29] "[I]mpartiality means that an arbitrator 'is not partial – or biased – in favor of, or against, a particular party or its case, while an independent arbitrator is one who has no close relationship – financial, professional or personal – with a party or its counsel." Constantine Partasides, *The Selection, Appointment and Challenge of Arbitrators,* 5 VINDOBONA JOURNAL OF INTERNATIONAL COMMERCIAL LAW AND ARBITRATION 217, 219 (2001). *See also* Henry Gabriel & Anjanette H. Raymond, *Ethics for Commercial Arbitrators: Basic Principles and Emerging Standards,* 2 WYOMING LAW REVIEW 453, 457 (2017) ("An impartial arbitrator is an arbitrator who is not biased in favor of, or prejudiced against, a particular party or the party's case. In contrast, an independent arbitrator is an arbitrator who has no close relationship; financial, professional, or personal, with a party or the party's counsel").
[30] Similarly, Diego M. Papayannis, *Independence, Impartiality and Neutrality in Legal Adjudication,* 28 REVUS: JOURNAL FOR CONSTITUTIONAL THEORY AND PHILOSOPHY OF LAW 33, 47 (2016) ("Impartiality is an attitude towards the parties involved and the subject matter of the dispute. Impartial adjudicators have an unprejudiced view of all parties and have no personal interest in the outcome of the dispute").

hybrid concept and are not two distinct and separable elements.[31] Almost all laws and rules pertaining to the assessment of bias tend to use these two notions as a "package."[32]

2.3 Reflections from Legal Theory

Arbitration requires, even more than other disciplines, a serious analysis from the standpoint of legal theory.[33] In Ronald Dworkin's terminology, rules apply in an all-or-nothing fashion. When a valid rule applies in a given case, it is conclusive. Because valid rules are conclusive reasons for action, they cannot be in conflict. If two rules conflict, then one of them cannot be a valid rule. By contrast, principles do not dispose of the cases to which they apply. They lend justificatory support to various courses of actions, but they are not necessarily conclusive. Valid principles, therefore, often conflict. Moreover, in contrast to rules, principles have weight. When valid principles conflict, the proper method for resolving the conflict is to select the position supported by the principles that have the greatest aggregate weight.[34]

Applying the previous distinction to international arbitration, we can affirm that, in practice, the duties of independence and impartiality seem to work more as principles rather than as rules, depending on the context. The suggestion that the circumstances of the case must be weighed in order to determine whether an arbitrator who has preexisting professional relationships with one of the parties is in violation of his or her duty of independence or impartiality indicates that these duties do not operate as conclusive or binding guidelines.[35] National constitutions[36] and human rights treaties contain norms from which principles are constructed. The principles of independence and impartiality are reflections of constitutional and human rights norms, such as equality under the law and due process.

---

[31] In this sense, Christopher Koch, *Standards and Procedures for Disqualifying Arbitrators*, 4 JOURNAL OF INTERNATIONAL ARBITRATION 325, 331 (2003), states that: "I do not believe that the difference is material. By looking at 'independence' one is really trying to measure the probability of 'bias.' On the other hand, even though impartiality as a subjective standard dealing with the arbitrator's state of mind, the English courts developed the notion of 'apparent bias,' a fact-based test, to determine impartiality. Independence and impartiality are two ways of looking at the same thing."

[32] *See, e.g.*, Matheus López, *supra* note 15, at 182–183. Similarly, *e.g.*, CLEIS, *supra* note 4, at 22, states that:

> In practice, distinctions between independence and impartiality are often overlooked, and the terms are used interchangeably. This considerably complicates the interpretation of challenge decisions. Terminologically distinguishing the terms, however, is less important and conducive to determining the scope of the concepts, than defining their common purpose. Looking beyond linguistic and conceptual differences, the notions of independence and impartiality are complimentary, and pursue the same goal.

[33] In this sense, EMMANUEL GAILLARD, ASPECTS PHILOSOPHIQUES DU DROIT DE L'ARBITRAGE INTERNATIONAL 18 (2008).

[34] Ronald Dworkin sees rules as "applicable in an all-or-nothing-fashion," while he defines

> legal principles as not setting out legal consequences that follow automatically when the conditions provided are met. A principle states a reason that argues in one direction, but it does not prescribe a particular decision. Because principles have less specificity in this way, unlike rules principles can conflict. Decision makers assign weights to principles to resolve such conflicts.

> Scott J. Shapiro, *The Hart–Dworkin Debate: A Short Guide for the Perplexed*, in 25–26 RONALD DWORKIN (Arthur Ripstein ed., 2007). *See also* John Braithwaite, *Rules and Principles: A Theory of Legal Certainty*, 27 AUSTRALIAN JOURNAL OF LEGAL PHILOSOPHY 47–82, 50 (2002).

[35] In this sense, *e.g.*, Papayannis, *supra* note 30, at 41.

[36] *See* ROBERT ALEXY, EL CONCEPTO Y LA VALIDEZ DEL DERECHO 73–85 (2004). *See also* MATTHIAS KLATT, INSTITUTIONALIZED REASON: THE JURISPRUDENCE OF ROBERT ALEXY (2012) (affirms that "Alexy uses constitutional rights to justify his non-positivistic concept of law. In his view, constitutional rights are principles, that is, optimization requirements, and as such should be distinguished from rules").

3 NATIONAL ARBITRATION LAWS AND RULES

3.1 *National Arbitration Laws*

Several examples illustrate the redundant character of the terms independence and impartiality discussed in the in the previous part. On the one hand, the English Arbitration Act uses only the term *impartiality*. Section 24(1) (a) reads as follows: "A party to arbitral proceedings may apply to the court to remove an arbitrator ... [where] circumstances exist that give rise to justifiable doubts as to his *impartiality*." On the other hand, Switzerland's Federal Code on Private International Law uses only the term *independence*. Article 180 Section (1) (c) reads as that "an arbitrator must be challenged ... If the circumstances permit legitimate doubt about his *independence*."

On the other hand, the Model Law on International Commercial Arbitration of the UN Commission on International Trade Law (UNCITRAL Model Law) has influenced many national arbitration laws. Sections (1) and (2) of Article 12 state:

> (1) When a person approached in connection with his possible appointment as an arbitrator, he shall disclose any circumstances likely to give rise to justifiable doubts as to his *impartiality or independence*. An arbitrator, from the time of his appointment and throughout the arbitral proceedings, shall without delay disclose any such circumstances to the parties unless they have already been informed of them by him.
>
> (2) An arbitrator may be challenged only if circumstances exist that give rise to justifiable doubts as to his *impartiality or independence*, or if he does not possess qualifications agreed to by the parties. A party may challenge an arbitrator appointed by him, or in whose appointment he has participated, only for reasons of which he becomes aware after the appointment has been made.

Following the UNCITRAL Model Law, Section 6 of the Irish Arbitration Act of 2010, in Part 2 states:

> Subject to this Act, the Model Law shall have the force of law in the State and shall apply to arbitrations under arbitration agreements concerning – (a) international commercial arbitrations, or (b) arbitrations which are not international commercial arbitrations.

Article 12 paragraphs (1) and (2) refer to impartiality and independence. The Irish Arbitration Act of 2010 incorporates the UNCITRAL Model Law.[37] Rule 77 of the Scottish Arbitration Act of 2010 states that "an arbitrator is not *independent* in relation to an arbitration if – (a) the arbitrator's relationship with any party, (b) the arbitrator's financial or other commercial interests, or (c) anything else, gives rise to justifiable doubts as to the arbitrator's *impartiality*."

In the same vein, Section 12 of the Danish Arbitration Act 2005 Section 12 states that:

> (1) When a person is approached in connection with a possible appointment as an arbitrator, that person shall disclose any circumstances likely to give rise to justifiable doubts as to his or her *impartiality or independence* ...
>
> (2) An arbitrator may be challenged only if circumstances exist that give rise to justifiable doubts as to the arbitrator's *impartiality or independence*.

Article 12 sections (1) and (2) of the Costa Rican Arbitration Law of 2011 state:

> 1. When a person is approached in connection with his possible appointment as an arbitrator, he shall disclose any circumstances likely to give rise to justifiable doubts as to his *impartiality or*

---

[37] The Act also includes the text of the UNCITRAL Model Law in Schedule 1.

independence. An arbitrator, from the time of his appointment and throughout the arbitral proceedings, shall without delay disclose any such circumstances to the parties unless they have already been informed of them by him.

2. An arbitrator may be challenged only if circumstances exist that give rise to justifiable doubts as to his *impartiality or independence*, or if he does not possess qualifications agreed to by the parties. A party may challenge an arbitrator appointed by him, or in whose appointment he has participated, only for reasons of which he becomes aware after the appointment has been made.

The countries of Angola,[38] Argentina,[39] Australia,[40] Cyprus, Fiji,[41] Ghana,[42] Japan,[43] Kenya,[44] Myanmar,[45] New Zealand,[46] Peru,[47] Qatar,[48] the Russian Federation,[49] Saudi Arabia,[50] South Korea,[51] Turkey,[52] and the United Arab Emirates[53] have similar provisions in their arbitration laws.

3.2 ICSID Convention and Rules

The International Centre for Settlement of Investment Disputes Convention (ICSID Convention) provides another example of the redundant nature of independence and impartiality. The ICSID Convention is similar to Switzerland's Federal Code on Private International Law in that it uses only the term *independence*. Article 14(1) of the ICSID Convention states: "Persons

---

[38] Article 10 of The Angola Voluntary Arbitration Law of 2003 (same).

[39] Articles 27 and 28 of the Argentina International Commercial Arbitration Act of 2018 ("arbitrator shall disclose any circumstances likely to give rise to justifiable doubts as to his impartiality or independence; challenged only if circumstances exist that give rise to justifiable doubts as to his impartiality and independence").

[40] Section 18A of the Australia International Arbitration Act of 1974:

1. ... there are justifiable doubts as to the impartiality or independence of a person approached in connection with a possible appointment as arbitrator only if there is a real danger of bias on the part of that person in conducting the arbitration. 2. ... there are justifiable doubts as to the impartiality or independence of an arbitrator only if there is a real danger of bias on the part of the arbitrator in conducting the arbitration.

[41] Article 17 of the Fiji International Arbitration Act of 2017 (same).

[42] Article 12(4)(d) of the Ghana Alternative Dispute Resolution Act of 2010:

person or the institution vested with the power of appointment shall have regard to: (a) the personal, proprietary, fiduciary or financial interest of the arbitrator in the matter to which the arbitration relates; (b) the relationship of the arbitrator to a party or counsel of a party to the arbitration; (c) the nationalities of the parties; and (d) other relevant considerations to ensure the appointment of an independent and an impartial arbitrator.

[43] Article 18(1ii)(3) of the Japan Arbitration Law of 2003 ("party may challenge an arbitrator ... if circumstances exist that give rise to justifiable doubts as to its impartiality or independence").

[44] Article 13 of the Kenya Arbitration Act of 1995 (same).

[45] Section 14(a)(c) of the Myanmar Arbitration Act of 2016 (same).

[46] New Zealand Arbitration Act of 1996, Schedule 1 ("correspond, for the most part, to the provisions of the Model Law on International Commercial Arbitration adopted by the United Nations Commission on International Trade Law on 21 June 1985").

[47] Article 28 section (1) of the Peru Arbitration Law of 2008 ("Arbitrators must be and must remain during the whole proceedings independent and impartial. Persons approached in connection with a possible appointment as arbitrators must disclose any circumstances likely to give rise to justifiable doubts as to their impartiality and independence.").

[48] Article 11 (3) and (12) of the Qatar Arbitration Law of 2017 ("arbitrator shall, upon nomination, disclose in writing any circumstances that may cast doubts on his/her impartiality and/or independence").

[49] Article 12 of the Russian Federation Arbitration Law of 2016 (same).

[50] Article 16 of the Saudi Arabia Arbitration Law of 2012 ("arbitrator is precluded ... under the same circumstances as those that preclude a judge from the same").

[51] Article 13 of the South Korea Arbitration Act of 2016 (same).

[52] Article 7C of the Turkey International Arbitration Law of 2001 (same).

[53] Articles 10(4) and 14(1) of UAE Arbitration Law of 2018 ("disclose in writing anything likely to give rise to doubts as to his impartiality or independence").

designated to serve on the Panels shall be persons of high moral character and recognized competence in the fields of law, commerce, industry or finance, who may be relied upon to exercise independent judgment."

The requirement of the arbitrator's "independent judgment" implicitly includes both independence and impartiality. The Spanish version of Article 14, section 1 of the ICSID Convention refers to impartiality of judgment (*imparcialidad de juicio*). In comparison, the English version of this article speaks of independent judgment. The French version alludes to the guarantee of independence (*garantie d'indépendance*). According to a note to Article 75 of the ICSID Convention, all three versions are equally authentic. Article 57 of the ICSID Convention deals with the challenge of the arbitrator: "A party may propose to a Commission or Tribunal the disqualification of any of its members on account of any fact indicating a manifest lack of the qualities required by paragraph (1) of Article 14."[54]

3.3 UNCITRAL Arbitration Rules

Like the UNCITRAL Model Law, the UNCITRAL Arbitration Rules use both terms – independence and impartiality – as a package. Article 6, section 7 states that:

> The appointing authority shall have regard to such considerations as are likely to secure the appointment of an *independent and impartial* arbitrator and shall take into account the advisability of appointing an arbitrator of a nationality other than the nationalities of the parties.

Article 12, section 1, reads: "Any arbitrator may be challenged if circumstances exist that give rise to justifiable doubts as to the arbitrator's impartiality or independence."

3.4 Institutional Rules

The Arbitration Rules of various arbitral institutions follow the UNCITRAL Model Law, by using the terms *independence* and *impartiality* like a package. Articles 11(1) and 14(1) of the Arbitration Rules of the International Chamber of Commerce of 2017 (the ICC Rules) state: (1) 11(1) "arbitrator must be and remain *impartial and independent* of the parties" and (2) 14(1) "challenge of an arbitrator, whether for an alleged lack of impartiality or independence." Other arbitral associations have adopted similar rules, which follow the framework of the UNCITRAL Model Law. The following is a sampling of institutional rules that follow the Model Law's approach: 2014 Arbitration Rules of the London Court of International Arbitration (LCIA Rules),[55] Stockholm Chamber of Commerce Arbitration Rules of 2017 (SCC Rules),[56] International Arbitration Rules of the International Center for Dispute Resolution of 2014 (ICDR Rules),[57] Arbitration Rules of the Singapore International Arbitration Centre of 2016 (SIAC Rules),[58] Arbitration Rules of the Kuala Lumpur Regional Centre for Arbitration of 2017

---

[54] Likewise, Rule 9, section 1, of the Arbitration Rules establishes that: "A party proposing the disqualification of an arbitrator pursuant to Article 57 of the Convention shall promptly, and in any event before the proceeding is declared closed, file its proposal with the Secretary General, stating its reasons therefore."

[55] Articles 5(3): "All arbitrators shall be and remain at all times impartial and independent of the parties; and none shall act in the arbitration as advocate for or representative of any party. No arbitrator shall advise any party on the parties' dispute or the outcome of the arbitration."

[56] Article 18, section 1: "Every arbitrator must be impartial and independent"; Article 19, section 1: "give rise to justifiable doubts as to the arbitrator's impartiality or independence or if he/she does not possess qualifications agreed by the parties."

[57] Articles 13(2) and 14(1).

[58] Articles 13 and 14.

(KLRCA Rules),[59] Arbitration Rules of the Dubai International Arbitration Centre of 2007 (DIAC Rules),[60] Arbitration Rules of the Vienna International Arbitral Centre of 2018 (VIENNA Rules),[61] Arbitration Rules of the German Arbitration Institute (Deutsche Institution für Schiedsgerichtsbarkeit) of 2017 (DIS Rules),[62] Administered Arbitration Rules of the Hong Kong International Arbitration Centre of 2018 (HKIAC Rules),[63] Commercial Arbitration Rules of the Japan Commercial Arbitration Association of 2019 (JCAA Rules),[64] International Arbitration Rules of the Korean Commercial Arbitration Board of 2016 (KCAB Rules),[65] and Arbitration Rules of the China International Economic and Trade Arbitration Commission (CIETAC Rules).[66] These rules incorporate two basic concepts. First, the arbitrator's impartiality or independence must exist throughout the arbitration process. Second, a party can challenge an arbitrator only if there is evidence of justifiable doubts as to the arbitrator's impartiality and independence.

4 STANDARDS FOR ASSESSING INDEPENDENCE AND IMPARTIALITY

There are two standards for assessing "justifiable doubts" regarding independence and impartiality – the subjective and the objective standard.[67] When considering the subjective standard, what matters is seeking the person's true intentions, a compromising event that indicates the existence of the arbitrator's guilt. The objective standard relates to appearance of bias and not the arbitrator's intentions. Situations or relationships are compromising when certain characteristics are present. Various arbitration laws, international conventions and institutional rules choose to adopt one or the other of these standards. The expression "justifiable doubt," or similar phrases, refers to a doubt that can be justified, making it undoubtedly an objective assessment.[68]

Some arbitration laws vary slightly in their wording but the idea is the same. For example, the Switzerland's Federal Code on Private International Law uses the phrase "permit legitimate doubt." Ghana's Alternative Dispute Resolution Act uses the wording "give rise to reasonable cause to doubt." Angola's Voluntary Arbitration Law uses the phrases "that may raise doubts" and "justified doubts." Saudi Arabia's Arbitration Law uses the phrase "giving rise to serious doubts." Qatar's Arbitration Law uses the wordings "that may cast doubts" and "reasonable doubts." The UAE Arbitration Law uses the phrases "give rise to doubts" and "that give rise to justifiable doubts." The DIS Rules use the words "has failed to comply," while the ICC Rules use the term "alleged lack."

The ICSID Convention follows the subjective standard.[69] Article 14, Section 1 uses the phrase "who may be relied upon to exercise independent judgment." It refers to an intimate and

---

[59] Article 5, section 1 and Article 12, section 1.
[60] Articles 9(1) and 13(3).
[61] Article 20, section 1.
[62] Articles 9.1 snf 15.1.
[63] Article 11 (1) and (6).
[64] Articles 24(1) and 34(1).
[65] Articles 10(1) and 14(1).
[66] Article 32, section 2.
[67] MATHEUS LÓPEZ, *supra* note 15, at 208.
[68] The countries that have adopted the justifiable doubts and objective standards include Argentina, Costa Rica, Cyprus, Denmark, Fiji, Ireland, Japan, Kenya, Myanmar, New Zealand, Peru, Russia, South Korea, Turkey, and the United Kingdom as well as arbitration associations, as noted in Section 3.4, including UNCITRAL Model Law, UNCITRAL Arbitration Rules, CIETAC Rules, LCIA Rules, SCC Rules, ICDR Rules, SIAC Rules, KLRCA Rules, DIAC Rules, VIENNA Rules, HKIAC Rules, JCAA Rules, and KCAB Rules.
[69] See Loretta Malintoppi, *Independence, Impartiality, and Duty of Disclosure of Arbitrators*, in 826 OXFORD HANDBOOK OF INTERNATIONAL INVESTMENT LAW (Peter Muchlinski, Federico Ortino, & Christoph Schreuer eds., 2008). *See also*

personal condition, requiring a subjective assessment.[70] However, most arbitration laws use the objective standard because of the influence of the UNCITRAL Model Law.

As a final observation, the subjective standard provides decision makers less discretion (narrower scope) in determining arbitrator bias than does the objective standard. This is because in the objective standard it is enough that there are circumstances that prove there is a breach, appearance, or risk of a breach of the arbitrator's duty of independence and impartiality.[71] Under the objective standard, questioning of the independence and impartiality of arbitrators is more frequent, given that in the objective standard the arbitrator's good or bad faith is immaterial.[72]

5 COMPLEMENTARY ELEMENT: DUTY OF DISCLOSURE

The duty of disclosure is a preventive means that aims to limit the risk of challenges to the arbitrator and/or annulment of the arbitral award, based on questions of independence and impartiality requirements. In order to help the parties determine the independence and impartiality of the arbitrator, there needs to be complete transparency regarding relationships that the arbitrator may have with the parties or the controversy. This is the main function of the duty of disclosure. The arbitrator's duty of disclosure, even though it works in the same way, does not replace the arbitrator's independence and impartiality. An arbitrator's failure to disclose relevant information does not automatically justify a challenge. A challenge is justified if the circumstances not disclosed question the arbitrator's independence and impartiality.[73] In other words, the mere omission of the duty of disclosure does not per se suggest the existence of partiality or dependence on the arbitrator. The undisclosed circumstances must raise a justifiable doubt about the independence or impartiality of the arbitrator. In a seminal case, the Peru Supreme Court of 2017 confirmed the importance of linking undisclosed circumstances to the partiality or dependence of the arbitrator.[74]

Various national arbitration laws and institutional arbitration rules prescribe a duty of disclosure, at the outset and throughout the proceeding, of "any circumstances likely to give rise to justifiable doubts as to his impartiality and independence." The texts include variations but are very much in line with the UNCITRAL Model Law.[75] Likewise, the expression "justifiable doubts," or similar phrasing, related to duty of disclosure refers to a making an objective assessment.[76]

Andrew Lotbinière Mcdougall & Ank Santens, *ICSID Amends Its Arbitration Rules*, 4 INTERNATIONAL ARBITRATION LAW REVIEW 119, 120 (2006).

[70] Notwithstanding the foregoing, many decisions on the independence and impartiality of the arbitrator, issued by various ICSID tribunals, ad hoc committee members or the chairman of the Administrative Council, repeatedly indicate that the standard for assessing the independence judgment of the ICSID arbitrators is one of objective character. See CARLOS A. MATHEUS LÓPEZ, LA INDEPENDENCIA E IMPARCIALIDAD DEL ÁRBITRO EN EL SISTEMA CIADI 23–242 (2013).

[71] See, e.g., MATHEUS LÓPEZ, supra note 15, at 6.

[72] "A lower standard will make it easier to disqualify and remove arbitrators. A more stringent standard will make it more difficult to disqualify arbitrators." KAREL DAELE, CHALLENGE AND DISQUALIFICATION OF ARBITRATORS IN INTERNATIONAL ARBITRATION 218 (2012).

[73] See CARLOS A. MATHEUS LÓPEZ, LA INDEPENDENCIA E IMPARCIALIDAD DEL ÁRBITRO 241 (2009).

[74] Peruvian Supreme Court of 27 November 2017 (Cassation No. 2267-2017, Lima). See Carlos A. Matheus López, *Should Arbitrators Come from Utopia Island?*, KLUWER ARBITRATION BLOG (Dec. 6, 2018), http://arbitrationblog.kluwerarbitration.com/2018/12/06/should-arbitrators-come-from-utopia-island.

[75] See Ciancio, supra note 10, at 448.

[76] See, e.g., MATHEUS LÓPEZ, supra note 15, at 248.

Finally, when deciding what to reveal, it is advisable for the arbitrator to disclose all the possible circumstances that may raise suspicions about the arbitrator's independence and impartiality. One must also be aware that excessive disclosure can generate as many problems as that of insufficient character, because if a scrupulous arbitrator discloses links that normally would not generate doubts, this could cause the parties to wonder if there is anything beyond what seems apparent.[77] Notwithstanding the foregoing, if an arbitrator has any doubt about whether or not disclose certain information, then is best that the arbitrator disclose the information.[78]

6 EFFORTS TO SYSTEMATIZE REGULATIONS

The most important effort to confront problems related to conflicts of interest in international arbitration was the publication of the IBA Guidelines on Conflicts of Interest in International Arbitration of 2004 (amended in 2014) (IBA Guidelines). A working group drafted the IBA Guidelines at the request of the IBA Arbitration and ADR Committee.[79] The IBA Guidelines set arbitrary limitation periods for different types of potential conflicts. For example, disclosures listed in the orange list expire after three years.[80] The IBA Guidelines are not comprehensive in that they do not cover all circumstances that may give rise to conflicts of interest.[81]

In another effort to define conflicts of interest, the International Chamber of Commerce (ICC) published three reports containing summaries of its challenge decisions. The summaries disclose the decisions but not the reasons for the decisions. The 1991 Bond Report revealed the outcome of objections or challenges in specific situations or scenarios.[82] The 1995 Hascher Report focused on a number of examples, grouped in paragraphs that made it difficult to distinguish particular cases.[83] Finally, the 2008 Whitesell Report contains case summaries that make it possible to organize the data and patterns reflecting the actual situations that arise regarding conflicts, but without the full detail needed to permit a deeper understanding of the cases.[84]

The ICC published the "Note to Parties and Arbitral Tribunals on the Conduct of the Arbitration," which went into effect on January 1, 2019. The note provides detailed guidance on the 2017 ICC Arbitration Rules, including on the issue of independence and impartiality of arbitrators. Paragraph 23 of the note establishes a nonexhaustive list of circumstances that affect the independence and impartiality of the arbitrator.

The London Court of International Arbitration (LCIA) published "sanitized" digests of its challenge decisions, together with commentary summarizing their highlights by Thomas Walsh and Ruth Teitelbaum. These digests are unique because they take the form of reasoned written opinions.[85] Despite the digests' significance as a source on conflicts of interest, they are limited

---

[77] See, e.g., Park, supra note 6, at 677.
[78] See M. Scott Donahey, *The Independence and Neutrality of Arbitrators*, 4 JOURNAL OF INTERNATIONAL ARBITRATION 31, 38 (1992).
[79] See Otto De Witt Wijnen, Nathalie Voser, & Neomi Rao, *Background Information on the IBA Guidelines on Conflicts of Interest in International Arbitration*, 5 BUSINESS LAW INTERNATIONAL 433, 436 (2004).
[80] See, e.g., Trakman, supra note 16, at 360.
[81] See Edna Sussman, *Ethics in International Arbitration: Soft Law Guidance for Arbitrators and Party Representatives*, in 248 SOFT LAW IN INTERNATIONAL ARBITRATION (Lawrence W. Newman & Michael J. Radine eds., 2014).
[82] See James H. Carter, *Reaching Consensus on Arbitrator Conflicts: The Way Forward*, 6 DISPUTE RESOLUTION JOURNAL 17, 21–23 (2012).
[83] Id.
[84] Id.
[85] See, e.g., Carter, supra note. 82, at 24–25. See Margaret L. Moses, *Reasoned Decisions in Arbitrator Challenges*, 3 YEARBOOK ON INTERNATIONAL ARBITRATION 199, 205–206 (2013) ("The LCIA reasoned decisions make a strong contribution to the transparency needed to promote confidence in the arbitral process.").

because English law was the only applicable law. It is important that arbitral associations publish more materials in this area. This information is vital for "parties in determining their future actions both with regard to selecting arbitrators and deciding whether to challenge an arbitrator. It can also be useful to arbitrators in knowing when they should refuse to accept an appointment, what kinds of information they should disclose, and what kind of conduct is expected from them while serving as an arbitrator."[86]

The Indian Arbitration and Conciliation (Amendment) Act proves an interesting example of guidance as to what constitutes conflict of interest or an appearance of a conflict. It lists thirty-four grounds that can give rise to justifiable doubts as to the independence or impartiality of arbitrators and provides explanations on the application of these grounds.[87] The thirty-four grounds are categorized into seven subject areas: (1) arbitrator's relationship with the parties or counsel, (2) relationship of the arbitrator to the dispute, (3) arbitrator's direct or indirect interest in the dispute, (4) previous services for one of the parties or other involvement in the case, (5) relationship between an arbitrator and another arbitrator or counsel, (6) relationship between arbitrator and party and others involved in the arbitration, and (7) other circumstances. These amendments to India's arbitration law, influenced by the Part 2 of the IBA Guidelines, represents the most extensive promulgation regulation of grounds to challenge to the independence and impartiality of the arbitrator in the world.

The United Arab Emirates' Penal Code makes it a crime to violate the duty of "integrity and impartiality":[88]

> Any person who issues a decision, gives an opinion, submits a report, addresses a case or proves an incident for the benefit or against a person, failing to maintain the requirements of integrity and impartiality, in his capacity as an *arbitrator*, expert, translator or fact finder, appointed by administrative or judicial authority or selected by parties, shall be sentenced to temporary imprisonment.[89]

Obviously, this rule has aroused concern in the arbitration community and may deter arbitrators from accepting appointments in the UAE. Fortunately, in October 2018, the United Arab Emirates amended its Penal Code, with the new wording that removes the word *arbitrator* from the quoted provision.[90]

7 NEED TO SET LIMITS

It is necessary to put limits on the requirements for arbitrators' independence and impartiality in order to avoid challenges that seek only to delay arbitral proceedings[91] or overturn a legitimate

---

[86] Id.
[87] Explanation 1 of the amendments to Section 12 of the 1996 Act (2015).
[88] Federal Law No. 7/2016, with effect from Oct. 29, 2016, amendment to article 257 of the United Arab Emirates' Penal Code.
[89] Articles 28 and 68 of the United Arab Emirates' Penal Code define "temporary imprisonment" for a term between three and fifteen years (emphasis added).
[90] The amendment also reduces the penalty from three to five years in prison to one to five years. However, any prison term is draconian if applied to arbitrators.
[91] See Mark Baker & Lucy Greenwood, *Are Challenges Overused in International Arbitration?*, 2 JOURNAL OF INTERNATIONAL ARBITRATION 101, 101–102 (2013), states that

> Challenges are freely available under most arbitration laws and rules and, increasingly, parties are availing themselves of these procedures. Challenges do not require significant briefing, therefore are not a particularly onerous or expensive undertaking for a party and they can either 'succeed', in which case the offending individual (usually an arbitrator, but on occasion counsel or expert witness) is removed, or 'fail' in which case

award. The next sections will discuss the distinction between necessary disclosures and excessive disclosure.

7.1 Scope of Possible Relationships

As previously noted, a standard of absolute independence or impartiality is impractical given the nature of the arbitration communities. Such arbitrators would reside in Thomas More's *Utopia*. According to his story, neighboring countries would borrow Utopian magistrates to lead them:

> In this they seem to have fallen upon a very good expedient for their own happiness and safety; for since the good or ill condition of a nation depends so much upon their magistrates, they could not have made a better choice than by pitching on men whom no advantages can bias; for wealth is of no use to them, since they must so soon go back to their own country, and they, being strangers among them, are not engaged in any of their heats or animosities.[92]

Arbitrators are not humans isolated in some strange land disconnected from the world. Given the tightness of the arbitration community and the ubiquitous nature of social media, it is increasingly easy to make alleged connections between the arbitrator and the parties. Social media tools such as Facebook, Twitter, Instagram, and LinkedIn or, in China, Tencent QQ, Sina Weibo, and WeChat, create virtual relationships.[93]

The first principle of the IBA International Principles on Social Media Conduct for the Legal Profession, states that:

> Social media creates a context in which lawyers may form visible links to clients, judges and other lawyers. Before entering into an online 'relationship', lawyers should reflect upon the professional implications of being linked publicly. Comments and content posted online ought to project the same professional independence and the appearance of independence that is required in practice.

The theory of "six degrees of separation" underlies the mechanics and success of social networks. The theory hypothesizes that everyone in the world is connected to every other person through a chain of acquaintances that has no more than five intermediaries.[94] First, numerous persons participate in the network. Second, there is at least one relationship between persons on the network. Third, there is an assumption of nonrandomness or locality. This condition is

---

the individual stays on. In both cases, the arbitration is disrupted. In short, challenges can be a cost-effective way to ensure an expensive delay.

[92] THOMAS MORE, UTOPIA 66 (2017) (1516).
[93] "With the rapid development of communications technology and the ever-expanding role of social media, there is now an unprecedented number of channels for arbitration practitioners to advertise their skills and express their views in real time, with the potential to reach an extremely large audience. Social media also threatens to blur the line between private and public information." See Loretta Malintoppi & Alvin Yap, *Challenges of Arbitrators in Investment Arbitration: Still Work in Progress?*, in 180 ARBITRATION UNDER INTERNATIONAL INVESTMENT AGREEMENTS: A GUIDE TO THE KEY ISSUES (Katia Yannaca-Small ed., 2018). Similarly, Ruth V. Glick & Laura J. Stipanowich, *Arbitrator Disclosure in the Internet Age*, Feb.–Apr. DISPUTE RESOLUTION JOURNAL 1–7, 6 (2012), ("The Internet is a powerful game changer in regard to arbitrator disclosure. Arbitrators should monitor information that is available about them on the Internet, and control the information they post online, especially on social media sites.")
[94] See JURE LESKOVEC, ANAND RAJARAMAN, & JEFF ULLMAN, MINING OF MASSIVE DATASETS 356 (2014). Hungarian author Frigyes Karinthy proposed this theory in 1929. See also, ALBERT-LÁSZLÓ BARABÁSI, LINKED: THE NEW SCIENCES OF NETWORKS 26 (2002).

the hardest to formalize, but the intuition is that relationships tend to cluster. If person A has a connection to B and C, then there is a higher probability than average that B and C are related. Facebook has lowered the degree of separation to 3.57![95] An example where this theory is used is found in the ICSID case of *Suez, Sociedad General de Aguas de Barcelona S.A., and Vivendi Universal S.A. v. The Argentine Republic*.[96] The proposal for the disqualification of a member of the arbitral tribunal refers to the six degrees of separation theory stating that: "While the validity of this theory certainly remains to be proven, its application does demonstrate how easily one may make connections between one person and another through the process of identifying real or alleged links."

An example of an arbitrator who was challenged based on a virtual relationship is found in the ICSID case of *Fábrica de Vidrios Los Andes v. Venezuela*.[97] Venezuela challenged the arbitrator based on a posting of the arbitrator's assistant that stated the assistant "has been working since August 2013 until the present day as an attorney in the international arbitration practice of the law firm Norton Rose Fulbright LLP." On that basis, Venezuela complained that the law firm (not counsel in the arbitration) would have access to the assistant's files. The two unchallenged arbitrators said that:

> a serious question would arise concerning the integrity of the information exchanged in these proceedings as it would have to be assumed that a law firm, which is not a counsel of record in this case, was able to access the record of the arbitration through the employment of [Assistant] and her access to the Box folder would arise over the integrity of the proceedings if Venezuela's assertions were true.

The two unchallenged arbitrators ruled that Venezuela had a legitimate interest in receiving more information on this relationship. After further inquiry found the assistant was not a member of the law firm; the assistant's "original LinkedIn profile was inaccurate." The two unchallenged arbitrators accepted the arbitrator's explanation and rejected Venezuela's challenge on that basis. In sum, the mere fact of the connection or "friendship" established through these social networks does not constitute a per se conflict of interest. The IBA Guidelines lists such a connection in its green list, stating that: "The arbitrator has a relationship with one of the parties or its affiliates through a social media network." However, the information contained in these social networks is useable to sustain, together with other evidence, a challenge against an arbitrator.[98]

---

[95] In this sense, Ruggero G. Pensa, Gianpiero Di Blasi, & Livio Bioglio, *Network-Aware Privacy Risk Estimation in Online Social Networks*, 9 SOCIAL NETWORK ANALYSIS AND MINING 1, 1 (2019):

> Online social networks are permeating most aspects of our life. More than two billions active social accounts are producing petabytes of behavioral and interaction data daily. At the same time, the famous "six degrees of separation" theory has been far exceed in Facebook, where an average degree of 3.57. This massive interconnectiv[ity] intrinsically exposes social network users to the risk of privacy leakage.

[96] Suez, Sociedad General de Aguas de Barcelona S.A. and InterAguas Servicios Integrales del Agua S.A. v. The Argentine Republic, ICSID Case No. ARB/03/17, Decision on a Second Proposal for the Disqualification of a Member of the Arbitral Tribunal, 18 (May 12, 2008), https://www.italaw.com/sites/default/files/case-documents/ita0812.pdf.

[97] Fábrica de Vidrios Los Andes v. Venezuela, ICSID Case No. ARB/ 12/ 21, Decision on the Proposal to disqualify L. Yves Fortier, Arbitrator (May 5, 2017), https://www.italaw.com/sites/default/files/case-documents/italaw8815.pdf.

[98] *See, e.g.*, Malintoppi & Yap, *supra* note 94, at 181, which states that: "[The] members of the arbitration community should be mindful that the information uploaded on social media profiles may be used against them or others."

7.2 Model Proposal

Potential conflicts of interest are detectable using the following steps:[99] (1) Determine the circumstance that gave rise to justifiable doubts as to the arbitrator's impartiality or independence. Being able to use for this, practical factors of analysis, such as the IBA Guidelines.[100] (2) Verify that the existence of such a circumstance (evidence).[101] (3) Determine whether the conflict is partial and whether it presents sufficient relevance or is an insignificant link[102] or de minimis.[103] For this purpose, the absence of independence or impartiality should always be viewed in conjunction with specific circumstances.[104] (4) Once it has been established that the partiality or dependence is sufficiently relevant, the challenge to the arbitrator must be weighed.

A beneficial amendment to the UNCITRAL Model Law would be to grant a margin of discretion to national courts to decide annulment of awards, to avoid defeating the object and purpose of the remedy or erode the binding force and finality of the award. Article 52(3) of ICSID Convention adopts such a rule.[105] This amendment to the UNCITRAL Model Law would encourage similar amendment of national arbitration laws. Such a margin of discretion would allow annulment if a conflict of interest affected, inter alia, the decision making of the arbitral tribunal.[106] It would also allow for a rejection of the annulment request, notwithstanding

---

[99] Which is consistent with the nature of the principle of independence and impartiality of the arbitrator (see 2.1.3.) and, therefore, its application in a particular case creates an argumentative problem, for whose resolution it becomes useful to distinguish various phases or steps. Similarly, MANUEL ATIENZA, CURSO DE ARGUMENTACIÓN JURÍDICA 647 (2013).

[100] See Carlos A. Matheus López, *Independence and Impartiality of Arbitrators: A Comparative Perspective*, in 120–123 CHINA AND INTERNATIONAL COMMERCIAL DISPUTE RESOLUTION (Qiao Liu & Wenhua Shan eds., 2016).

[101] One might do this using burden of proof rules.

[102] See also, Jan Havlíček, *The Partiality of Arbitrators*, in 147 CZECH (& CENTRAL EUROPEAN) YEARBOOK OF ARBITRATION (Alexander J. Bělohlávek, Naděžda Rozehnalová, & Filip Černý eds., 2014).

[103] See MATHEUS LÓPEZ, supra note 70, at 25–26 (better understanding of the issue in the ICSID Jurisprudence); CLEIS, supra note 4, at 20–21.

[104] See Alexander J. Bělohlávek, *Subjective and Objective Impartiality of Arbitrators and Appointing Authorities as a Part of Procedural Public Policy (Ordre Public)*, in 58 CZECH (& CENTRAL EUROPEAN) YEARBOOK OF ARBITRATION (Alexander J. Bělohlávek, Naděžda Rozehnalová, & Filip Černý eds., 2014).

[105] See Nicolás E. Lozada Pimiento, *El Mecanismo de Anulación de los Laudos Arbitrales del CIADI: Qué es y Para Dónde va*, 55 REVISTA DE DERECHO PRIVADO 1, 12 (2016) ("The ad hoc Committee could refrain from annulling the award provided that, despite the existence of the grounds invoked, the integrity of the arbitration procedure has not been substantially compromised. The ad hoc Committee, therefore, would have the discretion to decide if it is necessary or not to annul the award and would only be obliged to do so when the annulment was the remedy that, according to the circumstances, would be required to safeguard the due process of the parties."). See also Maritime International Nominees Establishment v. Republic of Guinea, ICSID Case No. ARB/84/4, Decision on the Application by Guinea for Partial Annulment of the Arbitral Award Jan. 6, 1988, para. 4.10, in which the ad hoc committee states that: "An ad hoc Committee retains a measure of discretion in ruling on applications for annulment. Its discretion ... should not be exercised to defeat the object and purpose of the remedy of annulment. [However, refusal] to exercise its authority to annul an award [is warranted] when the remedy[ing of] procedural injustice [would] unjustifiably erode the binding force and finality of ICSID awards." Similarly EDF International S.A., SAUR International S.A. and León Participaciones Argentinas S.A. v. Argentine Republic, ICSID Case No. ARB/03/23, Decision on Annulment Feb. 5, 2016, para. 73, in which the ad hoc committee states that:

> The Committee concludes that, even if an Article 52(1) ground is made out, it nevertheless retains a discretion as to whether or not to annul the award. Its discretion [does not] mean unlimited and must take account of all relevant circumstances, including the gravity of the circumstances which constitute the ground for annulment and whether or not they had – or could have had – a material effect upon the outcome of the case, as well as the importance of the finality of the award and the overall question of fairness to both Parties.

[106] The de lege ferenda proposal would constitute an additional fifth step to the proposed model.

the partiality or dependence of the arbitrator in cases where the award is unanimously approved by the other arbitrators.[107]

8 CRITERIA TO CHALLENGE AN ARBITRATOR

In assessing the strength of a prospective challenge to an arbitrator, certain factors or criteria need to be analyzed. First, review of the arbitrator's curriculum vitae and disclosures. Facts disclosed by the arbitrator could evidence circumstances that may affect the arbitrator's independence and impartiality. Likewise, the arbitrator's curriculum vitae may reveal professional, academic, and business ties that could lead to the arbitrator's disqualification. If, after consideration of the arbitrator's curriculum vitae, it arises that one of the arbitrator's clients is a company associated to one of the parties to the dispute, this could lead to the arbitrator's disqualification. Second, an investigation of the arbitrator's family and personal connections should be undertaken. The arbitrator's family and friendship ties are often discoverable by reviewing the arbitrator's disclosures and curriculum vitae as well as by word of mouth and performing internet searches.

Due diligence in finding conflicts of interest includes inquiring about the arbitrator's reputation in the profession (word of mouth). Counsels and parties in previous cases are a good source of information. It is useful to verify the previous arbitral awards written by the arbitrator. It is also worth checking the arbitrator's media postings and academic opinions. If the parties or advisers hear through word of mouth that the arbitrator is a friend of the counsel or of one of the parties, one should investigate the length, frequency, and quality of the contacts to determine if this circumstance could lead to his or her disqualification.

Review the arbitrator's previous arbitrations, including any previous disclosures, relating to the arbitrator's previous appointments by the same party to determine, among other things, if the appointments indicate economic dependence between the arbitrator and the party. Review the published awards of the arbitrator. Finally, analyze the arbitrator's past books, articles and other publications, and speeches. The arbitrator's curriculum vitae lists these items. Follow up internet searches can uncover items not listed in the curriculum vitae. Opinions and positions taken in these materials that are relevant to the current dispute could lead to his or her disqualification.

---

[107] See Compañía de Aguas del Aconquija S.A. and Vivendi Universal S.A. v. Argentine Republic (ICSID Case No. ARB/97/3) (Annulment Proceeding), Decision on the Argentine Republic's Request for Annulment of the Award rendered on Aug. 20, 2007 10 August 2010, Para. 232–39. *See* Matheus López, *supra* note 70, at 223–227.

3

Exploring the Parameters of Conflicts of Interest

Nathalie M-P Potin and Tunde Ogunseitan

1 INTRODUCTION

As arbitration specialists (arbitrators and practicing lawyers) build their credentials, their paths often cross in scholarship, conferences, and arbitral proceedings. Depending on their relationships with one another, both professional and personal, an appearance of impropriety (conflict of interest) may appear. This appearance is often more an illusion than reality because to the uninitiated the arbitral process seems to be the domain of a secretive group of insiders. In fact, there is a high level of transparency in the selection of arbitrators. Required disclosures flesh out any potential conflict of interest between the arbitrators and the parties. Most arbitrators will voluntarily remove themselves from consideration in order to ensure their professional integrity in the arbitration community. This is especially the case when there are justifiable doubts as to their independence and impartiality. Also, parties may challenge the appointment or retention of an arbitrator in cases of apparent bias.

There is a clear lack of consensus in the arbitration community as to what constitutes conflicts. The first part of the chapter examines some of the current parameters of conflict of interest in international arbitration and how they affect the arbitration process. The second part focuses on the approaches to conflicts in two prominent jurisdictions – English and French courts. The third and final part of this chapter discusses current trends related to conflicts of interest, including attempts to establish a code of conduct for arbitrators and the relationship between third-party funding and conflicts of interest.

1.1 *Definition*

Black's Law Dictionary defines conflict of interest as "a real or seeming incompatibility between the interests of two of a lawyer's clients such that the lawyer is disqualified from representing both clients if the dual representation adversely affects either client or if the clients do not consent."[1] In the present context, the essence of an effective arbitration lies in the core belief in the impartiality and independent tribunal. The words *impartial* and *independent* are different and yet complementary constructs. The duty of independence consists of resisting pressure from any of the parties, including third parties, related to the dispute. The duty of impartiality imposes on the arbitrator the obligation to set aside personal biases and interests in order to apply

---

[1] GARNER BLACK'S LAW DICTIONARY 363 (Bryan A. Garner ed., 10th ed. 2014).

objective reasoning in making a decision.[2] In order to ensure the enforceability of arbitral awards, arbitral tribunals must be seen as independent and impartial, resulting in a fair process without procedural irregularities. Finally, the impartiality and independence are verified by pre-appointment disclosures. But there remains confusion relating to what type of information should be disclosed and what constitutes an appearance of a conflict of interest (requiring disclosure). These determinations can be a daunting task for the individual arbitrator in deciding what information to disclose.[3]

1.2 Soft Law to Regulate Independence and Impartiality

Countries have different standards of conflict of interest. To solve the problem of multiple standards of conflict of interest, the International Bar Association (IBA) published the IBA Guidelines on Conflicts of Interest in International Arbitration (IBA Guidelines)[4] to ensure uniformity and procedural fairness. The original 2004 IBA Guidelines were drafted by a working group of nineteen experts from fifteen countries, while the 2014 IBA Guidelines were drafted by an expanded Conflicts of Interest Subcommittee representing "diverse legal cultures and a range of perspectives including counsel, arbitrators and arbitration users."[5] The IBA Guidelines define what a conflict of interest entails.[6] These guidelines do not override any applicable national law or arbitral rules chosen by the parties.[7] It is the hope of the IBA that the guidelines be applied with "robust commonsense and without unduly formalistic interpretation."[8]

Various institutions have drafted model codes of ethics for arbitrators. For instance, the American Arbitration Association/American Bar Association (AAA/ABA) Code of Ethics for Arbitrators (Code) sets out "generally accepted" standards of "ethical conduct" for commercial disputes in the hope of contributing to "the maintenance of high standards and continued confidence in the process of arbitration."[9] The Code recognizes that arbitrators are drawn from a pool of industry experts as well as legal experts and that distinguishes them from judges. To that end, the Code establishes the principle that arbitrators should accept an appointment only "if fully satisfied"[10] that they can serve impartially and independently. Further, the Code notes

---

[2] D. M. Papayannis, *Independence, Impartiality and Neutrality in Legal Adjudication*, 28 Revus J. Const. Theory & Phil. Law 33 (2016), DOI: 10.4000/revus.3546.

[3] R. Merkin & L. Flannery, Arbitration Act 1996 87 (5th ed. 2014).

[4] International Bar Association, IBA Guidelines on Conflicts of Interest in International Arbitration (2014), https://www.ibanet.org/Document/Default.aspx?DocumentUid=e2fe5e72-eb14-4bba-b10d-d33dafee8918.

[5] *Id.* at ii.

[6] (a) An arbitrator shall decline to accept an appointment or, if the arbitration has already been commenced, refuse to continue to act as an arbitrator, if he or she has any doubt as to his or her ability to be impartial or independent. (b) The same principle applies if facts or circumstances exist, or have arisen since the appointment, which, from the point of view of a reasonable third person having knowledge of the relevant facts and circumstances, would give rise to justifiable doubts as to the arbitrator's impartiality or independence, unless the parties have accepted the arbitrator in accordance with the requirements set out in General Standard 4. (c) Doubts are justifiable if a reasonable third person, having knowledge of the relevant facts and circumstances, would reach the conclusion that there is a likelihood that the arbitrator may be influenced by factors other than the merits of the case as presented by the parties in reaching his or her decision. (d) Justifiable doubts necessarily exist as to the arbitrator's impartiality or independence in any of the situations described in the Non-Waivable Red List.

[7] *Id.* at 3.

[8] *Id.*

[9] AAA/ABA *Code of Ethics for Arbitrators* (2004), https://www.adr.org/sites/default/files/document_repository/Commercial_Code_of_Ethics_for_Arbitrators_2010_10_14.pdf.

[10] *Id.* at Canon I.

that a person should avoid "entering into any business, professional, or personal relationship, or acquiring any financial or personal interest, which is likely to affect impartiality or which might reasonably create the appearance of partiality."[11] Canon II sets out that an arbitrator should disclose "any interest or relationship likely to affect impartiality or which might create an appearance of partiality."[12] The Code takes a pragmatic approach to managing the conduct of arbitrators at the start and during the proceedings. Canon I restricts arbitrators' conduct after the case. Practitioners have attempted to get around the requirements of Canon I through the use of advance waivers.

At the international level, investor–state dispute settlement reform[13] is centered in the Working Group of the UNCITRAL, which works under the mandate that "in order to be considered effective, the ISDS framework should not only ensure actual impartiality and independence of arbitrators and decision makers, but also the appearance of those qualities."[14] The 2018 Proposed Amended ICSID Rules contemplate the inclusion of a future code of conduct.[15] Similarly,

---

[11] *Id.*

[12] A. Persons who are requested to serve as arbitrators should, before accepting, disclose: (1) any known direct or indirect financial or personal interest in the outcome of the arbitration; (2) any known existing or past financial, business, professional or personal relationships which might reasonably affect impartiality or lack of independence in the eyes of any of the parties. For example, prospective arbitrators should disclose any such relationships which they personally have with any party or its lawyer, with any co-arbitrator, or with any individual whom they have been told will be a witness. They should also disclose any such relationships involving their families or household members or their current employers, partners, or professional or business associates that can be ascertained by reasonable efforts; (3) the nature and extent of any prior knowledge they may have of the dispute; and (4) any other matters, relationships, or interests which they are obligated to disclose by the agreement of the parties, the rules or practices of an institution, or applicable law regulating arbitrator disclosure.

B. Persons who are requested to accept appointment as arbitrators should make a reasonable effort to inform themselves of any interests or relationships described in paragraph A.

C. The obligation to disclose interests or relationships described in paragraph A is a continuing duty which requires a person who accepts appointment as an arbitrator to disclose, as soon as practicable, at any stage of the arbitration, any such interests or relationships which may arise, or which are recalled or discovered.

D. Any doubt as to whether or not disclosure is to be made should be resolved in favor of disclosure.

E. Disclosure should be made to all parties unless other procedures for disclosure are provided in the agreement of the parties, applicable rules or practices of an institution, or by law. Where more than one arbitrator has been appointed, each should inform the others of all matters disclosed.

F. When parties, with knowledge of a person's interests and relationships, nevertheless desire that person to serve as an arbitrator, that person may properly serve.

Id. at Canon II.

[13] UN Commission on International Trade Law, *Draft Report of Working Group III (Investor-State Dispute Settlement Reform) on the Work of Its Thirty-Sixth Session* [advance copy], UN GENERAL ASSEMBLY (Nov. 6, 2018), https://uncitral.un.org/sites/uncitral.un.org/files/draft_report_of_wg_iii_for_the_website.pdf. UN Commission on International Trade Law Working Group III (ISDS Reform) Thirty-Eighth Session, *Possible Reform of Investor–State Dispute Settlement (ISDS), Background Information on a Code of Conduct: Note by the Secretariat*, UN GENERAL ASSEMBLY (July 31, 2019), https://undocs.org/en/A/CN.9/WG.III/WP.167.

[14] UN General Assembly, *Report of Working Group III (Investor-State Dispute Settlement Reform) on the Work of Its Thirty-Fifth Session (New York, 23–27 April 2018)*, A/CN.9/934, May 2018, see para. 53, https://documents-dds-ny.un.org/doc/UNDOC/GEN/V18/029/59/PDF/V1802959.pdf?OpenElement.

[15] International Centre for Settlement of Investment Disputes, *Proposals for Amendment of the ICSID Rules – Working Paper*, Volume 3, ICSID Secretariat, Aug. 2018, at para. 298, p. 148, https://icsid.worldbank.org/en/Documents/Amendments_Vol_Three.pdf. This approach is preferable because it has the potential to memorialize a uniform set of ethical expectations for ISDS generally. Once final, this code of conduct should be attached to the Arbitrator Declaration in Schedule 2. International Centre for Settlement of Investment Disputes, *Proposals for Amendment of the ICSID Rules – Working Paper*, Volume 4, ICSID Secretariat, Feb. 2020, https://icsid.worldbank.org/en/Documents/WP_4_Vol_1_En.pdf; see discussions about code of conduct in relation to Arbitration Rule 19 at 293 and 299.

countries have worked on codes of conduct relating to dispute resolution in Free Trade Agreements.[16] Codes of conduct provide standards for how arbitrators conduct themselves, their duties in managing arbitral proceedings, and the disclosure of their obligations. Most codes offer a single remedy – replacement of the arbitrator on demand of one of the parties. Whether other remedies or sanctions should be made available against arbitrator malfeasance will be discussed later in this chapter.[17]

1.3 Disclosures under the IBA Guidelines and Consequences of Breach of Duty to Disclose

Arbitrators are required to provide all relevant information to the parties and the arbitration association in order to allow them to assess the suitability of the arbitrator for a particular dispute, safeguard arbitrators against possible subsequent challenge, and stimulate transparency and confidence in the arbitration process.[18] Among other sanctioning instruments, the breach of the duty of disclosure on the part of the arbitrator may lead to an annulment of the award.[19]

Part I of the IBA Guidelines sets out standards regarding independence,[20] impartiality, and disclosure and aims to address specific situations that might or might not indicate potential conflicts of interest with a color-coded system (Non-Waivable Red List,[21] Waivable Red List, Orange List,[22] and Green List[23]). The guidelines aim to enumerate relations and scenarios that

---

[16] See, for instance, the European Union-Singapore Free Trade Agreement (Annex 15-B, Code of Conduct for Arbitrators and Mediators, version as of May 2015) and Canada-European Union Comprehensive Economic Trade Agreement (CETA) (Annex 29-B, Code of Conduct for Arbitrators and Mediators).

[17] See Part (c) Disclosures under the IBA Guidelines and Consequences of Breach of the Duty to Disclose.

[18] C. A. Rogers, *Regulating International Arbitrators: A Functional Approach to Developing Standards of Conduct*, 41 STANFORD J. INT'L. L., 53 (2005).

[19] Ch. Séraglini, *Droit du Commerce International*, in DROIT DU COMMERCE INTERNATIONAL 980–988 (J. Béguin & M. Menjuncq eds., 3d ed. 2005); Ph. Fouchard, *Le statut de l'arbitre dans la jurisprudence française*, 3 REVUE ARB. 364 (1996).

[20] The 1996 Arbitration Act does not require the independence for arbitrators.

[21] The Red List is a nonexhaustive enumeration of specific situations that give rise to justifiable doubts as to the arbitrator's impartiality and independence, including the following situations: no one is allowed to be his or her own judge where there is identity between an arbitrator and a party; where the arbitrator is a manager, director, or member of the supervisory board or has a controlling influence on one of the parties or an entity that has a direct economic interest in the award to be rendered in the arbitration; where the arbitrator has a significant financial or personal interest in one of the parties or the outcome of the case; or where the arbitrator or his or her firm regularly advises the party or an affiliate of the party and the arbitrator or his or her firm derives significant financial income therefrom. Examples of Non-Waivable Red List situations are (1) current representation by an arbitrator of one of the parties or its affiliate if the representation is "regular" and "that arbitrator or his or her firm derives a significant financial income therefrom"; (2) the arbitrator is a manager, director, or member of the supervisory board or has a controlling influence on one of the parties or an entity that has a direct economic interest in the award to be rendered in the arbitration; and (3) the arbitrator has a significant financial or personal interest in one of the parties or the outcome of the case. Waivable Red List situations cover the relationship of the arbitrator to the dispute, including (1) the arbitrator has given legal advice, or provided an expert opinion, on the dispute to a party or an affiliate of one of the parties; (2) the arbitrator had a prior involvement in the dispute; (3) the arbitrator has direct or indirect interest in the dispute where the arbitrator holds shares, either directly or indirectly, in one of the parties or is an affiliate of one of the parties, this party, or an affiliate being privately held; and (4) the arbitrator is a close family member of one of the parties or has a significant financial interest in the outcome of the dispute.

[22] The Orange List is a nonexhaustive enumeration of specific situations, which in the eyes of the parties may give rise to justifiable doubts as to the arbitrators' impartiality or independence. Orange List situations are generally not subject to disclosure.

[23] The Green List contains situations where no appearance of (actual) conflict of interest arises from objective points of view. Green List situations are not subject to disclosure either.

constitute justifiable doubts as to the arbitrator's impartiality or independence. Such situations impose an ethical obligation on the arbitrator to disclose relevant information.[24]

However, the standard of bias applies before and after the appointment of an arbitrator. Thus the principle of disclosure applies if facts or circumstances exist or have arisen since the appointment that give rise to justifiable doubts as to the arbitrator's impartiality, from the perspective of a reasonable third person (objective test).[25] Doubts are justifiable if a reasonable person, having knowledge of the relevant facts and circumstances, would reach the conclusion that there is a likelihood that the arbitrator will be influenced by factors other than the merits of the case.[26] The arbitrator shall disclose such facts or circumstances to the parties, arbitration institution, and co-arbitrators prior to accepting the appointment or, if thereafter, as soon as the arbitrator learns of the new information. However, it is to be noted that the disclosure does not, by itself, imply the existence of a conflict of interest.[27] Arbitrators have an ongoing duty to disclose any conflict of interest.[28] However, attempts have been made to mollify the harm of partial disclosures in order diminish negative reputational effects on the arbitration process.[29]

Arbitrators in disclosing information may state that they are impartial and independent of the parties, despite the disclosed facts; would have declined the nomination if the new information had been known at that time; or resign.[30] Arbitrators are expected to make reasonable enquiries to investigate any potential conflict of interests. Failure to disclose a conflict is not excused by lack of knowledge, if the arbitrator failed to perform reasonable enquiries.

The IBA Guidelines merely provide guidance; they do not impose obligations and are not meant to be exhaustive in coverage. Although they are widely recognized, their application has been affected by regional and cultural differences. Potential arbitrators can follow IBA Guidelines but they are responsible and alone. Is it enough? It seems that more needs to be done. But what should be done?

What good is a code without consequence? The writers believe that there must be consequence given the implications to the parties in terms of time and expenditure when arbitrators

---

[24] This is mentioned in the Explanation to General Standard 2, clarifying that an arbitrator shall decline to accept an appointment or, if the arbitration has already commenced, refuse to continue to act as an arbitrator if he or she has any doubt as to his or her ability to be impartial or independent. See IBA Guidelines, supra note 4, at 5–6.

[25] General Standard 2 of the IBA Guidelines, supra note 4, at 5. The test in section 24(1)(a) is an objective one and was approved by the House of Lords in Porter v. Magill (2002) 2 AC 357. It was confirmed by the Court of Appeal in Locabail (UK) Ltd. v. Bayfield Properties Ltd. (1999) EWCA Civ 3004 and in AT&T Corporation v. Saudi Cable Co. (2000) EWCA Civ 154 that the test applies to arbitrators as well as to judges. The common law test for apparent bias is reflected in section 24 of the Arbitration Act 1996.

[26] General Standard 2 of the IBA Guidelines, supra note 4, at 6.

[27] Id. at 8.

[28] For instance, Article 12(1) UNCITRAL Arbitration Rules of 2013:

Any arbitrator may be challenged if circumstances exist that give rise to justifiable doubts as to the arbitrator's impartiality or independence; Article 14(1) of ICC Rules of 2014: A challenge of an arbitrator, whether for an alleged lack of impartiality or independence, or otherwise, shall be made by the submission to the Secretariat of a written statement specifying the facts and circumstances on which the challenge is based.

Article 1456, para. 2 of the French Code of Civil Procedure requires arbitrators to disclose all circumstances that may give rise to reasonable doubt regarding their independence or impartiality. In England, section 24 of the 1996 Arbitration Act provides that the court has power to remove an arbitrator on the grounds: "(1)(a) that circumstances exist that give rise to justifiable doubts as to his impartiality" and section 33 of the Act imposes a duty on arbitrators to "act fairly and impartially as between the parties."

[29] See the trend in investment arbitration, A. Roberts & Z. Bouraoui, UNCITRAL and ISDS Reforms: Concerns about Arbitral Appointments, Incentives and Legitimacy, EJIL: TALK! (June 6, 2018), https://www.ejiltalk.org/uncitral-and-isds-reforms-concerns-about-arbitral-appointments-incentives-and-legitimacy.

[30] Id.

have been found to be in breach of simple disclosure obligations or there is a risk of bias. In real terms, there is already a sanctions regime in place. Arbitration is a business where the reputation of the arbitrator is linked to his success. It has become very transparent with cases previously though independent becoming headline news once there is anything of interest to be discussed. The standards for independence and impartiality are individually determined, each arbitrator having to assess them conscientiously, and there is a subjective element relating to the parties' perspective of what are acceptable conflicts.[31] The IBA has done what it is able to in the face of the regional and cultural differences. Given the soft law nature of the guidelines and the uncertain consequences if they are violated, agreement needs to be reached as to the penalties or remedies applicable when arbitrators have been found to be in breach of disclosure obligations or there is a risk of bias. In real terms, the most powerful effect of violations is damage to the reputation of the arbitrator. An arbitrator's reputation is vital to acquiring future appointments.

In institutional arbitration, the coercive aspect of improper or partial disclosure is apparent. Arbitration institutions will usually not confirm arbitrators who do not fully disclose pertinent information in order to protect the integrity of the proceedings. If it becomes apparent that an arbitrator has failed to disclose potential conflicts, the parties have recourse to challenge the arbitrator and have him or her removed and replaced.[32] This is the substance of the current debate and awaited judgment of the UK Supreme Court *Halliburton Company* v. *Chubb Bermuda Insurance Ltd.*[33] The final step of the sanctions regime is arbitrator misconduct (nondisclosure), which is a ground for courts to set aside the award.[34] In ad hoc arbitration, this system is even more complex. First, courts enforcing an award use their own local rules to determine whether to set it aside an award. Secondly, courts will construe what constitutes arbitrator misconduct differently.

In order to avoid different outcomes involving similar fact patterns, a harmonization of the concept of disclosure is needed at the international level. However, an international agreement of the requirements of disclosure and the resulting consequences is likely to be both broad and rigid. Such a system is antithetical to arbitration, which is supposed to be highly flexible, private, and based upon the autonomy of the parties. Parties' autonomy, which is a core element of arbitration, might be ultimately compromised while seeking clarity on who can sit on the cases the parties want to bring. Cases and arbitration practice involving arbitral institutions and courts (relating to annulment of awards) show that the Guidelines have attained significant prestige, making them something more than a simple guide.[35] The next two parts of this chapter examine the English and French approaches to these issues.

---

[31] J. Fry & S. Greenberg, *The Arbitral Tribunal: Applications of Articles 7–12 of the ICC Rules in Recent Cases*, 20 ICC Int'l Arb. Bull. 18 (2009).
[32] *See* Articles 14 and 15 of ICC Arbitration Rules.
[33] Halliburton Company (Appellant) v. Chubb Bermuda Insurance Ltd (Formerly known as Ace Bermuda Insurance Ltd) (Respondent) (2018), https://www.supremecourt.uk/cases/uksc-2018-0100.html.
[34] *See* Section 68 of the 1996 Arbitration Act and Article 1520 French Code of Civil Procedure.
[35] *See, e.g.,* E. Rushton, *England and Wales: Hidden Conflicts in Arbitration – W Limited v M SDN BHD*, Ins. Bull., Apr. 22, 2016, at 4–5. Mr. Justice Knowles noted that:

> It would be possible simply to say that the 2014 IBA Guidelines are not a statement of English law and then not enter into any examination of them. However, the present arbitration is international, and parties often choose English Law in an international context. Thus, the role of this Court has an international dimension. I therefore prefer to consider the 2014 IBA Guidelines, as I have done, and explain why I do not, with respect, think they can yet be correct.

EWHC 422 (Comm) (2016), https://www.bailii.org/ew/cases/EWHC/Comm/2016/422.html.

2 ENGLISH COURTS' PERSPECTIVE

There has been a long string of English court decisions dealing with conflicts of interest, tracing back to the 1993 case of *Regina v. Gough*,[36] which provided guidance on dealing with the bias of jury members. The House of Lords set out the test for bias – whether there was a "real danger" that the defendant had been denied a fair trial.

Lord Woolf stated:

> When considering whether there is a real danger of injustice, the court gives effect to the maxim, but does so by examining all the material available and giving its conclusion on that material. If the court having done so is satisfied there is no danger of the alleged bias having created injustice, then the application to quash the decision should be dismissed. (...) that there was no danger of the justices' decision being contaminated by the possible bias of the clerk.[37]

Lord Goff of Chieveley argued that the standard should be applied to bias in arbitration cases: "it [is] possible, and desirable, that the same test should be applicable in all cases of apparent bias, whether concerned with justices or members of other inferior tribunals, or with jurors, or with arbitrators."[38] Interestingly, Lord Goff poses a variation of the reasonable person standard in that the construction of a reasonable person was not necessary: "because the court in cases such as these personifies the reasonable [person]; and in any event the court has first to ascertain the relevant circumstances from the available evidence, knowledge of which would not necessarily be available to an observer in court at the relevant time."[39] Otherwise, Lord Goff preferred to state the test in terms of "real danger rather than real likelihood," to ensure that the court was thinking in "terms of possibility rather than probability of bias."[40] He suggested that the court should ask whether, "there was a real danger of bias on the part of the relevant member of the tribunal in question, in the sense that he might unfairly regard (or have unfairly regarded) with favour, or disfavour, the case of a party to the issue under consideration by him."[41]

In *Laker Airways Inc. v. FLS Aerospace Ltd & Anor*,[42] the Commercial Court dismissed a request to remove an arbitrator under section 24(1) a of the English Arbitration Act on the basis

---

[36] Regina v. Gough (1993) UKHL 1, https://www.bailii.org/uk/cases/UKHL/1993/1.html. Robert Brian Gough appealed on the ground of a risk of bias. The question arose whether the courts should conclude that, by reason of the presence of Mrs. Smith on the jury, there was such a possibility of bias on her part against the appellant that his conviction should be quashed. The Court of Appeal answered in the negative. Mr. Robert Brian Gough was convicted of robbery and sentenced to fifteen years of imprisonment. The prosecution contended that Robert Brian Gough (the appellant) and his brother David Stephen Gough had committed the robberies. During the trial, photographs of both brothers had been produced to the jury and retained by them. The defence case was based on the premise that David Stephen Gough was one of the robbers. It had transpired after the sentencing that a member of the jury was David Stephen Gough's next door neighbor. After sentence was passed, David Stephen Gough, who was then present in court for the first time, started shouting; and it was at this point that the juror, Mrs. Smith, recognized him. He in his turn informed the defence that one member of the jury was his neighbor. The judge was informed of this fact, but he decided that he was functus officio. However, the juror was later interviewed by the police and subsequently swore an affidavit indicating that when the juror (Mrs. Smith) began her service she did not recognize the name "Gough" as she knew her neighbor as "Steve." Similarly, she knew David's wife as "Elaine" during the two years that they had been her neighbors. The juror did not recognize David on the police photographs of the appellant during trial. The Court of Appeal revealed that differing criteria had been applied in the past when considering the question of bias: (1) whether there was a real danger of bias on the part of the person concerned or (2) whether a reasonable person might reasonably suspect bias on his part. The Court of Appeal applied the real danger test. The House of Lords dismissed the appeal.
[37] *Id.* at 17.
[38] *Id.* at 14.
[39] *Id.*
[40] *Id.*
[41] *Id.*
[42] Laker Airways Inc. v. FLS Aerospace Ltd & Anor (1999) CLC. 1124; (2000) 1 WLR 113.

of circumstances that existed giving rise to justifiable doubts as to the arbitrator's impartiality. The case involved the appointment of a barrister from One Essex Court. A new member of the arbitrator's chambers unknown to the arbitrator had already been consulted by the same party. The other disputing party brought a challenge against Mr Burnton from One Essex Court. At the time Mr Sullivan, who had recently joined One Essex Court, the set of chambers where Mr Burnton also practiced, had already been instructed in the dispute on behalf of FLS. As a new member in the Chambers, Mr Sullivan did not know and had not met Mr Burnton. The arbitrator argued that that barristers are self-employed and share only office space and clerks and that a Chinese wall was in place to prevent the passing of information or the holding of informal discussions within the chambers. The challenging party argued that: (1) "circumstances exist that give rise to justifiable doubts as to Mr Burnton's impartiality, the circumstances being that he practices at the Bar from the same set of Chambers as the advocate instructed in the arbitration and in parallel litigation on behalf of [the other party]";[43] (2) it is "unthinkable for two lawyers from the same firm to assume roles in the same matter where an actual or potential conflict of interest arises";[44] and that any award "could not be regarded as just, and the decision of such a tribunal would not be respected in the U.S. as rendered by a just and impartial tribunal."[45]

In rebuttal, the arbitrator provided a witness statement clarifying that: (1) "their rooms are in different buildings"; (2) they are served "different teams of clerks"; (3) "their documents are kept in different rooms"; (4) "they do not have access to each other's computers"; (5) "it is common for members of their chambers to appear on different sides in the same litigation, [which] is the case in all large set of commercial and specialist chambers"; (6) the "administrative staff is experienced in dealing with that situation and in ensuring that no misdelivery of documents or leakage of information"; and (7) "there had never been an incident in chambers of such misdelivery or leakage."[46]

Justice Rix reasoned that Section 24(1) of the Arbitration Act reflected the principles laid out in *Reg. v. Gough*:[47]

> whether circumstances exist that give rise to justifiable doubts as to an arbitrator's impartiality. The test is thus objective in at least two respects: the court must find that circumstances exist, and are not merely believed to exist (although I suppose that a belief may itself be a circumstance); and secondly, those circumstances must justify doubts as to impartiality. An unjustifiable or perhaps unreasonable doubt is not sufficient: it is not enough honestly to say that one has lost confidence in the arbitrator's impartiality. On the other hand, doubts, if justifiable, are sufficient: it is not necessary to prove actual bias.[48]

In sum, the three principles of *Reg. v. Gough* should be applied when considering bias: (1) actual bias always disqualifies, (2) the importance of public confidence is such that even the appearance of bias will disqualify, and (3) disqualification follows if there is real danger of bias.[49] Further, Justice Rix added that this objective test reflected the common law in England and also applies to

---

[43] *Id.* at 115.
[44] *Id.* at 116.
[45] *Id.*
[46] *Id.*
[47] He asserts that: "the test laid down in section 24 reflects the test in *Reg. v. Gough*. Plainly, if that test were met, there would be no need in any event to go on to ask whether there was actual bias. I would accept, however, that the three principles apply equally to arbitration, even though it might be said that only the third of them is expressly reflected in the wording of section 24(1)." *Id.* at 118.
[48] *Id.* at 117.
[49] Peter J. Rees QC, Judicial Decisions on Arbitrator Independence presented at the ICC Arbitration Day: Arbitrator Independence, Paris June 4, 2010, 5.

arbitration proceedings: "it would be strange if the test in arbitration were different from that which applies generally in the administration of justice."[50] In sum, actual bias is only one ground to challenge an arbitrator's impartiality, but it is not required to find a case of conflict of interest.

Since the challenging party made no allegation of actual bias, the challenge had to rest on an alternative ground – appearance of bias or real danger of bias. The court noted that a judge cannot be said "to be judge in his own cause because he knows the advocate, even if he knows him well, or shares or has shared tenure in the same set of chambers with him."[51] As a result, the court focused on the third ground or principle of whether there was real danger of bias or apparent bias, as expressed in the terms of Section 24(1).[52] For the purposes of section 24(1)(a), the challenging party needed to show that the organization of chambers would give rise to justifiable doubts about an arbitrator's impartiality because of the danger of accidental or improper dissemination of confidential information or there was a danger that the arbitrator and barrister would commit misconduct by discussing the case.[53] The court dismissed the challenge reasoning that the challenging party had not shown that there was a real risk of breach of confidentiality, that the arbitrator's judgment would be colored by familiarity, and that the chambers system was made of individual barristers with separate reputations who shared neither career nor remuneration.

In *Locabail (UK) Ltd v. Bayfield Properties Ltd*,[54] the Court of Appeal reaffirmed the "real danger of bias" standard set forth in *Reg. v. Gough*. This case was instructive in explaining where bias occurred and when disclosure should be made. The court considered if judges could or should disqualify themselves from sitting on grounds of bias. The case involved a deputy High Court judge - a partner in a firm of solicitors - who became aware that his firm was acting for clients in a litigation for the enforcement of financial claims and of bankruptcy against the partner's former spouse. He immediately disclosed that connection. Neither party raised any objection. The judgment was latter challenged on the grounds of bias because the judge should have disqualified himself from further involvement in the case. The judge concluded that his firm's relationship to one of the parties had not created a conflict of interest to warrant disqualification.

The Court of Appeal disagreed, reasoning that the judge had a direct personal interest, which was not *de minimis* in the outcome of the proceedings, and therefore, a presumption of bias existed. Second, the court held that where apparent bias was asserted, it was for the reviewing court, personifying the reasonable person with knowledge to assess whether there was a real danger of bias. The court would enquire whether the judge knew of the matter relied on as undermining his impartiality.[55] Lord Bingham held that:

> Provided that the court, personifying the reasonable man, takes an approach which is based on broad common sense, without inappropriate reliance on special knowledge, the minutia of court procedure or other matters outside the ken of ordinary, reasonably well informed member of the public, there should be no risk that the courts will not ensure both that justice is done and that it is perceived by the public to be done.[56]

---

[50] Laker Airways, *supra* note 41, at 113, 117.
[51] *Id.* at 119.
[52] *Id.* at 118.
[53] *Id.* at 124.
[54] In Locabail (UK) Ltd v. Bayfield Properties Ltd (2000) QB, 451., L and litigants in a number of joined cases, brought appeals claiming direct or potential partiality and bias on the part of the judges or tribunal chairmen in their respective cases. The court of appeal considered the various situations.
[55] *Id.*
[56] *Id.* at 477.

In another case, a recorder, a member of the bar specializing in personal injury cases, had made regular contributions to specialist literature and showed support for the claimants in obtaining damages. The court held where the judge had knowledge of his interest, he should recuse himself at the earliest possible stage. However, the terms in which the recorder had expressed views critical of the defendants and their insurers gave rise to the possibility that he was biased. The court concluded therefore that there was a real danger of bias, which required the court to set aside the judgment.[57] Finally, the court held that solicitors should conduct "careful conflict search" within their firms for any associations, discovered during the hearing, to be disclosed to the parties to assess whether a real danger of bias arose.

The court in *AT & T Corporation Lucent Technologies Inc v. Saudi Cable Company*[58] involved the revocation and removal of a chairman of an ICC tribunal and the setting aside of three partial awards in favor of the Saudi Cable Company (SCC). AT&T was unaware that the chairman was a nonexecutive director of a competitor company (Nortel).[59] Due to an administrative error, the chairman's curriculum vitae sent to the parties did not contain this information. The claimant challenged the chairman, complaining that he had failed to disclose important facts or circumstances, so as to call into question the chairman's independence in the eyes of the parties and that the nondisclosed information would have given rise to reasonable doubts as to the arbitrator's impartiality. The ICC court rejected the challenge without setting out its reasons.[60] Following the ICC's dismissal of its challenge, AT&T commenced legal proceedings[61] for the revocation and removal of the chairman's appointment and for the setting aside of the awards.

The court considered that "the actual evidence of unconscious bias was no more than [the chairman's] non-executive directorship and his small shareholding in Nortel." The court observed that "nothing that he had said or done in the arbitration proceedings had shown any bias of any kind." The judge rejected the submission that, "even if there were no ground for complaint in relation to the First Partial Award, [the chairman's] should have excused himself at the later stages when confidential information was ordered to be disclosed."[62] The court found that the chairman was not guilty of misconduct because of an error and the risk of "making disclosure of confidential information to Nortel, consciously or unconsciously, is sufficiently remote to be ignored."[63] Further, there was no actual bias as Nortel was not party to the proceedings. Also, the chairman was not a "judge of his own cause" and that bias was not established "by a large margin."[64] The court noted that AT&T's concern involved disclosure of confidential information to a nonexecutive director of a competitor rather than the independence of the chairman as an arbitrator.[65] Although the court agreed that there was a "persuasive" case that his nonexecutive directorship might be of such a nature as to call into question his

---

[57] *Id.* at 454.
[58] AT & T Corporation Lucent Technologies Inc v. Saudi Cable Company (2000) 2 Lloyd's Rep. 217, https://www.bailii.org/ew/cases/EWCA/Civ/2000/154.html.
[59] Nortel was not simply a commercial rival of AT&T in the field of telecommunications. It had also been a disappointed bidder for the contract out of which the disputes being arbitrated arose and could be a competitor for further contracts.
[60] At the time, the ICC did not communicate its reasons.
[61] Pursuant to Sections 1 and 23 of the Arbitration Act 1950.
[62] AT & T Corporation, *supra* note 57, at para. 30.4.
[63] *Id.* at para. 54.
[64] *Id.* at para. 75.
[65] *Id.*

independence "in the eyes of [one] of the parties," this was not enough to justify the revocation and removal of the chairman and the setting aside of the award.[66]

In *ASM Shipping Ltd v. TTMI Ltd England*,[67] ASM applied to the court under section 68 of the English Arbitration Act to have an interim award annulled on the grounds that Mr. Matthews QC should have recused himself due to his prior and recent involvement as an advocate in legal proceedings in which serious allegations were made against a key witness in the present arbitration.[68] Upon discovery of this fact, TTMI requested that Mr. Matthews QC recuse himself. He denied on the grounds that he had a limited involvement in the previous arbitration. Justice Morison refused to annul the award holding that ASM had waived its right to object. The court opined that "the independent observer would share the feeling of discomfort ... and concluded that there was a real possibility that the tribunal was biased."[69] As to Mr. Matthews QC's independence, Justice Morison observed:

> It is true that in specialist arbitrations prior contact between parties and their lawyers and arbitrators is to be expected. The mere fact, for example, that a person selected as arbitrator had previously had a trade dispute with one of the parties would not thereby have caused an objectionable situation. But even in such a case, much would depend on the facts: if the dispute had involved allegations of dishonesty of a similar nature to the allegations in the second arbitration, the position could well be different. Again, there would be no problem with a barrister sitting as an arbitrator in a case in which an expert witness whom he had previously cross-examined was to give evidence. But, again, if the contact had been a short time before, and allegations of dishonesty had been made, the position could be different. The Armageddon theory espoused by Mr Croall, were this application to succeed, is unreal. In this case there was a pattern of complaint amounting to dishonesty in relation to disclosure being made by the same solicitors in each case; and X QC had played a part in the B disclosure exercise 7 months before the arbitration. The nature of the allegations; the pattern of them; the involvement of the same solicitors; X QC's involvement in the disclosure process a short time before sitting as an arbitrator in judgment on the alleged dishonest party persuades me, for the reasons I have given that X QC should have recused himself after objection was taken.[70]

Justice Morison concluded that: "In my view, given the facts and conclusions I have stated, Mr. Matthews QC should not continue to act in this matter. I have not heard argument about the continuation of the other two arbitrators but would express the hope that they could continue."[71]

In a case involving the removal of the sole arbitrator in a challenge to a LCIA partial award, the arbitrator remained involved with a party connected to the arbitration in an unrelated litigation for a different client.[72] During the arbitration, the arbitrator remained instructed by Dewey & LeBoeuf in an unrelated litigation for a different client. The claimants argued that this relationship violated a Waivable Red List situation and was evidence of "unconscious bias" on the part of the arbitrator who failed to disclose the relationship until after the hearing but before the issuance of the award.[73] The court rejected the application and deemed that the case of

---

[66] *Id.*
[67] ASM Shipping Ltd v. TTMI Ltd England (2005) EWHC 2238 (Comm), https://www.bailii.org/ew/cases/EWHC/Comm/2005/2238.html.
[68] *Id.* at para. 12.
[69] *Id.* at para. 42.
[70] *Id.* at para. 43.
[71] *Id.* at para. 50.
[72] A and others v. B and another (2011) EWHC 2345 (Comm), https://www.bailii.org/ew/cases/EWHC/Comm/2011/2345.html.
[73] A and others v. B and another (2011) EWHC 2345 (Comm), para. 58.

unconscious bias was not proven.[74] It held that the arbitrator's failure to disclose his involvement until after the hearing could give rise to a real possibility of apparent or unconscious bias.[75] But the court refused to accept that a late disclosure was "a serious irregularity which caused substantial injustice to the Claimants within the meaning of section 68 of the Act."[76] The court rejected the argument that the arbitrator committed a "serious irregularity" within the meaning of section 68 of the Act.[77]

In 2016, English courts considered several cases of apparent bias. In *Cofely Ltd* v. *Anthony Bingham and Knowles*,[78] the parties were embroiled in a contract dispute. Cofely applied to remove Bingham as an arbitrator on the grounds that there were circumstances giving rise to justifiable doubts as to his impartiality. Cofely subsequently learned of Bingham's repeated appointments by Knowles – Bingham had acted as an arbitrator or adjudicator for twenty-five cases involving Knowles. Cofely relied on subsections 3.1.3 and 3.1.5 of the Orange List to show that there was an apparent bias. The High Court noted that while only three of the twenty-five cases involved Knowles as a party, this was sufficient to trigger disclosure pursuant to the Orange List. Eighteen percent of Bingham's arbitrator appointments and 25 percent of his income as an arbitrator over three years derived from cases involving Knowles. As such, the court ordered Bingham to be removed since Cofely established the requisite grounds for apparent bias.

In *W Ltd* v. *M Sdn Bhd*,[79] the Commercial Court entertained a challenge of two arbitral awards on the grounds of apparent bias on the part of the arbitrator. The claimant asserted that a serious irregularity caused injustice under section 68 of the Arbitration Act. The sole arbitrator was a partner in a law firm whose regular client included a company that, following an acquisition, had the same corporate parent as the defendant. The arbitrator's conflict check did not reveal that his firm regularly advised a subsidiary of the defendant. The sole arbitrator did not regularly advise the defendant or its subsidiary. The claimant argued that the conflict of interest fell within paragraph 1.4 of the Non-Waivable Red List.[80] Justice Knowles acknowledged that the arbitrator's law firm regularly advised an affiliate of the defendant and the arbitrator's firm derived substantial financial income from advising the affiliate, but held that "the fair minded and informed observer would not conclude that there was a real possibility that the [arbitrator] was biased or lack independence or impartiality."[81] It noted that the arbitrator had carried out a conflict check and had made all necessary disclosures. The court was satisfied that he "could not have been biased by reason of the firm's work for the client: that work was not his mind at all, if it had been, he would have disclosed it."[82]

The case is interesting since Justice Knowles dismissed the challenge despite the fact the situation was "fairly and squarely"[83] within the Non-Waivable Red List. The judge was critical of the IBA Guidelines arguing that where "the facts fit Paragraph 1.4 [IBA Guidelines] cause a party to be led to focus more on assumptions derived from that fact, and to focus less on a case-specific

---

[74] *Id.* at para. 70.
[75] *Id.* at para. 71.
[76] *Id.* at para. 89.
[77] *Id.* at para. 91.
[78] Cofely Ltd v. Anthony Bingham and Knowles (2016) EWHC 240 (Comm).
[79] W Ltd v. M Sdn Bhd (2016) EWHC 422 (Comm).
[80] Paragraph 1.4 of the Non-Waivable Red List of the 2014 IBA Guidelines states that "the arbitrator or his or her firm regularly advises the party, or an affiliate of the party, and the arbitrator or his or her firm derives significant financial income therefrom."
[81] W Ltd v. M Sdn Bhd (2016) 1 CLC 437, 445.
[82] *Id.* at 438.
[83] Nick Longley, *IBA Guidelines on Conflict of Interest: The Traffic Lights Flash Amber*, HOLMAN FENWICK WILLAN (Apr. 2016), http://www.hfw.com/IBA-guidelines-on-conflict-of-interest-April-2016.

judgement."[84] Even if he agreed that the facts in question fell within the Non-Waivable Red List, he held that the situation under consideration was "not near to the situation where a person is his or her own judge, or where there is identity between an arbitrator and a party."[85] The decision casts doubt on the guidelines[86] since the challenge was denied even though the situation fell within the Non-Waivable Red List.[87]

In *H v. L, M, N, P*,[88] the court considered a challenge to an arbitrator stemming from his repeat appointments by a party. H sought coverage from its insurance company, L, under a Bermuda form insurance policy with respect to a US judgment against H and two other companies, R and Q. After the insurance company's denial of insurance coverage, H commenced arbitration, and after the parties failed to agree on a third arbitrator, the High Court appointed M. H sought the removal of M after discovering that M accepted appointments in two other arbitrations in which R sought insurance coverage arising out of an incident involving the US judgment. In one of those arbitrations, M was appointed by the insurance company through Clyde & Co., who also served as L's solicitors in the *H v. L* arbitration. H relied on the guidelines to argue that pursuant to the Orange List, M should have disclosed his intention to accept the appointments. M took the position that while it did not occur to him that he was under any obligation to disclose, he in hindsight should have. Nevertheless, M did not see a conflict and attempted to assure H that he would remain independent and impartial. The High Court agreed with M, finding that the IBA Guidelines did not represent English law of apparent bias and that none of the grounds advanced by H gave rise to any justifiable doubts as to M's impartiality.

Cofely v. *Bingham* and *H* v. *L* were mentioned in *Aldcroft* v. *International Cotton Association Ltd*.[89] The International Cotton Association (ICA) serves as an association of companies and individuals involved in the trade of raw cotton, with 80 to 85 percent of international trade in raw cotton carried out in accordance with the ICA bylaws and rules. Aldcroft was a full-time arbitrator, who sued the ICA after the introduction of the "3 and 8" rule.[90] The ICA adopted that rule in response to perceptions that the arbitration process had a pro-merchant bias, particularly where merchants repeatedly selected the same arbitrator. Aldcroft argued that the ICA rule constituted a restraint of trade. The court examined the issue of repeat appointments in arbitration. Looking to the guidelines, the court acknowledged paragraphs 3.1.3 and 3.1.5 of the Orange List, which function similarly to the ICA's 3 and 8 rule. The court recognized the opposite outcomes in *Cofely* v. *Bingham* and *H* v. *L* as demonstrating the lack of a clear resolution of conflicts stemming from repeat appointments. The court dismissed Aldcroft's claims because the ICA rule was a reasonable mechanism that promoted the legitimate objectives of the ICA.

In *P* v. *Q*,[91] an English commercial court considered if an arbitral tribunal had improperly delegated its duties to the tribunal secretary. In this case, the chairman mistakenly sent an email intended for the tribunal secretary to the claimant. In that email, he asked the tribunal secretary: "Your reaction to this latest from the [claimant]?" The claimant then brought a challenge

---

[84] W Ltd, *supra* note 80, at 437, 444.
[85] *Id.* 445.
[86] Longley, *supra* note 82.
[87] *Id.*
[88] H v. L, M, N, P (2017) EWHC 137 (Comm).
[89] Aldcroft v. International Cotton Association Ltd. (2017) EWHC 642 (Comm).
[90] As such, in 2014, the ICA revised their arbitrators' code of conduct to provide "In order to avoid the perception of bias, impartiality or justifiable doubts, an arbitrator may only accept up to and including 3 appointments for a party or related party to act as arbitrator from a claimant/appellant or respondent, per calendar year. An arbitrator should not be able to have more than 8 active first tier cases open at any one time."
[91] P v. Q, R, S and U (2017) EWHC 194 (Comm).

seeking to have all three members of the tribunal removed on the basis, among others, of improper delegation to the secretary. The LCIA court heard the challenge and analyzed the time spent by the secretary and all arbitrators on three procedural decisions and determined that there had not been an improper delegation. The commercial court reached the same conclusion. It noted that the courts should be slow to deviate from the determination of the challenge by the LCIA court, which was the parties' chosen forum for the resolution of such challenges. Following the judgment, the LCIA changed its approach in relation to tribunal secretaries. A tribunal wishing to appoint a secretary is now required to outline the tasks to be conducted by the secretary and the parties must expressly consent to the tasks proposed.

Similarly, Russia sought an annulment at Hague District Court pertaining to the *Yukos* awards.[92] It argued the fact that the tribunal assistant had drafted the award was an improper delegation of authority.[93] According to the guidance published by various institutions on best practice for arbitrators and tribunal secretaries, challenges on the basis of improper delegation must show that the arbitrators delegated their decision making to a third party. The ICC Note on the Conduct of the Arbitration states: "Under no circumstances may the Arbitral Tribunal delegate decision-making functions to an Administrative Secretary. Nor should the Arbitral Tribunal rely on the Administrative Secretary to perform any essential duties of an arbitrator."[94]

Recently, the Court of Appeal revisited *H* v. *L* and addressed the repeat appointments issue. The 2018 case of *Halliburton Company* v. *Chubb Bermuda Insurance Ltd and others*[95] dealt with disclosure relating to overlapping references. Following the explosion on the *Deepwater Horizon* oil rig, the United States and individual claimants made numerous claims against BP (lessee of the rig), Transocean (owner of the rig), and Halliburton (cementing and well-monitoring services provider to BP). Following a liability trial in US federal court, Halliburton made a claim against Chubb, its liability insurer. Halliburton commenced arbitration when Chubb refused to pay the claim. The parties failed to agree on the third arbitrator. The High Court appointed M who had disclosed that he had previously acted as arbitrator in a number of arbitrations in which Chubb was a party, including appointments by Chubb, and that he was currently appointed as arbitrator in two pending cases in which Chubb was involved.[96] When Halliburton's lawyers questioned M's failure to disclose these other cases, referring to the IBA, M answered that: "I do not think and did not think that the above circumstances put any obligation upon me to make any disclosure to you or your clients ... I appreciate, with the benefit of hindsight, that it would have been prudent for me to have informed your clients through your firm, and I apologise for not having done so."[97] Subsequently, Halliburton asked M's removal.

The High Court addressed the three elements of M's conduct, which Halliburton believed gave rise to an appearance of bias: (1) acceptance of the appointments in the Transocean arbitrations, (2) failure to disclose those appointments to Halliburton, and (3) the response to the challenge to the arbitrator's impartiality.[98] It dismissed Halliburton's application, which revolved around the contention that the judge failed to have proper regard to the unfairness

---

[92] Hulley Enterprises Limited (Cyprus) v. The Russian Federation (PCA Case No. AA 226); Yukos Universal Limited (Isle of Man) v. The Russian Federation (PCA Case No. AA 227); Veteran Petroleum Limited (Cyprus) v. The Russian Federation (PCA Case No. AA 228) awards of July 18, 2014.

[93] The point was not decided upon by the District Court as it annulled the award for lack of jurisdiction.

[94] ICC Note to Parties and Arbitral Tribunals on the Conduct of the Arbitration of 2019, para 184.

[95] Halliburton Company v. Chubb Bermuda Insurance Ltd and others (2018) EWCA Civ 817, https://www.bailii.org/ew/cases/EWCA/Civ/2018/817.html.

[96] *Id.* at para. 25.

[97] *Id.* at para. 18.

[98] *Id.* at para. 11.

that may arise when an arbitrator accepts appointments in overlapping references with one common party. The court reviewed the case law and referenced *Guidant LLC v. Swiss Re International SE*[99] and *Beumer Group UK Ltd v. Vinci Construction UK Ltd*.[100] The legitimate concern identified in both cases can be construed as being one of "inside information" or "inside knowledge."[101] The High Court accepted that: "inside information and knowledge may be a legitimate concern for the parties to have in overlapping arbitrations involving a common arbitrator but only one common party. We agree, however, ... that, in itself, it does not justify an inference of apparent bias."[102] It then held that: "these comments are equally applicable to arbitrators ... The mere fact of appointment and decision making in overlapping references does not give rise to justifiable doubts as to the arbitrator's impartiality."[103] The court took the view that "the mere fact that an arbitrator accepts appointments in multiple references concerning the same or overlapping subject matter with only one common party does not of itself give rise to an appearance of bias." The court clarified that "[s]omething more is required" and that must be "something of substance."[104]

The *Halliburton* case clarified that arbitrators can accept several appointments with overlapping subject matters, without necessarily giving rise to doubts about their impartiality. It confirmed "disclosure should be given of facts and circumstances known to the arbitrator," which according to section 24 of the Act, "would or might give rise to justifiable doubts as to his impartiality. Under English law this means facts or circumstances which would or might lead the fair-minded and informed observer, having considered the facts, to conclude that there was a real possibility that the arbitrator was biased."[105] The court rejected the argument that the multiple appointments with only one common party would "give rise to justifiable doubts as to the arbitrator's impartiality,"[106] even though they could justify an inference of apparent bias.[107]

---

[99] In Guidant LLC v. Swiss Re International SE (2016) EWHC 1201 Leggatt J observed that "If the same person were to be appointed, there would be a legitimate concern that that person would be influenced in deciding the Swiss Re arbitrations by arguments and evidence in the Markel arbitration." In the light of these considerations, Leggatt J did not appoint Guidant's requested arbitrator as the third arbitrator in the exercise of his discretionary powers under section 18 of the Act. At the same time, he recognized, however, that the appointment of a common arbitrator did not justify an inference of apparent bias. Thus he noted that the fact that Guidant had appointed the same arbitrator in all three arbitrations was not a ground upon which disqualification could be sought. In Beumer Group UK Ltd v. Vinci Construction UK Ltd (2016) EWHC 2283, Fraser J held that the appointment of the common adjudicator and the conduct of that adjudication with all that involved, in terms of contact and the running of inconsistent cases, without all that involved, in terms of contact and the running of inconsistent cases, without notifying the other party meant that this was a case of apparent bias. Fraser J observed that

> If all that takes place secretly, in the sense that the other party does not know it is even taking place, then that runs an obvious risk in my judgment of leading the fair minded and informed observer to conclude that there was a real possibility of bias. All of this can be avoided by disclosing the existence of the appointment at the earliest opportunity.

See Halliburton, *supra* note 94, at para. 45.
[100] Beumer Group, *supra* note 98, at para. 47.
[101] *Id.* at para. 48.
[102] *Id.* at para. 50.
[103] *Id.* at para. 51.
[104] *Id.* at para. 53.
[105] *Id.* at para. 71.
[106] *Id.* at para. 51.
[107] The Supreme Court heard the appeal Halliburton Company (acting as the Appellant) v. Chubb Bermuda Insurance Ltd (formerly known as Ace Bermuda Insurance Ltd) (acting as the Respondent) on Nov. 12 and 13, 2019, https://www.supremecourt.uk/cases/uksc-2018-0100.html. L. Flannery, Duncan Bagshaw, & Amir Mahdavi, *Deepwater Horizon Case on Actual or Apparent Bias to Go to the English Supreme Court*, STEPHENSON HARWOOD (Jan. 29, 2019), https://www.shlegal.com/insights/deepwater-horizon-case-on-actual-or-apparent-bias-to-go-to-the-eng

The English courts have emphasized the standard of apparent bias instead of actual bias. The case of *Soletanche Bachy France SAS v. Aqaba Container Terminal (Pvt) Co*[108] typifies the scope and the importance of ongoing disclosure and the importance of transparency. The arbitration concerned a contract by which the claimant building contractor agreed to construct an extension to a container port in Jordan on behalf of the respondent over a period of several years. The respondent subsequently decided to terminate the claimant's employment under the contract due to substantial delays in the construction. The respondent then employed an alternative contractor, BAM International (BAM) to complete the works. The respondent made a counterclaim to recover damages related to the hiring of BAM and the completion of the construction. The claimant asserted that the counterclaim was suspect because BAM was hired without a tender, BAM's pricing was unreasonable, and the construction was different from the one described in the claimant's contract.[109]

Arbitrator X initially disclosed that he was advising BAM in relation to a dispute on an entirely separate construction project. On the first day of hearing, Arbitrator X indicated that he was "instructed by BAM in a joint venture in relation to a project in Australia, totally unrelated to this. I have not met anyone from BAM, I have only dealt with the solicitors, who are not involved in this, to answer certain legal questions, but I am actually currently retained by them."[110] The parties did not take issue with Arbitrator X's disclosure at the hearing. The claimant commenced proceedings seeking to set aside the award on the grounds that Arbitrator X's failed to fully disclose his relationship with BAM and that this constituted a serious irregularity pursuant to section 68 of the English Arbitration Act. The court rejected the impartiality challenge, reasoning that the scope of disclosure obligations was ongoing and broad, but the courts are not required to apply an unrealistic or unduly rigorous standard when assessing alleged failures to disclose. Sir Michael Burton QC indicated that he had "no difficulty whatever in concluding that once it was known that he was retained and instructed by BAM in relation to a dispute, the fact that the dispute subsequently became active, in the sense of an arbitration, made no material change whatever. It had been disclosed."[111]

The court clarified the circumstances in which there might be a duty on an arbitrator to give further disclosure. Although the claimant pleaded that Arbitrator X should have, subsequent to the initial disclosure, disclosed to the parties that his involvement in BAM's other dispute had become more extensive, the court concluded that there was no need for him to provide further details to the parties. In sum, the initial disclosure was sufficient and there was no need for further disclosure on the matter.

The recent English decisions highlighted in this section provide guidance as to how the English courts have approached accusations of conflicts of interest while addressing such issues with reference to the IBA Guidelines. For arbitrators and counsel, the decisions suggest that it would be wise to err on the side of disclosure of the facts constituting a potential conflict to decrease the possibility of future challenges.

---

lish-supreme-court. The Supreme Court's decision will be welcome in clarifying several issues (1) disclosure obligations, (2) if disclosure must include disclosure of related arbitrator appointments, and (3) guidance when arbitrators fail to abide by the requisite standards even if it is unintentional. *See* Lee Carroll & Joshua Paffey, *The UK Supreme Court to Hear Deepwater Horizon Appeal Seeking Removal of an Arbitrator*, Kluwer Arbitration Blog (June 1, 2019), http://arbitrationblog.kluwerarbitration.com/2019/06/01/the-uk-supreme-court-to-hear-deepwater-horizon-appeal-seeking-removal-of-an-arbitrator.

[108] Soletanche Bachy France SAS v. Aqaba Container Terminal (Pvt) Co (2019) EWHC 362 (Comm) (Jan. 17, 2019).
[109] *Id.* at para. 11.
[110] *Id.* at para. 13.
[111] *Id.* at para. 27.

3 FRENCH COURTS' PERSPECTIVE

French courts have strictly interpreted the scope of arbitrators' conflicts of interest – arbitrators are required to be independent and impartial and appear to be.[112] Both independence and impartiality are "of the essence of their jurisdictional functions."[113] Article 1456, paragraph 2 of the Code of Civil Procedure (CPC)[114] requires arbitrators to disclose all circumstances that may give rise to reasonable doubt regarding their independence or impartiality[115]. In one instance, an arbitrator failed to disclose that he was the father-in-law of one of the parties' counsel. The Paris Court of Appeal annulled the award.[116] In another case, the arbitrator declared that he had been appointed by the same party on several occasions, but failed to disclose that he had been appointed eighteen times by this party before he rendered the award in 2002 and was appointed another sixteen times subsequently, resulting in the annulment of the award by the Reims Court of Appeal.[117]

In *Société Dukan de Nitya v. Société VR Services*, the arbitrator had omitted to disclose a close professional relationship with one of the party's counsel. He was chosen from a short list of people from various professional organizations pursuant to the arbitration agreement. This fact was available from the professional organization website. The Cour de Cassation observed that the arbitrator had "deliberately" issued a "truncated and reductive" declaration of independence. It clarified that the parties did not have an obligation to investigate the arbitrator's declaration even where information putting his independence and impartiality into question was publicly available. The Cour de Cassation confirmed the Court of Appeal's decision to annul the award on the grounds that the missing information on the disclosure could create a reasonable doubt in regard to the impartiality and independence of the arbitrator.[118] In *Sociétés Colombus v. Société AGI*,[119] the Cour de Cassation again showed the broad scope of the arbitrator's disclosure obligation. The disclosure must include (1) not only to direct links of the arbitrator with one of the parties but also to links of its colleagues and/or the law firm in which he works with one of the parties, (2) not only to the parties themselves but also to persons and entities related to the parties, and (3) information that is publicly available.[120] The Cour de Cassation essentially ruled that parties should be aware of all information that could potentially affect the arbitrator's independence or impartiality.

---

[112] Elie Kleiman & Yann Dehaudt-Delville, *Independence and Impartiality: Supreme Court Confirms Stern Approach to Duty of Disclosure*, FRESHFIELDS BRUCKHAUS DERINGER LLP NEWSLETTERS (Apr. 21, 2016), https://www.internationallawoffice.com/Newsletters/Arbitration-ADR/France/Freshfields-Bruckhaus-Deringer-LLP/Independence-and-impartiality-Supreme-Court-confirms-stern-approach-to-duty-of-disclosure# .

[113] A. Mourre, 'Conflicts Disclosures: The IBA Guidelines and Beyond, *in* EVOLUTION AND FUTURE OF INTERNATIONAL ARBITRATION, International Arbitration Law Library, vol. 37, 357 (Stavros L. Brekoulakis et al. eds., 2016).

[114] Article 1456, para. 2 CPC states "Il appartient à l'arbitre, avant d'accepter sa mission, de révéler toute circonstance susceptible d'affecter son indépendance ou son impartialité. Il lui est également fait obligation de révéler sans délai toute circonstance de même nature qui pourrait naître après l'acceptation de sa mission." [It can be understood that an arbitrator shall disclose any circumstance, before accepting a mandate, which may affect his or her independence or impartiality. He or she also shall disclose promptly any such circumstance that may arise after accepting the mandate.]

[115] See French cases: Cass Civ 1, Mar. 16, 1999, Etat du Qatar v. Société Creighton, 96-12748 (1999) REVUE DE L'ARBITRAGE, 308; CA Paris, Sept. 9, 2010, Consorts Allaire v. SAS SGS Holding France (2011) REVUE DE L'ARBITRAGE, 686; CA Paris, Mar. 10, 2011, Société Nykcool AB v. Société Dole France et al., 09/21413 (2011) REVUE DE L'ARBITRAGE, 732; and Cass Civ 1, Oct. 10, 2012, Société Tesco v. Société Neoelectra Group, 11-20299.

[116] CA Paris, Jan. 12, 1999, Société Milan Presse v. Société Média Sud Communication (1999) REVUE DE L'ARBITRAGE, 381.

[117] CA Reims, Jan. 31, 2012, Mr and Ms X v. SAS Prodim et al. 10/03288.

[118] Cass Civ 1, Société Dukan de Nitya v. Société VR Services, Dec. 18, 2014, 14-11085, http://www.legifrance.gouv.fr/affichJuriJudi.do?oldAction=rechJuriJudi&idTexte=JURITEXT000029934460.

[119] Case no. 14-26279.

[120] In this case the information had been published in 2010 on the law firm's website and also in the legal press.

In the case of *Avax* v. *Tecnimont*,[121] the French court examined whether an award should be set aside due to an arbitrator's gradual and incomplete disclosure. The case involved an arbitration where the counsel of one of the parties discovered that the arbitrator's law firm was providing advice to a company that was later acquired by the parent company of Tecnimont. The arbitrator provided additional information upon the party's request. Subsequently, the independence and impartiality of the arbitrator was challenged before the ICC Court of Arbitration which it dismissed without disclosing its reasons. Avax continued to participate in the arbitration while reserving its rights. In December 2007, the arbitral tribunal issued a partial award on liability in Tecnimont's favour.[122]

The judicial saga regarding the extent of the arbitrators' duty to disclose continued in the French court system. In 2009, the Paris Court of Appeal annulled an award based on the arbitrator's failure to disclose his law firm's representation, during the proceedings, of companies affiliated with one of the parties to the arbitration. The court held that the arbitrator's activities created a conflict of interest even if those activities started well after the chairman's appointment.[123] In 2010, the Cour de Cassation vacated the Paris Court of Appeal's decision and remitted the case for retrial to the Reims Court of Appeal,[124] which annulled the award again in 2011. The Reims Court held that the ICC decision on the challenge was administrative in nature and had no res judicata effect. The ICC Rules imposed a thirty-day time limit for challenging the arbitrator after his confirmation or knowledge of events that can lead to a challenge. The court did not consider the ICC time period to be "binding" on the *juge d'appui* (judge dealing with annulment).[125] The decision of the Reims Court of Appeal was subsequently quashed by the Cour de Cassation,[126] which held that if a party failed to exercise its right to challenge an arbitrator within the time limit specified by the relevant arbitration rules (ICC Rules) it is deemed to have waived its right to have the award set aside.[127]

---

[121] See various French courts decisions and comments published in French: Paris, Feb. 12, 2009, no. 07/22164, T. Clay, (2009) Recueil Dalloz 2959; T. Clay (2009) Revue de l'Arbitrage 186; P. Schweizer (2009) ASA Bulletin 520; on the Paris Court of Appeal decision J&P Avax SA v. Tecnimont SPA, Feb. 12, 2009; the Cour de Cassation decision: Civ. 1st, Nov. 4, 2010, no. 09-12.716, T. Clay (2010) Dalloz, 2933; T. Clay (2010) Cahiers de l'Arbitrage 1147; T. Clay (2010) Dalloz. 2939; the Reims Court of Appeal decision setting aside the award again: Reims Court of Appeal, Nov. 2, 2011, no. 10/02888, T. Clay, (2011) Dalloz, 3023; E. Loquin (2012) Revue Trimestrielle Droit Commercial 518; T. Clay (2011) Cahiers de l'Arbitrage, 1109; D. Bensaude (2012) Gazette du Palais, no. 22-24, 15; a second decision of the Cour de Cassation: Cass. Civ. 1st, June 25, 2014, no. 11-26.529, Tecnimont SPA (Sté) v. J&P Avax [Sté], T. Clay, (2014) Cahiers de l'Arbitrage, 547; J.-J. Arnaldez & A. Mezghani (2015) Revue de l'Arbitrage, 85; Paris Court of Appeal, Apr. 12, 2016, no. 14/14884, T. Clay (2016) Dalloz, 2589; E. Loquin (2017) Revue de l'Arbitrage, 234; Cour de Cassation: Cass Civ. 1st, Dec. 19, 2018, FS-P+B+I, no. 16-18.349, J. Jourdan-Marques, *Chronique d'arbitrage: La fin de la saga Tecnimont*, Dalloz Actualité, Jan. 29, 2019; C. Debourg, *Obligation de révélation de l'arbitre et obligation de s'informer à la charge des parties: Un équilibre encore perfectible* Dalloz Actualité, Feb. 1, 2019.

[122] It was done long after the expiry of the 30-day time limit set forth by the then Article 11 of the 1998 ICC Rules.

[123] Paris Court of Appeal, Feb. 12, 2009, no. 07/22164, T. Clay, (2009) Recueil Dalloz 2959; T. Clay (2009) Revue de l'Arbitrage 186. A commentator considered that the duty to disclose disappeared to the profit of the duty to react. See T. Clay, *Dissolution de l'obligation de révélation dans le devoir de réaction,* Paris Appeal Court, Apr. 12, 2016, no. 14/14884, (2016) Cahiers de l'Arbitrage, 447.

[124] Cass. Civ. 1st, Nov. 4, 2010, no. 09-12.716 T. Clay, (2010) Dalloz, 2933, T. Clay, *L'obligation de révélation de l'arbitre au prisme de l'indiscipline de la cour d'appel de Paris*, Cahiers de l'Arbitrage 1147, https://www.legifrance.gouv.fr/affichJuriJudi.do?idTexte=JURITEXT000023013868.

[125] Reims Appeal Court, Nov. 2, 2011, no. 10/02888, M. Henry (2012) Revue de l'Arbitrage, 11; T. Clay (2011) Cahiers de l'Arbitrage, 1109.

[126] Tecnimont SPA, *supra* note 121, https://www.courdecassation.fr/jurisprudence_2/premiere_chambre_civile_568/758_25_29578.html.

[127] The *Cour de cassation* judgment answers the concerns of commentators. It is now clear that a judgment reviewing an award which fails to take into account the time limits set forth in the ICC Rules (or any other

The case was sent back again to the Paris Court of Appeal, and this time it upheld the award,[128] reasoning that the facts that lead to the challenge were in the public domain and easily accessible and, further, that those facts – Sofregaz/EDF (which took control of Tecnimont's parent in 2005) was among the clients of the chairman's firm in 2005 – were not sufficient to raise doubts on the independence and impartiality of the arbitrator. Finally, it noted that the first challenge before the ICC was filed after the expiration of the relevant deadline.[129] Again, the case was brought on appeal to the Cour de Cassation. On December 19, 2018, the Cour de Cassation rendered its latest decision.[130] It quashed the appeal for the third time. It reaffirmed, inter alia, that if an arbitrator has a duty to disclose his or her conflict of interest and the parties have an obligation to act if they harbour any doubt as soon as possible and within the time limit set out by the arbitration rules. Should they fail to act diligently, they will be deemed to have waived their right to challenge the award on that ground.[131] In doing so, the court announced a new requirement that the request for challenge of the arbitrator and the request for setting aside the award must be similar in content and have a parallel structure.[132] In addition, it confirmed the Paris court's position that the arbitrator should disclose only information that is not publicly known.[133] Firstly, this position is astonishing because the arbitrator was unaware of those facts; second, the disclosure of facts not publicly known means that an arbitrator could exclude facts that link him to one of the parties. It has been suggested that the ruling goes against the principle of transparency[134] and is contrary to the trend in international arbitration of extending the scope of the arbitrator's duty to disclose.[135] It has been argued that the decision allows arbitrators to be less precise in their disclosure in spite of French jurisprudence reinforcing the duty of disclosure. At the other end of the spectrum, the question is whether or not the arbitrator is expected to scrutinize all aspects his or her life: all the people encountered in a professional setting, all the

---

institutional rules for that matter), which are binding on the parties, will be overturned. This does not mean, however, that the judge, when reviewing the award, is bound by the substantive decision of the ICC Court under the ICC Rules (that is, a decision whether or not to uphold the challenge to an arbitrator). Rather, it is only the failure to comply with the ICC Rules themselves, which amounts to a breach of the contract between the parties, which a French judge is not entitled to rectify.

L. Franc-Menget, *New Ruling of the French Cour de Cassation in the Tecnimont Judicial Saga on Challenge of an Arbitrator*, ARBITRATION NOTES (July 3, 2014), https://hsfnotes.com/arbitration/2014/07/03/new-ruling-of-the-french-cour-de-cassation-in-the-tecnimont-judicial-saga-on-challenge-of-an-arbitrator.

[128] Paris Court of Appeal, Apr. 12, 2016, no. 14/14884, D. Bensaude, *Aggravation significative (ou non) des doutes d'une partie sur l'indépendance et l'impartialité de l'arbitre*, GAZETTE DU PALAIS, July 12, 2016, 268.

[129] C. Fouchard, *Tecnimont Saga: Episode V – The Paris Court Strikes Back*, KLUWER ARBITRATION BLOG (Aug. 3, 2016), http://arbitrationblog.kluwerarbitration.com/2016/08/03/tecnimont-saga-episode-v-the-paris-court-strikes-back/?print=print.

[130] Cass Civ. 1st, Dec. 19, 2018, FS-P+B+I, no. 16-18.349, https://www.courdecassation.fr/jurisprudence_2/premiere_chambre_civile_568/1220_19_40991.html.

[131] *See* H. Barbier, *Le devoir de réaction du contractant: Essor et limites* (2016) REVUE TRIMESTRIELLE DROIT CIVIL, 856.

[132] *See* "la solution conduit à faire peser une obligation de parallélisme de formes entre la requête en récusation et le recours en annulation. Une telle exigence est dépourvue d'un quelconque fondement juridique et interdit aux parties d'affiner leur argumentation, ce qui laisse sceptique." Jourdan-Marques, *supra* note 120.

[133] Attendu … que, de ces énonciations et constatations, la cour d'appel, qui n'était pas tenue d'effectuer les recherches prétendument omises que celles-ci rendaient inopérantes, a exactement déduit, sans inverser la charge de l'obligation de révélation, que la requête en récusation était tardive pour avoir été introduite plus d'un mois après que la société Avax eut reçu les renseignements qui auraient altéré sa confiance dans le président du tribunal arbitral, et sans qu'aucune information complémentaire, qui ne fût notoire, ait été entretemps découverte de sorte que cette société n'était plus recevable à invoquer à l'appui du recours en annulation de la sentence les faits sur lesquels cette requête se fondait.

Cass Civ. 1st, Dec. 19, 2018, FS-P+B+I, no. 16–18.349.

[134] *Id.*

[135] Jourdan-Marques, *supra* note 121.

people he or she participated with at a conference; the people he or she wrote an article with or a book without forgetting his family, his or her connections, etc.[136]

In another case, between the Republic of Equatorial Guinea (Guinea) and Orange,[137] the Paris Court of Appeal strictly applied ICC Rules. The court refused to set aside an award on the grounds that the arbitral tribunal had been unlawfully constituted.[138] The chairman failed to mention that he had sat as an arbitrator in a previous arbitration involving Orange. He also failed to disclose he was an arbitrator in an award granted by a tribunal in favor of Orange. Finally, one of the arbitrators reported in a dissenting opinion the partiality of the chairman. Guinea subsequently challenged the chairman, which was dismissed by the ICC. In the subsequent court claim, the court denied the application to set aside and held that, in the course of the arbitration proceedings, Guinea had received sufficient information on the arbitrator in a letter sent by the other party. Even if such information had been insufficient for Guinea to fully understand the involvement of the arbitrator in the former arbitration, additional information was easily accessible within one month from the receipt of the letter. The court added that because Guinea did not raise the issue in a timely manner during the arbitral proceedings it was barred from raising that issue before the French courts.[139] French law takes a strict stance in terms of the timing of challenges to arbitrators.

The parameters of independence and impartiality remain intact in French law. However, the number of repeat appointments that constitute conflict is uncertain. In *Époux X v. Prodim/ Logidis*,[140] the Cour de Cassation annulled a decision of the Douai Court of Appeal of that refused to set aside an arbitral award rendered by an arbitrator who had not disclosed that he had been appointed thirty-four other times by companies of the same group as one of the parties. In *Somoclest v. DV*,[141] the Cour de Cassation annulled a decision of the Versailles Court of Appeal that dismissed a challenge to an arbitrator who had not disclosed that he had been appointed fifty-one times by companies affiliated to one of the parties. The Cour de Cassation quashed the award because of the systematic character of the designation of a particular person by the companies of the same group, its frequency and regularity over a long period of time in comparable contracts, which created the conditions of a flow of business between that person and the group of companies party to the proceedings.[142] The facts in *Serf v. DV*[143] was similar to those in *Somoclest v. DV Construction*. The Court of Appeal of Paris set

---

[136] *Id.*
[137] Orange is a French telecommunication company.
[138] Paris Appeal Court, Sept. 22, 2015, no. 14/17200.
[139] Jean-Christophe Honlet, Bartum Legum, Anne-Sophie Dufetre, & Annelise Lecompte, *France*, in THE INTERNATIONAL ARBITRATION REVIEW 209–210 (James H. Carter ed., 7th ed. 2016), https://www.dentons.com/.../2016/.../canada-the-international-arbitration-review-7th-edition.
[140] Époux X v. Société Prodim and Société Logidis, Cass. (1st Civ. Ch.), Judgment no. 962 (09-68.131), Oct. 20, 2010. The arbitral award was eventually set aside by the Reims Court of Appeal, and the French Supreme Court confirmed this decision, Société Logidis et al. v. M. M. Batard et al., Cass. Civ (1st Civ. Ch.), (2013) 2 REVUE DE L'ARBITRAGE, 531–532; full text of the decision is available at http://www.legifrance.gouv.fr.
[141] Société Somoclest v. Société DV Construction, Cass. (1st Civ. Ch.), Judgment no. 963 (09-68.997), Oct. 20, 2010.
[142] Judgment of the Cour de Cassation, Oct. 20 2010, no. 963, no. 09-68.997, https://www.courdecassation.fr/jurisprudence_2/premiere_chambre_civile_568/963_20_17862.html:

> 'Qu'en statuant ainsi, alors que le caractère systématique de la désignation d'une personne donnée par les sociétés d'un même groupe, sa fréquence et sa régularité sur une longue période, dans des contrats comparables, ont créé les conditions d'un courant d'affaires entre cette personne et les sociétés du groupe parties à la procédure de sorte que l'arbitre était tenu de révéler l'intégralité de cette situation à l'autre partie à l'effet de la mettre en mesure d'exercer son droit de récusation, la cour d'appel a violé les textes susvisés.

[143] SA Serf v. Société DV Construction, Paris CA (1st Civ. Ch.), Jan. 29, 2004 (2005) 3 REVUE DE L'ARBITRAGE, 709–713. On the doubts that the behavior of the challenging party in this case raises (it did not challenge the arbitrator despite

aside the arbitral award because the arbitrator that had obtained fifty-one appointments from a group of companies related to a party to the arbitration. In *STPIF v. Ballestero*,[144] the Paris Court of Appeal decided to appoint an expert to determine the number of repeat appointments of a sole arbitrator.

In sum, there is no clear threshold of the number of repeat appointments that should normally justify the disqualification of an arbitrator. This is made clear in two similar cases with different outcomes. In the first case, an arbitration under the aegis of the Stockholm Chamber of Commerce (SCC), the SCC upheld the challenge of a party-appointed arbitrator who had been appointed eight times by the same party and six times by companies associated with that party within a period of two years. In the second case, an ad hoc arbitration, the arbitral tribunal and later a national court rejected the challenge of a party-appointed arbitrator who had been appointed ten times in a nearly ten-year period.[145] In *Korsnäs v. AB Fortum*,[146] the court dismissed a party's application to set aside an arbitral award on the grounds of the appointment of the same arbitrator by the same law firm in three other cases during the previous three years. In the *Frémarc* case,[147] however, the Cour de Cassation annulled a decision by the Paris Court of Appeal to dismiss an application to set aside an arbitral award, which was based on the repeat appointment of a party-appointed arbitrator in three other cases.

French courts follow a strict application of law and limitation periods. They show great deference to arbitrators in order to enforce awards and maintain the sanctity of the process. This is especially the case in challenges to arbitrators raised after the limitation period. In cases of repeated appointments, the courts generally defer to the arbitrator unless other factors also pertain to the independence and impartiality of the arbitrator. At the same time, French law also recognizes an obligation on arbitrators to disclose the potential conflict of interest.

4 DUTY OF DISCLOSURE FOR THIRD-PARTY FUNDING

Third-party funding (TPF) has become a major trend, which allows parties greater access to justice. After fighting the barriers of legitimacy and legality, third-party funding has become common but also raises issues of conflict of interest. The funder is not a formal party to the proceeding and therefore has no blanket obligation to disclose its involvement. Under the IBA Guidelines, disclosure of a third-party funder is required only when a previous relationship exists between an arbitrator and the funder.[148]

The role and impact of third-party funders in international arbitration is a contentious matter. The majority view is that the greater involvement by any funder poses a risk to the integrity of arbitration. For instance, the counsels are bound by the ethical obligations to act in the best interest of their clients, however, third-party funders currently operate under no such rules.

---

knowing of eight out of the fifty-one repeat appointments), M. Henry, *Pluralité de désignation et devoir d'indépendance et d'impartialité de l'arbitre*, comment under case analysis Paris, 1re Ch. C, Jan. 29, 2004, Feb. 10 and 17, 2005; Trib. com. Paris), July 6, 2004 (2005) 3 Revue de l'Arbitrage, 727

[144] STPIF v. SB Ballestero, Paris CA (1st Civ. Ch.), May 16, 2002 (2003) 4 Revue de l'Arbitrage 1231–1240.

[145] *See* Alfonso Gomez-Acebo, *Problems of Bias in Party-Appointed Arbitrators*, in Party-Appointed Arbitrators in International Commercial Arbitration, International Arbitration Law Library, vol. 34, 97–144 (Alfonso Gomez-Acebo ed., 2016).

[146] Korsnäs Aktiebolag v. AB Fortum Värme samägt med Stockholms stad, Svea Court of Appeals, and obs. in IBA Conflicts of Interest Subcommittee, *The IBA Guidelines on Conflicts of Interest in International Arbitration: The First Five Years 2004–2009*, 4, no. 1 Disp. Resol. Int'l. 17–18 (2010).

[147] Frémarc v. ITM Entreprises, Cass. (2nd Civ. Ch.), Dec. 6, 2001, (2003) 4 Revue de l'Arbitrage, 1231–1233.

[148] IBA Guidelines, General Standard (7)(a).

Instead the interactions between the funder and a party are dictated by the terms of the funding agreement, including disclosure restrictions, confidentiality,[149] and the funder's level of control over arbitral strategy.[150]

Arbitral tribunals have no jurisdiction to address concerns relating to third-party funding agreements.[151] Thus the arbitral tribunal cannot independently force a party to disclose a third-party funding agreement.[152] This is problematic since such disclosures would help prevent conflicts of interest. Such conflicts are likely since the arbitration community has many repeat players in a highly specialized field. In the last few years, third-party funding has attracted significant interest in relation to conflict of interest. In 2018, the ICCA-Queen Mary Task Force issued its report on "Third-Party Funding in International Arbitration."[153] The report noted that there is "nearly universal agreement"[154] in favor of the disclosure of the identity of funders to arbitrators so that they can assess potential conflicts of interest. However, the report also noted that there was "somewhat less consensus about how and when"[155] such disclosures should be made.

Several arbitral institutions have adopted rules for investment arbitration on disclosure of third-party funding.[156] The Singapore International Arbitration Centre and China International Economic and Trade Arbitration Commission adopted provisions requiring disclosure of the identity of funders. However, the ICC does not require the disclosure of third-party funders in relation to the appointment, confirmation, or challenge of arbitrators.[157] The ICC recommends

---

[149] Jennifer A. Trusz, *Full Disclosure? Conflicts of Interest Arising from Third-Party Funding in International Commercial Arbitration*, 101 GEO. L.J. 1649, 1675 (2013).

[150] Victoria Shannon, *Judging Third Party Funding*, 63 UCLA L. REV. 388, 394 (2016; Gary J. Shaw, *Third-Party Funding in Investment Arbitration: How Non-disclosure Can Cause Harm for the Sake of Profit*, 33 ARB. INT'L. 109–120 (2017).

[151] For an in-depth discussion of these issues, *see* Selvyn Seidel, *Third-Party Investing in International Arbitration Claims to Invest or Not to Invest? A Daunting Question*, in THIRD-PARTY FUNDING IN INTERNATIONAL ARBITRATION 16, 24 (A. Dimolitsa & B. M. Cremades eds., 2013); ERIC DE BRABANDERE & JULIA LEPELTAK, THIRD PARTY FUNDING IN INTERNATIONAL INVESTMENT ARBITRATION 5 (Grotius Centre, Working Paper No. 2012/1, June 5, 2012), http://ssrn.com/abstract=2078358.

[152] When a party has disclosed a third-party funder for purposes of cost allocation, tribunals have refused to consider the funding agreement, stating that it knew "of no principle why any ... third party financing arrangement should be taken into consideration in determining the amount of recovery." Ioannis Kardassopoulos and Ron Fuchs v. Georgia, ICSID Case No ARB/05/18 and ARB/07/15, Award, Mar. 3. 2010, para 691.

[153] Report of ICCA Queen Mary Task Force on Third-Party Funding in International Arbitration of 2018, International Council for Commercial Arbitration, https://www.arbitration-icca.org/media/10/40280243154551/icca_reports_4_tpf_final_for_print_5_april.pdf.

[154] *Id.* at 98.

[155] *Id.*

[156] See Singapore International Arbitration Centre (Article 24 of the Investment Arbitration Rules of 2017 grants the power of the arbitral tribunal order the disclosure of the existence of a party's third-party funding arrangement and/or the identity of the third-party funder and, where appropriate, details of the third-party funder's interest in the outcome of the proceedings and/or whether or not the third-party funder has committed to undertake adverse costs liability); China International Economic and Trade Arbitration Commission (CIETAC) (Article 27 of the International Investment Arbitration Rules of 2017 requires the party accepting the funding to notify in writing, without delay, to the other party or parties, the arbitral tribunal, and the IDSC or the CIETAC Hong Kong Arbitration Center that administers the case of the existence and nature of the third-party funding arrangement and the name and address of the third-party funder. The arbitral tribunal shall have the power to order the disclosure by the party accepting the funding of any relevant information of the third-party funding arrangement).

[157] The ICC Note to Parties and Arbitral Tribunals on the Conduct of Arbitration of 2019 states:

> For the scope of disclosures, an arbitrator will be considered as bearing the identity of his or her law firm, and a legal entity will include its affiliates. In addressing possible objections to confirmation or challenges, the Court will consider the activities of the arbitrator's law firm and the relationship of the law firm with the arbitrator in each individual case. Arbitrators should in each case consider disclosing relationships with another arbitrator or counsel who is a member of the same barristers' chambers. Relationships between arbitrators, as well as

that an arbitrator in deciding whether or not to disclose, "should consider relationships with non-parties having an interest in the outcome of the arbitration."[158] This is clearly an indirect relationship to parties and is not construed as an express requirement by the parties and arbitrators to disclose relations with third-party funders.

The task force recommended that the parties voluntarily disclose the existence of a third-party funding arrangement and the identity of the funders. It also suggests that arbitrators, arbitral institutions, or appointing authorities require that parties disclose the third-party funder. The general feeling is that arbitral institutions or arbitrators should compel parties to disclose the participation of a third-party funder however remote.[159]

Even though third-party funders are now prominent in the field of international arbitration they prefer exerting control behind the scenes, while not being disclosed in the arbitrations they are funding. Also, a party may not want the other party to know that it has engaged third-party funder for tactical reasons. It is still yet to be determined whether parties who have third-party funding arrangements are obliged to disclose them. One view is that the current jurisprudence obligates parties to disclose. This view is supported by the argument that failure to disclose third-party financiers is a breach of procedural good faith. An ancillary issue relates to the level of control that third-party funders have in the selection of arbitrators It is clear that funders now heavily impact the choice and strategy in most arbitrations. As funders build up a body of experience in their ranks, it is likely that they will weigh in more on the choice of arbitrators. This is a role traditionally left to the counsel of the parties, but there may exist a blurring of the line between the outcome desired by the party and the one desired by the funder. The IBA rules allocate the power to nominate arbitrators to legal counsel. However, since funders prefer working behind the scenes if disclosures are not provided, the lack of transparency allows them to covertly influence the selection of arbitrators. This increases the risk of abuse where preferred arbitrators are appointed over and over again.

As discussed, the risk of suspect behavior by third-party funders should require that their role in the arbitration be disclosed. The party using a funder should be obligated to disclose its identity and any relations of the funder that may indicate conflicts of interest. It has also been argued that the creation of a general duty to disclose all third-party funding arrangements is unnecessary and time consuming. The balance to be struck is the disruption of the arbitration proceedings with challenges to arbitrators and the need to ensure impartiality, as well as the veracity and comprehensiveness of the arbitrator's disclosure, including contacts with third-party funders. In 2014, the IBA Guidelines examined third-party funding and its impact on conflicts of interest. General Standard 6(b) refers to a *direct economic interest* in the award of third-party funders and insurers,[160] as the reason for greater disclosure. Thus the IBA Guidelines contemplate two levels of disclosure: the parties' disclosure to arbitrators that the party is using a funder and the arbitrators' disclosure of any potential conflict of interest in line with the IBA

---

relationships with any entity having a direct economic interest in the dispute or an obligation to indemnify a party for the award, should also be considered in the circumstances of each case.

At para. 28. Although the wording is wide, the ICC does not refer to third-party funding.

[158] *Id.* at para. 24.

[159] *See* Burcu Osmanoglu, *Third-Party Funding in International Commercial Arbitration and Arbitrator Conflict of Interest*, 32 J. INT'L. ARB. 325–350 (2015).

[160] General Standard 6(b) "If one of the parties is a legal entity, any legal or physical person having a controlling influence on the legal entity, or a direct economic interest in, or a duty to indemnify a party for, the award to be rendered in the arbitration, may be considered to bear the identity of such party." The explanation to General Standard 6(b) clarified that "Third-party funders and insurers in relation to the dispute may have a direct economic interest in the award, and as such may be considered to be the equivalent of the party." IBA Guidelines, 14.

Guidelines.¹⁶¹ Accordingly, an arbitrator has a duty to "make reasonable enquiries" to identify any conflict of interest as well as any facts or circumstances that may reasonably give rise to doubts as to the impartiality or independence of an arbitrator (related to the third-party funder). General Standard 7(d) further clarifies that the arbitrator's failure to disclose a conflict is not excused by lack of knowledge, if the arbitrator does not perform reasonable enquiries.

A number of laws have been adopted providing rules on third-party funding. The 2019 Hong Kong Code of Practice for Third Party Funding in Arbitration requires a funded party to disclose in writing the existence of a funding agreement and the name of the third-party funder to the other party and the arbitration body.¹⁶² Similarly, legal practitioners regulated by the Singapore Legal Profession Rule¹⁶³ are under a strict obligation to disclose to the court or tribunal (and the other parties) the existence of any third-party funding contract and the identity and address of the funder. In sum, there are different parameters for different stakeholders relating to disclosure obligations, and it depends on the respective jurisdiction's rules whether non-disclosure of third-party funders can be the basis for challenging the impartiality of an arbitrator.

5 CONCLUSION

The analysis in this chapter shows that there are no uniform or universally recognized rules on determining the independence and impartiality of arbitrators. Nonetheless, tribunals and parties to arbitrations have to be cautious while dealing with situations and circumstances that might lead to an allegation of bias and/or a lack of independence and impartiality. It is clear that the obligation to disclose is not all encompassing as it should be. Even if the time for disclosure is extended pursuant to the suggestions of the ICSID, it will not settle all the issues associated with disclosure. The courts in the two jurisdictions we have examined have already indicated arbitrators need only disclose relevant information. If the arbitrator uses proper judgment, then he or she is not obliged to make disclosures seemingly irrelevant to the case. No matter how small the error in non-disclosure, it can only be said to be incomplete but not that it was never made at all.

When weighing such considerations against practical implications, arbitrators must be alert to the potential conflicts that any specific appointment may raise. First, as a matter of law or arbitral

---

[161] General Standard 7 (a) suggests disclosure along these levels:

> A party shall inform an arbitrator, the Arbitral Tribunal, the other parties and the arbitration institution or other appointing authority (if any) of any relationship, direct or indirect, between the arbitrator and the party (or another company of the same group of companies, or an individual having a controlling influence on the party in the arbitration), or between the arbitrator and any person or entity with a direct economic interest in, or a duty to indemnify a party for, the award to be rendered in the arbitration. The party shall do so on its own initiative at the earliest opportunity. (b) A party shall inform an arbitrator, the Arbitral Tribunal, the other parties and the arbitration institution or other appointing authority (if any) of the identity of its counsel appearing in the arbitration, as well as of any relationship, including membership of the same barristers' chambers, between its counsel and the arbitrator. The party shall do so on its own initiative at the earliest opportunity, and upon any change in its counsel team.

> IBA Guidelines, 15.

[162] The EW Code is silent on the parties' disclosure obligations. The inclusion of a disclosure requirement in the HK Code provides a clarity that the EW Code does not. See P. Hirst & M. Yeo, *Comparing Hong Kong Code of Practice for Third Party Funding Arbitration with the Code of Conduct in England & Wales*, KLUWER ARBITRATION BLOG Feb. 4 2019), http://arbitrationblog.kluwerarbitration.com/2019/02/04/comparing-hong-kong-code-of-practice-for-third-party-funding-arbitration-with-the-code-of-conduct-in-england-wales/, P. Teo, *Hong Kong Passes Law to Allow Third Party Funding for Arbitration and Related Proceedings*, BAKER MCKENZIE RECENT DEVELOPMENT (July 7, 2017), https://www.bakermckenzie.com/en/insight/publications/2017/07/hong-kong-thirdparty-funding.

[163] Singapore Legal Profession Act 2001 (Cap. 161), Sections 11, 15, 130I, section 49A; Singapore Legal Profession (Professional Conduct) Rules 2015, Section 3, "Application of Parts 2 to 5" (as amended Mar. 1, 2017).

practice, the issue of arbitrators' conflicts is complicated and far from resolved. Matters such as the extent of disclosure, the efficacy of conflicts checks, and the standard upon which impartiality is assessed are currently divergent across international arbitration. Second, guidelines are just that. Flexibility is one of the key remaining attractions of international arbitration. Care must be taken in drawing from advisory guidelines so as not to place too much emphasis on them, unless they have been specifically adopted as binding in particular proceedings. Third, in light of the differences and nuances from one jurisdiction to another, the exact same issues before different adjudicating bodies under different standards will yield different outcomes.

Finality is arguably the most attractive feature of international arbitration. The regularity of challenges, annulments, or refusals to enforce undermines the entire system. It follows that large international firms must employ more effective means of conflict searches if they do not wish to waste time and costs in dealing with objections to appointment or challenging arbitrators. Arbitrators are also encouraged to be more forthcoming: when in any doubt disclose!

4

Procedural Irregularities and Arbitrator Misconduct during Proceedings

Alexander J. Bělohlávek

1 INTRODUCTION

Arbitration is prized as a cost-effective, confidential dispute resolution process, where the parties have considerable autonomy in deciding how the procedure should take place. On the international level, compared to litigation, it has the additional benefit of being easily enforceable in states that are members of the New York Convention.

Perhaps the most significant difference between arbitration and litigation, is the finality of arbitration, with limited grounds for appeal. From this difference, the question arises, how does the arbitration process protect a party from arbitrators who are either outright biased, do not follow the procedure agreed upon by the parties, or otherwise prevent parties from a fair hearing? This chapter will aim to answer this question by looking at a number of issues. First, it will examine how the arbitration process should be conducted – namely what arbitrators should avoid doing, and the procedure they must follow. Second it will examine the remedies that parties have against procedural irregularities and arbitrator misconduct. It will also explore specific examples of procedural irregularities and arbitrator misconduct and how they are treated at each stage of the arbitral process, with particular emphasis on the decisions of the International Chamber of Commerce (ICC) and the London Court of International Arbitration (LCIA).[1] Last this chapter will analyze whether the current regime addressing procedural irregularity and arbitrator misconduct could be improved.

2 PROCEDURAL IRREGULARITIES AND ARBITRATOR MISCONDUCT: REMEDIES

This section examines recognized procedural irregularities and arbitrator misconduct during the arbitral proceedings. The areas covered include remedies for misconduct, bias, prejudgment, ex-parte communications, and language of animosity and concludes with a short case study.

2.1 *During Proceedings*

The first remedy against procedural irregularities and arbitrator misconduct is challenging an arbitrator during the proceedings themselves. Both national arbitration rules and arbitral

---

[1] *See* LCIA, https://www.lcia.org.

institutional rules provide for mechanisms to remove arbitrators on certain grounds, some rules are more expansive than others, providing grounds for removal that others do not. To illustrate, on the one end of the spectrum, we have the United States, whose domestic arbitration laws do not provide a general right to remove an arbitrator for misconduct or otherwise during arbitration proceedings.[2] The UNCITRAL Model Law, which influenced many national arbitration law,s provides: "An arbitrator may be challenged only if circumstances exist that give rise to justifiable doubts as to his impartiality or independence."[3] Swiss Law provides that an arbitrator may be challenged if "circumstances exist that give rise to justifiable doubts as to his independence."[4] French Law contains a similar provision. On the other end of the spectrum we have English arbitration law, which grants English courts the power to remove an arbitrator for a failure to "properly conduct the proceedings."[5] English courts have applied this provision in removing an arbitrator for, inter alia, making a peremptory order without first issuing directions and permitting exceptional delays.[6]

In arbitration proceedings under the auspices of an arbitration institution, parties also have the option of challenging arbitrators directly by petitioning the institution. Under the ICC Arbitration Rules, an arbitrator can be removed by the ICC for "an alleged lack of impartiality or independence, or otherwise."[7] Under the LCIA Arbitration Rules, the LCIA Court can revoke an arbitrator's appointment when "circumstances exist that give rise to justifiable doubts as to that arbitrator's impartiality or independence."[8] The updated 2014 rules also allow the LCIA Court to revoke an arbitrator who "does not conduct or participate in the arbitration with reasonable efficiency, diligence and industry."[9]

There is a trade-off in including additional grounds for challenging an arbitrator during the proceedings. On the one hand, if arbitrators can be challenged for their incompetence to manage the proceedings effectively, this can arguably ensure the efficiency of arbitration. On the other hand, it provides parties the opportunity to frustrate the proceedings by challenging arbitrators over frivolous matters. Gary Born argues that it is important that the grounds for removing an arbitrator be specific and accurately applied.[10] Removing arbitrators on frivolous grounds would open the floodgates for petty challenges intended to frustrate the course of the proceedings. By applying the grounds strictly and only in situations where removing an arbitrator is justified, parties will be deterred from making unmeritorious challenges. Furthermore, the ICC's rules do allow arbitrator challenges based on "other" grounds, but only when an arbitrator impartiality or independence is at issue.[11] As will be demonstrated throughout this chapter, procedural irregularities and arbitrator misconduct are at issue when they are inconsequential to the outcome of the case, do not amount to circumstances creating a danger of lack of independence and impartiality, or do not infringe on the rights of either of the parties (such as, right to be heard, equal treatment, and so forth.)

---

[2] The Federal Arbitration Act does not expressly grant courts with the power to remove an arbitrator.
[3] UNCITRAL Model Law on International Commercial Arbitration (1985), with amendments as adopted in 2006, Article 12(2).
[4] Swiss Federal Statute on Private International Law, Article 80.
[5] Arbitration Act 1996, Section 24(d)(i)
[6] Wicketts and Sterndale v. Brine Builders (2002) CILL 1805 (QB) (English High Ct.).
[7] ICC Arbitration Rules in force as from Mar. 1, 2017, Article 14(1).
[8] LCIA Arbitration Rules, Article 10(1).
[9] *Id.* at Article 10(2).
[10] GARY B. BORN, CHALLENGE AND REPLACEMENT OF ARBITRATORS IN INTERNATIONAL ARBITRATION, INTERNATIONAL COMMERCIAL ARBITRATION 1938 (2d ed. 2014).
[11] WILLIAM T. O'BRIEN & SANDEEP N. NANDIVADA, ARBITRATOR CHALLENGES: WARRANTED OR ABUSE? 2 (2014).

Born asserts that arbitral institutional authorities should be empowered to remove arbitrators for misconduct or incompetence that is not necessarily related to them being independent or impartial. The benefit of institutional arbitration is that parties have access to an institutional authority. There is no reason why an arbitrator should not be removed for procedural irregularities or misconduct that is unrelated to a lack of independence or impartiality. The only caveat is that the procedural irregularity or misconduct rises to the level of seriously impacting the fairness of the proceeding. The ICC Court has been successful in correctly distinguishing between misconduct that is regrettable but does not meet a certain threshold to warrant removal and misconduct that is serious enough to warrant removal.

The ICC Court has been reluctant to second-guess the procedural decisions of arbitrators. The tribunal is most familiar with the circumstances of the case and is therefore most suitable to make procedural decisions, for example, to balance the right of a party to be heard and the efficiency of the proceedings.[12] Instead, as will be shown in the next section, the ICC and the LCIA Courts have taken the approach of removing arbitrators for only "manifestly" improper conduct.

If parties do not choose institutional arbitration, they still have the option to challenge an arbitrator in the courts at the seat of arbitration. The viability of this option depends on whether the particular domestic arbitration rules empower domestic courts to remove arbitrators for procedural irregularities and the courts' willingness to do so. The English Courts for example, have the power to remove an arbitrator for refusal or failure "to properly conduct the proceedings." But removal of an arbitrator for procedural misconduct is allowed only when "substantial injustice" has been or will be caused to the applicant. Thus many challenges to procedural irregularities are dismissed for failing to meet the threshold of substantial injustice. In a recent case, the applicant had made the argument that there was a failure to properly conduct the proceedings because the arbitrator had acted contrary to his own orders.[13] The court dismissed the challenge since it considered the arbitrator to have correctly applied his discretion when he granted an extension of time. One commentator noted that the case was an example of the applicant failing to prove substantial injustice.[14] On the contrary, the court's reasoning found that the decision of the arbitrator was well within his power and the substantial justice standard was not relevant to its decision. Alternatively stated, the application for an extension of time, at issue in the case, was not considered a procedural irregularity.[15]

In sum, challenging an arbitrator on a procedural irregularity will succeed only when the irregularity is of such a severe nature that it is deemed to be outside the discretion granted to arbitrators. Furthermore, courts will also be unwilling to interfere with the arbitral process unless the conduct or procedural decision of the arbitrator actually causes injustice to the applicant. This concept is discussed later in the chapter.

2.2 ICC and LCIA Challenges against Arbitrators during the Proceedings

This section assesses the ICC and LCIA's approach to determining the types of procedural irregularities and misconduct that can result in the removal of an arbitrator. Particularly this

---

[12] ERIC A. SCHWARTZ & YVES DERAINS, GUIDE TO THE ICC RULES OF ARBITRATION 187 (2d ed. 2005).
[13] Enterprise Insurance Co Plc v. U-Drive Solutions (Gibraltar) Ltd [2016] EWHC 1301 (QB); [2016] 6 WLUK 324.
[14] Mark Edmonds, *How Easy Is to Remove an Arbitrator?*, GRIFFIN LAW (Mar. 20, 2017), https://www.griffin.law/easy-remove-arbitrator.
[15] Enterprise Insurance Co Plc v. U-Drive Solutions (Gibraltar), paras. 76–79.

section examines how bias is assessed, including the scenarios of prejudgment, inappropriate ex-parte communications, and to what extent crude language by arbitrators be tolerated.

2.2.1 *Bias*

The crux of challenges to an arbitrator's conduct during the proceedings relates to the question of impartiality. The challenge must demonstrate that a fair minded and informed observer would conclude that there is a substantial possibility of bias from the arbitrator.[16] Bias is often determined by how the arbitrator conducts the arbitral proceedings.

LCIA bias claims have been founded on the arbitrators' consideration of evidence, the scheduling of hearings, and denial of additional time for submissions. These challenges have been overwhelmingly unsuccessful due to the discretion afforded to arbitrators to conduct the proceedings. A successful challenge, however, was made against an arbitrator who had unilaterally instructed the deletion of parts of the hearing transcript. The fact that the arbitrator had a duty to keep a record of the hearing under the applicable UNCITRAL rules, along with the fact that the counsel had objected to the deletions, was sufficient to convince the LCIA that there was a real possibility of bias.[17]

Many other challenges have failed in cases of arbitrator mistake. One challenge was made against an arbitrator who rejected the respondent's application for extending a deadline for document production, without actually reading the application. The arbitrator read only the claimant's opposition. The LCIA labeled the conduct of the arbitrator as a "regrettable mistake" and a "mishap"; however, it did not accept the challenge because it came to the conclusion that the arbitrator would have made the same decision even if he had read the application. The court also rejected a challenge of an arbitrator for allegedly favoring the party that appointed him by not consulting with her co-arbitrators. The court opined that an arbitrator is not always required to consult their co-arbitrators and that the challenged arbitrator had in fact consulted the other arbitrators when it was required. Thus no real danger of bias was established.

Another challenge was rejected where the claimant-appointed arbitrator was accused of bias for allegedly asking easily answerable questions to the claimant's counsel in a manner that the counsel was able to simply respond "exactly, yes, or absolutely." The LCIA found that this exchange formed only a small part of the hearing and only the recurrence of such actions throughout the hearing would trigger doubt as to the impartiality of the arbitrator.

The ICC Court has consistently applied a high threshold for procedural misconduct. In one challenge[18] regarding drawing up the terms of reference, the court rejected the respondent's challenge of the chairman due to changes made in the terms of reference in favor of the claimant. The court considered that the tribunal had taken into account several of the issues raised by the respondents in the terms of reference and that most of the changes were administrative in nature. In another challenge, the court rejected a challenge that was based on the allegation of bias due to the fact that the parties did not have a reasonable opportunity to present their cases due to short deadlines. The court considered that the decisive issue is whether the arbitrators' acts were to such a degree "to disadvantage one party over another."

An example that illustrates the broad discretion a tribunal has in making procedural orders can be found in a challenge[19] that was made against an entire tribunal. The tribunal had been

---

[16] THOMAS W. WALSH & RUTH TEITELBAUM, THE LCIA COURT DECISIONS ON CHALLENGES TO ARBITRATORS: AN INTRODUCTION 284 (2011).
[17] LCIA Reference No. UN3490.
[18] Unpublished.
[19] Unpublished.

accused of favoring the claimants for approving a document production request made by the claimant that the respondent considered to be unnecessarily broad. The tribunal made its decision without providing reasons. The court found that that such an order did not constitute a violation of the parties' rights and that the tribunal was not required to provide reasoning when giving an interlocutory order such as a document production request, unlike what is considered reasonable in the granting of an award.

2.2.2 Prejudgment

A challenge aimed at removing an arbitrator because of an exhibition of prejudgment is usually made when arbitrators express their conclusion about an issue prematurely – that is before the issue has been subjected to evidentiary hearings.[20] That said, the LCIA has accepted that a degree of prejudgment is sometimes necessary, observing that when deciding whether to order interim measures, an arbitrator or tribunal is forced to take some provisional views on the merits of the dispute. In this case, the LCIA noted that the challenged arbitrator had clearly expressed that his current understanding and interpretation of the applicable contract had led him to deny the request for interim measures but had not formed a final view of the contract dispute.

A well-known LCIA decision on the issue of prejudgment is *National Grid* v. *Argentina*. In this case, during a cross-examination of the claimant's expert witness, the claimant-appointed arbitrator made the unfortunate remark, "everyone present knows the facts in general, that there has been an important damage or a very important change in the expectations of the investor." Taking this statement in isolation, there is no doubt that a fair-minded and informed observer would conclude that the arbitrator had already reached a conclusion on an issue in dispute. When looking at the statement in its context, however, it is far less clear. This is because the arbitrator made the statement in the context of whether certain questions were suitable to be asked of the legal expert. Furthermore, after making this remark, the arbitrator explained the statement by providing examples of hypothetical questions that could be answered by the expert. The LCIA concluded that the followup questioning had eliminated any appearance of bias. Moreover, it considered that the actual remark was perhaps confusing because the arbitrator made the remark in Spanish, which was not her native tongue.[21]

The ICC Court has also been hesitant to remove an arbitrator for allegations of prejudgment. In one decision,[22] the court rejected a challenge against a sole arbitrator brought by the claimant based on the arbitrator's decision not to accept new evidence. The claimant argued that the arbitrator's decision to reject the evidence for lack of relevance constituted a prejudgment on the merits of the case. The court here considered that the sole arbitrator's decision seemed to be based on the fact that the evidence was not produced in a timely manner and the main reason for rejecting it was that the claimant had knowledge of the new evidence at a much earlier time. However, the court noted that the arbitrator's additional reason that the evidence lacked relevancy was "an unfortunate formulation." In another decision,[23] the ICC Court rejected a challenge based on allegations that the arbitrator issued procedural orders before hearing the arguments of the other party and for not requesting a break at the hearing to reflect upon them, thus demonstrating prejudgment. The court noted that the arbitrator had reviewed the evidence before the hearing.

---

[20] William W. Park, *Arbitrator Integrity: The Transient and the Permanent*, 46 SAN DIEGO L. REV. 629, 683 (2009) ("saying too much too early").
[21] SAM LUTTRELL, BIAS CHALLENGES IN INTERNATIONAL COMMERCIAL ARBITRATION 59 (2009).
[22] Unpublished.
[23] Unpublished.

2.2.3 Ex-Parte Communication

Ex-parte communication refers to any communication between an arbitrator and a representative of only one of the parties. The LCIA has held that not all meetings with a single party are "absolutely unacceptable,"[24] but that meetings with just one party that address issues in the dispute are a "step too far."[25] It issued a guidance resulting in the removal of an arbitrator who had twice spoken privately to one of the counsels on issues material to the dispute. It noted that the meetings demonstrated an appearance of bias. It also removed an arbitrator who had indicated to the claimant (the party that had appointed the arbitrator) that the award would be partially favorable to the claimant while the award was still pending.[26]

The ICC Court has demonstrated similar reasoning on this issue, stressing that it is necessary to consider the content and purpose of such communications and whether it was such as "to disadvantage one party over another."[27] It has also confirmed the notion that ex parte communication between an arbitrator and a party does not automatically disqualify the arbitrator, especially where such ex parte communications were brief and did not concern the merits of the case.[28]

2.2.4 Language of Animosity

The LCIA has distinguished between language used by an arbitrator that expresses personal animosity toward a counsel and language that merely expresses that an arbitrator had formed a lesser opinion of counsel. Animosity toward a counsel has been considered to be one of the core reasons for removing an arbitrator, while something less than animosity is insufficient to warrant removal.[29] The LCIA found this distinction accurately drawn in an English case where the court held:

> It is inevitable that Judges and Arbitrators will form opinions as to the professional skills and integrity of those who appear before them; they are bound to find some advocates easier to listen to, and likely, therefore, to be more persuasive than others. But the existence of such views whether held in private or, as in this case made known to others, cannot, without, more be sufficient to constitute bias against that advocate's client.[30]

In one case, the LCIA found the arbitrator's language toward counsel to be "vicious" and "fictitious, false and malevolent," and sufficient to establish animosity and grounds for removal.[31]

The ICC Court dealt with a similar situation where a respondent introduced a challenge against the claimant's arbitrator on various grounds. One of the grounds related to the arbitrator's comments on the evidence behind the challenge, which allegedly showed that the arbitrator was no longer impartial. The court accepted the challenge because it found that the language used by the arbitrator was disrespectful and stemmed from personal animosity, which give rise to concerns about the arbitrator's impartiality. The arbitrator used words in reference to the counsel such as "ignorant of the law," "stubborn," and "hardly going to have the intellectual flexibility to admit its mistake."[32]

In other decisions, the courts have rejected such a challenge, despite the arbitrator using rather harsh language. In one case where the arbitrator in his partial award used phrases such as

---

[24] LCIA Reference No. UN 3490, para. 6.6.
[25] Id. at para. 6.7.
[26] LCIA Reference No. UN 0252.
[27] Unpublished.
[28] Unpublished.
[29] LCIA Reference No. 5665.
[30] Fletamentos Maritimos S.A. v. Effjohn Int'l B.V. (No.2), 2 Lloyd's Rep. 302, 310 (1997).
[31] LCIA Reference No. 5665, para. 1303.
[32] Unpublished.

"obviously wrong" and "simply wrong" when addressing the respondent's arguments. The court did not find this sufficient to give rise to serious concerns about the arbitrator's impartiality. In another case, where, despite the arbitrator using questionable language when drafting a procedural order, the court noted that the sole arbitrator had carefully considered the parties' arguments.

2.2.5 Case Study

It is apparent from the examples used that the courts of arbitral institutions do not entertain frivolous challenges and in cases of doubt are generally reluctant to remove arbitrators. The courts have rejected challenges where there is evidence that arbitrators are sympathetic with the position of one of the parties. In short, unless a procedural irregularity or misconduct gives rise to concerns about an arbitrator's impartiality or is "so manifestly improper as to raise due process concerns" an arbitrator will not be removed. Courts will sometimes label conduct of arbitrators as "regrettable" or "unfortunate," but below the threshold for removal.

The frequency of challenges is low given the high standard for proving arbitrator misconduct, which ensures that only meritorious challenges are brought forward. This is conducive to ensuring that challenges during arbitral proceedings remain a rarity. Frivolous challenges are also deterred because the applicant party pays the institutional costs of an unsuccessful challenge[33] as well as their own legal costs. Thus there is little incentive to challenge an arbitrator for frivolous reasons, unless delaying the proceedings is the goal.

3 SETTING ASIDE AND PREVENTING ENFORCEMENT

After an award is rendered, a party may apply to have an award set aside due to procedural irregularities or arbitrator misconduct at a judicial court at the seat of the arbitration (provided they have not waived their right to do so). Other avenues to contesting an award include where the assets are located or to resist enforcement in another jurisdiction via one of the grounds in Article V of the New York Convention.

3.1 Contracting Out of Challenging an Arbitral Award?

In line with the public policy favoring the finality of awards, some jurisdictions have provided parties the opportunity to waive their right to challenge the arbitral award. For example, the Swiss Private International Law Act (PILA) provides:

> If none of the parties have their domicile, their habitual residence, or a business establishment in Switzerland, they may, by an express statement in the arbitration agreement or by a subsequent written agreement, waive fully the action for annulment or they may limit it to one or several of the grounds listed in Art. 190(2).[34]

This possibility equally exists in Belgian,[35] French,[36] and Swedish[37] arbitration law.[38] If parties choose to include such a provision in their arbitration agreement they cannot apply to set aside

---

[33] WALSH & TEITELBAUM, *supra* note 16, at 312–313.
[34] Swiss Federal Statute on Private International Law Article 192(1).
[35] Belgian Judicial Code, Article 1718.
[36] French Code of Civil Procedure, Article 1522.
[37] Swedish Arbitration Act, Section 51.
[38] Catherine A. Kunz, Waiver of Right to Challenge an International Arbitral Award Is Not Incompatible with ECHR: Tabbane v Switzerland, 5 EUROPEAN INTERNATIONAL ARBITRATION REVIEW 125(2016).

awards on the grounds listed in the arbitration laws of the seat of arbitration. They can only resist the enforcement of the award under the NY Convention.[39]

3.2 Grounds for Setting Aside Awards and Resisting Enforcement under the New York Convention

There are multiple grounds for setting aside or nonenforcement of arbitral awards under national laws and the New York Convention. This chapter focuses only on the grounds related to procedural irregularities and arbitrator misconduct. In Switzerland, an award can be challenged for the following procedural irregularities and arbitrator misconduct: (1) if the arbitral tribunal's decision went beyond the claims submitted to it or failed to decide one of the items of the claim, (2) if the principle of equal treatment of the parties or the right of the parties to be heard was violated, and (3) if the award is incompatible with public policy.[40]

In the United States, an award can be challenged for the following procedural irregularities and arbitrator misconduct: (1) there was evident partiality or corruption in the arbitrators or either of them; (2) the arbitrators were guilty of misconduct in refusing to postpone the hearing upon sufficient cause shown, or in refusing to hear evidence pertinent and material to the controversy, or of any other misbehavior by which the rights of any party have been prejudiced; and (3) the arbitrators exceeded their powers or so imperfectly executed them that a mutual, final, and definite award upon the subject matter submitted was not made.[41]

In England, an award can be challenged for the following procedural irregularities and arbitrator misconduct: (1) failure to comply with the general duty of the tribunal; (2) the tribunal exceeding its powers, (3) failure by the tribunal to conduct the proceedings in accordance with the appropriate procedure, (4) failure by the tribunal to deal with all the issues that were put before it, (5) any arbitral or other institution or person vested by the parties with powers in relation to the proceedings or the award exceeding its powers, (6) failure to comply with the requirements as to the form of the award, or (7) any irregularity in the conduct of the proceedings or in the award that is admitted by the tribunal or by any arbitral or other institution or person vested by the parties with powers in relation to the proceedings or the award. These grounds are only sufficient if the court considers that the irregularity or misconduct "has caused or will cause substantial injustice to the applicant."

In ICSID arbitration, the relevant grounds available for annulment for procedural irregularities and arbitrator misconduct include (1) that the tribunal has manifestly exceeded its powers, (2) that there has been a serious departure from a fundamental rule of procedure, and (3) that the award has failed to state the reasons on which it is based. Finally, the UNCITRAL Model Law, which has been adopted as the domestic arbitration law of numerous countries, provides the following grounds for challenging an award based on procedural irregularities and arbitrator misconduct: (1) party making the application was not given proper notice of the appointment of an arbitrator or of the arbitral proceedings or was otherwise unable to present his case; (2) award deals with a dispute not contemplated by or not falling within the terms of the submission to arbitration or contains decisions on matters beyond the scope of the submission to arbitration,

---

[39] Parties cannot waive their right to oppose enforcement of an award in advance. Catherine Bratic, *The Parties Hereby Waive All Recourse ... but Not That One: Why Parties Adopt Exclusion Agreements and Why Courts Hesitate to Enforce Them*, INTERNATIONAL BAR ASSOCIATION (Oct. 5, 2018), https://www.ibanet.org/Article/NewDetail.aspx?ArticleUid=c8d82ee3-cb34-4113-a63c-7fff919639ee.
[40] PILA, Article 190(2)(c–e).
[41] FAA Section 10(2–4).

provided that, if the decisions on matters submitted to arbitration can be separated from those not so submitted, only that part of the award that contains decisions on matters not submitted to arbitration may be set aside; (3) composition of the arbitral tribunal or the arbitral procedure was not in accordance with the agreement of the parties, unless such agreement was in conflict with a provision of this law from which the parties cannot derogate or, failing such agreement, was not in accordance with this law; or (4) award is in conflict with the public policy of the state.

The New York Convention provides the same grounds for refusing enforcement as the Model Law provides for setting an award aside. The UNCITRAL Model Law is an almost verbatim copy of Article V of the New York Convention.

3.3 General Observations

When examining the grounds that can be used as a basis for nonrecognition of an award, international and domestic arbitration laws often do not explicitly include the grounds of lack of independence or impartiality of arbitrators. The English Arbitration Act is an exception where independence and impartiality are recognized as a general duty of the tribunal and a lack thereof is grounds for setting aside the award.

It is equally apparent that an arbitrator's lack of independence or impartiality can be used as evidence of recognized procedural grounds for setting aside or not enforcing an award.[42] The first ground is the lack of due process, also encompassing, inter alia, equal treatment of parties, a lack of fair hearing, inability to present a case, and violation of right to heard. The second ground is fundamental or significant departure from the agreed to rules of procedure. These two grounds have considerable overlap as, for example, the violation of the right to be heard would generally be impossible without also violating the mandatory rules of national arbitration law and hence would also be a fundamental or significant departure from the rules of procedure. Thus an arbitrator's lack of independence or impartiality is often captured under one of these grounds. These grounds, however, encompass more than a lack of independence or impartiality and deserve examination in greater detail.

The distinction between the grounds for removing an arbitrator and the grounds for setting aside an award exists due to their purpose. The grounds for removing an arbitrator are generally formulated to remove arbitrators who are not capable of acting in an independent and impartial arbitrator manner or incapable of properly conducting the proceedings or making an award. The grounds for setting aside or not enforcing an award are generally formulated to invalidate awards that are not compatible with the parties' arbitration agreement or otherwise are prejudiced against one of the parties.

The third common ground for refusing an award based on procedural irregularities and arbitrator misconduct is when the tribunal exceeds its powers. A tribunal should decide only on matters that were submitted to it and that it has the competence to rule over. As will be explored in the following, the difference between excess use of power and mistake of law is not easy to delineate.

3.4 Are the Differences in Grounds Important?

The differences in the formulation of the grounds for setting aside and for nonrecognition of awards between domestic laws are slight. This is because courts generally refrain from setting

---

[42] BORN, *supra* note 10, at 1242.

aside or refusing to recognize an award due to slight violations of due process. To provide some background, the predecessor to the New York Convention, the 1927 Geneva Convention on the Execution of Foreign Arbitral Awards omitted arbitrator misconduct as a ground for challenge.[43] During the drafting of the New York Convention, the delegates did not intend minor violations to be a ground for invalidating an award unless they altered the outcome of the arbitral proceedings. Accordingly, a violation of one of the grounds stipulated in Article V(1) should not prevent the enforcement of an award if a violation is minimal and does not alter the outcome of the proceedings. Otherwise, Article V(a)(d) would be problematic if interpreted to make small deviations from the arbitration procedure grounds for nonenforcement of awards.[44] The purpose of Article V was to ensure the right to due process and not act as a de facto appeal mechanism. The US Supreme Court has stressed that the grounds for setting aside an award have been designed for cases of "extreme" or "outrageous" arbitral misconduct.

4 VIOLATION OF DUE PROCESS

To ensure a fair and proper arbitration process, certain minimum procedural standards need to be observed that is best captured by the term *due process*. These minimum standards are needed to secure that parties are treated equally and are given a fair hearing.[45] Their exact formulation is different depending on the applicable national law. Generally, however, the principles are relatively similar – they require a party to be heard, to attend fair hearings, to have access to legal representation, to present evidence, and so forth. When arbitrators fail to ensure these principles, they expose the award to being challenged.

Nonetheless, national courts do view challenges for procedural grounds with great suspicion. They recognize that it is extremely enticing for an unsuccessful party to attempt to avoid compliance with an award by alleging a violation of procedural standards. For example, the Swiss Federal tribunal held that an award could not be set aside for the mere violation of a procedural rule.[46] In another decision, it held that a party to an arbitration did not possess an absolute right to hear a witness orally.[47]

Courts, however, can and do intervene by setting aside an award if the parties did not have the opportunity to present their case. For example, US federal courts have held that the failure to hold an oral hearing when requested by one of the parties is a fundamental violation of due process, and a valid ground for setting aside or not recognizing an award.[48] Civil law systems require that evidence should not be the basis of a decision unless the other party had an opportunity to comment.[49] The ICSID annulment committee has also held that a tribunal must allow both parties to make submissions when it receives new evidence it perceives to be relevant. The failure to do so cannot be excused by the fact that both parties were denied the

---

[43] Sundaresh Menon, *Adjudicator, Advocate, or Something in Between? Coming to Terms with the Role of the Party-Appointed Arbitrator*, 34 J INT'L ARB. 3, 35 (2017).
[44] MARIKE R. P. PAULSSON, THE 1958 NEW YORK CONVENTION IN ACTION 174–175 (2016).
[45] Alan REDFERN & Martin HUNTER, INTERNATIONAL ARBITRATION 587(6th ed. 2015).
[46] Decision of July 1, 2004, Case No. 4p_93/2004 (2005) 1 ASA Bulletin 139.
[47] Decision of Jan. 7, 2004, Case No 4P_196/2003(2004) 3 ASA Bulletin 592.
[48] Parsons Whittemore Overseas Co. Inc. v. Societe Geneale de l'Industrie du Papier (RAKTA) 508 f.2D 969 (2nd Cir. 1974).
[49] REDFERN & HUNTER, *supra* note 45, at 588.

opportunity.[50] Some courts also view certain procedural irregularities as violating public policy. For example, the Tokyo District Court when annulling an award, held that a tribunal treating a disputed fact as an undisputed fact was a procedural irregularity so serious, that recognizing the award would offend Japanese public policy.

4.1 Departure from Rule of Procedure

The procedure adopted in an arbitration should conform to the agreement of the parties and, in the absence of such agreement, with the laws of the seat of arbitration. When there is a specific agreement as to arbitral procedure, the tribunal must follow the agreed to procedure, unless it is in conflict with mandatory provisions of the law of the seat. In that event, the tribunal must adopt the mandatory provisions. In the event that there is no agreement, the tribunal can adopt its own procedure, as long as it complies with the principle of due process outlined earlier.[51] The tribunal will not find much guidance from the rules of major arbitral institutions, as these rules are intentionally quite vague as to what procedure should be followed. The rules are designed to be used worldwide and must therefore be flexible enough to be compatible with different judicial systems.[52] It is a challenge for the arbitrator to keep the arbitral process as efficient as possible while ensuring its compatibility with the due process requirements of the seat of arbitration and international principles as well.

As a starting point, arbitrators should recognize that party autonomy is paramount and that the parties may have different views on evidentiary matters. They should therefore always seek input from the parties and try to reach a mutually acceptable agreement. The procedure should always follow the agreement of the parties except in truly exceptional circumstances where such agreement would be incompatible with principles of justice or cause severe delays. Arbitrators balance the importance of promoting efficiency and making procedural decisions that are unlikely to be challenged by the losing party.[53] For the same reason, a tribunal should also warn the parties that failing to meet certain evidentiary obligations will draw adverse inferences. This should encourage compliance while also reducing the opportunities for challenge. That said, a tribunal must be careful not to inappropriately draw adverse inferences, as this would rightfully expose the award to challenge. The tribunal can reduce procedural concerns by adequately notifying the parties of their evidence production obligations.[54]

On the topic of evidence, it should be noted that a due process challenge can arise whether a tribunal accepts evidence or rejects evidence. Tribunals can help alleviate some challenges by restricting submissions by setting strict deadlines, ideally with the agreement of the parties. By doing so, they eliminate the potential for due process arguments if new material is rejected.[55] Essentially the tribunal needs to be proactive by communicating to the parties what is expected of them and obtain agreement on deadlines. If the tribunal fails to set strict deadlines and monitor the proceedings closely, the arbitral process becomes chaotic and unpredictable for the parties, which can open it up to scrutiny.

---

[50] Fraport AG v. Republic of the Philippines, ICSID Case or ARB/03/25 (annulment proceedings), Decision of Dec. 23, 2010, chapter IV. B (119–247); discussed in ICSID Annulment Proceedings based on Serious Departure from a Fundamental Rule of Procedure, Matthias Scherer.

[51] REDFERN & HUNTER, *supra* note 45, at 590.

[52] *Id.* at 588

[53] JEFFREY WAINCYMER, PROCEDURE AND EVIDENCE IN INTERNATIONAL ARBITRATION 752–753 (2012).

[54] *Id.* at 778.

[55] *Id.* at 824.

In terms of the time that tribunals allocate parties for submissions and hearing, tribunals should ensure that both parties have a reasonable opportunity to present their case. This might not always result in both parties having equal time. It is difficult to argue unequal treatment, when both parties had an adequate opportunity to present their case. Due to these uncertainties, it makes more sense for a tribunal to clearly indicate from the outset that the aim of the proceedings is to provide both parties with an adequate opportunity to present their cases and not to rigidly allot an equal amount of time.[56] When it comes to scheduling, a key challenge is that time limits should be as short as possible while guaranteeing due process. This is best achieved by communicating with the parties' counsel from the outset so that they can express how much time they need and why they need that amount of time. Also, tribunals should not overly restrict written submissions, as parties should be able to present arguments that they may not have time to expound upon during the oral hearing.

As for the oral hearings, when tribunals are generous in time allocation, it can allow parties to present their case before their allocated time expires, this helps limit the potential for challenges on the ground that a party was not afforded the right to be heard.[57] Furthermore, after the conclusion of the oral hearing, it is advisable for arbitrators to obtain a clear statement from the parties that they are satisfied with how the hearing was conducted. Such statements help protect the final award from challenge. If a party does declare a concern, the tribunal has the opportunity to address it before issuing its final decision. Often a concern will be declared by the party expecting to lose on the merits, in an attempt to taint the proceedings, claiming that the hearing was not conducted fairly. This point should be recognized by the other party, who should understand that the tribunal is sometimes being generous to the other party in order to protect an eventual award. When an award gets set aside for a procedural defect, the award is unenforceable in the country that sets it aside, and the vacated award is generally unenforceable elsewhere.[58] This is highly undesirable, and it is therefore preferable to appease the losing party by accommodating their procedural requests. In order to improve its chances to challenge an award, a party should object to any perceived procedural irregularities from the outset. The failure to do so will be interpreted as a waiver of the right to object, as most courts will not accept challenges based on procedural defects when a party did not raise the issue during the proceedings.[59]

4.2 Exceeding Powers

Another ground for challenging an award is where a tribunal, despite having jurisdiction, exceeds its powers by rendering an award that deals with matters that were not submitted by the parties. Sometimes such a situation can be easily identified such as when the Paris Cour d'Appel determined that a tribunal exceeded its mandate by awarding significantly higher damages than were actually claimed.[60] Other times, however, such overreaching is not easy to distinguish from a tribunal making an error of law. An error of law committed by a tribunal, while certainly unfortunate and undesirable, is generally not challengeable. If errors of law were challengeable, then the mechanism for challenging awards would function as an appeal

---

[56] *Id.* at 730.
[57] *Id.* at 731.
[58] REDFERN & HUNTER, *supra* note 45, at 601–602.
[59] MATTHIAS SCHERER & SAM MOSS, RESISTING ENFORCEMENT OF A FOREIGN ARBITRAL AWARD UNDER THE NEW YORK CONVENTION 20 (2018).
[60] Paris Lapeyre v. Sauvage (2001) Rev Arb 806.

mechanism, which would be in direct contradiction to one of the main principles of arbitration, the finality of awards.

4.3 Lesotho Case

The *Lesotho Highlands and Development Authority* v. *Impregilo Spa* case[61] illustrates the difficulty courts can have in discerning an error of law committed by a tribunal apart from a tribunal exceeding its powers. The crux of the challenge was that the tribunal had rendered its award in British pounds despite the fact that the amount due under the applicable contract was in Lesotho maloti. The tribunal relied on the English Arbitration Act, which provides that "unless otherwise agreed by the parties,"[62] "the tribunal may order the payment of a sum of money, in any currency."[63] The tribunal justified its decision by pointing to the fact that while the contract provided for payment in Lesotho maloti, it was silent regarding the currency in which an arbitral award was to be rendered. Given that the Lesotho maloti had severely depreciated since the payment under the contract ought to have been made, the tribunal opted to order the payment of the award in pounds. The judge at first instance and subsequently the court of appeal unanimously held that the tribunal had exceeded its powers by ordering the payment of the award in a currency other than that stipulated in the contract.[64]

The House of Lords, however, took a different view. The majority agreed that the tribunal wrongly rendered the judgment in a currency other than that agreed to by the parties; however, they considered that this was a case involving an error of law, a misreading of the Section 48(4) of the English Arbitration Act, which is not appealable. Lord Phillips, however, took the view that the English Arbitration Act does not empower an arbitrator to ignore the explicitly mentioned currency in the applicable contract and concluded that the tribunal had exceeded its powers. He nonetheless agreed that given the circumstances, there was no substantial injustice and therefore a challenge of the award could not be upheld.[65]

The case illustrates the issue of how difficult it is to discern between error of law and a tribunal exceeding its powers. The tribunal had a valid reason to render the award in a currency other than the Lesotho maloti; it wanted to rectify the depreciation of the contract currency. In doing so, however, it made the award susceptible to a challenge. It demonstrates how arbitrators can be challenged for conduct and decisions that they undertake in the interest of justice. Ultimately, the House of Lords found that the rendering of the award in the wrong currency was not a case of misconduct. The case reaffirms that courts will defer to the arbitral tribunal unless the misconduct leads to "substantial injustice" but not when there is simply a negative effect on the challenging party. In sum, the case unquestionably involved a misapplication of law, but the award was upheld since it secured a just outcome.

4.4 Occidental Case: Partial Annulment

While appellate courts may correct a decision of a lower court that was wrongly decided, arbitral awards are not subject to a traditional appellate review by another arbitral tribunal or a

---

[61] Lesotho Highlands and Development Authority v. Impregilo Spa and Others, (2003) 2 Lloyd's Rep 497.
[62] Arbitration Act, Section 48(2).
[63] *Id.* at Section 48(4).
[64] Lesotho Highlands, paras. 30–34.
[65] Robert Merkin & Louis Flannery, Arbitration Act 1996 216 (2014).

national court. The review of an arbitral award is a much more limited in scope than traditional judicial review. Awards generally cannot be vacated or annulled for errors of law.[66] As mentioned earlier, however, the line between an error of law and excess of power can be hard to delineate. In the *Occidental v. Ecuador Case*,[67] the tribunal had awarded the claimant compensation for its entire investment, despite the claimant having transferred 40 percent of its economic interests in the investment to a third party. The majority of the tribunal decided that since the assignment of the economic interests was not authorized, the claimant was entitled to compensation for 100 percent of its investment. The annulment committee, however, did not agree on this interpretation of Ecuadorian contract law and found that the tribunal had exceeded its powers by "compensating a protected investor for an investment which was beneficially owned by a non-protected investor."[68]

This partial annulment in *Occidental* is controversial because in order to establish that the tribunal manifestly exceeded its powers, the committee had to perform an extensive analysis of Ecuadorian contract law. This extensive analysis might appear incompatible with the requirement of the excess of powers being "manifest," which the parties agreed meant "perceived without difficulty."[69] In this respect, the committee noted that the term *manifest* does not prevent requiring "an extensive argumentation and analysis to prove that the misuse of powers has in fact occurred."[70]

5 CONCLUSION

The current mechanism addressing procedural irregularities and arbitrator misconduct is not inherently incompatible with the "spirit or arbitration." This is because without certain checks and balances, arbitration would have the potential to be abusive toward one party. That said, this mechanism should not affect the efficiency of the arbitral process. While it is true that any challenge of an arbitrator or the resisting of the enforcement of an award due to procedural irregularities and arbitrator misconduct slows down the arbitral process, arbitral institutions and national courts have done a good job at generally not allowing frivolous challenges to succeed. This reality, on top of the fact that an unsuccessful challenging party bears the cost of the challenge, has prevented frivolous challenges from becoming a significant issue in international arbitration.

Arbitral institutions, arbitration rules, and domestic arbitration laws provide different grounds for challenging procedural irregularities and arbitrator misconduct at different stages of the arbitral process. Party autonomy ensures that parties can choose particular arbitration rules for an arbitration seated in a particular jurisdiction, under the auspices of a particular arbitral institution, or for ad hoc arbitration, the combination of which most accurately reflects their idea of how procedural irregularities and arbitrator misconduct should be recognized and handled.

Arbitrators removed for committing procedural irregularities or misconduct may be denied their fees by the arbitral association. This is a useful tool to encourage arbitrators to strictly

---

[66] Tai-Heng Cheng, *Precedent and Control in Investment Treaty Arbitration*, in INVESTMENT TREATY LAW: CURRENT ISSUES. REMEDIES IN INTERNATIONAL INVESTMENT LAW EMERGING JURISPRUDENCE OF INTERNATIONAL INVESTMENT LAW 149, 158 (Andrea K. Bjorklund, Ian A. Laird, & Sergey Ripinsky eds., 2009).
[67] Occidental Petroleum Corporation and Occidental Exploration and Production Company v. Republic of Ecuador (II)(ICSID Case No. ARB/06/11).
[68] *Id.* Decision on Annulment of the Award dated Nov. 2, 2015, para. 266.
[69] *Id.* at para. 57.
[70] *Id.* at para. 267.

conform to their mandates. However, there is no agreement on how best to sanction arbitrators for incompetency or misconduct. Some commentators have proposed the creation of a disciplinary body for arbitrators. For example, the Chartered Institute of Arbitrators could offer arbitral institutions "an outsourced disciplinary adjudication process in respect of complaints against arbitrators." The proposed system would be capable of removing an arbitrator from an institution's list of arbitrators due to misconduct, and the misconduct could be published or posted for other institutions to see. Due to its neutrality, the Chartered Institute of Arbitrators would be a suitable organization to create such a disciplinary body. Other commentators, such as Alexis Mourre, have argued that such a disciplinary body is premature and should be considered only after agreement is reached on an internationally recognized ethical code for arbitrators. Such a universal code would require substantial cooperation between arbitral institutions. The importance of such a code before any trans-institutional disciplinary board is a strong argument. For now, procedural irregularities and arbitrator misconduct are the domain of arbitral institutions and national courts. The fact that arbitrators are not sufficiently sanctioned for misconduct under the current system is not an indictment of arbitration; it is more a reflection of the system in general.

PART II

Enforcing Commercial Arbitration Awards

5

Arbitrator Independence in Three Dimensions

Inter-arbitration Association Conflict

Richard Happ

1 INTRODUCTION

In 1884, Edwin Abbott published his novel *Flatland*, in which he described a two-dimensional word with two-dimensional people.[1] The story is told from the perspective of the novel's main character, a square. One day, he is visited by a being from a three-dimensional world, a ball. Being unable to understand and believe the existence of a third dimension, the ball tears the square out of its two-dimensional life and shows it Flatland from above. Upon returning from the third dimension, and wanting to tell his fellow flatlanders about it, the square is frowned upon and not believed.

The topic of this chapter is about a flatland-like experience in the area of conflict of interest in international arbitration. Flatlanders who practice or teach international commercial arbitration tend to believe that they know and understand the rules on conflict of interest. That is until the day they meet something inexplicable and strange such as commodity, sports, or investment arbitration. The study of other types or industry-specific arbitration provides a new and refreshing view on the conflicts-of-interest issue. It shows that conflict of interest is not two-dimensional but has at least three dimensions.

Section 2 will discuss the classical two dimensions of conflicts of interest, with its vertical dimension (within a state) and the horizontal dimension (across several states), Section 3 sketches the unique features of commodity arbitration. Sections 4 and 5 discuss and analyze the issue of potential conflicts between generic arbitration rules and specialized arbitration rule systems. Section 6 offers some findings and conclusions.

2 CLASSICAL TWO-DIMENSIONAL FRAMEWORK FOR CONFLICTS OF INTEREST

International commercial arbitration has a two-dimensional legal framework for conflicts of interest: the vertical dimension describes the legal framework within a state. In international commercial arbitration, the vertical dimension is insufficient because standards might be different in across countries and, therefore, also includes a horizontal dimension that provides a legal framework for the enforcement and recognition of foreign arbitral awards.[2]

---

[1] EDWIN A. ABBOTT, FLATLAND: A ROMANCE OF MANY DIMENSIONS (2d ed. 1884), https://epdf.pub/edwin-a-abbott-flatland.html.
[2] For a fuller discussion see Chapters 2 and 3.

2.1 Vertical Dimension

The starting point for any analysis is the agreement of the parties. The parties may agree on certain criteria for conflicts of interest, either directly or by selecting a set of model or institutional arbitration rules. Institutional arbitration rules provide explicitly that arbitrators must be independent and impartial, but do not substantiate in detail the content of those requirements. Examples include:

> Article 11.1 ICC Rules 2017: "Every arbitrator must be and remain impartial and independent of the parties involved in the arbitration."
>
> Article 9.1 of the 2018 DIS Arbitration Rules: "Every arbitrator shall be impartial and independent of the parties throughout the entire arbitration."
>
> LCIA Rules 2014: "5.3 All arbitrators shall be and remain at all times impartial and independent of the parties; and none shall act in the arbitration as advocate for or representative of any party."

Similar provisions are found in other major arbitration rules in that they set out general principles but very little in content as to the meaning of independence and impartiality. To compound the dearth of content, full decisions of institutional bodies are rarely published except for short abstract summaries. Gary Born called for the publication of decisions relating to challenges of arbitrators:

> In addition, all arbitral institutions should regularly publish summaries of the reasoning underlying their decisions on arbitrator challenges. Evidently, such reasons would need to be published in a way that safeguards the confidentiality of the arbitration (i.e. by providing generic descriptions of the issues in question). Publishing the reasons underlying a decision regarding a challenge would augment the presently limited jurisprudence available, providing more information to bodies ruling on challenges to arbitrators, and it is likely this would increase the predictability and consistency of challenge decisions.[3]

Subsequently, arbitral institutions such as the International Chamber of Commerce (ICC),[4] London Court of International Arbitration (LCIA),[5] and Stockholm Chamber of Commerce (SCC)[6] started publishing decisions. Challenge decisions are also published in academic newspapers.[7] Besides the arbitration rules chosen by the parties, the law at the place of the seat of the arbitration (*lex loci arbitri*) also contains standards on arbitrator independence and impartiality. In Chapter 2, Carlos Matheus López reviews numerous national arbitration laws. Most of them are based on the UNCITRAL Model Law of 1985 (amended 2006), including

---

[3] Gary Born, *Institutions Need to Publish Arbitrator Challenge Decisions*, KLUWER ARBITRATION BLOG (May 10, 2010), http://arbitrationblog.kluwerarbitration.com/2010/05/10/institutions-need-to-publish-arbitrator-challenge-decisions.

[4] "Providing reasons as to Court decisions will further enhance the transparency and clarity of the ICC arbitration process. This new service is a sign of our commitment to ensuring that ICC arbitration is fully responsive to the needs of our users the world over," ICC NEWS (Oct. 8, 2015), https://iccwbo.org/media-wall/news-speeches/icc-court-to-communicate-reasons-as-a-new-service-to-users.

[5] "Written challenge decisions are an invaluable resource for users, counsel, and arbitrators – they give guidance in relation to standards of conduct and provide a greater understanding of the reasoning applied by the Court." *LCIA Releases Challenge Decisions Online*, LCIA NEWS (Feb. 12, 2018). https://www.lcia.org/News/lcia-releases-challenge-decisions-online.aspx.

[6] *SCC Board to Provide Reasoned Decisions on Arbitrator Challenges*, SCC NEWS (Nov. 8, 2017), https://sccinstitute.com/about-the-scc/news/2017/scc-board-to-provide-reasoned-decisions-on-arbitrator-challenges.

[7] *See* Steffen Pihlblad & Johan Tufte-Kristensen, *Challenge Decisions at the Danish Institute of Arbitration*, 33 J. INT'L. ARB. 577–652 (2016).

Article 12 (2), which states: "An arbitrator may be challenged only if circumstances exist that give rise to justifiable doubts as to his impartiality or independence, or if he does not possess qualifications agreed to by the parties."[8] Unfortunately, the Model Law fails to elaborate on the meaning of *reasonable doubts* and the lack of elaboration is replicated in national arbitration laws,[9] which, not surprisingly, has resulted in a degree of nonuniformity when the reasonable doubts standard is applied by arbitration bodies and national courts.[10]

A review of Swiss and French law illustrates how the application of same standard can result in different outcomes:

> However, despite this common statutory approach, the record suggests that Swiss and French outcomes differ considerably: a French court is more likely to remove an arbitrator than a Swiss court hearing the same matter.[11]

Sam Luttrell concludes, with respect to the UNCITRAL Model Law and its requirement of independence and impartiality, that:

> But despite its virtual universality, this expression is read in different ways, and with different results. This is because municipal laws of apparent bias guide state courts in their interpretation of the expression 'justifiable doubts'. In seats with lower thresholds for the appearance of bias – including France, the Netherlands, Sweden, and Singapore – the Black Art of tactical challenge is clearly on the rise and has been for some time.[12]

In sum, while there seems to be a general consensus that the standard test of justifiable doubts is the view of a reasonable third party, the laws give little meaningful guidance in specific cases.

2.2 Horizontal Dimension

While there is universal agreement that arbitrators must be independent and impartial, there is little agreement as to what these principles actually mean. What might constitute a conflict of interest in the eyes of an American-trained lawyer may not be viewed as such by a German-trained lawyer. That is, of course, a problem for international commercial arbitration proceedings. With different standards for independence and impartiality, unnecessary differences arise between arbitration

---

[8] UNCITRAL Model Law on International Commercial Arbitration, 1985 (as amended 2006), http://www.uncitral.org/pdf/english/texts/arbitration/ml-arb/07-86998_Ebook.pdf.

[9] A notable exception is section 8 of the 2019 Swedish Arbitration Act (https://sccinstitute.com/media/408924/the-swedish-arbitration-act_1march2019_eng.pdf), which imposes very specific tests:

> An arbitrator shall be impartial and independent. If a party so requests, an arbitrator shall be released from appointment if there exists any circumstance that may diminish confidence in the arbitrator's impartiality or independence. Such a circumstance shall always be deemed to exist:
> 1. if the arbitrator or a person closely associated with the arbitrator is a party, or otherwise may expect noteworthy benefit or detriment as a result of the outcome of the dispute;
> 2. if the arbitrator or a person closely associated with the arbitrator is the director of a company; or any other association which is a party, or otherwise represents a party or any other person who may expect noteworthy benefit or detriment as a result of the outcome of the dispute;
> 3. if the arbitrator, in the capacity of expert or otherwise, has taken a position in the dispute, or has assisted a party in the preparation or conduct of its case in the dispute; or
> 4. if the arbitrator has received or demanded compensation in violation of Section 39, second paragraph.

[10] GARY BORN, INTERNATIONAL COMMERCIAL ARBITRATION 1774 (2d ed. 2014).

[11] SAM LUTTRELL, BIAS CHALLENGES IN INTERNATIONAL COMMERCIAL ARBITRATION: THE NEED FOR A "REAL DANGER" TEST 127 (2009).

[12] *Id.* at 278.

regimes. This issue becomes especially problematic in international arbitration proceedings that take place in different states. Thus there is a necessity for a horizontal dimension to conflicts of interest.

In 2004, the Arbitration Committee of the International Bar Commission published the IBA Guidelines on Conflicts of Interest in International Arbitration (IBA Guidelines).[13] The IBA Guidelines consist of seven general standards, with explanations, as well as "traffic light" lists of specific situations in which disclosure of potential conflicts is required and when disqualification of arbitrators is necessary. The 2014 revised version states that:

> If the Guidelines are to have an important practical influence, they should address situations that are likely to occur in today's arbitration practice and should provide specific guidance to arbitrators, parties, institutions and courts as to which situations do or do not constitute conflicts of interest, or should or should not be disclosed. For this purpose, the Guidelines categorise situations that may occur in the following Application Lists. These lists cannot cover every situation. In all cases, the General Standards should control the outcome.[14]

The *Red List* consists of two sections, the non-waivable Red List and the waivable Red List. The non-waivable Red List concerns situations where even disclosure does not cure a conflict of interest, in particular where there is a substantial relationship between an arbitrator and a party, while the waivable Red List requires full disclosure but allows the parties to agree on a way to cure the alleged conflict. These situations in which a relationship between the arbitrator and a party to the dispute is considered to be substantial include:

> 2.3 Arbitrator's relationship with the parties or counsel
> 2.3.1 The arbitrator currently represents or advises one of the parties, or an affiliate of one of the parties.
> 2.3.2 The arbitrator currently represents or advises the lawyer or law firm acting as counsel for one of the parties.
> 2.3.3 The arbitrator is a lawyer in the same law firm as the counsel to one of the parties.
> 2.3.4 The arbitrator is a manager, director or member of the supervisory board, or has a controlling influence in an affiliate of one of the parties, if the affiliate is directly involved in the matters in dispute in the arbitration.
> 2.3.5 The arbitrator's law firm had a previous but terminated involvement in the case without the arbitrator being involved himself or herself.
> 2.3.6 The arbitrator's law firm currently has a significant commercial relationship with one of the parties, or an affiliate of one of the parties.
> 2.3.7 The arbitrator regularly advises one of the parties, or an affiliate of one of the parties, but neither the arbitrator nor his or her firm derives a significant financial income therefrom.
> 2.3.8 The arbitrator has a close family relationship with one of the parties, or with a manager, director or member of the supervisory board, or any person having a controlling influence in one of the parties, or an affiliate of one of the parties, or with a counsel representing a party.
> 2.3.9 A close family member of the arbitrator has a significant financial or personal interest in one of the parties, or an affiliate of one of the parties.

---

[13] The IBA Guidelines were updated in 2014. The original version can still be found here: https://sccinstitute.com/media/37100/iba_publications_arbitration_guidelines_2004.pdf.
[14] IBA Guidelines on Conflicts of Interest, 2014 ed., Part II no. 1.

The *Orange List* "is a non-exhaustive enumeration of specific situations which (depending on the facts of a given case) from the view of one of the parties gives rise to justifiable doubts as to the arbitrator's impartiality or independence."[15] These situations relate to previous or current services obtained by a party, or involve the relationship between an arbitrator and another arbitrator or counsel. Disclosure of these relationships is required as they might give rise to justifiable doubts about the arbitrators' independence and impartiality. If no objection is made by the parties, then they are deemed to have accepted the arbitrator. Such situations include repeat appointments by a party. The IBA Guidelines state that the "arbitrator has, within the past three years, been appointed as arbitrator on two or more occasions by one of the parties, or an affiliate of one of the parties" or the "arbitrator has, within the past three years, been appointed on more than three occasions by the same counsel, or the same law firm."[16]

The *Green List* is non-exhaustive list of situations where no conflict of interest exists and no disclosure is required, for example in cases of unavoidable contacts between arbitrators and counsel for one of the parties:

> 4.3.1 The arbitrator has a relationship with another arbitrator, or with the counsel for one of the parties, through membership in the same professional association, or social or charitable organisation, or through a social media network.
>
> 4.3.2 The arbitrator and counsel for one of the parties have previously served together as arbitrators.
>
> 4.3.3 The arbitrator teaches in the same faculty or school as another arbitrator or counsel to one of the parties or serves as an officer of a professional association or social or charitable organisation with another arbitrator or counsel for one of the parties.
>
> 4.3.4 The arbitrator was a speaker, moderator or organiser in one or more conferences, or participated in seminars or working parties of a professional, social or charitable organisation, with another arbitrator or counsel to the parties.

The Working Group that adopted the first version of the IBA Guidelines emphasized the nonexhaustive and non-legal nature of its provisions. Further, the guidelines were meant to cover typical situations and not to override national law or agreed-upon arbitration rules. The Working Group noted that the IBA Guidelines should be "applied with robust common sense and without unduly formalistic interpretation." The application of the IBA Guidelines raises other interesting issues, such as the relationship between disclosure of potential conflicts and the separate question of whether a conflict actually exists. Unfortunately, these issues are outside the scope of the chapter.

What is relevant is that the IBA Guidelines have been widely recognized since they provide specific guidance in the application of the principles of impartiality and independence. In 2007, Judith Gill discussed a review undertaken by the IBA Arbitration Committee:

> The results from the monitoring exercise are clearly mixed. Many differing views are taken as to the correct role for the Guidelines and of their usefulness in resolving conflicts of interest in international arbitration. The Guidelines range from being used almost conclusively by tribunals or the courts in some jurisdictions, to being cited in submissions in others, to not being referred to at all in still others.[17]

In 2015, *Redfern and Hunter on International Commercial Arbitration* concluded that the IBA Guidelines had gained general acceptance and that they were heavily relied on in challenged

---

[15] *Id.* at Part II, para. 3.
[16] *Id.* at 3.1.3 and 3.3.8.
[17] Judith Gill, *The IBA Conflicts Guidelines – Who's Using Them and How*, 1 Disp. Resol. Int'l. 58, 71 (2007).

proceedings.[18] In 2016, the *Report on the Reception of the IBA Arbitration Soft Law Products* summarized the impact of the IBA Guidelines as follows:

> The results of the survey, together with the Country Reports, suggest that, when acting as counsel, practitioners consulted or relied on the Conflicts of Interest Guidelines in the selection of arbitrators even more often than the Guidelines were generally referenced in arbitrations. At the global scale, counsel made use of the Conflicts of Interest Guidelines when appointing arbitrators in 67 per cent of all reported cases. Arbitrators also appeared to make frequent use of the Conflicts of Interest Guidelines across all regions.[19]

In a report about its decisions on arbitrator challenges, the Stockholm Chamber of Commerce considers that the IBA Guidelines "have gained wide acceptance within the international arbitration community since their first issuance in 2004. Arbitrators commonly rely on the Guidelines when making decisions about prospective appointments and necessary disclosures, and the Guidelines are frequently cited in challenges. The SCC Board also routinely consult the Guidelines when deciding challenges under the SCC Rules and the UNCITRAL Rules."[20] The EU–Canadian Comprehensive Economic and Trade Agreement (CETA) requires members of its tribunals to comply with the IBA Guidelines.[21] The guidelines have also been frequently relied on in ICSID arbitrations. The IBA Guidelines have given the abstract principles of impartiality and independence form and substance. Even where parties, arbitrators, and institution disagree with them, especially the items on Orange List, they often use the IBA Guidelines in applying the abstract principles in practical situations.

3 COMMODITY ARBITRATION

For a practitioner of international commercial arbitration, commodity arbitration is an undiscovered country. It proclaims to be arbitration, and its awards are enforceable under the New York Convention, but its procedures are subject to different rules. This section provides an overview of major commodity trading associations, before explaining the peculiarities of commodity arbitration, in particular in regard to the independence and impartiality requirements for arbitrators.

3.1 History

Commodity arbitration developed within the tight framework of commodity trading associations. These associations set up rules and regulations for the trade, including standard contracts for respective commodity transactions among their members, and offer services for the resolution of disputes. These disputes initially concerned the quality or condition of delivered commodities (rice, grain, sugar), and the arbitrators where elected from members of the organization with

---

[18] NIGEL BLACKABY & CONSTANTINE PARTASIDES, REDFERN AND HUNTER ON INTERNATIONAL ARBITRATION para. 4.88 (6th ed. 2015).
[19] IBA Arbitration Guidelines and Rules Subcommittee, *Report on the Reception of the IBA Arbitration Soft Law Products* (2016), para. 100, https://www.ibanet.org/Document/Default.aspx?DocumentUid=105d29a3-6261-4437-84e2-1c8637844beb.
[20] SCC Practice Note, *SCC Board Decisions on Challenges to Arbitrators 2016–2018* (August 2019), https://sccinstitute.com/media/795278/scc-practice-note_scc-decisions-on-challenges-to-arbitrators-2016-2018.pdf.
[21] Comprehensive Economic and Trade Agreement (CETA) between Canada and the European Union and Its Member States, OJ L 11, Jan. 14, 2017, p. 23.

sufficient experience in particular trade. Over the years, the disputes moved away from pure quality arbitration to include disputes over technical and legal issues.[22]

3.2 Major Commodity Trading Associations

Most international commodity trading associations offer arbitration in London.[23] The historical reasons for the venue of these arbitrations in London lies in the fact that since England was the first industrial nation and the heart of the British Empire, a major part of the international trade in commodities was actually based on transactions emanating from London. Another major venue for commodity arbitration is Hamburg, Germany, which is a major port for the trading of commodities. It currently still has six commodity trading associations offering their own arbitration rules.[24] Four trading associations offering arbitration rules and proceedings will be examined here: Refined Sugar Association (RSA); Grain and Feed Trade Association (GAFTA); Federation of Oils, Seeds and Fats Associations Ltd. (FOSFA); and Warenverein Hamburg.

The RSA was founded in 1891 "for the purpose of establishing the Rules and Regulations required for the proper conduct of the white refined sugar trade in the United Kingdom and international markets."[25] The RSA provides contract terms as well as arbitration services. It is a rather small and exclusive organization with about 100 members[26] and a list of twenty-two arbitrators. GAFTA has a much larger membership, currently numbering over 1,800 members in ninety-five countries.[27] It develops "the standard forms of contracts on which it is estimated that 80% of the world's trade in grain is shipped." They also operate an arbitration service for parties using their standard forms.[28] The third major commodity institution is the FOSFA. It provides standard forms of contracts for sales of such goods and claims that 85 percent of the global trade in oils and fats are based on FOSFA contracts.[29] It offers its own arbitration rules and list of arbitrators.

The Warenverein Hamburg was founded in 1900 and represents the interests of German companies active in the foreign and wholesale trade in canned products, frozen products, dried fruit, edible nuts, spices and other goods. Its relevance in international trade stems not only from representing companies from Europe's largest economy but also from Hamburg being Germany's largest and Europe's third largest port.[30] The Hamburg Warenverein offers its own arbitration rules and arbitration court, which has international reach. A third of its arbitration cases involve a non-German party.[31]

---

[22] The historical development is well described in the classic treatise by DEREK JOHNSON, INTERNATIONAL COMMODITY ARBITRATION (1991).
[23] For a detailed list, see Michael Swangard & Tamsyn Pickford, *The Arbitration Agreement and Arbitrability, Commodity Arbitrations*, in AUSTRIAN YEARBOOK ON INTERNATIONAL ARBITRATION 29, 31 (Christian Klausegger, Peter Klein, Florian Kremslehner, et al. eds., 2016).
[24] See Donata von Enzberg & Jade Timmermann, *Hamburg – A German Hotspot for Arbitration*, 81–85 SCHIEDS VZ [German Arbitration Journal] (2019).
[25] See the Refined Sugar Association, http://www.sugarassociation.co.uk/rsa.php.
[26] The list of members is published on their website and covers eight pages. (http://www.sugarassociation.co.uk/documents/rsa%20rules/RSA%20Effective%20March%202018%20Rules%20&%20Regulations.pdf).
[27] See Gafta, https://www.gafta.com/Membership.
[28] For a detailed overview, see Iryna Polovets, Matthew Smith, & Bradley Terry, *GAFTA Arbitration as the Most Appropriate Forum for Dispute Resolution in Grain Trade*, 30 ARIZ. J. INT'L COMP. L., 569 et seq. (2013).
[29] See FOSFA, https://www.fosfa.org/about-us/.
[30] See Port of Hamburg, WIKIPEDIA, https://en.wikipedia.org/wiki/Port_of_Hamburg (last updated Sept. 24, 2019).
[31] In 2017 and 2018, I represented a US company (from California) in a lawsuit under Californian law against another US company from California. The dispute concerned the almond trade, and the jurisdiction of the tribunal was based on

3.3 *Commodity Arbitrations Are Similar but Different*

Commodity arbitration rules all show a peculiar set of features that differentiate them from "standard" international arbitration rules.[32] Those accustomed to only mainstream arbitration rules may wonder whether dispute resolution in the commodity trade should be classified as arbitration at all.

3.3.1 *Procedural Peculiarities*

The first peculiarity is that nearly all of these arbitral institutions provide for an appeal system on the merits (RSA being an exception). Such appeals are not to national courts, but to the association's appeal board or tribunal. GAFTA Arbitration Rule 10.1 states:

> Save as provided in Rules 6.4, 8.1(b), 8.2, 19 and 21, either party may appeal against an award to a board of appeal provided that the following conditions are complied with: – (a) Not later than 12 noon on the 30th consecutive day after the date on which the award was made the appellant shall: (i) ensure that a written notice of appeal is received by Gafta, (ii) serve a notice of his intention to appeal on the other party and ensure receipt of a copy by Gafta, and (iii) ensure Gafta have received cleared funds of the appeal deposit stated on the award of arbitration on account of the costs, fees and expenses of the appeal, otherwise the right of appeal shall be deemed to be waived and barred.

The GAFTA rules regulate the composition of boards of appeal (Rule 11), appeal procedure (Rule 12), withdrawals of appeals (Rule 13), appeals on string contracts (Rule 14 disputes between without direct contractual relationship in the supply chain) and appeal awards (Rule 15). FOSFA (Rules 7–10) and Warenverein Hamburg rules (sections 28–33) contain similar mechanism.

For many arbitration practitioners, an oral hearing is an indispensable cornerstone of due process. In commodity arbitration, that is not always the case. The arbitral tribunal "may grant an oral hearing"[33] but may refuse under FOSFA Rule-4c, which states that the "holding of a hearing shall be at the absolute discretion of the arbitrators"[34] or RSA Rule 10 which requires the party requesting an oral hearing to petition the secretary and council of the association.[35]

In contrast to mainstream international commercial arbitration, legal counsel is not always admitted to hearings. FOSFA Rule 10 states that:

> The holding of a hearing shall be at the absolute discretion of the arbitrator/s and who shall decide on its procedural conduct. If after application, and determined by the arbitrator/s to hold a hearing the arbitrator/s shall give reasonable notice to the parties of the date, time and place for the hearing when any oral evidence or additional submissions may be heard and both parties to

---

the general conditions for the almond exporters, which provided that for all almonds to be exported to Europe, dispute settlement would be arbitration under Warenverein Hamburg rules.

[32] For a detailed review, *see* Swangard & Pickford, *supra* note 23, at 29–46; and the (even if outdated) classic treatise by Johnson, *supra* note 22.

[33] GAFTA Arbitration Rule 4.8.

[34] FOSFA Arbitration Rules 2018, Rule 4c.

[35] *See* RSA Arbitration Rule 10: "Should either or both parties require an oral hearing they shall make their request, in writing, to the Secretary. The Council may grant or refuse such request in its absolute discretion and without assigning any reason."

the arbitration or their authorised representatives may attend any such hearing but may not have present or be represented by counsel, solicitor or any member of the legal profession wholly or principally engaged in private legal practice.[36]

In mainstream international commercial arbitration, parties expect that the arbitral tribunal will deliberate on the evidence and arguments submitted to it by the parties, that it will not consider facts outside the record and that no other persons will be allowed to participate in the deliberations. That is not always the case in commodity arbitration. RSA Arbitration Rule 10 states:

> The Council or Secretary may also, on its or his own behalf, whether in relation to a case decided on documents or an oral hearing, consult the legal advisers of the Association and unless otherwise agreed by the Council any information, opinion or advice offered by such person/s whether or not in writing shall be for the sole use of the Council and shall not be made available to the parties.

The Warenverein Hamburg rules provide for a permanent legal adviser with the task of assisting the tribunal, the role of the association's legal counsel being described as follows:

> shall participate as Advisor in all negotiations which take place within the Arbitral Tribunal, before the Arbitral Tribunal or before a member of the Arbitral Tribunal. On his motion he is to be given the floor. On his motion the Arbitrators shall retire for secret consultations from negotiations which take place before the Arbitral Tribunal.

There is a certain justification for this, and that is that arbitrators in commodity disputes are usually merchants without in-depth legal expertise. It makes sense to have a legal expert advising them. However, the parties have no role in selecting the legal expert, have little knowledge of the expert's views, and have no rights to question the expert or to know what advice the expert provides to the tribunal. This is a bit analogous to the role of tribunal secretaries in mainstream arbitration, as the "fourth member of a tribunal," a practice that under ethical rules is considered not to be permissible.[37]

Finally, nearly all trade associations follow a practice of "public shaming"[38] as an out-of-court enforcement mechanism. The names and identities of parties not complying with an award are communicated to the members of the association or publicly announced on the website of the trade association. Section 8 (3) of the Arbitration Rules of the Warenverein Hamburg states that:

> On request of a party the Board of the Association is empowered to inform the members of the Waren-Verein der Hamburger Börse e.V. and of European and international branch associations about the name of a company which has not fulfilled an admitted obligation, or an obligation found by an arbitral award.

Similar provisions can be found in section 24.1 GAFTA (Arbitration Rule No. 125) and Section 16 of the RSA arbitration rules.

---

[36] FOSFA Arbitration Rules 2018, Rule 4c; *see also* GAFTA Arbitration Rule 4.8. Cf. the excellent discussion, including historical background, in Yulia Chernykh, *The Last Citadel: The Restricted Role of Lawyers in Soft Commodity Arbitration*, 4 TRANSNAT'L. DISP. MGMT. (2017). She notes (p. 8) that "The 'delawyering' of soft commodity arbitration thus originates in the nature of the disputes and the precise technical mandate initially imposed on arbitrators."

[37] Cf. Michael Polkinghorne and Charles Rosenberg, *The Role of the Tribunal Secretary in International Arbitration: A Call for Uniform Standard*, INTERNATIONAL BAR ASSOCIATION (Oct. 2014), https://www.ibanet.org/Article/NewDetail.aspx?ArticleUid=987d1cfc-3bc2-48d3-959e-e18d7935f542. In commodity arbitration, such external legal advice is not uncommon, cf. Johnson, *supra* note 22, at 8.

[38] See Polovets et al., *supra* note 28, at 579.

3.3.2 Requirements for Arbitrators

Commodity arbitration historically is more commercial than legal in nature, which has implications for the selection of arbitrators. The pool of possible arbitrators is limited. The range of restriction on qualified arbitrators varies across commodity associations. At one end, the Warenverein Hamburg whose rules merely require that: "Only proprietors, directors, managers, personally liable partners, authorized signatories or executives of firms whose subject matter is the commerce with goods or the mediation or the closing of merchandise-contracts ... may be appointed by a party or on behalf of a party"[39] Other commodity arbitration rules are much stricter. GAFTA requires party-appointed arbitrators to select only "Gafta qualified," arbritrators who are described as "actively engaged in the grain and feed trade for at least ten years. Experience in the trade plus the training and examinations ensures the required level of expertise and commercial aptitude in determining the range of issues put to Gafta Arbitrators." Similarly, parties wishing to submit a dispute to FOSFA must select the members of the tribunal from among FOSFA members: "Only Trading, Full Broker and Full Non-Trading Members or their nominated representative/s to the Federation shall have the right to act as arbitrators . . . . No person wholly or principally engaged in private legal practice shall be eligible to act as an arbitrator."[40] Similar rules apply in RSA arbitration, where the arbitration tribunal is to be selected from the RSA Panel of Arbitrators, which in turn is appointed by the members of the RSA.

The rules thus do not exclude lawyers as arbitrators per se, but instead require that an arbitrator should have significant commercial and trading experience. Thus in-house counsels and academics might qualify as arbitrators.[41] Also, the size of pool of arbitrators is enhanced due to limited (narrow) rules of independence and impartiality. The RSA Arbitration Rules in Clause 9 simple requires that "[n]o such person shall act in an arbitration where he is, or becomes, directly or indirectly interested in the subject matter in dispute." Similarly, FOSFA Arbitration Rule 2b states that "No person shall be eligible to act who, or whose company or firm has any direct or indirect interest in the transaction in the dispute." A bit more specific rule is found in Section 3.7 of the GAFTA Arbitration Rules, which states:

> An arbitrator appointed under these Rules shall be a Gafta Qualified Arbitrator and shall not be interested in the transaction nor directly interested as a member of a company or firm named as a party to the arbitration, nor financially retained by any such company or firm, nor a member of nor financially retained by any company or firm financially associated with any party to the arbitration.

Among the most detailed rules on the impartiality and independence of arbitrators is found in the Arbitration Rules of the Warenverein, which provide in section 4 that:

> (4) The following are excluded from the office of Arbitrator:
>
> 1. Anyone who has been engaged or is still engaged as an Expert in the same case,
> 2. anyone who has mediated in a transaction underlying the dispute or a coherent covering transaction or anyone who belongs to an enterprise which mediated in one of these transactions, or at least temporarily belonged to that enterprise since mediation of the respective transaction,

---

[39] Warenverein Arbitration Rules 4 (2).
[40] FOSFA Arbitration Rule 2b.
[41] Chernykh, *supra* note 36, at 5.

3. anyone who is married to or has been married to a party or to the legal representative of a party,
4. anyone who is, in the sense of section 41 of the German Code of Civil Procedure (Zivilprozeßordnung [ZPO]), related to, an in-law of, or bound by adoption to a party or to the legal representative of a party."

4 CONFLICTS BETWEEN RULES

According to a popular theory developed in the 1960s, everyone is distanced from anyone else in the world by at most six degrees of separation.[42] Modern social networks such as Facebook and LinkedIn build on that premise which sometimes is also called the "small-world problem." In the field of commodity arbitration, this small-world problem creates conflicts recognized under IBA Guidelines. As explained, the commodity arbitration rules require significant experience to qualify as an arbitrator. Irrespective of where the parties are coming from, the arbitrators need either to be members of the commodity institution, or appointed to their panel of arbitrators, or to have significant commercial experience. This severely limits the pool of arbitrators available for any given case and makes business contacts or dealings between arbitrators and parties more likely.

One Warenverein Hamburg case involved a Chinese party as respondent. The Chinese party failed to select an arbitrator in a timely manner, leading to the Warenverein Hamburg appointing an arbitrator on its behalf. A close review of the arbitrator revealed that he was a direct competitor to the respondent and very likely doing business with the claimant, which was not disclosed. The respondent filed a challenge but in the flatland of commodity arbitration the Higher Regional Court dismissed the challenge, reasoning that it was established practice that arbitrators need to have specialized knowledge and that this results in the pool of arbitrators being small and regular business contacts between participants are inevitable.

A similar decision was given by the English High Court Decision in *Rustal Trading Ltd v. Gill & Duffus SA*, which concerned an arbitration under the RSA rules. The Court noted that:

> it can fairly be assumed that one of the reasons why the parties have agreed to trade arbitration is that they wish to have their dispute decided by people who are themselves active traders and so have direct knowledge of how the trade works. However, if the arbitrators are themselves to be active traders there is every likelihood that at least one member of the tribunal will at some time have had commercial dealings with one or both of the parties to the dispute ... (T)here are many ... features of commercial arbitration which find no parallel in the more formal procedures in Courts ... They are known to and accepted by the parties and many people number them among the advantages of arbitration ... In the case of a trade tribunal the fact that an arbitrator has previously had commercial dealings with one or both parties has never been regarded as sufficient of itself to raise a doubt about his ability to act impartially.[43]

5 ANALYSIS

The IBA Guidelines do not directly relate to commodity arbitration. They have been developed by lawyers for lawyers and presume that the arbitrators who will be appointed are lawyers. Consequently, the rules on business relationships relate to relationships between the arbitrator

---

[42] *Cf.* https://en.wikipedia.org/wiki/Small-world_experiment.
[43] Rustal Trading Ltd v. Gill & Duffus S.A (2000) 1 Lloyds Rep. 14.

and the arbitrator's law firm and one of the parties to the arbitration. In commodity arbitration, arbitrators usually are experienced businessmen and not lawyers, thus it is impractical to expect them to comply with the IBA Guidelines.[44] Rigorously applying the rules found in the guidelines to commodity arbitration would create serious problems due to the limited pool of arbitrators. FOSFA, for example, has 1,150 members in 89 countries, but only 46 listed arbitrators. As arbitrators must be representatives of the members of FOSFA, chances are high that they will be appointed in disputes involving FOSFA members or nonmembers with which they have business relationship. Similarly, GAFTA has 1,800 members and only 83 arbitrators.

A footnote in Rule 3.1.3 of the IBA Guidelines deals with the issue of repeated appointments and reads as follows:

> It may be the practice in certain types of arbitration, such as maritime, sports or commodities arbitration, to draw arbitrators from a smaller or specialised pool of individuals. If in such fields it is the custom and practice for parties to frequently appoint the same arbitrator in different cases, no disclosure of this fact is required, where all parties in the arbitration should be familiar with such custom and practice.[45]

This statement recognizes that a general rule applicable to mainstream commercial arbitration may not be a good fit for specific types of arbitration, which have different understandings of what *impartial* and *independent* mean. An arbitrator who could be challenged in an international commercial arbitration for not having disclosed repeat appointments or for being in continuing regular contractual relationship with a party, very likely would not need to disclose this information in commodity arbitration proceedings. It is to be noted that a different threshold for disqualification for repeat appointments is also seen in investment arbitration. An ICSID tribunal, in *OPIC Karimun*, rejected a challenge against a well-known academic based on multiple appointments.[46]

Notions of impartiality and independence thus have a third dimension outside mainstream arbitration, found in the different meanings applied in the contexts of industry-specific arbitration. Simply speaking, not every dispute which involves businesses is international commercial arbitration. This idea was aptly explained by Charles Brower:

> To my mind, there are at least four types: first, domestic arbitration between individual consumers and service providers, to which most, [all persons] have consented at various times, sometimes more knowingly than at others, or between two commercial entities engaged in

---

[44] For example, if the substance of the IBA Guidelines were to be transported into commodity arbitration, those rules would disqualify an arbitrator regularly doing business with a party (cf. Rule 2.3.7, waivable Red List), or that an arbitrator would have to disclose whether the arbitrator had been appointed as arbitrator, within the past three years, on two or more occasions by one of the parties, or is an affiliate of the parties (cf. Rule 3.1.3, Orange List).

[45] On the potential problems with this footnote 5, *see inter alia* Hansjörg Stutzer & Michael Bösch, *Footnote 5 of the Revised IBA Guidelines on Conflicts of Interest in International Arbitration or: CAS quo vadis?*, THOUVENIN RECHTSANWÄLTE KLG (Mar. 7, 2016), https://thouvenin.com/arbitration-newsletter-switzerland-footnote-5-revised-iba-guidelines-conflicts-interest-international-arbitration-cas-quo-vadis-2/. The reasoning from footnote 4 has also been applied in purely "commercial arbitrations" where the issue at hand was highly complex; cf. the report about a Lisbon Court of Appeal judgment (of 1.2.2018, in case no. 1320/17.0YRLSB-8, www.dgsi.pt) dealing with an arbitrator who had been appointed eleven times in three years, *see* http://www.marcalliance.com/brief-overview-of-a-recent-portuguese-state-courts-decision-regarding-the-application-of-iba-guidelines-on-conflicts-of-interests-in-international-arbitration/.

[46] OPIC Karimum Corporation v. The Bolivarian Republic of Venezuela, ICSID Case No. ARB/10/14, Decision on the Proposal to Disqualify Professor Philippe Sands, Arbitrator, May 2, 2011, paras. 44–57; see also Tidewater Investment SRL and Tidewater Caribe, C.A. v. Bolivarian Republic of Venezuela, ICSID Case No. ARB/10/5, Decision on Claimant's Proposal to Disqualify Professor Brigitte Stern, Arbitrator, Dec. 23, 2010, para. 64. For an in-depth review of the recent case law, *see* MARIA NICOLE CLEIS, THE INDEPENDENCE AND IMPARTIALITY OF ICSID ARBITRATORS (2017).

business (e.g., franchise agreements or sales contracts); second, arbitration within trade or industry-specific contexts, such as maritime disputes and commodity sales, where the arbitrators most often are experts in the field who have earned the trust of their peers for their knowledge and fairness; third, international investment arbitration, arising out of either arbitration clauses in contracts for large investments or dispute resolution provisions in bilateral or multilateral investment treaties; and fourth, non-investment related international arbitration, which typically arises out of non-investment commercial transactions and on-going business relationships. Each of these types entails similar, yet distinct, processes that involve different (but sometimes overlapping) actors, regimes and constituencies, whose relationships, in turn, implicate different public policy questions and prescriptions. Thus, while these different contexts may offer each other useful lessons, a set of pressing concerns in one context does not necessarily apply as forcefully or at all in another.[47]

6 INTERDIMENSIONAL CONFLICTS

The standards of neutrality in arbitration (impartiality and independence of arbitrators) are universal but have different meanings in different contexts. There can be no conflict of rules as long as both parties are aware of the specific rules that apply to their arbitration. The meanings of *impartiality, independence*, and, more specifically, *conflict of interest* are contextualized determinations. The fact is that the meaning and rules applying to conflicts of interest of arbitrators are different, depending on the type of arbitration. For example, independence and impartiality of arbitrators also have special meanings in sports arbitration and, to a limited extent, in investment arbitration. These forms of arbitration operate on and within the general legal framework of the *lex arbitri* and the New York Convention (with the exception of ICSID arbitration), but the meanings of these core principles differ from each other.

Given these differences practitioners and parties to arbitration need to be aware that special rules might exist, and not presume that all arbitrations are conforming to the same rules or give the same meaning to the words found in the different sets of arbitration rules. Commodity arbitration very much resembles early commercial arbitration before it became highly formalized and legalized. This type of arbitration reminds us of the origins of our practice and should encourage us to revisit some of what we now consider to be standard, common, and ordinary.

---

[47] Charles Brower, *The Ethics of Arbitration: Perspective from a Practicing International Arbitrator*, 5 PUBLICIST 1 (2010) [downloaded from HeinOnline].

6

Requirements for the Enforceability of Arbitral Awards: A Comparative Overview

Dário Moura Vicente

1 THE PROBLEM DEFINED

1.1 *The Rationale for the Enforceability of Arbitral Awards and the Legal Challenges It Faces*

Arbitration is a form of administration of justice that is distinguished from that administered by state courts fundamentally in that the basis of the arbitrators' jurisdiction – at least in the case of voluntary arbitration – is the consent of the parties in dispute.

Arbitration is thus an expression of party autonomy. In their arbitration agreement, parties not only decide to resort to arbitrators they themselves appoint (or allow arbitral institutions to designate) in respect of an existing dispute or of the disputes potentially emerging from a given legal relationship, but they are also free to stipulate when and how those adjudicators will resolve their dispute.

Notwithstanding its contractual basis, the essence of the arbitrators' activity is jurisdictional in nature, and in this respect, arbitration is broadly comparable with judicial proceedings. The effects of the arbitral award – notably its binding force upon the parties and its enforceability – are analogous to those of judgments emanating from courts.[1]

By virtue of its binding nature, an arbitral award that has acquired the status of *res judicata* may serve as the basis for the rejection of the same claim if resubmitted to a state court. In terms of enforceability, specific performance of the award may be demanded by the successful party from the defaulting one, if necessary, by coercive means.

Both effects generally require the cooperation of state courts or other public entities. The principal challenge faced by the enforcement of an arbitral award lies precisely in ensuring that cooperation.

Ordinarily, such cooperation should be granted as a form of recognition of private ordering, which is inherent to a liberal society and required by the proper functioning of a market economy. Concerning the enforcement of foreign awards, the needs of international trade, which demand the mobility of judgments and awards across national borders, also play a decisive role. But perhaps the most compelling reason for the enforcement of arbitral awards is the respect owed to party reliance. In fact, if States allow parties, under prescribed conditions, to agree on arbitration as an alternative dispute resolution mechanism, then it would frustrate their

---

[1] *See*, on this, GARY BORN, INTERNATIONAL COMMERCIAL ARBITRATION 216 f. (2d ed. 2014); NIGEL BLACKABY, et al., REDFERN AND HUNTER ON INTERNATIONAL ARBITRATION 27 (6th ed. 2015).

legitimate expectations if public judicial bodies were to deny enforcement of arbitral awards validly rendered pursuant to such an agreement.

However, in order that state courts may lend their coercive powers to the enforcement of arbitral awards, the arbitration agreement, the arbitral proceedings, and the award must meet certain minimum requirements. The crux of the matter lies in determining precisely what those requirements should be and the extent to which the arbitral award is to be scrutinized by state courts in order to ensure compliance with them. The responses to these issues, as discussed in this chapter, are varied and may differ depending often on whether the award was rendered by a tribunal seated in the country where the enforcement is requested or seated abroad – in short on whether the award is domestic or foreign.

Paradoxically, in order to enforce an arbitral award, litigation before state courts – which parties originally intended to avoid by resorting to arbitration – often becomes inevitable and may lead, as we shall see, to different results according to where it is conducted.

This in essence will be the subject matter of this paper. Considering the international context in which the problems alluded to increasingly arise, we shall concentrate on the enforcement of foreign arbitral awards, although reference will also be made as necessary to the enforcement of domestic awards.

1.2 Relevant Legal Sources and Their Interaction

As a preliminary step, our topic requires determination of the relevant legal sources and consideration of the way in which they interact.

It is a well-known fact that the enforcement of foreign arbitral awards is now largely regulated by international sources. Most notably, there is the 1958 New York Convention on the Recognition and Enforcement of Foreign Arbitral Awards (New York Convention), which reached the 60th anniversary of its entering into force on 7 June 2019 and now has 164 signatories.[2] As a *double convention*, in the sense that it deals with both the adjudicatory authority of arbitrators and the recognition and enforcement of their awards, the New York Convention has secured almost worldwide efficacy for arbitration as an alternative dispute-resolution mechanism. This is no small achievement, considering that it has no parallel in terms of the enforcement of judgments from state courts.

Even so, the New York Convention does not entirely render redundant national laws in respect to the enforcement of arbitral awards. In fact, pursuant to the principle of national treatment enshrined in Article III of the Convention, member states are to enforce those awards in accordance with the rules of procedure of the territory where the award is relied upon, albeit under the conditions laid down in its subsequent provisions. Furthermore, by virtue of Article VII(1) of the New York Convention, its provisions do not deprive an interested party of the right it may have to avail herself of an arbitral award in the manner and the extent allowed by the law or the treaties of the country where its enforcement is sought.

The New York Convention thus leaves significant leeway to national laws with respect to the enforcement of foreign arbitral awards. Due to the "porosity" of the New York Convention,

---

[2] *See* Convention on the Recognition and Enforcement of Foreign Arbitral Awards, New York, June 10, 1958, in force June 7, 1959 (1959) 330 UNTS 3. For a comparative overview of the New York Convention's interpretation and application in its signatory jurisdictions, *see* RECOGNITION AND ENFORCEMENT OF FOREIGN ARBITRAL AWARDS. THE INTERPRETATION AND APPLICATION OF THE NEW YORK CONVENTION BY NATIONAL COURTS (George A. Bermann ed., 2017).

differences between national approaches regarding the enforcement of arbitral awards have often resurfaced over the past six decades in cases falling within its scope of application.

1.3 Scope and Outline of the Chapter

This chapter will basically seek to point out the principal differences that exist between national legal systems with respect to the enforcement of arbitral awards, notwithstanding the purported degree of uniformity introduced in this field by the New York Convention.

As a first step, the fundamental approaches to arbitration as adopted by various national jurisdictions will be examined, which in turn will account for differences in enforceability practices. These approaches can be referred to as the *territorialist*, the *autonomist*, and the *pluralistic*. The most relevant expressions of these approaches will then be analyzed with regard to three crucial aspects of the legal framework of the enforcement of foreign arbitral awards, namely the need for an exequatur from a national state court, the enforceability of foreign annulled awards, and the public policy exception.

In this chapter, our comparison is necessarily confined to a selected number of legal systems embodying the identified approaches: the English and German systems as representatives of the territorialist approach; the French and Swiss systems as examples of the autonomist approach; and the Portuguese system for the pluralistic approach.

A final reflection will be devoted to the issue of whether and to what extent a compromise between these approaches is feasible under the current state of the law and whether such a compromise is indeed necessary or even desirable.

2 FUNDAMENTAL APPROACHES UNDERLYING NATIONAL RULES ON ENFORCEABILITY OF ARBITRAL AWARDS

2.1 Lex Facit Arbitrum

In an oft-quoted essay published over half a century ago, F. A. Mann put forward the view that "arbitration, like any other institution of municipal law, requires a firm legal basis, which can be found in the recognition and implementation of the idea of *lex facit arbitrum*."[3]

According to this idea, "every arbitration as a national arbitration, that is to say, subject to a specific system of national law." Indeed, as the learned author submitted,

> [n]o one has ever or anywhere been able to point to any provision or legal principle which would permit individuals to act outside the confines of a system of municipal law; even the idea of the autonomy of the parties exists only by virtue of a given system of municipal law and in different systems may have different characteristics and effects.

Similarly, the author went on to say, "every arbitration is necessarily subject to the law of a given state." This law would be the lex arbitri, which in most countries is assumed, as stated by Mann, to be the law of the arbitral tribunal's seat. According to this view, arbitrators are thus inevitably subject to the legislative jurisdiction of country in which they operate, which lays down whether and on what conditions arbitration is permitted at all. More specifically, Mann claimed that "[t]he law of the arbitral tribunal's seat initially governs the whole of the tribunal's life and work. In particular, it governs the validity of the submission, the creation and composition of the

---

[3] *See* Francis A. Mann, Lex Facit Arbitrum, *in* INTERNATIONAL ARBITRATION: LIBER AMICORUM FOR MARTIN DOMKE 241 ff. (Pieter Sanders ed., 1967).

tribunal, the rules of the conflict of laws to be followed, its procedure, the making and publication of its award." At no point, the author submitted, is it possible or desirable to leave the firm ground of a specific legal system and to have resort to some "droit anational." This, he concluded, almost certainly expressed the English approach at the time of his writing: "an arbitration having its seat in England is always and necessarily governed by English rules of procedure."

This view was upheld a decade and a half later by the English Court of Appeal in the case of *Bank Mellat v. Helleniniki Tecchniki S.A.*,[4] decided in 1983, in which Lord Kerr stated:

> Despite suggestions to the contrary by some learned writers under other systems, our jurisprudence does not recognize the concept of arbitral procedures floating in the transnational firmament, unconnected with any municipal system of law.

This approach to arbitration, which has often been described as a form of *territorialism*, still prevails to a large extent in English law. It was in fact enshrined in the 1996 UK Arbitration Act, albeit in a rather attenuated form, inter alia by stating in section 2(1) that the provisions of its Part I "apply where the seat of the arbitration is in England and Wales or Northern Ireland."[5]

A similar rule can be found for example in section 1025(1) of the German Civil Procedure Code,[6] according to which: 'The provisions of this Book apply if the place of arbitration, as referred to in section 1043 subsection 1, is situated in Germany.' This rule also reflects the dominant opinion among German scholars, which Leo Raape famously epitomized in his *Private International Law (Internationales Privatrecht)*,[7] by stating that: "The arbitral tribunal does not throne above the Earth, nor does it float in the air, it must 'land' somewhere." A more recent formulation of the same idea is found in Pieter Sanders's monograph entitled *Quo Vadis Arbitration?*, in which the renowned Dutch author and practitioner wrote that "arbitration can only exist and as such be recognised when based on a law, which regulates this private form of dispute settlement and exercises control over it as, in the case of arbitration, the jurisdiction of the court is ousted."[8]

2.2 Arbitral Awards as Expressions of an Autonomous Legal Order

A fundamentally different view has prevailed in France, at least in what concerns international arbitration, which Berthold Goldman defined in his 1963 Hague lectures[9] as "celui dont la procédure échappe ... à l'application d'un droit étatique." An entire school of thought flowed from Goldman's thesis. Shortly after the cited writing, Philippe Fouchard defined international arbitration in his 1965 doctoral thesis as "un arbitrage détaché de tous les cadres étatiques, soumis à tous égards à des normes et à des autorités véritablement internationales, c'est à dire, ... supra-nationales, extra-nationales, ou mieux, anationales."[10] This concept of international

---

[4] [1984] Q.B. 291. See Francis A. Mann, *England Rejects "Delocalized" Contracts and Arbitration*, 33 INT'L. COMP. L. Q. 193 (1984).
[5] See V. V. Veeder & Ricky H. Diwan, *England & Wales*, in INTERNATIONAL HANDBOOK ON COMMERCIAL ARBITRATION 36 (Lise Bosman ed., 2018), Kluwer Law International, Suppl. 98.
[6] See Stefan Michael Kroll, *Germany*, in INTERNATIONAL HANDBOOK ON COMMERCIAL ARBITRATION 27 f. (Lise Bosman ed., 2018), Kluwer Law International, Suppl. 98.
[7] See LEO RAAPE, INTERNATIONALES PRIVATRECHT 557 (5th ed. 1961).
[8] PIETER SANDERS, QUO VADIS ARBITRATION? SIXTY YEARS OF ARBITRATION PRACTICE 248 (1999).
[9] Berthold Goldman, *Les conflits de lois dans l'arbitrage international de droit privé*, in 109 RECUEIL DES COURS DE L'ACADÉMIE DE LA HAYE DE DROIT INTERNATIONAL 351 ff., 359 (1963-III).
[10] PHILIPPE FOUCHARD, L'ARBITRAGE COMMERCIAL INTERNATIONAL 23 (1965).

arbitration had its most recent exposition in Emmanuel Gaillard's book on legal theory of international arbitration, originally published in 2008,[11] in which the author argued for a "representation" of arbitration:

> qui accepte de considérer que la juridicité de l'arbitrage puisse être puisée non dans un ordre juridique étatique, qu'il s'agisse de celui du siège ou de celui du ou des lieux d'exécution, mais dans un ordre juridique tiers, susceptible d'être qualifié d'ordre juridique arbitral.[12]

This view, according to Professor Gaillard, would correspond to "a strong perception among international commercial arbitrators that they do not administer justice on behalf of a given State, but rather that they exercise a jurisdictional function in the service of the international community."[13]

Ultimately, this approach to international arbitration entered the case law of the French *Cour de Cassation*, which stated in the 2007 *Putrabali* case[14] that:

> La sentence internationale ... n'est rattachée à aucun ordre juridique étatique, est une décision de justice internationale dont la régularité est examinée au regard des règles applicables dans le pays où sa reconnaissance et son exécution sont demandées.

The provisions on arbitration of the French Code of Civil Procedure, last amended in 2011, have largely enshrined this view. International arbitration is indeed defined in Article 1504 of the code as "L'arbitrage qui met en cause des intérêts du commerce international." Pursuant to Article 1518 of the code, awards rendered in such arbitrations may only be the object of a request for annulment: no appeal from those arbitral awards thus lies in the French courts.

However, parties may exclude the possibility of such an annulment by a special agreement. According to Article 1522, section 1 of the code: "Par convention spéciale, les parties peuvent à tout moment renoncer expressément au recours en annulation." By allowing parties to opt out of the jurisdiction of French courts, even in cases that might otherwise justify annulment of the award, the *Code de Procédure Civile* in fact permits them to exclude the applicability of any provisions of French procedural law regarding international arbitrations held in France. The 'delocalization' of those arbitrations, long advocated by French Twentieth century legal scholarship, was thus accomplished.[15]

Swiss federal law followed suit, albeit in a somewhat more restrictive fashion, by providing in Article 192(1) of the Federal Private International Law Act:[16]

> Si les deux parties n'ont ni domicile, ni résidence habituelle, ni établissement en Suisse, elles peuvent, par une déclaration expresse dans la convention d'arbitrage ou un accord écrit ultérieur, exclure tout recours contre les sentences du tribunal arbitral; elles peuvent aussi n'exclure que pour l'un ou l'autre des motifs énumérés à l'article 190, 2e alinéa.

---

[11] EMMANUEL GAILLARD, ASPECTS PHILOSOPHIQUES DU DROIT DE L'ARBITRAGE INTERNATIONAL (2008) [also available in English as *Legal Theory of International Arbitration* (2012)].
[12] *Id.* at 60.
[13] *Id.* (author translation).
[14] Arrêt No. 1021 du 29 juin 2007, Cour de cassation, Première chambre civile, www.courdecassation.fr.
[15] *See*, for a detailed account of the jurisprudential developments that led to this result, Arthur Taylor von Mehren, *International Commercial Arbitration: The Contribution of the French Jurisprudence*, 46 LA. L. REV. 1045 (1986).
[16] For a critique of this rule, see JEAN-FRANÇOIS POUDRET & SÉBASTIEN BESSON, DROIT COMPARÉ DE L'ARBITRAGE INTERNATIONAL 828 f. (2002).

2.3 A Third Way

A third approach to arbitration, positioned somewhere between the other two visions, has increasingly gained ground.

One of its foremost proponents is Jan Paulsson, who dedicated a few enlightening pages to this issue.[17] His starting point is *legal pluralism* – a notion espoused by many comparatists, including the present author.

Despite all efforts aimed at the harmonization or the unification of the law (of which the UNCITRAL Model Law on International Commercial Arbitration provides a prominent example in the field covered by this chapter)[18], our "globalized" world is still characterized by a plurality of legal systems, which to a large extent reflect the idiosyncrasies and the particular sense of justice of national and local communities.

A plurality of legal orders – not just the lex arbitri, as advocated by Mann, but also not necessarily a single autonomous, supranational legal order, like that devised by Goldman, Fouchard and Gaillard – may accordingly give effect to arbitration. Perhaps the most apt normative expression of this idea is the New York Convention itself. While not espousing the notion of an "international arbitration award," as originally proposed, the Convention allows the enforcement of foreign arbitral awards without requiring their approval by the courts of their countries of origin: such is the consequence of the abolition of the double exequatur, as postulated by the 1927 Geneva Convention on the Execution of Foreign Arbitral Awards.[19]

Admittedly, the New York Convention allows denial of the enforcement of foreign arbitral awards where (i) the arbitration agreement on which they were founded is invalid under the law of the country where the award was made (Article V(1)(a)), (ii) the arbitral procedure has failed to conform with the law of the country where the arbitration took place (Article V(1)(d)), or (iii) the award has yet to become binding on the parties or alternatively has been set aside or suspended by a competent authority of the country in which, or under the law of which, that award was made (Article V(1)(e)). In this way the drafters of the New York Convention gave some degree of acknowledgment to the lex arbitri.[20]

At the same time, as already mentioned, the Convention also allows an involved party to avail itself of the more favorable rules of the lex loci executionis (Article VII(1)). In any event, the final word in respect of arbitrability and public policy issues raised by the award is given to the law of the country of enforcement under Article V(2) of the New York Convention.

Thus no single legal system – be it either the lex arbitri or an overarching 'ordre juridique arbitral' –, but rather a multitude of systems is competent to decide on the enforceability of the arbitral award. Consequently, under the New York Convention, enforcement of an award may be denied in one country but upheld in another. This conclusion may seem rather disappointing – given the undeniable complexities it may lead to –, but it is certainly more realistic than those reached by either of the former approaches.

---

[17] JAN PAULSSON, THE IDEA OF ARBITRATION 29 ff. (2013).
[18] *See* UNCITRAL Model Law on International Commercial Arbitration, adopted by the UN Commission on International Trade Law on June 21, 1985, with amendments adopted on July 7, 2006, www.uncitral.org.
[19] *See* Convention on the Execution of Foreign Arbitral Awards, Geneva, Sept. 26, 1927 (1929–1930) 92 League of Nations Treaty Series 301.
[20] *See*, for a thorough discussion of this issue, ALBERT JAN VAN DEN BERG, THE NEW YORK ARBITRATION CONVENTION OF 1958, TOWARDS A UNIFORM JUDICIAL INTERPRETATION esp. 275 ff., 391 f. (1981).

When looking for a national legal system that has adopted this third pluralist approach, then the Portuguese Voluntary Arbitration Law of 2011 (PVAL) may be cited as an example.[21] Based upon the UNCITRAL Model Law, the PVAL devotes an entire chapter to international arbitration, which Article 49 (1) defines, in characteristically French style, as follows: "An arbitration is considered international when international trade interests are at stake."

All the same, the PVAL does not adhere to the delocalization approach advocated in French legal literature since the 1960s, as Article 61 of the PVAL expressly states that: "The present Law is applicable to all arbitrations that take place in Portuguese territory, as well as to the recognition and enforcement in Portugal of awards made in arbitrations seated abroad." Thus, under the Portuguese Act it is not possible to opt out of the jurisdiction of Portuguese courts in what concerns the annulment of awards rendered in arbitrations that take place in Portugal.

At the same time, a significant caveat was introduced in Article 54 concerning the annulment of awards rendered in international arbitrations taking place in Portugal on the grounds of breach of public policy:

> An award made in Portugal, in an international arbitration in which non-Portuguese law has been applied to the merits of the dispute, may be set aside on the grounds provided for in article 46, and also, if such award is to be enforced or produce other effects in national territory, whenever such enforcement leads to a result that is manifestly incompatible with the principles of international public policy.

By virtue of this provision, the international public policy of the Portuguese state may be invoked only in annulment proceedings if the award is to be enforced or produce other effects in the national territory.[22]

The Portuguese arbitration statute has thus made a considerable concession to the pluralistic approach to arbitration, in that it allows awards rendered in Portugal in international arbitrations to remain immune to annulment, even if contrary to Portuguese public policy, insofar as they are not intended to be enforced in the country, but rather elsewhere.

3 REQUIREMENTS FOR THE ENFORCEABILITY OF ARBITRAL AWARDS IN THE LIGHT OF THE VARIOUS APPROACHES TO THE PROBLEM: SELECTED ASPECTS

3.1 Need for Exequatur versus Direct Enforcement

In light of the three approaches discussed earlier, this section will focus on the specific requirements for the enforceability of arbitral awards.

First and foremost, the question arises of whether and to what extent an act of exequatur should be deemed necessary in order that an arbitral award may be enforced by the courts of a given country.

The response is categorically in the affirmative in legal systems that promote the *delocalization* of international arbitration. Under that approach, if arbitral awards can be rendered within the territory of the forum state without any regard to local rules concerning the arbitration

---

[21] *See*, for an English translation and analysis of this law, Dário Moura Vicente, *Portugal*, in INTERNATIONAL HANDBOOK OF COMMERCIAL ARBITRATION (Lise Bosman ed., 2014), Kluwer Law International, Suppl. 82.

[22] *See*, for a broader discussion of this provision, Dário Moura Vicente, *Impugnação da sentença arbitral e ordem pública*, in II ESTUDOS EM HOMENAGEM A MIGUEL GALVÃO TELES 327 ff. (2012); ANTÓNIO SAMPAIO CARAMELO, A IMPUGNAÇÃO DA SENTENÇA ARBITRAL 85 ff. (2014).

agreement or the arbitral procedure and if parties may opt out of local court jurisdiction to set aside arbitral awards, then the enforcement of such awards in that state must necessarily be preceded by an act aimed at verifying whether the award meets a number of minimum requirements.

Such is the position of French law, which expressly requires an act of exequatur in respect of all awards rendered abroad or in international arbitrations that take place in France.[23] This is the main purpose of Article 1516, section 1, of the French Code of Civil Procedure, which states:

> La sentence arbitrale n'est susceptible d'exécution forcée qu'en vertu d'une ordonnance d'exequatur émanant du tribunal de grande instance dans le ressort duquel elle été rendue ou du tribunal de grande instance de Paris lorsqu'elle a été rendue à l'étranger.

In France, an arbitral award rendered in an international arbitration, even if conducted on French soil, is thus equated with a foreign arbitral award. If parties have renounced their right to request the annulment of the award, pursuant to Article 1522, section 1, they are entitled to an appeal from the *ordonnance d'exequatur*, pursuant to Article 1522, section 2, of the Code.

A similar regime applies in Switzerland, whenever the parties have excluded the possibility of setting aside arbitral awards rendered in the country. To this end, Article 192(2) of the Federal Private International Law Act provides that:

> Lorsque les parties ont exclu tout recours contre les sentences et que celles-ci doivent être exécutées en Suisse, la convention de New York du 10 juin 1958 pour la reconnaissance et l'exécution des sentences arbitrales étrangères s'applique par analogie.

Accordingly, in France and Switzerland the requirement of an exequatur in respect of awards rendered in the forum state in international arbitrations is the price to be paid for the delocalization of such arbitrations in those jurisdictions.

A different stand is taken by countries that have not adopted delocalization theory. Such is the case of Portugal, where awards rendered in arbitrations conducted in the national territory are directly enforceable by state courts, notwithstanding their international nature. This is ensured by Article 42(7) of the PVAL (which applies to international arbitration by virtue of the referral to the rules governing domestic arbitration contained in Article 49(2) of the Law), according to which: "An arbitral award that cannot be appealed and that is no longer subject to amendments under article 45 has the same binding effect on the parties as the final and binding judgement of a State court and is enforceable as a State court judgement."

This rule, however, does not extend to the enforcement of foreign awards, as the Supreme Court decided in its ruling of February 18, 2014,[24] according to which: "A foreign arbitral award is not automatically enforceable in Portuguese territory (it does not constitute an enforceable title) without being previously submitted to revision and confirmation by the competent court in light of the national legal system, in spite of the fact that it is covered by the [New York] Convention." This differentiation can be readily explained. Awards rendered in arbitrations seated in Portugal, even if they fall within the notion of international arbitration as defined in Article 49 of the PVAL, are as a matter of law subject to control of their formal regularity through the setting aside procedure provided in Article 46 of the PVAL. Foreign awards, by contrast, are by their nature exempt from such a control and accordingly should not be enforced in Portugal without having first been reviewed by an appropriate national court.

---

[23] *See*, on this, PHILIPPE FOUCHARD, EMMANUEL GAILLARD, & BERTHOLD GOLDMAN, TRAITÉ DE L'ARBITRAGE COMMERCIAL INTERNATIONAL 901 (1996).

[24] Case No. 1630/06.2YRCBR.C2.S1, www.dgsi.pt.

3.2 Enforceability versus Non-enforceability of Foreign Annulled Awards

The three basic approaches have equally relevant consequences regarding the fate of arbitral awards that have been annulled in their country of origin.

Whereas according to the territorial approach such awards should necessarily be denied enforcement in the forum state, since they are devoid of any effect under the lex arbitri, the autonomous approach, on the contrary, is prone to disregard this circumstance and to assess enforceability of the award with complete independence from the arbitral law.

This was the conclusion reached by the French Supreme Court in the already mentioned *Putrabali* case, in which the court held that an arbitral award rendered and annulled in England could be enforced in France on the following terms:

> en application de l'article VII de la Convention de New-York du 10 janvier 1958, la société Rena Holding était recevable à présenter en France la sentence rendue à Londres le 10 avril 2001 conformément à la convention d'arbitrage et au règlement de l'IGPA, et fondée à se prévaloir des dispositions du droit français de l'arbitrage international, qui ne prévoit pas l'annulation de la sentence dans son pays d'origine comme cause de refus de reconnaissance et d'exécution de la sentence rendue à l'étranger.

Although the French Court invoked the more favorable rights provision of the New York Convention, the major premise of its ruling was, as mentioned above, the notion that "la sentence internationale ... n'est rattachée à aucun ordre juridique étatique."[25]

This, however, is not a notion that one may derive from the New York Convention. As Pieter Sanders, its founding father, has pointed out, "[o]n the basis of the [Convention] the judge must refuse leave for enforcement of an annulled award,"[26] except when the interested party relies on Article VII(1) of the Convention. In such a case, however, as Sanders also noted, "we leave the domain of the [Convention] and enter into the domain of national arbitration law or the domain of a treaty."[27]

Hence, a *pluralistic approach* to arbitration affords a degree of leeway to the enforcement of foreign annulled awards; but that enforcement will be based neither on the New York Convention itself nor on a supranational arbitration law of sorts, but rather on the law of the country where the enforcement is sought.

As rightly noted by George Bermann in his 2017 Hague lectures, Article VII of the Convention "suggests that a court may, and indeed must, recognize and enforce a foreign award – even if the Convention would itself allow non-recognition or non-enforcement – as long as domestic law would require its recognition and enforcement."[28]

This includes cases in which the foreign annulment order would not be recognized in the country where enforcement of the arbitral award is requested, as happened in the ruling rendered by the Amsterdam Court of Appeal in the *Yukos* case, subsequently affirmed by the Dutch Supreme Court.[29] However, in such cases enforcement of the annulled award remains firmly grounded on the domestic law of the country of exequatur, notably its public policy

---

[25] For a critical assessment of this ruling, *see* Richard W. Hulbert, *When the Theory Doesn't Fit the Facts. A Further Comment on Putrabali*, 25 ARB. INT'L. 157 (2009).
[26] *See* SANDERS, *supra* note 8, at 414.
[27] *Id.* at 76.
[28] *See* GEORGE A. BERMANN, INTERNATIONAL ARBITRATION AND PRIVATE INTERNATIONAL LAW 544 n. 1485 (2017).
[29] Hoge Raad, OAO Rosneft v. Yukos Capital S.à.r.l., ruling of June 25, 2010, www.rechtspraak.nl. For a comment, *see* Albert Jan van den Berg, *Enforcement of Arbitral Awards Annulled in Russia. Case Comment on Dutch Supreme Court of 25 June 2010*, 28 J. INT'L. ARB. 617 (2011).

exception. This may justify denying effects to the foreign judgment annulling the award, for example because it was politically motivated, obtained through corruption, or failed to guarantee due process.

3.3 Domestic versus International versus Transnational Public Policy

A final point of fracture between the three basic approaches to arbitration concerns the public policy exception. Pursuant to Article V (2) (b) of the New York Convention:

> Recognition and enforcement of an arbitral award may also be refused if the competent authority in the country where recognition and enforcement is sought finds that ... the recognition or enforcement of the award would be contrary to the public policy of that country.

But this begs the question of what, for the purposes of this provision, is to be understood as the public policy of the country of enforcement.

According to one possible view, this notion equates with domestic public policy, i.e. the sum of the mandatory rules of that country. Any award that violates such rules should accordingly be denied enforcement. This is the understanding of that notion implied by a strictly territorial approach to arbitration.

Such an application of the public policy exception is found in the English case of *Soleimany v. Soleimany*,[30] in which the High Court held that "the enforcement here is governed by the public policy of the *lex fori*.' Subsequently, in *IPCO (Nigeria) Ltd.* v. *Nigerian National Petroleum*,[31] the court held that "the relevant public policy is English public policy" and that the analysis should be whether the "enforcement of the award would offend against English public policy."

The contrary view, stemming from the autonomist approach, construes the said notion as referring instead to *transnational public policy*. This would comprise certain basic legal tenets that have purportedly acquired universal acceptance and are part of the so-called ordre juridique arbitral. As Gaillard[32] puts it:

> dans l'ordre juridique arbitral, la constatation que le droit choisi par les parties contrevient aux valeurs fondamentales de la communauté internationale permet aux arbitres de faire prévaloir ces valeurs sur les dispositions de la *lex contractus*. La protection de ces valeurs est assurée par des règles, constitutives de l'ordre public réellement international, dégagées à partir de la constatation que les États s'accordent, même s'ils ne sont pas nécessairement unanimes, à condamner certaines pratiques telles que la corruption, le trafic de stupéfiants ou d'organes humains, à protéger certaines parties jugées faibles ou même, comme dans le cas d'embargo décrétés par la communauté internationale, à promouvoir certaines politiques destinées à assurer la paix et la sécurité internationales.

The problem with this view of public policy is that it presupposes a consensus among national legal systems that actually does not exist. Suffice it to mention in this respect the duty to act in accordance with good faith during contractual negotiations. This notion is close to the hearts of several civil law countries, whose Civil Codes expressly enshrine it. The notion was rejected, however, by the Judicial Committee of the English House of Lords (the precursor of the UK Supreme Court) in *Walford* v. *Miles*, on the grounds that it "is inherently repugnant to the

---

[30] [1999] Q.B. 785.
[31] [2017] UKSC 16.
[32] GAILLARD, *supra* note 11, at 177.

adversarial position of the parties when involved in negotiations. Each party to the negotiations is entitled to pursue his (or her) own interest, so long as he avoids making misrepresentations."[33]

Again, a third way is provided by the *pluralistic approach* to arbitration, according to which the notion of public policy, as enshrined in Article VII(1) of the New York Convention, refers neither to domestic public policy nor to transnational public policy, but rather to *international public policy*. This expression is best understood as comprising those legal principles of national law that cannot be derogated from even in international situations, in spite of the fact that a judgment or award has been rendered abroad.

The distinction between this pluralistic notion of public policy and the territorial approach has been neatly drawn by the Portuguese courts. In a 2014 ruling, the Lisbon Court of Appeal[34] held that Article 33 of the Portuguese law regulating commercial agency contracts,[35] which grants agents the right to goodwill compensation ("indemnização de clientela") in case of contract termination, is a rule of internal as opposed to international public policy. Accordingly, the rule does not prevent the recognition and enforcement in Portugal of a foreign arbitral award that denies the right to goodwill compensation to a commercial agent acting in Portugal on behalf of a foreign company. The Supreme Court confirmed this ruling on October 23, 2014.

The PVAL gave normative expression to this view, by stating in Article 56(1)(b)(ii) that the recognition and enforcement of a foreign arbitral award may be denied if the court finds that: "The recognition or enforcement of the award would lead to a result clearly incompatible with the international public policy of the Portuguese State."[36] Internal, or domestic, public policy is thus clearly distinguishable from international public policy, which is a considerably more restrictive notion.

Yet, each state is entitled to maintain its own notion of international public policy, and as such the concept is eminently susceptible to variations in interpretation from country to country. In fact, international public policy may be described as the kernel of each legal system: those rules and principles that will under no circumstances yield to foreign divergent rules or principles. Although it should not be confused with national mandatory rules, the public policy exception so understood may therefore have different meanings in each contracting state of the New York Convention.

4 CONCLUSION: A PERENNIAL PROBLEM?

The analysis presented in this chapter has shown that, despite the significant efforts undertaken over the past century or so to unify, or at least harmonize, this field of the law, a uniform set of rules governing the requirements for the enforceability of arbitral awards is still nonexistent. In fact, enforceability requirements vary considerably between countries, and to a large extent this is owing to the different approaches to arbitration that prevail in those countries.

One may, of course, identify a trend, which globalization and the advent of the information society have largely promoted, to move away from the strict territorialism that still prevailed in this legal domain into the mid-twentieth century. But we are still far from the universal recognition of a single, transnational legal order governing arbitration in general and the enforcement of foreign arbitral awards in particular.

---

[33] [1992] 1 All ER 453.
[34] Case No. 1036/12.4YRLSB.S1 of Jan. 16, 2014, www.dgsi.pt.
[35] *See* Decree-Law No. 178/86, of 3 July 1986, amended by Decree-Law No. 118/93 of Apr. 13, 1993.
[36] *See*, on this provision, LEI DA ARBITRAGEM VOLUNTÁRIA ANOTADA 191 ff. (Dário Moura Vicente ed., 4th ed. 2019), with further references.

The question nevertheless remains of whether, and to what extent, a compromise between the above-mentioned legal regimes can and should be sought.

However, one may doubt this is feasible in the current state of the law. The differences revealed by legal comparison in this field are not of a purely technical nature, but rather, as this chapter has sought to demonstrate, the result of deeply-rooted divergences in respect of the sources of arbitrators' adjudicatory powers and of the extent to which national courts should give effect to their awards.

A pluralism of legal systems is thus, to a large extent, inevitable in the field of international arbitration. Such a pluralism, ultimately, is nothing more than a consequence of the cultural nature of the law and of the inescapable diversity of its expressions across national borders.

Private International Law nevertheless ensures an "orderly pluralism" ("un pluralisme ordonné") in the sense given to that expression by Mireille Delmas-Marty.[37] That is precisely the type of pluralism that the New York Convention allows in respect to the enforcement of foreign arbitral awards.

---

[37] *See* Mireille Delmas-Marty, Les forces imaginantes du droit, II, Le pluralisme ordonné 26 ff. (2006).

PART III

Scope and Interpretation of Arbitration Clauses

7

Judicial Interpretation of Standard Clauses

Rocío Digón, Kamil Mehiz, and Tony Cole

1 INTRODUCTION

Arbitration is routinely said to be based on consent. Indeed, the consensual nature of arbitration is perhaps its most influential feature, operating both to restrict domestic court involvement in arbitral proceedings as well as limit the review of awards by national courts of law. It is also the consensual nature of arbitration, however, that justifies a domestic court's power to review an arbitral agreement, especially when a party against whom arbitration is brought denies that it agreed to arbitrate a dispute. In essence, the argument has long been that because arbitration is based on consent, parties that have not agreed to arbitrate should not be required to do so. However, as long as only parties who have agreed to arbitrate are required to do so, there are few legitimate reasons for court involvement in the arbitral process or court review of arbitral awards. The parties agreed to arbitrate and thus should live with the consequences of that agreement.

Perhaps the most notable aspect of this traditional approach to arbitration is how it balances support of arbitration with a cautious wariness of its possible misuse. In essence, courts in many jurisdictions perceive their role as equivalent to that of gatekeepers to a secret garden. Their role is to remain at the gate and ensure that only those who had genuinely agreed to arbitrate their disputes were allowed to pass through the gate and access arbitration.

This balance between careful scrutiny of arbitration agreements, and limited review of arbitral procedures and awards, laid the foundation for the development of arbitration from a niche method of dispute resolution into one of the primary methods through which international commercial disputes are resolved. It created a balance through which parties were given the autonomy to decide for themselves how their dispute would best be resolved, while providing assurance that if they still wanted to go to court, they merely had to avoid agreeing to arbitrate.

Traditionally, this gatekeeping role was performed by domestic courts through careful analysis of arbitration agreements. Famously, for example, English courts would often place great weight on such minor variations in contractual language as whether an arbitration agreement covered disputes "arising under" or "arising out of" the contract, with the former often being interpreted as covering a narrower range of disputes than the latter.[1]

Any views in this publication are those of the author and should not be attributed in any way to White & Case LLP, Jones Day or any affiliated partnerships, companies and entities. Due to the general nature of the chapter its content should not be regarded as legal advice. The authors wish to thank Chloe Do for her assistance in preparing this chapter.

[1] *See, e.g.*, Heyman v. Darwins Ltd [1942] AC 356 at 399. *But see* Union of India v. E B Aaby's Rederi A/S [1975] AC 797 at 814, 817 (rejecting this distinction).

However, the growth of international commercial arbitration since the late twentieth century has unquestionably resulted in an adjustment to the traditional balance. Arbitration came to be acknowledged as a professionalized field of legal practice, which in turn reduced concerns that requiring parties to arbitrate meant subjecting them to an unknown process that might work well but also might result in appalling injustice. In sum, the gatekeepers took a glimpse into the garden and concluded that perhaps they did not need to be monitoring the gate as strictly as they had been previously.

This change was perhaps most famously exhibited in the 2007 decision by the United Kingdom's House of Lords in *Fiona Trust & Holding Corp v. Privalov*.[2] While England and Wales had long established itself as a leading arbitration forum, English courts had traditionally paid close attention to the language of the contract (i.e., parsing of the words of the agreement) in order to precisely determine the scope of the parties' agreement to arbitrate. The 2007 *Fiona Trust* decision, however, represented a sea change in English arbitration, with the Court rejecting this longstanding approach and adopting instead a broad presumption that commercial parties, "as rational businessmen, are likely to have intended any dispute arising out of the relationship into which they have entered ... to be decided by the same tribunal."[3] In short, as long as commercial parties have agreed to arbitrate, they should be assumed to have agreed to arbitrate all of the disputes that arise from the same commercial relationship, subject only to a clearly expressed intention to do otherwise.

The importance of this change was not that British courts were now directed to adopt a more expansive interpretation of the language of arbitration agreements but rather that language itself became less important than the expressed intention of parties. Given the inherent uncertainty involved in third parties (i.e., judges) interpreting contracts, it thereby signified an acceptance of arbitration as a means of resolving disputes. In essence, while close attention to contractual language says "we need to ensure that no-one is sent to arbitration unless they agreed to arbitrate, even if this means sometimes not sending people to arbitration who did agree to do so," the new presumption equates to "we need to ensure that arbitration agreements are enforced, even if this means sometimes sending people to arbitration who did not actually agree to arbitrate."

Nonetheless, despite the increased acceptance of arbitration and the resulting broad interpretation given to arbitration clauses, this has certainly not been universal. Indeed, in two large-scale surveys of arbitration practitioners in 2014 and 2016, only practitioners in twenty-two of fifty-three countries described courts in their jurisdictions as taking a, to some degree, "liberal" approach to interpreting the scope of arbitration clauses, with practitioners in twelve other countries describing their courts as taking to some degree a "strict" approach.[4]

In England and Wales, an insistence on the need for the traditional balancing has remained, as seen in the decision by the English Court of Appeal in *Michael Wilson & Partners, Ltd v. John Forster Emmott*.[5] There, the court placed an important qualifier on the *Fiona Trust*'s presumption and found that a broad arbitration clause providing for "all and any disputes" to be referred to arbitration in London nonetheless did not cover the dispute in question, because it was

---

[2] Fiona Trust & Holding Corp v. Privalov [2007] UKHL 40.
[3] Id. at para. 13.
[4] Tony Cole, Ilias, Bantekas, Federico Ferretti, Christine Riefa, Barbara Warwas, & Pietro Ortolani, *Legal Instruments and Practice of Arbitration in the EU*, EUROPEAN PARLIAMENT THINK TANK (2014), http://www.europarl.europa.eu/thinktank/en/document.html?reference=IPOL_STU(2015)509988; Tony Cole, Pietro Ortolani, Pinar Karacan, & Stephanie Trindade Cardoso, *Arbitration in the Americas*, UNIVERSITY OF LEICESTER (Apr. 2018), https://www2.le.ac.uk/departments/law/research/arbitration.
[5] Michael Wilson & Partners, Ltd v. John Forster Emmott, [2018] EWCA Civ 51.

"highly unlikely" that at the time the parties entered into the arbitration agreement they had intended for that agreement to cover the type of dispute at hand.[6] Importantly, this holding did not result from the language of the clause but rather resulted from the court's interpretation of the parties' intent.

This leads to an important issue within the interpretation of arbitration agreements – namely how expansive such interpretation should be. Acceptance of arbitration as a valid form of dispute resolution argues in favor of broad interpretation of arbitration agreements, while traditional concerns about parties losing access to court argues in favor of attending closely to the language used. As this chapter demonstrates, jurisdictions around the world are steadily moving toward the former approach, focusing on identifying the intentions of the parties on the basis that arbitration is acceptable as a mechanism for dispute resolution. While this is not yet a universal position, even those jurisdictions that have traditionally been resistant to arbitration can now be seen to be moving toward this position.

Nonetheless, as recognized by the English Court of Appeal, there is a difference between simply deciding that all disputes should be sent to arbitration as long as the parties entered into an arbitration agreement and focusing on the most likely intentions of the parties. Ultimately, if arbitration is to remain consistent with its foundation in party autonomy, only the latter approach is genuinely acceptable.

This chapter addresses this issue through a comparative analysis of the judicial interpretation of standard arbitration clauses. A short overview of standard arbitration clauses is provided (Section 2), followed by a description of the relevant New York Convention provisions courts apply to the interpretation of such clauses (Section 3). The chapter then analyzes and compares the approach taken by courts in France, the United States, Hong Kong and mainland China, and Argentina (Section 4) before offering conclusions (Section 5).

2 OVERVIEW OF STANDARD CLAUSES

Standard arbitration clauses are common in international arbitration, although such clauses are often drafted with slight differences in formulation. The most frequently used standard arbitration clauses are ones emanating from arbitral institutions themselves, which promote their standard arbitration clauses on their websites and in the annexes to their arbitration rules.[7] Similarly, corporations also constitute another source of standard arbitration clauses by, for instance, including standard dispute resolution clauses in their standard contracts.

Nowadays, although parties have a wide variety of sample clauses to consider when drafting their dispute resolution clauses, unfortunately only very little attention is given by contracting parties.[8] In our view, this finding is a cause for concern because when a dispute arises, it is the language of that clause, and that language alone, that a court will assess to determine the scope of the arbitral tribunal's jurisdiction. As such, and given the increasing complexity of legal disputes, we believe that great care should be given to the drafting of dispute resolution clauses

---

[6] Id. at para. 46.
[7] *See, e.g.*, model arbitration clauses contained in the arbitration rules of the International Chamber of Commerce (ICC), London Court of International Arbitration (LCIA), Stockholm Chamber of Commerce (SCC), Hong Kong International Arbitration Centre (HKIAC), and International Center for Dispute Resolution (ICDR).
[8] *See* Richard Summerfield, *Before Midnight – Practical Approaches to Dispute Resolution Clauses*, in COMPENDIUM 2015: LITIGATION & ALTERNATIVE DISPUTE RESOLUTION 114 (Navigant Consulting ed., 2015). *See also* Hon. Nancy Holtz (Ret.), *Beware the Midnight Clause: Hold the Champagne?*' JAMS (Feb. 19, 2016), https://www.jamsadr.com/files/uploads/documents/articles/holtz-insidecounsel.com-beware-the-midnight-clause.pdf.

so as to ensure that the protection granted to the parties is the one that they envisioned when they initially concluded their contract.

The standard arbitration clauses of leading dispute resolution institutions all have comparable language. For example, the standard International Chamber of Commerce (ICC) dispute resolution clause provides, "[a]ll disputes arising out of or in connection with the present contract shall be finally settled under the Rules of Arbitration of the ICC by one or more arbitrators in accordance with the said Rules."[9] Similarly, the London Court of International Arbitration (LCIA) recommended clause states, "[a]ny dispute arising out of or in connection with this contract, including any question regarding its existence, validity or termination, shall be referred to and finally resolved by arbitration under the LCIA Rules."[10] Finally, the Hong Kong International Arbitration Centre (HKIAC) model clause – more complex than that of either ICC or the LCIA – provides in relevant part that "[a]ny dispute, controversy, difference or claim arising out of or relating to this contract, including the validity, interpretation, performance, breach or termination thereof or any dispute regarding non-contractual obligations arising out of or relating to it shall be referred to and finally resolved by arbitration."[11] As a general matter, arbitral institutions encourage parties to adopt institutional clauses to help ensure the arbitrability of the dispute and the ultimate enforceability of the award. All of these considerations allow for greater efficiency and predictability of the dispute by notably ensuring that the parties' time and money are not wasted on unnecessary jurisdictional hurdles.[12]

Corporations also heavily rely on standard arbitration clauses, although the language of such clauses may vary depending on the industry, the parties involved in the transactions, and the nature of the disputes. Yet, most of these clauses are carefully drafted and often appear to share overlapping language with institutional model clauses. For example, the standard arbitration clause contained in the consumer contract of AT&T provides that:

> [The parties] agree to arbitrate all disputes and claims between [them]. This agreement to arbitrate is intended to be broadly interpreted. It includes, but is not limited to:
> (1) Claims arising out of or relating to any aspect of the relationship between [the parties], whether based in contract, tort, statute, fraud, misrepresentation or any other legal theory;
> (2) Claims that arose before this or any prior Agreement (including, but not limited to, claims relating to advertising);
> (3) Claims that are currently the subject of purported class action litigation in which [the customer is not] a member of a certified class; and
> (4) Claims that may arise after the termination of this Agreement.[13]

Similarly, the dispute resolution clause contained in the 1999 FIDIC standard contract provides in relevant part that "[u]nless settled amicably, *any* dispute in respect of which the DAB's

---

[9] *See Standard ICC Arbitration Clauses (English Version)*, INTERNATIONAL CHAMBER OF COMMERCE, https://iccwbo.org/publication/standard-icc-arbitration-clauses-english-version/.

[10] *See Recommended Clauses*, LONDON COURT OF INTERNATIONAL ARBITRATION, https://www.lcia.org/Dispute_Resolution_Services/LCIA_Recommended_Clauses.aspx.

[11] *See Model Clauses*, HONG KONG INTERNATIONAL ARBITRATION CENTRE, https://www.hkiac.org/arbitration/model-clauses#Arbitration%20under%20the%20HKIAC%20Administered%20Arbitration%20Rules.

[12] Poor drafting of dispute resolution clauses often results in complex jurisdictional challenges where both parties spend a great amount of time and resources to determine whether a claim or a party fall within the jurisdiction of the tribunal. *See, e.g.*, Mediterranean Enterprises v. Ssangyong Corporation, 708 F 2d 1458, 1465 (9th Cir. 1983).

[13] *See AT&T TV Terms of Use*, AT&T, https://www.att.com/legal/terms.attTVDeviceTOU.html (last visited May 15, 2020).

decision (if any) has not become final and binding shall be finally settled by international arbitration."[14]

The frequency of use of standard dispute resolution (or form) clauses, such as the ones cited here, have come to the center of scholarly and institutional debates. A 1990 survey of ICC dispute resolution clauses found that "the standard ICC clause, with perhaps minor variations in wording, was used in 47 arbitration clauses (20 percent) in 1987 and in 21 arbitration clauses (10 percent) in 1989, generally with the addition of the place of arbitration."[15] A more recent survey of international supply contracts collected from SEC filings over the four-year period from 2011 to 2015 found similar divergences in clauses. Of the eighty-six arbitration clauses identified in 157 total contracts, the authors found that the dispute resolution clauses "departed in notable ways from the standard language suggested by international arbitration institutions" and "contained 70 different formulations of scope language."[16] Notably, and relevant to the discussion of the present chapter, in referring to the "dispute," the contracts included twenty-nine references to "dispute or disputes," twenty-three references to "dispute, controversy, or claim," and eleven references to "controversy or claim."[17] Similarly, in describing the source of the dispute, in thirty-one clauses the parties involved referred to "contract" or "agreement" and ten clauses referred to "contract, or breach thereof."[18] There were twenty-one different variations of how the relationship between the dispute and its source was described, with thirty-one clauses invoking the term "arising out of or relating to" and eleven clauses invoking the phrase "arising out of or in connection with."[19] Despite the differences highlighted by Bond, Coyle, and Drahozal in their respective studies, other scholars mostly involved in complex international disputes have noted that "[i]n the overwhelming majority of cases, ... international arbitration agreements are straightforward exercises, adopting either entirely or principally the model, time-tested clauses of a leading arbitral institution."[20] Whether or not this is true, and whether or not an arbitration agreement is "standard," it is certainly true that certain phrases and words often appear in arbitration agreements. As reflected below in this chapter, it is the court's interpretation of these phrases, and that interpretation alone, that ultimately matters.

As the examples have shown, the language of standard arbitration clauses may vary slightly with the use of terms such as *any and all claims related*, *all disputes*, and *any disputes arising from*. The difference between *arising under* and *relating to* has been one of the most discussed in national jurisprudence. With little exception, domestic courts tend to interpret arbitration agreements, in line with the proarbitration stance most countries have now adopted, in an attempt to enforce the parties' true intent to arbitrate, as opposed to strictly focus on the language of the clause.[21] Notwithstanding, there are nuances and differences in how certain phrases are interpreted: this notion is developed in Section 3 below.

---

[14] INTERNATIONAL FEDERATION OF CONSULTING ENGINEERS (FIDIC), CONDITIONS OF CONTRACT FOR CONSTRUCTION, Cl. 20.6 (1999), http://site.iugaza.edu.ps/kshaath/files/2010/12/FIDIC-1999-RED-BOOK.pdf (emphasis added).
[15] Stephen R. Bond, *How to Draft an Arbitration Clause (Revisited)*, in TOWARDS A SCIENCE OF INTERNATIONAL ARBITRATION: COLLECTED EMPIRICAL RESEARCH 69–70 (C. R. Drahozal & R. W. Naimark eds., 2005).
[16] John F. Coyle & Christopher R. Drahozal, *An Empirical Study of Dispute Resolution Clauses in International Supply Contracts*, 52 VANDERBILT JOURNAL OF TRANSNATIONAL LAW 323, 327 (2019).
[17] Id. at 351.
[18] Id. at 352.
[19] Id.
[20] GARY B. BORN, INTERNATIONAL COMMERCIAL ARBITRATION 212 (2014).
[21] Even jurisdictions that were once very restrictive in their approaches, such as China and Argentina, are now starting to prefer a more encompassing approach. *See* Section 3.

3 INTERPRETING STANDARD CLAUSES

The starting point for considering the scope of any arbitration clause, including standard clauses, is the New York Convention,[22] and any applicable provisions of domestic arbitration laws.

Article II of the New York Convention, which refers expressly to arbitration agreements, provides that:

1. Each Contracting State shall recognize an agreement in writing under which the parties undertake to submit to an arbitration all or any differences which have arisen or which may arise between them in respect of a defined relationship, whether contractual or not, concerning a subject matter capable of settlement by arbitration.
2. The term 'agreement in writing' shall include an arbitral clause in a contract or an arbitration agreement, signed by the parties or contained in an exchange of letters or telegrams.
3. The court of a Contracting State, when seized of an action in a matter in respect of which the parties have made an agreement within the meaning of this article, shall, at the request of one of the parties, refer the parties to arbitration, unless it finds that the said agreement is null and void, inoperative or incapable of being performed.[23]

This article thus gives effect to the scope of an arbitration agreement and sets forth the requirements of a valid agreement to arbitrate. Articles II(1) and II(2) introduce a requirement that the agreement to arbitrate must be in writing, and Article II(3) requires that the courts of a contracting state refer parties to arbitration unless the agreement is "null and void, inoperative or incapable of being performed."[24] Such defects of formation are understood to include internationally recognized and generally applicable contract law defenses such as incapacity, duress, mistake or fraud, among others.[25]

Article V(1)(a) of the New York Convention also has an important role in assessing standard clauses at the time of award enforcement. This article provides, in relevant part, that:

Recognition and enforcement of the award may be refused ... [if] [t]he parties to the agreement referred to in Article II [i.e., the agreement to arbitrate] were, under the law applicable to them, under some incapacity or the said agreement is not valid under the law to which the parties have subjected it or, failing any indication thereon, under the law of the country where the award was made.[26]

Therefore, pursuant to Article V(1)(a) – which places the parties' consent at the center of the analysis – the invalidity of an arbitration agreement is a ground to refuse enforcement of an arbitral award. This article must be read together with Article II, given the cross-reference in the

---

[22] Convention on the Recognition and Enforcement of Foreign Arbitral Awards, June 20, 1958, 21 UST 2517 (hereinafter New York Convention). As of July 2019, the New York Convention has been ratified by 160 contracting states (Papua New Guinea being the latest state to have deposited its instrument of accession on July 17, 2019).
[23] New York Convention, Art. II.
[24] New York Convention, Art. II (3).
[25] BORN, *supra* note 20, at 3470–3471 (citing, *e.g.*, Bautista v. Star Cruises, 396 F 3d 1289, 1301 (11th Cir. 2005) ("The limited scope of the Convention's null and void clause 'must be interpreted to encompass only those situations – such as fraud, mistake, duress, and waiver – that can be applied neutrally on an international scale.'") (internal citation omitted) (emphasis added); Rhône Méditerranée Campagnia Francese Di Assicurazioni E Riassicurazoni v. Lauro, 712 F 2d 50, 53 (3rd Cir. 1983) ("An agreement to arbitrate is 'null and void' only (1) when it is subject to an internationally recognized defense such as duress, mistake, fraud, or waiver, or (2) when it contravenes fundamental policies of the forum state.")).
[26] New York Convention, Art. V (1)(a).

text. Parties, and their counsel, should thus carefully review the drafting of their arbitration clauses to ensure insofar as possible that all of the parties' disagreements are resolved in a single forum,[27] namely arbitration.

4 COMPARATIVE ANALYSIS OF COURT INTERPRETATIONS OF STANDARD CLAUSES

A comparative analysis of the interpretation of standard clauses in multiple jurisdictions offers distinct insights into the shift to a broad interpretation of standard clauses that many jurisdictions now embrace. We have chosen the courts of four jurisdictions – France, the United States, Hong Kong and mainland China, and Argentina – as demonstrative evidence of the ways in which various jurisdictions (from the more liberal to the more restrictive ones) interpret arbitration clauses.

4.1 Interpretation of Standard Arbitration Clauses in France

France has long established itself as one of the most arbitration-friendly fora. It thus comes as no surprise that French courts have taken a very liberal approach to interpreting arbitration agreements. In this context, very little importance is given to the fact that the arbitration clause is a standard one, as opposed to the actual language being used. Indeed, French courts apply an *in concreto* approach aimed at giving effect to the intent of the parties rather than focusing strictly on the exact language of the agreement.[28] Therefore, defective clauses – i.e., poorly drafted clauses, indefinite in their scopes – may survive in France while they, most likely, would not in other jurisdictions. The rationale behind this approach lies in the normalization of international arbitration as the primary means of solving international disputes, and thus – according to French courts – there can be no justification to restrict the interpretation of arbitration agreements.[29]

French courts have long applied pro-arbitration policies,[30] whereby arbitrators have jurisdiction only over disputes that the parties have agreed to bring before them. To ensure that the parties' intent to arbitrate is respected, French courts rely on a combination of various legal principles aimed at materializing the exact intent of the parties, and so notwithstanding the language of the clause at issue. Therefore, when tasked with determining the scope *ratione materiae* of an arbitration agreement, French courts have rejected the principle of strict interpretation and instead have commonly relied on the principle of good faith, as well as the doctrines of *contra proferentem* and *effet utile*.[31] Together, these legal principles ensure that

---

[27] BORN, *supra* note 20, at 1352.
[28] *See, e.g.*, Municipalité de Khoms El Mergeb v. Société Dalico, French Cour de cassation, First Chamber, Dec. 20, 1993, 1994 REV. ARB. 116, 117 (holding that the existence and validity of an arbitration agreement should be determined primarily in light of the common intent of the parties).
[29] *See, e.g.*, CHRISTOPHE SERAGLINI & JÉROME ORTSCHEIDT, DROIT DE L'ARBITRAGE INTERNE ET INTERNATIONAL 207 n. 136 (2013), ("[L]'arbitrage est le mode ordinaire de règlement des différends; il ne serait donc pas justifié de restreindre l'interprétation des conventions d'arbitrage qui prévoient d'y recourir.") (International arbitration is the ordinary means of solving disputes; it would therefore not be justified to restrict the interpretation of the arbitration agreements which provide for it.).
[30] Id.
[31] *See, e.g.*, id. at 207; EMMANUEL GAILLARD & JOHN SAVAGE, FOUCHARD GAILLARD GOLDMAN ON INTERNATIONAL COMMERCIAL ARBITRATION 257–260 (1999).

(1) the initial intent of the contracting parties is respected,[32] (2) the ambiguity of the clause does not benefit the drafter at the expense of the other party,[33] and (3) "where [an arbitration] clause can be interpreted in two different ways, the interpretation enabling the clause to be effective should be adopted in preference to that which prevents the clause from being effective."[34]

Such an interpretive approach has allowed French courts to extend the scope of arbitration agreements to tortious claims where the agreement *solely* provided for the arbitrability of disputes "relating to the present contract," "arising out of the contract," or "in connection with the present contract."[35] Similarly, in cases where arbitration clauses provide for the arbitrability of "disputes arising *from the execution of the contract*," "all disputes arising during the performance of the present contract," or "in connection with the present contract," French courts have recognized that the arbitrators could entertain quasi-contractual claims related to the wrongful termination of the contract.[36]

In *Sineco v. Société Shure Brothers Incorporated*,[37] for instance, the Paris Court of Appeal considered the following arbitration clause: "all disputes, differences or questions arising from or in relation with the present contract, its validity, interpretation, or lack thereof, or a violation or a rescission of the contract, shall be finally and only settled in arbitration in Chicago, Illinois in accordance with the rules of arbitration of the AAA."[38] The court was tasked to consider whether the arbitration agreement was manifestly inapplicable and if so, whether the court of Bobigny had jurisdiction over the dispute. While claimant argued that the arbitration clause was inapplicable because the dispute related to extra-contractual breaches arising from the economic public order, rather than contractual breaches resulting from one party's failure to renew the contract, the court rejected this argument and went on to find that such claims ultimately fell within the scope of the arbitration agreement.

Similarly, when analyzing the standard ICC arbitration clause that provides that "[a]ll disputes arising out of or in connection with the present contract shall be finally settled under the Rules of Arbitration of the International Chamber of Commerce by one or more arbitrators appointed in accordance with the said Rules," the French Supreme Court held more than forty

---

[32] *See, e.g.*, GAILLARD & SAVAGE, id. at 257 (noting that "a party's true intention should always prevail over its declared intention, where the two are not the same" and that "when interpreting a contract, one must look for the parties' common intention, rather than simply restricting oneself to examining the literal meaning of the terms used").

[33] *See, e.g.*, id. at 259; UNIDROIT Principles of International Commercial Contracts, May 2016, Art. 4.6 ("If contract terms supplied by one party are unclear, an interpretation against that party is preferred.") (hereinafter UPICC).

[34] *See, e.g.*, GAILLARD & SAVAGE, *supra* note 31, at 258 n. 83 (noting that "[t]his provision has been contained in the French Civil Code since its initial publication in 1804. Since then it has been adopted in a large number of jurisdictions"); UPICC Art. 4.5 ("Contract terms shall be interpreted so as to give effect to all the terms rather than to deprive some of them of effect.").

[35] *See* SAS Merial v. Société Klocke Verpackungs, Cour d'appel de Paris, Mar. 17, 2011, discussed in the Revue de l'arbitrage (2011) at 575. *See also* SERAGLINI & ORTSCHEIDT, *supra* note 29, at 209 n. 148; GAILLARD & SAVAGE, *supra* note 31, at 307 (citing ICC Case Award No. 5779 (1988) and Bureau de recherches géologiques et minières v. Patino International N.V., Cour d'appel de Paris, Dec. 11, 1981, and the opinion of the advocate general J.-C. Lecante).

[36] Seraglini & Ortscheidt, *supra* note 29, at 207 n.139; GAILLARD & SAVAGE, *supra* note 31, at 307 (citing ICC Case Award No. 5779 (1988) and Bureau de recherches géologiques et minières v. Patino International N.V., Cour d'appel de Paris, Dec. 11, 1981, and the opinion of the advocate general J.-C. Lecante).

[37] Sineco v. Société Shure Brothers Incorporated, Cour d'appel de Paris, June 2, 2004.

[38] Id. (Tous les litiges, différends, ou questions nées ou en relation avec le présent contrat, sa validité, son interprétation, un manquement, ou une violation ou une résiliation de ce dernier, devront finalement et uniquement être déterminés et réglés par arbitrage à Chicago, Illinois, conformément aux règles d'arbitrage de l'Association d'arbitrage américaine) (unofficial translation).

years ago that the scope of such an agreement extended to noncontractual disputes.[39] This finding has been upheld in subsequent decisions before French courts.[40]

It follows that a careful review of arbitration clauses with a seat in France is essential. Indeed, the French pro-arbitration policy has a significant impact on the parties most notably because French courts will give meaning to the clause so as to ensure that most disputes not expressly excluded by the parties be subject to arbitration.[41] It is thus of paramount importance that parties and, a fortiori their counsel, properly understand the intention of the parties and draft the arbitration clause accordingly. Given the liberal approach of French courts, parties willing to exclude noncontractual claims from the jurisdiction of the arbitrators may want to expressly provide in their agreement that, for instance, "tortious disputes should not be subject to arbitration, and that such claims fall within the exclusive jurisdiction of the national court of law where the damage occurred."

4.2 Interpretation of Standard Arbitration Clauses in the United States

In the United States, chapter 2 of the Federal Arbitration Act (FAA), which incorporates the New York Convention, regulates the interpretation and enforcement of international arbitration agreements and foreign arbitral awards. At the outset, it is worth noting that we recognize that the FAA may apply in state courts and that states are not preempted from applying either state arbitration laws or state rules of procedure where the latter do not conflict with the FAA or its policies, but we have decided to solely focus the analysis in this section on the federal court's interpretation of the FAA in recognition of the dominance of the FAA in US jurisprudence.

The United States has long established itself as an arbitration-friendly forum, where courts have commonly refused to interfere with the arbitral process and where arbitration agreements are interpreted in a broad and liberal manner. However, unlike the French approach, the American approach is more focused on the actual language of the clause. This pro-arbitration stance originates from a 1973 landmark decision in which the US Supreme Court recognized that "the principle purpose underlying American adoption and implementation of [the Federal Arbitration Act] ... was to encourage the recognition and enforcement of commercial arbitration agreements in international contracts and to unify the standards by which agreements to arbitrate are observed."[42] Applying this new ruling, the highest court of the land later rejected the "old hostility toward arbitration" and instead enacted a "national policy favoring arbitration."[43]

The Supreme Court's pro-arbitration stance has likewise been affirmed by federal courts, which have, for instance, found that chapter 2 of the FAA "generally establishes a strong presumption in favor of arbitration of international commercial disputes"[44] as well as establishing, "as a matter of federal law, [that] any doubts concerning the scope of arbitrable issues should

---

[39] See French Court of Cassation, Commercial Chamber dated July 9, 1974, cited in the French Rev arb 1976, p. 107, note Phillipe Fouchard.

[40] See, e.g., supra note 22.

[41] French Courts even go as far as to cure "pathological clauses" – i.e., clauses suffering from essential defects hindering the harmonious progress of arbitration resulting from, among other things, an incorrect reference to the arbitral institution or a defecting appointment for choosing arbitrators – because "when inserting an arbitration clause in their contract the intention of the parties must be presumed to have been willing to establish an effective machinery for the settlement of disputes covered by the arbitration clause. See GAILLARD & SAVAGE, supra note 31, at 262–264.

[42] Scherk v. Alberto-Culver, 417 US 506, 520 n. 15 (1973).

[43] Southland Corp. v. Keating, 465 US 1, 10, 14 (1984).

[44] Trifonov v. MSC Mediterranean Shipping Co. SA, 590 F Appx 842, 843 (11th Cir. 2014).

be resolved in favor of arbitration."[45] Against this backdrop, US courts have developed a singular approach to the interpretation of standard arbitration clauses, which since the early 1980s has included the categorization of arbitration agreements as either broad or narrow. This categorization by courts is relevant when, for instance, courts assess whether an arbitration clause extended to extra-contractual claims or to multiparty disputes. However, the courts of many circuits have started to abandon such a categorization in favor of a more all-encompassing analysis.

The evolution and approach of US courts' interpretation of the scope of arbitration clauses may be understood through the lens of how the term *arising hereunder* has been analyzed. Historically, US courts have found that the term *arising hereunder* is synonymous with "arising under the agreement" and has been considered to be relatively narrow insofar as standard arbitration clauses are formulated. An oft-cited case supporting this position is the Ninth Circuit's *Mediterranean Enterprises* v. *Ssangyong*, where the district court was asked to consider the scope of an arbitration clause providing that "*any disputes arising hereunder* or following the formation of a joint venture shall be settled through binding arbitration pursuant to the Korean-US Arbitration Agreement with arbitration to take place in Seoul, Korea."[46]

Following a hearing on the scope of the arbitration clause, the court found that the breach of contract claims and the breach of fiduciary duty claims were arbitrable and therefore decided to stay the litigation while the arbitration was pending. Ssangyong appealed the decision and both parties made arguments concerning the meaning of *arising hereunder*. According to Ssangyong, the arbitration clause extended to "'any' disputes between the parties," while according to Mediterranean Enterprises, "arising hereunder" meant "arising under the contract itself" and did not include "matters or claims independent of the contract or collateral thereto."[47]

The Ninth Circuit agreed with Mediterranean Enterprises and specifically relied on Second Circuit precedent to find that "arising hereunder" was synonymous with "arising under the [a]greement."[48] While "arising under" has been considered a narrower construction than "arising out of or relating to,"[49] this approach has largely been rejected by other federal courts.[50] In *Prima Paint*, the US Supreme Court clarified the US position and unsurprisingly found that the use of "any controversy or claim arising out of or relating to this Agreement" in a clause results in a broad, all-encompassing clause.[51]

---

[45] Doe v. Princess Cruise Lines, Ltd., 657 F 3d 1204, 1213 (11th Cir. 2011). It bears mention that the FAA has been found to apply in both federal and state courts, but nothing appears to prevent a state court from applying state arbitration law and state rules of procedure where they do not conflict with the FAA. See Southland Corp. v. Keating, 465 US 1, at 10, 12, 16 (1984) (holding that "[t]he Arbitration Act creates a body of federal substantive law ... applicable in state and federal court"; "Congress declared a national policy favoring arbitration and withdrew the power of the states to require a judicial forum for the resolution of claims which the contracting parties agreed to resolve by arbitration"; and "[i]n holding that the Arbitration Act preempts a state law that withdraws the power to enforce arbitration agreements, we do not hold that [state courts are bound by the act's procedural rules]." See also Christopher R. Drahozal, *The New York Convention and the American Federal System*, 2012 JOURNAL OF DISPUTE RESOLUTION 101, 111–114 (2012).

[46] Mediterranean Enterprises v. Ssangyong Corporation, 708 F 2d 1458, 1465 (9th Cir. 1983) (emphasis added).

[47] Id. at 1463.

[48] Id. *See, e.g.,* In re Kinoshita & Co., in which the Second Circuit held that when an arbitration clause refers to "disputes or controversies 'under' or 'arising out of the contract," arbitration is restricted to "disputes and controversies relating to the interpretation of contract and matters of performance." 287 F 2d 951, 953 (2nd Cir. 1961).

[49] In re Kinoshita & Co., 287 F 2d 951, 953 (2nd Cir. 1961).

[50] *See, e.g.,* Gregory v. Electro-Mechanical Corp., 83 F 3d 382, 386 (11th Cir. 1996) ("This Court has not drawn a distinction between the words 'arising under' and 'arising out of.'"); Battaglia v. McKendry, 233 F 3d 720 (3rd Cir. 2000) (using both phrases interchangeably); Oldroyd v. Elmira Sav. Bank, FSB, 134 F 3d 72 (2nd Cir. 1998).

[51] Prima Paint Corp. v. Flood & Conklin Mfg. Co., 388 US 395, 404 (1967). Arguably, the Second Circuit may be moving closer to the majority position, as it has held that, "to ensure that an arbitration clause is narrowly interpreted, contracting parties must use ['arising under'] or its equivalent, although the better course, obviously, would be to specify exactly which claims are and are not arbitrable." *See* S.A. Mineracao da Trindade-Samitri v. Utah Int'l, Inc. 745

A comprehensive overview of the current US circuit courts' position on the interpretation of the "arising under" clause can be found in the 2018 Colorado Court of Appeals decision, *Digital Landscape Inc v. Media Kings*.[52] There, the court noted that out of the eight circuits considered, five circuits concluded that the mere use of the "arising under" language in a dispute resolution clause could not narrow the scope of an arbitration agreement.[53] In sum, while the language of standard arbitration clauses has been heavily discussed in US jurisprudence, interested parties should pay close attention to the following observations. First, "any and all disputes" has commonly been interpreted as extending the tribunal's jurisdiction to any disputes having any factual or legal connection to the parties' agreement or their dealings. The rationale behind this conclusion is that US courts view the use of "all" or "any" as determinative evidence that parties intended to give broad discretionary powers to the arbitral tribunal.[54] Second, for the sake of clarity, the word *disputes* may be preferable to the word *controversy*, but no real distinction exists among the two since they both cover *every* circumstance in which one party is demanding something and the other party refuses, fails, or is unable to provide for it. US courts have therefore commonly rejected attempts to limit the scope of arbitration agreements based on this artificial distinction.[55] Third, the use of "related to" has the effect of allowing a tribunal to have jurisdiction over a broad range of disputes. In this regard, US courts have almost entirely confirmed that using "related to" in an arbitration agreement permits a tribunal to consider both the parties' contractual and noncontractual claims. Most notably, that particular language allows a tribunal to "reach [] any disputes that 'touch' or have a factual relationship with the parties' contract,"[56] as well as "all disputes having a significant relationship to the parties' underlying contract, regardless of whether those claims implicated the terms of the consulting agreement."[57]

F 2d 190, 194 (2nd Cir. 1984). *See also* Louis Dreyfus Negoce S.A. v. Blystad Shipping & Trading, Inc., 252 F 3d 218, 225 (2nd Cir. 2001).

[52] Digital Landscape Inc. v. Media Kings LLC, 440 P 3d 1200, 1213 (Colo. App. 2018).

[53] Id. at 1210.

[54] Notwithstanding the usefulness of the "any" and "all" language, some arbitral institutions (such as the LCIA) have provided additional security in their standard arbitration clause in order to ensure that a tribunal's powers would not be restricted to a limited set of issues. The LCIA therefore recommends to explicitly state that "any question regarding [the arbitration agreement's] existence, validity or termination" falls within the arbitral tribunal's jurisdiction. While this language is not mandatory, and may appear as overzealous, we believe that principles of efficiency and predictability may warrant such additional language especially in cases in which, for instance, the arbitration is seated in a forum where (1) little arbitral jurisprudence exists or is accessible or (2) domestic courts are known to be reluctant to enforce all-encompassing clauses. *See Recommended Clauses*, THE LONDON COURT OF INTERNATIONAL ARBITRATION, https://www.lcia.org/Dispute_Resolution_Services/LCIA_Recommended_Clauses.aspx.

[55] *See, e.g.*, Public Serv. Elec. & Gas Co. v. Local 94 IBEW, 140 F Supp 2d 384, 395 (D.N.J. 2001); BORN, *supra* note 20, at 1348 (citing Caithness P.I. Corp. v. Prod. Inc., 1992 WL 266316 (D. Kan.); Cales v. Armstrong World Indus., Inc., 2003 WL 1798671, at *15-21 (Ohio Ct. App.); Nanosolutions, LLC v. Prajza, 793 F Supp 2d 46, 57 (D.D.C. 2011) (noting that the term *conflict* has similarly been interpreted expansively)).

[56] *See* BORN, *supra* note 20, at 1349 (citing Pennzoil Exploration & Prod. Co. v. Ramco Energy Ltd, 139 F 3d 1061, 1068 (5th Cir. 1998) ("relating to" language in arbitration agreement is "broad"; clause not limited to claims under contract, and also reaches claims that "'touch' matters covered by" contract); Swensen's Ice Cream Co. v. Corsair Corp., 942 F 2d 1307, 1309 (8th Cir. 1991); In re Kinoshita & Co., 287 F 2d 951, 953 (2nd Cir. 1961); Nokia Corp. v. AU Optronics Corp. (In re TFT–LCD (Flat Panel) Antitrust Litg.), 2011 WL 2650689, at *5 (N.D. Cal.) ("relating to" interpreted broadly to cover all disputes "touching" contractual relationship between parties, including antitrust claims); Tigra Tech. v. Techsport Ltd, 2011 WL 2710678, at *2 (C.D. Cal.) ("any dispute arising from or relating to this Agreement" is broad, covering disputes that "touch[ed] matters" related to underlying contract); McDonnell Douglas Corp. v. Kingdom of Denmark, 607 F Supp 1016, 1019 (E.D. Mo. 1985) ("'[R]elating to' is generally regarded as broad rather than narrow language.")).

[57] *See* BORN, *supra* note 20, at 1349 (citing Am. Recovery Corp. v. Computerized Thermal Imaging, 96 F 3d 88, 93 (4th Cir. 1996). *See also* Doe v. Princess Cruise Lines, Ltd, 657 F 3d 1204, 1218 (11th Cir. 2011) (arbitration agreement ("any and all disputes ... relating to or in any way arising out of or connected with") was "broad, but not limitless"; court required that claims be foreseeable or have some direct relationship to performance of duties under contract)).

4.3 Interpretation of Standard Arbitration Clauses in Hong Kong, SAR and China

Although Hong Kong and mainland China share a common cultural tradition and history, their approaches to international arbitration (and a fortiori the way in which each interpret international arbitration agreements) differ significantly. Indeed, while arbitration has long been used as a means of solving disputes in mainland China,[58] Chinese courts have traditionally been more reluctant to effectively let parties access private tribunals for the resolution of international disputes.[59] In fact, it was only in 1994, with the internationalization of disputes and the rise of "foreign-related and civil and commercial transactions," that the Chinese arbitration law was finally codified.[60] In sharp contrast, Hong Kong, owing much to its British colonial past, has traditionally been considered an arbitration-friendly jurisdiction primarily because of its "legislation based on the UNCITRAL Model Law, decades of jurisprudence, and good lawyers and judges."[61] While these differences may in part lie with the difference in legal tradition (i.e., common law in Hong Kong and civil law in mainland China), the following analysis limits itself to presenting and analyzing the way in which arbitral agreements have been interpreted and enforced in each jurisdiction.

In our view, this analysis is essential, especially at a time when Hong Kong and mainland China continue to play an increasing role in the Asia Pacific region and the interaction between the two jurisdictions is growing. On January 18, 2019, for instance, Hong Kong and mainland China signed the Arrangement on Reciprocal Recognition and Enforcement of Judgments in Civil and Commercial Matters, which provides for reciprocal enforcement and recognition of judgments covering monetary and nonmonetary relief and updates an older 2006 arrangement.[62] The same year, on April 2, 2019, the two also entered into an arrangement in which Chinese courts would recognize and enforce interim measures in arbitrations seated in Hong Kong, applicable to only certain institutions and primarily to measures against assets or property.[63] The move toward greater judicial cooperation between mainland China and Hong Kong will likely expand in the months and years to come[64] and will undoubtedly affect the development of arbitral jurisprudence relating to the enforcement of arbitration agreements.

---

[58] *See* Song Lianbin, Zhao Jian, & Li Hong, *Approaches to the Revision of the 1994 Arbitration Act of the People's Republic of China*, 20 JOURNAL OF INTERNATIONAL ARBITRATION 169 (2003).

[59] Kong Yuan, *Revision of China's 1994 Arbitration Act – Some Suggestions from a Judicalization Perspective*, 22 JOURNAL OF INTERNATIONAL ARBITRATION 323 (2005).

[60] Zhu Weidong, *Determining the Validity of Arbitration Agreements in China: Towards a New Approach*, 6 ASIAN INTERNATIONAL ARBITRATION JOURNAL 44 (2010).

[61] Charles W. Allen, *Disputes Resolution in Hong Kong: Time to Go Back to Basics*, MONDAQ (July 25, 2017).

[62] *See, e.g., Hong Kong and China Sign New Arrangement on Reciprocal Recognition and Enforcement of Judgments in Civil and Commercial Matters*, BAKER MCKENZIE (Jan. 29, 2019).

[63] *See* Peter Yuen, Helen Shi, Damien McDonald, Olga Boltenko, & Matthew Townsend, *Hong Kong and Mainland China Agree upon Bilateral Arrangement Regarding Interim Measures for Arbitration*, KLUWER ARBITRATION BLOG (Apr. 2, 2019), http://arbitrationblog.kluwerarbitration.com/2019/04/02/hong-kong-and-mainland-china-agree-upon-bilateral-arrangement-regarding-interim-measures-for-arbitration/.

[64] In our view, the interaction between China and Hong Kong will continue in the years to come in part because of China's continued commitment to develop the Belt and Road Initiative, and Hong Kong's being one of the major financial players in the development of the project. All together, these initiatives evidence the desire from both mainland China and Hong Kong to create an environment more suitable to the resolution of international disputes. Hong Kong's financial institutions, along with other major financial institutions from the United Kingdom, France, Singapore, Pakistan, the United Arab Emirates, among others, have signed up to the Green Investment Principles for Belt and Road Development aimed at promoting green investment for Belt and Road project. *See, e.g., List of Deliverables of the Second Belt and Road Forum for International Cooperation*, THE SECOND BELT AND ROAD FORUM FOR INTERNATIONAL COOPERATION (Apr. 27, 2019), https://www.beltandroad.news/2019/04/28/joint-communique-of-the-leaders/.

4.3.1 *Hong Kong*

Hong Kong has long established itself as one of the most arbitration-friendly forums, making it in 2018 the fourth most preferred seat of international commercial arbitration in the world, behind Paris, London, and Singapore.[65] While this will come as no surprise for practitioners in the Asia Pacific region, the overwhelming success of Hong Kong as an arbitration hub is, for the most part, attributable to its modern arbitration law – conforming closely to the UNCITRAL Model Law on International Commercial Arbitration – as well as "the aggressive 'pro-arbitration' stance of Hong Kong's first-rate judiciary, [which builds] on similar trend[s] in other jurisdictions with legal systems based on English common law; and the Hong Kong International Arbitration Centre, known for its innovation, internationalism and world-class secretariat."[66] Additionally, and most relevant to this chapter, any domestic judgment on the scope of an arbitration agreement in Hong Kong now benefits from the liberal approach of English courts, which emphasizes the importance of the parties' intent in interpreting arbitration clauses.

Unlike courts in mainland China, Hong Kong courts have put the will of the parties at the forefront of their analysis, hence giving "great deference to party autonomy in determining whether a valid arbitration agreement exists" and with "a strong inclination toward overcoming defects in such agreements where the parties clearly intended to arbitrate their disputes."[67] In *Schindler Lifts (Hong Kong) Ltd v. Sui Chong Construction Engineering*,[68] for instance, the Hong Kong District Court confirmed this position when it ordered a stay of an action pending referral of the dispute to arbitration, despite the defendant having filed a defense in Hong Kong's trial courts.

There, the arbitration agreement provided, in relevant part, that "[i]f a dispute arises under or in connection with the [Contract] the parties agree to resolve the dispute in accordance with the dispute settlement procedures in clause 42 [of the Contract]."[69] The dispute settlement provision of clause 42, in turn provided "for the referral of the dispute to the parties' designated representatives and for mediation," otherwise (1) "either party may give a notice to the other party, by special delivery, to refer the dispute to arbitration and the person to act as the arbitrator shall be agreed between the parties"; and (2) "[t]he arbitration shall be a domestic arbitration conducted in accordance with the Arbitration Ordinance."[70]

Unsurprisingly, and consistent with its general pro-arbitration stance, the Hong Kong court, inter alia, held that noncompliance with a multitier dispute resolution mechanism, which provides for mandatory recourse to mediation before arbitration, could not render the arbitration agreement "inoperative or incapable of being performed."[71] Similarly, the court reaffirmed its position that a party's use of "in connection with" or "connected therewith" in their arbitration agreements will force the court to apply an all-encompassing approach that "will cover all disputes other than those entirely unrelated to the transaction covered by the contract."[72]

---

[65] *See* Paul Friedland, *2018 International Arbitration Survey: The Evolution of International Arbitration*, WHITE & CASE (May 9, 2018).

[66] *See* Steven Nelson & Michael Robbins, *Hong Kong – The Gold Standard of International Arbitration in Asia*, DORSEY & WHITNEY (Oct. 7, 2016), https://www.dorsey.com/newsresources/publications/client-alerts/2016/10/hong-kong-golden-international-arbitration.

[67] Id.

[68] Schindler Lifts (Hong Kong) Ltd v. Sui Chong Construction and Engineering Co Ltd [2014] HKEC 1967.

[69] Id. at para. 22 (emphasis added).

[70] Id.

[71] Id. at para. 54.

[72] Id. at para. 57 (citing Tommy CP Sze v. Li & Fung [2003] 1 HKC 418).

While Hong Kong is now a preferred forum for solving international disputes, it will undoubtedly become an even more attractive forum for parties involved in arbitration in years to come since Hong Kong's jurisprudence now benefits from the landmark *Fiona Trust* judgment, which – as discussed in the introduction to this chapter – creates a rebuttable presumption of consent to arbitrate in cases of ambiguity.[73] Indeed, the *Fiona Trust* court examined the language of the standard arbitration agreement and concluded that "[i]t may be a great disappointment to the judges who explained so carefully the effects of the various linguistic nuances if they could learn that the draftsmen of so widely used [standard arbitration agreements] obviously regarded the expressions 'arising under this charter' ... and 'arisen out of this charter' ... as mutually interchangeable."[74]

Parties, however, should not be misled by this language and should keep in mind that limitations do in fact exist. This has recently been confirmed by the 2019 *Dickson Holdings Enterprise Co Ltd v. Moravia CV and Others* decision. There, the Court of the Hong Kong Special Administrative Region was tasked to consider, among other factors, the scope of the HKIAC's standard arbitration agreement when deciding whether to stay the proceeding while the arbitration was pending.[75] More specifically, the court examined whether the dispute between the parties concerning (1) the transfer of 225,000 shares that formed part of an addendum to a shareholders' agreement and (2) the forfeiture of 275,000 shares fell within "the ambit of the arbitration agreement."[76] To answer this question, the judge had to consider if, in any event, the dispute could be considered within the scope of the phrase "dispute, controversy or claim arising out of or relating to [the shareholders' agreement], or the breach, termination or invalidity thereof."[77] The judge responded in the negative because:

> It has to be borne in mind that the arbitration clause ... applies to disputes arising out of or relating to the *Shareholders' Agreement* or the breach, termination or invalidity thereof, *not* arising out of or relating to any *affairs of the Company*. If the parties had intended otherwise, they could have easily devised an arbitration clause that expressly applied to any dispute between them relating to any affair of the Company.[78]

In short, although Hong Kong is a forum where arbitration agreements are interpreted quite liberally, parties to a contract ought to be careful when choosing the language to be inserted in their dispute resolution clauses. Indeed, Hong Kong courts will try to extend the scope of the agreement as much as they possibly can. They will not, however, completely disregard the language of the clause when making their assessments.

4.3.2 Mainland China

Chinese courts have traditionally been reluctant to "depart from a largely court-driven justice system" mostly because they view arbitration "as procedurally unsound, based on a perception that arbitration cannot guarantee due process."[79] As such, a number of specific court procedural rules are incorporated into arbitral proceedings, which in turn places a number of inappropriate

---

[73] *See* Premium NAFTA Products Ltd. v. Fili Shipping Co. Ltd. [2007] UKHL 40.
[74] Id.
[75] The arbitration clause at issue provided in relevant part that "[a]ny dispute, controversy or claim arising out of or relating to this Agreement, or the breach, termination or invalidity thereof, shall be settled by arbitration under the Hong Kong International Centre Administered Arbitration Rules in force at the date of this Agreement." *See* Dickson Holdings Enterprise Co Ltd v. Moravia CV and Others [2019] HKCFI 1424.
[76] Id.
[77] Id.
[78] Id. (emphasis added).
[79] Yuan, *supra* note 59, at 323.

restrictions on the parties involved in the arbitration.[80] In recent years, however, Chinese courts have leaned toward a more liberal approach, enforcing ambiguous arbitration agreements that nonetheless reflect a clear intention to arbitrate. As always and as further described in the following, changes go only so far and limits do remain.

Nowadays, when courts in mainland China are asked to interpret the scope of arbitration agreements involving domestic arbitral institutions, they generally adopt a pro-arbitration stance. In an unpublished case, for instance, the Supreme People's Court (SPC), in response to a query from the Gansu Higher People's Court, held that the terms "disputes arising out of the contract performance" referred to "[a]ll disputes between the two parties to a contract over matters such as the existence of a contract, the time of its establishment, interpretation of the contents of a contract, implementation of a contract, liability for breach of contract, as well as disputes over the amendment, suspension, assignment, dissolution or termination of a contract."[81]

Similarly, arbitral clauses providing that "all disputes arising from the contract," "in connection with the contract," or "arising out of the performance of the contract" have been interpreted by courts in mainland China as allowing for the adjudication of both tortious and quasi-contractual claims.[82] Moreover, Chinese courts have repeatedly dismissed cases where a validly formed arbitration agreement has been found[83] and have, for instance, recognized the validity of an arbitration clause in a standard-form electronic contract.[84] In *Zhejiang Yisheng Petrochemical v. INVISTA Technologies*,[85] the Intermediate People's Court of Ningbo Municipality recognized, for the first time, the validity of a clause in which parties to a contract agreed to have a permanent arbitration institution in China manage an arbitration process in accordance with the [UNCITRAL]

---

[80] Id. (noting that "[f]or example, parties in arbitrations governed by the 1994 Act enjoy less freedom and flexibility than they would under other legislation where parties choose arbitrators, the place of arbitration, as well as the procedural rules and substantive law governing their relationship, rights, and obligations").

[81] LIN YIFEI, JUDICIAL REVIEW OF ARBITRATION: LAW AND PRACTICE IN CHINA 65 (2018).

[82] See W. SUN & M. WILLEMS, ARBITRATION IN CHINA 84 (2015), p. (citing Best (USA) Enterprise Co., Ltd. v. Anhui Hotel, Zongkui HE, Fucheng ZHANG, and Others [2005] Min Si Ta Zi No. 9); Yifei, *supra* note 81, at 66:

> ([T]he Response of the Supreme People's Court to Certain Questions Concerning the Application of the Foreign Economic Contract Law shall apply, which provides that: "The term 'disputes arising from the contract' as stated in Article 5 of the Foreign Economic Contract Law shall be understood in the general sense. All disputes between the two parties to a contract over matters such as the existence of a contract, the time of its establishment, interpretation of the contents of a contract, implementation of a contract, liability for breach of contract, as well as disputes over the amendment, suspension, assignment, dissolution or termination of a contract shall be included under this term." (In China, "disputes" in arbitration agreement, whether arising from the main contract or in connection with the contract, should be construed expansively according to the above opinion by the Supreme People's Court.).

[83] See, e.g., Yifei, *supra* note 81.

[84] Zheng Jianfang v. Jindao Precious Metal Co. Ltd., Case No. (2016) Min Shen 2368, Fujian High People's Court (June 18, 2016) (decision in Chinese). Argentina has similarly shown its desire to create a friendlier environment for the resolution of international disputes in Argentina. Indeed, while Argentinean courts have traditionally been known for their hostility toward international arbitration, a major shift in the legislation occurred on July 4, 2018. The Argentine National Congress passed a new arbitration act that largely mirrors the UNCITRAL Model Law and abandons the "problematic amendments introduced in 2015." For example, the new law adopts a broad definition of *commercial* and requires arbitration agreements to be in writing. Ideally, the new law will have the effect of promulgating a more stable and predictable enforcement regime in Argentina. It remains to be seen, however, whether this effect will be realized. See, e.g., Noiana Marigo, Maria J. Milesi, Ezequiel Vetulli, *New Signs of Good Prospects for International Arbitration in Argentina*, KLUWER ARBITRATION BLOG (Sept. 12, 2018), http://arbitrationblog.kluwerarbitration.com/2018/09/12/new-signs-of-good-prospects-for-international-arbitration-in-argentina/.

[85] *Zhe Jiang Yisheng Petrochemical Co., Ltd. v. Invista Technologies S.à.r.l., Luxembourg, A Case of an Application to Affirm the Invalidity of an Arbitration Clause* (2014), Intermediate People's Court of Ningbo Municipality, Zhejiang Province (Mar. 17, 2014), STANFORD LAW SCHOOL CHINA GUIDING CASES PROJECT (Mar. 1, 2018), https://cgc.law.stanford.edu/wp-content/uploads/sites/2/2016/11/CGCP-BR-English-Typical-Case-6.pdf.

Arbitration Rules and clarified that what was agreed upon by this clause was institutional arbitration, rather than ad hoc arbitration.[86] This decision is significant as it showcases the Intermediate People's Court of Ningbo Municipality's willingness to "adopt[] the teleological method of interpretation that was conducive to realizing the parties' wishes to arbitrate"[87] rather than declare the agreement as "null and void, inoperative or incapable of being performed."[88]

There are limits, however, to the Chinese courts' willingness to enforce poorly drafted clauses. In *Wicor Holding AG v. Taizhou Haopu Investment Co Ltd*, for instance, the SPC denied enforcement of an ICC award on public policy grounds because it concluded that the arbitration agreement, under which the award was based, was in fact invalid due to poor drafting.[89] There, the parties agreed to have their disputes arbitrated "in accordance with ICC mediation and arbitration rules" and "if one party initiates the arbitration, the other party shall choose the seat of arbitration."[90] The lower court rendered a judgment in 2012 declaring the arbitration agreement invalid as it failed to specify an arbitral commission (as required by Article 16 of the Arbitration Law of the People's Republic of China),[91] a decision that was later endorsed by the SPC.

Interestingly enough, the SPC's reasoning in declaring the arbitration clause invalid appeared to be based on the circumstance that the arbitration commission could not be "ascertained" from the ICC Arbitration Rules.[92] Clarity in drafting is therefore key. Ambiguous language should be avoided because an ambiguous arbitration agreement may be found invalid and unenforceable in China, despite the seat being located outside of the country.

The Chinese approach to assessing the scope of arbitration agreements in mainland China has also been overshadowed by the difficulties faced by both international arbitral institutions and non-Chinese parties willing to arbitrate disputes seated in China. While several positive developments have taken place over the years,[93] including the one described earlier, we believe that further changes need to take place.[94]

---

[86] Id.
[87] Id.
[88] New York Convention, Art. II.
[89] Hogan Lovells, James Kwan, & Mariel Dimsey, *One Step Forward, Two Steps Back – PRC Court Refuses to Enforce an ICC Award on the Ground of Public Policy*, LEXOLOGY, ARBLOG (Sept. 20, 2016), https://www.lexology.com/library/detail.aspx?g=7f8d397c-9921-4bec-a4b2-8dd11fa73559 (citing Wicor Holding A.G. v. Taizhou Haopu Investments Limited (Civil Action (2015), Tai Zhong Shang Zhong Shen Zi No. 00004 (June 2, 2016)).
[90] Id.
[91] Arbitration Law of the People's Republic of China, Art. 16, http://www.arbiter.com.sg/pdf/laws/China%20Arbitration%20Law.pdf.
[92] Lovells et al., *supra* note 89.
[93] For example, on Aug. 6, 2019, the State Council of China published the "General Planning of the New Area of the China (Shanghai) Pilot Free Trade Zone Program," under which, reputable overseas arbitration and dispute resolution institutions will be allowed to "set up business organisations in the new area [of the China (Shanghai Pilot Free Trade Zone)] and conduct arbitration businesses in relation to civil and commercial disputes arising in the areas of international commerce, maritime affairs, investment, etc." and the relevant bodies will "support and assure the application and enforcement of interim measures by Chinese and foreign parties before and during the arbitration proceedings, such as asset preservation, evidence preservation and action preservation." A number of international arbitral institutions, including the ICC, the HKIAC, and the SIAC currently maintain representative offices in the Shanghai Free Trade Zone. While these representative offices are limited to liaison and marketing purposes only and do not administer cases in mainland China, "Article 4 of the General Planning [of the New Area of the China (Shanghai) Pilot Free Trade Zone Program] now appears to have given a green light for foreign arbitration institutions to administer arbitration cases seated in mainland China in the future." *See* Michelle Li, Stella Hu, & Weina Ye, *State Council of China Announced Ground-Breaking Policy to Allow Foreign Arbitration Institutions to Set Up Businesses in Shanghai Free Trade Zone to Administer Cases in Mainland China*, HERBERT SMITH FREEHILLS (Aug. 9, 2019), https://hsfnotes.com/arbitration/2019/08/09/state-council-of-china-announced-ground-breaking-policy-to-allow-foreign-arbitration-institutions-to-set-up-businesses-in-shanghai-free-trade-zone-to-administer-cases-in-mainland-china/.
[94] *See, e.g.*, Sarah Grimmer, *Distinction and Connection: Hong Kong and Mainland China, a View from the HKIAC*, GLOBAL ARBITRATION REVIEW (May 24, 2019), https://globalarbitrationreview.com/insight/the-asia-pacific-arbitration-

In that regard, two cases are worth considering: the 2009 *Duferco* case and the 2013 *Longlide* case. *Duferco* was the first reported case from mainland China enforcing an arbitration agreement providing for a foreign arbitral institution – the ICC – with a seat in China. The Ningbo Intermediate People's Court characterized the award as "non-domestic" and applied the New York Convention to conduct its analysis. The precedential value of the case has been questioned, as "the case was concluded on the basis of the respondent's waiver without discussing much about the status of ICC arbitration seated in Mainland China."[95]

In 2013, however, further light was shed on the issue when Chinese courts were again asked to scrutinize the text of an arbitration agreement and consider the enforceability of an arbitration clause providing that "all disputes" be submitted to ICC arbitration with a seat in Shanghai. In the *Longlide* case, the Anhui Provincial Higher People's Court consulted the SPC on three issues: (1) whether the ICC was a validly designated arbitration institution, (2) whether Chinese public policy was violated by the ICC's administration of a case seated in mainland China, and (3) whether any arbitral award should be considered domestic such that the New York Convention would be inapplicable to enforcement issues.[96] The SPC considered only the first question and ultimately held that the ICC was a validly "designated arbitration institution." The court, however, failed to address the questions of public policy and the status of the award under the New York Convention. According to Chinese scholars, the court's reluctance to address the two remaining questions rests on the fact that an answer in the affirmative "would have a huge influence on [the] Chinese arbitration market."[97] This careful holding is, in the authors' view, welcome because such an impactful policy decision for the Chinese market should be reserved to the legislature and not a court of law.[98]

Taken together, the *Duferco* and the *Longlide* decisions address two key developments for the arbitration landscape and the interpretation of arbitral agreements in mainland China: (1) the designation of an award with a seat in China as non-domestic under the New York Convention and (2) the ability for the ICC to be considered a "valid designated arbitration institution" for arbitrations seated in mainland China.

The two cases reflect the courts' desire to render mainland China a more attractive forum to solve international disputes.[99] The scope of these decisions, along with the courts' interpretative approach and the strict requirements of the arbitration law,[100] however, illustrate why parties, and a fortiori their counsels, should be cautious when drafting an arbitration clause with a nexus to mainland China. In our view, and in order to avoid unnecessary procedural hurdles, proper time and effort should be given when drafting such a clause.

---

review-2020/1193369/distinction-and-connection-hong-kong-and-mainland-china-a-view-from-the-hkiac. For a more moderate approach, *see* Gu Weixia, *The Developing Nature of Arbitration in Mainland China and Its Correlation with the Market: Institutional, Ad Hoc, and Foreign Institutions Seated in Mainland China*, 10 CONTEMPORARY ASIA ARBITRATION JOURNAL 257 (2017).

[95] Weixia, *supra* note 94, at 270.
[96] Id.
[97] Id. at 271.
[98] China is a civil law country. In civil law jurisdictions, including China and France, it is traditionally accepted that judges do not make the law but merely apply and interpret it. Major changes in the law thus need to be made by legislators. In common law jurisdictions, such as the United States, England, and Hong Kong, judges do, in contrast, hold such powers. In fact, it is often said that in these jurisdictions the judges make the law.
[99] *See* Mu Xuequan, China Improves Arbitration System to Strengthen Credibility Xinhuanet (Apr. 16, 2019).
[100] *See, e.g.*, Arbitration Law of the People's Republic of China, Art. 16 (requiring the designation of an arbitration commission in the arbitral agreement for it to be valid).

4.3.3 Interpretation of Standard Arbitration Clauses in Argentina

Argentina has long had considerable name recognition within international arbitration community, derived largely from its participation as respondent in a series of investment arbitrations arising out of the economic crisis it experienced at the turn of the century. However, while this engagement with arbitration has at least contributed to the existence of an active community of arbitration practitioners in Argentina, Argentine law has placed restrictions on arbitration. Indeed, in a 2016 survey of Argentine arbitration practitioners, only twenty-one percent of respondents stated that they would recommend Argentina as one of five recommended seats for an international arbitration, placing it behind other South American countries such as Uruguay, Chile, and Peru.[101] Consistent with this overall concern about arbitration in Argentina, respondents described the approach of Argentine courts to the interpretation of the scope of arbitration agreements as "strict" and focused on a narrow interpretation of the clause's language.[102]

Arguably the foundational decision of a restrictive approach to the interpretation of arbitration agreements in Argentina was the 1994 decision of the Commercial Court of Appeals of the City of Buenos Aires in *Compañía Naviera Pérez Companc v. Ecofisa*.[103] In *Ecofisa*, the court addressed a situation in which the parties had agreed to arbitrate all their disputes in accordance with the ICC Arbitration Rules. Under these Rules, the parties and tribunal were required to agree upon "terms of reference," specifying which matters were to be submitted to the tribunal. The parties disagreed on what matters had been submitted to arbitration, and so in the absence of party agreement, the tribunal (in accordance with the ICC Rules) finalized the terms of reference itself. The difficulty this created, in the view of the court, was that as drafted the terms of reference did not clearly preclude the tribunal from evaluating the validity of Argentine laws and regulations, something that was precluded by Argentine public policy. While no attempt had yet been made to require the tribunal to do this, the Court determined that it had the power to redraft the terms of reference to explicitly exclude this possibility, then allowing the arbitration to proceed.

While on one level this decision represented a moderate approach to judicial supervision of arbitration agreements, as the court intervened only to protect what it saw as a matter of public policy, it nonetheless reflects an ongoing strain in Argentine caselaw over the following two decades, in which Argentine courts often viewed themselves as possessing a supervisory role with respect to arbitration. This conception was most famously enunciated in the decision of the Argentine Supreme Court in *José Cartellone Construcciones Civiles SA v. Hidroeléctrica Norpatagónica SA o Hidronor SA*, which announced that Argentine courts were able to annul arbitration awards if they were found to be "unconstitutional, illegal or unreasonable."[104]

In accordance with this conception of courts as supervisors of arbitration, Argentine courts largely proceeded to adopt what has been referred to as a "restrictive criterion" with respect to arbitration agreements.[105] For example, in 2014, in *Supermarkets Norte Investments B.V. v. Carrefour S.A. y otros s/ ordinario*,[106] the National Court of Appeals in Commercial Matters, when addressing an arbitration clause that submitted to arbitration "any dispute, divergence, claim or doubt regarding the interpretation and/or application of this Contract," with specified

---

[101] Cole et al., *supra* note 4.
[102] Id.
[103] Compañía Naviera Pérez Companc v. Ecofisa, CNCom, Panel B, LL 1994-A, 139.
[104] José Cartellone Construcciones Civiles SA v. Hidroeléctrica Norpatagónica SA o Hidronor SA, CSJN, 2004, 7.
[105] Diego Arroyo & Ezequeil Vetulli, *The New Argentinian Arbitration Law: A Train in an Unknown Direction?*, 32 ARBITRATION INTERNATIONAL 357–335 (2016).
[106] Supermarkets Norte Investments B.V. v. Carrefour S.A. y otros s/ ordinario, CNCom, sala F, Expediente N° 9120/2011, 2017, 2.

exceptions, emphasized that "[i]t is necessary to start from the following basic premise: compromissory clauses constitute a contractual convention, which by implying a waiver of the general principle of submission of conflicts to judges, deserve to be interpreted restrictively."[107]

Nonetheless, while such decisions may have represented the dominant approach to the interpretation of arbitration agreements in Argentina, there were also contrary decisions, adopting a more expansive approach. Perhaps more importantly, however, recent years have seen an increasing acceptance of arbitration by Argentine legislators. Before 2015 there was no single national arbitration law in Argentina, with the legislation applicable to arbitration being found in a variety of laws and in the procedural codes of Argentina's provinces. In 2015, however, a new National Civil and Commercial Code (NCCC) was adopted, based to a significant degree on the UNCITRAL Model Law, with Article 1656 expressly adopting the principle that an arbitration agreement should always be interpreted so as to ensure its effectiveness.[108] Here, though, the traditional approach remained, with Article 1656 also including the express affirmation that the right of parties to challenge in court an arbitral award that contravened the legal order could not be waived. Subsequent case law, however, addressed even this concern by holding that this restriction related only to the possibility of applications for annulment, not to substantive review of the award.[109] These steps toward aligning Argentina's approach to arbitration with that of the dominant trend among arbitration jurisdictions was then further solidified in 2018, when Argentina adopted a new arbitration act that largely mirrors the UNCITRAL Model Law.

While it is too early to determine the impact of these legislative changes on the approach of Argentine courts to the interpretation of arbitration agreements, the steady movement in recent years of Argentine legislation toward the norms of international commercial arbitration, combined with the restrictive approach given to the interpretation of the "no waiver" clause in Article 1656 of the NCCC, provides some ground for concluding that Argentina will now also move toward acceptance of the broad approach to the interpretation of arbitration agreements that has now become the dominant approach around the world.[110]

5 CONCLUSION

The particular language of standard dispute resolution clauses may have significant interpretive consequences depending on the jurisdiction in which the clause is being analyzed. As the discussion in this chapter indicates, countries around the world are now increasingly adopting policies favoring a broad interpretation of arbitration clauses and a decreasing number of jurisdictions remain in which arbitration clauses are interpreted narrowly. Some jurisdictions, like the United States and Hong Kong, continue to move toward an expansive interpretation of arbitration agreements, while other courts, such as those of France, have adopted an approach that most strongly favors the will of the parties. Even courts in jurisdictions that traditionally interpreted arbitration clauses narrowly, such as mainland China and Argentina, seem to have embraced this change and are now moving toward interpreting clauses more liberally.

---

[107] Id.
[108] "En caso de duda ha de estarse a la mayor eficacia del contrato de arbitraje."
[109] *See* Federico Campolieti & Santiago Pena, *Argentina, in* THE INTERNATIONAL ARBITRATION REVIEW (James H. Carter ed., 10th ed. 2019), https://thelawreviews.co.uk/edition/the-international-arbitration-review-edition-10/1195825/argentina.
[110] Landmark Investors SRL v. Emprendimientos Inmobiliarios Arenales S.A. s/ordinario, CNCom, sala C, Expte. nro. 14807/2015 (enforcing an arbitration agreement, but without expressly referring to the provisions of the new law).

Reflecting on this chapter, we welcome these changes but believe that a careful balance has to be struck where only disputes intended to be resolved by arbitration ultimately fall outside the hands of domestic courts. This is because, if courts want to enhance the rule of law and honor the parties' intent, "any and all" claims cannot fall within an arbitral tribunal's jurisdiction if the contracting parties did not so intend. As such, drafters of arbitration clauses should be attentive to the subtle distinctions between jurisdictions when choosing the terms of a clause, whether or not the arbitration clauses are standard. Particular importance should be paid to limiting the scope of the clause, where desired, given the increasing tendency of courts around the world to broadly interpret arbitration clauses.

8

Industry-Specific Clauses and Their Interpretation

Alexandra-Luiza Ionescu (Mareş)

1 INTRODUCTION

Some industries have avoided using standard or generic arbitration clauses by developing industry-specific clauses. This chapter focuses on the energy sector and its view of arbitration as reflected in its widely used arbitration clause. Given the specificity and uniqueness of the industry, energy disputes are mostly settled through alternative dispute resolution methods. From a legal standpoint, the regulations and practices related to the energy sector are complex and chaotic due to the technical nature of the energy industry. In such a context, energy dispute resolution cases are unusually complex. Large energy transactions, projects or contracts almost always have an international dimension, and the preferred means of dispute resolution is international arbitration. One legal professional notes that:

> If the premise that international energy contracts should include enforceable, effective arbitration agreements is not yet axiomatic, it is at least widely accepted. More importantly, it is true. If arbitration did not already exist, it would have had to be invented for international energy projects to thrive.[1]

This observation is especially pertinent given the global nature of the energy industry.

1.1 Dispute Resolution in the Energy Sector

International energy contracts inherently involve substantial levels of risks. First, such contracts involve long-term agreements, as well as the expenditure of large amounts of financial resources. To be successful such contracts need to be strategic in balancing the concerns and interests of both parties in order to provide a stable environment for their project. Energy companies seek to isolate their capital investments from the uncertainties of foreign courts. In some cases, the counterparty is a state-owned or state-controlled company. In such situations the investor energy company will want a high degree of protection for its investment. For this reason, one of the more important clauses in such contracts refers to dispute resolution.

Energy contracts reviewed include oil extraction, power plant construction, mining, gas sales agreements, and other energy projects that have an international dimension. Before entering

---

[1] Jennifer L. Price, *Drafting Dispute Resolution Provisions for International Oil and Gas Contracts*, in LEADING PRACTITIONERS' GUIDE TO OIL & GAS ARBITRATION 813 (James M. Gaitis ed., 2015).

such contracts, the parties expect that the fiscal, regulatory and legal conditions remain stable throughout the duration of the project. Stability, at some point, becomes harder to maintain as disputes arise. Energy companies are aware of the high stakes and risks involved as well as the importance of clear and unambiguous provisions in their transactional documents; however, such contracts sometimes do not incorporate a customized arbitration clause.

It is prudent to negotiate a multilayered arbitration clause precisely to ensure dispute resolution during the performance of the contract when the contract becomes imbalanced. It is of prime importance to establish the guidelines and details for potential disputes during the negotiating of the contract:

> [G]iven the international scope and complexity of energy industry contracts, disputes frequently arise. When they do, the dispute resolution clause, together with the governing law clause, provide the basic rules of engagement. Any contract negotiator must view dispute resolution clauses in this light when sitting down to negotiations.

An effective dispute resolution in the transaction documents[2] are pivotal to both avoiding the escalation of disputes early in a manner which best protects the parties' commercial interests. An organizational approach to the drafting of such clauses is a best practice: "Having a dispute resolution policy in place which sets out an organisation's approach to the drafting of these clauses is therefore integral to good risk management."[3] The dispute resolution clause as well as the dispute resolution mechanism need to be tailored in the light of the industry's specificity and include all the technical requirements related to it being a regulated industry. The dispute resolution clause in the energy sector needs to track the requirements for an industry-specific clause.

1.2 Governing Law and Dispute Resolution Clauses

1.2.1 Governing Law Clause

The governing law clause provides the applicable law to be used in case of dispute. The governing law provision in energy contracts is especially important since the parties are often from numerous jurisdictions. When one of the parties is a state-owned company or the state itself, negotiations of choice of law are more difficult. The best solution is not the adoption of the state party's law but a compromise choice of law for a neutral jurisdiction. The first step is the determination of the type of legal system that better fits the contract – civil or common law system. Surveys[4] have shown that English law is one of the most popular neutral country systems used because many international energy contracts are written in English and English law is considered to be certain, predictable, and well developed.[5]

---

[2] Domenico di Pietro, *Incorporation of Arbitration Clauses by Reference*, 21 J. INT'L ARB. 439 (2004).
[3] Mark Clarke & Jessica Neuberger, *Drafting Effective Dispute Resolution Clauses*, in DISPUTE RESOLUTION IN THE ENERGY SECTOR, A PRACTITIONER'S HANDBOOK 7 (Ronnie King ed., 2012).
[4] THE 2010 INTERNATIONAL ARBITRATION SURVEY: CHOICES IN INTERNATIONAL ARBITRATION, conducted by the School of International Arbitration at Queen Mary, University of London.
[5] There are other reasons for preferring English law, and the list below provides a guide to choosing the governing law: (1) English law is largely settled and predictable – principles of English law have developed over an extended period through case law. As commercial realities have changed through centuries, this case law has been refined and adapted to suit. As a result, there tends to be a greater degree of certainty as to how contracts will be interpreted by the courts than in civil law jurisdictions; (2) It is flexible and commercial – it seeks to uphold the freedom of the parties to contract as they see fit; (3) It is suited to oil and gas agreements. The existence of significant case law on issues arising under commonly used oil and gas agreements means that parties can better predict how a court will interpret the agreement; and (4) English law imposes no obligation of good faith and

1.2.2 *Dispute Resolution Clause*

The dispute resolution clause has to be constructed with clear and unambiguous language. A major issue in such clauses is the scope of the disputes to be captured by the clause. As such, parties must ensure that the scope of the dispute, as established and identified in the dispute resolution clause, reflects the intent of the parties in a clear and precise manner. Parties may decide to define the "dispute" narrowly and be aware of the issues subject to arbitration or to use a broad clause by extending the scope through the use of standard phrasing, such as "arising out of or in connection with the contract" or "arising out of or relating to."[6]

Besides the costly and time-consuming dispute resolution methods of litigation or arbitration, the parties should consider a broader range of dispute resolution mechanisms, including nonbinding dispute resolution forms, such as negotiation, mediation, and early neutral evaluation (mini-trials). Evidence shows that meditation–arbitration clauses result in a majority of disputes being settled during the lower-cost mediation phase. In sum, parties instead of providing a single option of arbitration should draft dispute resolution clauses that include a hierarchical menu of alternative dispute resolution mechanisms (tiered clauses). Negotiation and mediation are the most commonly used nonbinding alternative dispute resolution (ADR) procedures. Whether the parties draft standard, customized, or multitiered clauses, the dispute resolution clause should reflect the characteristics of the project and particularities of likely disputes.[7]

In drafting the dispute resolution clause, parties must first adopt the preferred resolution mechanism according to which ones are best suited to the contract and the contractual relationship. For example, arbitration may be a good fit in contracts between parties transacting for the first, while negotiations and mediation may be more suited to parties with a long-term relationship or repeat players. Broadly, in formal resolution processes, the parties must choose

---

> restricts the ability of parties to evade contractual obligations (such as, invocation of the doctrine of hardship found in many civil law jurisdictions).

Clarke & Neuberger, *supra* note 3, at 8.

[6] Arbitral institutions worldwide have inserted such phrases in their standard arbitration clauses, as has been recommended for parties choosing to submit a dispute to be settled according to the rules of such arbitral institutions. For example, the International Chamber of Commerce (ICC) recommends the following standard arbitration clause that parties may insert in their contract as such or adapt according to the circumstances that best describe their contractual framework: "All disputes arising out of or in connection with the present contract shall be finally settled under the Rules of Arbitration of the International Chamber of Commerce by one or more arbitrators appointed in accordance with the said Rules."

[7] The following is an example of a simply drafted multitier dispute resolution clause, including the mechanism of structured negotiations to be held at the level of the senior management of the companies, thus with a view to settle the dispute in an amicable manner at the management level:

> Any controversy that may arise among the parties with respect to the legal relation arising out of this Agreement shall be submitted to senior management representatives of the parties who will attempt to reach an amicable settlement within fourteen (14) calendar days after submission. If an amicable solution cannot be reached by negotiation, the dispute shall be finally settled by arbitration by a panel of one (1) arbitrator, which shall be appointed by both parties. In the event the parties fail to appoint the arbitrator within the following fifteen (15) days as of the initiation of the arbitration, such arbitrator shall be designated by the International Chamber of Commerce, Paris, who conducted in accordance with the Rules of Conciliation and Arbitration of the International Chamber of Commerce, Paris. The site of the arbitration shall be Mexico City, and the language to be used in the arbitration shall be the English Language. The award of the arbitrator shall be final and binding upon both parties, and neither party shall seek recourse to a court of law or other authorities to appeal for revision of such award or any other ruling of the arbitrators. The cost of the arbitration shall be borne by both parties in equal amounts.

ICC Case No. 9977, in Dyalá Jiménez Figueres, *Multi-Tiered Dispute Resolution Clauses in ICC Arbitration*, ICC BULL. 84 (2003).

between litigation, arbitration, or other types of expert determination[8] that offer a binding resolution of the dispute. In the energy industry, when deciding upon the mechanism to be adopted for obtaining a final and binding resolution of a dispute, arbitration is highly preferred for numerous reasons, which are discussed in the following sections.

2 ARBITRATION IN THE ENERGY SECTOR: OVERVIEW

2.1 *Choice of Law*

Few industries have an international flavor as intense and complicated as the energy sector. As a consequence, the business community in the energy sector in its majority prefers arbitration as the main method of resolving international disputes. Depending on the nature of the business relationship and the parties involved, the preference toward arbitration may be due to different reasons. In some cases, such as in investment arbitration, the investor seeks to protect the long-term agreement and its substantial capital investment from being subject to a decision in an unfamiliar jurisdiction. Other companies involved in international energy transactions choose arbitration for the resolution of a potential dispute arising under the international agreement precisely because they seek flexibility, a time-efficient procedure, and high degree of enforceability. Since the parties are free to tailor the rules of the proceedings as to fit their requirements, they will also agree upon the language of the arbitration, the seat and the law governing the arbitration, the procedural rules, the characteristics of the arbitrators, and whether to pursue institutionalized or ad hoc arbitration.

2.2 *Type of Arbitration: Ad Hoc versus Institutional*

Although arbitration clauses are common in energy contracts, there still are situations when the decision to refer a dispute to arbitration is agreed upon by the parties after that particular dispute has arisen. Important to be highlighted is that once an arbitration agreement has been concluded by the parties, it cannot be withdrawn in a unilateral manner, such as any other contract under the principle of *pacta sunt servanda* principle. Parties willing to organize and conduct the arbitration themselves may chose ad hoc arbitration and tailor the rules and proceedings in accordance with the objectives they find important to be targeted in the arbitration. The most frequently adopted ad hoc arbitration rules are the UNCITRAL Model Rules.[9]

On the other hand, institutional arbitration provides a process that is managed and supervised by an institution; such specialized institutions provide an established arbitration framework, including arbitration rules and standard arbitration clauses. Given the complexity of the projects in the energy industry, parties together with their advisers tailor the arbitration clause, even if they choose institutional arbitration.[10]

---

[8] Especially because the energy industry is the loop of the analysis and referring technical issues to expert determination, given the high level of complexity in energy-related issues, has become a common solution for many companies in the sector.

[9] *See* 31 U.N. GAOR, Supp. No. 17 U.N. Doc. A/31/17 at 33 1976, reprinted in 15 I.L.M. 701 (1976).

[10] A good ad hoc arbitration can be tailored specifically to dispute, after dispute arises. The parties can frame their own methodology for resolving the issues between them. However, if there is significant tactical advantage to one party in insisting on one element (multiple arbitrators or disclosure), this benefit maybe lost. The parties may agree about how best to proceed, leading to delays. Conversely, ad hoc arbitrations are most susceptible to obstructive parties that seek to frustrate the arbitration proceedings (although once an arbitrator or tribunal is appointed, there is much less scope for this). Institutional arbitration is better suited to avoiding such tactics. Cost may be harder to control in ad hoc arbitration. By contrast, leading institutions such as the ICC and all

2.3 Drafting a Suitable Arbitration Agreement

In order to have an effective and enforceable arbitration agreement, the parties must include essential elements for creating a clear framework for resolving disputes. Essential elements of an arbitration clause include (1) expressly specifying that the arbitration agreement represents joint consent to submit any dispute to binding arbitration,[11] (2) selection of the type of arbitration and corresponding rules, (3) choice of venue or seat of the arbitration, (4) scope of the arbitration agreement, (5) language of the arbitration, (6) characteristics of arbitrators, and (6) number of arbitrators and the appointment method.

2.3.1 Scope of Express Agreement to Arbitrate

As a general rule, even if it is clear that the parties' intent was to resolve any disputes between them through binding arbitration, it is advisable to include a statement of intent in the dispute resolution clause in unambiguous and clear wording. The submission agreement should be placed at beginning of the paragraph of the arbitration clause, especially when the clause is lengthy and complex.

It lies within the parties' consent to determine the scope of the arbitration clause. As such, the parties may choose a broad type of clause that is applicable to any type of dispute, controversy, claim, or disagreement or draft a narrow arbitration agreement that limits the ambit of the matters that are subject to arbitration. Due to the complexity of energy contracts, the risks are high that disputes will entail interpretation gaps, multiple controversies, and disagreements; therefore, use of a broad arbitration clause is most appropriate. Drafting a clause that narrows the scope of the arbitration agreement may result in undesired consequences. Narrow arbitration clauses are more likely to be scrutinized by national courts relating to particular issues in dispute.

While the majority of jurisdictions have a tradition in favoring arbitration,[12] if an issue of determining the scope of the arbitration clause arises, the national court hearing the matter will primarily decide if the clause is broad or narrow. Such decisions will be based on the

---

LCIA provide schedule of fees which enable parties to estimate how much the proceedings will cost. The reputation of a leading arbitration institution may make it easier to enforce an arbitral award in certain jurisdictions. Both the ICC and the LCIA have significant name recognition globally, lending authority to any award issued in their names.

Contract negotiators often favour institutional arbitration. It provides a "safety net" in the event of anything going wrong, such as a difficult party refusing to participate in the process. In addition, the comfort provided by the oversight of an institution is likely to make the arbitration exercise more certain and less stressful. That said, as with any aspect of the dispute resolution procedure, circumstances may dictate a different approach. Thus, many of the disadvantages of ad hoc arbitration are less of a consideration in contracts between sophisticated, substantial contractual parties with long-term aligned interests, such as major oil and gas companies.

Clarke & Neuberger, *supra* note 3, at 16–17.

[11] As there are many jurisdictions and legal systems that do not recognize parties' consent to arbitrate unless expressly set forth.

[12] English courts, for example, use much the same language of deference to arbitration as do the U.S. federal courts, but come to more generous conclusion. Courts in England construe arbitration agreements liberally, without parsing the language to infer limitations on scope unless clearly intended and stated. They adopt the view that commercial parties who provide for arbitration are likely to have intended to use arbitration as the sole forum for binding resolution of all disputes regarding their relationship, regardless of their choice of phrasing such as "arising out of," "arising under," or "in connection with" to express that intention. The scope of the clause will be deemed to be narrower in scope than broad-form clause only if the parties clearly express that intent. In any event, parties should be very careful in imposing any limitations on the scope of their

rules applicable in that specific jurisdiction. This may not be the applicable law chosen by the parties.

2.3.2 Seat of Arbitration

As noted, the determination of the seat or place of the arbitration is of major importance as it provides the procedural rules governing the arbitration and the rules as to the competency or grounds that provide for judicial intervention. Parties should carefully choose the seat of the arbitration, since the mandatory national laws of one state (the state chosen as the seat of arbitration) become ipso facto applicable to the arbitration. If the parties have not chosen the rules governing the arbitration, then the applicable law will likely be the seat of the arbitration. However, it is rare to find an energy contract that fails to expressly state the applicable rules of arbitration. Also, when choosing the arbitration seat, parties should consider an arbitration friendly jurisdiction.[13] The place for vacation or annulment of an award is commonly the seat of arbitration since the New York Convention provides few exceptions for the foreign court of enforcement to disregard the award.[14] As a consequence, parties should ab initio agree upon a seat of arbitration that they are most comfortable with, considering all the particularities relating to the choice.

2.3.3 Language of the Arbitration

It is important to specify the language of the arbitration, as that will be the language for the proceedings, the oral and written submissions, and the hearings. The arbitration language is also important for the choice of arbitrators since they will need to be fluent in that language. Not choosing a "major" language reduces the individuals who may be appointed as arbitrators in the given dispute. Since most disputes involve the interpretation of a contract, the language of the arbitration should be the language of the contract.

2.3.4 Composition of Arbitration

In specialized industries, especially those with a thick texture of trade usage and commercial practices, such as the energy sector, the arbitrators should have in-depth knowledge of that particular industry. First, each type of arbitration and each institution has its own specific rules and procedure for the appointment of the arbitral tribunal. The parties should determine which set of rules best suits their needs for the selection and appointment of arbitrators. Beyond the selection of suitable arbitration rules, the parties should describe with specificity the characteristics of the arbitrators in their arbitration agreement to ensure the arbitrators possess the qualifications, expertise, and knowledge of the energy industry.

---

agreements, including particularly any expressed carve-outs of issues subject arbitration. The nature and scope of any carve-outs, whether issues to be submitted for expert determination or for some reason reserved to the courts, must be carefully and precisely defined. Significant disputes are rarely limited to single, narrow issue, and any lack of clarity in the scope of the arbitration provision and any carve-outs set up a virtually inevitable fight over the scope of the provision and whether some or all of the issues in dispute are subject to arbitration.

Price, *supra* note 1, at 829–830.

[13] France, England, Singapore, Switzerland, Hong Kong, and New York are on the top of the most arbitration-friendly jurisdictions and widely chosen as seat of arbitration in agreements in the energy sector.

[14] Convention on the Recognition and Enforcement of Foreign Arbitral Awards, New York, June 10, 1958, UNTS (New York Convention).

3 PATHOLOGICAL CLAUSES

3.1 *How Pathological Can an Arbitration Clause Be?*

Used for the first time in 1974, the label *pathological clauses* refers to arbitration clauses that are deficient, particularly clauses that are defective in various ways.[15] Pathological clauses may result in disruptions in the arbitration process. If substantially defective the arbitral tribunal or national court may have no option other than to void the arbitration clause. If, for example, the clause provides for arbitration, but fails to provide details as to the place of arbitration, the arbitration rules to be applied, and a mechanism for the appointment of the arbitrators, then the arbitration clause is likely to fail due it its vagueness or indeterminacy. Other flaws include providing incorrect reference to an arbitral institution or the selection of an arbitral institution that is no longer in existence.[16]

In most jurisdictions, in cases of pathological or hopelessly vague clauses, it will be the province of the courts to determine the meaning and enforceability of such a clause. Ultimately whether a pathological arbitration clause is enforceable will rest on the arbitral body or court's consideration of the parties' intention. If that intention is not discernible, then the arbitration clause is not enforceable.[17] However, if the parties demonstrated an intent to resolve their disputes through arbitration the courts will try to salvage the clause by implying the necessary details into the clause such as, type of arbitration, arbitration rules, seat of arbitration, scope of the arbitration clause, the language of arbitration, and number and appointing mechanism of the arbitrators. But courts may decide that determining the implication of such terms or all the important details is a step too far and void the clause due to indefiniteness. In the end, defective arbitration clauses are rarely found in the energy industry. This does not mean that defective clauses do not occur from time to time. A seminal case involving a pathological arbitration clause is discussed in the next section.

3.2 *SIAC's* Insigma v. Alstom

An arbitration agreement should not mix different arbitral institutions and the applicable arbitration rules. Each arbitral institution is the administrator of its own set of rules and

---

[15] The honorary Secretary General of the ICC, Frédéric Eismann, used the label *pathological clauses* to encompass all the defective dispute resolution clauses, especially the arbitration clauses that were tainted in a manner that would alter the process of arbitration.

[16] The agreement may ... provide that certain issues (such as the validity of the contract) are not to be dealt with by the arbitrators, despite the fact that such issues are closely related to the dispute which the arbitrators are called upon to decide. Another example is an agreement that permits an appeal from the award before national courts in cases where the subject-matter is international. At best, these defects will give rise to associated litigation, fuelling the arguments of the party attempting to avoid arbitration and making the overall process more time-consuming and expensive. At worst, the defect will prevent the arbitration form taking place at all. This will be the case where it is impossible to infer an intention which is sufficiently coherent and effective to enable the arbitration to function.

EMMANUEL GAILLARD & JOHN SAVAGE, INTERNATIONAL COMMERCIAL ARBITRATION 263 (1999).

[17] The essential core of an arbitration agreement, pursuant to its definition, is relatively simple: it consists of nothing more than an obligation to resolve certain disputes with another party by "arbitration" and the right to demand that such disputes be resolved in this fashion. These rights and duties can be contained in nothing more than the word "arbitration" included in a contract, letter, or fax, by which the parties commit to resolve disputes relating to their transaction by arbitration. Moreover, as discussed above, even if the word "arbitration" is not used, an arbitration agreement can be concluded by agreement to a dispute resolution mechanism with the characteristics of arbitration.

GARY B. BORN, I INTERNATIONAL COMMERCIAL ARBITRATION 655–656 (2009).

has drafted and organized such rules with due regard to the tradition and specificity of the institution.

Consequently, attention should be paid to the link between an administrative body and the set of rules when drafting an arbitration clause. To commingle institutions with different arbitral rules may give rise to a pathological clause. Such a hybrid arbitration clause that was the core issue in the case of *Insigma Technology Co. Ltd. v. Alstom Technology Ltd (Insigma v. Alstom)*.[18] In June 2009, the Singapore Court of Appeal upheld the arbitration agreement, which set forth that all disputes should be ultimately resolved "by arbitration before the Singapore International Arbitration Centre (SIAC) in accordance with the Rules of Arbitration of the International Chamber of Commerce."[19] Alstom initially commenced the arbitration before an ICC court, but Insigma challenged the jurisdiction of the ICC and argued that the competent arbitral institution was SIAC. Subsequently, Alstom, withdrew its application to the ICC and commenced a new arbitration at SIAC. Then, Insigma objected SIAC tribunal's jurisdiction arguing that the arbitration clause was void.[20]

The Singapore Court of Appeal in *Insigma v. Alstom* upheld the hybrid (pathological) clause in favor of arbitration and affirmed that SIAC had jurisdiction to manage the arbitration according to the parties' intent as reflected in the arbitration agreement. The arbitration-friendly approach of the Singapore Court of Appeal was highlighted in this case:

> where the parties have evinced a clear intention to settle any dispute by arbitration, the court should give effect to such intention, even if certain aspects of the agreement may be ambiguous, inconsistent, incomplete or lacking in certain particulars so long as the arbitration can be carried out without prejudice to the rights of either party and so long as giving effect to such intention does not result in an arbitration that is not within the contemplation of either party. This approach is similar to the "principle of effective interpretation" [found] in international arbitration law.[21]

The principle of effective interpretation of arbitration agreements was inspired by national laws, such as Article 1157 of the French Civil Code, according to which "where a clause can be interpreted in two different ways, the interpretation enabling the clause to be effective should be adopted in preference to that which prevents the clause from being effective." This commonsense rule whereby, if in doubt, one should "prefer the interpretation which gives meaning to the words, rather than that which renders them useless or nonsensical" is widely accepted by the courts and arbitrators. Thus, it reaches the level of a "universally recognized rule of interpretation." To give just one example of the application of this principle, an arbitral tribunal

---

[18] Insigma Technology Co. Ltd. v. Alstom Technology Ltd. [2009] SGCA 24.
[19] "This attempt to mix and match arbitral rules and institutions predictably proved itself an invitation to delay, use of guerrilla tactics, and controversy going well beyond the case itself." Price, *supra* note 1, at 836.
[20] Insigma argued that only the ICC Court could conduct an arbitration under the ICC Rules, in part because SIAC does not have the equivalent structure to perform the roles of the ICC Secretariat, ICC Secretary General, and the ICC Court as contemplated by the ICC Rules. These bodies are integral to the functioning of the ICC Rules, being charged with handling a number of procedural matters and, unique to the ICC Court, scrutiny of the draft awards for potential procedural defects that might affect enforceability. Upon the tribunal's enquiry, SIAC confirmed that it could administer the arbitration in accordance with the ICC Rules, and would replicate the functions of the ICC bodies through the SIAC Secretariat, the SIAC Registrar, and the SIAC Board of Directors, respectively. The tribunal found it had jurisdiction, a decision Insigma challenged in Singapore courts.

Id. at 837.
[21] Citing para. 20.017 2 HALSBURY'S LAWS OF SINGAPORE (2003 *reissue*); GAILLARD & SAVAGE, *supra* note 16, at 258 (discussion of principle of effective interpretation).

interpreting a pathological clause held that: "when inserting an arbitration clause in their contract the intention of the parties must be presumed to have been willing to establish an effective machinery for the settlement of disputes covered by the arbitration clause."[22]

The Singapore courts did not invalidate the arbitration clause, although it was pathological in nature; a defective clause does not ipso facto obliterate the parties' agreement and, depending on the substance of the pathology the intention of the parties – namely the existence of the arbitration clause – may still be enforceable. The *Insigma v. Alstom* case not only recognized the enforceability of a hybrid or pathological clause but provided a set of principles that could be applied in future cases, including

> (i) where the parties have evinced a clear intention to settle any dispute by arbitration, the court should give effect to that intention even if certain aspects of the agreement are ambiguous, inconsistent or incomplete; (ii) where a clause can be interpreted in two different ways, the interpretation enabling the clause to be effective should be adopted in preference to that which prevents the clause from being effective; (iii) as far as possible, a commercially logical and sensible construction is to be preferred over another that is commercially illogical; (iv) there was no reason why a clause providing for the rules of one arbitral institution to be applied by a similar institution should be too uncertain to be given effect to; (v) a defect in an arbitration clause does not necessarily render it unworkable, since it may often be cured by the assistance of state courts, arbitral institutions and arbitrators, and in this case the clause was rendered workable by the SIAC agreeing to administer the arbitration in accordance with the ICC Rules; and (vi) no policy considerations would bar the SIAC from agreeing to administer an arbitration under the ICC Rules.[23]

Although controversial, the Singapore Court of Appeal ruling in favor of the parties' autonomy to tailor their dispute resolution clauses ultimately lead the ICC to amend its rules to explicitly provide that the arbitrations under the ICC Arbitration Rules shall be administered only by ICC Courts.[24]

4 MEDIATION CLAUSES IN ENERGY CONTRACTS

First and foremost, mediation is a type of ADR that may be regarded as an assisted negotiation. In other words, mediation, at its core, is a type of negotiation that is conducted with the support of an objective third party in order to reach a mutually satisfactory settlement. As opposed to an arbitrator or a judge, the third party in mediation (mediator) has no power to order a specific conduct from the parties or capacity to enforce the result of the mediation. The nonbinding nature of mediation is problematic for parties wanting a binding and enforceable decision. That said, once the parties sign a settlement agreement based on the mediation that agreement becomes a binding, enforceable contract.

The business community in general, but particularly the energy sector prefers mediation as an alternative dispute resolution mechanism – namely as an alternative to arbitration or litigation. Among the other ADR mechanisms, such as expert determination, early neutral evaluation, and

---

[22] Insigma v. Alstom [2009] SGCA 24, para. 31.
[23] *See* Richard Hill, *Hybrid ICC/SIAC Arbitration Clause Upheld in Singapore*, KLUWER ARBITRATION BLOG (June 10, 2009), http://arbitrationblog.kluwerarbitration.com/2009/06/10/hybrid-iccsiac-arbitration-clause-upheld-in-singapore.
[24] ICC Rules as revised in 2012, Art. I (2): "The Court is the only body authorized to administer arbitrations under the Rules, including the scrutiny and approval of awards rendered in accordance with the Rules. It draws up its own internal rules, which are set forth in Appendix II (Internal Rules)."

adjudication,[25] mediation is highly preferred, and mediation clauses are frequently inserted in agreements across different jurisdictions. The best practice is to agree on a mediation–arbitration (med–arb) clause, where the parties must in good faith seek mediation before pursuing a claim in arbitration.[26]

Unfortunately, because of their nonbinding nature, mediation clauses are often not drafted and designed with the same care as arbitration clauses. They also present the problem of determining whether a party mediated in good faith, which gives the parties another issue to dispute. Mediation clauses are more commonly used at the domestic level but is more problematic in international disputes due to differences in culture (different views of the meaning and importance of mediation) and language, distance, and lack of confidence in the mediation process. However, sometimes disputes are caused by cultural misunderstandings and may best be resolved by mediation or conciliation. A successful mediation is dependent on the parties' willingness to focus on their mutual interests, objectives, and continuing an undertaking or preserving the contractual relationship, rather than on the strict enforcement of legal entitlements and rights.

The disregard for mediation in international arbitration clauses is a missed opportunity to resolve disputes faster and cheaper, given the high rate of successful settlements through mediation. Mediation clauses also serve as signals that the parties expect to work together in good faith, which creates the context for prospective and more amicable settlements. To ensure a good faith attempt to settle disputes through mediation, the mediation clause must state that mediation is mandatory and provide some guidance as to the criteria for a good faith mediation (involvement of top executives, schedule, minimal hours for mediation, and possibly a selection of institutional mediation or conciliation rules[27]). Also, the parties may consider granting greater power to the mediator than is customary, such as the ability to propose a settlement. In specialized industries that would require the appointment of a mediator with knowledge and who is skilled in specific technical competencies of the given industry. Mediation has many advantages for long-lasting business relationships, but mediation clauses that are not tailored or customized for contracts relating to highly complex and technical disputes (as is in the energy industry), will largely be ineffective.

In the end, while drafting a complex agreement in the energy sector, it is important to consider incorporating a mediation clause that would benefit the parties and their contractual relationship. Due consideration should be given, as mentioned, to the nonbinding nature of the procedure, the lack of active involvement of the mediator, the characteristics of the mediator

---

[25] Steven C. Nelson, *Alternatives to Litigation of International Disputes*, 23 INT'L LAWYER 187 (1989).

[26] An example of a Med-Arb clause is provided by the World International Property Organization (WIPO):

> Any dispute, controversy or claim arising under, out of or relating to this contract and any subsequent amendments of this contract, including, without limitation, its formation, validity, binding effect, interpretation, performance, breach or termination, as well as non-contractual claims, shall be submitted to mediation in accordance with the WIPO Mediation Rules. The place of mediation shall be [specify place]. The language to be used in the mediation shall be [select language]. If, and to the extent that, any such dispute, controversy or claim has not been settled pursuant to the mediation within ___ days of the commencement of the mediation, it shall, upon the filing of a Request for Arbitration by either party, be referred to and finally determined by arbitration in accordance with the WIPO Arbitration Rules.

> *Recommended WIPO Contract Clauses and Submission Agreements*, WIPO www.wipo.int/amc/en/arbitration/contract-clauses/clauses.html.

[27] *See, e.g.*, ICC Rules of Optional Conciliation. For a discussion of these Rules, see Eric A. Schwartz, *International Conciliation and the ICC* 5 INT'L CHAMBER COM. INT'L. CT. ARB. BULL. 5 (1974).

(in terms of knowledge and competencies), and at what stage of the dispute would mediation be required.

5 CONCLUSION

Given the complexity of the energy industry, arbitration in this sector is prolific. Disputes in this sector are almost always time consuming and involve large sums of money. These characteristics of energy contract disputes are intimately connected in that time-consuming disputes on high-value projects result in extremely expensive cost overruns. It is among the reasons why contracting parties are pressured to reach an early settlement. These reasons also make it imperative that the parties and their lawyers use due diligence in negotiating a well-drafted arbitration clause, which should be the foundation of good preparation and attentive risk management, ensuring a smooth resolution of a possible dispute. Instead, it is still common to use model form clauses.

The energy industry has been greatly influenced by geographical, political, economic, and environmental factors that create a high risk of uncertainty in most projects. This uncertainty is compounded through litigation using courts with little experience in specialized industries. Resorting to national courts for the resolution of an energy dispute offers few chances of resulting in a good solution.

9

Drafting, Interpretation, and Enforcement of Commercial Arbitration Clauses

A Practitioner's Perspective

Philippe Cavalieros

1 INTRODUCTION

An arbitration agreement is an agreement between parties to a legal relationship to submit an existing or any future disputes to arbitration. It follows that an agreement of the parties to arbitrate is the cornerstone of arbitration, as it contains the consent of the parties to submit their dispute to arbitration. There are two basic types of arbitration agreements. The first one is a submission agreement, which consists in an agreement to submit an existing dispute to arbitration. The second is an arbitration clause, which consists in an agreement to submit a future dispute to arbitration.[1]

In practice, submission agreements are relatively rare, because once a dispute arises, it is in general difficult for the parties to reach an agreement on any issue. Nevertheless, a submission agreement may be considered less dangerous for a 'weak party' such as an employee or a consumer. When a dispute arises, such party is given the opportunity to assess the consequences of bringing the case before an arbitral tribunal rather than going before a judge, without being necessarily pressured by the other party.[2]

In any case, whether it be a submission agreement or an arbitration clause, the drafting stage is essential because it ensures that the parties have agreed on the way arbitration will be conducted for settling an existing or a future dispute. As a result, some instruments have created guidelines on how to draft arbitration agreements. This is the case of the New York Convention on the Recognition and Enforcement of Foreign Arbitral Awards, concluded in 1958 (Hereinafter 'the New York Convention'), and the UN Commission on International Trade Law Model Law (hereinafter 'the UNCITRAL Model Law'), initially concluded in 1985 and amended in 2006.[3] Both instruments play an important role in improving the framework of international trade through the elaboration of international legislative rules to be used by states and therefore contribute to modernising arbitration.

Depending on the way an arbitration agreement is drafted, it may give rise to various interpretations. As such, arbitrators have an important role to play and may rely on various principles of interpretation and presumptions to guide their analysis. Finally, after an arbitral award has been rendered, a party may challenge said award before a state judge. This chapter

---

[1] I INTERNATIONAL COMMERCIAL ARBITRATION §2.02, 241 (Gary B. Born ed., 2d ed. 2014).
[2] DROIT DE L'ARBITRAGE INTERNE ET INTERNATIONAL 14–15 (Christophe Seraglini & Jerôme Ortscheidt eds., 2013).
[3] UN Commission on International Trade Law Model Law, Vienna, in force June 21, 1985, amended July 7, 2006, General Assembly Resolution 40/72 (1985), General Assembly Resolution 61/33 (2006).

describes the process of drafting, interpreting and enforcing arbitration agreements, with a focus on commercial arbitration agreements. Section 2 provides information on the way an arbitration agreement should be drafted in practice by the parties regarding an existing or a future dispute. Section 3 analyses the arbitrators' interpretation of an arbitration agreement. Section 4 finally describes certain grounds on which a party may rely to challenge the validity of an arbitration agreement before a state court and the role of judiciary in this regard.

2 DRAFTING AN ARBITRATION AGREEMENT

2.1 Negotiation

In general, contracting parties tend to focus on negotiating the commercial substance of such contract; clauses related to price or liability are clauses which are thoroughly negotiated between the parties. By contrast, a clause, which is often neglected despite its important consequences on the parties is the arbitration clause. In this respect, some authors have pointed out that:

> [M]ost international arbitrations take place pursuant to an arbitration clause in a commercial contract. These clauses are often 'midnight clauses', i.e. the last clauses to be considered in contract negotiations, sometimes late at night or in the early hours of the morning. An insufficient thought is given as to how disputes are to be resolved (possibly because the parties are reluctant to contemplate falling into dispute) and an inappropriate and unwieldy compromise is often adopted.[4]

One logical explanation to the poor drafting of arbitration clauses is that, at the negotiation stage, parties are thinking about developing their commercial relationship rather than foreseeing potential disputes.

However, there is of course always a risk that disputes may arise between the parties to a contract. The advantage of having recourse to arbitration is that the parties are autonomous in deciding on the way they wish to settle their dispute. At the same time, there are pitfalls to be avoided when drafting an arbitration agreement.

2.2 Formal Requirements

Parties to a contract are advised to rely on the New York Convention for drafting their arbitration agreement because it provides useful indications on the formal elements of an arbitration agreement.

2.2.1 New York Convention

The formal requirements governing arbitration agreements under most national legislations are inspired by the provisions of the New York Convention governing the international recognition and enforcement of foreign arbitral awards. The New York Convention is a well-known instrument for arbitral matters, and its application is widespread, thanks to the fact that it has been adopted by more than 160 member states.[5] Therefore, it is recommended that the arbitration agreement follow the convention's formal requirements, because if not, there is a risk that the

---

[4] REDFERN AND HUNTER ON INTERNATIONAL ARBITRATION 72–73 (Nigel Blackaby & Constantine Partasides, with Alan Redfern & Martin Hunter eds., 6th ed. 2015).
[5] New York Convention on the Recognition and Enforcement of Foreign Arbitral Awards, New York, June 10, 1958, in force June 7, 1959, 330 UNTS 38; 21 UST 2517; (1968) 7 ILM 1046.

resulting award would not be enforceable. In practice, even if it is not compulsory, many states explicitly require that arbitration agreements respect those formal requirements, by incorporating them into domestic law. The formal requirements for drafting an arbitration agreement are provided in Articles II(1) and V(1)(a) of the New York Convention.

2.2.2 *Article II(1) of the New York Convention*

Article II(1) of the New York Convention provides four main formal requirements, as follows: 'Each Contracting State shall recognize an agreement in writing under which the parties undertake to submit to arbitration all or any differences which have arisen or which may arise between them in respect of a defined legal relationship, whether contractual or not, concerning a subject matter capable of settlement by arbitration.' Therefore, the convention establishes that an arbitration agreement needs to be drafted in writing rather than orally, it needs to cover either existing or future disputes, the parties need to be part of a defined legal relationship and, finally, the dispute must be capable of arbitration.

2.2.2.1 AGREEMENT IN WRITING Due to its probative value, the fact that an arbitration agreement must be in writing is probably the most important requirement provided by Article II(1) of the New York Convention. Such requirement is also provided for by the UNCITRAL Model Law in Article 7. Under French Law, pursuant to a 1981 Decree and a 2011 revision of the French arbitration legislation, Article 1507 of the Code of Civil Procedure provides that 'the arbitration agreement shall not be subject to any requirement as to its form'.[6] This was upheld by the Paris Court of Appeal, which provided that the New York Convention imposed only a 'minimum' requirement, which French national law could not supplement or expand.[7] Sweden,[8] Scotland,[9] Singapore,[10] Hong Kong[11] and New Zealand[12] have also decided to abolish the written form requirements.[13] By contrast, section 2(1) of the Irish Arbitration Act 2010, section 5 of the English Arbitration Act 1996, section 1031 of the German ZPO and section 2 of the US Federal Arbitration Act[14] all require a written arbitration agreement.

The requirement of an agreement in writing is supposed to be a 'maximum' form requirement, preventing domestic law from imposing stricter writing requirements than those under the Convention.[15] As a result, an arbitration agreement can be recorded in any form; even a simple electronic communication is sufficient for the agreement to be considered as a written agreement. The UNCITRAL Model Law itself illustrates this flexibility, by asserting that an agreement is in writing 'if its content is recorded in any form, whether or not the arbitration agreement or contract has been concluded orally, by conduct or by other means'. The UNCITRAL Model Law also explicitly provides that an arbitration agreement is in writing when it is 'met by electronic communication, if the information contained therein is accessible so as to be

---

[6] French Code of Civil Procedure, Article 1507.
[7] Paris Court of Appeal, Judgment of Jan. 20, 1987, Société Bomar Oil NV v. Entreprise Tunisienne d'Activités Pétrolières, Rev Arb 482, 485.
[8] Swedish Arbitration Act 2019, § 1(1).
[9] *Id.* at § 4.
[10] Singapore International Arbitration Act 2012, § 2A (4).
[11] Hong Kong Arbitration Ordinance 2013, Article 19 (1).
[12] New Zealand Arbitration Act 1996, Schedule 1, Article 7(1).
[13] Born, *supra* note 1, at vol. I, §5.02, 708.
[14] US Federal Arbitration Act of 1925, Pub L No 68-401, 43 Stat. 883 (1925), codified at 9 U.S.C. ch 1 (1926).
[15] Born, *supra* note 1, vol. I, §5.02, 669.

useable for subsequent reference'.[16] Most states respect this maximum requirement and do not require the agreement to be signed; in fact, as long as there is a written evidence of the existence of this agreement, an exchange of correspondence is sufficient.

2.2.2.2 EXISTING OR FUTURE DISPUTES An arbitration agreement must deal either with existing or future disputes; indeed, there are two possibilities offered to the parties when drafting such agreement, either to insert an *arbitration clause* within the main contract, for dealing with *future* disputes or to conclude a *submission agreement* to submit to arbitration an *existing* dispute. As such, under French Law, Article 1442 of the Code of Civil Procedure gives the possibility to insert an arbitration clause (*clause compromissoire*) within the main contract for dealing with future disputes or concluding a submission agreement (*compromis*) for submitting an existing dispute before an arbitral tribunal.[17] Similarly, the Swiss federal statute on Private International Law (hereinafter 'the PILA') provides in its Article 178 (3) that 'an arbitration agreement cannot be contested on the grounds ... that the arbitration agreement concerns a dispute which has not as yet arisen';[18] this allows for either existing or future disputes to be settled by arbitration.

2.2.2.3 DEFINED LEGAL RELATIONSHIP Parties to an arbitration agreement should have a defined business relationship, whether contractual or not, which has led or might lead to a dispute. One commentator explains this requirement as follows: 'Parties cannot enter into an unlimited agreement that any controversy that should ever arise between them is subject to arbitration. There must be some degree of specificity in defining the kind of controversy one undertakes to submit to arbitration'.[19] In practice, this requirement is of limited importance. There are no reported cases in which an arbitration agreement was held to be invalid on the ground that it did not involve a 'defined relationship' between the parties. In addition, this requirement does not imply that the arbitration agreement needs to have a defined scope.[20] In practice, arbitration clauses usually contain broad scope formulas, to avoid any issue in this respect.

2.2.2.4 SUBJECT MATTER CAPABLE OF SETTLEMENT BY ARBITRATION When a subject matter is capable of being submitted to arbitration, it is arbitrable. Notwithstanding the arbitration agreement between the parties and their autonomy, objective arbitrability or arbitrability *ratione materiae* prevents certain types of claims from being resolved through arbitration.[21] According to Gary B. Born, arbitrability 'rests on the notion that some matters so pervasively involve public rights, or interests of third parties, which are the subjects of uniquely governmental authority, that agreements to resolve such disputes by "private" arbitration should not be given effect'.[22] Thus, the main criterion for determining the arbitrability of a dispute is whether the matter involves public rights or third parties' rights.

Each country decides which matters may or may not be resolved by arbitration in accordance with its own political, social and economic rules. Certain disputes are therefore not arbitrable,

---

[16] UNCITRAL Model Law, Article 7.
[17] French Code of Civil Procedure, Article 1442.
[18] Swiss Private International Law Act 2018, Article 178 (3).
[19] LAURENCE CRAIG, WILLIAM PARK, & JAN PAULSSON, §6.02, 86 INTERNATIONAL CHAMBER OF COMMERCE ARBITRATION (3d ed. 2000).
[20] Born, *supra* note 1, at vol. I, §2.03, 295.
[21] *Id.* at vol. I, §6.01, 944.
[22] *Id.* at vol. I, §5.04, 768.

depending on the applicable law, such as criminal matters, those, which affect the status of an individual or a corporate entity (such as bankruptcy or insolvency) and even at times disputes involving patents and trademarks.[23] Countries need to find the right balance between, on the one hand, reserving matters of public interest to state courts and, on the other hand, favouring trade and autonomous dispute settlement.[24] Under French Law, Article 2059 of the French Civil Code provides that 'all persons may enter into arbitration agreements relating to the rights that they may freely dispose of';[25] this provision clearly favours commerce and trade. However, another article restricts the possibility to submit to arbitration certain disputes, notably in family law matters and more generally in matters related to public order.[26] In contrast, Swiss law is broader on the matters that may be subject to arbitration; it requires only the dispute to involve a 'financial interest',[27] without defining what constitutes a financial interest.

2.2.3 Article V(1)(a) of the New York Convention

Article V(1)(a) provides two additional requirements by stipulating that the recognition and enforcement of an award may be refused if it is proven that 'The parties to the agreement referred to in Article II were, under the law applicable to them, under some incapacity, or the said agreement is not valid under the law to which the parties have subjected it or, failing any indication thereon, under the law of the country where the award was made'. Thus, it is important at the drafting stage to pay attention to the parties' legal capacity in entering the arbitration agreement, as well as to the overall validity of such agreement.

2.2.3.1 PARTIES' LEGAL CAPACITY The parties' legal capacity to enter into an arbitration agreement relates to general requirements for entering into any contract.[28] The New York Convention provides that the parties' capacity is governed by 'the law applicable to them'.[29] This concept does not appear in the UNCITRAL Model Law, which, deliberately, does not provide any criteria for determining an individual's capacity to conclude an arbitration agreement. Thus, one needs to rely on each state's domestic rules. As a result, there is no uniform understanding concerning the law applicable to the legal capacity of individuals. The prevailing concept is that legal capacity should be governed by the *personal law* of each party, which opens up many possibilities since personal law may involve the law of the parties' nationality or the law of their domicile.[30] In any case, many states have adopted common standards of legal capacity, prohibiting the conclusion of agreements (including arbitration agreements) by individuals such as minors or those suffering from mental illness.

2.2.3.2 VALIDITY OF THE ARBITRATION AGREEMENT The validity of the arbitration agreement is assessed under the law chosen by the parties or, failing any indication on their part, under the law of the country where the award was made. Under the New York Convention, validity encompasses all the requirements at the domestic level, which apply in addition to the

---

[23] *Id.* at vol. I, §6.01, 945.
[24] *Id.* at vol. I, §6.03, 963.
[25] French Code of Civil Procedure, Article 2059.
[26] *Id.* at Article 2060.
[27] Swiss Private International Law Act 2018, Article 177 (1).
[28] UN Conference on Trade and Development, Dispute Settlement – International Commercial Arbitration – The Arbitration Agreement (2005) UNCTAD/EDM/Misc.232/Add.39.
[29] Article V(1)(a) of the New York Convention.
[30] *Supra* note 28.

requirements provided in the convention itself. In addition to formal requirements, parties to an arbitration agreement are strongly advised to agree on certain additional components.

2.3 *Practical Requirements*

It is particularly important for the arbitration clause to contain some practical information which guarantees the smooth conduct of the arbitration, because once the dispute arises, there is a risk that parties will not agree on the settlement of any issue related to arbitration. As such, there are elements which are indispensable to any arbitration agreement, and some others which are only recommended or even optional, but which may nonetheless be of practical use.

2.3.1 *Essential Elements*

Some elements, if not agreed upon by the parties, make the arbitration process uncertain. As such, it is essential for the clause to explicitly refer to arbitration and strongly recommend providing for the seat of arbitration.

2.3.1.1 EXPRESS REFERENCE TO ARBITRATION An arbitration agreement is unclear if it does not expressly contain the word *arbitration*. In addition, an issue may arise where the arbitration agreement states that the parties 'may' refer a dispute to arbitration. This allows a party to argue that it is not bound by the arbitration process. Under French Law, an arbitration clause has a mandatory character (*force obligatoire*), because parties 'commit to submit the disputes arising out of the contract to arbitration'.[31] This idea of commitment to arbitration prevents any ambiguity. Under Swiss Law, the arbitration clause must clearly express the parties' intent to submit any dispute covered by the arbitration agreement.[32] Similarly, under English case law, it is widely accepted that the term *may* turns into a mandatory provision if either party seeks to arbitrate a dispute.[33] A similar view is adopted in most common law countries including the United States, Canada, Australia and Singapore.[34]

2.3.1.2 SEAT OF ARBITRATION Although not mandatory as such, it is paramount to provide the seat of arbitration in the arbitration agreement. Indeed, the seat of arbitration has many consequences on the conduct of arbitration and on the parties. As such, the choice of the seat of arbitration is strategic. Firstly, it is recommended that the place of the seat of arbitration be a signatory of the New York Convention, in order for the arbitration agreement to benefit from the provisions regarding reciprocity. The principle of reciprocity in general involves that a state offers certain privileges to another state on the condition that its subjects enjoy the similar privileges in the other state;[35] as for arbitration, states must favour the recognition and enforcement of foreign arbitral awards in their own jurisdiction pursuant to the rules of the convention.[36]

Secondly, the seat of arbitration determines which judge will have a supervisory control over the conduct of arbitration. As such, it is recommended to choose a seat in a state in which courts

---

[31] French Code of Civil Procedure, Article 1442.
[32] *See, e.g.,* First Civil Law Court, Judgment of June 3, 2015, 4A_676/2014.
[33] *See, e.g.,* Anzen Limited and others v. Hermes One Limited [2016] UKPC 1.
[34] Narges M. Kakalia & Terry McMahon, *Mandatory vs. Permissive Arbitration Clauses: A Survey of the Laws of Other Common Law Countries*, MINTZ (Mar. 27, 2017) www.mintz.com/insights-center/viewpoints/2196/2017-03-mandatory-vs-permissive-arbitration-clauses-survey-laws.
[35] Young-Joon Mok, *The Principle of Reciprocity in the United Nations Convention on the Recognition and Enforcement of Foreign Arbitral Awards of 1958*, 21 CASE WESTERN RESERVE JOURNAL OF INTERNATIONAL LAW 124–125 (1989).
[36] *Id.* at 125–126.

are experienced in the field and supportive of arbitration. Indeed, such state's procedural rules will govern the arbitral proceedings, the selection, the qualification and removal of arbitrators, the arbitrators' power to order provisional measures or disclosure, the conduct of counsel representatives in the arbitration or even the form and publication of the arbitral award and, last but not least, the recourse against the award.[37]

Finally, although the choice of the seat of arbitration is not necessarily intended to favour or disadvantage one party over the other. In practice, parties frequently insist that the arbitral seat be 'neutral', meaning that it should not be the home jurisdiction of either party because there is a perceived risk that the court of the seat may be biased in favour of the party established therein. The parties will thus choose the seat of arbitration depending on the experience and perceived neutrality of the state courts among the potential arbitral seats under consideration.[38] Corruption affecting the judicial system is another factor to consider.[39]

Countries that clearly cope with the considerations related to the seat of arbitration and which, in addition, are experienced in complex commercial matters, include the United States, England, France, Switzerland, Austria, Belgium, the Netherlands, Sweden, Canada, Singapore, Hong Kong, Australia and New Zealand. In practice, successful seats of arbitration are Paris, London, Geneva, Zurich and Singapore.[40]

2.3.2 *Recommended Elements*

In addition to the mentioned essential provisions, parties are advised to insert some elements in the clause to ensure the smooth procedural conduct of arbitration.

2.3.2.1 NUMBER OF ARBITRATORS The parties may decide on the number of arbitrators. Parties mainly choose between having one or three arbitrators (an arbitral tribunal composed of five arbitrators being relatively rare). Having three arbitrators may present several advantages. Each party can appoint one co-arbitrator and the presiding arbitrator may be appointed by such two arbitrators in consultation with the parties. Having three arbitrators also may lead to a shared burden, reducing the risk of error or accidental omissions. It may also lead to a more balanced outcome (whether appropriate or not).

On the other hand, the advantages of having one arbitrator is that in theory, the sole arbitrator would not feel 'indebted' to either party, contrary to a co-arbitrator who may feel some sense of duty towards the party that appointed him or her. Moreover, proceedings are generally more cost and time effective.[41]

2.3.2.2 INSTITUTIONAL VERSUS AD HOC ARBITRATION The parties to a contract may choose to submit a future or existing dispute to an institution specialised in arbitration,[42] such as the International Chamber of Commerce (hereinafter 'the ICC'), the London Court of International Arbitration (hereinafter 'the LCIA'), the Singapore International Arbitration Centre (hereinafter 'the SIAC'), the Dubai International Arbitration Centre (hereinafter 'the DIAC') or the American Arbitration Association (hereinafter 'the AAA'). Conversely, parties can choose to

---

[37] Born, *supra* note 1, at vol. II, §14.02, 2057.
[38] *Id.* at vol. II, §14.02, 2061.
[39] *Id.* at vol. II, §26.04, 2061.
[40] ICC Statistics on the Seat of Arbitration 2016.
[41] Ben Giaretta & Akshay Kishore, *One Arbitrator or Three?* ASHURST (Sept. 1, 2015) www.ashurst.com/en/news-and-insights/legal-updates/one-arbitrator-or-three/.
[42] Born, *supra* note 1, at vol. I, §1.04, 169.

submit a dispute to an ad hoc arbitral tribunal – namely a tribunal which is constituted independently of any institution and which is tailored to dealing with the dispute at hand.[43]

It is highly recommended that the parties specify in the clause whether they prefer an institutional or an ad hoc arbitration. Indeed, having an institutional or ad hoc arbitration determines the applicable procedural rules to the arbitral process. If the parties have chosen an institutional arbitration, then the procedural rules of the institution apply. As such, arbitral institutions have developed their own arbitration rules such as the 2017 ICC Arbitration Rules.[44] As for ad hoc arbitration, in principle the parties can adopt their own procedural rules.

Institutional or ad hoc arbitration both have their own advantages and drawbacks. The arguments in favour of an ad hoc arbitration include, notably, its flexibility – it is suitable for all types of claims and parties freely decide on the procedure. Another nonnegligible consideration is costs, because there are no administrative fees payable to an institution; only the fees for remunerating the arbitrators, lawyers and representatives will have to be paid by the parties, which may in theory be cost-effective as such fees can be negotiated. In practice, the reality is quite different.

However, ad hoc arbitration also has important drawbacks, which often lead the parties to an arbitration agreement to favour institutional arbitration. In practice, parties have difficulty agreeing on the different aspects of an arbitration once a dispute has arisen. There is a risk of misunderstanding and reluctance to cooperate, especially between parties from different cultures and backgrounds. Moreover, the parties usually lack the knowledge to anticipate all the potential issues, which may arise during the conduct of arbitration. Finally, it may not be much cheaper compared to an institutional arbitration, because if the parties cannot reach an agreement on the procedure, the local courts' intervention may be required, incurring further legal costs in the arbitral proceedings.

In the end, it is often argued that ad hoc arbitration works effectively only when the parties cooperate, have sufficient knowledge of the arbitral process and rely on experienced counsel and arbitrators.[45] In the opinion of some authors, it is believed that ad hoc arbitration is better suited to parties having a dispute involving small claims.[46] It is very difficult, if not impossible, to anticipate all the potential problems which may arise when drafting an arbitration agreement, and as such, Gary Born believes that institutional arbitration is valuable because it ensures that the staff has an experience or institutional resources for dealing with arbitration.[47]

2.3.2.3 CHOICE OF LAW The parties to an arbitration agreement can decide on the law applicable to the contract and on procedural law, and also on the law applicable to the arbitration agreement. National legal systems take different approaches to the choice of the law governing the formal validity of the arbitration agreement; they frequently rely on the law of the putative arbitral seat, failing which the law of the underlying contract.[48] In case the parties have agreed on the applicable law governing the arbitration agreement, then the law selected by the parties applies to this agreement.[49] As for procedural law, some authors suggest parties decide on which

---

[43] *Id.* at vol. I, §1.04, 170.
[44] International Chamber of Commerce Arbitration Rules, Paris, 2012, amended Mar. 1, 2017.
[45] Sundra Rajoo, *Institutional and Ad-hoc Arbitrations: Advantages and Disadvantages*, 2 THE LAW REVIEW 547–549 (2010).
[46] *Id.*
[47] Born, *supra* note 1, at vol. I, §1.04, 171.
[48] *Id.* at vol. I, §5.04, 742.
[49] *Id.* at vol. I, §5.02, 722.

law should apply in their agreement. If the parties disagree on it once a dispute arises, there is a risk of having to wait for the arbitral tribunal's decision thereon, which will involve costs and delay in the conduct of arbitration.[50]

2.3.2.4 LANGUAGE For practical reasons, it is important to agree on the language of the arbitration in advance, especially when the parties come from different countries. The parties can choose one of the parties' native languages or a different language. English is often favoured in international commercial disputes.[51] The chosen language will be used in written and oral submissions, though the parties can also specify certain derogations, i.e., whether evidentiary exhibits or testimony may be submitted in different languages without the need for translations.

2.3.2.5 EXCLUSION OF A COURT REMEDY Parties choosing to submit disputes to arbitration intend for the resulting arbitral award to be final and binding. The parties may wish to go a step further and exclude challenges to the arbitral award before state courts, either by waiving their rights to bring an annulment action (at the seat) or to appeal an enforcement order (in any jurisdiction where an enforcement order is granted). The validity of such waivers depends on the domestic law of the countries in which the parties intend to enforce such waiver. For example, under French Law, the parties may expressly waive their rights to bring an action for annulment but may not waive their right to appeal an enforcement order.[52]

2.3.3 *Optional Elements*

In addition to the recommended elements, parties may choose to be even more explicit when drafting their arbitration clause by inserting provisions which are not indispensable but may nevertheless facilitate the conduct of the arbitration.

2.3.3.1 APPOINTMENT OF ARBITRATORS Arbitrators are not necessarily lawyers, they can also be technical experts (for example, engineers, architects and scientists). If the contract from which the parties' legal relationship arises involves a particularly technical or niche sector, the parties may want to specify in the arbitration agreement certain qualifications that they wish the arbitrator(s) to have. Parties should however be wary of not imposing too stringent conditions.

More generally, the parties may want to agree on the method of constitution of an arbitral tribunal. In an institutional arbitration, the applicable institutional rules usually provide for the procedure to be followed in the absence of party agreement (including deadlines for nominations of arbitrators, powers of the institution to nominate, etc.). Otherwise, recourse to a state court may be necessary to assist in the constitution of the tribunal. However, it is not recommended to appoint specific arbitrator(s) by name in the agreement, as contracts may be concluded over a long duration, and the situation and availability of an arbitrator may change. Moreover, the identified arbitrator may decline to hear the dispute when it arises, even if he or she expressly agreed thereto at the time of conclusion of the arbitration agreement.

---

[50] Diana-Loredana Hogas, *Considerations about Drafting Arbitration Clauses*, 8 JOURNAL OF PUBLIC ADMINISTRATION FINANCE AND LAW 126–127 (2015).
[51] Born, *supra* note 1, at vol. II, §15.06, 2231.
[52] French Code of Civil Procedure, Article 1522.

2.3.3.2 CONFIDENTIALITY One of the most well-known advantage of arbitration is confidentiality; parties usually agree to arbitrate on the understanding that information regarding the proceedings will not be disclosed to third parties. However, contrary to a popular belief, most national arbitration legislations and institutional arbitration rules are silent on the issue of confidentiality, and parties wishing to keep their arbitration confidential will need to conclude express agreements to such effect. Under French law, unless the parties agree otherwise, domestic arbitrations are subject to confidentiality (but not international arbitrations),[53] and in all instances, 'the arbitral tribunal's deliberations shall be confidential'.[54]

2.3.4 *Templates*

Parties to a contract are advised to rely on one of the various recommended arbitration clauses provided by international conventions or arbitral institutions. For example, the UNCITRAL Model Law provides the following suggested wording:

> Any dispute, controversy or claim arising out of or in connection with this contract, including any question regarding its existence, validity or termination, shall be referred to and finally resolved by arbitration in accordance with the Rules of [choose the set of Rules/institution], which Rules are deemed to be incorporated by reference into this clause. The seat of the arbitration shall be [city, country]. The language of the arbitration shall be [language]. The number of arbitrators shall be [one or three].

Similarly, the ICC for instance has its own standard arbitration clause, which states 'All disputes arising out of or in connection with the present contract shall be finally settled under the Rules of Arbitration of the International Chamber of Commerce by [one or more arbitrators] appointed in accordance with the said Rules'.

3 INTERPRETING AN ARBITRATION AGREEMENT

Once a dispute arises, parties may disagree on the interpretation of the arbitration agreement. Frequently, the main issue relates to the interpretation of the scope of the agreement itself. In addition, the competence–competence doctrine allows the arbitral tribunal to notably rule on the existence and validity of the arbitration agreement.[55]

3.1 *Existence, Validity and Scope of the Arbitration Agreement*

At the interpretive stage – in addition to procedural issues or issues related to the applicable institutional rules or the arbitral seat, for example – issues often relate to the scope of the arbitration agreement. This requires considering what the parties consented to at the drafting stage.[56] Most international arbitration conventions do not expressly address how to interpret the scope of an arbitration agreement. Although the New York Convention acknowledges the necessity of interpreting such scope,[57] it does not expressly provide for any rule governing

---

[53] *Id.* at Article 1464.
[54] *Id.* at Article 1479.
[55] Born, *supra* note 1, at vol. I, §7.01, 1047.
[56] *Id.* at vol. I, §7.01, 1047.
[57] Articles II(1) and II(3) of the New York Convention.

the same. Similarly, the UNCITRAL Model Law does not specify any rule for construction of this interpretation.[58]

Arbitrators can rely on the applicable general principles of national contract law. Those canons of contract interpretation are often derived from several national legal systems. As an illustration, in ICC Award No 7929, the arbitrator asserted that 'an arbitral tribunal should construe the validity and scope of an arbitration clause in accordance with the general principles of the interpretation of contracts, i.e., seeking the real and common intent of parties, based on the wording of the clause, and the principle of confidence or good faith'.[59] National courts in both common law and civil law jurisdictions almost uniformly apply ordinary rules of contract interpretation, by notably looking at the parties' intent.[60] Arbitrators may also have recourse to the principle according to which "it is better for a thing to have effect than to be made void" (*ut res magis valeat quam pereat*). This is a pro-arbitration principle, which is widely applied.[61] This principle, which is initially a generally applicable rule of contract construction, has become a presumption in arbitration in many jurisdictions.

Certain states adopt a pro-arbitration presumption regarding international arbitration agreements. For instance, the Swiss Federal Tribunal held in a judgment of March 1990, that 'if it is established that an arbitration clause exists, there is no reason to interpret that clause restrictively' as it had to be 'assumed that the parties wished for an embracing jurisdiction of the arbitral tribunal, given that they have concluded an arbitration agreement'.[62] An arbitral tribunal adopted the same approach in a 2010 ICC award, by asserting that

> Pursuant to Swiss case law, when the existence of an arbitration clause is established, as it is the case here, there is no ground for a restrictive interpretation. Quite to the contrary, one must consider that the parties want that the arbitral tribunal be vested with a general jurisdiction, and, in case of doubt, that they did not intend to refer to arbitration only their dispute relating to the implementation of their respective obligations, but also the ones concerning the validity of the agreement that embodies such obligations.[63]

In addition, Swiss Law has adopted the principle of presumptive validity of international arbitration agreements (*in favorem validitatis* rule). Pursuant to Article 178 (2) PILA,[64] an arbitration agreement is valid if it complies either with the law chosen by the parties or with the law governing the subject matter of the dispute or with Swiss law. This illustrates the arbitration friendliness of the PILA.[65]

By contrast, some arbitral tribunals, as illustrated by two older ICC cases from 1998[66] and 1976,[67] also held that an arbitration clause needs to be interpreted 'strictly' and not 'expansively'. However, these decisions reflect a minority position, not the current trend. In the end, there is support in favour of an expansive interpretation of an arbitration agreement, because it serves the public interest, by avoiding costly and unproductive litigation.[68] It also encourages international

---

[58] Born, *supra* note 1, at vol. I, §9.02, 1318.
[59] Final Award in ICC No 7929, XXV YB Comm Arb 312, 317 (2000).
[60] Born, *supra* note 1, at vol. I, §9.02, 1322.
[61] *See, e.g.*, Partial Award in ICC No 7710 128 JDI 1147, 1151 (2001).
[62] Swiss Federal Tribunal, judgment of Mar. 15, 1990, Sonatrach v. KCA Drilling Ltd, Rev arb 921, 923, 3 (b), 923.
[63] Final Award in ICC No 14046, XXXV YB Comm Arb 241, 246 (2010).
[64] Swiss Private International Law Act 2018, Article 178 (2).
[65] ARBITRATION IN SWITZERLAND, A PRACTITIONER'S GUIDE 63 (Manuel Aroyo ed., 2013).
[66] Partial Award in ICC No 7920, XXIII YB Comm Arb 80, 81 (1998).
[67] Award in ICC No 2321, I YB Comm Arb 133, 133 (1976).
[68] JURISDICTIONAL PROBLEMS IN INTERNATIONAL COMMERCIAL ARBITRATION – A STUDY OF BELGIAN, DUTCH, ENGLISH, FRENCH, SWEDISH, SWISS, U.S. AND WEST GERMAN LAW 123–124 (Adam Samuel ed., 1989).

trade, by guaranteeing the efficiency of the arbitral process.[69] According to Gary Born, this pro-arbitration interpretation expands to both contractual and noncontractual claims (torts, breach of fiduciary duty, etc.).[70]

3.2 The Role of the Arbitrator

Having described the various interpretative methods, it is necessary to consider the role of arbitrators over court judges in determining the existence, validity and scope of an arbitration agreement.

3.2.1 Exclusivity of Arbitration Agreements

A preliminary issue arises as to whether an arbitration agreement is an exclusive remedy for the parties to settle their dispute, meaning whether it confers jurisdiction on arbitrators only or also on local courts. The New York Convention itself assumes that an arbitration agreement is exclusive,[71] and it is unlikely and, in fact, not advised to provide in an arbitration agreement that arbitration is a nonexclusive remedy. This is because such wording may cast doubts on whether the agreement constitutes a valid arbitration agreement, which is binding on the parties. If the parties preserved their right to bring their dispute before a judge, this would contradict the principle of having a final and binding arbitral award.[72] That is why, in case of doubt, it is generally presumed that arbitration agreements constitute exclusive remedies.

3.2.2 Competence–Competence

Once the parties have agreed to submit their dispute to arbitration by concluding an existing and valid arbitration agreement, arbitrators, rather than national courts, are empowered in the first instance to resolve disputes over the scope of the arbitration agreement.[73] The competence–competence doctrine is almost universally accepted and is given effect by leading international arbitration conventions. Articles V(1)(a) and V(1)(c) of the New York Convention contemplate that an arbitral tribunal would have addressed any objections to the existence, validity and scope of the arbitration agreement within its arbitral award.[74] Similarly, Article 16 of the UNCITRAL Model Law expressly grants arbitrators powers of competence–competence to consider challenges to their own jurisdiction, including those arising from the validity of arbitration agreements.[75]

Under French law, the competence–competence doctrine is set out in Article 1448 of the Code of Civil Procedure. Firstly, there is a positive aspect – namely, the authority designated for dealing with a dispute has the power to determine its own jurisdiction. Secondly and more importantly, there is also a negative aspect to the principle, pursuant to which an authority, which is not designated for dealing with a dispute, must let the designated authority decide on its own competence. In that sense, the article creates a prima facie test, following which, unless an

---

[69] Born, *supra* note 1, at vol. I, §9.02, 1344.
[70] *Id.* at vol. I, §9.02, 1357.
[71] Article II(3) of the New York Convention.
[72] Born, *supra* note 1, at vol. I, §8.03, 1275.
[73] *Id.* at vol. I, §7.01, 1047.
[74] Article V(1)(a) and V(1)(c) of the New York Convention.
[75] UNCITRAL Model Law, Article 16.

arbitration clause is obviously not applicable or manifestly void, the judge must decline its own competence and let the arbitral tribunal decide.[76] The main advantage of a prima facie test is that it ensures the efficiency of the arbitral proceedings. French courts have upheld this principle consistently. For example, in a recent decision from the Cour de cassation, the judges recalled that pursuant to the principle of competence–competence, the arbitral tribunal determines its own jurisdiction, unless the arbitration clause is manifestly null or void. Applying this principle, the Cour de cassation found that because the parties agreed to submit their dispute to arbitration in Hamburg pursuant to the German Maritime Arbitrators Association, the victims of the loss caused by the destruction of a dam were bound by the arbitration agreement concluded with their insurers.[77] Under Swiss law, the PILA also guarantees the application of the competence–competence doctrine,[78] which is also consistently upheld by the Swiss courts in express terms, in both domestic and international matters.[79] Switzerland also limits the role of the judge to a prima facie test as to whether an existing and valid arbitration agreement was concluded.

Some countries, on the contrary, do not adopt the negative effect of the competence–competence doctrine. For example, under Swedish law, a challenge to the existence, validity and scope of an arbitration agreement before the judge is permitted at any time, including prior to an arbitral tribunal's jurisdictional decision.[80] In the words of the Swedish Arbitration Act, 'the arbitrators may rule on their own jurisdiction to decide the dispute. The aforesaid shall not prevent a court from determining such a question at the request of a party .... Notwithstanding that the arbitrators have, in a decision during the proceedings, determined that they possess jurisdiction to resolve the dispute, such decision is not binding'.[81]

Similarly, under English law, notwithstanding the recognition of the arbitral tribunal's competence–competence, the Arbitration Act gives the right to a party, in the absence of any contrary agreement, to challenge the validity of an arbitration agreement before the judge without having to challenge it before the arbitral tribunal beforehand.[82] As an illustration, an English lower court decided, in a relatively recent case, that 'despite the doctrine of competence-competence ... , the English courts retains the jurisdiction to determine the issue as to whether there was ever an agreement to arbitrate ... The Act does not require a party who maintains that there is no arbitration agreement to have that question decided by an arbitral tribunal.'[83] However, when the judge is seized prior to the arbitral tribunal, he or she may still decide to defer the issue to the tribunal; this is notably the case when it seems quite certain that there is an arbitration agreement.[84] Conferring to the judge the power to interpret arbitration agreements may be seen as favouring an economy of means. Indeed, after the judge has rendered a final decision on the validity of an arbitration agreement, it may deter the parties to challenge the validity of the arbitration agreement in the future.[85]

---

[76] French Code of Civil Procedure, Article 1448.
[77] Cour de cassation, 1e ch, Dec. 19, 2018 No 17-28.951.
[78] Swiss Private International Law Act 2018, Article 186 (1).
[79] See, e.g., Swiss Federal Tribunal, judgment of Oct. 16, 2001, DFT 128 III 50, 59.
[80] Swedish Arbitration Act 2019.
[81] Id. at §2.
[82] English Arbitration Act 1996, §31.
[83] Excalibur Ventures LLC v. Texas Keystone Inc. [2011] EWHC 1624 (Comm); [2011] 2 Lloyd's Rep 289 §57.
[84] Born, supra note 1, at vol. I, §7.01.
[85] Id. at vol. I, §9.02, 1343.

3.2.3 *Examples*

There are many situations where the arbitration agreement is unclear in its wording and leads to difficulties of interpretation. In such situations, the agreement is considered as pathological.[86] For instance, the clause 'In the event of any unresolved dispute, the matter will be referred to the International Chamber of Commerce' was rejected, because it did not appear to make arbitration mandatory.[87] In contrast, an English court has upheld the clause stating, 'English law – arbitration, if any, London according to ICC Rules', finding that it did refer disputes to arbitration.[88] An arbitration agreement may also be considered pathological due to an ambiguity in the arbitral institution being designated.[89] This is for example the case with the following clauses: 'the official Chamber of Commerce in Paris, France', 'the Arbitration Commission of the Chamber of Commerce and Industry of Paris' and 'a Commission of arbitration of French Chamber of Commerce, Paris'.[90] Therefore, it is highly recommended to rely on model clauses, at least for institutional arbitration.

4 ENFORCEMENT OF AN ARBITRATION AGREEMENT

One of the parties may challenge the validity of an arbitration agreement before the arbitral tribunal or a state court, based for instance on the invalidity of the underlying contract, the non-arbitrability of the dispute or arguing that the clause binds nonconsenting parties.

4.1 *Separability*

One party to a dispute may claim before the arbitral tribunal or the judge that an arbitration clause is invalid because the matrix contract in which it is inserted is invalid. However, the principle of separability will prevent the upholding of such claim. This principle applies when an arbitration clause is inserted in a contract, prior to any dispute. As such, an arbitration agreement is treated as presumptively 'separate' or 'autonomous' from the commercial or other contract within which it is contained, otherwise known as the separability doctrine, or separability presumption.[91]

Most international instruments provide for the separability principle. As such, even if the New York Convention does not expressly impose or require the application of the doctrine, this implicitly stems from its definition of an arbitration agreement.[92] The UNCITRAL Model Law goes further, by explicitly stating that 'an arbitration clause which forms part of a contract shall be treated as an agreement independent of the other terms of the contract. A decision by the arbitral tribunal that the contract is null and void shall not entail ipso jure the invalidity of the arbitration clause'.[93]

---

[86] Frédéric Eisemann, *La Clause d'Arbitrage Pathologique*, in COMMERCIAL ARBITRATION ESSAYS IN MEMORIAM (Eugenio Minoli ed., 1974).
[87] LAW AND PRACTICE OF INTERNATIONAL COMMERCIAL ARBITRATION 166 (Alan Redfern, Martin Hunter, Nigel Blackaby, & Constantine Partasides eds., 4th ed. 2004).
[88] Arab-African Energy Corp Ltd v. Olieprodukten Nederland BV [1983] 2 Lloyd's Rep 419.
[89] Shaun Lee, *Pathological Arbitration Clauses*, SINGAPORE INTERNATIONAL ARBITRATION BLOG (Mar. 8, 2013), https://singaporeinternationalarbitration.com/2013/03/08/pathological-arbitration-clauses.
[90] Redfern et al., *supra* note 87.
[91] Born, *supra* note 1, at vol. I, §3.01, 350.
[92] New York Convention, Articles II and V(1)(a).
[93] UNCITRAL Model Law, Article 16(1).

The separability principle is of paramount practical and analytical importance regarding the enforcement of the arbitration agreement. Indeed, an arbitration agreement may remain valid, notwithstanding the possible invalidity, illegality or termination of the parties' underlying contract and vice versa.[94] Despite the fact that they are distinct principles which do not rely on one another,[95] the separability doctrine also supports the doctrine of competence–competence, in the sense that arbitrators determine their own jurisdiction when an arbitration agreement exists prima facie.[96] Under French law, the separability doctrine has been recognised since 1963 by the Cour de cassation for international arbitration agreements.[97] Article 1447 of the Code of Civil Procedure now provides that an arbitration agreement is independent from the underlying contract and that it is not impacted if such contract is found to be void.[98] However, according to Gary Born, one should be careful not to consider the 'separability' principle as a principle of 'autonomy' or 'independence'. French courts have in some cases asserted the autonomy of international arbitration agreements from national legal systems and rules of international law.[99] However, Gary Born argues that those two expressions can create misimpressions and suffer from imprecisions. Indeed, the arbitration clause is not wholly or necessarily autonomous or independent from the matrix contract, because it is still related to such contract and has an 'interrelated, supportive function' for that contract.[100] An ICC tribunal also questioned the complete autonomy of the arbitration agreement.[101] Thus, the term *separability* can be favoured, precisely because the arbitration agreement cannot be entirely separated from the underlying contract. Under Swiss law, the doctrine is widely recognised. The concept is that, procedurally, the arbitration agreement is 'an independent agreement of a special nature'.[102] Article 178 of the PILA codifies the doctrine: 'The arbitration agreement cannot be contested on the grounds that the main contract is not valid'.[103]

4.2 Arbitrability

A party to a dispute may challenge the validity of the arbitration agreement by claiming that it covers a non-arbitrable dispute. Arbitrability determines the categories of subjects or disputes, which are deemed by a particular national law to be incapable of resolution by arbitration, even if the parties have agreed otherwise in their arbitration agreement. In some jurisdictions, this is referred to as objective arbitrability or arbitrability *ratione materiae*.[104]

In addition to having a subject capable of settlement by arbitration, which is a requirement of the New York Convention,[105] an arbitration agreement cannot be enforced against certain individuals or moral entities. This prohibition is not based on those persons' legal incapacity but rather on the non-arbitrability of the dispute towards them; thus, this relates to subjective arbitrability or arbitrability *ratione personae*. As a result, if an arbitration agreement is enforced

---

[94] Born, *supra* note 1, at vol. I, §3.01, 351.
[95] Seraglini & Ortscheidt, *supra* note 2, at 90.
[96] Born, *supra* note 1, at vol. I, §3.01, 351.
[97] Cour de cassation, Civ 1e, judgment of May 7, 1963, Ets Raymond Gosset v. Carapelli, (1963) JCP G, II, 13 §405.
[98] French Code of Civil Procedure, Article 1447.
[99] Paris Court of Appeal, judgment of Apr. 20, 1988, Société Clark International Finance v. Société Sud Matériel Service, Rev arb 570, 572.
[100] Born, *supra* note 1, at vol. I, §3.01, 352.
[101] Final Award in ICC No 8938, XXIV YB Comm Arb 174, 175 (1999).
[102] Swiss Federal Tribunal, judgment of Oct. 7, 1933, Tobler v. Justizkomission des Kantons Schwyz, DFT 59 I 177, 179.
[103] Swiss Private International Law Act 2018, Article 178.
[104] Born, *supra* note 1, at vol. I, §6.01, 944.
[105] New York Convention, Article II(1).

against or in favour of an individual or an entity where the applicable law to the dispute expressly prohibits it, the arbitration agreement, when challenged, could be held null and void. An interesting example relates to consumers in arbitration – namely when there is a dispute between a consumer and a merchant or commercial party.[106] French law was initially reluctant to enforce an arbitration agreement concluded between a consumer and a merchant. However, pursuant to a 2016 Act,[107] Article 2061 of the French Code of Civil Procedure was reformed and now provides that when a consumer has accepted an arbitration agreement, then this agreement is valid.[108]

4.3 Nonsignatories

Another issue may arise as to whether an arbitration agreement can be extended to nonsignatories. In principle, pursuant to the principle of party consent to arbitrate, only parties who signed the agreement should be bound by it. As a result, binding nonsignatories is considered to be one of the most delicate issues in international commercial arbitration.[109] However, no international arbitration convention or national arbitration legislation provides any express guidance in identifying the parties to an international arbitration agreement. The New York Convention provides only that an arbitration agreement binds its parties, without providing a definition of what is a party to an arbitration agreement,[110] similarly to the UNCITRAL Model Law.[111] It is thus left to national courts and arbitral tribunals to decide on a case-by-case basis whether nonsignatories may be bound by the arbitration agreement.

One of the most commonly used theories is the group of companies' doctrine. Professor William Park explains that a common example is that of a claimant with a dispute under contract between itself and the subsidiary of a major international corporation. The contract contains an arbitration agreement, and so arbitration can be compelled against the subsidiary company; but the claimant would very much like to bring the parent company into the arbitration, so as to improve its chances of being paid, if it succeeds in its claim.[112]

There are two well-known ICC arbitral awards in which the 'group of companies' doctrine was relied upon to extend an arbitration agreement to nonsignatories. In *Dow Chemical Company v. Isover Saint Gobain*,[113] Dow Chemical was the parent company of a group in which one subsidiary concluded an arbitration agreement. Dow Chemical was thus a third party to an arbitration agreement. The tribunal ultimately considered that it was nevertheless bound by the agreement, because it had participated in the negotiation, performance and termination of the underlying contract and there was evidence of a mutual intent of Dow Chemical and its subsidiary to perform the contract. Another ICC tribunal also considered that an arbitration agreement was binding on a nonsignatory party belonging to a company group on the ground that it was to safeguard 'the security of international commercial relations'.[114] The aim of such extension was to ensure solidarity between all the companies of a group in the payment of one's debts.

---

[106] Born, *supra* note 1, at vol. I, §6.02, 1014.
[107] Law No 2016-1547 of Nov. 18, 2016, on the modernisation of twenty-first-century justice, Article 11.
[108] French Code of Civil Procedure, Article 2061.
[109] Born, *supra* note 1, at vol. I, §10.01.
[110] New York Convention, Article II.
[111] UNCITRAL Model Law 2006.
[112] WILLIAM W. PARK, NON-SIGNATORIES AND INTERNATIONAL CONTRACTS: AN ARBITRATOR'S DILEMMA §1.56 (2009).
[113] Award in ICC No 4131, Dow Chemical Company and Others v. ISOVER Saint Gobin (1982) YCA 1984, at 131 et seq.
[114] Award in ICC No 5103, (1998) Clunet, 1206 et seq.

A nonsignatory public entity can also be considered as a party to an arbitration agreement when it is involved in the performance of the underlying contract. A famous illustration of this theory is the *Dallah* case in which the government of Pakistan was sued in a situation where a contract had been concluded between two companies, Dallah Real Estate and Tourism Holding Co. The Paris Court of Appeal held that the Pakistani government intended to be bound by the clause and that not considering it as a true party to the arbitration agreement would result in a 'denial of Justice'.[115] By contrast, the English judge, a year earlier, had rejected the possibility to bind the Pakistani government to the arbitration agreement, because it considered that the principle of party consent to arbitrate had to be applied strictly and prevented an extension of an arbitration agreement to nonsignatories.[116]

These cases show that the possibility of extending an arbitration agreement to nonsignatories will depend on the applicable law. As for the group of companies' doctrine, there is no consensus on the criteria to be met to justify binding nonsignatories. In any event, it remains essential to make a case-by-case analysis, considering in detail the circumstances in which the agreement was concluded and performed.[117]

4.4 Judicial Review

An arbitration agreement must exist in order for the parties to validly refer a dispute to arbitration. If an arbitral award is rendered on the basis of an arguably invalid arbitration agreement, it may be refused recognition and/or enforcement. The New York Convention provides that 'recognition and enforcement of an award may be refused, at the request of the party against whom it is invoked, only if that party furnishes to the competent authority where the recognition and enforcement is sought, proof that: ... the said agreement is not valid under the law to which the parties have subjected it'.[118] Thus, the court before which recognition and enforcement of an award is sought has a role to play in determining whether, under the applicable law, the arbitration agreement underlying the award is valid.

Most domestic arbitration legislations at least indirectly provide that the nullity of an arbitration agreement constitutes a ground for refusing recognition and enforcement of an award. However, they are silent on the standards of judicial review to be applied by the judge. The legal standards of judicial review have been developed mostly through international case law. At the pre-award stage, it is possible to adopt one of the two types of legal standards of judicial review:[119] a full judicial review, where the court makes a final determination on the existence of an arbitration agreement, or a prima facie judicial review, where the court refers the matter to the arbitral tribunal for determination, after having made a rapid and succinct test concerning the existence of the arbitration agreement. As mentioned, French law adopts the second option – namely a prima facie test pursuant to which the judge has jurisdiction only when an arbitration agreement is 'manifestly null or manifestly inapplicable.'[120]

It is only at the post-award stage – namely after the arbitral tribunal has ruled on the challenge raised by a party in an arbitral award making such determination – that the parties can challenge

---

[115] Paris Court of Appeal, judgment of Feb. 17, 2011, Gouvernement du Pakistan – Ministère des Affaires Religieuses v. Dallah Real Estate and Tourism Holding Company (Case No 09/28533).
[116] Dallah Real Estate and Tourism Holding Co v. Government of Pakistan [2010] UKSC 46; [2011] 1 AC 763.
[117] Interim Award in ICC No 9517 (2000).
[118] New York Convention, Article V(1)(a).
[119] Born, *supra* note 1, at vol. I, §7.02.
[120] French Code of Civil Procedure, Article 1448.

the validity of the agreement before the judge, relying one of the grounds of Article 1520 of the Code of Civil Procedure. Among the grounds are the situations in which the arbitral tribunal wrongly upheld and declined jurisdiction, or where the arbitral tribunal has been irregularly constituted. These grounds may be raised to assert that an arbitration agreement is null and void. The judge analyses the case de novo, by seeking, on legal and factual grounds all the elements concerning any alleged defects in the arbitration agreement raised by one party.[121] By contrast, Article 7 of the Swiss PILA provides that 'if the parties have concluded an arbitration agreement covering an arbitrable dispute, a Swiss court seized shall decline jurisdiction unless ... the courts find that the arbitral agreement is null and void, inoperative or incapable of being performed'.[122]

According to Gary Born, contrary to French law, the language adopted by the PILA could appear to grant parties access to interlocutory judicial determinations of jurisdictional objections at a pre-award stage.[123] Thus, the literal interpretation of this provision seems to provide that contrary to French law, it is not necessary to challenge the validity of the agreement before the arbitral tribunal prior to doing it before the judge. However, Swiss courts have been more inclined to limit the judicial role prior to the arbitral tribunal's award. Rather, they tend to ascertain the prima facie existence and validity of the arbitration agreement where the arbitration seat was in Switzerland (but not where the seat was abroad).[124] This approach parallels the one of the French courts.[125]

5 CONCLUSION

Parties wishing to submit their existing or future disputes to arbitration, rather than to court litigation, must clearly express such consent through careful drafting, also anticipating the different issues that may arise when arbitral tribunals or courts are called upon to interpret or enforce the arbitration agreement. At the drafting stage, it is highly advised to rely on the rules provided by the New York Convention and in particular the requirement to have an arbitration agreement in writing. In addition, there are many elements to be inserted in the clause as a matter of best practice. For instance, it is important to determine the seat of arbitration, because it has multiple consequences on the conduct of arbitration, including as to which State courts will have supervisory jurisdiction.

Among the recommended elements to include in the arbitration agreement, are practical matters such as the number of arbitrators, an institutional or ad hoc arbitration, the choice of law or the language of the proceedings. If a dispute arises between parties regarding, for example, the existence, validity or scope of the arbitration agreement, arbitrators will interpret the clause and may rely on different principles and presumptions, in the exercise of their powers under the competence–competence doctrine, it being clear that state courts usually retain the final say in this respect.

---

[121] Cour de cassation, Civ 1e, judgment of Jan. 6, 1987, Southern Pacific Properties Ltd v. République Arabe d'Egypte, 26 Int'l Legal Mat 1004, 1006.
[122] Swiss Private International Law Act 2018, Article 7.
[123] Born, *supra* note 1, at vol. I, §7.03, 1118.
[124] *See, e.g.*, Swiss Federal Tribunal, judgment of Aug. 6, 2012, DFT 4A_119/2012.
[125] Born, *supra* note 1, at vol. I, §7.03, 1118.

PART IV

Judicial Control of Arbitral Awards

Country Reports

10

Judicial Control of Arbitral Awards in Argentina

Maria Beatriz Burghetto

1 INTRODUCTION

In the past four years, Argentina embarked on a significant modernisation of its arbitration law, including the aspect of judicial control over arbitration. This is important to practising lawyers, courts and scholars, given that the legislative reform has provided better defined parameters to assess courts' intervention in arbitration. Indeed, court's intervention may manifest itself as a valid implementation of court's powers of control over arbitration or, in its negative aspect, as definite undue interference with arbitration. The latter would now be undoubtedly in violation of the current applicable law on arbitration, which presently sets forth the principle of minimal court intervention in support of arbitration or to control that due process is respected and there is no violation of public policy.

This chapter therefore analyses the impact that the recent legislative reforms have or may have on the practice of arbitration in Argentina and whether such reforms are sufficient or, at the very least, effective in order to neutralise some negative aspects of courts' treatment of arbitration in Argentina, when exercising their essential but limited role of control over arbitration. This chapter provides general background on Argentinean arbitration law and its recent reforms, especially the adoption in 2018 of an arbitration law modelled after the UNCITRAL Model Law on International Commercial Arbitration (1985) (UNCITRAL Model Law),[1] for international arbitration. This chapter then looks at Argentinean court decisions rendered in the recent past, in connection with several stages or aspects of judicial control over arbitration, as a historic foundation for the problems over which the current arbitration law may have an impact.

The instances of judicial control over arbitration upon which we focus can be broadly categorised in two parts. First are those related to the interpretation of arbitration agreements and the conduct of arbitration (Section 4); courts deal with the interpretation of arbitration agreements either before the arbitral proceedings have started or once the final award has been rendered. Once the arbitral tribunal is in place and the arbitral proceedings are in progress, courts may need to deal with issues related to arbitrator disqualification, although this is generally dealt with by arbitral institutions or by the arbitrators themselves, depending on the applicable arbitration rules. Some Argentinean case law also provides examples of undue interference in the form of anti-arbitration injunctions. Second are those related to the control

---

[1] Law No. 27, 449 adopted by the Argentinean Federal Congress on July 4, 2018, and promulgated on July 25, 2018.

of the validity of arbitral awards (Section 5), when faced either with applications for setting aside awards rendered in Argentina or for enforcement of foreign arbitral awards.

For each of these instances, this chapter explores how the current Argentinean law on (international) arbitration may shape the scope of courts' control over arbitration in the future. In doing so, I refer briefly to the practice of international arbitration in Chile, by way of comparison. Chile modernised its arbitration law in 2004 in a similar way to Argentina. Chile adopted the UNCITRAL Model Law, implemented measures, including the training of the judiciary and displayed a concerted governmental effort,[2] hoping to become an attractive international arbitration venue. These analyses and comparisons highlight how Argentina could develop a more autonomous arbitration process with the courts' support.

2 BACKGROUND ON ARGENTINEAN ARBITRATION LAW

2.1 Evolution of Argentinean Law of Arbitration

Argentina has traditionally integrated arbitration rules in the various codes of civil and commercial procedure applicable in its territory, notably at the federal level and in the codes of civil and commercial procedures of the major provinces,[3] which have copied the Federal Code of Civil and Commercial Procedure. Although initially Argentina had a favourable attitude towards arbitration, as reflected in a previous version of the Federal Code of Civil and Commercial Procedure and courts' practice,[4] this gave way to distrust from the beginning of the twentieth century. The legislation enacted at that time and that which followed, until 2015, designated arbitration as a special version of the judicial procedure and not as a stand-alone means of dispute resolution and, therefore, became outdated with time.[5]

Until now, the rules applicable to arbitration in Argentinean law were found (1) in the Federal Code of Civil and Commercial Procedure (CPCCN, in its acronym in Spanish) as well as in the codes of procedure of some provinces[6] and (2) as from August 2015, in the Civil and Commercial Code (CC Code), which modernised Argentina's arbitration law. A more recent reform, in July 2018, saw Argentina's adoption of the UNCITRAL Model Law, with amendments as adopted in 2006 and with further additions, in the form of a federal law applicable to international arbitration only.

---

[2] See Section 6.
[3] Being a federal republic, Argentina has legislatures at the federal and state or provincial levels that have power to legislate in different areas. More specifically, pursuant to the Argentinean federal constitution, modelled after the US Constitution, the provinces have the power to establish their own codes of procedure. This allows for the possibility of having contradictory treatment of arbitration at different levels (i.e., federal and state levels, or even between two provinces). Because of this possibility of inconsistency, there have been proposals for a federal statute on arbitration. Contrary to the United States, however, only the federal congress has the power to enact the substantive codes (civil code, penal code) and related laws, which means that only one civil code applies in all the Argentinean territory. The civil code was unified with the Code of Commerce in 2015.
[4] See Horacio A. Grigera Naón, *Arbitration and Latin America: Progress and Setbacks*, 21 ARBITRATION INTERNATIONAL, 127–176, 141–143 (2005).
[5] It requires the parties, for example, to execute a submission agreement as a condition to a valid arbitration, even in the presence of an arbitration clause.
[6] The major provinces have copied the CPCCN, while some of the others have included no arbitration rules in their codes of civil procedure. Indeed, pursuant to the Argentine federal constitution, modelled after the US Constitution, each of the twenty-three provinces in Argentina has the power to enact its own codes of procedure. This allows for the possibility of having contradictory treatment of arbitration at different levels (i.e., federal and state levels, or even between two provinces). Because of this possibility of inconsistency, there have been proposals for a federal statute on arbitration.

Despite the archaic arbitration rules in force for most of the twentieth century, Argentinean courts, especially those with jurisdiction over commercial matters, had realised that such rules were not suitable for international arbitration.[7] Accordingly, they had recognised the essential pillars of arbitration, such as separability of the arbitration agreement, which is valid and consistent with the spirit of Argentinean law. In addition, parties' choice of modern institutional arbitration rules allowed them to bypass the inauspicious national arbitration rules, in practice.[8]

2.2 *Judicial and Governmental Attitudes towards Arbitration*

Nevertheless, certain judgments at all levels still show the Argentinean judiciary's lack of familiarity with (international) arbitration or some form of mistrust, especially in matters where the Argentinean State is involved.[9] Argentinean judges have expressed certain negative preconceptions about arbitration, such as that it is (1) a 'privatisation' of justice, (2) a means of oppression by large companies over companies in emerging countries, (3) a way to circumvent the application of mandatory state legislation (or public policy), and (4) a means of dispute resolution where the decision makers (arbitrators) are not independent of the parties.[10] Another element contributing to this state of affairs is the backlash suffered by arbitration in Argentina as a result of the record number of investment arbitration proceedings brought against the country, pursuant to governmental measures taken during the 2001–2002 economic crisis. All these factors have contributed to the perpetuation of outdated arbitration rules, despite the proposals for reform made by arbitration specialists.[11]

Another factor that should be taken into account is the Argentinean judiciary's relative lack of independence of the executive power. Although judicial independence is a pillar of the democracy in the Argentina's federal constitution, it is in practice seriously compromised by the 'politicisation' of the relationship between the judiciary and the administration.[12] Judges, including those of the Supreme Court, have suffered political pressure in recent times. This fact, combined with the paralysis of the Council of the Judiciary (the 'Council') has led to significant delays in filling judicial vacancies. In many cases, acting judges have filled those vacancies. This has led to the manipulation of appointments. This holds true especially since 2006, when the number of politicians sitting on the Council increased, resulting in an overrepresentation of the contemporaneous political majority. The Council has also neglected its

---

[7] See Welbers, S.A., Enrique C. v. Extrarktionstechnik Gesellschaft Fur Anlagenbav M.B.M. (Federal Court of Appeal on commercial matters, Branch E, Sept. 26, 1988, La Ley, 189-E, 302), where the court rejected a defence of lack of jurisdiction based on the CPCCN, on the grounds that the specific section mentioned therein referred to domestic arbitrations and was not applicable to international commercial arbitrations.

[8] The requirement of the execution of a submission agreement has nevertheless caused delays and contributed to the general unfavourable views on the efficiency of arbitration proceedings in Argentina (*see* Roque Caivano, *Argentina Needs to Improve Its Arbitration Law* [in Spanish], LA LEY, Mar. 18, 1994, at 141).

[9] See the cases cited in Section 4, for example, where some Argentinean courts issued anti-arbitration injunctions.

[10] See Julio César Rivera, *Arbitration and Judicial Power, Judges Prejudices Regarding Arbitration*, 5 INTERNATIONAL REVIEW ON ARBITRATION 193 (2006).

[11] In 2003, the Argentina federal Ministry of Justice introduced a rather innovative arbitration bill modelled after the UNCITRAL Model Law in its third attempt at reforming Argentinean arbitration law. A working group formed by prestigious specialists in arbitration and private international law prepared said bill, which was approved with some changes by both chambers of the Federal Congress. It was expected to be enacted as law after the last changes were approved by the Senate. However, this never took place. It was probably due to the prevailing arbitration hostile mood at the time.

[12] *See*, Association for Civil Rights and Citizen Power (Poder Ciudadano – the Argentinean chapter of Transparency International), *Current Status of Judiciary Independence in Argentina*, Nov. 2015, 42, http://poderciudadano.org/wp-content/uploads/2013/06/indep-5.pdf.

disciplinary functions, all of which has caused grave deficiencies in the performance of judges' duties.[13] This situation may explain certain judges' tendencies to embrace the administration's negative attitude towards arbitration in general, in particular where the State is directly or indirectly concerned.

2.3 Arbitration-Related International Treaties Ratified by Argentina

Despite its changing attitude towards arbitration, Argentina has ratified numerous international treaties on arbitration and arbitration-related matters, such as (1) the 1958 Convention on the Recognition and Enforcement of Foreign Arbitral Awards ('New York Convention') in 1988; (2) the 1975 Panama Inter-American Convention on International Commercial Arbitration in 1989; (3) the 1979 Inter-American Convention on Extraterritorial Validity of Foreign Judgments and Arbitral Awards in 1983; (4) the 1889 and 1940 Montevideo Treaties; (5) the Protocol on Jurisdictional Cooperation and Assistance in Civil, Commercial, Labour and Administrative Matters within the Mercosur; and (6) the 1965 Washington Convention on the Settlement of Investment Disputes between States and Nationals of Other States in 1994, as well as some bilateral treaties on judicial cooperation (with France, for example), fifty-six bilateral investment protection treaties (BITs) and eighteen other treaties with investment provisions (TIPs).

2.4 Recent Reforms to Argentinean Arbitration Law

As noted, Argentinean arbitration law has gone through two recent reforms: the first one, in 2015, introduced the 'arbitration contract' in the new (unified) CC Code, which is substantive law applicable in the whole country and the more recent one, in 2018, when the adoption of a law modelled after the UNCITRAL Model Law took place, whereby the law applicable to international arbitration was harmonised in the whole territory of the country. As a result of the latter reform, the rules on the arbitration contract of the CC Code have been deemed to apply to domestic arbitration only.

While these reforms have significantly updated Argentinean arbitration law, it is worth exploring not only the impact of these changes on the Argentinean arbitration regime but also whether the adoption of more modern arbitration legislation will suffice in itself or will be the main factor when establishing at least the basis for Argentina to become an attractive, reliable, jurisdiction for arbitration. Or, alternatively, whether other measures or developments are still necessary to achieve such goal. This chapter focuses principally on *international* commercial arbitration, although we make some observations on the impact of the 2015 legislative reform on domestic arbitration as well.

3 IMPACT OF RECENT REFORMS

3.1 *2015 Reform: Modernisation of the Rules of Arbitration*

In August 2015, Argentina's nineteenth-century Civil Code of 1871 and Code of Commerce of 1862 were unified and replaced with the CC Code, which regulates several specific contracts that had not been included in the original codes. One of those contracts is the 'arbitration contract', to which the CC Code devotes seventeen articles in its chapter 29 (1649–1665).

---

[13] Id. at §3.2, 17–22.

A positive aspect of the reform is that it expressly integrates the concepts of separability of the arbitration clause (Article 1653), kompetenz–kompetenz (Article 1654)[14] and the interpretative rule of *favor arbitri* (Article 1656, para. 2). Concerning the validity requirements of the arbitration agreement, it prohibits arbitration agreements granting one of the parties a privileged position with respect to the constitution of the arbitral tribunal (Article 1661).[15]

As far as arbitrability is concerned, it expressly dispels doubts about the arbitrability of corporate disputes (Article 1650).[16] However, as a result of changes made to the bill by the executive power before it was submitted to Congress, Article 1651 limits objective arbitrability, excluding for example family law disputes or those arising out of adhesion contracts. Also, when defining *arbitration contract*, Article 1649 includes the requirement that the dispute that is submitted to arbitration must arise out of a legal relationship regulated by private law in which public policy is not directly implicated. However, public policy permeates areas of the law that are deemed to be of a 'private' – in contrast with 'administrative' or 'public' – character, such as the law of contracts. Thus, this provision may in theory lead to the exclusion of contractual matters from arbitration, to the extent public policy is concerned. It therefore reflects poor legislative technique.

Concerning the grounds for setting aside arbitral awards, Article 1656, para. 3, allows parties to challenge arbitral awards before the courts of the seat, if it is in Argentina, arguing that it is 'contrary to the [Argentinean] legal system', which implies the revision of the merits by the state courts.[17] A reform bill submitted by the executive branch in March 2017[18] intends to correct the negative points referred to here, among others. In any event, pursuant to the 2018 reform of Argentinean international commercial arbitration law, which applies exclusively to international arbitration, these rules apply at present to domestic arbitration, together with those contained in the CPCCN and the codes of procedure at the provincial level, although the rule on arbitrability has a bearing in international arbitrations where the place of arbitration is in Argentina.

3.2 2018 Reform: New Federal Law on International Arbitration

3.2.1 General Aspects

The new Argentinean Federal Law on International Arbitration (the 'ALIA'), applicable throughout the country, is practically identical to the UNCITRAL Model Law, with some additions. It establishes a dualist treatment of arbitration in Argentina, given that it regulates

---

[14] These two concepts had been recognised by case law, although they were not explicit in the CPCCN.

[15] Another positive feature is that it describes arbitrators' duties in a clear and precise manner (Article 1662), including their duty to reveal 'any circumstance that exists prior to the acceptance of the designation or that arises afterwards that is capable of affecting their independence and impartiality' (para. a) and to 'guarantee party's equal treatment and due process, as well as giving each of them sufficient opportunity to assert their rights' (last paragraph).

[16] These disputes were deemed arbitrable under the previous legislation, although they were rarely submitted to arbitration.

[17] Fortunately, Argentinean courts have interpreted this provision of the CC Code only as a reference to the application for setting aside that is available to parties in the CPCCN and other codes of procedure, as opposed to some kind of new 'appeal'; see Leandro Caputo, *Apuntes sobre la reciente Ley de Arbitraje Comercial Internacional* (Notes on the new Law on International Commercial Arbitration), La Ley, vol. 2018-E, 1–4, citing judgments issued by the Buenos Aires Court of Appeal on commercial matters, in Olam Argentina SA v. Cubero, Alberto Martín et al on appeal by complaint, Branch E, Dec. 22, 2015; Díaz, Rubén Héctor v. Techint CIA. Técnica Internacional SACEI on appeal by complaint, Apr. 12, 2016 (Branch B) and Amarilla Automotores SA v. BMW Argentina SA on appeal by complaint, Apr. 12, 2016 (Branch D).

[18] See Francisco Amallo, *Las reformas al régimen jurídico del arbitraje: La nueva ley y los proyectos de ley* (The Reforms to the Legal Regime of Arbitration: The New Law and the Bills), 78 Revista del Colegio de Abogados de la Ciudad de Buenos Aires 44, 44 (2018).

only international arbitration, excluding all other national legislation, but without prejudice to the application of international treaties ratified by Argentina on the subject (Article 1, ALIA). Concerning the scope of its application, it adheres to an objective notion of *international arbitration*[19] and a broad characterisation of a *commercial relationship*.[20]

Other modern provisions as to the form of the arbitration agreements included in the ALIA expressly require it should be in writing and that written arbitration agreements may take different formats (arbitration clause, submission agreement, agreement by reference, etc.) and can be transmitted electronically (Articles 14-18, ALIA).[21] Interim measures and preliminary orders are extensively regulated, by adhering to the regime inserted in 2006 in the UNCITRAL Model Law (Title V, Articles 38–61, ALIA). Finally, as to the applicable law to the merits of the dispute, the ALIA expressly allows arbitrators, in the absence of an agreement by the parties, to apply the rules of law they consider appropriate to the merits of the dispute (Article 80, ALIA), thus adopting the approach of the ICC Arbitration Rules (Article 21(1)).[22]

3.2.2 ALIA and Judicial Control of Arbitration

Article 24, para. 2 of the ALIA, prohibits all arbitration agreements from granting one of the parties any advantage concerning the selection of arbitrators. Regarding the challenge of arbitral awards, the ALIA, following the UNCITRAL Model Law in this aspect, grants Argentinean courts the power, 'where appropriate and at the request of a party, to stay setting aside proceedings for a period of time determined by it in order to give the arbitral tribunal an opportunity to resume the arbitral proceedings or to take such other action that, in the arbitral tribunal's opinion, will eliminate the grounds for setting aside'.[23]

---

[19] Under Article 3 of the ALIA, an arbitration is international when the parties' places of business are in different countries at the time of conclusion of the contract or when either the place of arbitration, the place of performance of a substantial part of the commercial relationship or the place with the closest connection to the subject matter of the dispute are situated outside the country where the parties have their places of business. In other words, parties are not allowed to categorise their arbitration as international merely by mutual agreement, in the absence of these objective factors.

[20] The ALIA integrates the UNCITRAL Model Law's guidelines on interpretation of this term, i.e., the relationship may be contractual or noncontractual (see note 2 to Article 1 of the UNCITRAL Model Law, which also contains a nonexhaustive list of transactions to be deemed commercial). It further adds that the legal relationship in question must be ruled mainly by 'private' law, as per the Argentinean legal system, as opposed to other types of law, for example, administrative law (Article 6 of the ALIA).

[21] Although the ALIA does not accept an oral arbitration agreement, it does recognise that an arbitration agreement may be considered to be 'in writing' 'if its content is recorded in any form', which implicitly accepts agreements that may originally be oral, for example, where the voices are recorded; see Roque J. Caivano & Verónica Sandler Obregón, *La nueva Ley argentina de arbitraje comercial internacional* (The new law on international commercial arbitration), 11 ARBITRAJE 575–600, 582 (2018).

[22] In contrast, the UNCITRAL Model Law prefers a conflict of laws approach, by referring the arbitral tribunal to 'the law determined by the conflict of laws rules which it considers applicable' (Article 28.2).

[23] Article 101 of the ALIA. The ALIA expressly provides for this possibility by allowing arbitrators to continue in their functions in the event that a party's request to have the annulment proceedings suspended is admitted and the arbitrators are granted the opportunity to remedy what may cause the setting aside of the award (Article 92, ALIA). Parties may also ask arbitrators to correct calculation, typographical or other mistakes in the award (or arbitrators may do it on their own initiative), to interpret the award or to render a supplementary award to deal with claims not included in the award (Articles 93 to 97 of the ALIA). Parties must be mindful of this feature in order to make the necessary arrangements – for example, in the Terms of Reference, if any are drawn, or in the procedural timetable – in cases where the place of arbitration is located in Argentina, so that their intent to apply this provision to their arbitration prevails over any contrary or incompatible rule of the arbitral institution that administers the arbitration (for example, the rule whereby, once the final award is rendered and the time limit for the parties to request correction or interpretation of the award expires, the arbitral tribunal becomes *functus officio*). The current version of the ICC Arbitration Rules provides in Article 36(4) for the arbitrators' power to continue acting as such in the event the court remits the award to them.

3.2.3 Principles of Courts' Minimal Intervention under ALIA

Under Article 12 of the ALIA, which reproduces the wording of Article 5 of the UNCITRAL Model Law, Argentinean courts' intervention is restricted to

1. Referring the parties to arbitration, where appropriate (Article 19, ALIA).
2. Issuing interim measures, either before the commencement of the arbitral proceedings or during those proceedings (Article 21, ALIA).
3. Appointing arbitrators, deciding on a challenge against them or removing them, where appropriate (Articles 24, 25, 26, 31 and 32, ALIA).
4. Deciding on whether the arbitrators have jurisdiction, after they have ruled in favour of their own jurisdiction as a preliminary matter (Article 37, second paragraph, ALIA).
5. Assisting the arbitrators in the enforcement of interim measures (Articles 56 to 61, ALIA).
6. Assisting the arbitrators or a party, with the arbitrator's approval, in taking evidence (Article 78, ALIA).
7. Dealing with an application for setting aside an award (Articles 99 and 100, ALIA).
8. Dealing with a request for enforcement of a foreign arbitral award (Articles 102, 103 and 104, ALIA).

By restricting courts' intervention, Article 12 of the ALIA should act as deterrent to Argentinean courts' undue interference in arbitral proceedings. Thus, no Argentinean court could validly order the stay of arbitral proceedings while the court establishes the contents of the terms of reference, as some courts have done in the past,[24] given that such kind of interference is not included among the instances where court intervention is allowed under the ALIA. Conversely, if an Argentinean court has to deal with a challenge against an arbitrator or has to decide whether the arbitrators have jurisdiction, it would a priori seem convenient in general to stay the arbitral proceedings, pending the court's decision. Such a measure would need to be taken by the arbitral tribunal, however, since the court itself has no power to order the stay of the arbitral proceedings in such cases, under the ALIA. In contrast to Argentinean courts, Chilean courts appear to restrain themselves from interfering with arbitration with less reluctance than Argentinean courts.[25] Finally, the ALIA has added two grounds for the challenge of arbitrators, which will be discussed in the following sections.

4 JUDICIAL CONTROL OF ARBITRATION AGREEMENT AND ARBITRAL PROCEEDINGS

This section explores how Argentinean courts approach the crucial task of interpretation of the terms and scope of the arbitration agreement and the impact the ALIA will have on this, the two additional grounds for the challenge of arbitrators added by the ALIA and the risk of their misuse by courts and some instances of undue interference in arbitral proceedings by Argentinean courts.

---

[24] See Section 4.3 (anti-arbitration injunctions).
[25] See the commentary to EGI-VSR v. Río Bonito, a judgment by the Santiago Court of Appeals rendered in Sept. 2013, Francisco González & Andrés German, *Minimal Intervention and Public Policy*, INTERNATIONAL LAW OFFICE (June 4, 2015), https://www.internationallawoffice.com/Newsletters/Arbitration-ADR/Chile/Barros-Letelier-Gonzlez/Minimal-intervention-and-public-policy.

4.1 Interpretation of Arbitration Agreements

In some cases, arbitrators are required to interpret the terms of a given arbitration agreement in order to establish its scope and, as a result, the scope of their own jurisdiction. An arbitrator's interpretation may be called into question before Argentinean courts where one party challenges an arbitral award on the basis of the arbitrator's lack of jurisdiction or even before the arbitration has been brought. Argentinean courts may therefore exercise their control function in either or both those instances, under Articles 19 and 37 of the ALIA, to a certain extent and under certain conditions established therein. The previous Argentinean arbitration law already included grounds for challenge that may be related to the interpretation of the arbitration agreement, i.e., the case where 'the arbitrators have dealt with issues that have not been submitted to arbitration'.[26] At present, Article 99(a) III of the ALIA provides that an arbitral award that 'deals with a dispute not contemplated by or not falling within the terms of the submission to arbitration or contains decisions on matters beyond the scope of the submission to arbitration'[27] may be challenged before the Argentinean courts.

The kompetenz–kompetenz principle should lead Argentinean courts to give precedence to arbitrators in the interpretation of the scope of the arbitration agreement. Argentinean courts may exercise their interpretative function before arbitrators in exceptional circumstances, if the court finds that the agreement is 'null and void, inoperative or incapable of being performed'.[28] Such finding must be the result of a cursory scrutiny of the terms of the arbitration agreement leading to a preliminary finding on the validity of the arbitration agreement.[29]

Traditionally, Argentinean courts have favoured a restrictive interpretation of arbitration agreements. They funded such approach on the parties' waiver of their constitutional right to submit their disputes to Argentinean courts[30] Argentinean courts have recently taken upon themselves to determine the scope of the arbitration agreement even before the arbitrators were able to make a determination on the same. In *Rivadeneira*,[31] the Buenos Aires Court of Appeals on commercial matters held that it had jurisdiction to hear the parties' contractual dispute, despite the presence of an arbitration clause in the contract. The court further held that the unusual economic cataclysm, which had occurred after the conclusion of the contract,[32] did not

---

[26] Article 760, para. 2, CPCCN.
[27] This also constitutes grounds for refusing recognition or enforcement of a foreign arbitral award, under Article 104(a) III of the ALIA.
[28] Article II (3), New York Convention; Article 19 of the ALIA (copied from Article 8(1) of the UNCITRAL Model Law).
[29] See Jeffrey Waincymer, *How Should a Court Asked to Apply Article 8 of the Model Law Approach Its Task: Challenges for the Arbitral/Court Interface (I)*, KLUWER ARBITRATION BLOG (June 1, 2018), http://arbitrationblog.kluwerarbitration.com/2018/06/01/court-asked-apply-article-8-model-law-approach-task-challenges-arbitralcourt-interface/. Waincymer submits that courts should 'take a deferential approach and simply determine whether the arbitration agreement may reasonably be valid in cases where court proceedings are opposed on the basis of a submitted arbitration agreement'. Courts should 'seek at most a reasonable indication of a valid arbitration agreement'. This is because these kinds of jurisdictional objections are normally made by preliminary applications; therefore, courts should not seek to make a definitive ruling on the validity of the arbitration agreement without a full body of evidence and also at the risk of duplicating the arbitral proceedings, within which arbitrators have the power to decide on their own jurisdiction with priority over national courts (Article 37, para. 2, ALIA).
[30] See Julio C. Rivera *Interpretación restrictiva de la cláusula arbitral en la jurisprudencia argentina* (Restrictive Interpretation of the Arbitration Clause in Argentinean Case Law), 1 REVISTA DE LOS CONTRATOS, LOS CONSUMIDORES Y DERECHO DE LA COMPETENCIA 3 (2010).
[31] Rivadeneira, Hugo Germán v. ABN AMRO Bank N.A. et al. on ordinary proceedings, Buenos Aires Court of Appeal on commercial matters, Branch D, Feb. 28, 2008, published on www.eldial.com AA46F6 on Apr. 30, 2008.
[32] This was in reference to the 2001–2002 economic and financial crisis that led to Argentina's enacting emergency legislation and defaulting on its sovereign debt.

allow the court 'to consider that it was the will of the contracting parties to leave to the judgment of arbitrators ... the interpretation of the laws and other emergency economic rules and the fixing of the damages that they claim to have suffered'.[33] The court stressed that arbitration clauses must be construed in a restrictive manner, which is commonplace in Argentinean case law.[34] However, it added that this leads to the conclusion that arbitral jurisdiction must be admitted for those issues 'in which the discussion is about interpretation of contract clauses or verification of matters of fact certain and determined, excluding those other hypotheses in which it deals with questions of rights or of application of the law, whose knowledge is reserved exclusively to judges'.[35]

Rivadeneira contradicted other precedents of another branch of the same Court of Appeal and of the Argentinean Supreme Court, as the Buenos Aires Court of Appeal expressly acknowledged in its judgment.[36] The justification, in the eyes of that court, seems to be the extraordinary character of the circumstances giving rise to the dispute. However, this does not seem appropriate or even accurate, especially in a country that has suffered multiple economic crises in the past two centuries.[37]

---

[33] See Id.
[34] See Julio C. Rivera, Comentarios a la jurisprudencia argentina en materia de arbitraje comercial (Commentary on Argentinean Case Law on Commercial Arbitration), in 3 ARBITRAJE: REVISTA DE ARBITRAJE COMERCIAL Y DE INVERSIONES 899–932, 901 (Evelio Verdera y Tuells & José Carlos Fernández Rozas eds., 2010).
[35] Rivadeneira, supra note 31. Another federal court located in the province of Buenos Aires had previously issued a similar decision in Peyras, Hernán Matías v. Nordelta Constructora S.A., Court of Appeal of San Isidro on civil and commercial matters, Branch II, Dec. 23, 2004, holding, also with respect to the 2001–2002 emergency legislation, that the parties could not have envisaged this crisis at the time of conclusion of the arbitration agreement and that they could not have left to the arbitrators to decide on whether the emergency legislation was constitutional or unconstitutional. This is even though, in Argentina, any judge at any level is competent to declare a piece of legislation unconstitutional (as opposed to a specific court, as is the case in other countries, such as France), which would rather lead to the conclusion that arbitrators also have such power.
[36] Rivadeneira, supra note 31: 'This [Court of Appeal] Chamber does not ignore the argument contained in the memorial nor does it fail to observe that in similar cases there were judicial rulings that supported the solution advanced by the appellants' (citing Porcelli, Daniel v. ABN Asset Management Arg. SG on ordinary proceedings, Court of Appeal on commercial matters, Branch B, Dec. 16, 2005 judgement in full: elDial – AA3273); Llanos, Miguel v. Santander Investment Soc. Gerente on ordinary proceedings, Court of Appeal on commercial matters, Branch C, 23 Aug. 2006 and Basf Argentina S.A. v. Capdevielle Key y Cía. S.A. on jurisdiction, Supreme Court, May 11, 2004. See also a later judgment of the same branch of the same court of appeal, which held:

> Arbitration clauses that imply a waiver of the general principle of submission of disputes to ordinary judges must be interpreted restrictively (Court of Appeal on commercial matters, Branch D, 3 March 2008, Lorusso, Elba Susana and another v. Gioffre, Angel Antonio et al, on ordinary proceedings; Court of Appeal on commercial matters, Branch A, 14 February 2006, Constructora Iberoamericana S.A. v. Sociedad de Inversiones Inmobiliarias S.A., on ordinary proceedings; among others), limiting their admissibility to those cases in which the discussion is about the interpretation of contractual clauses or the verification of certain and determined factual issues, excluding those other cases which deal with legal issues or the application of the law, which pertains exclusively to judges' jurisdiction. (citing Rivadeneira and Cooperativa Agropecuaria de la Violeta v. Nidera S.A., on ordinary proceedings, Court of Appeal on commercial matters, Branch C, Oct. 25, 1996).

Captec SRL v. Constructora San José Argentina S.A., on ordinary proceedings, Court of Appeal on commercial matters, Branch D, Oct. 3, 2012.
[37] See Congressional Research Service, Argentina's Economic Crisis, https://fas.org/sgp/crs/row/IF10991.pdf. According to this paper, 'Argentina has a long history of economic crises. It has defaulted on its external debt (debt held by foreigners) eight times since independence in 1816. Argentina has also entered into 21 IMF programs since joining the international organization in 1956.' This would render such events somewhat predictable to a certain extent, especially by relatively experienced businessmen.

Another example of this inappropriate exercise of the courts' interpretative power can be found in *Supermarkets Norte v. Carrefour et al.*[38] In that case, the Buenos Aires Court of Appeal on commercial matters decided that the claimant's multiple claims had to be heard by Argentinean courts, despite the fact that the parties had agreed in the arbitration clause to submit only one type of claim to litigation, i.e., any claim related to price adjustment, while all the other claims had to be arbitrated.[39] The court reasoned that the claimant's claims touched upon both a matter that had to be submitted to litigation and also concerned matters to be submitted to arbitration. Consequently, arbitral jurisdiction had to be disregarded, in order to 'avoid an impractical double treatment of aspects concerning the same problem' and as a corollary of the principle of restrictive interpretation of arbitration agreements. Thus, the court of appeal ignored its obligation, under Article II(3) of the New York Convention and under Article 19 of the ALIA, to let the arbitrators decide on the scope of the arbitration agreement, pursuant to the kompetenz–kompetenz principle. The court issued its judgment despite the principle being part of Argentinean case law long before the ALIA came into force.[40]

One could argue that the operation of both Articles 19 and 35, together with that of Article 12, that confines all 'intervention' of the national courts to only those cases where the ALIA provides for such intervention, would suffice to prevent Argentinean courts from issuing decisions on the scope of the arbitration agreement prior to arbitrators. However, unless Argentinean courts abandon their restrictive interpretation of arbitration agreements, they will very likely feel compelled to continue ignoring the rules mentioned here in those cases where they consider that the parties have not waived their right to 'ordinary' judges in favour of arbitration, which would appear to be those where there are complex or extraordinary rules or where the frontier between matters to be submitted to arbitration and those to be litigated before the courts is not clear-cut.

4.2 Arbitrator Disqualification: Conflict of Interest

The ALIA includes two additional grounds for the challenge of arbitrators that are not part of the UNCITRAL Model Law adopted by it. Thus, a party may challenge an arbitrator if he or she or members of that arbitrator's law firm, consulting firm or other entity of that kind to which the arbitrator is a member:

1. acts as counsel or representative(s) to one of the parties to the arbitration where the arbitrator is being challenged, in another arbitration or litigation, regardless of the issue under discussion, or
2. if such other arbitration or legal proceedings have the same cause or purpose as the arbitration in which the arbitrator in question is acting, and the arbitrator himself or the other persons mentioned above act as counsel or representative(s) to a third party.

---

[38] Court of Appeal on commercial matters, Branch F, Nov. 27, 2014, available at Abeledo Perrot No. AR/JUR/90086/2014.

[39] In the arbitration agreement, the parties had agreed to submit to arbitration 'any controversy, divergence, claim or doubt regarding the interpretation and/or the application of this Contract, except for ... (ii) the determination of the Final Adjustment Amount', which had to be litigated before the national courts.

[40] *See* Guido Santiago Tawil & Federico Campolieti, *Arbitration Guide* (IBA Arbitration Committee: ARGENTINA, 2018), 9. This principle is currently enshrined in Article 35 of the ALIA, which reproduces Article 16 of the UNCITRAL Model Law: 'The arbitral tribunal may rule on its own jurisdiction, including any objections with respect to the existence or validity of the arbitration agreement'.

In these two specific situations, a challenge to the independence or the impartiality of an arbitrator must be admitted *without the possibility of proof to the contrary*,[41] thus providing concrete examples to the general formulation of the grounds for challenge included in the UNCITRAL Model Law, i.e., the existence of 'circumstances giving rise to legitimate doubts' as to the impartiality or independence of an arbitrator, 'or if he does not possess the qualifications agreed by the parties'.[42]

These additions denote bad legislative technique, given that they appear both unnecessary and excessive. Indeed, a similar scenario to the first ground for challenge is included among the scenarios foreseen in the IBA Guidelines on conflict of interest in international arbitration,[43] while the second ground for challenge actually goes far beyond the IBA Guidelines, because it provides for an arbitrator or one of their colleagues who represents a third party (as opposed to a party to the arbitration) in an arbitration or in judicial proceedings with the same object or subject matter as the arbitration where the arbitrator in question is being challenged. By contrast, the IBA Guidelines do not refer to just any third party, but to 'an affiliate' of the party to arbitration.[44] In addition, the reference to proceedings having 'the same cause or purpose' is too vague. These additions seem to be a gut rejection of the situations encountered in investment arbitrations against Argentina, where some arbitration specialists acted at the same time as arbitrators in one of those cases and as counsel to an investor in another arbitration against Argentina, both arbitrations then being based on the same facts, i.e., the aftermath of the economic and monetary crisis Argentina went through in 2001–2002.

Other grounds for challenge based on unfair conduct of the arbitration are generally dealt with, at least initially – and, in most cases, exclusively – by arbitral institutions.[45] However, some of them may give rise to the annulment of an award, for instance, for violation of due process. There is not a lot of Argentinean case law on this particular issue. However, in *Pan American Energy LLC (Sucursal Argentina) v. Metrogas SA (Chile)*,[46] the court of appeal observed, *obiter*, that the decision by the arbitrators to reject the production of certain evidence requested by one of the parties was not enough to have the award set aside, given that such decision had been taken *after* hearing the parties and, in the court's view, parties must be able to make a sufficient, but not necessarily thorough, presentation of their case for the requirement of due process to be deemed to have been complied with.[47]

4.3 Anti-arbitration Injunctions

There are some examples of cases where the Argentinean state was a party to a commercial or an investment arbitration and there was undue interference by some Argentinean courts. Certain courts have issued injunctions ordering the arbitrators to stay the arbitral proceedings, in cases

---

[41] Article 28 para. 2 of the ALIA.
[42] Article 12.2 of the ALIA.
[43] *See* section 2.3.6 of the Waivable Red List: 'The arbitrator's law firm currently has a significant commercial relationship with one of the parties, or an affiliate of one of the parties'.
[44] *See, e.g.,* section 2.1.1 of the Waivable Red List: 'The arbitrator has given legal advice, or provided an expert opinion, on the dispute to a party or an affiliate of one of the parties.'
[45] It should be noted, however, that national courts may have to deal with challenges against arbitrators in some cases: Article 31 of the ALIA grants jurisdiction to national courts to deal with a challenge against an arbitrator if a challenge under any procedure agreed upon by the parties or under the procedure set out in Article 30 of the ALIA is not successful.
[46] Buenos Aires Court of Appeal on commercial matters, Branch D, La Ley, Mar. 7, 2018, 8.
[47] Id.

where the state (or state entity) has had a disagreement with the arbitrators and the opposing party on certain aspects of the proceedings.

4.3.1 Court's Order to Stay the Arbitral Proceedings while the Court Deals with the Terms of Reference

In 1990, in *Compañía Naviera Pérez Companc v. Ecofisa*,[48] the Buenos Aires Court of Appeal, Branch B, held:

> Where there is no agreement between the parties on the issues to be solved and when a mandatory provision of the Argentinean State is involved, Article 740 of the Code of Procedure must apply, in order to render the judicial control of the arbitration agreement admissible, so that it is possible, with the intervention of the commercial judge, to establish the content of the 'terms of reference', thus avoiding future annulments, thereby facilitating the correct development of the arbitral proceedings [and] safeguarding at the same time the parties' right of defence and the indispensable transparency of the contents of the matters to be submitted to arbitration.[49]

In 1993, another court issued a judgment in the same case, whereby the contents of the terms of reference were definitively set out.[50] Both these judgments were obviously wrong. They blatantly ignored the parties' agreement to submit their arbitration to the ICC Arbitration Rules. The ICC Rules provide that the ICC Court shall examine and approve the terms of reference where the parties are not in agreement on its contents.[51]

In an ICC arbitration, the state entity, which was a binational one from Argentina and Paraguay, wished to add certain language to the terms of reference that had already been agreed upon by the parties and later approved by the ICC Court. An Argentinean first instance court with jurisdiction on administrative matters[52] issued an injunction granting the state entity's application. It also ordered the arbitrators to suspend the arbitral proceedings until a court decision could be made on (1) the final wording of the document setting forth the terms of reference and (2) the challenge of arbitrators.[53] Such injunction ignored the arbitrators' power to conduct the arbitration and the finality of ICC Court's decision on challenges of arbitrators.[54] This unfortunate decision was based on obiter dictum in a Supreme Court judgment. Said judgment authorised judicial intervention where the arbitrator's decision is 'unconstitutional, illegal or unreasonable'.[55]

---

[48] Court of Appeal on commercial matters, Branch B, Aug. 10, 1993, La Ley 1994-A, 139.

[49] Cited in Julio C. Rivera (j), *Interferencias judiciales en el arbitraje* (Judicial Interference in Arbitration), La Ley, Dec. 6, 2006.

[50] Judgment issued on Aug. 10 1993, La Ley, 1994-A, 139, cited in Rivera, Id.

[51] Article 23(3) of the ICC Arbitration Rules.

[52] In Argentina, a separate set of courts deals with matters to which the Argentinean state is a party.

[53] Entidad Binacional Yacyretá v. Eriday et al s/ proceso de conocimiento, First instance court on administrative litigation matters No. 3, Sept. 27, 2004, available in MJJ3299.

[54] The ICC Court had previously rejected the challenges against the arbitrators and the ICC Court's reasoning had not been communicated to the parties, in accordance with its practice at the time. This also weighed in the Argentinean court's decision to grant the interim relief to the binational state entity; *see* Víctor Gustavo Parodi, The 'Yacyretá' Case (or How to Go Back Eighty Years), Fores (Feb. 29, 2016), https://foresjusticia.org/2016/02/29/el-caso-yacireta-o-como-retroceder-80-anos/.

[55] José Cartellone Construcciones Civiles S.A. v. Hidroeléctrica Norpatagónica S.A. o Hidronor S.A., Supreme Court, June 1, 2004, Jurisprudencia Argentina (JA) 2004-III-48: We analyse this precedent further in Section 5.1. Annulment of awards on the grounds of public policy violation.

4.3.2 Court's Order to Stay the Arbitral Proceedings while the Court Deals with the Challenge of an Arbitrator

In an ad hoc investment arbitration under the UNCITRAL Arbitration Rules,[56] the Argentinean state challenged the ICC Court's decision rejecting the state's challenge against the chairman of the arbitral tribunal before the Argentinean courts.[57] The state applied for a stay of the arbitral proceedings pending a decision on the challenge filed by the state. The court issued the injunction ordering (1) the arbitrators to stay the arbitral proceedings, postponing the scheduled evidentiary hearing, pending a court decision on the challenge filed by the State and (2) the investor, claimant in the arbitration, to refrain from any act aimed at pressing the proceedings forward. The arbitrators and the claimant in the ad hoc arbitration ignored the Argentinean court's injunction.

In contrast, the *Yacyreta* case,[58] which was an ICC arbitration where the place of arbitration was the city of Buenos Aires showed a different outcome. Indeed, the Argentinean first-instance court issued an injunction ordering the arbitrators and the parties to stay the arbitration and supplemented this order with a penalty of 7 million USD in case of noncompliance, to be incremented by 1 million USD for every day of delay in complying. Eventually, the non-state-owned party in the *Yacyreta* case withdrew its nomination of a new arbitrator, after the Argentinean arbitrators had been removed from the arbitral tribunal,[59] Both the state entity's challenge and the court decision were highly criticised by scholars and practitioners. The critics of this case referred to the dilatory and baseless nature of the challenge. They have also criticised the granting of the injunction as ignorant of the essential principles of arbitration and as reflecting 'anachronistic positions that show a lack of knowledge of the reality of international business'.[60] I am not aware of any other recent unwarranted intervention of that kind.

5 JUDICIAL CONTROL OF ARBITRAL AWARDS

The ALIA sets out a restrictive list of grounds for annulment of an arbitral award. Some of these grounds, including arbitrability and public policy violation, have given rise to court decisions that raise the question whether Argentina is a suitable venue for arbitration, especially for arbitrations where the Argentinean state is involved. It is surprising that the Buenos Aires Court of Appeal[61] decided that it had jurisdiction to hear an application for setting aside an award in an arbitration where the place of arbitration was located in Uruguay, even if the parties had included a choice-of-forum clause designating Argentinean courts to hear any application for

---

[56] In this ad hoc case, National Grid Transco plc (United Kingdom) v. The Argentine Republic -UNC 72/CCO, the ICC Court acted as appointing authority for the purpose of dealing with the Argentinean state's challenge against the president of the Arbitral Tribunal, Andés Rigo Sureda, who had been appointed by the co-arbitrators. The ground for challenge was that Mr Rigo Sureda was acting at the time as president of other arbitral tribunals who were dealing with two ICSID cases against Argentina. The ICC Court rejected such challenge, which prompted the Argentinean state to challenge its decision before the branch of the Buenos Aires Court of Appeal that deals with matters in which the Argentinean state is involved. The Argentinean State also applied for injunctive relief from such court of appeal, with the view to having the arbitration stayed, pending the resolution of the challenge against the ICC Court's decision on the challenge against Mr Rigo Sureda.

[57] Procuración del Tesoro v. Cámara de Comercio Internacional, court of appeal on administrative litigation matters, Branch IV, July 3, 2007, http://fallos.diprargentina.com/2007/07/procuracin-del-tesoro-c-cmara-de.html.

[58] See *supra* note 53.

[59] See Rivera, *supra* note 49, section IV, f (v).

[60] See Parodi, *supra* note 54, section V, Conclusions; see also Gary B. Born, INTERNATIONAL ARBITRATION AND FORUM SELECTION AGREEMENTS: DRAFTING AND ENFORCING 37–116, tip 3 (2010).

[61] As noted, this is the court with jurisdiction to hear disputes when the Argentinean state is involved.

annulment of the award.[62] This decision is based on the French doctrine of 'de-localization' of arbitration. Such a liberal approach shows a promising respect of party autonomy and will hopefully pave the way for a modernisation of the Argentinean case law.

5.1 Annulment of Arbitral Awards Rendered in Argentina

5.1.1 General Grounds for Annulment

Article 98 of the ALIA provides that the only recourse against an arbitral award is an application for setting it aside, on the grounds listed in Article 99 of the ALIA. This application must be brought within the time limits mentioned in Article 100 of the ALIA.[63] The grounds for challenge of arbitral awards under the ALIA are identical to those of the UNCITRAL Model Law, which in turn are the same as the grounds under the New York Convention.[64]

Under the old regime, replaced by the ALIA as far as international arbitration is concerned and thus currently applicable only to domestic arbitration, the grounds for challenge included two other grounds that are not present in the ALIA: (1) arbitrators' failure to issue the award within the agreed time limit and (2) inconsistent decisions in the dispositive part of the award.[65] Conversely, the ALIA has added two grounds: a party's lack of capacity or the agreement not being valid under the law chosen by the parties or under Argentinean law and the composition of the arbitral tribunal or arbitral procedure not being in accordance with the agreement of the parties.[66] The grounds for challenge based on the non-arbitrability of the subject matter of the arbitration or the violation of Argentinean public policy have been applied by Argentinean courts in the past and have justified courts' review of the merits of awards in certain cases.

---

[62] YPF S.A. v. AES Uruguaiana Emprendimientos S.A. et al on appeal by complaint, Court of Appeal on administrative litigation matters, Branch IV, Oct. 7, 2014, http://fallos.diprargentina.com/2014/10/ypf-c-aes-uruguaiana-emprendimientos-s.html. The court upheld the parties' choice of jurisdiction clause, where they had agreed upon Argentinean courts' jurisdiction to hear applications for the setting aside of the award, on the grounds that the arbitration procedure is flexible and no arbitration is bound to a given forum, based on the French de-localisation theory.

[63] The application for setting aside must be filed within one month (as opposed to three months, as per Article 34.3 of the UNCITRAL Model Law) from the date on which the party making the application receives the award or, if a request for correction and interpretation of the award or for an additional award, from the date on which that request is disposed of by the arbitral tribunal.

[64] Article 99 of the ALIA reads:

> Article 99. An arbitral award may be set aside by the court specified in article 13 only if: a) The party making the application furnishes proof: I. That a party to the arbitration agreement referred to in article 14 was under some incapacity; or the said agreement is not valid under the law to which the parties have subjected it or, failing any indication thereon, under Argentinean law; or II. That the party making the application was not given proper notice of the appointment of an arbitrator or of the arbitral proceedings or was otherwise unable to present his case; or III. That the award deals with a dispute not contemplated by or not falling within the terms of the submission to arbitration, or contains decisions on matters beyond the scope of the submission to arbitration, provided that, if the decisions on matters submitted to arbitration can be separated from those not so submitted, only that part of the award which contains decisions on matters not submitted to arbitration may be set aside; or IV. That the composition of the arbitral tribunal or the arbitral procedure was not in accordance with the agreement of the parties, unless such agreement was in conflict with a provision of this law from which the parties cannot derogate, or, failing such agreement, was not in accordance with this law; or b) The court finds: I. That the subject-matter of the dispute is not capable of settlement by arbitration under Argentinean law; or II. That the award is in conflict with Argentinean public policy.

[65] Articles 760 and 761 CPCCN; see Guido Santiago Tawil *National Report for Argentina*, in ICCA International Handbook on Commercial Arbitration 1–44, 38 (Jan Paulsson & Lise Bosman eds., 1984).

[66] Article 99(a) I and IV of the ALIA.

5.1.2 *Arbitrability*

Following the UNCITRAL Model Law, the ALIA contains no provision on arbitrability. Therefore, one has to look for guidance in the Argentinean CC Code. When dealing with non-arbitrable matters between private parties, Article 1649 of the CC Code refers to disputes that have arisen or may arise between parties to a particular legal relationship of private law, contractual or noncontractual, 'in which no public policy is involved'. And Article 1651 of the CC Code casuistically enumerates the disputes that are non-arbitrable,[67] unlike the CPCCN, which simply excludes, as non-arbitrable, those 'issues that may not be the subject of a settlement'.

A reform bill of chapter 29 of the CC Code is currently under consideration by the Argentinean Congress (mentioned in Section 3.1). It proposes the repeal of the controversial provision of Article 1649 and a return to the generic formulation of the CPCCN. The reform bill also makes the effort to clarify that where mandatory rules apply to the merits of the dispute, it does not necessarily mean that the subject matter of the dispute is not arbitrable. This appears to be a reaction to certain federal case law that reached the opposite conclusion.[68]

Fortunately, some Argentinean courts are aware of this; an example of this is the Supreme Court of the province of Cordoba's upholding of the defendant's motion to dismiss the plaintiff's lawsuit in a case where the contract contained an arbitration clause. The court held in that case that the fact that the subject matter of the dispute was related to mandatory rules – i.e., the emergency legislation enacted in Argentina further to its economic and financial crisis in 2002 – did not render the award null and void. Moreover, the court found that arbitrators, just like judges, may decide on the constitutionality of laws, as long as such issue is related to the controversy submitted to arbitration. In addition, given that the dispute was in connection with pecuniary matters, the court found it was arbitrable.[69] The Buenos Aires Court of Appeal reached the same conclusion in *Francisco Ctibor S.A.C.I. Y F. v. Wall-Mart Argentina S.R.L.* on ordinary proceedings.[70]

5.1.3 *Public Policy Violation*

5.1.3.1 DEFINITION OF PUBLIC POLICY Argentinean law contains no definition of *public policy* for the purpose of the judicial control of arbitral awards. Argentinean courts tend to assimilate the concept of public policy to mandatory rules. Alternatively, they refer to 'a set of (extra-juridical) principles',[71] as opposed to black letter law, but 'which apply to certain laws and make them imperative'.[72] Public policy can be of a political, economic, moral or religious

---

[67] Article 1651 of the CC Code lists the following disputes as non-arbitrable: (1) those connected to the family status or the capacity of a person, (2) family disputes, (c) those connected to the rights of users and consumers (N.B.: this is not correct as far as consumers are concerned, given that a National System of Consumer Arbitration exists in Argentina, which is voluntary and free), (4) those arising out of adhesion contracts irrespective of their subject matter and (5) those arising out of labour relationships.
[68] CRI Holding Inc Sucursal Argentina v. Compañía Argentina de Comodoro Rivadavia Explotación de Petróleo S.A., Court of Appeal on commercial matters, Branch C, Oct. 5, 2010, (2011) La Ley, 2011-A-555, with commentary by Julio César Rivera.
[69] *See* Oliva, Oscar v. Disco SA, Supreme Court of Cordoba, Mar. 14, 2013, note in BERETTA GODOY NEWSLETTER Apr. 10, 2013.
[70] Judgment dated Dec. 20, 2016, 20/12/2016, https://ar.vlex.com/vid/francisco-ctibor-saci-f-656106605.
[71] *See* Noiana Marigo *Argentina & Uruguay* 2 (memorandum dated Sept. 4, 2015, presented as part of the work of the IBA Recognition and Enforcement of Arbitral Awards Subcommittee).
[72] *Id.*

nature and generally affects the collective interest.[73] It is a flexible, contingent and relative concept that is applied by courts on a case-by-case basis[74] and even ex officio.[75]

5.1.3.2 ASSIMILATION OF THE DOCTRINE OF ARBITRARY JUDGMENT The Argentinean Supreme Court has unfortunately imported into the judicial control over arbitration a long-standing doctrine that it applies to the control of lower courts' judgments. This twentieth-century doctrine allows the Supreme Court to set aside lower courts' judgments that it deems arbitrary. The origin of this doctrine can be found in the expansion by the Supreme Court of its own jurisdiction on 'extraordinary appeal', which it exercises as guardian and ultimate interpreter of the Argentinean constitution. The rationale behind the Supreme Court's power is that such 'arbitrary judgments' may have an impact on the interpretation or application of federal law, an international treaty or the Argentinean Constitution.[76] Thus, the Supreme Court annulled certain final judgments on the basis of an old precedent, in the framework of 'extraordinary appeals', even though they did not fall within the scope of such appeals per black letter law. The Supreme Court's rationale for this is that those judgments were arbitrary[77] to such a significant extent that they did not deserve to be considered as judgments, because (1) they were unfounded or because (2) they ignored the law that was undoubtedly applicable to the case, be it because they departed from the proven facts of the case or because they were affected by other equally serious vices.[78] The Supreme Court has stressed that this doctrine was not about correcting judicial errors but it was rather about eliminating decisions which contained grave omissions and should be disqualified as judicial decisions.[79]

In contrast, the Argentinean Supreme Court had developed a theoretical framework in the 1990s that favoured arbitration as an autonomous means of dispute resolution contractually chosen by the parties that did not deprive them from their right to access justice and that was guaranteed by the Argentinean Constitution. Accordingly, judicial control of awards was 'limited to certain eminently formal aspects ... which tend to circumscribe to procedural errors'.[80]

---

[73] See CRI Holding, supra note 68.

[74] See Compañía Naviera Pérez Companc et al v. Ecofisa S.A. et al, Court of Appeal on commercial matters, Branch B, Aug. 10, 1993, (1994) La Ley 1994-A, 139.

[75] Techint Compañía Técnica Internacional S.A.C.E. e I. v. Empresa Nuclear Argentina de Centrales Eléctricas in liquidation and Nucleoeléctrica Argentina S.A., Supreme Court, May 8, 2007.

[76] The final judgment in question must decide (1) against the validity of an international treaty or of federal law or an authority exercised in the name of the nation or (2) in favour of the validity of a law, decree or authority of a province, where it has been questioned under the pretence of being repugnant to the Argentinean constitution, to an international treaty or laws of the National Congress or (3) where the intelligence of some clause of the Argentinean constitution, or of a treaty or law of the National Congress or a commission exerted in the name of the national authority has been questioned and the decision is against the validity of the title, right, privilege or exemption that is based on said clause and is a matter of litigation (Article 14, Law 48, Aug. 25, 1863).

[77] An '[a]rbitrary judgment is one that lacks reasonableness and is not the consequence or logical derivation of due consideration of the issue under debate, of the right invoked, of the applicable law, of the facts that motivate it or of the evidence produced or offered.' An 'arbitrary judgment' is therefore 'an unconstitutional judicial act, to the extent that it violates rights and guarantees recognised by the Constitution" see GREGORIO BADENI, TRATADO DE DERECHO CONSTITUCIONAL TOMO II (Treatise on Constitutional Law Volume II) 1245 (2006).

[78] See Genaro R. Carrió, Sobre la competencia de la Suprema Corte argentina y su necesaria y urgente modificación (On the Supreme Court's Jurisdiction and Its Necessary and Urgent Reform), 1990 REVISTA DEL CENTRO DE ESTUDIOS CONSTITUCIONALES, 9–43, 21 (1990).

[79] See in re Allaría Amézaga de Munilla Lacasa, María Clara v. Palma, José Marcial, Supreme Court, 1959 Revista Fallos 244: 384, among many others, cited in Roque J. Caivano, Alcances de la revisión judicial en el arbitraje (Comentario a la sentencia de la Corte Suprema de Justicia Argentina in re "Cartellone"), 2005 REVISTA BRASILEIRA DE ARBITRAGEM 159–192 (2005).

[80] Justice Boggiano's vote, in re Color S.A. v. Max Factor Sucursal Argentina, Supreme Court, Nov. 17, 1994, Revista Fallos 317: 1527.

However, in 2004 the Supreme Court opened the door to the judicial review of arbitral awards on the grounds of arbitrariness, thus allowing the review of the merits of the case, as seen in the following sections.

5.1.3.3 THE *CARTELLONE* CASE In *Cartellone*,[81] the Argentinean Supreme Court held that an arbitral award is subject to judicial review if it is 'unconstitutional, illegal or unreasonable', even if the parties have waived their right of appeal:

> It may not be lawfully interpreted that the waiver of the right to appeal against an arbitration decision extends to cases in which the award is contrary to public order, since it is not logical to foresee, when formulating a waiver with such scope, that the arbitrators will adopt a decision that incurs in that defect. It should be recalled in this regard that the assessment of the facts and the regular application of the law are functions of the arbitrators and, consequently, the award they issue will be unappealable under those conditions, but, on the other hand, their decision may be challenged judicially when it is unconstitutional, illegal or unreasonable. (Fallos: 292:223)

The Supreme Court decided to disregard the parties' waiver, which was highly criticised by scholars.[82] It also indirectly invoked the 'arbitrary judgment' doctrine and applied it to arbitral awards. Although it rendered its judgment in the context of a domestic arbitration in very particular circumstances,[83] the Supreme Court confirmed that it can review the merits of an arbitration, on the ground that the award violates Argentinean public policy.

While the Supreme Court's control of arbitrary judgments may be justified, the review of the merits of the individual cases appears unwarranted when applied to arbitral awards and could lead to excesses. A former justice of the Supreme Court held,

> courts must respect the parties' waivers – of the ordinary judicial jurisdiction, in general, and of the subsequent review by the state courts, in particular – ignoring the subsequent retractions that the parties may tentatively attempt as a result of an adverse resolution, at the risk of denaturing arbitration, by depriving it of its most precious benefits ... In this sense, once a judgment is rendered setting aside an arbitral award by the superior court of the case and provided the other formal and substantial requirements of admissibility required by this exceptional federal instance are met, this Court may only conduct a very limited review on the possible violation of the rights and constitutional guarantees the award may have incurred in. If the parties freely and in matters they are allowed to do so, have subtracted themselves from the decision-making authority of state courts, it is not within the powers of this Court to supply, through the indirect means of a comprehensive review of the judgment of the inferior court – comprehensive of the award itself – the deficiencies of judgment or criterion of the arbitrators, the greater or lesser fairness of its pronouncement or its accuracy or error.[84]

In many cases, the frontier between judicial error and outright arbitrariness may be blurred and, ultimately, whether a judgment is 'arbitrary' may be a somewhat subjective consideration. The framework of very limited judicial control displayed in the annulment procedure of

---

[81] José Cartellone Construcciones Civiles S.A. v. Hidroeléctrica Norpatagónica S.A. o Hidronor S.A., Supreme Court, June 1, 2004 (2004) Jurisprudencia Argentina (JA) 2004-III-48.

[82] *See*, among others, Héctor O. Méndez, *Impugnación judicial de laudos arbitrales. El caso "Cartellone": Un lamentable retroceso* (Judicial Challenge of Arbitral Awards. The 'Cartellone' Case: A Regrettable Setback), 1 JURISPRUDENCIA ARGENTINA 1312 (2005).

[83] Award rendered by the defunct Public Works Arbitral Tribunal. This tribunal had jurisdiction in matters concerning public works, and its jurisdiction was compulsory for the Argentinean state, if the contractor chose to submit the dispute to said tribunal.

[84] *See* Justice Boggiano's vote, *supra* note 80.

arbitral awards should not lead to the review of the decision on the merits made by the arbitrators, under the pretence that the decision is arbitrary or conflicts with the public policy of the state where the award has been rendered.[85] In other words, only flagrant violations of the state's public policy should be disallowed. This calls for a very restrictive application of the public policy exception. There is another feature of the Argentinean constitutional system that has contributed to certain Argentinean courts' tendency to interfere with certain arbitral awards. In Argentina, any court may declare a piece of legislation unconstitutional. By analogy, some court of appeal judgments have interpreted that courts have the power and the duty to decide whether arbitral awards are arbitrary – hence, contrary to Argentinean public policy – and, in the affirmative, to set them aside. By contrast, some scholars have attempted to restrict the impact of the Supreme Court's judgment in *Cartellone* by recommending that its particular characteristics should be borne in mind.[86]

5.1.3.4 CASE LAW INSPIRED BY THE *CARTELLONE* CASE The lower courts, however, have followed the *Cartellone* judgment in relation to the enforcement of international awards[87] and also in annulment cases.[88] In my opinion, arbitrariness could be validly understood to be comprised only within the public policy ground for annulment included in the ALIA, if the award was so repugnant to 'fundamental principles of law and justice in substantive as well as procedural respects'[89] of the Argentinean legal system that it did not deserve to be considered as such.

In more recent judgments, the Supreme Court rejected the parties' application filed directly against certain 'arbitral decisions', because the parties had waived their right to appeal. It stated that the only recourse available to the parties was the application for setting aside, set out in Section 760 of the CCNPC.[90] Given that the Supreme Court rejected these 'extraordinary

---

[85] *See* Santiago L. Capparelli, *Necesarias aclaraciones de la Corte sobre el control judicial al arbitraje* (Necessary Clarifications by the Court on Judicial Control on Arbitration) (2008) La Ley, 2008–C, 258 ss and the other scholarly articles cited in Leandro Caputo, *La nulidad es el único remedio procesal contra un laudo arbitral. Su alcance restrictivo también alcanza al Estado (clarificaciones de un caso argentino)*, 11 ARBITRAJE 847–860, 849 n. 4 (2018) (The application for setting aside is the only procedural remedy against an arbitral award. Its restrictive scope also applies to the state (clarifications by Argentinean case law)).

[86] In *Cartellone*, the award had been issued by the Public Works Arbitral Tribunal in an arbitration that was compulsory for the state, which rendered its decisions subject to judicial review. In fact, the issue of the admissibility of judicial review of the awards of this arbitral tribunal had been discussed by the Supreme Court in a previous judgment and the court had decided against it by majority, thus indirectly confirming the arbitral award issued by the Public Works Arbitral Tribunal against the state; *see* Meller Comunicaciones S.A. UTE v. Empresa Nacional de Telecomunicaciones, Nov. 5, 2002. This led to the impeachment of the Supreme Court justices who issued the majority vote in that case; *see* Méndez, *supra* note 82, at 2–4).

[87] *See* Milantic Trans SA v. Ministerio de la Producción, La Plata Court of Appeal on administrative litigation matters, Aug. 30, 2007, La Ley 2008-A, 72 — DJ 06/02/2008, 287 – La Ley 04/07/2008, 6, with commentary by Hernán Cruchaga.

[88] *See* EDF International S.A. v. Endesa Internacional (España) et al. on arbitration, Court of Appeal on commercial matters, Branch C, Dec. 9, 2009.

[89] This is the interpretation of the public policy concept included in the UNCITRAL Commission's Report on the UNCITRAL Model Law (Supplement No. 17 (A/40/17). However, the UNCITRAL Secretariat in its explanatory note on the UNCITRAL Model Law stated that the violation of public policy of the state where the award has been rendered 'is to be understood as serious departures from fundamental notions of procedural justice' (*See* Explanatory Note by the UNCITRAL Secretariat on the 1985 Model Law on International Commercial Arbitration as amended in 2006, at 12) The explanatory note is not an official commentary on the UNCITRAL Model Law and refers for such a commentary to the UNCITRAL document A/CN.9/264. This document, in turn, explains that the notion of public policy is essentially as found in Article V of the 1958 New York Convention, which is a 'familiar' notion that 'require[s] no detailed explanation' (at 73, para. 10 – document, https://undocs.org/en/a/cn.9/264).

[90] *See* Cacchione, Ricardo C. v. Urbaser Argentina S.A., Supreme Court, Aug. 24, 2006, El Dial Express, Dec. 6, 2006, and Pestarino de Alfani v. Urbaser Argentina, Supreme Court, Mar. 11, 2008.

appeals' because they were inadmissible, it did not need to analyse the parties' arguments. Although those decisions were welcomed by the arbitration community, they do not provide detailed insight on the Supreme Court's position in this regard.

In the *EDF Internationale* annulment case,[91] the Buenos Aires Court of Appeal referred to *Cartellone*. It considered that the arbitrators had not applied Argentinean law, which applied to the merits by the parties' agreement and set aside an award rendered in an international arbitration with Buenos Aires as the seat. In fact, the arbitrators had analysed in detail the applicable Argentinean law in the award. They had favoured the claimant's thesis on the timing when a certain piece of legislation had been repealed, which was in fact a mixed question of fact and law with a significant bearing on the merits of the claimant's claim.

An extraordinary appeal before the Supreme Court is available to the party against judgments like the one mentioned. When exercising its writ of certiorari, the Supreme Court may reject extraordinary appeals that carry insufficient, unsubstantial or irrelevant federal issues, by applying its 'sound discretion' and relying on the applicable procedural rule.[92] In practice, the Supreme Court refuses to hear most of the extraordinary appeals lodged by parties.[93] Consequently, there is a potentially high risk that annulment judgments issued by the court of appeal become final.[94]

In both the *Cartellone* and the *EDF International* cases, the state was either directly involved or indirectly, respectively. With respect to the former, the reversal of its own jurisprudence by the Argentinean Supreme Court in that case was more in harmony with the prevailing political and economic ideas of the Argentinean administration of the time. It was also a response to previous harsh criticism of an earlier Supreme Court judgment in which it had refused to review an application for setting aside an award that was contrary to the interests of the Argentinean state and had been rendered by the same Public Works Arbitral Tribunal that later rendered the award at the centre of the *Cartellone* case.[95]

5.1.3.5 SUPREME COURT'S RESTRICTIVE VIEW OF THE GROUNDS FOR ANNULMENT OF AWARDS In recent cases concerning domestic arbitration, the Supreme Court in *Ricardo Agustín López*[96] and *Estado Nacional*[97] confirmed its position that the only recourse available against an arbitral award is the application to set aside under Article 760 of the CPCCN, where the parties have waived their right to lodge an appeal against it. State courts may not review the arbitrators' decision on the merits, unless it is contrary to Argentinean public policy. Such violation was established in none of these cases.

In *Ricardo Agustín López*, the losing party challenged the award before the Buenos Aires Court of Appeal on commercial matters on the grounds of breach of due process or fundamental procedural defect. The party argued that the arbitral tribunal had refused to stay the arbitral

---

[91] EDF International, *supra* note 88.
[92] See Leandro J. Giannini, *Supreme Courts: 'Filters' and Case Selection. Argentina's Writ of Certiorari in a Comparative Perspective*, 9 EUROPEAN AND REGULATORY PROCEDURAL LAW 249–266 (2017) (in VVAA, Loïc Cadiet, Burkhard Hess, & Marta Requejo Isidro eds., *Approaches to Procedural Law. The Pluralism of Methods*. Studies of the Max Planck Institute Luxembourg for International).
[93] *Id.*
[94] This is exactly what happened in the *EDF International* case.
[95] See Méndez, *supra* note 82.
[96] Ricardo Agustín López, Marcelo Gustavo Daelli, Juan Manuel Flo Díaz, Jorge Zorzópulos v. Gemabiotech SA s/ organismos externos, Supreme Court, Sept. 5, 2017.
[97] EN-Procuración del Tesoro Nacional c. (nulidad del laudo del 20-III-09) s. recurso directo, Supreme Court, Nov. 6, 2018.

proceedings pending the outcome of criminal proceedings initiated against the claimant. To justify the refusal, the arbitral tribunal had held that the civil and the criminal proceedings were unrelated. Therefore, the arbitral tribunal was under no obligation to stay the arbitral proceedings. The court of appeal held that the party's application to set aside the award was not the proper forum to evaluate all the arbitrators' arguments. It also held that a mere disagreement of the applicant with the arbitral tribunal's assessment of the evidence could not lead to the conclusion that there had been a due process violation. The court, however, set aside the award. It considered that the arbitral tribunal had failed to postpone the issuance of the final award until the outcome of the criminal proceedings was known in breach of the Argentinean Civil Code.[98] When reviewing the annulment, the Supreme Court noted that neither the party challenging the award, nor the court of appeal had justified how the complainant's disagreement with the manner in which the arbitral tribunal had interpreted the applicable law and assessed the evidence could be considered grounds for annulment in the restricted list of Article 760 of the CPCCN. The Supreme Court held that the court of appeal had rather reassessed the evidence when deciding that the arbitrators should have stayed the arbitral proceedings. According to the Supreme Court, however, the arbitrators had not breached due process. They had simply chosen an alternative manner to solve the motion to stay the arbitral proceedings. The court of appeal had therefore exceeded its power of review.[99]

In *Estado Nacional*, the state entity challenged the award before the Buenos Aires Court of Appeal, invoking the doctrine of arbitrary judgment applied in *Cartellone*, on the following grounds: (1) disregard of the law applicable to the contract and deviation from the contractual provisions that fixed the compensation, (2) error in the assessment of the evidence and (3) failure to apply Argentine emergency regulations on payment currency and debt consolidation by the state. The court of appeal set aside part of the award, on the grounds mentioned in (3) and rejected the other two. The court found that the validity of the arbitration agreement was not in question, and the correctness or error, or the justice or injustice, of the solution adopted by the arbitrator with respect to the contractual dispute, was not to be analysed by national courts in the framework of an application for setting aside. Such a full review would imply conferring the application to set aside the same scope as an appeal, whose purpose is the ex novo review of the controversy. The court of appeal held that the state entity had failed to show the arbitrary nature of the award.[100]

On appeal before the Supreme Court, the state entity alleged that the court of appeal's judgment was arbitrary. The state entity held that the court of appeal's judgment lacked foundation and failed to deal with questions that the state entity had introduced when challenging the arbitral award. The appellant submitted that in deciding in this way, the court of appeal had departed from the doctrine set forth by the Supreme Court in *Cartellone*. Under this doctrine, the parties' waiver of their right to appeal may not be extended to cases in which the award violates public policy. In those cases, the award may can be challenged before the courts when it is unconstitutional, illegal or unreasonable. The state entity reiterated its grievances. It further argued that the shortcomings of the award constituted a violation of due process[101] and as such, the award violated public policy.

---

[98] *See* Leandro Caputo & Martina Monti, *Ratificación de la Corte Suprema de Justicia de la Nación de causales de nulidad taxativas de laudos arbitrales bajo el Derecho argentino* (Confirmation by the Supreme Court of the Nation of the Restrictive Character of the Grounds for Annulment of Arbitral Awards under Argentinean Law), 11 ARBITRAJE 293–310, 308 (2018).
[99] Ricardo Agustín López, *supra* note 96.
[100] *See* EN-Procuración, *supra* note 97, at section 2.

The Supreme Court reiterated that the only recourse available against the award was the application for setting aside.[102] As to the scope of judicial review in the framework of an application for setting aside, the Supreme Court held it was very limited. It also held that it was prevented from reviewing the merits.[103] It referred to *Ricardo Agustín López* and held that such decision applied to the case under review, despite the fact that one of the parties was a state entity.[104] The Supreme Court concluded that the state entity had failed to show that the arbitrator had violated due process, given that such entity's complaints reflected only its disagreement with the arbitrator's decision as to the interpretation of the contractual stipulations and the assessment of the evidence. This showed that there had been no violation of due process as guaranteed by the Argentinean Constitution. The court particularly stressed that the state entity's request involved assimilating the application for setting aside to an appeal, which in fact exceeded the confines of the former. Second, the Supreme Court held that the state entity had failed to show that the arbitrator's interpretation of the contract and his assessment of the evidence had violated public policy 'whatever scope is given to such notion',[105] Consequently, the Supreme Court rejected the state entity's application for setting aside the award, by majority.[106]

5.1.3.6 FUTURE OF THE DOCTRINE OF ARBITRARY JUDGMENTS IN INTERNATIONAL CASES The Supreme Court's judgment in *Estado Nacional* has been interpreted as the abandonment by that court of the *Cartellone* doctrine.[107] However, it would have been desirable to see further elaboration of the relationship between the concepts of public policy and arbitrariness or at least a more general rejection of the application of the doctrine of arbitrariness to arbitral awards.

Despite the *Estado Nacional* judgment, it is unclear how the Supreme Court would decide an application to set aside an arbitral award under the ALIA in an international arbitration with the place of arbitration located in Argentina, in particular where the state or a state entity is a party. In such case, it is still unclear if the Supreme Court could find, when faced with an award that has failed to apply some provision of the applicable law, in particular if such law is Argentinean law, that such award is arbitrary and, therefore, violates public policy. It is not clear either, whether the Supreme Court assimilates the notion of 'mandatory provisions' to public policy or whether, in the case of international arbitration, the court would look at rules or principles that may be comprised within Argentinean international public policy. A deeper analysis of these two questions is necessary. In my opinion, a distinction should be made between judgments and arbitral awards, as far as the doctrine of arbitrariness is concerned. This doctrine should be used only for judgments and a minimum standard of review should be applied to awards, which glaringly violate either procedural or substantive Argentinean international public policy.

---

[101] Article 760 of the CPCCN.
[102] Supreme Court's judgment, *supra* note 90, at section 8, citing *Cacchione* and *Pestarino*.
[103] Here, the court cited a very old Supreme Court's precedent (Otto Frank, 1922) in support of its assertion that it had adopted a restricted view of the scope of the application for setting aside arbitral awards in the distant past already (and had maintained it).
[104] Citing its own case law in support of this (section 10 of the judgment).
[105] See section 13, para. 3 of the judgment.
[106] One of the justices issued a dissenting opinion based on noncompliance by the applicant with the requirements of the 'ordinary appeal' under the CPCCN. He nevertheless agreed with the majority in that the state entity's complaint reflected a mere disagreement with the decisions taken by the arbitrator on the merits; therefore, the applicant had not challenged the award in an effective manner. The dissenting opinion therefore reached the same ultimate solution as the majority's one: dismissal of the application for setting aside the award (*see* judgment, *supra* note 87, dissenting opinion by Justice Juan Carlos Maqueda, sections 6–8).
[107] See Caputo, *supra* note 85, at 857.

5.2 Enforcement of Foreign Arbitral Awards

Argentina ratified the New York Convention in March 1989. Pursuant to reservations it made, the New York Convention applies to arbitral awards rendered in disputes arising out of legal relationships, whether contractual or not, that are considered 'commercial' under Argentinean law and only to recognise and enforce awards made in the territory of other contracting states to the New York Convention (reciprocity). The ALIA has however extended the application of the same grounds for refusal of recognition or enforcement of foreign arbitral awards as those contained in the New York Convention to all foreign awards.[108] The ALIA has clarified that the classification of a legal relationship as commercial derives from the fact that it is governed, or predominantly governed, by private law and has prescribed that, in case of doubt, the relationship must be categorised as commercial.[109]

Unfortunately, the requirement for the commercial nature of the underlying legal relationship was misapplied in some cases by Argentinean courts in the past. In *Milantic*,[110] the La Plata Court of Appeal on administrative litigious matters refused to enforce an award rendered in London. The dispute arose out of an international contract entered into between a foreign company and an Argentinean provincial state entity. The first instance judge rejected a motion to refuse the enforcement of the award based on the allegation that the underlying contract was not of a commercial nature. However, the court of appeal found that the underlying contract could not be of a commercial nature because the contract was with a state entity. The court held that the provincial state had not acted as a commercial player, even if it was in an international contract. Such flawed reasoning should by no means prevail in international arbitration cases under the current law. As a result, Argentinean courts are now forced to categorise a relationship as commercial, even if one of the parties is an Argentinean state entity, provided that such relationship is governed by private law. Since this is the case in most international contracts entered into by the state or a state entity, the courts will have to find that such relationship is a commercial one, for the purpose of enforcing and recognising foreign arbitral awards.

Another application of the public policy exception in the context of recognition and enforcement of foreign awards may be found in *Ogden*.[111] In that case, the Buenos Aires Court of Appeal refused to enforce a foreign arbitral award issued in an ICC arbitration. It observed that the amount of the costs to be borne by the winning party exceeded the amount that the losing party had been ordered to pay as compensation to the former. The court of appeal followed the advocate general's opinion and held that such decision on costs violated the winning party's right of access to justice. It added that the arbitrator had offered no justification to his order that the costs had to be borne by the winning party. Although such an extreme decision on costs may shock or appear illogical or unfair, the court of appeal widened the scope of judicial scrutiny of foreign awards in an unjustified manner. There is no specific rule in Argentinean law that prohibits the amount of costs to be paid by one of the parties to exceed that of the compensation it is awarded. The ICC Arbitration Rules leave the allocation of the costs of the arbitration to the

---

[108] It has done so by expressly repealing an outdated regime that was still present in the CPCCN that involved a 'double exequatur' and applied to the recognition and enforcement of foreign judgments in the absence of a treaty.

[109] *See* Article 6 of the ALIA. This article does not exist in the UNCITRAL Model Law, except, partially, in the form of a footnote to the term *commercial* in 'international commercial arbitration' in Article 1(1) of the UNCITRAL Model Law, which has been integrated to Article 6 of the ALIA. The mandate to categorise relations as commercial in case of doubt is not present in the UNCITRAL Model Law.

[110] Milantic Trans SA, *supra* note 87.

[111] Ogden Entertainment Services v. Eijo, Néstor et al., Court of Appeal on commercial matters, Branch C, Sept. 20, 2004, (2005) La Ley 2005-B-21.

discretion of the arbitral tribunal, who 'may take into account such circumstances as it considers relevant'.[112] In sum, the court of appeal refused to enforce the award because it did not agree with the arbitrator's allocation of costs. This decision adopted a broad notion of public policy but ignored the fact that the parties had submitted all aspects of their dispute, including the allocation of costs, to arbitration.

In contrast, Chilean courts have interpreted the scope of public policy in a restrictive manner, distinguishing international from internal public policy, both when dealing with applications for setting aside arbitral awards[113] and for enforcing foreign arbitral awards.[114]

6 ATTRACTIVENESS OF A COUNTRY AS ARBITRATION VENUE

After commenting on the Argentinean arbitration law and practice, it seems appropriate to look briefly at what has been done in another South American country such as Chile in terms of modernisation of its arbitration legislation. The Chilean government and legislators seem to have become aware of the significance of international arbitration as a means of dispute resolution at the international level at the same time as they decided to open the country's economy to the world, in the first decade of the twenty-first century. Accordingly, Chile adopted the UNCITRAL Model Law in 2004 for international arbitration. In contrast, even if Argentina ratified the New York Convention in 1988, together with several BITs and TIPs submitting disputes to arbitration in the 1990s and the 2000s, Argentina kept its archaic arbitration rules, and its legislators refused to pass any modern arbitration bill until 2018.

A modern legal framework is a key contributing factor to the reliability of an arbitration venue. It is, however, not the only one. In this regard, Chile meets several criteria. It is an attractive international arbitration venue which attracts foreign investment. It has a rather stable economy, a good degree of international prestige (solid image of its public institutions, including its judiciary), thus generating confidence at the international level (transparency, low level of corruption); well prepared counsel and arbitrators; good arbitral institutions; and facilities at a relative low cost. Although Argentina also has experienced counsel and arbitrators, it is lacking all other parameters mentioned above.

The courts' positive attitude towards arbitration and their familiarity with its characteristics are other essential elements that must be present in order to create an arbitration-friendly environment. Chilean courts seem to be mindful of their relationship with the arbitration community. Judges receive training in arbitration. In contrast, some Argentinean courts are still reluctant to favour arbitration as the parties' choice in contractual matters or, generally, in matters where no general or community interest is involved.

Another feature that seems to have certain weight is the significant promotion of arbitration by local arbitral institutions in Chile, which administer numerous arbitrations. Argentina has

---

[112] See Article 38.5 of the ICC Arbitration Rules.
[113] See José Antonio Moreno Rodríguez, Memorandum on Chile, Paraguay-Mercosur, Peru, Venezuela, dated Oct. 20, 2014, prepared for the IBA Recognition and Enforcement of Awards Subcommittee, 9, citing Constructora Emex Limitada con Organización Europea para la Investigación Astronómica en el Hemisferio Sur, Apr. 10, 2014, Appeals Court of Santiago (First Chamber), where the court rejected an application for setting aside an arbitral award, finding that parties may stipulate on costs and fees for the arbitration specifically and, therefore, the costs and fees fixed by the arbitrators were not contrary to public policy, even where they were higher than those allowed by Chilean law.
[114] Id. at 9, citing Gold Nutrition Industria e Comercio v. Laboratorios Garden House S.A, Chilean Supreme Court, 6615–07, Sept. 15, 2008, where the Supreme Court ordered the enforcement of an award rendered in Brazil, by refusing to deal with the issue of whether the compound interest fixed by the arbitral tribunal was contrary to Chilean public policy, holding that to do so would be to deal with the merits of the award.

certain prestigious institutions, but lacks a concerted effort by the government, the arbitral institutions and other key players in the arbitration field, to make significant progress towards becoming a trustworthy arbitration venue.

7 CONCLUSION

In conclusion, although the legislative reform in Argentina is a significant step towards its consolidation as a reliable arbitration venue, there are still several areas where improvement is necessary. For instance, if Congress enacts the bill on the reform of the CC Code, before Congress since 2017, certain provisions that are unfavourable to arbitration will be eliminated. As seen in this chapter, this would affect not only domestic arbitration but also international arbitration in Argentina, because of the scope of arbitrable matters.

Unless Argentinean courts abandon (1) their *restrictive interpretation* of arbitration agreements, (2) the notion of arbitration as an exception to judicial litigation and (3) their inclination to intervene in arbitrations where the state is a party, Argentina will not become an attractive place for (international) arbitration. In other words, the careful guidance for courts contained in some of the provisions of the ALIA, aimed at curtailing abusive interference in arbitration by courts, does not appear to be sufficient.

I would hope that the judiciary, legislators, businesses and the public in general are trained to better understand to the real nature, purpose and finality of arbitration. All these players, judges included, should be made aware of the benefits that a stable framework for arbitration generates for the country and even justice in general:

- It makes the country more attractive to foreign investors.
- It contributes to the respect of the rule of law in the country.
- It renders justice more accessible to impecunious parties, given that they are more likely to obtain third-party funding if the jurisprudence of local courts is reliable and arbitration friendly.

In this regard, it is key that the judiciary's change of attitude is accompanied by a strong political will to instate (or restore) confidence in arbitration as a means of dispute resolution and also in the judiciary in general, by fostering courts' independence from the executive power. This evidently forms part of a much broader and significant task that is extremely and urgently necessary to undertake in Argentina.

11

Judicial Control of Arbitral Awards in Australia*

Nobumichi Teramura, Luke Nottage, and James Morrison

1 INTRODUCTION

Geographical remoteness has not prevented Australia from pursuing a persistent ambition to become a major hub for international commercial arbitration (ICA). While regional competitors in the Asia-Pacific region such as Singapore and Hong Kong have already achieved great success in the arbitration world, Australia's 'Tyranny of Distance'[1] requires that extra efforts be made to attract ICA cases. Recent marketing from Austrade within the Australian government[2] emphasises the relative strengths of ICA in Australia: (1) a harmonised legal framework for ICA in line with international standards, (2) sophisticated arbitration institutions and (3) some of the world's leading arbitration practitioners.

First, as to legal framework, although Australia is a federation of six states and two commonwealth (Cth) territories, it recently implemented 'a bifurcated but harmonised arbitration legislative regime governing arbitration matters'[3] that seeks to keep pace with global trends in ICA. On the one hand, the International Arbitration Act 1974 (Cth) (IAA) is a federal statute regulating ICA proceedings held in the territory of Australia. It gives force of law (s. 16) to the UNCITRAL Model Law on International Commercial Arbitration (Model Law) including almost all its 2006 revisions, with various other (mostly opt-out or default) provisions and elaborations. The IAA also implements the 1958 New York Convention on the Recognition and Enforcement of Foreign Arbitral Awards (NY Convention).[4] On the other hand, domestic arbitrations are governed by Uniform Commercial Arbitration Acts (Uniform Acts) enacted by each state and territory and which also give force of law to the Model Law. Section 2A of the Uniform Acts further provides that, in their interpretation, 'regard is to be had to the need to promote so far as practicable uniformity between the application of [the Uniform Acts] to domestic commercial arbitrations and the application of the provisions of the Model Law'.[5] The Uniform Acts therefore aim to

---

* A version of this chapter was presented at the University of Hong Kong, July 15, 2019, for its project co-funded with the University of Sydney on New Frontiers for International Arbitration in the Asia-Pacific Region (http://blogs.usyd.edu.au/japaneselaw/2019/02/new_frontiers_in_intlarb.html). We thank Christian Santos, Associate at the Australian Centre for International Commercial Arbitration (ACICA) for helpful editorial and research assistance.
[1] GEOFFREY BLAINEY, THE TYRANNY OF DISTANCE: HOW DISTANCE SHAPED AUSTRALIA'S HISTORY (2001).
[2] AUSTRALIAN TRADE AND INVESTMENT COMMISSION, AUSTRALIA'S CAPABILITY IN INTERNATIONAL COMMERCIAL ARBITRATION (2018).
[3] Albert Monichino & Luke Nottage, *Australia Country Update*, 2018 ASIAN DISPUTE REVIEW 131, 131 (2018).
[4] *Id.* at 132.
[5] *Id.*

promote the development of a single body of jurisprudence regulating commercial arbitration (both domestic and international) in Australia,[6] in conformity with international standards, the Model Law and the NY Convention.

Second, as to sophisticated arbitration institutions, several institutions do now offer dispute resolution service and facilities in the country's major cities: the Australian Centre for International Commercial Arbitration (ACICA), arguably the leading institution particularly for ICA; the Australian Maritime and Transport Arbitration Commission (AMTAC); the Australian Disputes Centre (ADC); the Melbourne Commercial Arbitration and Mediation Centre (MCAMC); the David Malcolm Justice Centre; Perth Centre for Energy and Resources Arbitration (PCERA); and Resolution Institute, recently incorporating the Institute of Arbitrators and Mediators Australia (IAMA). In addition, the Chartered Institute of Arbitrators (CIArb) Australia provides lawyers with training opportunities for arbitration practice, working closely with those arbitration institutions, but it does not offer dispute resolution service.[7] Having a spread of various dispute resolution service providers in the major cities brings geographical convenience for a large continent island-nation like Australia. However, it makes for a crowded market in contrast to regional neighbours such as Singapore, Hong Kong and Malaysia where most public and private sector resources and energy have been poured into one dominant international arbitration centre (respectively, SIAC, HKIAC, and AIAC – previously called the Kuala Lumpur Regional Centre for Arbitration). Nonetheless, Australian arbitration institutions, especially ACICA, have been diligently trying to improve Australia's arbitration industry.[8]

Third, as to leading arbitration practitioners, Australia has long 'exported' arbitration lawyers worldwide. A number of prominent arbitrators were recently highlighted in Austrade's promotional brochure released by the Australian government when Sydney hosted in 2018 the Congress of the International Council of Commercial Arbitration.[9] Statistics prepared by the International Chamber of Commerce (ICC) further show that thirty-nine Australian arbitrators were confirmed or appointed for ICC arbitrations in 2017.[10] Australian arbitrators make up only 2.6 per cent of total ICC appointments, but the population of the country is around 25 million and so much smaller than that of other major arbitration players such as the United Kingdom, France, the United States and Germany, which are also geographically much closer to the ICC headquarters in Paris.[11] Further, recent statistics from the London Court of International Arbitration show that in 2018 there were 317 cases, in which eleven Australian arbitrators were appointed.[12]

Overall, those three features of ICA in Australia do suggest that the country has considerable potential to attract ICA cases. To ensure that this goes beyond a mere possibility, the Australian government, judiciary and legal profession are making quite concerted efforts to expand the comparatively low numbers of Australia-seated ICA cases. The government has recently become more active in marketing Australia-based ICA in and out of the country.[13] The judiciary has

---

[6] *Id.*

[7] Luke Nottage & Richard Garnett, *Australian Centre for International Commercial Arbitration (ACICA), in* ENCYCLOPEDIA OF INTERNATIONAL PROCEDURAL LAW 12 (2019).

[8] ACICA is currently revising its 2016 arbitration rules.

[9] Australian Trade and Investment Commission mentions Gavan Griffith AO QC, Doug Jones AO, Peter McQueen, Karyl Nairn QC, Michael Pryles AO PBM, Kim Rooney, James Spigelman AC QC and Professor Jeffrey Waincymer.

[10] Julien Fouret, et al., *2017 ICC Dispute Resolution Statistics,* 2018 ICC DISPUTE RESOLUTION BULLETIN 51 (2018).

[11] *Id.*

[12] *See* 2018 Annual Case Work Report, LONDON COURT OF INTERNATIONAL ARBITRATION (Apr. 1, 2019), www.lcia.org/News/2018-annual-casework-report.aspx. Of the 317 cases, 19 involved Australian parties and 1 applied Australian law.

[13] Luke Nottage & Nobumichi Teramura, *Australia's (In)Capacity in International Commercial Arbitration,* KLUWER ARBITRATION BLOG (Sept. 20, 2018), http://arbitrationblog.kluwerarbitration.com/2018/09/20/australias-incapacity-international-commercial-arbitration/. For further indications of ICA cases involving hearings within (Western) Australia,

generally tried to issue pro-arbitration judgments particularly over the last ten years, and in public speeches or publications leading judges have been actively summarising and promoting Australian developments both domestically and worldwide.[14] However, the court system has structural challenges, due to the shared ICA jurisdiction of state and territory courts alongside the federal courts, compared to the unitary system in Hong Kong and Singapore. Statistical evidence revealed that case disposition times in court-related ICA matters under the IAA did not improve markedly after its 2010 amendments, even in the Federal Court of Australia.[15] However, comparable statistics are unavailable regarding ICA-related court proceedings in major regional venues such as Singapore or Hong Kong, and perfection is never attainable anyway.

As for the legal profession, ICA has been actively promoted by the overarching Law Council of Australia,[16] various state-based law societies[17] and recently the Australian Bar Association (ABA). In December 2018 the ABA announced that its past president and former judge of the Federal Court, Hon Roger Gyles AO QC, would lead an inquiry into challenges and opportunities for Australian barristers engaging in ICA both within Australia and abroad, especially in the Asia-Pacific region. His report was due by May 1, 2019, and reportedly[18] this initiative builds on the recent Austrade Report on Australia's Capability in International Commercial Arbitration and is consistent with the government's push for the expansion of the export of Australian services into the Asia and Pacific regions. At the recent national conference of the Australian Bar Association calls were made by Federal Court Chief Justice James Allsop AO and leading Australian silk,

---

compared to more plentiful opportunities for Australian lawyers becoming involved in other ICA (and domestic arbitration) related proceedings, *see also WA Arbitration Initiative: Perth Arbitration Survey*, FRANCIS BURT CHAMBERS (2019), https://www.francisburt.com.au/waarbitrationinitiative.

[14] See Chief Justice James Allsop, *The Role of Law in International Commercial Arbitration* FEDERAL COURT OF AUSTRALIA (speech, Chartered Institute of Arbitrators Inaugural Annual Lecture, Oct. 15, 2018), www.fedcourt.gov.au/digital-law-library/judges-speeches/chief-justice-allsop/allsop-cj-20181015; Chief Justice James Allsop, *Commercial and Investor-State Arbitration: The Importance of Recognising Their Difference* FEDERAL COURT OF AUSTRALIA (speech, ICCA Congress, Apr. 16, 2018), www.fedcourt.gov.au/__data/assets/pdf_file/0003/49413/16_April_2018.pdf; Chief Justice James Allsop & Justice Clyde Croft, *The Role of Courts in Australia's Arbitration Regime* FEDERAL COURT OF AUSTRALIA (speech, Commercial CPD Seminar Series, Nov. 11, 2018), www.fedcourt.gov.au/digital-law-library/judges-speeches/chief-justice-allsop/allsop-cj-20151111; Chief Justice Allsop, *International Commercial Arbitration – The Courts and the Rule of Law in the Asia Pacific Region* FEDERAL COURT OF AUSTRALIA (speech, Annual Global Arbitration Review, Nov. 11, 2014), www.fedcourt.gov.au/digital-law-library/judges-speeches/chief-justice-allsop/allsop-cj-20141111; and Chief Justice James Allsop & Justice Clyde Croft, *Judicial Support of Arbitration* FEDERAL COURT OF AUSTRALIA (speech, APRAG Tenth Anniversary Conference, Mar. 28, 2014), www.fedcourt.gov.au/digital-law-library/judges-speeches/chief-justice-allsop/allsop-cj-20140328.

[15] Diana Hu & Luke Nottage, *The International Arbitration Act Matters in Australia: Where to Litigate and Why (Not)*, 35 THE ARBITRATOR AND MEDIATOR 91 (2016), https://ssrn.com/abstract=2862256.

[16] For example, through submissions to parliamentary inquiries to amend the IAA and Uniform Acts, and events including annual conferences: *see 6th International Arbitration Conference*, LAW COUNCIL OF AUSTRALIA (Oct. 17, 2018), www.lawcouncil.asn.au/event/6th-international-arbitration-conference.

[17] *See, for example*, chapter 9 of *FLIP: The Future of Law and Innovation in the Profession*, LAW SOCIETY OF NEW SOUTH WALES (2017), https://lawsociety.cld.bz/online-flip-report.

[18] See *Inquiry by Roger Gyles QC on International Arbitration*, AUSTRALIAN BAR ASSOCIATION (Dec. 13, 2018), https://austbar.asn.au/news-media/inquiry-by-roger-gyles-qc-on-international-arbitration. Some preliminary views were outlined in *Inquiry by Hon. Roger Gyles AO QC on International Arbitration*, AUSTRALIAN BAR ASSOCIATION (July 9, 2019), https://austbar.asn.au/uploads/pdfs/conference-papers/Hon_R_Gyles_AO_QC_Report_09_07_19.pdf. Recommendations included: promoting a whole-of-government approach, such as public contracts specifying Australia as seat, hearing venue and/or governing law; practical reforms (including visas and taxation of arbitrators, amendments to 'consumer' law); better facilities (new, or upgraded in Sydney, Melbourne and perhaps Perth); possible use of Federal Court facilities for hearings and its sole jurisdiction in international arbitration matters; and a wider role for ACICA (including even possibly a move to the national capital in Canberra). *Compare also* generally, Allsop, 'International Commercial Arbitration' *supra* note 14.

Allan Myers AC QC for the ABA to lead a national approach in the area of international practice and arbitration in particular.

Against this backdrop, the rest of this chapter argues that Australia has significantly improved the legal environment for ICA in line with international standards, focusing on the main topics identified for this cross-jurisdictional research: arbitrator bias, conflicts of interests, procedural irregularities and arbitrator misconduct during proceedings, arbitrability (objective arbitrability), judicial interpretation of arbitration clauses (subjective arbitrability) and enforceability of arbitral awards.

2 ARBITRATOR BIAS

In line with Art. 12 of the Model Law, under the IAA, arbitrators (including prospective ones) are required to disclose any circumstances likely to give rise to justifiable doubts as to their impartiality, independence and bias; similar requirements apply, for example, where parties adopt the ACICA Arbitration Rules.[19] This disclosure obligation continues throughout arbitral proceedings, and challenges can be made (only) if circumstances exist giving rise to justifiable doubts.[20]

The 'justifiable doubts' test is defined in s. 18A of the IAA, added in the 2010 reform: there must be a 'real danger' of bias on the part of the arbitrator(s) in conducting the arbitration.[21] The latest and fullest analysis of this test can be found in *Hui v. Esposito Holdings Pty Ltd*.[22] The award debtors in an ICA seated in Melbourne, Australia, applied to set aside parts of two partial awards and remove the sole arbitrator, alleging that the arbitrator prejudged the subject matter under Arts. 12 and 34(2)(b)(ii) of the Model Law. Partially accepting the allegation, Beach J held that the correct approach for examining whether there is a 'real danger of bias' is to be done from the perspective of a 'reasonable bystander', instead of the perspective of the court.[23] Accordingly, the applicable legal test is 'whether a reasonable person would no longer have confidence in the arbitrator's ability to come to a fair and balanced conclusion on the issues if remitted'.[24] That test was well satisfied in this case because the arbitrator: 'stepped well outside the bounds of the preliminary hearing', 'decided various substantive questions in a final manner without giving some of the parties an opportunity to be heard' and 'offered a retrospective analysis and in some respects a questionable recounting of what had previously occurred'.[25]

This judgment does not necessarily indicate that Australian courts are reverting to interpreting the arbitration legislation in a way inimical to arbitration or in a parochial way. The applicable legal test taken by Beach J is similar in approach to the one taken in United Kingdom. Beach J, citing *Lovell Partnerships (Northern Ltd v. AW Construction plc*,[26] agreed with the test and approach applied by Mance J (as he then was).[27] Beach J carefully pointed out that a supervisory court, in determining whether to vacate an ICA award or to remove an arbitrator, must understand that only consequences with real unfairness or real practical injustice may justify

---

[19] International Arbitration Act 1974 (Cth) s 18A; and Art. 16.3 of ACICA Arbitration Rules.
[20] Art. 12(2) of the Model Law.
[21] See generally Sam Luttrell, *Recent Developments in Model Law Plus Lawmaking: Australia Enacts the 'Real Danger' Test for Bias Challenges to Arbitrators*, 26 ARBITRATION INTERNATIONAL 625–632 (2010).
[22] [2017] FCA 648.
[23] However, he admitted that this difference in perspective may not cause any practical consequences.
[24] [2017] FCA 648 at [242].
[25] *Id.* at 247.
[26] (1996) 81 BLR 83.
[27] [2017] FCA 648 at [242].

such a remedy, because of the consensual nature of and the need for commercial efficiency in ICA. Exceptionally, however, Beach J concluded that 'even accommodating such robustness underpinned by the necessary commercial conservatism to ensure that contracting parties are bound to their choice of mechanism, I cannot overlook the significant flaws in the present arbitral process'.[28]

Australian courts' cautious attitude towards bias challenges was also expressed in *Sino Dragon Trading Ltd* v. *Noble Resources International Pte Ltd*.[29] The contract contained an arbitration clause requiring that disputes be resolved by arbitration in Australia. Despite the fact that Sino Dragon (a Hong Kong party) was uncooperative in appointing the arbitrators and ignored communications from Noble Resources (a Singaporean party) and the appointing authority (New Zealand arbitrator David Williams QC who was designated by the secretary general of the Permanent Court of Arbitration at Hague), Sino Dragon later filed a challenge against the three arbitrators[30] with the appointing authority on the grounds of alleged cultural bias (the three arbitrators were living in Sydney but Sino Dragon was a Hong Kong incorporated company), potential conflict of interest (all of the arbitrators and counsel for Noble, incorporated in Singapore, had offices in Sydney) and other procedural issues. Being unsuccessful in the challenge procedure before the appointing authority, Sino Dragon sought removal of one arbitrator through the Federal Court of Australia. Edelman J (later promoted to the High Court of Australia) refrained from reexamining the bias challenge, pointing out that Sino Dragon failed to observe the challenge procedure agreed by the parties under Art. 13 of the Model Law. Counsel for Sino Dragon nevertheless submitted that the court had a common law power to remove an arbitrator. Edelman J rejected such an argument because such an implied common law power would be contrary to Art. 5 of the Model Law, which provides that in 'matters governed by this Law, no court shall intervene except where so provided in this Law', and to recognise an unrestricted common law regime to challenge an arbitrator would undermine the efficacy of the carefully constructed Art. 13 of the Model Law.[31]

Sino Dragon raised the issue of arbitrator impartiality again in its challenge to the final award in *Sino Dragon Trading Ltd* v. *Noble Resources International Pte Ltd*.[32] In that case, the Hong Kong party claimed that as there was a reasonable apprehension of bias in the two arbitrators (Mr Bonnell and Mr Hoyle), the award was in conflict with the 'public policy' of Australia under Art. 34(2)(b)(ii) of the UNCITRAL Model Law. Beach J rejected the allegation, noting: '[t]he vague connections between King & Wood Mallesons (KWM) China and Mr Bonnell are insufficient to create a real danger of bias' because Mr Bonnell was a partner of KWM Australia, which was financially independent from KWM China that acted in a separate proceeding on behalf of a different subsidiary of the Noble Group. Further, Mr Hoyle had not worked for Mr Bonnell in the predecessor law firm of KWM Australia since 2009 and had no connection with KWM China or Noble Resources when appointed as chairperson by Mr Bonell and the other Sydney-based arbitrator.

---

[28] *Id.* at 6.
[29] [2015] FCA 1028.
[30] Sydney barrister Terry Mehigan, Sydney arbitration lawyer Max Bonnell and Sydney-based barrister Jonathan Kay Hoyle.
[31] However, some Australian commentators suggest that Art. 5 of the Model Law does not prohibit national courts from staying arbitral proceedings where procedural unfairness would occur. The appropriate scope of the national courts' residual authority is still under debate. *See, generally,* Sam Luttrell & Isuru Devendra, *Inherent Jurisdiction and Implied Power to Stay Proceedings in Aid of Arbitration: 'A Nice Question*, 32 JOURNAL OF INTERNATIONAL ARBITRATION 493 (2015).
[32] [2016] FCA 1131.

3 CONFLICT OF INTEREST

Australian jurists and practitioners have been well aware of the IBA Guidelines on Conflicts of Interest in International Arbitration, first published in 2004, as parameters addressing conflicts of interest in ICA. Article 11.4 of the ACICA Rules 2016 provides that '[on the issue of appointment of arbitrators], the Arbitral Tribunal and the parties may have regard to the International Bar Association Guidelines on Conflicts of Interest in International Arbitration in the version current at the commencement of the arbitration'. This express reference was quite innovative when the ACICA Rules came into force in 2005.[33] Although the rules were developed by a drafting committee, the then ACICA board president had been involved in the IBA Working Group for the preparation of the guidelines.[34]

Australian case law has referred to the IBA Guidelines, but only recently and occasionally. This may due to the limited numbers of ICA cases filed annually in Australia and even fewer challenges in courts, although there are significant numbers of judgments contesting enforcement of foreign awards that might raise objections to arbitrator neutrality based, for example, on public policy grounds. Notably, in *Sino Dragon Trading Ltd v. Noble Resources International Pte Ltd*,[35] Beach J referred to the IBA Guidelines to confirm the qualification of Mr Bonnell as an arbitrator, stating that 'the matters raised by Sino Dragon against Mr Bonnell fell into the "Green List" as matters not requiring disclosure let alone disqualification'.[36] It seems that other IAA judgments have not referred to the IBA Guidelines, and Australia certainly has no equivalent to the 2016 English High Court judgment questioning automatic disqualification in a 'non-waivable Red List' situation.[37]

4 PROCEDURAL IRREGULARITIES AND ARBITRATOR MISCONDUCT DURING PROCEEDINGS

Both the IAA and the Uniform Acts are based on the Model Law, so a party may request an Australian court to set aside an arbitral award under Art. 34. For example, he or she may invoke, as a ground to annul the arbitral award, a lack of due process (or violation of procedural public policy) during arbitral proceedings (Art. 34(2)(a)(ii) and Art. 34(2)(b)(ii)) or the award being beyond the terms of the submission to arbitration (Art. 34(2)(a)(iii)). Like in other jurisdictions, various parties have attempted to vacate an arbitral award on such grounds. But they have usually failed because Australian courts have construed those grounds narrowly, particularly over the last decade.

---

[33] Nottage & Garnett, *supra* note 7, at 32; and Björn Gehle, *The Arbitration Rules of the Australian Centre for International Commercial Arbitration*, 13 The Vindobona Journal of International Commercial Law and Arbitration 251, 266 (2009).

[34] Leon Trakman, *The Impartiality and Independence of Arbitrators Reconsidered*, 10 International Arbitration Law Review 124, 124 (2007) (referring to Doug Jones).

[35] [2016] FCA 1131.

[36] *Id.* at 194.

[37] W Ltd v. M SDN MHD [2016] EWHC 422 (Comm), involving a barrister/arbitrator allegedly falling within para. 1.4 of the Guidelines ('the arbitrator or his or her firm regularly advises the party, or an affiliate of the party, and the arbitrator or his or her firm derives significant financial income therefrom'). For a critique of this judgment by an English lawyer, subsequently based in Sydney and a member of the ACICA Rules Committee, *see* Nick Longley, *IBA Guidelines on Conflict of Interest: The Traffic Lights Flash Amber*, HFW (Apr. 2016), http://www.hfw.com/IBA-guidelines-on-conflict-of-interest-April-2016.

4.1 Evidence and Hearings

A landmark case in Australia is *TCL Air Conditioner (Zhongshan) Co Ltd v. Castel Electronics Pty Ltd*.[38] TCL (a Chinese company) sought to set aside an arbitral award issued in Australia, arguing that the tribunal in a Victoria-seated arbitration breached the rules of natural justice (and therefore public policy, as discussed Section 6.2). This was allegedly due to making findings of fact on the assessment of damages in the absence of probative evidence, or without affording the appellant the opportunity to make submissions in respect of the proposed findings. The Full Court upheld the Federal Court's rejection of this challenge, stating:

> One can, at the outset, accept without the slightest hesitation, that the making of a factual finding by a tribunal without probative evidence may reveal such a breach. This would be so when the fact was critical, was never the subject of attention by the parties to the dispute, and where the making of the finding occurred without the parties having an opportunity to deal with it. That is unfairness; the parties have not been given an opportunity to be heard. *It does not follow, however, that any wrong factual conclusion that may be seen to lack probative evidence (and so amount to legal error) should necessarily, and without more, be characterised as a breach of the rules of natural justice in this context.*[39]

The Full Court continued that an international arbitration award would not be annulled unless there was 'real unfairness or real practical injustice' in the conduct of the arbitration in lieu of established rules of natural justice or procedural fairness. However, the Full Court emphasised that this would not ordinarily involve a detailed reexamination of evidence or the tribunal's fact-finding process and reasoning.

This case clarified that a lack of evidence does not automatically trigger a breach of the rules of natural justice, and, from a broad perspective, the pro-arbitration approach adopted by the Federal Court of Australia.[40] Other Australian courts have followed the judgment, even if not bound to do so. One of the most recent examples, although brought under the Queensland enactment of the Uniform Acts, is *Mango Boulevard Pty Ltd v. Mio Art Pty Ltd & Anor*.[41] In this case, the arbitration arose from a joint venture for the development of land, which included a share sale agreement. At first instance,[42] Mango sought unsuccessfully to set aside the award, relying on Arts. 34(2)(a)(ii) and 34(2)(b)(ii) of the Commercial Arbitration Act 2013 (Qld), based on Art. 34 of the Model Law. Mango then sought to overturn the first-instance decision in the Queensland Court of Appeal. The point at issue was the fact that the arbitrator adopted a share-valuation methodology not advanced by either party and, from Mango's view, that fact amounted to the violation of due process (natural justice) and public policy. The court dismissed the appeal and maintained the arbitral award, carefully relying on the 'real unfairness or real practical injustice' test developed in the *TCL* case. The majority of the court held that the

---

[38] [2014] FCAFC 83. The many court cases associated with this quite rare example of an Australia-seated ICA are outlined in Luke Nottage, *International Commercial Arbitration in Australia: What's New and What's Next?*', 30 JOURNAL OF INTERNATIONAL ARBITRATION 465 (2013), with a longer version at Luke Nottage, *International Commercial Arbitration in Australia: What's New and What's Next?*, in INTERNATIONAL COMMERCIAL LAW AND ARBITRATION: PERSPECTIVES 30–341 (Nye Perram ed., 2014), https://ssrn.com/abstract=2393232.
[39] Nottage, *supra* note 38, at 83 (emphasis added).
[40] Albert Monichino & Alex Fawke, *International Arbitration in Australia: 2013/2014 in Review*, 25 AUSTRALIAN DISPUTE RESOLUTION JOURNAL 187, 195 (2014).
[41] [2018] QCA 39.
[42] Mango Boulevard Pty Ltd v. Mio Art Pty Ltd [2017] QSC 87.

arbitrator clearly mentioned the possibility of his reasoning during final addresses and that 'it could not be said that ultimately, the appellant was denied an opportunity to argue a case in response to it'.[43]

Amasya Enterprises Pty Ltd v. Asta Developments (Aust) Pty Ltd[44] is another recent example indicating how the restrictive interpretation of public policy developed in IAA case law is being paralleled even in judgments under the Uniform Acts. Amasya and Asta entered into a building contract containing an arbitration clause. The building project stalled and an arbitration was commenced under the law of Victoria. The sole arbitrator decided in favour of Asta so that the company applied to enforce the award under the Commercial Arbitration Act 2011 (Vic). Amasya requested to set aside the award under s. 34 of the Act, and alternatively sought to resist enforcement of the award under s. 36 (ss. 34 and 36 of the Commercial Arbitration Act are based on Arts. 34 and 36 of the Model Law). In particular, Amasya argued that it was not given a reasonable opportunity to present its case under ss. 34(2)(a)(ii) and 36(1)(a)(ii), and claimed that the lack of procedural fairness in relation to issuing the award implied that the award conflicted with the public policy of Victoria under ss. 34(2)(b)(ii) and 36(1)(b)(ii). The main point of Amasya's allegation was that the award was neither based on facts articulated in Asta's notice of dispute nor argued during the hearing. Croft J rejected these arguments and granted Asta's application for enforcement. Deciding in the framework of 'real unfairness or real practical injustice' test,[45] Croft J concluded that Amasya had the chance to deal with Asta's new argument in the one-day oral hearing but decided to ignore it for its own reasons. Like the other two cases mentioned, '[t]his decision demonstrates that the objecting party must be able [to] demonstrate real practical unfairness before it can succeed on [the ground that the losing party has not been afforded a reasonable opportunity to present its case]'.[46]

4.2 Exceeding Power

Australian courts are cautious in deciding that an arbitral tribunal exceeded its authority to determine disputes. However, in *Hui v. Esposito Holdings Pty Ltd*,[47] an issue was whether the arbitrator stepped beyond the scope of the preliminary hearings and thereby exceeded his jurisdiction. Accepting this allegation by Hui, the court decided to set aside part of the first partial award and removed the arbitrator. Closely examining the facts, Beach J first pointed out that the arbitrator repeatedly confirmed before and during the preliminary hearing that he would not adjudicate on the merits of set-off defences raised by Hui.[48] However, as Beach J noted, there was a stark contrast between the arbitrator's first set of reasons in the first partial award and Esposito's written submissions filed before the preliminary hearing. His Honour then stated that '[t]hat contrast alone is a powerful demonstration that the arbitrator travelled well beyond what was contemplated as the scope of the preliminary hearing'.[49] Once again, however, this case was quite exceptional. The arbitral procedure adopted by the arbitrator had inherent

---

[43] Mango Boulevard Pty Ltd v. Mio Art Pty Ltd [2017] QSC 87 at [106].
[44] [2016] VSC 326.
[45] *Id.* at 48.
[46] Albert Monichino & Alex Fawke, *International Arbitration in Australia: 2015/2016 in Review*, 27 AUSTRALIAN DISPUTE RESOLUTION JOURNAL 211 (2016).
[47] [2017] FCA 648.
[48] *Id.* at 162.
[49] *Id.* at 94.

dangers in that he sought to determine certain questions before the filing of defences by Hui.[50] That is why Beach J cautiously held that the tribunal exceeded jurisdiction.

4.3 Other Matters

The rigorous application of grounds for vacating awards nowadays is based on the expectation of Australian courts that arbitrators in the country maintain high professional standards. For instance, the bar association and law societies in Australian states and territories regulate the conduct of legal practitioners in each jurisdiction (e.g., barristers' rules and law society's code of conduct for solicitors). Lawyers acting as arbitrators need to follow these professional rules, and most arbitrators in Australia are lawyers or former judges.

5 OBJECTIVE ARBITRABILITY

The scope of what matters are subject to settlement in arbitration is not defined in the IAA and the Uniform Acts.[51] Accordingly, arbitrability must be decided 'by examining express or implied legislative intent across the statute book, as well as the background common law'.[52] A useful starting point is provided by the Australian High Court in *Tanning Research Laboratories Inc v. O'Brien*.[53] The apex court held that to be arbitrated 'the controversy must be one falling within the scope of the arbitration agreement and, perhaps, *one relating to rights which are not required to be determined exclusively by the exercise of judicial power*'.[54]

The discussion on arbitrability was further refined in *Comandate Marine Corp v. Pan Australia Shipping Pty Ltd*.[55] The Full Federal Court elaborated on the notion of arbitrability under the IAA, in relation to the NYC and the Model Law:[56]

> First, the common element to the notion of non-arbitrability was that there was a sufficient element of legitimate public interest in these subject matters making the enforceable private resolution of disputes concerning them outside the national court system inappropriate. Secondly, the identification and control of these subjects was the legitimate domain of national legislatures and courts. Thirdly, in none of the *travaux préparatoires* [of the NY Convention and the Model Law] was there discussion that the notion of a matter not being capable of settlement by arbitration was to be understood by reference to whether an otherwise arbitrable type of dispute or claim will be ventilated fully in the arbitral forum applying the laws chosen by the parties to govern the dispute in the same way and to the same extent as it would be ventilated in a national court applying national laws.

In other words, the court admitted that whether subject matters are capable of arbitration depends on whether they involve a sufficient element of public interest, and clarified that the

---

[50] Albert Monichino & Alex Fawke, *International Arbitration in Australia: 2016/2017 in Review*, 28 AUSTRALIAN DISPUTE RESOLUTION JOURNAL 215 (2018).
[51] Even though at least one public submission called for a listing to be included in the amendments enacted in 2010. See Luke Nottage & Richard Garnett, *The Top 20 Things to Change in or Around the Australia's International Arbitration Act*, in INTERNATIONAL ARBITRATION IN AUSTRALIA 179–184 (Luke Nottage & Richard Garnett eds.,2010).
[52] James Morrison & Luke Nottage, *Country Report on Australia for: International Commercial Arbitration – An Asia-Pacific Perspective*, 14 SYDNEY LAW SCHOOL RESEARCH PAPER 1, 48 (2014).
[53] (1990) 169 CLR 332.
[54] (1990) 169 CLR 332 (emphasis added).
[55] [2006] FCAFC 192 (Dec. 20, 2006).
[56] *Id.* at 200.

sufficiency is determined by national legislatures and municipal courts. Nonetheless, Australian judges have addressed non-arbitrability claims in a rigorous manner, as the following discussion demonstrates.

5.1 Competition Law Issues

Pure competition law issues have normally been regarded as involving wider public interests – this being non-arbitrable – due to their impact on third parties.[57] For instance, again in *Comandate Marine Corp* v. *Pan Australia Shipping Pty Ltd*,[58] Allsop J remarked that '[t]he types of disputes which national laws may see as not arbitrable ... are disputes such as those concerning ... anti-trust and competition disputes'.[59] Later, in *Nicola* v. *Ideal Image Development Corporation Incorporated*,[60] Perram J held that '[s]uits concerning competition law have frequently been cited as examples of claims unsuitable, by reason of public policy, for arbitration'.[61] According to commentators, examples of 'pure competition law issues' under Australian case law include, provisions regulating exclusive dealing, resale price maintenance, horizontal conduct or cartel conduct.[62]

By contrast, disputes unrelated to 'pure competition issues' may be regarded by Australian judges as subject to arbitration. For instance, in *Casaceli* v. *Natuzzi S.p.A.*,[63] the Australian dealer Casaceli alleged various violations of the Trade Practices Act 1974 (Cth) (TPA)[64] and its successor Australian Consumer Law (ACL),[65] including the legislative Franchise Code, in relation to an exclusive distributorship agreement with the Italian supplier Natuzzi S.p.A. providing for arbitration in Italy. Casaceli argued that the TPA and ACL claims were non-arbitrable, invoking the notion of arbitrability explained in *Comandate* case, but the court dismissed these objections and stayed its proceedings.[66] Jagot J stated:

> [T]he applicants sought to surround their claims with an aura of important public policy issues when, in substance, the dispute is a commercial cause between two companies involved in the international furniture trade by which one company seeks damages from another. The idea that a dispute of this character is only capable of resolution by an exercise of judicial power is far-fetched. Although the source of the claims is Australian legislation which serves important public policy objectives it is difficult to accept that the matter in this case is not precisely the type of matter where effect should be given to the intention of the parties to submit disputes between them arising out of contract regulating their overall commercial dealings, the Dealership Agreement, to arbitration. It is well settled that such claims are capable of settlement by arbitration.[67]

---

[57] Morrison & Nottage, *supra* note 52, at 49.
[58] [2006] FCAFC 192 (Dec. 20, 2006).
[59] *Id.* at 200.
[60] [2009] FCA 1177.
[61] [2009] FCA 1177 at [56].
[62] Morrison & Nottage, *supra* note 52, at 49; and Colette Downie, *Will Australia Trust Arbitrators with Antitrust?*, 30 JOURNAL OF INTERNATIONAL ARBITRATION 221 (2013).
[63] [2012] FCA 691 (June 29, 2012).
[64] Renamed the Competition and Consumer Act 2010 (Cth).
[65] Contained in Schedule 2 of the Competition and Consumer Act 2010 (Cth).
[66] [2012] FCA 691 (June 29, 2012).
[67] *Id.*

5.2 Consumer Transactions

Arbitrability of consumer transactions, namely business-to-consumer (B2C) contracts, is still open to debate in Australia. As mentioned, both the IAA and the Uniform Acts do not contain a provision defining arbitrability. The Model Law is not particularly useful to examine arbitrability of consumer transactions because it applies only to 'commercial arbitration' and the broad nonexclusive definition of *commercial* under the Model Law does not refer to B2C transactions.[68] In addition, the Australian Consumer Law (ACL) does not address arbitrability of consumer transactions. Further, the applicability of arbitration to B2C transactions is an issue that has not yet arisen in Australian municipal courts.[69] This is so at least in the context of a supplier dealing with a 'consumer' in the usual or narrow sense (as found, for example, generally in European Union consumer law), of an individual transacting for a nonbusiness purpose. The ACL (and earlier the TPA) is comparatively unusual in extending protection for 'consumer' transactions to various types of business-to-business (B2B) transactions,[70] where public interests are likely different from those in true B2C transactions. Overall, to analyse the arbitrability of consumer transactions requires, in accordance with the comment by Allsop J in the *Comandate* case, an examination of whether claims and rights on consumer transactions contain 'a sufficient element of legitimate public interest in these subject matters making the enforceable private resolution of disputes concerning them outside the national court system inappropriate'.[71]

Following Professor Richard Garnett,[72] the following sections examine three sets of issues arising under the ACL, especially in a cross-border context: misleading and deceptive conduct, consumer guarantees and unfair contract terms. The following discussion focuses on the most likely or controversial scenario involving an overseas-seated arbitration where parties have also agreed to apply a foreign law to their contract.

Similar problems afflict an Australia-seated ICA where the parties agree on foreign law, especially if they further specify that this is to the exclusion of the ACL. In fact, because the arbitrators may be more concerned about a successful challenge in local Australian courts over arbitrability (and public policy of the seat) if they uphold the parties' express choice of governing law, compared to arbitrators abroad if the parties instead chose a seat outside Australia, some commentators have long urged legislative reform to the IAA and/or the ACL to clarify the situation and thereby promote more Australia-seated arbitrations.[73] Along similar lines, in a very recent speech by a past president who prompted the ABA to commence an inquiry into means of

---

[68] Article 1(1) of the Model Law provides:

> Relationships of a commercial nature include, but are not limited to, the following transactions: any trade transaction for the supply or exchange of goods or services; distribution agreement; commercial representation or agency; factoring; leasing; construction of works; consulting; engineering; licensing; investment; financing; banking; insurance; exploitation agreement or concession; joint venture and other forms of industrial or business cooperation; and carriage of goods or passengers by air, sea, rail or road.

> It is evident that consumer transactions are not included in this list. Moreover, the drafters of the Model Law stated that the exclusion was deliberate. *See* HOWARD M. HOLTZMANN, A GUIDE TO THE UNCITRAL MODEL LAW ON INTERNATIONAL COMMERCIAL ARBITRATION: LEGISLATIVE HISTORY AND COMMENTARY (1989).

[69] Richard Garnett, *Arbitration of Cross-Border Consumer Transactions in Australia: A Way Forward?*, 39 SYDNEY LAW REVIEW 569, 569 (2017).
[70] Luke Nottage & Justin Malbon, *Introduction, in* CONSUMER LAW AND POLICY IN AUSTRALIA AND NEW ZEALAND 3–38 (Justin Malbon & Luke Nottage eds., 2013).
[71] (2006) 157 FCR 45 at 98.
[72] Garnett, *supra* note 69, at 578.
[73] Nottage & Garnett, *supra* note 51; Nottage, *supra* note 38; Luke Nottage & James Morrison, *Accessing and Assessing Australia's International Arbitration Act*, 34 JOURNAL OF INTERNATIONAL ARBITRATION 963 (2017).

expanding ICA work for Australian lawyers, Allan Myers argued that ACL provisions on misleading conduct were 'a reason many persons do not wish to have disputes determined according to Australian Law or in Australia'. Accordingly, he argued they should be amended to 'not apply to "commercial" as opposed to "consumer" transactions which have an international character, in each case where the transactions are regulated by agreements which exclude the effect of the statutory provisions' of the ACL.[74]

By contrast, no problem would arise regarding consumer protection if an Australian court recognises arbitrability of ACL claims in the context of domestic arbitration or Australia-seated ICA in which parties have agreed to apply the law of an Australian state or territory to govern their contract. In either of those situations, arbitral tribunals are required to apply Australian rules regulating pure-consumer transaction issues.

5.2.1 *Misleading and Deceptive Conduct*

Section 18 of the ACL (formerly s. 52 of the TPA) prohibits misleading and deceptive conduct by suppliers in trade or commerce, whether or not the counterparty is another commercial supplier or a consumer. (In some countries outside Australia, this sort of prohibition may be incorporated within competition law.) But it is still controversial whether this provision has an adequate public interest element. Similar issues arise concerning the provisions in the TPA, and since 2010 the ACL (ss. 20–22), which have gradually from the 1980s expanded the statutory prohibition of 'unconscionable conduct' in trade to B2B as well as B2C transactions.

In *Comandate*, Allsop J (as he then was) identified two kinds of policy considerations competing for application regarding the prohibition of misleading and deceptive conduct in trade. On the one hand, he acknowledged that the TPA is 'a statute of the highest importance' in the sphere of consumer protection in Australia. On the other hand, he also admitted that the requirement to enforce foreign arbitration agreement in s. 7 of the IAA (giving effect to NYC Art II) may trump the policy in the TPA.[75] The policy behind the IAA was based on international commercial considerations including the global support for ICA as a dispute settlement method bringing certainty for parties with respect to the agreed forum for dispute resolution. From Allsop J's view, the pro-arbitration policy under the IAA may prevail over the 'consumer' protection policy under the TPA (or now ACL).

However, that decision was made concerning B2B transactions instead of B2C transactions in the narrower (EU-like) sense. For the latter, the balance of competing public policy considerations identified by Allsop J would probably fall on the side of consumer protection, rather than of certainty of dispute resolution. As Garnett states, 'the drastic consequences to a consumer of losing their s 18 [of the ACL] rights in a foreign arbitration with (likely) no equivalent cause of action available under the governing law of the contract'.[76] Therefore, arbitrability of s. 18 ACL claims would not be justified in such a situation. This view can be supported by court forum selection cases such as *Knight v. Adventure Associates Pty Ltd*[77] and *Quinlan v. Safe International Forsakrings AB*.[78] In these cases, the courts refused to stay local court proceedings commenced by consumers for violation of s. 18 of the ACL, mainly because the consumers would be unable to invoke their s. 18 rights in the nonlocal proceedings.

---

[74] A. J. Myers, Commercial Law Stream Opening Address, Australian Bar Association and NSW Bar Association Biennial Conference, Sydney (Nov. 16, 2018), [37].
[75] (2006) 157 FCR 45 at 96.
[76] Garnett, *supra* note 69, at 578.
[77] [1999] NSWSC 861 (27 August 1999).
[78] [2005] FCA 1362 (Dec. 20, 2005).

In *Walter Rau Neusser Oel und Fett AG v. Cross Pacific Trading Ltd*,[79] which involved an agreement for arbitration with the seat outside Australia, the Federal Court granted a stay of court proceedings subject to the parties agreeing to resolve their ACL claims before the arbitral tribunal abroad. The case has been criticised by several commentators. Holmes and Brown argue the consequence of that decision is that the court can 'dictate to the parties what form their arbitration agreement would take as a condition [of] allowing them to arbitrate in accordance with their original agreement'.[80] It would also be practically difficult to confirm that the parties and foreign tribunal would follow such a requirement imposed on them by courts in Australia. Garnett points out that it is impossible for Australian courts to order foreign tribunals to apply a specific provision of law.[81] However, this approach could be followed by a future court (or law reformer) faced with narrowly defined B2C transactions raising misleading conduct allegations by individual consumers engaged in nonbusiness purposes.

Another argument that may allow arbitrability of s. 18 ACL claims even for such B2C transactions is to adopt the 'second-look' doctrine suggested in obiter dicta by the US Supreme Court in *Mitsubishi Motors Corp v. Soler Chrysler-Plymouth Inc*.[82] On this approach, an Australian court, after it has stayed its proceedings despite ACL allegations, may refuse to recognise or enforce any subsequent award on the grounds of public policy if the foreign arbitral tribunal in fact fails to apply ACL provisions.[83] However, this approach may not sufficiently address the imbalance between individual consumers and businesses because the former may be required to undertake expensive arbitration proceedings in a foreign country. This is particularly problematic if such consumers have assets there or in another (especially NY Convention) state, so the award creditor might seek to enforce the award there rather than in Australia.

In *Kraft Foods Group Brands LLC v. Bega Cheese Ltd*,[84] there was an application for an anti-arbitration injunction restraining an arbitration seated in New York, United States, while a parallel s. 18 ACL Australian Federal Court proceeding was commenced. The dispute centred on the ownership of the 'trade dress' or 'get up' of a particular design of peanut butter jar, which Kraft licensed to Mondelez International Inc. (Mondelez) in a Master License and Ownership Agreement (Master Agreement) that contained an arbitration agreement. Bega purchased Mondelez, including the peanut butter business and acquired the rights and obligations in respect of the brand license under the Master Agreement. It is alleged that Bega advertisements, which included the Kraft trademark being replaced with the Bega trademark, contained false or misleading representations. Kraft commenced Australian Federal Court proceedings for contravention of s. 18 of the ACL and later commenced an arbitration against Bega. Prompted by Kraft's arbitration, Bega immediately filed an application in the Australian Federal Court for an anti-arbitration injunction.

O'Callaghan J held that the ownership of the goodwill and trade dress was central to both the alleged breach of the Master Agreement in the arbitration and whether the alleged representations were false or misleading in breach of the ACL. Further, O'Callaghan J held that there was substantial degree of overlap between the two proceedings, if they both continued, there would be a real risk of inconsistent findings on the critical question of who owns the goodwill in the

---

[79] [2005] FCA 1102 at [111] (Aug. 15, 2005).
[80] MALCOLM HOLMES & CHESTER BROWN, THE INTERNATIONAL ARBITRATION ACT 1974: A COMMENTARY 57 (2d ed. 2015).
[81] Garnett, *supra* note 69, at 579.
[82] 473 US 614 (1985).
[83] Nottage & Garnett, *supra* note 51, at 166.
[84] [2018] FCA 549.

trade dress or get up. This risk justified an anti-arbitration injunction to protect the Federal Court's proceedings. In finding there was a substantive nexus between the Master Agreement and the contraventions of the ACL, O'Callaghan J reviewed recent Australian case law which made clear the correct general approach to the construction of arbitration clauses, including that (1) parties do not intend to have possible disputes that may arise heard in two places; and (2) arbitration agreements should be construed with a broad, liberal and flexible approach.

5.2.2 Consumer Guarantees

The second issue that may affect the discussion on arbitrability of ACL claims is consumer guarantees. ACL provides mandatory 'consumer guarantees', for example that goods be of acceptable quality (s. 54) and fit for pre-disclosed purpose (s. 55). These apply not only to B2C but also many B2B transactions (e.g., where each supply of goods is under a statutory threshold value and not for resupply or using up in manufacturing.) Section 64 of the ACL states that the guarantees cannot be excluded, restricted or modified by contract. One question is whether s. 64 is violated if an agreement is added providing for arbitration abroad, where a tribunal may potentially ignore the ACL. The problem becomes acute if the parties also add a governing law provision requiring the tribunal to apply a specified foreign law (perhaps even stating: only that law, and to the exclusion of the ACL). In the latter respect, however, s. 67 of the ACL does state:

(a) the proper law of a contract for the supply of goods or services to a consumer would be the law of any part of Australia but for a term of the contract that provides otherwise; or
(b) a contract for the supply of goods or services to a consumer contains a term that purports to substitute, or has the effect of substituting, the following provisions for all or any of the provisions of this Division:
  (i) the provisions of the law of a country other than Australia;
  (ii) the provisions of the law of a State or a Territory;
  (iii) the provisions of this Division apply in relation to the supply under the contract despite that term.

It would seem from s. 67(a), unchanged from the TPA, that the legislature intended some scope for parties to choose the application of a foreign law. But a recent decision of Edelman J (before his promotion to the High Court), which was upheld by the Full Federal Court, found that s. 67(b) prevails as a mandatory rule and so an Australian court must always apply the ACL consumer guarantees.[85] Edelman J the legislative intention of protecting consumers, which in this case were individuals purchasing online gaming services. A different result might apply in a case involving B2B rather than B2C transactions. That said, even in respect of a B2C transaction, the New South Wales Supreme Court was recently prepared to stay its proceedings in deference to an agreement entered into by an individual consumer in Australia (booking a hotel room in Paris) consenting to the exclusive jurisdiction of the courts and the governing substantive law of Singapore.[86]

5.2.3 Unfair Contract Terms

The situation is also uncertain regarding provisions rendering void unfair standard-form contract terms, inspired by EU consumer law, which were extended nationwide in 2010 through the ACL

---

[85] Australian Competition and Consumer Commission (ACCC) v. Valve Corp (No 3) (2016) 337 ALR 647; and [2016] FCA 196.
[86] Gonzalez v. Agoda Company Pty Ltd [2017] NSWSC 1133.

(Part 2-3). There is no provision like s. 67 attempting to deal with agreements purporting to apply a foreign governing law. Nor is there any provision regarding parties' choice of foreign arbitration (or choice of foreign court). There is only s. 25(k) indicating that 'a term that limits, or has the effect of limiting, one party's right to sue another party' *may* be unfair under the general test set out in s. 24. A party seeking to void a clause providing for foreign arbitration under s. 23 is likely to be more successful if an individual consumer contracting for a nonbusiness purpose (to which this Part 2-3 has applied from its inception) as opposed to a 'small business' (to which Part 2-3 was extended by amendment in 2016).

5.3 *Other Arbitrability Issues*

Arbitrability concerning other subject matters in Australian courts is also somewhat complicated. Some state courts have allowed arbitrability, without paying detailed attention to practical considerations. For instance, in *Rinehart* v. *Welker*,[87] involving a domestic arbitration with one of Australia's richest businesspeople in a dispute with family members, the New South Wales Court of Appeal held that a dispute concerning removal of trustee was arbitrable, in spite of the arbitrator lacking practical authority to remove the trustee. Moreover, in *Larkden Pty Ltd* v. *Lloyd Energy Systems Pty Ltd*[88] adopting the CAA 2010 (NSW), the New South Wales Supreme Court held that the arbitrators could decide the rights and obligations of parties to a licensing contract regarding ownership of patents, despite the fact that only the commissioner of patents could actually grant such patents under *the* Patents Act 1900 (Cth).[89]

In contrast, some other state courts have interpreted arbitrability restrictively, without adequately respecting the express terms of relevant statutes. In *Siemens Ltd* v. *Origin Energy Uranquinty Power Pty Ltd*,[90] the New South Wales Supreme Court denied the arbitrability of applications by contactors to recover unpaid amounts under s. 15(2)(a)(i) of the Building and Construction Industry Security of Payment Act 1999 (NSW) (SOP), although this provision did not expressly exclude arbitration and other provisions of the Act had expressly permitted arbitration.[91] The observation below by Ball J is difficult to follow (emphasis added):

> [Section] 15(2)(a)(i) specifically says that the claimant may bring proceedings in any court of competent jurisdiction. In doing so, it gives the claimant a right. Section 34 of the SOP ... makes it clear that the claimant cannot contract out of that right. Elsewhere, the [SOP] recognises that disputes under construction contracts may be the subject of arbitration. In particular, ... , s 32(3) confers powers on arbitrators (as well as courts). However, s 15(2)(a)(i) confers a right to bring a claim in a court. It makes no reference to arbitration. If the legislature had intended the section to include an arbitration, it would have specifically said something about arbitration in the section, as it did in s 32(3). In my opinion, a provision of an arbitration agreement that prevents a party from exercising a right under s 15(2)(a)(i) to bring proceedings in a court of competent jurisdiction is, to that extent, void under s 34 of the SOP.[92]

His Honour's point seems to be that the subject matter is not arbitrable because s. 15(2)(a)(i) of the SOP does not expressly confer on parties the right to bring claims in arbitration. Yet, as stated

---

[87] [2012] NSWCA 95 (New South Wales Court of Appeal).
[88] (2011) 279 ALR 772 (New South Wales Supreme Court).
[89] Nottage & Morrison, *supra* note 73, at 987.
[90] (2011) NSWLR 398 (New South Wales Supreme Court).
[91] (2011) NSWLR 398 at [41] (New South Wales Supreme Court; and Building and Construction Industry Security of Payment Act 1999 (NSW) s. 32.
[92] (2011) NSWLR 398 at [45].

earlier, if the legislature had intended the section to exclude arbitration, it would have specifically expressed the exclusion in that section. Section 15 (2)(a)(i) certainly gives parties a right to bring proceedings in any competent court, but it does not prohibit them from resorting to arbitration.

Other courts have interpreted objective arbitrability broadly, by cautiously assessing policy assessment in relation to arbitrability. In *ACD Tridon* v. *Tridon Australia*[93] decided under the Corporations Act 2001 (Cth) and the CAA 1984 (NSW), the New South Wales Supreme Court stated in *obiter* that, as a general rule, but with certain exceptions, the statutory powers of a court under the Corporations Act, including the authority to issue a winding-up order or rectify the share register of a company, are comparable to that of exercised by a court under the general law. They are generally not special powers to be exercised referring to specialist public interest criteria. The public policy considerations applicable to, for example, a disputed claim to wind up a company, would not always bar the parties from referring to arbitration a claim for some merely inter parte relief under the oppression provisions of the Corporations Act (although the arbitration agreement was not effective in doing so in this case), or a claim for access to corporate information under s. 247A.[94]

5.4 Statutory Limitations on Objective Arbitrability

There are a few statutes that expressly limit arbitrability in Australia. Predispute arbitration agreements relating to certain insurance contracts are completely 'void' under s. 43 of the Insurance Contracts Act 1984 (Cth) or 'do not bind the insured' under s. 19 of the Insurance Act 1902 (NSW). Moreover, both pre- and post-arbitration agreements concerning certain carriage of goods transactions have 'no effect' under s. 11 of the Carriage of Goods by Sea Act 1991 (Cth), unless the arbitration 'is conducted in Australia'.[95]

6 SUBJECTIVE ARBITRABILITY: JUDICIAL INTERPRETATION OF ARBITRATION CLAUSES

Australian national courts have increasingly adopted a broad and expansive approach to interpret arbitration clauses, especially when parties adopt the generic language of any dispute 'arising out of', 'in connection with' or 'relating to' the contract.[96] A landmark case was, again, *Comandate Marine Corp* v. *Pan Australian Shipping Pty Ltd*[97] in 2006 where the Full Federal Court stated the importance of adopting a liberal and flexible approach in construing the wording of arbitration agreements. It departed from restrictive approaches that had been adopted by some Australian courts, whereby wording in arbitration agreements referring to disputes

---

[93] [2002] NSWSC 896 (New South Wales Supreme Court).
[94] In general, about this case, *see* Nottage & Morrison, *supra* note 73, at 987. Supporting the suggestion that statutory shareholder oppression relief should be arbitrable, Australian commentators further claim that winding-up applications may also be arbitrable in some situations. *See* Alistair Marchesi & Kanaga Dharmananda, *The Arbitrability of Oppression and Winding-up Actions*, 87 AUSTRALIAN LAW JOURNAL 258, 266–269 (2013). *Compare* with a recent Singapore Court of Appeal judgment: Tomolugen Holdings Ltd and another v. Silica Investors Ltd and other appeals [2015] 1 SLR 373.
[95] However, it is unclear from the statutory language and history whether s. 11 means a seat or hearings in Australia, and the policy rationales anyway may need revisiting as Australia adopts a more internationalist outlook on arbitration: *see* Nottage, 20??, *supra* note 38.
[96] Garnett, *supra* note 69, at 572–573.
[97] [2006] FCAFC 192.

'arising under' the contract had been interpreted to prevent arbitrators from determining, for example, questions of fraud or other vitiating factors making the underlying contract void.[98] Allsop J held:

> The court should … construe the contract giving meaning to the words chosen by the parties and giving liberal width and flexibility to elastic and general words of the contractual submission to arbitration.
>
> This liberal approach is underpinned by the sensible commercial presumption that the parties did not intend the inconvenience of having possible disputes from their transaction being heard in two places … This approach conforms with a common-sense approach to commercial agreements, in particular when the parties are operating in a truly international market and come from different countries and legal systems and it provides appropriate respect for party autonomy.[99]

Allsop J concluded that the wide interpretation of disputes 'arising out of' the contract could include a controversy in connection with representations made before the conclusion of the contract.

Some commentators argue that Australian courts should adopt a more liberal approach[100] in line with the presumptive approach subsequently laid down in the United Kingdom by Lord Hoffmann in *Fiona Trust & Holding Corp v. Privalov*.[101] Lord Hoffmann suggested that the interpretation of an arbitration clause should start from the assumption that the parties have intended to solve any dispute arising out of or relating to their contract in the same tribunal, otherwise it is commercially irrational.[102] He pointed out that the parties, especially those in the case of international contracts, decide to resort to arbitration since they wanted a quick and efficient adjudication instead of time-consuming proceedings in a national court.[103] Leaving some disputes to arbitration tribunals and some other to national courts would contradict that expectation. Accordingly, Lord Hoffmann recommended to adopt the presumptive approach, instead of focusing primarily on the effects of linguistics nuances of 'arising out of' or 'in connection with' in arbitration agreements, 'unless the language [of the contract] makes it clear that certain questions were intended to be excluded from the arbitrator's jurisdiction'.[104]

This presumptive approach may be more expansive than the liberal approach recommended in *Comandate* case by Allsop J,[105] but it is unclear whether the latter falls significantly short of other liberal approaches worldwide.[106] In fact, in *Fiona Trust*, Lord Hope also noted that the

---

[98] For narrow approaches, see Hi-Fert Pty Ltd & Anor v. Kiukiang Maritime Carriers Inc & Anor [1998] FCA 1485; Allergan Pharmaceuticals Inc v. Bausch & Lomb Inc [1985] FCA 369. Compare also James Morrison, *Defining the Scope of Arbitrable Disputes in Australia: Towards a 'Liberal' Approach*, 22 JOURNAL OF INTERNATIONAL ARBITRATION 569 (2005).
[99] [2006] FCAFC 192 at [164]–[165]
[100] Joachim Delaney & Katharina Lewis, *The Presumptive Approach to the Consuruction of Arbitration Agreements and the Principle of Separability – English Law Post Fiona Trust and Australian Law Contrasted*, 31 UNSW LAW JOURNAL 341 (2008).
[101] [2007] UKHL 40.
[102] [2007] UKHL 40 at [13].
[103] [2007] UKHL 40 at [6].
[104] [2007] UKHL 40 at [13].
[105] Delaney & Lewis, *supra* note 100, at 357–358.
[106] In a recent comparative survey of enforcement under the New York Convention, for example, several national reports declared that under their respective domestic laws arbitral 'tribunals are entitled to a presumption – even a "powerful presumption" – that they acted within their powers': George Bermann, *Recognition and Enforcement of Foreign Arbitral Awards: The Interpretation and Application of the New York Convention by National Courts*, in RECOGNITION AND ENFORCEMENT OF FOREIGN ARBITRAL AWARDS; THE INTERPRETATION AND APPLICATION OF THE NEW YORK CONVENTION BY NATIONAL COURTS 47 (George Bermann ed., 2017).

broad approach in *Comandate* case was 'firmly embedded as part of the law of international commerce', bolstering the argument for England to accept a broad approach as part of English law.[107] Nonetheless, while various Australian courts have followed the liberal approach to construction of arbitration agreements, some of them have expressly stated that no legal presumption in favour of arbitration works to make the words of the agreement of the parties paramount.[108]

On May 8, 2019, the High Court of Australia, in *Rinehart v. Hancock Prospecting Pty Ltd*[109] involving a domestic arbitration associated with a family trust dispute, adopted an 'orthodox'[110] approach to interpretation, by which 'a commercial contract should be construed by reference to the language used by the parties, the surrounding circumstances, and the purposes and objects to be secured by the contract'.[111] Applying this approach to the facts, the High Court found that disputes 'under' the relevant agreements were intended to extend to questions as to its validity, so litigation alleging misconduct in securing the agreements should also be stayed in favour of confidential arbitration. It was therefore unnecessary for the High Court to clarify whether the Full Federal Court had been correct to apply a presumptive liberal approach (along the lines of *Fiona Trust*) to reach the same conclusion.[112] The trial judge had instead followed the orthodox approach adopted by the New South Wales Court of Appeal (explicitly refusing to follow the approach in *Fiona Trust*),[113] finding that arbitration clauses limited to disputes 'under' the relevant agreements did not encompass claims as to their validity.

The High Court's judgment has been claimed by some commentators, somewhat optimistically, as being pro-arbitration.[114] However, others are disappointed that the court did not expressly adopt a liberal approach.[115] In future cases, applying the 'orthodox' approach to interpreting commercial contracts in general might result in reduced scope of application for the arbitration, compared to jurisdictions that expressly espouse a liberal approach. The judgment also does not clearly resolve the precise contours of the 'orthodox' approach in Australia anyway, including the vexed question of whether evidence of 'surrounding circumstances' can be referred to only if contractual wording can be shown to be ambiguous.[116] Parties should be mindful of such

---

[107] [2007] UKHL 40 at [31].
[108] Rinehart v. Rinehart (No 3) [2016] FCA 539 at [101]; Rinehart v. Welker [2012] NSWCA 95; and TCL Airconditioner (Zhongshan) Co Ltd v. Castel Electronics Pty Ltd [2009] VSC 553 at [17]–[20].
[109] [2019] HCA 13, http://eresources.hcourt.gov.au/downloadPdf/2019/HCA/13.
[110] [2019] HCA 13 at [18].
[111] [2019] HCA 13 at [44].
[112] Hancock Prospecting Pty Ltd v. Rinehart [2017] FCAFC 170.
[113] Rinehart v. Welker [2012] NSWCA 95.
[114] Liam Prescott, Richard Edwards, et al., *High Court of Australia Affirms Liberal Pro-arbitration Approach and the Importance of Arbitration in Confidential Disputes*, DLA PIPER PUBLICATIONS (May 9, 2019), www.dlapiper.com/en/australia/insights/publications/2019/05/high-court-of-australia-affirms-liberal-pro-arbitration-approach.
[115] Albert Monichino, *Arbitration: The Australian Approach to the Interpretation of Arbitration Agreements*, COMMBAR MATTERS (May 14, 2019), http://www.commbarmatters.com.au/2019/05/14/arbitration-the-australian-approach-to-the-interpretation-of-arbitration-agreements; Monique Carroll & Albert Monichino QC, *The Proper Approach to the Interpretation of Arbitration Agreements: Australian High Court Speaks Out*, 2019 ACICA REVIEW 9 (2019) (with a version also at https://www.kwm.com/en/au/knowledge/insights/interpretation-of-arbitration-agreements-in-australia-new-high-court-authority-20190528).
[116] The key problem is an earlier High Court judgment stating that ambiguity is a prerequisite or gateway to examining surrounding circumstances (Codelfa, decided in 1985), which the court has subsequently refused to reconsider, while issuing judgments (like Woodside, decided in 2014 and cited in this latest judgment) stating simply that surrounding circumstances can be referred to when interpreting commercial contracts. See generally, e.g., John Eldridge, *Surrounding Circumstances' in Contractual Interpretation: Where Are We Now?*, 32 COMMERCIAL LAW QUARTERLY 3–11 (2018), https://papers.ssrn.com/sol3/papers.cfm?abstract_id=3252243. The latest judgment still does not expressly resolve this question. The result can be understood as following from the agreements themselves referring not just to

uncertainties when choosing Australia as a seat of arbitration, as this will also often result in Australian contract law principles being applied to determine the scope intended for the arbitration clause.

Another recent Australian case interpreting an arbitration agreement, without venturing into the vexed question of whether the approach to construction should be orthodox or liberal, is found in *Hurdsman & Ors v. Ekactrm Solution Pty Ltd*.[117] This involved an application by the defendant for a stay of court proceedings under s. 7 of the IAA or alternatively s. 5 of the CAA on the basis of an alleged agreement to arbitrate contained in a share sale agreement (SSA). The claimant argued that the dispute resolution clause was ambiguous and therefore could not justify a stay because it provided 'the parties must submit the Dispute to a mediator for determination in accordance with the Rules of the Singapore International Arbitration Centre (Rules), applying South Australian Law, which are to be taken as incorporated into this agreement'. The defendant argued that this was a typographical error and should have read 'arbitrator' otherwise unintended absurd consequences would follow. Kelly J resolved the issue as a matter of contractual interpretation, although it is unclear which law was applied in this regard: South Australian law (which governed the SSA) or Singaporean law (being the putative situs of the dispute resolution procedure). This included having recourse to the precontractual negotiations between the parties and a memorandum of understanding (MOU).

Kelly J found that while the dispute resolution clause in the earlier MOU did provide for arbitration, the subsequent reference to 'mediator' remained in five drafts of the SSA without any change to 'arbitrator'. Also, considering other clauses in the SSA, Kelly J found that certain other clauses in the SSA which contemplated court proceedings would be inconsistent with and without effect if the ambiguous clause were interpreted as an arbitration agreement. Considered as a whole, therefore, Kelly J dismissed the application for a stay of proceeding because the clause in the SSA was not an arbitration agreement.

7 REQUIREMENTS FOR ENFORCING AWARDS: PUBLIC POLICY AS A GROUND FOR REFUSAL

Both the IAA and the Uniform Acts adopt the Model Law and the NY Convention, so the legislative requirements for enforcing awards in Australia conform to international standards. In the past, there were some country-specific aspects to enforcement in Australia, but they have been rectified following several amendments of the IAA since 2010.[118] The following discussion demonstrates Australia's general compliance with international standards for recognition and enforcement of arbitral awards.[119]

In Australia, although there have been comparatively few locally ICA proceedings and therefore very few court decisions on challenges to award enforcement, the case law (often

---

confidential arbitration but also (in recitals) concerns about media and public scrutiny of the dispute, and hence the parties' intention to have widely applicable arbitration clauses to maintain confidentiality. Even if the High Court could be seen as considering wider 'surrounding circumstances', the wording ('under') could be viewed as ambiguous anyway.

[117] [2018] SASC 112.

[118] See Nottage & Morrison, *supra* note 73; and James Morrison, *Recent Developments in International Arbitration in Australia 2017/2018*, 36 JOURNAL OF INTERNATIONAL ARBITRATION 1 (2019).

[119] See generally also Luke Nottage & Chester Brown, *Interpretation and Application of the New York Convention in Australia*, in RECOGNITION AND ENFORCEMENT OF FOREIGN ARBITRAL AWARDS; THE INTERPRETATION AND APPLICATION OF THE NEW YORK CONVENTION BY NATIONAL COURTS 93 (George Bermann ed., 2017). An earlier manuscript available at https://ssrn.com/abstract=2340806.

invoking the public policy exception) does not suggest much significant difference between enforcing an international arbitral award issued in Australia compared to enforcing a foreign arbitral award rendered overseas. The former relies on Art. 34 of the Model Law, whereas the latter is based on ss. 8(5) and (7) of the IAA, which corresponds with Art. V of the NY Convention,[120] This is despite the theoretical possibility of adopting an even more restrictive approach to exceptions to enforcement for setting aside awards at the seat, because doing so will likely impede enforcement worldwide under the NY Convention, whereas refusal to enforce a foreign award in Australia does not prevent the award creditor seeking enforcement elsewhere. In the long-running dispute on an international award from an arbitration seated in Australia in *Castel Electronics Pty Ltd v. TCL Air Conditioner (Zhongshan) Co Ltd (No 2)*,[121] Murphy J at first instance did remark that 'an order refusing enforcement is effectively only in the State where enforcement is sought, whereas an order setting aside an award prevents its enforcement in all Convention countries',[122] but the potential significance of the distinction was not elaborated.

In addition, Murphy J stated in relation to the 'public policy' exception, including breaches of natural justice pursuant to s. 19 of the IAA, stated that:

> Although this interpretation might be said to lead to inconsistency with international decisions on the meaning of 'public policy', I consider that the plain words of s. 19(B) [of the IAA] unambiguously declare that if *any* breach of natural justice occurs in connection with the making of an award the ... the award is in conflict with or contrary to the public policy of Australia.[123]

This construction is in stark contrast to the overseas authorities Murphy J examined, which his Honour said 'that a Convention award is only in conflict with or contrary to public policy if it offends fundamental notions of justice and fairness'.[124] That seemed to indicate a narrower approach to the public policy exception being adopted overseas compared to Australia given the 'natural justice' gloss in s. 19 of the IAA (and in s. 8(7A) since its 2010 amendments). However, Murphy J nonetheless refused to set aside the award on the ground of public policy, and this decision was upheld by the Full Federal Court (as outlined in Section 3.1).[125] There are a number of other cases where the breach of natural justice gloss to the public policy exception has been seized upon by award debtors in Australia as the basis for resisting enforcement of awards, although almost always unsuccessfully. Overall, Australian courts have construed public policy narrowly especially over the last decade.[126]

However, it remains possible that they would refuse enforcement of awards that declined to apply the ACL on (substantive) public policy grounds as well as for lack of arbitrability (as discussed in Section 4). There also remains uncertainty about whether an award issued by arbitrators, after having failed to facilitate a settlement despite the parties having initially

---

[120] Michael Pryles, *National Report for Australia (2018)*, in ICCA INTERNATIONAL HANDBOOK ON COMMERCIAL ARBITRATION 1–64, 49 (Jan Paulsson & Lise Bosman eds., 2018). IAA s. 20 requires enforcement of foreign awards primarily under 8, but if unavailable under Art. 36 of the Model Law.

[121] [2012] FCA 1214.

[122] *Id.* at [21].

[123] *Id.* at [29].

[124] *Id.* at [30].

[125] Nottage, *supra* note 38, at 482.

[126] Comparing improvements in Australia, although mainly through cases involving enforcement of foreign awards under the NY Convention, *see* DEAN LEWIS, THE INTERPRETATION AND UNIFORMITY OF THE UNCITRAL MODEL LAW ON INTERNATIONAL COMMERCIAL ARBITRATION: FOCUSING ON AUSTRALIA, HONG KONG AND SINGAPORE (2016), http://blogs.usyd.edu.au/japaneselaw/2017/04/book_review_dean_lewis.html.

consented to them acting as mediators (Arb-Med), would be enforceable under the IAA if the arbitrators had caucused (meeting separately) with each party during the attempted mediation. For domestic arbitrations, due to concerns about procedural public policy as well as the mandatory requirement for equal treatment of parties under Art. 18 of the Model Law, s. 27D of the Uniform Acts added from 2010 a requirement that even if the parties expressly authorised Arb-Med in writing before the tribunal's settlement attempts, they must consent again in writing before the tribunal can revert to arbitration and issue an award following the tribunal's failed mediation. A recent decision of the New South Wales Supreme Court interpreted this 'dual written consent' requirement quite strictly[127] and was upheld on appeal.[128] The IAA still has no provisions whatsoever on Arb-Med, despite some longstanding calls for legislative reform.[129] Awards issued after failed Arb-Med attempts may therefore be open to challenge especially for locally seated international arbitrations that have involved caucusing without following the strict dual consent procedure required under the Uniform Acts for domestic arbitrations. However, the public policy exception may be interpreted more restrictively in enforcing foreign awards after failed Arb-Med, following the lead of case law in Hong Kong (which is now quite often cited in Australia).[130]

In general, an important example of Australia's more restrictive approach towards the public policy exception under the IAA came from the *Federal Court in Uganda Telecom Limited v. Hi-Tech Telecom Pty Ltd*.[131] Foster J emphasised that the rationale of the statute, and therefore the public policy of Australia, is to enforce foreign arbitral awards as much as possible, for the sake of supporting certainty and finality in international dispute resolution.[132] Referring to various judgments for example from the United States that interpreted public policy narrowly, Foster J cast doubt on the view that s. 8(7) of the IAA conferred a general discretion to refuse enforcement of foreign arbitral awards,[133] but favoured instead a narrow construction. This view was followed by the Full Federal Court in *TCL Air Conditioner (Zhongshan) Co Ltd v. Castel Electronics Pty Ltd*.[134] The court explained that public policy is 'limited to the fundamental principles of justice and morality of the state, recognising the international dimension of the context'.[135] The court further continued that arbitral awards are denied recognition or

---

[127] Ku-ring-gai Council v. Ichor Constructions Pty Ltd [2018] NSWSC 610 (8 May 2018).
[128] Ku-ring-gai Council v. Ichor Constructions Pty Ltd [2019] NSWCA 2 (5 February 2019). The court did not interfere with the trial judge's assessment that the second written consent had not been given and therefore the decision by McDougall J to terminate the arbitrator's mandate under s. 14(2) of the Commercial Arbitration Act 2010 (NSW). The Court of Appeal interpreted s. 14(3), which makes the decision 'final', as precluding an appeal. One reason given by Bathurst CJ (at [72]) was that s. 2A(1) requires the Uniform Acts to be interpreted as consistently as practicable with the Model Law as applied in the IAA, and Model Law Art. 14(2) states that decisions on terminating arbitrator mandates 'shall be subject to no appeal'. Another reason given (at [73]) is that s. 2A(3) of the Commercial Arbitration Act 2010 (NSW) allows reference to extrinsic materials produced by UNCITRAL, which clarified that the Model Law used this wording to clarify uncertainty about what might be meant by a 'final decision'. Bathurst CJ's judgment is also notably internationalist in referring (at [61]–[62]) to UNCITRAL's 2012 *Digest of Case Law on the Model Law on International Commercial Arbitration*, seemingly for the first time in Australian case law, along with other extrinsic material and Singaporean case law, to rule that the trial court's decision to terminate arbitrator's mandate could not be interpreted instead as an 'interim measure' under the Model Law (Art. 17J) or Uniform Acts (s. 17J).
[129] See, e.g., Nottage & Garnett, *supra* note 51, at 179–184.
[130] Gao Haiyan v. Keeneye Holdings Ltd [2011] HKCA 459, reversing the trial judge's decision to refuse enforcement of the award from mainland China.
[131] [2011] FCA 131.
[132] Id. at [126].
[133] Id. at [132].
[134] [2014] FCAFC 83.
[135] Id. at [76].

enforcement only when there is demonstrated real unfairness or real injustice in how the arbitration was conducted.[136]

Accordingly, Australian courts have accepted challenges to awards on public policy grounds only occasionally; courts intervene in arbitrations minimally in Australia. An example in this regard is *Armada (Singapore) Pte Ltd (under judicial management) v. Gujurat NRE Cole Ltd*.[137] A ground raised to resist award enforcement related to a declaration in the second arbitral award that purported to bind the parties in the future to pay damages for breach of contract at a time when those damages had not yet arose. The award debtor claimed that the declaration would be contrary to public policy under s. 8(7) of the IAA. Foster J's answer was negative. His Honour commented that the future declaration was on one view inappropriate, commenting that an Australian court would not make a similar declaration. However, he carefully declined to invoke the public policy ground, stating that '[t]he mere fact that enforcing such a declaration might not be consistent with principles developed in Australia for the exercise of an Australian Court's discretion to make declarations would not, of itself, be sufficient to constitute a reason for refusing to enforce the award on the grounds that to do so would be contrary to public policy'.[138]

More recently, in a case decided in record time in the context of a Formula One racing event, the Court of Appeal of the Supreme Court of Victoria in *Sauber Motor AG v. Giedo Van Der Garde BV* also rejected a public policy objection and followed the Full Federal Court decision in *TCL Air Conditioner*. Additional observations applied the narrow approach consistently with the minimal judicial intervention of Australian courts. The court held: 'Courts should not entertain a disguised attack on the factual findings or legal conclusions of an arbitrator dressed up as a complaint about natural justice. Errors of fact or law are not legitimate bases for curial intervention'.[139] In applying the 'real unfairness or real injustice' approach from *TCL*, the courts are also cognisant of attempts to resist enforcement on grounds not contravening fundamental notions of justice. The court further stated that 'unfairness in a particular case will depend upon context, and all the circumstances of that case'.[140] The standard and approach adopted by the Full Federal Court in *TCL* has also seen subsequent judgments reject attempts to resist arbitral awards on the basis of breaches of public policy.[141]

Interestingly, in obiter, the judgment of Croft J in *Indian Farmer Fertiliser Cooperative Ltd v. Gutnick* considered a circumstance in which public policy may be breached.[142] Croft J said 'if it were necessary for me to decide this point – I would be prepared to accept that, where an arbitral award allows for double recovery, or where enforcement would result in double recovery, fundamental principles of justice and morality may be engaged'.[143] The rule against double recovery, as a specific fundamental principle of public policy, is a rare instance in recent Australian case law of such a possible example being identified.[144] However, it is doubtful whether Australian courts will now multiply many categories that would be held as specific

---

[136] *Id.* at [55].
[137] [2014] FCA 636.
[138] *Id.* at [67].
[139] [2015] VSCA 37 at [8].
[140] *Id.* at [8].
[141] For example, Indian Farmers Fertiliser Cooperative Ltd v. Gutnick [2015] VSC 724; Gutnick v. Indian Farmers Fertiliser Cooperative Ltd [2016] VSCA 5; William Hare UAE LLC v. Aircraft Support Industries Pty Ltd [2014] NSWSC 1403; Giedo van der Garde BV v. Sauber Motorsport AG [2015] VSC 80; Liaoning Zhongwang Group Co Ltd v. Alfield Group Pty Ltd [2017] FCA 1223; ALYK (HK) Ltd v. Caprock Commodities Trading Pty Ltd [2015] NSWSC 1006; and Sino Dragon Trading Ltd v. Noble Resources International Pte Ltd (No 2) [2016] FCA 1169.
[142] [2015] VSC 724.
[143] *Id.* at [105].
[144] Monichino & Fawke, *supra* note 46, at 214.

instances of breaches of public policy. Although somewhat belatedly, Australian case law on the public policy exception has developed in a way that recognises the context and objects of international commercial arbitration and comity with other international authorities on the subject. Fewer challenges on this ground have reached Australian courts in recent years.

8 CONCLUSION

'The Lucky Country' is how some have described Australia since the 1960s. Many of those using the phrase believe that the implication is positive: the country has bountiful natural resources and is a fair distance from major geopolitical threats. However, the original meaning of the term coined by Donald Horne was instead rather negative: 'Australia is a lucky country run mainly by second rate people who share its luck. It lives on other people's ideas, and, although ordinary people are adaptable, most of its leaders (in all fields) so lack curiosity about the events that surround them that they are often taken by surprise'.[145]

This chapter has demonstrated that neither meaning of the Lucky Country applies to Australia in the context of ICA. Geographical remoteness has made the country a comparatively unfavourable venue in terms of increasing ICA caseloads. Yet this 'unlucky' aspect has generated world-class Australian arbitration experts contributing and responsive to progress outside the country and willing to improve the ICA industry. Australia has also gradually improved the legal environment for ICA locally, following international standards in regard to arbitrator bias, conflicts of interests, procedural irregularities and arbitrator's misconduct during proceedings, objective and subjective arbitrability and enforceability of arbitral awards. Without stressing too much over its unlucky location, in recent years Australia has been redoubling its efforts to become a leading regional venue for ICA.

---

[145] DONALD HORNE, THE LUCKY COUNTRY (6th ed. 2008).

12

Judicial Control of Arbitral Awards in Bulgaria

*Oleg Temnikov**

1 INTRODUCTION

Bulgaria has traditionally been an arbitration-friendly jurisdiction, both for domestic and international disputes.[1] Arbitration as a means of dispute resolution was first implemented in Bulgaria at the end of the nineteenth century with the first Civil Procedure Act (1892). At this time arbitration was used mainly to solve commercial disputes between merchants with the assistance of local and national chambers of commerce. In the first half of the twentieth century, arbitration was widely used to resolve both civil and commercial cases, and the arbitrators had extensive powers, including resolving disputes ex aequo et bono. Also during this period, the first reported international commercial arbitration proceedings involving Bulgarian parties occurred, mainly in the international trade and infrastructure construction sectors. Throughout the socialist period (1944–1989), arbitration was allowed only in respect of legal disputes between Bulgarian socialist organisations (i.e., state-owned entities engaged in industry and trade, such as industrial plants, foreign trade enterprises, tourist companies, state-owned banks, etc.) and foreign enterprises or entities, and it was the privileged dispute resolution mechanism for such disputes. The existence of this sort of arbitration allowed Bulgarian practitioners to conserve and develop their knowledge in the field during the socialist period. In particular, the Arbitration Court at the Bulgarian Chamber of Commerce and Industry allowed some prominent scholars and practitioners to regularly engage in domestic and international arbitration proceedings and to develop, as a follow up, domestic legislation and academic materials on the topic.

---

* The opinions and positions expressed by the author in this article are his personal scientific views on the topic. They are not to be attributed to Wolf Theiss Law Firm or its lawyers.
[1] For a general presentation, in English, of arbitration in Bulgaria, please see Anna Rizova-Clegg & Oleg Temnikov, *Chapter on Bulgaria*, in THE INTERNATIONAL ARBITRATION REVIEW (James H. Carter ed., 10th ed. 2019), thelawreviews. co.uk/edition/1001364/the-international-arbitration-review-edition-10; Assen Alexiev, *National Report for Bulgaria (2018)*, in ICCA INTERNATIONAL HANDBOOK ON COMMERCIAL ARBITRATION 1–67 (Lise Bosman ed., 2019), Supplement 100, August 2018; Deyan Draguiev & Assen Georgiev, *Chapter on Bulgaria*, in THE EUROPEAN, MIDDLE EASTERN AND AFRICAN ARBITRATION REVIEW 2016 (2016), at globalarbitrationreview.com/edition/1000135/the-european-middle-eastern-and-african-arbitration-review-2016; Assen Alexiev, *Arbitration Procedures and Practice in Bulgaria: Overview*, in PRACTICAL LAW – ARBITRATION GUIDE (2019), at practicallaw.com/arbitration-guide; Tsvetelina Dimitrova, *Bulgaria*, in THE ICLG ON INTERNATIONAL ARBITRATION LAWS AND REGULATIONS 2018 (2018), iclg.com/practice-areas/international-arbitration-laws-and-regulations/bulgaria. In the Bulgarian language, please see Венцислава Желязкова, *Арбитражът като способ за решаване на имуществени спорове* (2019); Живко Сталев, *Закон за международния търговски арбитраж* (1991); Живко Сталев, *Арбитраж по частноправни спорове* (1999).

The transition to the market economy at the end of the 1980s led to considerable development and modernisation of both domestic and international commercial arbitration, which remained and developed as a widely used dispute resolution mechanism. Currently, both domestic and international commercial arbitration is widely used as a dispute resolution mechanism.

1.1 National Legislation

Arbitration in Bulgaria is regulated mainly by the International Commercial Arbitration Act (ICAA).[2] Adopted back in 1988, the ICAA is largely based on the UNCITRAL Model Law on International Commercial Arbitration (1985), thus rendering Bulgaria one of the first Model Law jurisdictions. The 2006 amendments to the UNCITRAL Model Law have not yet been implemented in Bulgaria and currently there are no plans for their implementation. In addition to the ICAA, provisions of the Civil Procedure Code[3] (with respect to the scope of the arbitration agreement, arbitrability and seat of the arbitration) and the Private International Law Code[4] with respect to recognition and enforcement of foreign arbitral awards) are also applicable to arbitration proceedings.

1.2 International Conventions Concluded by Bulgaria

Bulgaria is a party to the most significant international conventions in the field of arbitration. With respect to recognition and enforcement, Bulgaria is a party to the Convention on the Recognition and Enforcement of Foreign Arbitral Awards (New York 1958) (the New York Convention)[5] and the European Convention on International Commercial Arbitration (Geneva 1961).[6]

In the field of international investment law, Bulgaria is party to the ICSID Convention[7] and the Energy Charter Treaty (ECT).[8] Bulgaria has also concluded 71 bilateral investment treaties (BITs),[9] including with all major investors' jurisdictions. With respect to investment protection, Bulgaria has been a member state of the European Union since January 1, 2007 and thus all legal issues arising in respect of the validity of intra-EU BITs would be relevant (see Section 3).

---

[2] International Commercial Arbitration Act (Закон за международния търговски арбитраж), published in State Gazette issue No. 60 Aug. 5, 1988, as amended (last amendment published in State Gazette issue No. 8 of Jan. 24, 2017).

[3] Civil Procedure Code (Граждански процесуален кодекс), published in State Gazette issue No. 59 of July 20, 2007, as amended time to time, last amendment and published in State Gazette issue No. 65 of 07 Aug. 7, 2018.

[4] Private International Law Code (Кодекс на международното частно право), published in State Gazette issue No. 42 of May 17, 2005, as amended (last amendment published in State Gazette issue No. 100 of Dec. 21, 2010).

[5] Convention on the Recognition and Enforcement of Foreign Arbitral Awards (New York, 1958), signed on Oct. 10, 1961, entered into force on Jan. 8, 1962, published in State Gazette issue No. 57 of Oct. 10, 1961. Please note that Bulgaria has made a reciprocity reservation under Article 1 of the New York Convention.

[6] European Convention on International Commercial Arbitration (Geneva, 1961), signed on Apr. 21, 1961, entered into force on May 13, 1964, published the State Gazette issue No. 57 of July 21, 1964.

[7] Convention on the Settlement of Investment Disputes between States and Nationals of Other States, signed on Mar. 21, 2000, entered into force on May 12, 2001, published in State Gazette issue No. 110 of Dec. 21, 2001.

[8] 1994 Energy Charter Treaty, signed on Dec. 17, 1994, entered into force on Apr. 16, 1998, published in State Gazette issue No. 64 of July 30, 1996.

[9] For a full up-to-date list, please see UNCTAD's Investment Policy Hub, investmentpolicy.unctad.org/international-investment-agreements/countries/30/bulgaria?type=tips.

1.3 ICAA Scope and Structure

Despite its name, the ICAA applies to both domestic and international arbitrations having a seat in Bulgaria. An arbitration is deemed international if one or all of the parties to it are seated (for legal entities) or resident (for individuals) outside of Bulgaria. Respectively, an arbitration is domestic when all parties are seated or resident in Bulgaria. This legislative solution – i.e., to have substantially the same set of rules applying both to international and to domestic cases – has proven to be efficient in Bulgaria. The rule provides, on the one side, a harmonized arbitration framework, easier to understand and be applied by parties, legal practitioners and courts, and on the other side, it allows practitioners and courts to cross use case law and academic writings in the field of domestic and international arbitration.

The ICAA is applicable also to arbitrations with a seat outside Bulgaria, but only with respect to (1) the effects of the arbitration agreement (duty of state courts to terminate a case if the dispute is subject to arbitration), (2) the possibility to request interim measures in support of an arbitration seated outside Bulgaria and (3) the recognition and enforcement of foreign arbitral awards (where the procedure is set in the Private International Code). Both institutional and ad hoc arbitration are regulated by the ICAA. The ICAA applies to private parties as well as to state or public entities having concluded arbitration agreements. The ICAA follows the Model Law's structure and covers the arbitration agreement, the composition of the arbitral tribunal, its jurisdiction and the competence–competence principle, the conduct of the proceedings, the arbitral award and its effects, the set-aside proceedings and the recognition and enforcement of arbitral awards.

1.4 Arbitrability under Bulgarian Law

The conditions of arbitrability under Bulgarian law are primarily addressed in Article 19 of the Civil Procedure Code.[10] Some other acts (such as the Concessions Act, the ICAA) also contain provisions which have effect on arbitrability. The parties to a dispute involving a pecuniary right that is 'disposable' (a right that parties may dispose of between themselves, for instance, by way of a settlement or a transaction) may agree to allow a dispute between them to be settled by arbitration with the exception of the following disputes: (1) disputes with respect to absolute rights over immovable property (i.e., ownership) or possession of immovable property (however, disputes involving relative contractual rights with respect to immovable property – such as lease agreements and their effects, vacation of premises disputes – are arbitrable); (2) disputes with respect to alimony (i.e., financial obligations arising out of divorce); (3) employment disputes (dispute arising out of an employment relationship in the meaning of the Bulgarian Labour Code. However, disputes under management agreements between companies or shareholders and their directors/managers are arbitrable since they are not considered as employment disputes); (4) disputes involving nonpecuniary rights; (5) administrative and other public law disputes; (6) disputes involving nontransferable personal rights and disputes in relation to personal or marital status and origin; (7) civil law disputes that may be initiated by

---

[10] Article 19 (Arbitration Agreement) of the Bulgarian Civil Procedure Code:

(1) The parties to a property dispute may agree that the said dispute be settled by an arbitration court, unless the said dispute has as its subject matter any rights in rem or possession of a corporeal immovable, maintenance obligations or rights under an employment relationship, or is a dispute one of the parties to which is a consumer within the meaning of § 13, Item 1 of the Supplementary Provisions of the Consumer Protection Act.

(2) The arbitration may have a seat abroad if one of the party has his, her or its habitual residence, registered office according to the basic instrument thereof or place of the actual management thereof abroad.

a prosecutor or where the participation of a prosecutor is required; (8) some disputes in relation to insolvency proceedings (such as disputes for declaratory judgments establishing the existence of receivables from an insolvent company that have not been accepted in the insolvency proceedings); (9) disputes in which one of the parties is a consumer in the meaning of the Consumer Protection Act; (10) hardship/adaptation of contract disputes under Art. 307 of the Commercial Act arising under privatization contracts;[11] and (11) concessions agreement without trans-border interest (in the meaning of EU Law).

The concept of arbitrability under Bulgarian law has evolved in the years since the adoption of the ICAA. At first the arbitrability of disputes was very strictly construed by courts. Then, at the beginning of the twentieth century, the case-law evolved towards a more pro-arbitration approach. Limitations, such as the ones applicable to consumer disputes and disputes involving some public contracts (concessions, privatizations agreements, etc.), were adopted by the legislator in order to protect particular public interests at a given moment.

1.5 Arbitration Agreement

The ICAA requires the arbitration agreement be in written form (art. 7 of the ICAA,[12] which follows closely art. 7 of the UNCITRAL Model Law). An arbitration agreement is considered to be in writing when the agreement is contained in a document signed by both parties; in an exchange of letters, faxes, telegrams or other means of telecommunication; or in general terms and conditions, to which the parties have referred in their contract. Any of the parties may raise an objection as to the form or existence of an arbitration agreement by the end of the first hearing. If no objection is made, it will be considered that there was a valid arbitration agreement. The ICAA provides that an arbitration agreement may be concluded before a dispute arises or afterwards. The latter option has arisen very rarely in practice.

Under Bulgarian law, arbitration agreements can cover both contractual and noncontractual disputes. Although this is expressly provided for in Art. 7 of the ICAA, arbitral tribunals and

---

[11] This limitation of arbitrability is not expressly provided for in the law but has been crystallized by courts practice. The Bulgarian Commercial Act provides that a court or arbitral tribunal may, upon request by one of the parties to a contract, amend or terminate it in full or in part when circumstances have arisen that the parties could not foresee and were not obliged to foresee, and the preservation of the contract is contrary to justice and good faith. In a recent controversial judgment (judgment No. 189/09.11.2017 under commercial case No. 1675/2017 of the Supreme Court of Cassation), the Supreme Court of Cassation ruled that disputes for revision of privatization agreements, based on the provision of Art. 307 of the Commercial Act, are not arbitrable. Its reasoning is based on the provision of Art. 32(5) of the Privatization Act, which prohibits the parties to privatization agreements to renegotiate them. According to the court, this prohibition not only limits the freedom of the parties and the possibility to dispose of their rights and obligations but also precludes them from agreeing to settle through arbitration a dispute for a revision of a privatization contract based on Article 307 of the Commercial Act.

[12] Article 7 of the ICAA:

(1) An arbitration agreement is the consent of the parties to entrust to the court of arbitration to solve all or certain disputes, which may arise or have arisen between them on the subject of a contract or non-contractual legal relations. The arbitration agreement may take the form of arbitration clause in another contract or a settlement agreement.

(2) The arbitration agreement shall be in a written form. An agreement is considered in a written form if it is contained in a document signed by the parties or in an exchange of letters, telexes, telegrams or other forms of communications.

(3) An arbitration agreement is considered concluded when the defendant in a written form or by a statement, included in the Minutes of the arbitration proceedings, agrees that the dispute be brought to arbitration or when the defendant takes part in the arbitration proceedings by depositing a written response, presenting evidence, filing of a counterclaim or sitting in an arbitration hearing without questioning the jurisdiction of the arbitration.

courts have applied this provision with some hesitation. In particular, the question where a noncontractual dispute may be subjected to arbitration (if this is not expressly provided for in the arbitration agreement) is still open in Bulgarian law, and some arbitral tribunals have refused to hear such cases on the grounds of a lack of an explicit agreement in this respect.[13] Also, under Bulgarian law, the doctrine of separability of the arbitration agreement is fully recognised, and the ICAA provides that an arbitration agreement included in a contract is independent of the other terms of the contract. The nullity of the contract does not automatically render the arbitration agreement contained in it also invalid. In some cases, a dispute with respect to a particular contract could be brought in arbitration on the basis of the arbitration agreement contained therein also in case the respective contract is terminated or annulled.

An interesting angle of analysis of the separability doctrine is how it affects acceptance of agreements by tacit consent. Under Art. 301 of the Bulgarian Commercial Act, a trader (a natural person, merchant or commercial legal entity) is considered to have accepted a transaction that was concluded on its behalf by an unauthorized person if the trader has not objected to the transaction immediately after it becomes aware of it. This way of acceptance of contracts is widely used in practice and the question arose whether this implies also the acceptance of the arbitration agreement. The Bulgarian Supreme Court of Cassation's case law[14] considers that since the arbitration agreement is independent of the main contract and is subject to specific requirements for formal validity, it cannot be validated by nonobjection to it as provided for under Art. 301 of the Bulgarian Commercial Act. Thus, this confirms that under Bulgarian law tacit acceptance of an arbitration agreement is not admissible.

Another aspect of the doctrine of separability of arbitration agreements under Bulgarian law is transferability of the arbitration agreement in case of transfer/assignment of the contract in which it is included. In particular, the Bulgarian Supreme Court of Cassation has considered[15] the question of whether an assignment of contractual receivables affects the rights under the arbitration agreement included in the respective contract. Surprisingly, the court considered that the assignment of receivables under a contract does not lead to the automatic transfer of the rights under the arbitration agreement contained therein, unless the debtor explicitly agrees to the assignment of the arbitration agreement. In other words, if a creditor assigns its rights under a loan agreement containing an arbitration clause, the acquirer of the receivables would not be able to bring a dispute before arbitration against the debtor. This judgment has been widely criticized by legal doctrine and practitioners, as it undermines transferability of contracts.

1.6 Mandatory Principles Applicable to the Arbitral Proceedings

Under the ICAA and case law, only a very limited number of mandatory procedural provisions could lead to setting aside the arbitral award, such as (1) parties must be treated equally (according to the principle of equal treatment of the parties), (2) each party must be given an equal opportunity to present its case, (3) arbitrators must be impartial and independent, (4) parties must be notified of the arbitration and the open hearings, and (5) requirements for

---

[13] Arbitral Award of Jan. 26, 1999 under domestic arbitration case No. 25/1998 of the AC at the BCCI, Arbitral Award of Apr. 4, 2002, under domestic arbitration case No. 99/2001 of the AC at the BCCI.

[14] Judgment No. 157 of Jan. 11, 2013, under commercial case No. 611/2012, judgment No. 117 of May 31, 2018, under commercial case No. 2592/2017 of the Supreme Court of Cassation of Bulgaria.

[15] Judgment No. 261 of Aug. 1, 2018 under commercial case No. 624/2017 of the Supreme Court of Cassation of Bulgaria (M.S.D. v. Credo Consult 55 OOD).

the form and the requisites of arbitral awards provided for in the ICAA should be met (i.e., the written form of the award, motives, signatures of the arbitrators).

1.7 Intervention by State Courts

The ICAA strictly limits the possibility of intervention by state courts in arbitration proceedings only if a dispute, subject to arbitration, is referred to a state court and no party objects to the state court proceedings by the reply to the statement of claim; to impose interim or conservatory measures (such as freezing of assets, collection of evidence, etc.) in support of a future or pending arbitration case (domestic or international); if there is a challenge to arbitrators in proceedings seated in Bulgaria; if there is need to assist the parties or an arbitral tribunal to collect evidence; in set aside proceedings; in proceedings for the issuance of a writ of enforcement for an arbitral award rendered in arbitrations seated in Bulgaria; and in proceedings for the recognition and enforcement of foreign arbitral awards.

Requests for interim measures or collection of evidence may be made before any competent Bulgarian court, and the Civil Procedure Code will apply. In practice, interim measures in support of arbitration are requested and granted regularly. Also, Bulgarian law allows parties to request interim measures to secure a procedure for the recognition and enforcement of an arbitral award rendered abroad.

With respect to the issuance of writs of enforcement on the basis of arbitral awards rendered in arbitrations seated in Bulgaria, the competent court would be the respective district court at the place of residence of the debtor. The procedure is conducted ex parte and is relatively quick and efficient. The state court does not review the arbitral award on the merits and performs only prima facie review of whether the award is enforceable (i.e., whether it has been served to the opposing party, whether it could be enforced with the means of the Bulgarian Civil Procedure Code, etc.). Upon issuance of the writ of enforcement the respective party may request a private enforcement officer or a public enforcement officer to enforce the arbitral award, as any ordinary writ of enforcement issued in Bulgaria.

Set-aside proceedings against an arbitral award rendered in Bulgaria may be initiated before the Bulgarian Supreme Court of Cassation within three months of the serving of the arbitration award to the respective party. The filing of a set-aside request does not stop the enforceability of the respective arbitral award unless a specific order in this respect is made by the Supreme Court of Cassation, and the requesting party establishes a security for the whole amount of the award. The scope of control in set-aside proceedings is limited exclusively to the strictly provided grounds in the ICAA and the Supreme Court of Cassation would not review the arbitral award on the merits. The judgment of the Supreme Court of Cassation on the set-aside request is not subject to appeals.

Requests for recognition and enforcement of foreign arbitral awards are to be brought before the Sofia City Court. Such requests follow the standard claim procedure and the first instance judgments are subject to appeals before the Sofia Court of Appeals and the Supreme Court of Cassation. The scope of control in recognition and enforcement proceedings is limited exclusively to the strictly provided grounds in the New York Convention or other applicable Acts. The Sofia City Court would not review the arbitral award on the merits.

1.8 Local Arbitration Institutions

In Bulgaria, more than forty arbitral institutions are active. This considerable number is due to the possibility until 2017 to include arbitration agreements in consumer contracts. This lead to the proliferation of institutions specialised in consumer disputes – such as disputes arising out of utilities contracts (electricity distribution, heating, mobile phones, water supply, etc.), consumer finance contracts and leasing agreements. Some of these institutions administered several thousand arbitration cases per year with, however, very low individual value.

As to commercial disputes, there are three major national arbitration institutions. The oldest and most prominent Bulgarian arbitral institution is the Arbitration Court (AC) at the Bulgarian Chamber of Commerce and Industry (BCCI),[16] which recently marked its 120th anniversary. The AC at the BCCI has considerable experience in dealing with domestic and international commercial disputes in a number of sectors, such as sale of goods, construction, electricity trade and distribution, leases, loan agreements, agriculture, public procurement and IT. It has a permanent secretariat with specialised staff and hearing facilities in Sofia. The AC at the BCCI Rules of Arbitration,[17] the tariff of arbitration fees and costs,[18] the recommended arbitration clause[19] and other documents are available in different languages and the institution has considerable experience in administering disputes in English, Russian and German. The AC at the BCCI implemented an online document management system, allowing the parties to proceedings to have full access to all documents in the proceedings (all parties' submission, orders or awards by the tribunal, correspondence and delivery receipts, transcript from hearings, etc.) via secure access on the website of the AC at the BCCI. The AC at the BCCI is by far the busiest arbitral institution in Bulgaria; for example, in 2017 it registered approximately 300 domestic and 50 international new arbitration cases. In addition to institutional arbitration, the AC at the BCCI may act as an appointing authority, providing administrative support to ad hoc arbitrations and mediation services. Other major Bulgarian arbitral institutions are the Arbitration Court at the Bulgarian Industrial Association,[20] the recently established KRIB Court of Arbitration[21] and the Arbitration Court at the Bulgarian–German Chamber of Commerce.[22]

1.9 Trends or Statistics Relating to Arbitration

Since 1990 arbitration in Bulgaria has been widely used both by local companies and international businesses. A considerable number of commercial contracts provide for arbitration and such disputes are very common. Arbitration is the most commonly used means to resolve commercial disputes in business transactions with an international element. The exact proportion of disputes settled through arbitration is unknown due to the lack of official statistics published by the various arbitration institutions in the country. Regarding foreign arbitral institutions, Bulgarian parties most often opt for ICC, VIAC, SCC or LCIA arbitration.

2 DEVELOPMENTS WITH RESPECT TO THE SCOPE OF ARBITRATION IN BULGARIA

The present section outlines the recent developments in Bulgarian law with respect to the scope of disputes which could be subject to arbitration, in particular those of the arbitrability of

---

[16] *See* www.bcci.bg/bcci-arbitration-court-en.html.
[17] *See* www.bcci.bg/rulescort-en.html.
[18] *See* www.bcci.bg/tariffcort-en-2015.html.
[19] *See* www.bcci.bg/clause-en.html.
[20] *See* en.bia-bg.com/service/view/21257/.
[21] *See* arbitration.bg/?lang=en.
[22] *See* bulgarien.ahk.de/bg/dienstleistungen/schiedsgericht/.

consumer disputes and the possibility of arbitration tribunals to hear claims or adaptations of contracts. As explained earlier, Bulgarian law has traditionally adopted a relatively wide definition of arbitrable disputes, including most of contractual and noncontractual commercial disputes. The limitations are in line with the usual in other EU member states. However, recent legislative changes have limited the availability of arbitration for consumer disputes where courts have further defined the conditions necessary to allow adaptation of contracts by arbitration tribunals.

2.1 Non-arbitrability of Consumer Disputes

The most important legislative development in the field of arbitration in Bulgaria in recent years is the amendment to the Civil Procedure Code and the ICAA of 2017 (the 2017 amendments).[23] Those amendments were initiated by the ombudsman with the aim of enhancing the protection of consumers. Indeed, during the past year Bulgaria experienced an impressive development of arbitration of consumer disputes. In particular, most utility companies (telecom operators, water companies, electricity companies) and consumer credit entities started to provide arbitration agreements in their standard form contracts or in their general terms and conditions applicable in relations with consumers. Those clauses, which were not subject to negotiation with consumers, provided for mandatory arbitration before dedicated arbitration institutions, mainly specialized in consumer disputes. Most of the time, the disputes were decided by sole arbitrators, which were repetitively nominated by the respective company – with some arbitrators deciding more than 2,000 cases with the same claimant per year. This lead to a widely spread filling of injustice and inherent bias of the arbitrators and resulted in the said amendments.

The first major development introduced by the 2017 amendments was the prohibition of arbitration of consumer disputes. This was achieved by extending the scope of Article 19 of the Civil Procedure Code[24] – the legislator added all disputes involving consumers to the list of disputes that are non-arbitrable. Under Bulgarian law, a 'consumer' is considered any natural person who acquires products or uses services for purposes that do not fall within his or her commercial or professional activity, and any natural person who acts outside his or her commercial or professional capacity. Thus, arbitration is no more available in respect of most of the contracts entered into by physical persons, such as utilities contracts (water, electricity, gas, heating, waste), telecom contracts, consumer finance contracts, purchase of goods by consumers and travel packs.

In order to ensure the effectiveness of the new provision, the new legislation also provides that arbitration clauses in consumer contracts are null and void, arbitral awards rendered in disputes that are non-arbitrable shall be considered as null and void, an express provision has been adopted obliging district courts to refuse issuance of writs of enforcement of arbitral awards that are rendered in disputes that are not arbitrable and arbitrators who render arbitral awards involving a consumer may be subject to financial sanctions amounting to up to BGN 2,500 (approximately EUR 1,300) and the arbitration institution could be fined up to BGN 5,000

---

[23] Act for amendment and supplementation of the Civil Procedure Code, published in State Gazette issue No. 8 of Jan. 24, 2017. Further analysis is available, in English, in the following articles: Angel Ganev& Tsvetelina Bayraktarova, *Key Amendments to Bulgarian Arbitration Law*, MONDAQ (Jan. 26, 2018), www.mondaq.com/x/650466/Arbitration+Dispute+Resolution/Key+Amendments+To+Bulgarian+Arbitration+Law; Deyan Dragiev, *Bulgaria Reforms Arbitration Law by Imposing More Control and Restrictions*, KLUWER ARBITRATION BLOG (Feb. 8, 2017), arbitrationblog.kluwerarbitration.com/2017/02/08/bulgaria-reforms-arbitration-law-by-imposing-more-control-and-restrictions/.

[24] Article 19 (Arbitration Agreement) of the Bulgarian Civil Procedure Code, on which *see supra* note 10.

(approximately EUR 2,600). this illustrates the firm will of the legislator to render impossible consumer arbitration in Bulgaria. Interestingly, the legislative provisions described here addressed not only the question of arbitrability but also provided express solutions for the conduct of such arbitration provisions (i.e., fines for arbitrators), the rendering of such awards (nullity) and their enforcement (impossibility for enforcement).

The case law of the courts in applying those provisions was consistent and in line with the intention of the legislator. The courts[25] not only fully applied the said provisions but also granted to them retroactive effect.[26] In particular, with respect to the provisions declaring such arbitral awards null and void and prohibiting courts to issue writs of enforcement, the courts have considered them as procedural rules and as such – with immediate application. In this way, the courts have set aside or refused issuance of writs of enforcement to arbitral awards rendered in arbitrations involving consumers, even if rendered before the 2017 amendments. This approach was widely criticized by Bulgarian legal doctrine,[27] as it led to adverse effects for legal security and put some claimants in situations of denial of justice, such as the expiration of claims due to limitation periods; thus under-effected arbitral awards were not able to initiate new claims before state courts.

Further, the provisions, with respect to fines to be imposed on arbitrators rendering arbitral awards involving consumers, have also been widely criticized. In particular, legal doctrine noted the extraordinary character of this provision, which subjects arbitrators to public law enforcement mechanisms in breach of the very idea of arbitration. To my best knowledge, no such sanctions have been imposed until now on arbitrators, and a number of authors have suggested the abolition of those fines.

2.2 Adaptation of Contracts

In its original wording, the ICAA expressly provides that arbitral tribunals may resolve disputes concerning filling gaps in a contract or its adaptation to newly arisen circumstances.[28] Although this power of arbitral tribunals is undisputed, recent case law of the Bulgarian Supreme Court of Cassation[29] (which is competent to hear set-aside cases) has specified that adaptation of contract is possible only if the arbitral tribunal is expressly empowered to do so by the parties.

The reasoning of the courts is based on the fact that adaptation of contract has been generally considered in Bulgaria not as a judicial activity (i.e., not as resolving a dispute on the basis of the law) but rather as a particular form of judicial administration. When it comes to arbitration, it is expected that the parties would most likely refer their disputes – i.e., the same scope of competence as the state courts in the context of a dispute would have between them. Thus, referral to arbitration, of matters which are not strictly speaking disputes, shall be explicit.

Thus, an arbitral tribunal in an international arbitration seated in Bulgaria would be allowed to fill gaps in a contract or adapt it to newly arisen circumstances only if this is expressly provided

---

[25] Judgment No. 315/17.12.2018 under commercial case No. 1374/2018 of the Supreme Court of Cassation.
[26] Judgment No. 36/28.06.2018 under commercial case No. 2798/2017 of the Supreme Court of Cassation.
[27] Желязкова, supra note 1, at 42 (2019).
[28] Article 1 (2) of the ICAA:

> The International commercial arbitration allows civil property disputes resulting from foreign economic relations as well as disputes for filling in the gaps in a contract or its adaptation to changed circumstances, if the domicile or the seat of at least one of the parties is not in the Republic of Bulgaria.

[29] Judgment No. 171 of Jan. 22, 2018, under commercial case No. 1791/2016 of 2nd Comm. division of the Supreme Court of Cassation.

for in the arbitration agreement. If the parties have not expressly authorized the arbitral tribunal to adapt or supplement the contract, this would be outside of the scope of the arbitration agreement and outside the scope of the powers of the arbitral tribunal. Another element of this particularity is that, according to Bulgarian legal doctrine,[30] an arbitral award where the tribunal has filled gaps in a contract or has adapted it to newly arisen circumstances would not have res judicata and most likely would not be enforceable as an arbitral award under the ICAA or the New York Convention.

Another question which arises with respect to adaptation of contracts is whether such claims are admissible in domestic arbitrations. Some authors consider that, on the ground of Art. 19 (1) of the CPC and Arts. 300 and 307 of the Commercial Act (dealing with the power of the court to fill gaps in a contract in case the parties do not reach an agreement on how to do this, and with the powers of the court to amend or terminate a contract in hardship situations, respectively), this should be possible if expressly provided for in the arbitration agreement.[31] However, the opposite opinion has also been expressed.[32] This issue is, thus, still debatable in Bulgarian case law and legal doctrine.

3 PUBLIC POLICY AND SET ASIDE OF AWARDS

Perhaps the most unexpected change introduced by the 2017 amendments was the reduction of the grounds for setting aside an arbitral award. The Bulgarian legislator deleted item 3 of Article 47 (1) of the ICAA, which provided that a breach of public policy is a ground for setting aside an arbitral award rendered by an arbitral tribunal seated in Bulgaria. Since the adoption of the ICAA in 1988, breach of public policy was one of the grounds for setting aside, as it is also under Art. 34 (2) (b) (ii) of the UNCITRAL Model Law. This ground for setting aside was widely used by the Supreme Court of Cassation and recognised by legal doctrine as an effective protection of parties in arbitration proceedings. However, during the past ten years, a number of arbitrators, practitioners and authors started complaining about the relatively active approach of the Supreme Court of Cassation in the course of set-aside proceedings. In particular, the Supreme Court of Cassation relatively often set aside arbitral awards rendered in proceedings involving consumers, for breach of procedural public policy.[33] Most of such cases indeed involved particularly severe breaches of the rights of fair proceedings. However, this ground for setting aside has also been sometimes used in more disputed circumstances to set aside arbitral awards rendered in a purely commercial context. For this reason, some arbitrators and authors[34] have suggested to either provide a stricter definition of public policy (which would then fragment the concept, which is used also in the New York Convention) or to simply delete it from the grounds for setting aside.

Nevertheless, this amendment was unexpected, as it was not sufficiently discussed by legal doctrine and was not related to the main purpose of the 2017 amendments (i.e., to enhance the protection of consumers) but, on the contrary, it seems to reduce the possibility for state courts to

---

[30] Assen Alexiev, *National Report for Bulgaria (2018 through 2019)*, in ICCA INTERNATIONAL HANDBOOK ON COMMERCIAL ARBITRATION 19 (Lise Bosman ed., 2019), Supplement No. 104, Feb. 2019.
[31] *Id.*
[32] Silvy Chernev, *Country Report on International Arbitration – Bulgaria*, in ARBITRATION LAW AND PRACTICE IN CENTRAL AND EASTERN EUROPE (2006).
[33] Judgment No. 8 of Feb. 4, 2013, under commercial case No. 1052/2012 of the Supreme Court of Cassation, Judgment No. 20 of Feb. 4, 2016 under commercial case No. 2893/2015 of the Supreme Court of Cassation, Judgment No. 33 of July 1, 2016, under commercial case No. 2620/2015 of the Supreme Court of Cassation.
[34] Желязкова, *supra* note 1, at 326.

control arbitral awards. Deleting the breach of public policy as a ground for setting aside immediately produced effects, the Supreme Court of Cassation extended the scope of other grounds for setting aside in order to prevent arbitral awards from producing unacceptable results.[35] In this respect, the reaction of the Supreme Court of Cassation shows that the balance between the limited review in set-aside proceedings and the powers of the courts, reached with the UNCITRAL Model Law and originally implemented in the ICAA, was in fact rather well working and efficient for the intended purposes. We would expect in the future an intensification of the reaction of the Supreme Court of Cassation in this respect to further legislative amendments to reestablish the ground for set aside for breach of public policy.

It is interesting to note that the 2017 amendments did not affect the application of the public policy grounds in matters of recognition and enforcement of foreign arbitral awards, which is governed by the New York Convention or the Bulgarian Private International Law Code (if the NY Convention is not applicable). This leads to the strange situation that an arbitral award (domestic or international) rendered in Bulgaria and breaching public policy could not be set aside, where an international or foreign arbitral award with similar content could have its recognition refused on the same ground. This could be potentially a shortcut to overturn Bulgarian public policy.

4 OTHER RECENT AMENDMENTS IN RELATION TO ARBITRATION

4.1 Control of Arbitral Institutions

Another major development is the introduction for the first time in Bulgarian law of a mechanism for control over arbitration institutions for compliance of their practices with the ICAA. Such control is to be exercised by an inspectorate with the Ministry of Justice. The inspectorate may initiate an inspection ex officio by way of decision by the minister of justice or upon complaint by interested parties. During an inspection, the arbitral institution shall ensure access to its premises and archives. Following the inspection, the inspectors may issue mandatory recommendations to the arbitral institution, where the noncompliance may lead to fines amounting to up to BGN 2,500 (approximately EUR 1,300). This mechanism applies exclusively to arbitral institutions seated in Bulgaria. Notwithstanding that, at first sight, it may seem a threat to the independence of arbitral institutions, the mechanism is intended primarily to ensure the compliance with the provisions protecting consumers, and until now it has not been enforced in practice.

4.2 Conditions and Qualifications for Arbitrators

The 2017 amendments introduced, for the first time in Bulgarian law, conditions to be met by arbitrators. Under the new Article 11 (3) of the ICAA, any natural person may be appointed as arbitrator, provided that the prospective arbitrator (1) has not been convicted of a premeditated crime, (2) holds a university degree, (3) has at least eight years of professional experience and (4) has high integrity. Similar conditions existed under some of the institutional arbitration rules but were not provided in the ICAA.

---

[35] For instance, Judgment No. 189 of Nov. 9, 2017, under commercial case No. 1675/2017 of the Supreme Court of Cassation, where an arbitral award was set aside on the ground that the award was dealing with matters outside the arbitration agreement, where before the amendments the SCC would probably have used the provision on breach of public policy.

The question arises what would be the sanction of noncompliance with this provision. The ICAA does not provide explicitly for the consequences if an arbitrator is appointed without having the due qualifications. In our view, the sanctions to be excluded are the set aside and nonenforceability of the arbitral award, as the grounds for such consequence are enumerated in the respective provisions of the ICAA and cannot be interpreted in an extensive way. A potential sanction could be the removal of the arbitrator in case of challenge; however, there is still no case law in this respect. A civil-law consequence of the breach of this provision could be potential liability for damages, although under Bulgarian law it would be difficult to establish the causal link between the potential breach and the respective damages in such a situation.

Although the ICAA does not explicitly provide whether this requirement is to be applied also to international arbitrations seated in Bulgaria, it should be considered also when appointing arbitrators for arbitrations with a seat in Bulgaria under foreign arbitration rules (for instance in case of an ICC arbitration seated in Bulgaria) or in international ad hoc cases seated in Bulgaria.

4.3 Obligation to Ensure Online Access to the Case File

Following the 2017 amendments, the parties in arbitration proceedings should have online access to the case file. Although such options existed for arbitration at the AC at the BCCI for a long time, applying this condition could create some practical issues in respect of ad hoc arbitrations or arbitrations administered by other institutions.

5 CONCLUSION

Arbitration remains a widely used and reliable venue for dispute resolution in Bulgaria. The Bulgarian arbitration legislation is generally arbitration friendly and supportive, and the local legislative framework and court practice are predictable with respect to arbitration. The core principles of separability of the arbitration agreement and of competence–competence are affirmed and respected.

The limitation of consumer disputes, although limiting the number of cases, may have positive effects in terms of credibility and integrity of arbitration. Lower fees of arbitration compared with state courts, a faster arbitration process and the considerable workload of state courts, which often impedes judges from going into the details of a dispute, are favourable conditions for commercial arbitration to expand in Bulgaria across sectors, including electricity and gas trade, construction and FIDIC disputes, and possibly post-M&A disputes, which some other countries have viewed as matters of public policy best reserved for the courts.

13

Judicial Control of Arbitral Awards in Mainland China

Chen Lei and Wang Hao

1 INTRODUCTION

Mainland China has not adopted the UN Commission on International Trade Law (UNCITRAL) Model Law, nor has it permitted ad hoc arbitration. Yet, arbitration in China is developing rapidly. According to the data released by the Ministry of Justice on March 2019, at the end of 2018 there were 255 arbitration commissions established with more than 60,000 staff members in mainland China.[1] The caseload of 2018 is 540,000, which was a 127 percent increase compared to that in 2017.[2] The stakes involved in 2018 are around 700 billion RMB.[3] Since the promulgation of the Chinese Arbitration Law (CAL) in 1994, domestic arbitral commissions have handled over 2.6 million cases involving more than seventy countries/regions.[4] Additionally, judicial review of arbitration in China has undergone changes over the last decades. The Chinese Arbitration Law has gone through heated discussions of amendment, and the Supreme People's Court's (SPC) judicial interpretations have contributed significantly to the development of Chinese arbitration. With the acceleration of open-up policy and the implementation of the Belt and Road Initiative (BRI), China endeavors to elevate its international image by providing fair, transparent, and efficient judicial services for international dispute resolution. Judicial attitude toward arbitration becomes more open minded than ever before. In earlier days, foreign investors had little information on the prospects of enforceability of arbitral awards in mainland China. The uncertainty inevitably affected their decisions on whether to choose arbitration as a dispute resolution mechanism when doing business with Chinese counterparts.

2 STATUTORY FRAMEWORK OF CHINESE ARBITRATION

2.1 Dual-Track System and Its Legal Basis

In mainland China, arbitral awards are normally categorized into three types, i.e., domestic awards, foreign-related arbitral awards, and foreign arbitral awards.[5] Domestic arbitral awards are

---

[1] A media report by the Ministry of Justice at the official website, www.moj.gov.cn/subject/content/2019-03/26/862_231600.html.
[2] Id.
[3] Id.
[4] Id.
[5] Chinese Civil Procedure Law stipulates different judicial criteria for enforcement of domestic, foreign-related, and foreign arbitral awards.

awards granted by Chinese arbitral institutions without foreign elements. Foreign-related awards are awards related to economic, trade, transportation, and maritime activities involving certain foreign elements. Foreign awards are granted by foreign arbitral institutions or ad hoc arbitration conducted outside mainland China. Hence, foreign-related arbitral awards are still domestic arbitral awards in a broad sense and subject to domestic laws.[6] The CAL set up separate criteria in regard to enforcement of domestic and foreign arbitral awards. For domestic awards, judicial supervision could be exercised over both procedural and substantive issues. Article 58 of the CAL grants the court power to control substantive aspects of domestic arbitral awards in certain circumstances.[7] Contrary to domestic awards, the court can only exercise judicial supervision over procedural issues in foreign arbitral proceedings pursuant to the UN Convention on the Recognition and Enforcement of Foreign Arbitral Awards 1958 (New York Convention). That is what we called the dual-track system.

2.2 Institutional and Ad Hoc Arbitration

Since the CAL makes the selection of arbitration institution a prerequisite for a valid arbitral agreement,[8] basically ad hoc arbitration is not permitted in mainland China.[9] However, according to the New York Convention, to which China is a contracting state, ad hoc commercial arbitration conducted outside mainland China could be recognized and enforced by Chinese courts.

2.3 Prior Reporting System

The prior reporting system (PRS) is the feature of judicial review of foreign and foreign-related arbitral awards that has the strongest Chinese characteristic. Article 2 of the Notice of the SPC on Handling Relevant Issues about Foreign-Related Arbitration and Foreign Arbitral Issues, which was issued by the SPC in 1995, requires any judicial decision of the Intermediate People's Court (IPC) to refuse recognition of foreign arbitral awards has to be reviewed by the Higher People's Court (HPC) and later by the SPC. This is a procedural mechanism to ensure a refused-recognition decision is well founded. Besides, such a mechanism also functions as a safeguard to ensure that arbitral awards' enforcement in Chinese courts effectively reduces

---

[6] Before 1996, only the China International Economic and Trade Arbitration Commission (CIETAC) and the China Maritime Arbitration Commission (CMAC) were permitted to do foreign-related arbitral cases in China. Other arbitration commissions were confined to do only domestic cases, even though these two kinds of arbitral awards are subject to the same applicable law, which is the Chinese arbitration law and the related SPC's judicial interpretations for judicial review. Due to this differentiation, when the SPC decided to apply the prior reporting system on judicial review of arbitral awards, both foreign awards and foreign-related awards were included and required to request approval from the SPC if the local courts held denial opinions toward these arbitral awards. Since CIETAC awards are deemed domestic awards regardless of whether they involve foreign elements, their enforcements in court are not pursuant to the New York Convention but to another set of domestic rules. Surveys mingling foreign awards and foreign-related awards granted by the CIETAC or other Chinese arbitration commissions are inaccurate for illustrating the application situation of the New York Convention in Chinese court.

[7] According to Article 58 of the Chinese Arbitration Law, arbitral awards can be set aside on the grounds of forged or hidden evidence.

[8] See Article 16 of the Chinese Arbitration Law.

[9] Article IV (9) of the Opinions of the SPC on Providing Judicial Guarantee for the Building of Pilot Free Trade Zones in 2016 provides that if two enterprises registered in the free trade zone (FTZ) agree that relevant disputes shall be submitted to arbitration at a particular place in the Chinese mainland, according to particular arbitration rules, or by particular personnel, the arbitration agreement may be determined as valid. So, under certain circumstances ad hoc arbitration might be conducted in the FTZs.

interventions caused by local protectionism. On the other hand, the PRS is very effective in providing guidance for local courts in regard to detailed issues or correct understanding of the New York Convention. The PRS was designed to apply to the enforcement of only foreign arbitral awards in order to decide the validity of arbitral agreements/clauses of foreign or foreign-related arbitral awards and whether to set aside or refuse the enforcement of foreign-related arbitration awards. It establishes a duty for the IPC to report and request approval from the HPC if the former intends to refuse enforcement of arbitral awards or deny the validity of arbitral clauses. If the HPC concurs with the position of the IPC, it must further report to the SPC. Theoretically, any refusal judgment should be requested by a local court and be approved eventually by the SPC. Since all the requests and replies are published in the journal *China Trial Guide on Foreign-Related Commercial and Maritime Trial* (edited by the 4th Civil Division of the SPC, which specifically deals with foreign-related civil and commercial cases and maritime disputes), the reasons of refusal and reasoning held by different levels of courts are comprehensively published and available to the public. This SPC system purports to both provide guidance for and supervision of local courts. At the end of 2017, the SPC released new judicial interpretations that extend the application of the PRS to domestic arbitration with slight differences. All refusal verdicts toward arbitral agreements or arbitral awards should be approved by the HPC; regardless of whether they involve domestic or foreign arbitrations. If the court intends to turn down a domestic arbitration on the basis of public policy or the dispute involving parties from another province, only the SPC has the final say upon the issue.

3 EMPIRICAL STUDY ON ENFORCEMENT OF FOREIGN ARBITRAL AWARDS

3.1 *Legal Basis*

China has adopted the New York Convention since 1987 with reciprocity reservation and commercial reservation. Awards would be recognized only if they are made in the territory of other contracting states and if the subject matters of the disputes are considered to be commercial under the laws of the People's Republic of China (PRC), excluding disputes between investors and foreign states. In 1987 the SPC issued a Notice of the SPC on Implementing the Convention on the Recognition and Enforcement of Foreign Arbitral Awards Acceded to by China (the "Notice"),[10] which served as the basis for the application of the New York Convention within Chinese jurisdiction. The Notice elaborates further on the definition of *commercial*,[11] including procedural details such as jurisdiction of the court and limitation period of application.[12] At the

---

[10] See No. 5 [1987] of the Supreme People's Court, Apr. 10, 1987.

[11] Article 2 of the notice provides that "[l]egal relationships, whether contractual or not, which are considered commercial" means the economic rights and obligations arising from contracts, torts, or relevant legal provisions such as purchase and sale of goods, lease of property, project contracting, processing, technology transfer, equity or contractual joint adventure, exploration and development of natural resources, insurance, credit, labor service, agency, consultation service, marine, civil aviation, railway or road passenger and cargo transportation, product liability, environment pollution, marine accident, and ownership disputes, except disputes between foreign investors and the host government.

[12] At that time, Article 169 of the Civil Procedure Law of the People's Republic of China (Trial Implementation) provided that

> [t]he time limit for an application for enforcement shall be one year, if both parties are individuals or either of them is an individual; or shall be six months if both parties are enterprises, public institutions, government agencies or social groups.

> This has been amended in Article 239 of the Civil Procedure Law of 1991 (as revised in 2017) and unified to two years.

time, China had neither arbitration law nor civil procedural law. For awards made in the Hong Kong Special Administrative Region (HKSAR), Macau Special Administrative Region (MSAR), and Taiwan, there are separate arrangements or directives to regulate the relevant issues.[13]

3.2 Empirical Studies

There have been many empirical studies on the recognition and enforcement of arbitral awards made by Chinese courts. Some of these studies were conducted by domestic arbitration institutions, and some were written by scholars in this field. For example, the Arbitration Research Institute (ARI) of the China International Economic and Trade Arbitration Commission (CIETAC) conducted two surveys, separately, in 1994 and 1996, finding that 71 percent of foreign arbitral awards were enforced by courts.[14] The results contained within these two surveys were widely cited and functioned as a reference for comparison by later empirical studies conducted by scholars to verify their empirical study outcomes. Peerenboom's study in 2001 was based on eighty-nine foreign and CIETAC reported cases and interviews of practitioners, which he approached by relying on his personal connections with foreign and PRC lawyers and academics.[15] In this study, he found that the general enforcement rate of foreign arbitral awards in Chinese courts was 52 percent, which was higher than the 47 percent success rate for CIETAC awards. Furthermore, investors could expect to recover 75–50 percent of the award amount in 34 percent of the cases and half of the award in at least 40 percent of the cases. There are a couple of studies made by judges from the SPC as well. One was conducted in 2007, which reviewed 610 cases involving foreign and foreign-related arbitral awards between 2002 and 2006 based on the data and reports provided by the local courts of major provinces.[16] This survey is based on co-operative research between the 4th Civil Division of SPC and Seventeen HPCs in PRC. Within this large subset of cases, seventy-four cases involved actions for the recognition and enforcement of foreign arbitral awards. Of these seventy-four cases, the survey found fifty-eight applications had been granted, six cases were withdrawn because of settlement or other reasons, five cases resulted in nonenforcement, and the other five cases were pending. According to this survey, the enforcement rate of foreign arbitral awards was around 78 percent. Another study made by the SPC judges was conducted in 2012 and reviewed fifty-six cases of SPC's review of lower court nonenforcement requests of foreign arbitral awards from 2000 to 2011.[17] Of these fifty-six proposed nonenforcement requests submitted by different local courts,

---

[13] For HKSAR, there is the SPC arrangement with respect to the Mutual Enforcement of Arbitral Awards by the mainland and the Hong Kong Special Administrative Region; for MSAR, there is the SPC arrangement with respect to the Mutual Acknowledgment and Enforcement of Arbitral Awards by the mainland and the Macau Special Administrative Region; for Taiwan, there are the SPC directives with respect to Acknowledgment and Enforcement of Arbitral Awards Rendered in Taiwan Region.

[14] Wang Shengchang, *Enforcement of Foreign Awards in the People's Republic of China*, in IMPROVING THE EFFICIENCY OF ARBITRATION AND AWARD: 40 YEARS OF APPLICATION OF THE NEW YORK CONVENTION 461–480, 482 (Albert Jan Van den Berg ed., 1998).

[15] The sixty-six cases Peerenboom obtained were through interviews; only eighteen cases were from reliable publications, and another five cases were from a combination of texts and interviews. See Randall Peerenboom, *Seek Truth from Facts: An Empirical Study of the Enforcement of Arbitral Awards in the PRC*, 49 AMERICAN JOURNAL OF COMPARATIVE LAW 249–328, 250 (2001).

[16] Yang Honglei (杨弘磊), *Research Report on Judicial Review of Foreign-Related Arbitration by the People's Court* (人民法院涉外仲裁司法审查情况的调研报告), 7 INTERNATIONAL LAW REVIEW OF WUHAN UNIVERSITY (武大国际法评论) 304–321 (2007) (China).

[17] Liu Guixiang & Shen Hongyu, *Recognition and Enforcement of Foreign Arbitral Awards: A Reflection on Court Practices*, 1 BEIJING ARBITRATION (北京仲裁) (China) 1 (2012).

the SPC confirmed nonenforcement in twenty-one cases. Generally, 62 percent of the nonenforcement requests submitted by local courts were denied or sent back to the relevant courts for further consideration by the SPC in its replies. The latest empirical study on the enforcement of foreign arbitral awards collected from China Judgment Online and PKU Lawinfor (Beida Fabao) covers eighty-one judgments of the Chinese courts from 2015 to 2017 and thirty-five replies made by the SPC before 2015.[18]

3.3 Empirical Survey

We have collected altogether 283 court decisions (239 cases on recognition and enforcement of foreign arbitral awards and 44 cases on the enforcement of HKSAR arbitral awards) from publicly available sources. The earliest court decision available was made in 1990 by the Guangzhou Maritime Court.[19] This study collected only concrete judgments that could be verified through open resources with docket numbers. No pending case was included. According to our survey, nearly 67 percent of foreign awards were enforced and around 65 percent of the HKSAR awards were enforced. The overall enforcement rate was 66.67 percent. This outcome was very similar to the survey on 98 court cases conducted in 2016 involving enforcement of foreign arbitral awards from 1994 to 2015. According to that survey, China courts recorded an overall average enforcement rate of 68 percent.[20]

The geographic distribution of cases is illustrated in Figure 13.1. As can be seen, the darker an area is colored, the more cases a relevant local court has adjudicated.

As indicated in the map, the geographic distribution of foreign and HKSAR arbitral awards enforcement is generally concentrated in the southern and eastern parts of China. This does not necessarily indicate that judicial capacity in these areas is superior to other parts of China. Since Art. 224 of Chinese Civil Procedure Law directs parties seeking enforcement of foreign arbitral awards to "apply to the intermediate people's court of the place where the party subjected to the enforcement has his domicile or wherever his property is located," most of these cases were adjudicated in provinces where the respondents resided or where their property located. Courts in areas bearing vigorous international commercial transactions naturally gain jurisdiction over these types of cases. The distribution on locations of these cases is a clear reflection of China's overall economic development. Coastal provinces such as Guangdong, Jiangsu, and Shandong have many more cases than Beijing largely due to import and export economic trade mode. It is worth noting that Hubei, as an inland province, has more cases than other inland provinces because it is where the Wuhan Maritime Court is seated. As arbitration is popularly selected as a form of dispute resolution in the maritime industry, enforcement of such cases would be handled in maritime courts subject to exclusive jurisdiction.

Under the CAL, the parties cannot freely choose the place of adjudication of an enforcement procedure.[21] Nonetheless, it may happen that parties try to create some connection with certain provinces, though most of them would fail. For example, in *Changsheng Trading Co. Inc*

---

[18] Liu Jingdong & Wang Lulu, *An Empirical Study on Recognition and Enforcement of Foreign Arbitral Awards in Our Country under the Initiative of "One Belt, One Road"* (一带一路"倡议下我国对外国仲裁裁决承认与执行的实证研究), 5 JOURNAL OF LAW APPLICATION (法律适用) (China) (2018), http://www.iolaw.org.cn/showArticle.aspx?id=5494.
[19] *See* (1990) Guang Hai Fa Shang Zi No. 31.
[20] *See* Meg Utterback, *Enforcing Foreign Arbitral Awards in CHINA – A Review of the Past Twenty Years*, KING & WOOD MALLESONS (Sept. 18, 2016), www.kwm.com/en/knowledge/insights/enforcing-foreign-arbitral-awards-in-china-20160915.
[21] Article 2 of the SPC Opinion on the Judicial Review of Arbitral Awards of 2017.

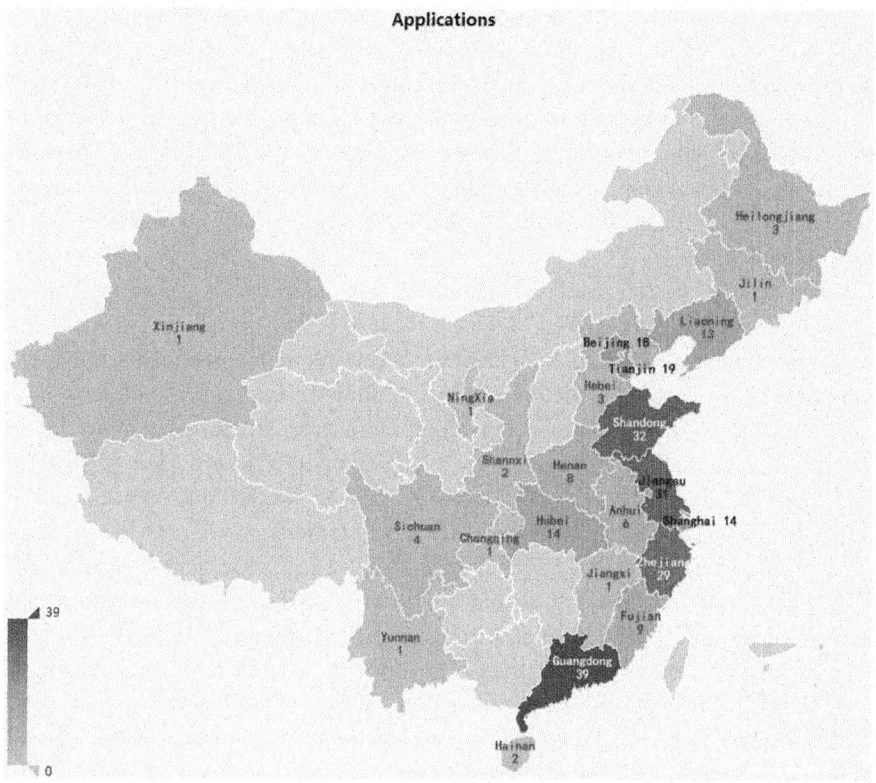

FIGURE 13.1 Geographic distribution of applications to recognize and enforce foreign arbitral awards

v. *Henan Jianghe Industrial Co., Ltd*,[22] the applicant presented its application for recognition and enforcement of a foreign arbitral award in Lianyungang Intermediate People's Court located in Jiangsu Province. The court dismissed the case on the ground of lack of jurisdiction. The court held that the respondent was registered in Henan Province, and there was no evidence proving that its property was located in Lianyungang City. Because the respondent was bankrupt, this case has been counted also as one of the nonenforcement cases in this study. Also, in *United Communications (Holdings) Corporation v. Weisheng Electronics Co. Ltd*,[23] the applicant tried to enforce a Hong Kong International Arbitration Centre (HKIAC) award in the Beijing No. 4 Intermediate Court. The respondent, a Taiwan registered company, raised an objection to jurisdiction. United Communications insisted that the Beijing Court had jurisdiction over the case since the respondent held 100 percent share of Viatechco Ltd., which held 100 percent of Viatechnologies (HK) Inc Ltd. – the only shareholder of ViaChina. Ltd., a company that was headquartered in Beijing. The court rejected the case for want of jurisdiction. The creation of a connection through indirect investment has not so far been accepted by courts.

Under the PRS, the refusal decisions made by IPCs usually went through scrutiny by the SPC. A simple comparison of the absolute refusal numbers or the ratios is not enough to draw a comprehensive conclusion. After the case-by-case analysis, we find that in a province such as Jiangsu, which had the highest number of refusal decisions, all of the refusal requests were

---

[22] *See* (2016) Su 07 Xie Wai Ren No. 1 [(2016) 苏07协外认1号].
[23] *See* (2015) Si Zhong Min Shang Te Zi No. 272.

double-checked and confirmed by the SPC. On the contrary, for a province such as Liaoning, which had only one refusal case and a quite low refusal rate (7.69 percent), we found upon closer scrutiny that three out of four requests the courts in the province submitted were denied by SPC. It is clear that, with the introduction of the PRS, a procedural safeguard has been in place to lower the refusal rate of many provinces. As far as all the SPC's replies are concerned, it indicates that, comparatively, courts in Jiangsu and Tianjin shared a similar understanding with the judges of the SPC in dealing with foreign (including HKSAR) arbitral awards enforcement applications.

It is notable that, in practice, the guidance provided by the SPC has its limits. For example, the SPC would make interpretations only on matters of law and leave great discretion to local courts on matters of fact. In that situation, many requests contain diverging opinions, and both majority and minority opinions were submitted. Taking a closer look into these requests and replies, we discover that some courts submitted requests even when the majority opinion actually supported the enforcement of the foreign arbitral award. Hence, the local court should have directly enforced the award without requesting the SPC to conduct a check.

Additionally, the SPC does not always provide final opinions on whether the awards should be enforced. For example, in *Ecom Agro Industrial Asia Pte Ltd* v. *Qingdao Golden River Group Penglai Textile Clothes Co., Ltd*,[24] the issue in question was on the validity of the arbitration agreement. The Shandong HPC formed two contradicting opinions, yet the SPC replied that the issue of whether there was an arbitration agreement in existence between the parties should be decided by HPC. The SPC did not provide a direct answer to the question in that reply. What if the HPC's decision is to refuse the enforcement based on the ground of validity of arbitration agreement? Does it mean HPC needs to submit the same case again to SPC for a final check? This would obviously generate some unnecessary delay.

Furthermore, there is no supervision mechanism or sanctions against breach of the PRS in the judicial interpretations. Sometimes it is unclear whether local courts have submitted all refusal decisions to the SPC as required. The requirement to report was made through a notice of the SPC rather than stipulated in law or judicial interpretations, which leaves some suspicion on the actual operation of the system. For example, in one of the refusal cases decided by the Xiamen Maritime Court,[25] we did not find any trace of the SPC's reply, but when we interviewed a judge in the Xiamen Maritime Court, we found that the SPC actually had given a reply regarding that case. We asked the judge from the Xiamen Maritime Court whether the Xiamen Maritime Court reported that case to the SPC. The judge gave us an affirmative answer and sent us a copy of the SPC's reply on that case,[26] though this request and reply were not publicly accessible. From this case, it can be inferred that failing to find corresponding SPC replies does not necessarily mean that the case did not comply with PRS. However, we also found some other cases that, in all likelihood (though lacking absolute certainty), were highly probably not reported to the SPC as required by PRS. For example, in *Chenco Chemical Engineering and Consulting GMBH* v. *Duofuduo Chemical Corp*, the Xinxiang IPC in Henan Province issued a refusal decision.[27] In that case, the Xinxiang IPC conducted a hearing on August 7, 2014, but issued a refusal decision on August 21, 2014. In less than fifteen days' time, it would have been impossible for the Xinxiang IPC to report to the Henan HPC, which

---

[24] *See* (2015) Min Si Ta Zi No. 29.
[25] *See* (2010) Min Min Ta Zi No. 1 [(2016)闽民他字第1号].
[26] *See* (2010) Min Si Ta Zi No. 67 [(2010)民四他字第67号].
[27] *See* (2014) Xin Zhong Min San Chu Zi No. 73 [(2014) 新中民三初字第73号].

subsequently reported to the SPC for approval. It is suspected that this refusal decision did not follow PRS as required. To tackle this problem, SPC issued a new judicial interpretation in 2017, which introduced the resultant disciplinary consequences as the local courts are duty-bound to comply with PRS.[28] However, the interpretation did not extend the reporting system as it might at first sight appear. Under the 2017 Interpretations, the PRS applied to domestic arbitrations only when: (1) the parties in dispute reside in different provinces or (2) the ground for refusing enforcement or setting aside the award is "infringement of public policy."[29] In those cases, it is mandatory to report to every level of higher court, up to and including the SPC. In all other domestic cases, the HPC will conduct the final review, without involving the SPC.

Finally, the PRS would inevitably prolong the already time-consuming judicial review process. Although the law prescribes a time limit for such cases, the mechanism does not provide a deadline for either reporting or replying. Two issues are at stake. First, sometimes the IPC may just take no action, neither enforcing nor requesting the SPC to verify its decision not to enforce. This surely prolongs the process and, therefore, affects the applicant's interests. Under the Chinese Civil Procedure Law, a case should be dealt with within the time frame.[30] But that mainly concerns domestic cases without foreign elements. For cases enforcing a foreign arbitral award, there is no hard and fast rule on time limit. Second, it is about the further delay caused by shortage of manpower at SPC. According to KWM survey, the average time taken to obtain a final order on enforcement from the time of application was 331 days.[31] In the case *Siemens International Trade Co., Ltd* v. *Shanghai Golden Landmark Co., Ltd*,[32] it took 293 days for the SPC to deny the refusal request made by Shanghai High People's Court. This may not strike one as an unduly long period of time. But when the PRS is also applied to enforce domestic arbitration awards under the new SPC initiative, this would bring new challenges. As all the cases dealing with enforcement of arbitral awards, whether foreign or domestic, will go to SPC, it is anticipated that the SPC's would be overburdened, thus causing further delay in the process.

4 CASE ANALYSIS OF NONENFORCEMENT IN CHINESE JUDICIAL PRACTICE

The grounds for refusal of both foreign and HKSAR arbitral awards are basically the same. Both the New York Convention and the HKSAR Mutual Arrangement[33] provide that arbitral awards can be refused on the following grounds: (1) lack of a valid arbitration agreement, (2) lack of notice, (3) the arbitration tribunal exceeded its authority, (4) defects in the composition of arbitral tribunal or arbitration procedures, (5) the arbitral award had been set aside or was not binding, (6) arbitrability, and (7) violation of public policy.

4.1 *Validity of Arbitral Agreement*

Under both the New York Convention and the HKSAR Mutual Arrangement, courts may refuse enforcement of a foreign or HKSAR arbitral award if the arbitration agreement is not valid or

---

[28] On Dec. 29, 2017, the SPC published two judicial interpretations, which came into force on Jan. 1, 2018.
[29] *Id.*
[30] Article 135 of the Chinese Civil Procedure Law.
[31] *See* Utterback, *supra* note 20.
[32] *See* [2015] Min Si Ta Zi No. 5 ([2015] 民四他字第5号).
[33] *See* Peerenboom, *supra* note 15.

if one of the parties to the agreement lacked the capacity to make the agreement.[34] The question of invalidity or incapacity is governed by the law chosen by the parties as stipulated in the agreement or, if no choice was made, by the law of the country where the award was made. The ground of validity of arbitral agreement can also be invoked to set aside domestic arbitral awards.

Validity has regularly been relied upon as a ground to refuse enforcement or set aside arbitral awards. For example, in *Proton Automobiles Ltd. v. Venus Heavy Industries Co., Ltd.*,[35] the parties had contracted to establish a Sino-foreign joint venture, and the contract stated that any dispute arising between the parties should be referred to the arbitral tribunal of the Singapore International Arbitration Center (SIAC) under UNCITRAL Arbitration Rules. A dispute arose between the parties, and Proton initiated arbitration against Venus. The SIAC later rendered an arbitral award in favor of Proton. When Proton initiated an application for enforcement in Dongguan IPC, Venus raised an objection on the ground that the arbitration clause in the joint venture contract had been substituted by a subsequently signed forum-selection clause. The court accepted the objection raised by Venus and refused to enforce the arbitral award granted by SIAC on the ground of invalid arbitration clause. The controversial issue was that the court drew this conclusion on the basis of the claimant's (i.e., Proton's) failure to provide sufficient evidence that the subsequent memorandum was fake, thus not following the burden of proof rules of Article V(1) of the New York Convention.[36]

In *Glencore Co., Ltd v. Chongqing Machinery and Equipment Import and Export Corporation*,[37] the SPC for the first time clarified that the capacity of the parties should be determined by private international law of the enforcement state. Whether Mr. Sun, as an employee of the respondent, has properly delegated authority to sign the contract for Chongqing Machinery and Equipment Import & Export Company is a question that should be answered by resorting to Chinese law. Since Mr. Sun was not authorized by his employer, and the contract also did not contain the official seal of the company, the respondent subsequently made a clear denial of such authorization. The contract and the arbitration clause therein contained were both invalid and the arbitral award granted on the basis of the arbitration clause should be refused in terms of enforcement.

In *Siemens International Trade Co. Ltd v. Shanghai Golden Landmark Co. Ltd.*,[38] the validity of the arbitration clause was quite open to question. The main issue was whether the contract in question involved foreign-related elements. Under Chinese law, only foreign-related disputes can be submitted to arbitration outside mainland China.[39] If it was a foreign-related dispute, the arbitration agreement would have been valid; otherwise it would have been invalid.[40] Since

---

[34] Article V 1 (a) of New York Convention provides that enforcement can be refused if a party furnishes proof that

the parties to the agreement referred to in article II were, under the law applicable to them, under some incapacity, or the said agreement is not valid under the law to which the parties have subjected it or, failing any indication thereon, under the law of the country where the award was made.

[35] Proton Automobiles Ltd. v. Venus Heavy Industries Co., Ltd. (宝腾汽车（中国）有限公司与金星重工制造有限公司申请承认和执行外国仲裁裁决纠纷案). *See* (2013) Min Si Ta Zi No. 28 [(2013) 民四他字第28号].

[36] According to Article V(1) of the New York Convention, the party who is against the enforcement of award and invokes a refusal procedure should furnish proof to the competent authority where the recognition and enforcement is sought.

[37] *See* [2001] Min Si Ta Zi No. 2 ([2001] 民四他字第2号).

[38] *See supra* note 32.

[39] *See* Article 128 of the Chinese Contract Law.

[40] According to Article 1 of the Interpretations of the Supreme People's Court on Several Issues Concerning Application of the Law of the People's Republic of China on Choice of Law for Foreign-Related Civil Relationships (I), when a civil relationship falls under any of the following circumstances, the people's court may deem it a foreign-related civil

Siemens and Golden Landmark were both Chinese legal persons, the Shanghai No. 1 IPC was about to refuse enforcement on the ground that the arbitration agreement was invalid. The Shanghai HPC intended to invoke public policy as a "safety valve" and to refuse enforcement as well. These propositions were both denied by the SPC which held that

> [t]he contract does not, *prima facie*, have any foreign-related elements. However, considering the parties to the contract, the specification of performance and other actual circumstances as a whole, this contract with unique features is obviously different from a purely domestic contract and can be deemed a foreign-related civil legal relationship.[41]

The case of *Siemens* has been taken as an example showing the gradually open and supportive attitude of the Chinese courts toward foreign arbitral awards. Yet, there are criticisms as well. The controversy sits on whether the validity of arbitration agreements should be judged according to Chinese domestic law. Since Article 2 of the New York Convention has clearly directed that the validity of arbitral agreement should be determined by the law the parties chose or the law of the seat of arbitration, there should be no room for direct application of domestic law. For example, in *Züblin International GmbH v. Wuxi Woke General Engineering Project Rubber Co., Ltd.*,[42] the parties consented to "Arbitration: ICC Rules, Shanghai shall apply." However, the court held that because, according to CAL, a clearly designated arbitration institution is required, the failure to name an arbitration commission in this arbitral clause rendered the clause invalid. In that case, the seat of arbitration was Shanghai; hence, Chinese law was the applicable law for determining the validity of the arbitration agreement. However, in *Siemens* and another case regarding a South Korean award enforcement,[43] the courts refused to enforce the awards by stating no foreign elements were involved in those cases and the relevant arbitral clauses were invalid. Since these two awards were not made within the PRC, the authors sustain that Chinese law should not be applicable here to determine the validity of the arbitration agreements.

4.2 Denial of Opportunity to Present Case

Due process applies to judicial control of both domestic and foreign arbitral awards. It means that recognition and enforcement can be refused if "the party against whom the award is invoked

---

relationship: (1) where either party or both parties are foreign citizens, foreign legal persons, or other organizations or stateless persons; (2) where the habitual residence of either party or both parties is located outside the territory of the People's Republic of China; (3) where the subject matter [of the relationship] is outside the territory of the People's Republic of China; (4) when the legal facts that lead to the establishment, change, or termination of the civil relationship happen outside the territory of the People's Republic of China; or (5) in other circumstances under which the civil relationship may be determined as a foreign-related civil relationship.

[41] The main reasons of the SPC are the following: (1) the parties to the contract were foreign-related to some degree. Although they were all Chinese legal persons, their registration place was in the Shanghai Free Trade Zone, and they are wholly foreign-owned enterprises. Because the sources of capital, ownership of ultimate interest and the governance of such companies were closely related to foreign investors, these two companies had foreign-related characteristics compared with normal domestic enterprises. (2) The performance of the contract had foreign-related characteristics. The goods that were the subject matter of this contract had to be imported from abroad to the Shanghai Free Trade Zone and went through a whole set of Chinese customs procedures, which was similar to an international sale of goods. The court, therefore, concluded that the contract dispute fell within the scope of Article 1(d) of the Interpretations of the Supreme People's Court on Several Issues Concerning Application of the Law of the People's Republic of China on Choice of Law for Foreign-Related Civil Relationships – that is, "other circumstances under which the civil relationship may be determined as a foreign-related civil relationship." The decision is published in 41 *Yearbook Commercial Arbitration* 96–98 (2016).

[42] *See* (2004) Xi Min San Zhong Zi No.1 [(2004) 锡民三仲字第1号].

[43] *See* (2013) Min Si Ta Zi No. 64 [(2013) 民四他字第64号].

was not given proper notice of the appointment of the arbitrator or of the arbitration proceedings or was otherwise unable to present his case."[44]

In *Aiduoladuo (Mongolia) Co., Ltd. v. Zhejiang Zhancheng Construction Group Co., Ltd.*,[45] the parties contracted for a construction project. Later when a dispute arose, *Aiduoladuo* initiated arbitration against *Zhejiang Zhancheng* in the Mongolian National Arbitration Center, which rendered a default award in favor of *Aiduoladuo*. When this award was submitted to the Shaoxing IPC for enforcement, the court refused to enforce the arbitral award on the ground that *Zhejiang Zhancheng* did not receive proper notice of the arbitral proceedings. *Aiduoladuo* presented to the court the DHL delivery record. In the delivery record, mail No. 1677283941 did not contain the notice of arbitral proceedings, and mail No. 1681469484 was marked as unable to reach the respondent and was finally abandoned by DHL with the consent of its sender.

The important issue in regard to all five grounds stipulated in Article V(1) of the New York Convention is that the burden of proof is still an unsolved problem in practice. In some cases, the SPC emphasized that where the respondent claimed that he had not received the notice of arbitral proceedings without providing any evidence to prove the proposition, the condition of Article V(1)(b) was not fulfilled, and the arbitral award should be recognized and enforced.[46] Still, there were many cases in which the court required the respondents to bear the burden of proof.

4.3 Excess of Authority

Excess of authority refers to an award that "deals with a difference not contemplated by or not falling within the terms of the submission to arbitration, or it contains decisions on matters beyond the scope of the submission to arbitration."[47] This ground may be invoked "where a valid arbitration agreement existed, but the issues and claims decided by an award exceeded or differed from those presented to the tribunal by the parties in the arbitration,"[48] or the "arbitral tribunal decided issues or claims that went beyond the scope of the original arbitration agreement."[49]

In *Gerald Metals Inc v. (1) Wuhu Smelter & Refinery Plant (2) Wuhu Hengxin Copper Group co., Ltd.*,[50] the parties concluded a sales contract containing an arbitration clause. When disputes arose, Gerald filed an application of arbitration to London Metal Exchange according to the arbitration agreement. The tribunal rendered an award in favor of Gerald. The Anhui High People's Court refused to recognize and enforce the award on the ground of Article V(1)(c) of New York Convention and held that the entire award should be turned down. The SPC rectified the local court's proposition and held that the part involving excessive authority could be separated and the remainder could be enforced.

---

[44] *See* Article V(1)(b) of New York Convention.
[45] *See* the Report of Not Recognition Mongolian National Arbitration Courts' No. 7323-06 Arbitration Award. (2009) Min Si Ta Zi No. 46 [(2009) 民四他字第46号].
[46] *See* (2014) Min Si Ta Zi No. 31([2014] 民四他字第31号), Reply of the Supreme People's Court to the Report of Non-Recognition and Enforcement of No. 2/11Arbitration Award of Hamburg Exchange Commodity Association by the Liaoning High People's Court (最高人民法院关于辽宁省高级人民法院不予承认及执行德国汉堡交易所商品协会仲裁法庭2/11号仲裁裁决请示一案的答复).
[47] *See* Article V(1)(c) of New York Convention.
[48] *See* GARY B. BORN, INTERNATIONAL COMMERCIAL ARBITRATION 3542 (2d ed. 2014).
[49] *Id.*
[50] *See* (2003) Min Si Ta Zi No. 12 [(2003) 民四他字第12号].

Sometimes an excess of authority could be misused by the respondents or even by the courts, and therefore in such cases the function of reporting mechanism is vital to the final result of the case. In *Paul Reinhart AG v. Hubei Qinghe Textile Corp.*,[51] the respondent did not invoke any ground listed in the New York Convention; instead, it merely stated its insolvency condition as a defense. The local court still submitted its refusal report to the SPC on the ground of excessive authority. The SPC concisely replied that since the respondent did not raise any concrete refusal proposition against the arbitral award on the basis of the New York Convention, the court should not initiate such judicial review. The arbitral award in this case was recognized even though the claimant might not be able to actually retain any property of the respondent due to the respondent's insolvency.

4.4 Defects in the Composition or Authority of Arbitral Tribunal

Procedural irregularities usually means that "the composition of the arbitral authority or the arbitral procedure was not the agreement of the parties, or, failing such agreement, was not in accordance with the law of the country where the arbitration took place."[52] For domestic arbitral awards, the arbitration procedure should follow both CAL as well as the applicable arbitration rules; otherwise, the court may set aside the arbitral awards if the violation leads to injustice of the outcome.[53]

In *Shin-Etsu Chemical Co., Ltd. v. Jiangsu Zhongtian Technology Co., Ltd.*,[54] Shin-Etsu and Jiangsu Zhongtian concluded a sales contract including an arbitration clause consenting to present disputes in Japan under the arbitration rules of the Japan Commercial Arbitration Association (JACC). After arbitration, JACC rendered an arbitral award in favor of Shin-Etsu, and the award was submitted to the Nantong IPC for enforcement. The case went all the way to the SPC, and the award was refused for enforcement on the ground of Article V(1)(d) of the New York Convention. According to the arbitration rules of JCAA, the arbitral award should be rendered within five weeks of the end of the arbitration proceedings – that is, before September 20, 2005. Since the award was rendered on February 23, 2006, the court held that the arbitral authority failed to comply with the time limit requirement as stipulated in the arbitral rules chosen by the parties; thus, it constituted a ground for refusal of enforcement.

In *Zhonghai Development Incorp. Cargo Ship v. Anhui Technological Import and Export Incorp.*,[55] the parties agreed to "Arbitration in Hong Kong, English law to apply. Other as per

---

[51] *See* (2016) Zui Gao Fa Min Ta No. 11 ([2016] 最高法民他11号), Reply of the Supreme People's Court on the Report Regarding the Application of Recognition and Enforcement of Foreign Arbitral Award between the Applicant Paul Reinhart AG and the Respondent Hubei Qinghe Textile Corp. (最高人民法院关于申请人保罗.赖因哈特公司与被申请人湖北清河纺织股份有限公司申请承认和执行外国仲裁裁决一案请示的答复). *Also see* (2016) Zui Gao Fa Min Ta No. 12 ([2016]最高法民他12号), Reply of the Supreme People's Court on the Report Regarding the Application for Recognition and Enforcement of Foreign Arbitral Award between the Applicant Noble Resources Pte Ltd. and the Respondent Hubei Qinghe Textile Corp. (最高人民法院关于申请人来宝资源有限公司与被申请人湖北清河纺织股份有限公司申请承认和执行外国仲裁裁决一案请示的答复).

[52] *See* Article V(1)(d) of the New York Convention.

[53] *See* Article 58 (3) of the Chinese Arbitration Law and Article 20 of Judicial Interpretation 2006.

[54] *See* [2007] Min Si Ta Zi No. 26 ([2007]民四他字第26号), Reply of the Supreme People's Court to the Report of Non-Recognition of No. 04-05 Arbitration Award of Japan Commercial Arbitration Association (Tokyo) (最高人民法院关于不予承认日本商事仲裁协会东京04-05号仲裁裁决的报告的复函).

[55] *See* [2008] Min Si Ta Zi No. 17 ([2008] 民四他字第17号), Reply of the Supreme People's Court on the Report of Zhonghai Development Incorp. Cargo Ship's Application for Recognition and Enforcement of London Arbitration Award) (最高人民法院关于对中海发展股份有限公司货轮公司申请承认伦敦仲裁裁决一案的请示报告的复函).

GENCON charter party 1994 with logical amendments." The SPC stated that the seat of arbitration was Hong Kong. When the parties failed to reach a consensus on the number of arbitrators, the parties should first apply to the HKIAC to decide whether there should be one or three arbitrators. If the HKIAC decided on an individual arbitrator, one party should apply to the commission and appoint the individual arbitrator pursuant to Article 11(3) of the UNCITRAL Model Law. In this case, the applicant did not apply to the HKIAC for appointing an arbitrator but directly appointed William Packard as an individual arbitrator who made the final award. This award was also refused for enforcement.[56]

In *ALSTOM Technology Ltd. v. Zhejiang Zheda Insigma Group Co., Ltd.*,[57] the parties agreed to arbitrate in SIAC under International Chamber of Commerce (ICC) rules, yet the arbitral commission appointed arbitrators in accordance with their own rules. The court refused to recognize and enforce the award granted by the SIAC, and this decision has been widely appraised. As pointed out by some commentaries, "any court would refuse enforcement in such circumstances."[58]

4.5 Defects on the Binding Force of Arbitral Award

The fifth refusal ground pursuant to Article V of the New York Convention is that "the award has not yet become binding on the parties, or has been set aside or suspended by a competent authority of the country in which, or under the law of which, that award was made."[59] So far, no case has been reported concerning refusal on this ground in mainland China.

4.6 Arbitrability

There are some issues that are simply beyond the capability of arbitral tribunals to resolve. Insolvency, real property, and intellectual property issues involving registration, family law, criminal law, succession, and rights in rem are generally considered beyond the realm of arbitration.[60] According to Article V of the New York Convention, arbitrability and public policy are two grounds that can be initiated by the court itself. The court can refuse enforcement where "the subject matter of the difference is not capable of settlement by arbitration under the law of that country." Tort disputes are arbitrable disputes under Chinese law. Articles 2 and 3 of the CAL provide the scope of matters arbitrable in mainland China. It permits the arbitral resolution of all disputes of a commercial nature while excluding administrative disputes, labor disputes, and disputes of personal rights such as marriage, adoption, guardianship, child maintenance, and inheritance. Special discussions might arise on arbitrability of disputes concerning intellectual property rights or securities regulation, which need further discussion; hence, we will not elaborate further here.

---

[56] It should be noted that, as a HKSAR award, the court should have applied the Mutual Arrangements. Yet, both the Hubei HPC and the SPC applied the New York Convention.

[57] See [2012] Min Si Ta Zi No. 54 ((2012)民四他字第54号), Reply of the Supreme People's Court with regard to ALSTOM Technology Ltd.'s Application for Recognition and Enforcement of Foreign Arbitral Award) (最高人民法院关于申请人ALSTOM Technology Ltd.与被申请人浙大网新科技股份有限公司申请承认和执行外国仲裁裁决一案请示复函).

[58] See Peerenboom, *supra* note 15, at 249–328, 250.

[59] See Article V(1)(e) of the New York Convention.

[60] Michael Hwang, *Commercial Courts and International Arbitration – Competitors or Partners?*, 31 ARBITRATION INTERNATIONAL 193–212 (2015).

Among all the foreign arbitral awards, there is only one case that invoked arbitrability as refusal ground for foreign awards enforcement.[61] In *Wu Chunying v. Zhang Guiwen*,[62] the SPC held that the main content of the arbitration award granted by the Mongolian National Arbitration Center was confirming Wu Chunying as successor in title at law of her deceased husband's investment property. According to Article 3 of the CAL, matters on inheritance were not arbitrable. On that basis, the SPC confirmed the refusal request submitted by the Shandong HPC. In the case of *ED & F*,[63] one defense raised by the respondent was that the futures contract signed by the parties was illegal. Hence, the subsequent disputes fell outside commercial disputes under Chinese law. The Beijing HPC held that there was no such stipulation in Chinese law to exclude illegal futures contracts as noncommercial contracts. The defense of lack of arbitrability was finally rejected.

4.7 Public Policy Exception

Public policy might be the most intriguing ground to either set aside or refuse enforcement of arbitral awards. Some scholars say that it is difficult for people to define the phrase *public policy*, but we can list what should not be within the scope of public policy. Dozens of cases initiated by lower courts requesting refusal approval from SPC on the ground of public policy were eventually rejected by the SPC. For example, in *Western Bulk Pte Ltd v. Beijing Zhonggang Tiantie Steel Trade Co., Ltd.*,[64] the local court found that the arbitral award was overtly unconscionable which constituted a violation of public policy. The SPC rejected this proposition and stated that public policy should be applied rigidly and cautiously. Obviously, unconscionability does not fall within the scope of this ground.

In China, there is no statutory definition of what constitutes "social and public interest." Yet, a notable interpretation by the SPC in the decision of *TCL Air-Conditioner (Zhongshan) Limited v. Castel Electronics Pty Ltd.*[65] stated:

> [t]he infringement of public interest shall be interpreted as a violation of the basic principle, infringement of the national sovereignty, jeopardizing public security, violation of public policy and other circumstances which will infringe the basic public interest.

Before 2018, only one foreign arbitral award was refused to be enforced by the Chinese court on the ground of public policy. In the case of (1) *Hemofarm D.D. Et al.*, (2) *MAG International Commerce Co.*, (3) *Sulame Media Co., Ltd. v. Jinan Yongning Pharmaceutical Co., Ltd*,[66] Hemofarm and Yongning entered into a contract stating that any disputes arising between the parties should be referred to the ICC in Paris for arbitration. On August 6, 2002, Yongning initiated civil proceedings regarding rental and leased property against Hemofarm before the Jinan Intermediate People's Court. Hemofarm challenged the jurisdiction of the court based on the arbitration clause. The court dismissed the objection and held that since Hemofarm was not

---

[61] *See* Article V(1)(e) of the New York Convention.
[62] *See* (2009) Min Si Ta Zi No. 33 [(2009)民四他字第33号].
[63] *See* (2003) Min Si Ta Zi No. 3 [(2003) 民四他字第3号].
[64] *See* [2012] Min Si Ta Zi No. 12 ([2012] 民四他字第12号), "Reply of the Supreme People's Court to the Application of Western Bulk Pte Ltd. for Recognition and Enforcement of a British Arbitration Award" (最高人民法院关于韦斯顿瓦克公司申请承认与执行英国仲裁裁决案的请示的复函).
[65] *See* [2013] Min Si Ta Zi No. 46 ([2013] 民四他字第46号).
[66] *See* [2008] Min Si Ta Zi No. 11 ([2008] 民四他字第11号), Reply of the Supreme People's Court to the Request for Instructions on the Non-Recognition and Non-Enforcement of an Arbitration Award of the ICC International Court of Arbitration (最高人民法院关于不予承认和执行国际商会仲裁院仲裁裁决的请示的复函).

a party to the joint venture contract that contained the arbitration clause, the court had jurisdiction over the dispute. The court granted property preservation initiated by Yongning and eventually ruled in favor of Yongning on the merits of the case. On September 3, 2004, Hemofarm initiated arbitration against Yongning according to the arbitration clause. The ICC tribunal stated that the property preservation in the previous litigation proceeding constituted a breach of the joint venture contract and hence rendered the award in favor of Hemofarm. When Hemofarm initiated an application for recognition and enforcement of the arbitral award in the Jinan IPC, the court refused to recognize and enforce the award on the ground of excess of authority as well as violation of public policy. This opinion was supported by the SPC, which held that the tribunal ignored the final judgment made earlier by the Chinese court was a violation of China's judicial sovereignty and, therefore, it amounted to a violation of China's public policy.

Still, this case does not serve as a settled law that a finding by the arbitral tribunal which is inconsistent with the previous court judgment would be deemed unenforceable. When a Chinese court has already made a decision on an issue before an award on the same issue was decided by a foreign arbitral tribunal, the foreign arbitral tribunal might be found to have interfered with China's judicial sovereignty, and, therefore, it is contrary to public policy to enforce the award. But the consequence is not absolute. The Chinese courts are still quite cautious in resorting to the public policy ground. In fact, there are enforcement orders granted because the awards were issued before court judgments were delivered, so the inconsistency between the awards and judgments did not give rise to public policy issue. In *TCL Air-Conditioner (Zhongshan) Limited v. Castel Electronics Pty Ltd.*, the SPC stated that the awards were rendered on December 23, 2010, and January 27, 2011, which is earlier than the Chinese court's verdict declaring the invalidity of the arbitral agreement. In addition, TCL did not raise any objection to jurisdiction during the arbitration proceeding. Rather, it submitted a counterclaim instead. Hence, the arbitral tribunal's confirmation of its jurisdiction over the matter did not violate China's judicial sovereignty.[67]

Although the Chinese courts have been quite cautious in applying public policy on arbitral awards enforcement, the criteria seem to be inconsistent between foreign awards and HKSAR awards. For example, in *Wicor v. Taizhou Hao Pu Investment Co., Ltd.*,[68] the SPC refused to enforce the arbitral award granted by ICC in HKSAR on the ground that the enforcement of the arbitral award would be contrary to the public interest of mainland China. In that case, the arbitral tribunal accepted Wicor's application for arbitration on November 4, 2011, and rendered an interim award confirming the validity of the arbitration agreement. The Taizhou IPC rendered a verdict on December 11, 2012, and declared the invalidity of the arbitral clause between Wicor and Taizhou Hao Pu. Later, the court sent the invalidity verdict to the Asian representative of ICC and notified it of the content. Yet, the ICC still maintained that the arbitral agreement was valid and granted an award on that basis. The SPC held that the enforcement of the relevant award would contradict the Chinese effective verdict, hence violating the social and public interests of mainland China.

---

[67] See supra note 65.
[68] See (2016) Zui Gao Fa Min Ta No. 8 [(2016)最高法民他8号].

5 CONCLUSION

In view of the recent efforts made by the SPC, Chinese judicial control over arbitration seems gradually becoming more and more arbitration friendly. However, problems still exist as to the variations among different provinces on judicial review of commercial arbitration. Overall, the prior reporting requirement set by the SPC as a procedural safeguard to ensure the compliance with the New York Convention is well-functioning enough to tackle these problems. Still, the PRS has its own drawbacks. For example, there is no supervisory mechanism to ensure all local courts report all of their refusal cases as required; there is no transparency on the sanctions against failure to comply with the prior reporting requirement by the lower level courts; and the extended application of PRS to domestic arbitral award enforcement might aggravate the already time-consuming PRS process. Finally, understanding as to many issues such as the relationship between domestic law and the validity of arbitral agreements and the application of public policy, and so forth are still unresolved.

14

Certain Aspects of Judicial Control of Arbitral Awards in France

Denis Bensaude

1 HISTORY AND FRENCH ARBITRATION LAW

France has always recognised arbitration as a mean of settling disputes.[1] Arbitration has long been and still is considered in France to actually be the 'normal mode of dispute resolution' in international commerce, and the French arbitration community was among the promoters of the New York Convention of 1958 on the recognition and enforcement of foreign awards (1958 New York Convention). The 1958 New York Convention entered into force in France on September 24, 1959.[2]

The French government codified by decree the French courts' rulings on arbitration in the French Code of Civil Procedure (CPC) and modernised French arbitration law in the 1980s.[3] The CPC was again amended and the provisions of the 1980s decrees were replaced by those of decree No. 2011-48 of January 13, 2011. This reform again codified French courts' case law and modernised international arbitration law through the insertion of the provisions of decree No. 2011-48 into Articles 1442 to 1527 of the CPC. These provisions are generally applicable as from May 1, 2011; however, the 2011 decree provides for a number of transitory provisions.[4]

Provisions on international arbitration may be found in Articles 1504 to 1527 CPC. Article 1506 CPC states that certain domestic arbitration provisions also apply to international arbitration unless the parties agree otherwise.[5] Article 1504 CPC defines international arbitration as one that 'involves the interest of international trade'. Specifically, the French courts consider

---

[1] C. Jallamion, *Tradition et modernité de l'arbitrage et de la médiation au regard de l'histoire*, GAZETTE DU PALAIS [hereinafter GAZ. PAL.], Jan. 16, 2009, at 3.
[2] Decree No. 59-1039 of Sept. 1, 1959.
[3] Decrees No. 80-354 of May 14, 1980, and No. 81-500 of May 12, 1981. For a commentary in English on the provisions of decree No. 81-500, regarding international arbitration, *see, e.g.*, D. Bensaude, *French Code of Civil Procedure*, in CONCISE INTERNATIONAL ARBITRATION 1133 (L. A. Mistelis ed., 2015).
[4] The 2011 decree provides in particular that (1) Articles 1442 to 1445, 1489 and 1505, paras. 2 and 3 CPC shall apply where the arbitration agreement was concluded after May 1, 2011; (2) Articles 1456 through 1458, as well as 1486, 1502, 1513 and 1522, CPC shall apply where the arbitral tribunal was constituted after May 1, 2011; and (3) Article 1526 CPC shall apply to arbitral awards rendered after May 1, 2011.
[5] Article 1506 CPC provides that, unless the parties have agreed otherwise and subject to the provisions of the title on international arbitration, the following domestic arbitration articles shall apply to international arbitration: (1) 1446, 1447, 1448 (paras. 1 and 2) and 1449 CPC, regarding the arbitration agreement; (2) 1452 to 1458 and 1460 CPC regarding the constitution of the arbitral tribunal and the procedure governing application to the judge acting in support of the arbitration; (3) 1462, 1463 (para. 2), 1464 (para. 3), 1465 to 1470 and 1472 regarding arbitral proceedings; (4) 1479, 1481, 1482, 1484 (paras. 1 and 2), 1485 (paras. 1 and 2) and 1486 regarding arbitral awards; (5) 1502 (paras. 1 and 2) and 1503 regarding means of recourse other than appeals or actions to set aside.

that arbitrations are international when they involve the economy of more than one country.[6] That is to say when the subject matter of the dispute submitted to arbitration is commercially connected with more than one country at the time the arbitration is commenced.

Applicable French arbitration regulations may also be found in international conventions. France is a party to the 1923 Geneva Protocol, the 1927 Geneva Protocol on the Enforcement of Arbitral Awards, the 1958 New York Convention, the European Convention on International Arbitration of 1961, the Agreement Relating to the Application of the Convention of 1962, the 1965 Convention on the Settlement of Investment Disputes between States and Nationals of other States, as well as a party to numerous bilateral agreements concerning the recognition of judicial decisions and awards.

Numerous arbitration institutions are established in France, among which is the International Court of Arbitration of the International Chamber of Commerce (ICC Court). The ICC Court has its headquarters in Paris and manages arbitrations taking place all over the world. Other notable institutions that handle international arbitrations are established in France and are either (1) specialised, for example, the Chambre Arbitrale Maritime de Paris (Paris Maritime Arbitration Chamber),[7] which handles maritime-related disputes, and the Chambre Arbitrale Internationale de Paris (Paris International Arbitration Chamber),[8] which handles disputes over the sale of grains); or (2) not specialised, such as the Association Française d'Arbitrage (French Association for Domestic and International Arbitration)[9] and the Centre de Médiation et d'Arbitrage de Paris,[10] which handle all type of business disputes.

The ICC Court deals with more than 800 cases a year and publishes statistics in its bulletin.[11] There are no other published statistics that would give a reasonable idea of the number of arbitration cases dealt with in France every year. The French Cour de cassation (the French Supreme Court) and the Paris Cour d'appel (Court of Appeal) render a dozen decisions a month that relate to arbitrations taking place in France and abroad, with particular regard to the recognition or setting aside of awards rendered in France. This figure is not in and of itself sufficient to evaluate the number of arbitrations that take place in France but shows how familiar the French courts are with arbitration in general.

The French courts, and in particular the Paris Court of Appeal and the French Supreme Court, are not only both very familiar with, but also very favourable to arbitration, and they both render numerous decisions on arbitration per year as evidence of the popularity of arbitration in France. Paris is frequently chosen as a seat in international arbitration. French companies involved in international business regularly use arbitration agreements in their international dealings, whether these transactions involve construction, commercial contracts, joint-ventures, sales of share, etc. This explains that, as of today, many international arbitrations take place in Paris without the parties or the dispute having any connection whatsoever with France and that is because, in France, arbitration is generally considered, by the public and the courts, as the normal means of resolving international business disputes.

---

[6] *See, e.g.*, CA Paris, Paris 25e ch. (section A), Jan. 28, 2009, Pacific Elysées v. Yemen Airways Co. (2009) 24(5) *Mealey's international arbitration report* [hereinafter *Mealey's Int'l Arb. Rep.*].
[7] *See* www.arbitrage-maritime.org/us/index.php.
[8] *See* arbitrage.org/us/Presentation/index.htm.
[9] Also known as AFA, www.afa-arbitrage.com.
[10] Also known as CMAP, www.cmap.fr. This institution is particularly renowned for its mediation practice and also administers domestic and international arbitrations at very reasonable costs when compared to the increasing arbitration costs of more renowned institutions. It is part of the Paris Chamber of Commerce and Industry. Several regional Chambers of Commerce and Industry in France offer similar arbitration services.
[11] The ICC Court Bulletin is published four times a year and is available at library.iccwbo.org/dr-bulletins.htm.

2 ARBITRATION AGREEMENTS

Arbitration is defined under French law as the process whereby one or more individuals are entrusted by parties with the power to decide a legal dispute by way of one or more binding and final decisions.[12] Under French arbitration law, an arbitration agreement may be in the form of an arbitration clause (*clause compromissoire*) or that of a submission agreement (*compromis*). The first is defined as the agreement by which parties to one or more contract(s) undertake to submit to arbitration disputes which may arise in relation to such contract(s), and the second as the agreement by which parties to an existing dispute submit such a dispute to arbitration (Article 1442 CPC). In investment arbitration, consent to arbitrate may be given in other instruments, such as a law or a treaty.[13]

The only requirement in international arbitration, in regard to the content of the agreement under French international arbitration law, is that the parties 'agree to arbitrate' their dispute. Actually, the word *arbitration* mentioned in a contractual document together with the indication of a place of arbitration is sufficient to create a binding arbitration agreement under French international arbitration law.[14] Moreover, Article 1507 CPC provides that an arbitration agreement shall not be subject to any requirements as to its form. Therefore, arbitration agreements do not have to be signed or in writing at all. The French courts will be satisfied that there is an arbitration agreement among parties where the court finds evidence of a 'common intent of the parties to arbitrate their dispute'. In the absence of writing, evidentiary issues concerning the existence, content and nature of such a common intent to arbitrate may of course arise. However, the absence of writing does not in and of itself render an international arbitration agreement void.[15]

As mentioned, an international arbitration agreement may be found wherever there is a 'common intent of the parties' to arbitrate. French courts will find such an arbitration agreement to exist where draft contracts or letters implementing a verbal contract that contains an arbitration clause were exchanged among the parties, so long as none of the parties raised any objection to that clause.[16] In other words, an arbitration clause will be given effect by the French courts where it is shown that the parties were aware of the content of that clause and accepted that clause, including through silence.

Where international arbitration is concerned, French courts may be considered to be very liberal in finding a 'common intent of the parties' to arbitrate. Common intent may, for instance, be found where a party against which an arbitration clause is invoked was aware (at the time of entering into a contract) of general conditions that contained an arbitral clause and accepted the incorporation of that clause in the contract, including by silence. Such reference may also be found, for example, in an invoice.[17]

---

[12] C. Jarrosson, La notion d'arbitrage (1987).
[13] On international commercial arbitration, *see* P. Fouchard, E. Gaillard, & B. Goldman, Fouchard, Gaillard, and Goldman on International Commercial Arbitration 194–195, para. 386 (1999).
[14] CA Paris, Oct. 23, 2008, Limak Insaat San Vetic v. Weatherford Kopp GmbH (2009) 24(2) Mealey's Int'l Arb. Rep.
[15] Fouchard, Gaillard, & Goldman, *supra* note 13, at 360, para. 590.
[16] E.g., Cass. com., July 15, 1987, Jezequel & Maury v. Brittania (1990) *Revue de l'arbitrage* [hereinafter *Rev. arb.*], 627; Cass. com., June 17, 1997, Négobeureuf v. Jouandin (1998) *Rev. arb.*, 539; Cass 2nd civ., Jan. 21, 1999, Coisplet v. CH Daudry Van Cauwenberghe (2003) *Rev. arb.*, 1341, note C. Legros.
[17] Cass. 1st civ., Nov. 9, 1993, Entreprise Tunisienne d'Activités Pétrolières (ETAP) v. Bomar Oil (1994) *Rev. arb.*, 108, note C. Kessedjian; CA Paris, Sept. 13, 2007, Comptoir Commercial Blidéen v. Union Invivo (2007) *Rev. arb.*, 649; and CA Paris, Oct. 15, 2009, Sanofi v. Scanpartners (2009) (24)12 *Mealey's Int'l Arb. Rep.*

The separability of arbitration agreements is codified in Article 1447, para. 1 CPC which provides that: 'An arbitration agreement is independent of the contract to which it relates [and] shall not be affected if such contract is void.' This principle is well recognised and applied by the French courts. Separability, under French international arbitration law, covers two distinct concepts. First, there is 'material separability', pursuant to which arbitration agreements are separable from the main contracts which they cover or are inserted in. Under this aspect of the separability doctrine under French arbitration law, enforceability of arbitration agreements is evaluated independently from the enforceability of the main contract to which they refer. As a consequence, the unenforceability of the main contract does not necessarily impair the enforceability of the arbitration agreement contained or referred to therein. Second, arbitration agreements are 'legally separable'. This means that the law applicable to the main contract does not apply to the arbitration agreement unless the parties have expressly provided so. French law goes even further; considering that in the absence of a choice of law specifically made applicable to the arbitration agreement by the parties, no domestic law will apply to the arbitration agreement.

Parties that intend for a particular law to govern their arbitration agreement, including the law applicable to the interpretation thereof, must expressly say so. If parties have not agreed on any such applicable law, as is often the case, the principle of 'legal autonomy' set out by the French courts also provides that no national law will govern the agreement to arbitrate, including its interpretation. Indeed, the French courts consider that international arbitration agreements are transnational instruments which, as such, are not subject to any national law.[18] Hence, when a party challenges the enforceability of an international award before the French courts for lack of jurisdiction, the courts will only examine whether – in all logic – there was a 'common intent of the parties' to arbitrate the dispute at stake. The interpretation of that intent, including its scope, shall, therefore, be conducted by the French courts without reference to any specific national law.

In principle, arbitration agreements are only binding on the parties thereto. However, there is a long line of French court decisions in both domestic and international arbitrations, based on the French courts' liberal approach in finding a common intent to arbitrate on the part of 'non-signatories', and according to which third parties may rely upon, or be bound by, arbitration agreements which they have not signed.[19] For instance, entities or persons designated as third party beneficiaries of a contract containing or referring to an arbitration agreement may be bound by that arbitration agreement. These third-party beneficiaries may also rely upon such agreement to arbitrate against parties to the contract.[20] Generally, entities directly involved in the performance of a contract which contains or refers to an arbitration clause, as well as in the dispute that may result from that contract, will often be considered bound by that arbitration clause.[21] For example, individuals involved in the management and liquidation of a corporation,

---

[18] Cass. 1st civ., Dec. 20, 1993, Municipalité de Khoms El Mergeb v. Dalico (1994) *Rev. arb.*, 116, note H. Gaudemet-Tallon.

[19] *See* generally on this issue, in regard to international arbitration, B. HANOTIAU, COMPLEX ARBITRATIONS MULTIPARTY, MULTI-CONTRACT, MULTI-ISSUE AND CLASS ACTIONS (2006).

[20] Cass. 1st civ., July 11, 2006, Banque Populaire Loire et Lyonnais v. Sangar (2006) *Rev. arb.*, 969, note C. Larroumet, (*contra* Cass. com., June 4, 1985, Sefimo v. Mrs B. (1987) *Rev. arb.*, 140, note J.-L. Goutal). On the issue of arbitration agreements and third party beneficiaries, *see* C. Larroumet, *Promesse pour autrui, stipulation pour autrui et arbitrage* (2005) *Rev. arb.*, 903.

[21] Cass. 1st civ., Mar. 27, 2007, Alcatel Business Systems (ABS) v. Amkor Technology et al. (2007) *Rev. arb.*, 785, note A. H. El Adhab; CA Paris, May 7, 2009, Suba France v. Pujol (2009) *Rev. arb.*, 439; CA Paris, May 5, 2011, Kosa France Holding and Invista v. Rhodia Operations and Rhodianyl (July 24, 2011) *Gaz. Pal.*, 13; and CA Paris, Dec. 18, 2018, New Europe Corporate Advisory et al. v. Avicena et al. (19 March 2019) *Gaz. Pal.*, 37.

who were not shareholders of that corporation, were held to be bound by the arbitration clause contained in the corporation's bylaws.[22] Always for example, the Paris Court of Appeal found a state to be bound by an arbitration clause signed by a trust it created because, during negotiation of the contract that contained the arbitration clause and after disappearance of this trust, the state was involved in the performance of the contract and acted as if the contract 'was its own'. Such involvement was evidence to the French Court, that the state was the actual party to the contract and related economic transaction.[23] French courts of appeal have discretion to determine the existence of the parties' intent to be bound by an arbitration agreement.[24]

Certain matters may not be subject to arbitration in France. In particular, any dispute concerning the personal status of individuals, such as their identity (name, nationality or filiations) may not be arbitrated. In the same vein, where certain matters are covered by the exclusive jurisdiction of national courts, arbitrators are deprived of all or part of their jurisdiction that infringes upon such exclusive jurisdiction. For example, arbitrators may not declare a company bankrupt or annul a patent or a trademark. However, disputes relating to the use of patents and trademarks are arbitrable. In this respect, arbitrators may decide in the body of their award on issues regarding the validity of a patent to settle a dispute. However, that decision will not be binding upon the parties.[25] Arbitrators may not order the levy of assets or the foreclosure of real estate. Although arbitrators may not decide disputes concerning the termination of marriage, divorced parties may arbitrate certain financial consequences of their divorce. Issues concerning child custody may not be arbitrated. Certain aspects of bankruptcy cannot be decided by arbitrators, such as the admissibility of a creditor's debt over a company undergoing bankruptcy. This does not mean that a company undergoing bankruptcy cannot arbitrate disputes. It only means that an award that orders payment against a French company undergoing bankruptcy, will, as the case may be, be set aside by the French courts if the award was rendered in France, or will be refused enforcement in France if rendered abroad.[26]

Certain rules and regulations protecting consumers at the European level may also affect the validity of arbitration agreements entered into by individuals in consumer contracts. Indeed, these clauses have been held to constitute unfair contractual terms that are void under such regulations.[27]

Of note, on May 17, 2010, the *Tribunal des conflits* (a jurisdiction in charge of deciding upon conflicts of jurisdiction between the French private and administrative body of courts) implicitly confirmed the arbitrability of contracts entered into by French public entities with foreign parties despite their administrative character when these contracts involve the interests of international trade.[28] However, that same decision also made the French administrative courts responsible for the enforcement and challenge of awards rendered in certain international arbitrations involving the French State and/or French public entities.

---

[22] CA Paris, May 22, 2008, Joseph Abela Family Foundation v. Albert Abela Family Foundation et al. (2008) *Rev. arb.*, 833.

[23] CA Paris, Feb. 17, 2011, Gouvernement du Pakistan v. Dallah real Estate and Tourism Holding Company (May 15, 2011) *Gaz. Pal.*, 16. Of note, seized with the same case and issues, and applying French arbitration law, the House of Lords in England reached the opposite conclusion: House of Lords, Nov. 3, 2010, *Supreme Court of the United Kingdom* [UKSC] 46, www.supremecourt.gov.uk/decided-cases/docs/UKSC_2009_0165_Judgment.pdf.

[24] Cass. 1st civ., June 29, 2011, Papillon Group Corporation v. République Arabe de Syrie (Nov. 11, 2011) *Gaz. Pal.*, 15–16.

[25] CA Paris, 1st Ch. C, Feb. 28, 2008, Liv Hidravlika DOO v. Diebolt (2009) *Rev. arb.*, 169, note Z. A. Azzi.

[26] Cass. 1st civ., May 6, 2009, Liquidateurs de Jean Lion v. Income (2009) 24(8) *Mealey's Int'l Arb. Rep.*

[27] EUCJ, Oct. 26, 2006, Elisa Maria Mostaza Claro v. Centro Móvil Milenium SL, C-168/05 (2007) *Rev. arb.*, 109, note S. Bollée.

[28] Tribunal des conflits, May 17, 2010, Inserm v. Fondation Letten F. Saugstad (2010) (25)6 *Mealey's Int'l Arb. Rep.*

More importantly, Articles 1448 and 1465 CPC establish the principle of competence–competence under French arbitration law. Article 1465 CPC, in particular, grants arbitral tribunals the jurisdiction to decide upon their jurisdiction and states that 'the arbitral tribunal has exclusive jurisdiction to rule on objections to its jurisdiction'. Article 1448 provides that:

> When a dispute subject to an arbitration agreement is brought before a [French] court, such court shall decline jurisdiction, except if an arbitral tribunal has not yet been seized of the dispute and if the arbitration agreement is manifestly void or manifestly not applicable. A court may not decline jurisdiction on its own motion.

The principle of competence–competence under French arbitration law confers the arbitral tribunal only with a priority to decide upon its jurisdiction and that is because any question as to the existence, scope or validity of an arbitration agreement must first be resolved by the arbitrator, and that arbitrator's decision on jurisdiction (to be rendered in the form of an award) may eventually be challenged before the courts. Actually, awards on jurisdiction may be reviewed (de novo) by the French courts once rendered.

According to Article 1448 CPC, when facing an objection to his jurisdiction based on the alleged existence of an arbitration agreement, the French judge must decline jurisdiction over a dispute already submitted to an arbitral tribunal. When such tribunal has not yet been constituted, the French judge must also decline jurisdiction unless he or she finds that the arbitration agreement relied upon is 'manifestly void' or 'manifestly inapplicable'. In deciding whether an arbitration agreement is manifestly void or manifestly inapplicable, the French judge is barred from carrying out a substantive, in-depth examination of the arbitration agreement. An arbitration agreement cannot be said to be manifestly void or manifestly inapplicable, where either party needs to carry a demonstration that the arbitration agreement is either void or inapplicable. In essence, any doubt regarding the existence, validity or scope of the arbitration agreement must, therefore, be first resolved by the tribunal.

3 ARBITRAL TRIBUNAL

Article 1508 CPC provides that: 'An arbitration agreement may designate the arbitrator(s) or provide for the procedure for their appointment, directly or by reference to arbitration rules or to procedural rules'. Under French arbitration law, parties may agree in the arbitration clause or otherwise, that the arbitrators to be appointed on the tribunal shall have certain qualifications (based on age, gender, training, diplomas, experience, nationality, language abilities and so forth). In such a case, the parties' agreement should be given full force and effect, and any arbitrator appointed in violation of this agreement may bear the risk of a successful challenge. Moreover, if objections are raised in due course, the award rendered by an irregularly constituted tribunal bears the risk of being set aside or refused enforcement.[29] Indeed, in case the procedure agreed upon by the parties for the appointment of the arbitrators is not followed, the validity and enforcement of the award may be at risk for the improper constitution of the tribunal. In all cases, the parties' agreement on the method for appointment of arbitrators must comply with the principle of equality of the parties in the constitution of the tribunal.

When the parties have not agreed on the procedure for constituting the tribunal, Articles 1452 to 1454 CPC generally grant authority upon the 'person responsible for administering the

---

[29] For an example of an international tribunal that was said to be irregularly constituted in violation of the parties' agreement, Cass. 1st civ., Dec. 4, 1990, ETPM and Ecofisa v. Gas del Estado (1991) *Rev. arb.*, 81, note P. Fouchard.

arbitration' that was chosen by the parties to rule upon issues affecting the constitution of the tribunal. Such person may either be an arbitration institution or, in case of an ad hoc arbitration, an authority that the parties have mutually chosen, or in the absence of such a choice, the judge acting in support of the arbitration (known as the supporting judge, or *juge d'appui*). Unless otherwise agreed upon, the *juge d'appui* is the president of the Tribunal de grande instance of Paris (First instance court in Paris) when: (1) the arbitration takes place in France, (2) the parties have agreed that French procedural law shall apply to the arbitration, (3) the parties have expressly granted jurisdiction to French courts over disputes relating to the arbitral procedure or (4) one of the parties is exposed to a risk of a denial of justice (Article 1505 CPC).

If there is to be a sole arbitrator and the parties fail to agree on the arbitrator, he or she shall be appointed by the person responsible for administering the arbitration or, where there is no such person, by the supporting judge (Article 1452-1 CPC). If there are to be three arbitrators, each side shall appoint one, and the two arbitrators so appointed shall appoint a third one. If a party fails to appoint an arbitrator within one month following receipt of a request to that effect from the other party, or if the two arbitrators fail to agree on the third arbitrator within one month of having accepted their mandate, the person responsible for administering the arbitration or, where there is no such person, the judge acting in support of the arbitration shall appoint the third arbitrator (Article 1452-2 CPC). If there are more than two parties to the dispute and they fail to agree on the procedure for constituting the tribunal, the person responsible for administering the arbitration or, where there is no such person, the supporting judge shall appoint the arbitrator(s) (Article 1453 CPC).

According to Article 1457 CPC, and where the tribunal was constituted after May 1, 2011, arbitrators are to carry out their mission to completion unless they become legally incapacitated or there is a legitimate reason for them to refuse to act or to resign. French law does not provide for what may constitute a valid reason for an arbitrator to resign, and the French courts have no specific power to force an arbitrator to act in an arbitration. Despite the absence of any particular provision regarding what may be a legitimate cause for resignation, an arbitrator may be liable and ordered to pay damages to either party for resignation without cause and/or for disorganising the arbitration. In case of disagreement as to the legitimacy of the reasons invoked, the person administering the arbitration or, where there is no such person, the supporting judge has jurisdiction to resolve the matter and must be seized within one month following the incapacity, refusal to act or resignation. Most institutional arbitration rules provide for both prior authorisation of the institution and a replacement procedure in case an arbitrator resigns.

In all cases, arbitrators must be and remain impartial and independent.[30] Article 1456 CPC, para. 2, provides that before accepting a mandate, an arbitrator has to disclose any circumstance that may affect his or her independence or impartiality. This duty to disclose remains after the arbitrator's acceptance of his or her mission and must be performed in a manner that allows the parties to exercise their right to challenge the arbitrator.[31] An arbitrator should disclose any fact or circumstances that may affect his or her judgment and provoke a reasonable doubt in the parties' mind concerning his or her impartiality and/or independence. The arbitrator's duty to disclose applies from appointment until the end of the arbitration.[32] The relationship of trust between an arbitrator and the parties must be continuously preserved, and the parties must

---

[30] CA Paris, 1st Ch. C, Apr. 9, 1992, Annahold et al. v. L'Oréal (1996) *Rev. arb.*, 483.
[31] Articles 1456, para. 3, and 1458 CPC provide that challenges must be filed within one month from disclosure or discovery of the facts giving rise to the challenge.
[32] CA Paris, 1st Ch. C, Jan. 12, 1996, Gouvernement de l'Etat du Qatar v. Creighton (1996) *Rev. arb.*, 427.

be informed throughout the arbitration of any relationship that may, in their eyes, affect an arbitrator's judgment or independence.[33]

There is no duty to disclose a notorious fact or a fact which may not influence the arbitrator's judgment.[34] A *courant d'affaires* (ongoing business relationship) between the arbitrator and a party must be disclosed. Such relationships may derive from the frequency or the regularity of appointments of the arbitrator.[35] Repetitive and frequent appointments of the same arbitrator by the same party in similar disputes may create a reasonable doubt as to the independence of that arbitrator that is sufficient to sustain a challenge.[36] An arbitrator who sits in two parallel arbitrations involving similar issues also runs a risk of challenge. If a party discovers, after an arbitrator is appointed, that the arbitrator breached his duty to disclose, that party may successfully challenge the arbitrator.[37] Such a breach may also prevent enforcement of the award or give rise to the liability of the arbitrator.[38]

Relationships between an arbitrator and a party's counsel should also be disclosed. In evaluating a challenge based on an arbitrator's alleged breach of duty to disclose, the French judge will consider both whether the information at issue was notorious or not and whether the facts at issue would have affected the arbitrator's judgment.[39]

So far as the procedure and deadlines for challenging an arbitrator are concerned, in case the parties have agreed that an institution is in charge of administering the arbitration or submitted their arbitration to specific arbitration rules, the procedures described under such rules will apply. In case the parties have not referred to arbitration rules, an arbitrator may be challenged before the person administering the arbitration designated in the arbitration agreement and, in the absence thereof, before the supporting judge. The failure to timely file a challenge amounts to a waiver of the right to later complain of the arbitrator's lack of independence.[40]

Article 1464, para. 3 CPC also provides that parties and arbitrators shall act diligently and in good faith in the conduct of the proceedings. Arbitrators may not be held liable for having erred in applying the law or for having misjudged the case.[41] Moreover, arbitrators belonging to a profession subject to rules of ethics, such as lawyers, must continue to abide by these rules when acting as arbitrators.

The primary duty of an arbitrator is to ensure that the parties are treated equally and to make sure that the principle of due process is abided by (Article 1510 CPC). Article 1464, para. 3 CPC also provides that arbitrators shall act with celerity and loyalty in the conduct of the proceeding. Although French international arbitration law does not impose a deadline for the completion of their mandate, arbitrators must abide by the contractual deadlines agreed upon by the parties or contained in the arbitration rules chosen by the parties. A breach of the deadline to render an award may give rise to the liability of arbitrators, subject to evidence being filed that a damage resulted from the personal misconduct of the arbitrator.

---

[33] CA Paris, 1st Ch. C, Feb. 12, 2009, J&P Avax v. Tecnimont (2009) 24(5) *Mealey's Int'l Arb. Rep.*
[34] E.g., CA Paris, Sept. 9, 2010, Consorts A. v. SGS (Feb. 6, 2011) *Gaz. Pal.*, 17–18; (2011) *ASA Bulletin* [*ASA Bull.*], 197, note P. Pinsolle.
[35] CA Paris, Oct. 20, 2010 (2 decisions) (Feb. 6, 2011) *Gaz. Pal.*, 18–19: the arbitrators had respectively been appointed as arbitrator 34 and 51 times by companies of the same group.
[36] Trib. com. Paris, July 6, 2004, Chomat v. A. (2005) *Rev. arb.*, 709, note A. Hory.
[37] CA Paris, 1st Ch. C, Feb. 12, 2009, J&P Avax v. Tecnimont (2009) 24(5) *Mealey's Int'l Arb. Rep.*
[38] CA Paris, 1st Ch. C, Apr. 9, 1992, Annahold et al. v. L'Oréal (1996) *Rev. arb.*, 483.
[39] CA Paris, pole 1, ch. 1, Oct. 14, 2014, Auto Guadeloupe Investissements et al. v. Colombus Acquisitions et al. (Nov. 21, 2014) *Gaz. Pal.*, 18.
[40] CA Paris, Feb. 22, 2007, Worms services maritimes v. CMA CGM (2007) *Rev. arb.*, 142.
[41] CA Paris, May 22, 1991, Bompard v. Consorts C. (1996) *Rev. arb.*, 476.

Certain arbitration rules restrict or exclude arbitrators' liability. The effect of such a restriction is limited under French law. For example, the French courts held that the waiver of liability provision in article 34 of the ICC Rules 1998 (now Article 41 of the 2017 ICC Arbitration Rules) is void ab initio under French law because it would otherwise allow the ICC to fail to perform its core obligations as a provider of arbitration services and, therefore, contradicts the essence of the arbitration contract entered into with the institution. More importantly, arbitrators have a jurisdictional immunity under French arbitration law, in the sense that they cannot be held liable for the manner in which they perform that function. The fact that an arbitrator may have reached the wrong solution to the dispute is not a ground for liability. An arbitrator may incur liability only in the event of gross negligence, fraud, or connivance with one of the parties.

In practice, tribunals sitting in France are free to determine the admissibility and assess the weight of the evidence. In practice, tribunals sitting in France often refer to and rely upon the IBA Rules on the Taking of Evidence in International Arbitration (IBA Rules 2010 on the Taking of Evidence). These rules provide that the tribunal is free to determine the admissibility, relevance, materiality and weight of the evidence submitted.[42] These rules also provide that the tribunal may draw an adverse inference from the failure of a party to either produce any requested evidence without satisfactory explanation or to object in due time. Article 1467, para. 3 CPC grants tribunals the power to order a party to submit an item of evidence, determine the terms and conditions for this submission and, if necessary, attach penalties to such order. If any such evidence is held by a third party, the tribunal may not directly order that third party to submit such evidence in the arbitration.

An arbitral tribunal sitting in France may order any conservatory or provisional measure that it deems appropriate under the conditions it determines and, as need be, under penalty. However, state courts have exclusive jurisdiction to order conservatory attachments and judicial securities. The arbitral tribunal may also take measures to (1) hear any person provide testimony, (2) order a party to submit an item of evidence and determine the terms and conditions of submission, if need be, under penalty (Article 1467 CPC) and (3) settle disputes concerning the authentication of handwriting or claims of forgery (Article 1470 CPC). Should a party allege in the course of the arbitration that a document submitted is forged, then the tribunal must stay the arbitration and decide on such a claim unless it finds the document irrelevant to decide the parties' dispute.

Under French arbitration law, arbitral tribunals and domestic courts have a so-called complementary jurisdiction to order conservatory and provisional measures.[43] For as long as the tribunal is not constituted, the existence of an arbitration agreement does not prevent a party from requesting the President of the First Instance Court (*Tribunal de grande instance*) or that of the Commercial Court (*Tribunal de commerce*) for measures in futurum relating to the taking of evidence envisaged under Article 145 CPC[44] and, where the matter is urgent, for provisional or conservatory measures (Article 1449 CPC). Nothing under French arbitration law prevents

---

[42] Article 9 of the IBA Rules on the Taking of Evidence 2010. See CA Paris, pole 1, ch. 1, Nov. 12, 2013, CIEC v. Carlson Anse Marcel (June 27, 2014) *Gaz. Pal.*, 17.

[43] See TGI Paris (Ord. Réf.), Mar. 29, 2010, République de Guinée équatoriale v. Fitzpatrick Equatorial Guinea (2011) *Rev. arb.*, 500, note D. Bensaude.

[44] According to which:

> If there is a legitimate reason to preserve or to establish, before any legal process, the evidence of the facts upon which the resolution of the dispute depends, legally permissible preparatory inquiries may be ordered at the request of any interested party, by way of a petition or by way of a summary procedure.

tribunals from ordering security for costs of arbitration. Article 1468, para. 2 CPC expressly provides that the state courts have exclusive jurisdiction to order conservatory attachments and judicial securities. More importantly, the French courts do not intervene in the tribunal's direction of the procedure in the course of arbitration and will generally refuse to do so.[45]

4 AWARD

Under French arbitration law, an award is any decision rendered by an arbitral tribunal which finally settles all or part of the parties' dispute submitted to it and which either addresses jurisdiction, all or part of the merits of the dispute, or a procedural issue that terminates the procedure.[46] This definition encompasses partial, interim and final awards. Arbitrators may, therefore, issue interim and partial awards unless otherwise agreed by the parties. A decision on provisional measures that touches upon the merits of a dispute may constitute an award under French law.[47] An award that settles only part of a dispute on jurisdiction or on the merits is considered an award under French international arbitration law. French law recognises parties' agreement that a tribunal is to rule on a dispute in separate awards. An award rendered in breach of such an agreement may be set aside or refused enforcement in France on the grounds that the tribunal exceeded its mission. However, this protection is limited to parties' directions that are sufficiently clear and precise.[48]

French arbitration law does not provide specific rules for default awards. It is generally accepted that a party's default does not, in and of itself, affect the award. Thus, arbitrators may issue an award even though a party has defaulted during the proceedings, as long as due process has been complied with. A French court rejected an action to set aside a default award on the basis that documents of the proceedings 'had invariably been sent to the defaulting party' and that the arbitration rules adopted by the parties had been complied with.[49] A party that does not participate in the arbitration is not barred from filing an action to set aside the award or barred from appealing the award's enforcement order (for awards rendered abroad).[50] If the award is rendered outside the time limit agreed upon by the parties, it may be set aside or refused enforcement[51] and the arbitrators held liable therefore.[52]

A principle of collegiality established by French case law also requires arbitrators to work together in organising the proceedings and deliberating together.[53] Article 1513, para. 1 CPC provides that:

> Where the arbitration agreement is silent, the award must be rendered by a majority of votes. The award shall be signed by all the arbitrators. However, should a minority among them refuse to sign the award, the other arbitrators shall mention it in the award. In the absence of a

---

[45] *E.g.*, CA Paris, Dec. 20, 2018, Etat du Cameroun v. Projet Pilote Garoube (Mar. 19, 2019) *Gaz. Pal.*, 35.
[46] CA Paris, Mar. 25, 1994, Sardisud v. Technip (1994) *Rev. arb.*, 391, note C. Jarrosson.
[47] CA Paris, Oct. 7, 2004, Otor v. Carlyle Holdings (2005) *Journal of International Arbitration [J. Int'l Arb.]*, 357, note D. Bensaude.
[48] CA Paris, Dec. 19, 1986, O.I.A.E.T.I. v. SOFIDIF (1987) *Rev. arb.*, 359, note E. Gaillard; and Cass. 1st civ., Mar. 8, 1988, SOFIDIF v. O.I.A.E.T.I. (1989) *Rev. arb.*, 481, note C. Jarrosson.
[49] CA Paris, Mar. 24, 1995, Bin Saud Bin Abdel Aziz v. Crédit industriel et commercial de Paris (1996) *Rev. arb.*, 259, note J.-M. Talau.
[50] CA Paris, June 23, 2011, La Bergousie v. Willex (Nov. 15, 2011) *Gaz. Pal.*, 19.
[51] CA Paris, Jan. 17, 1984, Bloc'h et Fils v. Delatrae Mockfjaerd (1984) *Rev. arb.*, 498, note P. Fouchard.
[52] CA Paris, Mar. 31, 2015, Banque Delubac v. MM. B., K., and R. (June 19, 2015) *Gaz. Pal.*, 20.
[53] CA Paris, 1st Ch. C, Jan. 1, 2003, Société internationale des télécommunications du Cameroun (Intelcam) v. France Télécom (2004) *Rev. arb.*, 369, note L. Jaeger.

majority, the President of the arbitral tribunal shall decide alone. If the other arbitrators refuse to sign the award, the President shall mention it in the award, which he or she shall then sign alone. The award rendered in the circumstances foreseen in one of the two preceding paragraphs shall produce the same effects as if it had been signed by all the arbitrators or rendered by a majority of votes.

It is generally admitted that dissenting opinions do not affect the validity of the award.[54] The Paris Court of appeal confirmed that dissenting or separate opinions do not violate French international public policy unless they evidence a breach of collegiality or a failure to deliberate on the part of the tribunal.[55]

4.1 Enforcement of Award

Awards must meet a certain number of formal requirements in order to be valid and enforceable. These requirements are set forth in Articles 1481 and 1482 CPC. Article 1481 CPC requires that awards mention the date on which they were made, together with the place where they were rendered. Awards must state the full names of the parties as well as their domicile or registered office. Omission of such items should not prevent the award from being enforceable.[56] The names of counsel or any other person who represented or assisted the parties during the proceedings as well as the names of the arbitrators who rendered the award, the date and the place of where the award was rendered should also be mentioned in the award.

Article 1482 CPC further requires that awards be reasoned and that they briefly mention the parties' respective claims and arguments. Unless the rules applicable to the arbitration provide that the award shall be reasoned, the failure to reason an international award rendered outside France is not, in and of itself, a ground to refuse enforcement of that award.[57] Generally, the judge in charge of annulment or enforcement and recognition of awards in France may verify only whether there is a reasoning, i.e., that the reasoning exists in the award but not whether that reasoning is pertinent and/or sufficient. Moreover, the lack of reasoning in an award is not in and of itself a ground for setting aside, or refusal to recognise and enforce, an international award in France. As a consequence, in the absence of a violation of due process or a violation of French international public policy, an award's reasoning cannot be reviewed or scrutinised by the French judge in charge of the setting aside, or recognition and enforcement, of the award. However, that judge must nevertheless verify that the arbitrators ensured that the parties were made aware in the award of the issues of fact and law considered for their decision(s). That being said, the judge's scrutiny does not extend to alleged mistakes of facts or mistakes of law in the award. In particular, erroneous or inconsistent reasoning does not affect an award's enforceability or validity in France. Indeed, French courts consider that arguments based upon such alleged mistakes or inconsistencies serve as a criticism of the arbitrators' reasoning and are therefore inadmissible.

Article 1511 CPC states that the arbitral tribunal must decide the dispute in accordance with the 'rules of law' chosen by the parties. The wording *rules of law* includes, but is not limited to, national law. Parties are also free to choose a law that is not connected with the contract or the dispute and may choose different laws to govern different aspects of the dispute (*dépeçage*).[58]

---

[54] *See* FOUCHARD, GAILLARD, & GOLDMAN, *supra* note 13, at 765, para. 1398.
[55] CA Paris, Apr. 7, 2011, Merial v. Klocke (July 24, 2011) *Gaz. Pal.*, 14.
[56] CA Paris, Mar. 22, 1985, Ets. Crucke v. Frahuil (1987) *Rev. arb.*, 78, note B. Moreau.
[57] Cass. 1st civ., Mar. 18, 1980, (1980) *Rev. arb.*, 496.
[58] FOUCHARD, GAILLARD, & GOLDMAN, *supra* note 13, at 793–794, paras. 1435–1436.

Parties may, therefore, agree upon the rules of law they wish the tribunal to apply, and this agreement will bind the tribunal whether or not those rules are connected to the parties' relationship. An award rendered in contradiction with the parties' choice of law may be set aside under Article 1520 (3) CPC for violation of the tribunal's mission. To satisfy the requirements of Article 1511 CPC, the arbitral tribunal needs merely to refer in the award to the selected rules of law.

Pursuant to Article 1512 CPC, the parties may entrust a tribunal with the mission to decide as amiable compositeur. The reference to amiable composition may not be explicit in the award and may emerge from the reasoning in the award.[59] Arbitrators acting as amiable compositeurs must confront their own sense of fairness to the solution that would have been reached from the mere application of the law or of the applicable contractual terms.[60]

Arbitrators have discretion in allocating the costs of the arbitration and are not bound by any rule or principle in this regard. There is no specific provision in French arbitration law as to decisions on attorneys' fees or a winning party's claim for legal costs. However, it is general practice in arbitrations with their seat in France that arbitrators tend to grant the winning party the 'reasonable legal and other costs incurred by the parties for the arbitration'. Again, tribunals sitting in France have discretion in this regard.

Upon application of a party, a tribunal sitting in France may interpret its award (Article 1485, para. 2 CPC). Interpretation of an award is limited to clarifying unclear or ambiguous provisions, and tribunals cannot alter their decision.[61] Arbitral awards shall be recognised or enforced in France if their existence is established by the party relying upon them and if said recognition or enforcement is not manifestly contrary to international public policy (Article 1514 CPC). Therefore, recognition and enforcement of foreign awards is subject only to the existence of the award and that, prima facie, recognition or enforcement of such award is not blatantly contrary to French international public policy. Article 1515 CPC provides that the existence of an arbitral award is established through the submission of the original thereof together with the arbitration agreement or copies of such documents satisfying the conditions required to ascertain their authenticity.

The enforcement is the process pursuant to which an exequatur is stamped on the award. According to Article 1516 CPC, the award may be enforced in France only pursuant to an enforcement order (exequatur) issued by a First Instance Court (*Tribunal de grande instance*). The procedure relating to the request for enforcement is conducted ex parte. The request for enforcement is to be filed by the most diligent party with the secretariat of the court together with the original of the award and of the arbitration agreement or copies satisfying the conditions required to ascertain their authenticity. The enforcement order is affixed on the original of the award or, if it is not produced, on the copy satisfying the conditions required to ascertain its authenticity. Where the award is not drafted in the French language, the enforcement order is also affixed on the translation. If the judge refuses to grant the exequatur on the award, the order shall be reasoned (Article 1517 CPC).

---

[59] Cass. 1st civ., Oct. 18, 2001, SARL société grenobloise d'investissement v. Eurovia et autres (2002) *Rev. arb.*, 359, note C. Jarrosson; CA Paris, Dec. 17, 2009, Gothaer (2010) *Cahiers de l'arbitrage* [hereinafter *Cah. Arb.*], 251; CA Paris, Oct. 6, 2011, Applications Générales des Polyesters v. Norpac (Nov. 15, 2011) *Gaz. Pal.*, 12 offers a rare example of the annulment of a domestic award for failure to decide ex aequo et bono in breach of the parties' agreement.

[60] CA Paris, Dec. 9, 2010, Energeia v. Wartsila France, and CA Paris, Jan. 6, 2011, M. T. and Damilo v. Norma (May 17, 2011), *Gaz. Pal.*, 13.

[61] J.-L. DELVOLVÉ, J. ROUCHE, & G. POINTON, FRENCH ARBITRATION LAW AND PRACTICE 191, para. 343 (2003); CA Paris, Apr. 18, 1991, Letierce et fils v. Stolz (1992) *Rev. arb.*, 631, note J. Pellerin.

Pursuant to Article 1525 CPC, the decision ruling on a request for recognition or enforcement of an arbitral award rendered abroad may be appealed. The appeal shall be filed within one month from service (by bailiff) of the award bearing the enforcement order. Parties may specifically agree upon another means of service. The court of appeal may only refuse recognition or the granting of an enforcement order on the arbitral award for the grounds set forth in Article 1520 CPC. Such an appeal does not stay the enforcement of the award. However, the First President ruling in expedited proceedings or, as soon as in charge, the judge in charge of the procedure before the court of appeal (*Conseiller de la mise en état*) may stay or impose conditions for enforcement of the award if such enforcement may 'seriously harm one of the parties' rights' (Article 1526 CPC).

The grounds for setting aside an international award rendered in France are listed in Article 1520 CPC and are exclusive. The French courts of appeal will not review an award's reasoning. That is because appeal of international award is not available under French international arbitration law. French courts regularly dismiss applications filed under Article 1520 CPC where the complaining party relies on alleged deficiencies in the arbitral tribunal's reasoning. Such arguments are simply inadmissible before French courts.

When seized with a request to set aside an award rendered in France, the courts of appeal have the power to examine any evidence and factual or legal submissions they consider relevant. The court has the power to review de novo any issue regarding jurisdiction, the regular constitution of the tribunal,[62] or an alleged violation of procedural international public policy.[63] However, in such cases, the courts often give a certain deference to the findings of tribunal, particularly with respect to questions of facts. The setting aside of a foreign award at the seat of arbitration is not, in and of itself, a ground for denying enforcement of that award in France.[64] Actions to either set aside international awards or appeal an enforcement order affixed on an international award, does not stay enforcement (Article 1526 CPC).[65] Parties may nevertheless request a stay of enforcement before the First President ruling in expedited proceedings or, as soon as in charge, the judge in charge of the procedure (*Conseiller de la mise en état*), who may suspend or set conditions for enforcement of the award if such enforcement may seriously harm one of the parties' rights (Article 1526 CPC).

4.2 Setting Aside Awards

Parties may also now waive their right to request the setting aside of an award rendered in France (Article 1522 CPC). In such a case, the parties will nevertheless be entitled to appeal the enforcement order granted on that award on either of the grounds provided for in Article 1520 CPC. Such an appeal shall be filed within one month from service of the award bearing the enforcement order. Parties may not expressly waive one or several specific grounds for the setting aside of an award rendered in France. Having said this, a party's conduct in the arbitration may lead a French court to consider such conduct as constituting a waiver of that party's right to invoke either of the grounds set in forth in Article 1520 CPC. Article 1466 CPC provides that a party that knowingly and without a legitimate reason fails to object to an irregularity before the tribunal in a timely manner shall be deemed to have waived its right to invoke such irregularity

---

[62] Cass. 1st civ., Jan. 6, 1987, Southern Pacific Properties Ltd and Southern Pacific Ltd v. République arabe d'Egypte (1987) *Rev. arb.*, 469, note P. Leboulanger.
[63] CA Paris, Mar. 23, 2006, SNF SAS v. Cytec Industries BV (2007) *Rev. arb.*,100, note S. Bollée.
[64] Cass. 1st civ., June 29, 2007, Putrabali Adyamulia v. Rena Holding, (2007) *Rev. arb.*, 517, note Gaillard.
[65] Article 1526 CPC applies to awards rendered after May 1, 2011.

at the time of challenge of the award. For example, a party that participates in the arbitration without raising any objection to jurisdiction shall be considered as having waived the right to eventually claim before the court of appeal, once the award is rendered, that the arbitration clause was null and void.[66] The signing of terms of reference with a mention that a party objects to jurisdiction does not constitute any such waiver.[67] The failure of a party to timely object that the tribunal was irregularly constituted,[68] or that an arbitrator lacked independence,[69] shall be considered as a waiver of that party's right to later complain on such basis. However, a party may not necessarily be considered as having waived its right to challenge an award merely because it did not repeatedly submit its objections before the tribunal. A party may be stopped from challenging an award only if its procedural conduct in this respect amounts to a change of legal position which misleads the other party as to its intentions.[70]

A party may waive a right only as from the time it had knowledge of the fact justifying the complaint,[71] and if the rules applicable to the arbitration afforded that party an opportunity to remedy the alleged irregularity.[72]

This being said, a party cannot waive its right to challenge an award on the ground that enforcement or recognition of such award would violate substantive French international public policy.[73] In particular, it is irrelevant to the admissibility of a challenge of an award for violation of international public policy whether the complaining party has raised an objection in this regard before the arbitrators. This is because the scope of the French court's control concerning any such violation should not be conditioned by the parties' conduct during the arbitration.[74]

4.3 Grounds for Setting Aside Awards

According to Article 1520-1 CPC, an international award rendered in France may be set aside in the following cases: 'The arbitral tribunal has wrongly retained or denied jurisdiction.' This may be the case where the court of appeal finds that (1) the dispute is not arbitrable or (2) the arbitration agreement is null and void, does not exist, does not apply to all or certain parties or does not cover all or part of the subject matters submitted to the tribunal.[75] This also encompasses cases where the tribunal denied jurisdiction, and the court of appeal nevertheless finds to the contrary in respect of this issue.[76]

In reviewing the tribunal's decision on jurisdiction, the French judge has a complete power to appreciate the existence, validity and scope of the arbitration agreement. In such a case, the

---

[66] Cass. 1st civ., Nov. 21, 2002, Gromelle v. Institut International des Techniques d'Organisation (2004) *Rev. arb.*, 283, note M. Bandrac; Cass. 1st civ., July 6, 2005, Golshani v. Gouvernement de la République islamique d'Iran (2005) *Rev. arb.*, 993, note P. Pinsolle.
[67] Cass 1st civ., Jan. 6, 1987, Southern Pacific Properties Ltd and Southern Properties, (SPP) v. République Arabe d'Egypte (1987) *Rev. arb.*, 469, note P. Leboulanger.
[68] CA Paris, July 11, 2002, Beugnet Acquitaine v. DV Construction (2004) *Rev. arb.*, 283, note M. Bandrac.
[69] CA Paris, Feb. 22, 2007, Worms services maritimes v. CMA CGM (2007) *Rev. arb.*, 142.
[70] Cass. 1st civ., Feb. 3, 2010, Merial v. Klocke Verpackungs-Service (2010) 25(3) *Mealey's Int'l Arb. Rep.*; (2010) *Rev. arb.*, 94, note L. Weiller.
[71] CA Paris, May 6, 2004, Malecki v. Long (2006) *J Int'l Arb.*, 81, note D. Bensaude.
[72] CA Paris, Jan. 21, 1997, Nu Swift v. White Knight et al. (1997) *Rev. arb.*, 429, note P. Derains.
[73] CA Paris, June 14, 2001, *Compagnie Commerciale André v. Tradigrain France* (2001) *Rev. arb.*, 773, note C. Seraglini.
[74] CA Paris, Oct. 22, 2009, Linde v. Halyvourgiki (2010) 25(3) *Mealey's Int'l Arb. Rep.*
[75] For an example of a partial setting aside CA Paris, Sept. 16, 2010, Evertrade v. Fertial (Feb. 6, 2010) *Gaz. Pal.*, 14.
[76] CA Paris, June 16, 1988, Swiss Oil v. Petrogab et République du Gabon (1989) *Rev. arb.*, 309, note C. Jarrosson; CA Paris, June 21, 1990, Compagnie Honeywell Bull (1991) *Rev. arb.*, 96, note J.-L. Delvolvé; Cass. 1st civ., Oct. 6, 2010, Joseph Abela Family Foundation v. Albert Abela Corporation (2010) *Rev. arb.*, 813, note F. X. Train; (Feb. 6, 2011) *Gaz. Pal.*, 14; *see also* J.-B. Racine, La sentence d'incompétence (2010) *Rev. arb.*, 729.

court's analysis is more extensive than at the time when a competence–competence issue arises since, at that stage, the French judge may decide only whether the arbitration clause at issue is 'manifestly void' or 'manifestly inapplicable'.[77]

4.3.1 Arbitral Tribunal Was Improperly Constituted

Under Article 1520-2, a tribunal may, for instance, be considered improperly constituted when: (1) it was not constituted in accordance with the parties' agreement,[78] (2) the parties did not have the opportunity to participate in an equal manner in the constitution of the tribunal,[79] (3) an arbitrator failed to disclose facts or circumstances that could raise reasonable doubts as to that arbitrator's independence and impartiality in the eyes of the parties or in case that arbitrator objectively lacked independence and/or impartiality[80] or (4) the arbitral institution in charge of administering the procedure wrongfully rejected a challenge against an arbitrator.[81]

4.3.2 Arbitral Tribunal Ruling Did Not Comply with Conferred Mission

The tribunal's mission is defined by the subject matter of the parties' dispute, which is determined by the parties' submissions during the course of the arbitration.[82] As a consequence, claims that are not expressly set out in terms of reference do not necessarily fall outside the arbitrator's mission.[83] An arbitral tribunal may fail to comply with its mission when it does not follow the rules agreed upon by the parties to govern the arbitration. For example, a tribunal vested with powers of amiable compositeur that does not make use of these powers fails to fulfill its mission.[84] Hence, the absence of reference to fairness and the strict application of contractual terms and legal provisions in an award rendered in amiable composition may justify the setting aside or prevent enforcement of the award in France.[85] The mere absence of a reference to powers of amiable compositeur in an award rendered in application of such powers is not, in and of itself, a ground for setting aside.[86] A tribunal may not act as an amiable compositeur if the parties did not entrust it with such power. In such a case, and if it appears from the terms of the award that the tribunal decided the dispute using powers of amiable compositeur, the award may be set aside or denied enforcement.[87]

Where parties agree that certain rules of law shall apply, the tribunal that entirely disregards those rules may also fail to comply with its mission. However, a court of appeal is unlikely to sanction a tribunal that does not make reference to the particular legal provisions upon which it relies to reach its decision.[88] In practice, it is sufficient for the tribunal to merely make reference to the applicable rules of law in its award. Again, the court of appeal will not examine whether or

---

[77] Cass. 1st civ., Mar. 9, 2011, CMA/CGM v. Hyundaï Nipo Dockyard (July 24, 2011) *Gaz. Pal.*, 12.
[78] Cass. 1st civ., Dec. 4, 1990, E.T.P.M. and Ecofisa v. Gas del Estado (1991) *Rev. arb.*, 81, note P. Fouchard.
[79] Cass. 1st civ., Jan. 7, 1992, BKMI & Siemens v. Dutco (1992) *Rev. arb.*, 470, note P. Bellet.
[80] CA Paris, pole 1, ch. 1, Oct. 14, 2014, Auto Guadeloupe Investissements et al. v. Colombus Acquisitions et al. (Nov. 21,2014) *Gaz. Pal.*, 18.
[81] CA Paris, July 3, 2007, Clal MSX v. Inwon (2007) *Rev. arb.*, 747.
[82] CA Paris, pole 1, ch. 1, Sept. 22, 2015, République de Guinée équatoriale v. Orange Middle East and Africa (Mar. 22, 2016) *Gaz. Pal.*, 29.
[83] Cass. 1st civ., Mar. 6, 1996, Farhat Trading Company v. Daewoo (1997) *Rev. arb.*, 70, note J.-J. Arnaldez.
[84] Cass. 1st civ., May 24, 2018, Époux X v. Sté toulousaine d'investissements Leroux (2018) *Gaz. Pal.*, 23.
[85] CA Paris, July 3, 2007, Leizer v. Bachelier (2007) *Rev. arb.*, 647.
[86] Cass. 1st civ., Nov. 28, 2007, C. v. S. (2008) *Rev. arb.*, 99, note V. Chantebout.
[87] Cass. 1st civ., Oct. 12, 2011, Groupe Antoine Tabet v. République du Congo (Jan. 24, 2012) *Gaz. Pal.*, 11.
[88] CA Paris, Dec. 11, 1997, Cubana v. Consavio International Ltd (1999) *Rev. arb.*, 121.

not the applicable rules were correctly applied by the tribunal.[89] A tribunal may fail to comply with its mission when it decides matters beyond those submitted by the parties (ultra petita). Then, only the part that decides ultra petita will be annulled.[90] When a tribunal fails to decide all the claims submitted to it (infra petita), the award may not be annulled on this ground since these claims may again be submitted to the tribunal.

The principle of collegiality, which is not expressly mentioned in the CPC, generally requires that all arbitrators be afforded the opportunity to participate in the tribunal's deliberations, and the breach of that duty may also constitute a ground for challenge of an award under Article 1520 (3) and (5) CPC.[91]

4.3.3 Violation of Principle of Due Process

Article 1510 CPC provides that: 'Whatever may be the chosen procedure, the arbitral tribunal shall ensure equality among the parties and abide by the principle of due process'. All parties must be afforded due process throughout the arbitration.[92] Under French law, due process requires that every party to an arbitration be given a reasonable opportunity to present its case. This means that all information submitted to the tribunal by a party must be provided to all other parties as well.[93] It also means that when the tribunal finds there is a factual or legal issue, which is of relevance to decide the merits of the case and which has not been raised by the parties, the tribunal should then raise the issue with the parties and take their comments into account before taking any decision on such issue.[94]

4.3.4 Enforcement of Award Contrary to International Public Policy

Generally, French courts avoid in-depth examination of the award[95] and will generally focus only on whether recognition and enforcement of the award in France would violate French substantive or procedural international public policy. In order to be admissible and successful under Article 1520(5) CPC, the alleged breach of international public policy must generally be actual and concrete.[96] Enforcement of an award may be contrary to French international public policy where an arbitrator lacked impartiality or independence or where a party was denied due process. Submission of false documents in the course of the arbitration constitutes

---

[89] Cass. 1st civ., Oct. 22, 1991, Compania Valenciana de Cementos Portland v. Primary Coal Inc. (1992) *Rev. arb.*, 457, note P. Lagarde.

[90] CA Paris, pole 1, ch. 1, Sept. 29, 2011, MM. S., T. and T., Mme B. and Quebec inc. v. Techman Head (Fim's) (Nov. 11–15, 2011) *Gaz. Pal.*, 16.

[91] CA Paris, July 1, 1997, Agence Transcongolaise des Communications-Chemins de fer Congo Océan (ATC-CFCO) v. Compagnie minière de l'Ogooué (Comilog) (1998) *Rev. arb.*, 131, note D. Hascher.

[92] CA Paris, June 12, 2003, Citel v. Mungovan (2004) *Rev. arb.*, 887, note D. Bensaude; CA Paris, Nov. 27, 1987, C.C.M. Sulzer v. Somagec, Saers et autre (1989) *Rev. arb.*, 62, note G. Couchez.

[93] CA Paris, Dec. 17, 2009, Fichtner GmbH & Co. KG v. Lksur SA (2010) 24(3) *Mealey's Int'l Arb. Rep.*

[94] CA Paris, June 14, 2007, Ciech v. Comexport Companhia de Comercio Exterior (2007) *Rev. arb.*, 644; CA Paris, Dec. 3, 2009, Engel Austria GmbH v. Don Trade (2010) 24(3) *Mealey's Int'l Arb. Rep.* Generally, *see* ILA 2008 report, *Ascertaining the Contents of the Applicable Law in International Commercial Arbitration*, Rio de Janeiro, www.ila-hq .org/en/committees/index.cfm/cid/19, and (2009) *Rev. arb.*, 445, note D. Bensaude.

[95] *See e.g.*, CA Paris, Nov. 18, 2004, Thalès v. Euromissile (2005) *J. Int'l Arb.*, 239, note D. Bensaude; (2005) *Rev. arb.*, 529, note L. Radicati di Brozolo; Cass. 1st civ., June 4, 2008, SNF v. Cytec (2008) *Rev. arb.*, 473, note I. Fadlallah; CA Paris, Oct. 22, 2009, Linde v. Halyvourgiki (2010) 25(3) *Mealey's Int'l Arb. Rep.*

[96] Cass. 1st civ., Mar. 21, 2000, Moreau v. Verhoeft (2001) *Rev. arb.*, 805, note Y. Derains; CA Paris, Nov. 18, 2004, Thalès v. Euromissile (2005) *J. Int'l Arb.*, 239, note D. Bensaude; *Rev. arb.*, 529, note L. Radicati di Brozolo; and CA Paris, P. 1, ch. 1, Oct. 22, 2009, Linde v. Halyvourgiki (2010) 25(3) *Mealey's Int'l Arb. Rep. See*, however, CA Paris, Jan. 17, 2012, Planor Afrique v. Etilsalat (May 2012) *Gaz. Pal.*, 16.

a fraud that is a breach of French procedural international public policy.[97] Fields, where violations of substantive public policy were found, are rare: money laundering,[98] corruption,[99] certain European regulatory provisions on the protection of consumers[100] and certain French rules on bankruptcy.[101]

5 CONCLUSION

French international arbitration law and practice are clear, simple and efficient. In recent years, many new places of arbitration have emerged due to the rise of this dispute resolution mechanism in a globalised world. In spite of this, Paris still is and remains a favorite seat for many international business lawyers and parties.

---

[97] CA Paris, Sept. 30, 1993, European Gas Turbine v. Westman International Ltd. (1995) *Rev. arb.*, 371, note D. Bureau; Cass. 1st civ., Dec. 19, 1995, Westman International Ltd v. European Gas Turbine (1996) *Rev. arb.*, 49, note D. Bureau.

[98] CA Paris, Sept. 30, 1993; Cass. 1st civ., Dec. 19, 1995; and CA Paris, Feb. 2017, République du Kirghizistan v. M. B. (July 18, 2017) *Gaz. Pal.*, 32.

[99] CA Paris, pole 1, ch. 1, May 28, 2019, Alstom Transport v. Alexander Brothers (July 2, 2019) *Gaz. Pal.*, 22.

[100] EUCJ, Oct. 26, 2006, Elisa Maria Mostaza Claro v. Centro Móvil Milenium SL (2007) *Rev. arb.*, 109, note S. Bollée.

[101] CA Paris, Feb. 16, 1989, Almira Films v. Pierrel ès qual. (1989) *Rev. arb.*, 711, note L. Idot; CA Paris, May 12, 2008, Accor v. Intertraff (July 24, 2011) *Gaz. Pal.*, 16.

15

Commercial Arbitration in Germany

Joseph Schwartz

1 INTRODUCTION

Subject to minor modifications, Germany has adopted an almost verbatim version of the UNCITRAL Model Law on International Commercial Law (Model Law) and is a signatory country to the New York Convention. This means that domestic discussions regarding the relevant and recurring topics, such as the arbitrator's potential bias and misconduct, the interpretation of arbitration clauses, and arbitrability and the enforcement of arbitral awards generally follow the international standard. Since the adoption of the Model Law in 1998, Germany has been regarded as an arbitration-friendly country and has increasingly attracted international arbitration cases.

It follows that the standards in regard to an arbitrator's independence and impartiality are very much in line with international expectations. Yet, in contrast to arbitrators and parties particularly from common law countries, arbitration practitioners from Germany tend to be more familiar with the concept of preliminary legal and factual assessments and the indication of the relevant issues by an arbitral tribunal. Reflecting the idea of a "communicative civil procedure," as rooted in the German Code of Civil Procedure and practiced by state courts, many German practitioners will likely perceive such conduct as means to increase the efficiency of proceedings, particularly during the oral hearing(s), as it allows the parties to focus on the issues that have been indicated as being decisive for the outcome of the case instead of having to safeguard their position for any eventuality by arguing each and every issue that may hypothetically become relevant.

When analyzing recent developments in the German arbitration practice, regard must be had to 2018 revision of the Arbitration Rules of the German Arbitration Institute (DIS) (2018 DIS Arbitration Rules). In 2016, the DIS began the revision process by reviewing the then-applicable version of its arbitration rules in order to define opportunities for improvement of the proceedings and enhance efficiency. In doing so, the DIS opted for a rather exceptional approach: instead of drafting a new version behind closed doors, the DIS decided to include the actual and potential users of the arbitration rules, allowing different stakeholders to contribute with their specific experience and feedback. For this purpose, the DIS established a reform commission of nearly 300 members who worked together for eighteen months in order to identify recent developments, problems and respective solutions. The commission was composed of legal scholars, arbitration practitioners – both regular arbitrators and party counsels – as well as company representatives. As a direct result of these efforts, the 2018 DIS Arbitration Rules came into force on March 1, 2018. While not being limited to these issues, one may name the new stipulations that explicitly govern the conduct of the first case management and the potential adjustment and adaptation of the arbitral proceedings to the individual case's particularities as examples of the 2018 DIS Arbitration Rules' approach to efficiency.[1] In addition, the new rules explicitly address the matter of potentially different views on an arbitral tribunal's duty and capacity to offer preliminary assessments of the case and its role in regard to settlement facilitation by providing opt-in/opt-out mechanisms to allow the parties to actively decide about the arbitral tribunal's role during the proceedings.

In addition, a working group has been tasked by the Federal Ministry of Justice and Consumer Protection with the purpose of reviewing the German Arbitration Law. While it is too early to report on any final results or decisions, one should expect rather considerate amendments and a tendency to remain close to the Model Law, while potentially undertaking means to further strengthen the attractiveness of Germany as a place of arbitration, e.g., by partially allowing English as a court language, reflecting on the applicability of soft law (such as the IBA Rules on the Taking of Evidence in International Arbitration) and promoting the publication of arbitral awards.

2 ARBITRATOR'S INDEPENDENCE AND IMPARTIALITY

2.1 *General Considerations*

2.1.1 *Legal Basis*

Under the German arbitration law, the requirement of the arbitrator's independence and impartiality is governed by Sec. 1036 Code of Civil Procedure (*Zivilprozessordnung*, ZPO). The provision is an almost verbatim adoption of Art. 12 of the Model Law[2] and stipulates:

> (1) When a person is approached in connection with his possible appointment as an arbitrator, he shall disclose any circumstances likely to give rise to doubts as to his impartiality or independence. An arbitrator, from the time of his appointment and throughout the arbitral proceedings, shall without delay disclose any such circumstances to the parties unless they have already been informed of them by him.
>
> (2) An arbitrator may be challenged only if circumstances exist that give rise to justifiable doubts as to his impartiality or independence, or if he does not possess qualifications agreed to by the parties. A party may challenge an arbitrator appointed by him, or in whose appointment he has participated, only for reasons of which he becomes aware after the appointment has been made.

While para. 1 stipulates the duties of disclosure, para. 2 governs the applicable standards for challenging an arbitrator. The only deviation from Art. 12 of the Model Law is the removal of the qualifying prerequisite of *justifiable* doubts in para. 1, so that (reasonable) "doubts" may suffice under Sec. 1036 (1) ZPO for a disclosure duty of the (prospective) arbitrator. Yet, as Art. 12 (2) of the Model Law has been adopted without any modifications as Sec. 1036 (2) ZPO, the standard for challenging an arbitrator is the same as under the Model Law and in many jurisdictions.

---

[1] *Cf.* Sec. 27.4 in connection with Annex 3 of the 2018 DIS Arbitration Rules.
[2] J. Münch, *Sec. 1036*, *in* MÜNCHENER KOMMENTAR ZUR ZPO vol. 3, para. 3 (T. Rauscher & W. Krüger eds., 5th ed. 2017).

2.1.2 *Purpose*

Sec. 1036 ZPO shall guarantee the independence of the arbitrators and thereby ensure procedural fairness and quality of decisions.[3] Eventually, the stipulations safeguard the well-established and fundamental general principles of the *equal treatment of the parties*, the *right to a fair trial*, and *nemo iudex in causa sua*, meaning that no one should be a judge in his or her own case.

In application of these principles, the German Federal Court of Justice (*Bundesgerichtshof*, BGH) recently decided that a decision board, which not only consists of neutrals but also of party representatives (which are, by nature, not independent), may not even qualify as an arbitral tribunal.[4] In the underlying case, the parties had agreed on a five-member "contract advisory board" (*Vertragsbeirat*) in their contract, to which the parties could refer disputes that would arise during the execution of the contract. By agreement, each party to the contract would appoint its managing director and its technical director to the contract advisory board, whereas these four persons would jointly appoint the presiding member of the board who had to be qualified for judicial office. In case a dispute was referred to the contract advisory board and could not be resolved amicably within two weeks, the contract advisory board was supposed to "decide the dispute as an arbitral tribunal in accordance with Sec. 1025 ZPO et seqq."

In the underlying previous decision, the court of second instance had held that the contract advisory board had not acted as an arbitral tribunal in accordance with Sec. 1025 et seqq. when rendering its decisions due to its personal composition:

> The principle that no one may be a judge in this own case also applies to arbitral proceedings, as it constitutes an inalienable component of every judicial system based on the rule of law. Accordingly, neither a party itself nor its legal representative may be an arbitrator.[5]

Irrespectively of any specific misconduct, the court of second instance held that the parties – despite the principle of party autonomy – could not validly deviate from such principles:

> In the absence of the parties' discretionary power over the prohibition of one judging one's own case that derives from the principle of the rule of law, it is furthermore irrelevant that the parties have, in full knowledge of the significance and scope of their decision, contractually and by an individual agreement agreed to the authority of the contract advisory board to decide as an arbitral tribunal in the meaning of §§ 1025 et seqq. of the German Civil Code. The contractual autonomy of the parties does not justify admitting decisions by partial arbitrators as jurisdiction.[6]

The Federal Court of Justice upheld this decision and reaffirmed that the independence and impartiality of arbitrators constitutes an indispensable and overriding principle.[7]

2.1.3 *General Requirements*

2.1.3.1 DISCLOSURE DUTY Sec. 1036 (1) ZPO states that any (potential) arbitrator has the duty to disclose any and all circumstances that might give rise to doubts as to their impartiality without undue delay. If the arbitrator violates the disclosure obligation, such violation itself is

---

[3] *Id.* at paras. 1, 2.
[4] Federal Court of Justice (BGH), decision dating Oct. 11, 2017, case. no. I ZB 12/17.
[5] Higher Regional Court (OLG) Frankfurt am Main, decision dating Feb. 2, 2017, case no. 26 Sch 6/16, para. 26.
[6] *Id.* at para. 30.
[7] *Supra* note 4.

considered to be an indication of bias.[8] As Sec. 1036 (1) ZPO has very slightly modified Art. 12 (1) of the Model Law and removed the qualification of *justifiable doubts* and merely requires *doubts*,[9] one may interpret the disclosure duties to be slightly broader than under the Model Law.

2.1.3.2 OBJECTIVE THRESHOLD FOR CHALLENGES Under Sec. 1036 para. 2 sentence 1, 1st alternative ZPO, an arbitrator may be challenged only if circumstances exist that give rise to justifiable doubts as to his or her impartiality or independence. According to the general understanding, the arbitrator is obliged to observe the rules applicable to a judge, in particular impartiality, independence and the observance of party rights. While impartiality is interpreted as being unbiased and unprejudiced toward the parties, independence shall secure that an arbitrator has no relationship to the parties or someone closely connected to them.[10] In addition, any connection or interest in regard to the matter in dispute may be regarded as lack of independence.[11] It is not necessary for the arbitrator to actually be partial or biased. Rather, a challenge is already justified if there are objective reasons that, from the point of view of the challenging party, could give rise to the fear that the arbitrator is not impartial and thus unbiased in the arbitration proceedings.[12] This threshold is generally in accordance with international standards. Section 2 of the 2014 IBA Guidelines on Conflicts of Interest in International Arbitration, for example, formulates a largely similar definition of impartiality.

2.1.3.3 IBA RULES ON CONFLICTS OF INTEREST Practical experience shows that, while constituting no binding law but *soft law* only, recourse is had to the IBA Guidelines on Conflicts of Interest in International Arbitration as guidance in many international cases.[13]

2.1.4 *2018 DIS Arbitration Rules: Impartiality and Independence*

Art. 9.1 of the 2018 DIS Arbitration Rules contains the relevant stipulations in regard to the independence and impartiality of arbitrator(s): "Every arbitrator shall be impartial and independent of the parties throughout the entire arbitration and shall have all of the qualifications, if any, that have been agreed upon by the parties." The provision, therefore, not only governs the impartiality and independence but adds the further prerequisite of "having all of the qualifications," in case the parties agreed on such.

2.2 *Application of Standards to Determine Arbitrator's Bias*

When applying the aforementioned standards, the following cases are being regularly discussed when determining the question of whether the challenge of an arbitrator is justified: relationships between the arbitrator and a party, relationships between the arbitrator and a party counsel, prior involvement of the arbitrator in or related to the dispute, prior statements or opinions by the arbitrator (e.g. publications or legal/expert opinions) that relate to the subject matter of the dispute, and the arbitrator's conduct in the arbitration proceedings. While the first three issues

---

[8] C. Wolf & N. Eslami, *Sec. 1037*, *in* BECKOK ZPO para. 19 (V. Vorwerk & C. Wolf eds., 31st ed. 2018).
[9] *Cf. id.* at para. 2.1.1.
[10] *Cf.* Art. 3.1 IBA Rules of Ethics for International Arbitrators.
[11] *Cf.* R. KREINDLER, J. SCHÄFER, & R. WOLFF, SCHIEDSGERICHTSBARKEIT – KOMPENDIUM FÜR DIE PRAXIS para. 530 (2006).
[12] Higher Regional Court (KG) Berlin, decision dating Feb. 12, 2018, case no. 13 SchH 2/17.
[13] Wolf & Eslami, *supra* note 8, at paras. 11 ff.; Münch, *supra* note 2, at para. 13.

may be considered standard issues in international arbitration, the latter two points may be elucidated in a bit more detail.

2.2.1 Challenges Due to Prior Statements or Opinions

While a prior involvement in or directly related to the individual dispute will regularly give justifiable doubts in regard to the impartiality of an arbitrator, it is being widely held that prior *abstract* legal positions, e.g., because the arbitrator has covered similar legal matters in publications or otherwise expressed his or her position unrelated to the concrete arbitration proceedings, must not be regarded as giving rise to justifiable doubts to his impartiality and independence.[14]

However, it should be noted that this position is being questioned by authors from time to time. It has recently been argued that prior abstract legal statements may constitute grounds for challenges at least for presiding and sole arbitrators, who are not chosen unilaterally and may, therefore, be expected to be exceptionally neutral.[15] This argument is met with the criticism that every arbitrator and every tribunal must meet the same requirements of neutrality and no different standard must be applied to party-appointed arbitrators.[16]

In addition, it may be of interest that the German Federal Court of Justice (*Bundesgerichtshof*) held in January 2017 that a court-appointed expert witness may be challenged for justifiable doubts in regard to his or her impartiality based on prior expert opinions in similar cases:

> An expert may also be rejected on grounds of bias if he has provided a private expert opinion for remuneration on a similar question in a similar case for a third party not directly or indirectly involved in the legal dispute and if the interests of the parties conflict comparably in both cases ... .
>
> Unlike in the case of a court appointment, the witness expert is contractually bound to one of the parties to the respective dispute in the case of a private expert opinion. If he later assesses the facts, that were the subject of the private expert opinion, differently, he may expose himself to the accusation – whether justified or unjustified – of his client that he did not properly conduct the private expert opinion or violate other contractual obligations ... . The possibility of a conflict between the expert's consideration towards his previous client and the obligation to provide an objective court-ordered expert opinion which is separate from the previous expert opinion, has the potential to undermine the trust of the challenging party in the impartiality of the expert opinion.[17]

While this case did not directly apply to arbitration proceedings or the impartiality of an arbitrator, one may still find it to be of significance for arbitration proceedings. This is due to the fact that arbitrators, court judges and court-appointed experts may be challenged for the exact same reasons: Justifiable doubts in regard to their impartiality. This follows under German law from Sec. 406 (1) ZPO, which states that: "An expert may be rejected for the same reasons for which a party is entitled to challenge a judge." In turn, Sec. 42 (2) ZPO provides the grounds for challenging the impartiality of court judges, which are very similar to the prerequisites for challenging arbitrators in accordance with Sec. 1036 ZPO:

---

[14] *Cf.* D. Effer-Uhe, *Schiedsrichterliche Unabhängigkeit bei wissenschaftlichen Äußerungen*, ZEITSCHRIFT FÜR SCHIEDSVERFAHREN [SCHIEDSVZ], 75, 80 (2018); KREINDLER, SCHÄFER, & WOLFF, *supra* note 11, at para. 534; O. Froitzheim, *Schiedsrichterliche Befangenheit durch Äußerungen zu Rechtsfragen – Eine Antwort auf Effer-Uhe*, 16 SCHIEDSVZ 10 (2019).

[15] *Cf.* Effer-Uhe, *supra* note 14, at 75.

[16] *Cf. id.* at 75, 78; Münch, *supra* note 2, at para. 30–31.

[17] Federal Court of Justice (BGH), decision of Jan. 20, 2017, case no. VI ZB 31/16, Neue Juristische Wochenschrift – Rechtsprechungs – Report Zivilrecht [NJW-RR] 2017, 569, 570.

Sec. 42 (2) Recusal of a judge from a case: A judge will be recused for fear of bias if sound reasons justify a lack of confidence in his impartiality.

Sec. 1036 (2) Recusal of an arbitral judge: The appointment of an arbitral judge may be refused only if any circumstances give rise to justified doubts as to his impartiality or independence, or if he does not meet the prerequisites established by the parties.

The Higher Regional Court (*Oberlandesgericht*) in Hamburg recently also confirmed that the challenge of arbitrators generally follows comparable standards as laid down in Sec. 42 ZPO.[18] Accordingly, while no such judgment has yet been rendered, the Federal Court of Justice's reasoning for finding a court-appointed expert to be prejudiced based on prior positions in different proceedings may – in theory – equally apply to arbitrators.

It should however be noted that, according to the Federal Court of Justice's decision, three specific prerequisites need to be fulfilled: (1) a previous issuance of a private expert opinion, (2) the opinion concerned a similar question in a similar case, and (3) the involved parties are subject to the same conflicting interests as those parties affected by the previous opinion.[19] A similar position on potential grounds for challenging an arbitrator had previously been expressed by Schwab and Walter, who held that the expression of a legal position or a publication on legal questions (as long as it is unrelated to the actual dispute) may not constitute grounds for challenging an arbitrator, whereas previous decisions in similar cases (e.g., by the arbitrator of an association) would be questionable.[20] It, therefore, remains to be seen whether similar reasoning as in the decision of the Federal Court of Justice regarding expert witnesses will also be applied to challenges of arbitrators.

2.2.2 Arbitrator's Conduct in Promotion of Settlements and Preliminary Assessments

Most arbitration practitioners with a common law background are reluctant to allow the arbitrator to engage in dispute settlement negotiations. According to the traditional common legal view, preliminary assessments and settlement proposals are irreconcilable with the arbitrator's duty to neutrality. From a German perspective, however, such conduct is understood to be one of the primary duties of courts and, respectively, of arbitral tribunals. This understanding is rooted in German procedural law and has been applied in practice in German domestic arbitral proceedings accordingly ever since. The ZPO reflects the idea of a "communicative civil procedure" and authorizes and obliges the court to give preliminary assessments of the legal and factual issues, to direct the parties to relevant aspects (Sec. 139 (2) and (3) ZPO) and even to actively promote settlements in all circumstances of the proceedings (see Sec. 278 (1) ZPO).

Many arbitration practitioners from Germany, therefore, perceive the preliminary assessment and the indication of the relevant issues by the decision-making body as a means to increase the efficiency of proceedings, particularly during the oral hearing(s). Instead of arguing any issue that the parties may consider as potentially relevant (and examining all witnesses at length to cover each hypothetical argument), the parties may focus on the issues that have been indicated as being decisive for the outcome of the case. Such conduct, however, is foreign to most common law jurisdictions, which follow, at least in this regard, a more adversarial approach. Any preliminary assessment or suggestion for a settlement by the court may be encountered with skepticism or be considered as an expression of bias from international practitioners, who may, therefore, perceive such conduct as incompatible with the arbitrator's neutrality duties.

---

[18] Higher Regional Court (OLG) Hamburg, decision of June 29, 2018, case no. 6 SchH 1/18.
[19] *Supra* note 17.
[20] K. H. SCHWAB & G. WALTER, SCHIEDSGERICHTSBARKEIT chap. 14, para. 8 (7th ed. 2005).

While it is generally up to the arbitrator(s) to adjust their conduct to the expectations from the parties (and many arbitration practitioners in Germany will do so in consideration of the parties' nationalities and the internationality of the proceedings), the newly adopted 2018 DIS Arbitration Rules aim to provide the parties with a general framework for the arbitrator's rights and obligations during a proceeding, which the parties may adjust to their needs and expectations using opt-in/opt-out mechanisms. Accordingly, Art. 26 of the 2018 DIS Arbitration Rules generally provides the arbitrator with a mandate to encourage amicable settlements at every stage of the proceedings, whereas any party may decide to object to such conduct: "Unless any party objects thereto, the arbitral tribunal shall, at every stage of the arbitration, seek to encourage an amicable settlement of the dispute or of individual disputed issues."

Where the parties do not opt-out from this provision, the 2018 DIS Arbitration Rules have elevated the tribunal's mandate to facilitate settlement from an encouragement ("should" in the 1998 edition) to an obligation ("shall" in the 2018 DIS Arbitration Rules). As a corrective of that change, the 2018 DIS Arbitration Rules explicitly state that any party may object to settlement facilitation. Similarly, the 2018 DIS Arbitration Rules oblige the arbitrator(s) to discuss certain means of increasing the efficiency of the proceedings during the case management conference, including the question whether the arbitrator(s) should provide the parties with preliminary nonbinding assessments of factual or legal issues in the arbitration, provided all of the parties consent thereto:

> During the case management conference, the arbitral tribunal shall discuss with the parties the following measures for increasing procedural efficiency: . . . Providing the parties with a preliminary non-binding assessment of factual or legal issues in the arbitration, provided all of the parties consent thereto.[21]

Accordingly, arbitrators may only provide their (nonbinding) preliminary assessments upon prior explicit consent of both parties.

2.3 Consequences of a Lack of Impartiality or Independence

In case of justifiable doubts as to the arbitrator's impartiality and independence, the procedure for challenging such arbitrator is stipulated by Sec. 1037 ZPO, which is an adoption of Art. 13 of the Model Law.[22] The provision provides for a two-tier procedure that allows parties to first challenge arbitrators within the arbitral proceedings (Sec. 1037 (2) ZPO) while the parties may freely define the requirements and organizational procedure for such a challenge (Sec. 1037 (1) ZPO). In proceedings administered by arbitral institutions, parties mostly rely on the respective institutional rules on the challenge and replacement procedures, such as Art. 15 of the 2018 DIS Arbitration Rules.

In this context, the 2018 DIS Arbitration Rules deviate from the common procedure that the arbitral tribunal itself will decide on such challenge, but rather attempts to provide for a more neutral approach:

Article 15 Challenge of an Arbitrator:

> (1) Any party who seeks to challenge an arbitrator, on the grounds that the arbitrator has failed to comply with one or more of the requirements of Article 9.1, shall file a request for challenge ('Challenge') pursuant to Article 15.2.

---

[21] Art. 27.4, in connection with Annex 3, lit. F. of the 2018 DIS Arbitration Rules.
[22] Wolf & Eslami, *supra* note 8, at paras. 1, 2.

(2) The Challenge shall describe the facts and circumstances on which it is based and shall specify when the party filing the Challenge first obtained knowledge of the same. The Challenge shall be filed with the DIS no later than 14 days after the party filing the Challenge first obtained knowledge of the facts and circumstances on which it is based.

(3) The DIS shall transmit the Challenge to the challenged arbitrator, the other arbitrators and the other party and shall set a time limit for comments. The DIS shall send any comments that it receives to the parties and to each arbitrator.

(4) The Arbitration Council shall decide upon the Challenge.

(5) The arbitral tribunal may proceed with the arbitration unless and until the Challenge is accepted.

As may be seen from Art. 15.4 of the 2018 DIS Arbitration Rules, the decision over the challenge of an arbitrator will not be made by the arbitral tribunal but by the DIS's Arbitral Council. The Arbitral Council consists of at least fifteen members from at least five different countries, who shall have practical experience in international and domestic arbitration[23] and are appointed by the DIS board of directors.[24] Hereby, the 2018 DIS Arbitration Rules aim to provide a more neutral approach by referring the decision over an arbitrator's challenge to another decision-making body. In a second step, if the arbitral tribunal (or in case of the 2018 DIS Arbitration Rules: the Arbitral Council) rejects the challenge, the party is entitled to file for the challenge before the competent state court, which has the authority to override the tribunal's (or Arbitral Council's) decision in this regard (Sec. 1037 (3) ZPO).

Lacking a valid reason for a challenge, most challenging procedures are unsuccessful. Professor Dr. Stefan Kröll, in a review of recent German arbitration-related jurisprudence, collects some of the decisions exemplifying this,[25] which are summarized as follows. The Higher Regional Court (*Kammergericht*) in Berlin recently decided over a number of challenges that concerned the language of the proceedings. The respondent in the case felt it had been treated unfairly by the arbitrator, who had ordered the counter-memorial to be submitted in both English and German, under an arbitration agreement that provided for the proceedings to be in "English or German." The party filing the challenge felt the arbitrator had been biased against it, as the choice for a language had been arbitrary and caused additional expenses on its counsel's part. Dismissing the challenges, the court stressed that such subjective and irrational perceptions could not constitute a reason for dismissal.[26]

Similarly, a challenge was unsuccessful that regarded an arbitrator who had, a few years prior to the proceedings in question, argued as counsel in a similar case. The court dismissed the challenge and held that generally not even prior involvement in a case regarding the same factual circumstances could prove an arbitrator's lack of impartiality. His role as counsel required different skillsets of him, which would not preclude his ability to be partial when acting in the role of an arbitrator. In any case, even if there was information relating to previous involvement that could be subject to a duty of disclosure, as for example under Sec. 3 of the IBA Guidelines on Conflicts of Interest in International Arbitration, this disclosure duty does not by itself indicate a lack of impartiality. The duties are merely indicators that influence a case-by-case analysis.[27]

Another decision of the Higher Regional Court (*Oberlandesgericht*) Frankfurt am Main confirms that challenges to arbitrators may not be instrumentalized to reprimand decisions

---

[23] Cf. Art. 3.1, Annex 1 to the 2018 DIS Arbitration Rules.
[24] Cf. Art. 3.2, Annex 1 to the 2018 DIS Arbitration Rules.
[25] S. Kröll, *Die schiedsrechtliche Rechtsprechung 2016 und 2017*, SCHIEDSVZ 61(2018).
[26] Higher Regional Court (KG) Berlin, decision dated June 29, 2015, case no. 20 SchH 1/15.
[27] *Supra* note 18.

one party might consider unfavorable. In the decision regarding an expert witness statement ordered by the tribunal that allegedly favored one side, the court dismissed the challenge and confirmed that the threshold for a lack of impartiality of an arbitrator will be met only when it can be substantiated that decisions result from arbitrariness or specifically from a bias in favor of one party.[28]

However, if an award is rendered under the participation of a successfully challenged arbitrator, the award is likely to be annulled. In an arbitration proceeding initiated in 2010, the defendant had challenged the presiding arbitrator. After the arbitral tribunal rejected the request, the defendant filed for a challenge before the Higher Regional Court of Munich. Just after the arbitral tribunal had rendered an award, the Higher Regional Court of Munich confirmed the reasons for a challenge. On this account, the defendant sought to annul the award. The claimant to the original proceeding argued that there was no causal link between the possible challenge of the presiding arbitrator and the content of the award. In support of the argument, the claimant presented a document signed by the other two arbitrators, stating that the decision was unanimous and would have been the same if a different presiding arbitrator had acted. The Federal Court of Justice, however, rejected the argument and held that the award had been based on an infringement of due process under Sec. 1059 (2) No. 1 lit. d ZPO,[29] which was causal for the following reasons:

> In arbitral proceedings with more than one arbitrator, pursuant to Sec. 1052 (1) ZPO, any decision of the Arbitral Tribunal shall be made by a majority of the votes of all members unless the parties have agreed otherwise. Even though the provision does not expressly state this, it presupposes a deliberation prior to voting. If a judiciary body composed of several judges decides by voting after a deliberation, it can never be ruled out that a certain decision has been reached due to the participation of one of these judges. It is always possible that the behaviour of one judge during deliberation and voting influences the formation of opinion and the voting behaviour of the other judges . . . .
>
> Since a decision may only be made after deliberation and it cannot, therefore, be ruled out for legal reasons that an arbitral tribunal in a different composition would have reached or would reach a different result, it is irrelevant whether the challenged arbitral award was made unanimously. Furthermore, it is therefore irrelevant that the adjudicating arbitrators declared that an identical award would be made with a different presiding arbitrator.[30]

3 ARBITRABILITY AND ENFORCEABILITY

3.1 Scope and Judicial Interpretation of Arbitration Agreements

Just like their 1998 predecessor, the new 2018 DIS Arbitration Rules recommend that the parties adopt the following model clause if they opt for arbitration proceedings administered by DIS:

> (1) All disputes arising out of or in connection with this contract or its validity shall be finally settled in accordance with the Arbitration Rules of the German Arbitration Institute (DIS) without recourse to the ordinary courts of law. (2) The arbitral tribunal shall be composed of [a sole arbitrator / three arbitrators]. (3) The seat of the arbitration shall be in [city and country]. (4) The language of the arbitration shall be in [language]. (5) The law applicable to the merits shall be [law / rules of law].

---

[28] Higher Regional Court (OLG) Frankfurt, decision dated Sept. 26, 2016, case no. 26 SchH 1/16.
[29] Federal Court of Justice (BGH), decision dated Dec. 11, 2014, case no. I ZB 23/14, *NJW-RR* 2015, 1087.
[30] Federal Court of Justice (BGH), decision dated Dec. 11, 2014, case no. I ZB 23/14, *NJW-RR* 2015, 1087, 1088.

This clause confirms the wording of the 1998 model clause, which has been successfully tested in practice over the past twenty years. The DIS also offers model clauses for expedited procedures and corporate disputes, which, as will be also discussed in this chapter, are subject to particular prerequisites in Germany. Following a pro-arbitration approach and the parties' underlying intention not to separate connected matters by referring disputes to different *fora*, it has been held that arbitration agreements are to be interpreted broadly.[31]

The usual phrasing of arbitration clauses ("arising out of this contract"), therefore, encompasses not only direct contractual claims but also inter alia the formation and validity of the contract;[32] subsequent deliveries under a framework agreement;[33] non-competition duties under a contract;[34] claims for damages,[35] including claims for cartel damages;[36] revocation of an agreement;[37] indemnification duties;[38] and claims between joint debtors under a contract.[39]

Furthermore, contradictory party's conduct may lead to the competence of arbitral tribunals or state courts. If one party has previously invoked the competence of another decision-making body to decide the dispute, it may be precluded to argue against such a previous position in front of the respective other decision-making body. The Federal Court of Justice recently held that a party may be precluded from relying on the relevant arbitration agreement if it has previously applied for a stay of arbitral proceedings in front of an ordinary court – even if the matter is covered by the arbitration agreement and generally arbitrable. This preclusion occurs because the behavior would otherwise constitute "an inadmissible exercise of rights on account of contradictory procedural conduct against the principles of good faith"[40] (*venire contra factum proprium*). In two related decisions, the court decided this for cases of contradictory conduct during the enforceability declaration procedure but clarified that the same applies for relying on the arbitration agreement in earlier stages of the proceedings, for example:

> if the defendant first asserts in the arbitral proceedings that it is not the arbitral tribunal but the state court which is competent to decide on the subject-matter of the dispute and then objects to the subsequently initiated proceedings before the ordinary courts by invoking the arbitration agreement.[41]

Regarding the *subjective scope* of the arbitral agreement, it may be held that generally only the contractual parties and their legal successors are bound to the arbitration agreement.[42] The Federal Court of Justice, in a decision regarding sports arbitration, confirmed the privity of arbitration agreements as contracts which only bind their signatories. It rejected as "alien" the

---

[31] Federal Court of Justice (BGH), judgments dating Feb. 27, 1970, case no. VII ZR 68/68, *Neue Juristische Wochenschrift* [NJW] 1970, 1046; and dating Oct. 4, 2001, case no. III ZR 281/00, NJW-RR 2002, 387, 387; Higher Regional Court (OLG) Munich, decision dating Dec. 18 2013, case no. 34 Sch 14/12, *Bech-Rechtsprechung, Datenbank* [BeckRS] 2014, 1197; R. Geimer, § 1029, *in* ZPO – ZIVILPROZESSORDNUNG: KOMMENTAR 2016 para. 78 (R. Zöller ed., 31 ed. 2015).

[32] *Cf.* Federal Court of Justice (BGH), judgment dating Oct. 29, 2008, case no. XII ZR 165/06, NJW-RR 2009, 637; case no. VII ZR 68/68, *supra* note 31.

[33] *Cf.* Federal Court of Justice (BGH), judgment dating Dec. 5, 1963, Case no. KZR 9/62, *Gewerblicher Rechtsschutz und Urheberrecht* [GRUR] 1964, 405.

[34] *Cf.* Federal Court of Justice (BGH), judgment dating Aug. 1, 2002, case no. III ZB 66/01, NJW-RR 2002, 1462.

[35] J.-P. Lachmann, *Klippen für die Schiedsvereinbarung*, 1 SCHIEDSVZ 28, 29 (2003).

[36] A. Weitbrecht, *Schiedsklauseln und Kartellschadensersatz*, 16 SCHIEDSVZ 159 (2018).

[37] Higher Regional Court (OLG) Frankfurt am Main, judgment dating Sept. 17, 2010, case no. 13 Sch 1/10.

[38] Higher Regional Court (OLG) Hamm, decision dating May 6, 2015, case no. 8 SchH 1/15.

[39] Higher Regional Court (KG) Berlin, judgment dating June 28, 2007, case no. 2 U 37/05.

[40] Federal Court of Justice (BGH), two decisions dating Mar. 16, 2017, case no. I ZB 49/16, *Zeitschrift für Erbrecht und Vermögensnachfolge* [ZEV] 2017, 416, 419; and case no. I ZB 50/16, NJW 2017, 2115, 2118.

[41] *Id.*

[42] C. Wolf & N. Eslami, Sec. 1029, *in* BECKOK ZPO para. 16 (V. Vorwerk & C. Wolf eds., 31st ed. 2018).

notion that the scope of potential claimants and respondents could be extended by way of a modification of the procedural rules:

> The dynamic reference [to the current Procedural Rules] is stretched beyond its limits if subsequent amendments to the Rules of Procedure violate the legitimate interests of one of the two parties to the arbitration agreement with regards to the principle of good faith. Specifically, such a violation against good faith exists if, with a view to subsequent amendments to the Rules of Procedure, the circle of persons entitled to bring an arbitration action is extended. Such an extension would exist due to NADA's right to bring an action. In the opinion of the court, it is alien to the nature of procedural rules to determine or change the group of possible claimants and respondents in an arbitration agreement.[43]

Limited exceptions include insolvency administrators, who are bound by the arbitration agreement concluded by the insolvent party:

> The parties, as insolvency administrators of the assets of [the companies], are bound by this arbitration agreement insofar as contractual claims are asserted with the arbitration action – as in the present case. Since the arbitration agreement is neither a mutual contract within the meaning of Sec. 103 German Insolvency Code nor a mandate within the meaning of Sec. 115 German Insolvency Code, the administrator may neither refuse performance nor is the arbitration agreement terminated by the commencement of insolvency proceedings.[44]

In addition, the Federal Court of Justice recently held that an arbitration agreement could validly extend to a third party if they were given a right to choose:

> There are no concerns against this result under the aspect of an unduly imposed obligation to arbitrate of uninvolved third parties. The insured are merely given a right to choose, so that they will not be subjected to arbitration proceedings, but are also free to initiate proceedings in front of a state court.[45]

Furthermore, as part of the current discussions regarding the revision of the German Arbitration Law (Sec. 1025 et seqq. ZPO), some commentators suggest lowering the formal threshold for arbitration clauses in order to facilitate multi-company disputes in proceedings regarding the involvement of different subsidiaries and legal entities.[46]

3.2 Arbitrability and Enforceability

Having ratified the New York Convention, the enforceability of arbitral awards in Germany follows well-known and established international standards, and German courts may be described as generally arbitration friendly. In regard to arbitrability, it follows from Sec. 1059 (2) no. 2 a) ZPO that an award may be set aside if the subject matter of the dispute lacks arbitrability. The question of arbitrability is regulated in Sec. 1030 ZPO, which stipulates:

> (1) Any proprietary claim may be the subject of an arbitration agreement. An arbitration agreement on non-proprietary claims shall have legal effect to the extent that the parties are entitled to conclude a settlement agreement on the subject matter of the dispute.

---

[43] Federal Court of Justice (BGH), decision dating Apr. 19, 2018, case no. I ZB 52/17, SchiedsVZ 2019, 41, 44.
[44] Federal Court of Justice (BGH), decision dating Aug. 9, 2016, case no. I ZB 1/15, NJW 2017, 488, 489.
[45] Federal Court of Justice (BGH), decision dating Nov. 8, 2018, case no. I ZB 24/18, BeckRS 2018, 40831.
[46] Cf. C. Benedict, *Mehrvertragsverfahren, Mehrparteienverfahren, Einbeziehung Dritter und Verbindung von Verfahren*, 16 SchiedsVZ 306 (2018); R. Wolff, *Empfiehlt sich eine Reform des deutschen Schiedsverfahrensrechts?*, 14 SchiedsVZ 293, 299 ff (2016).

(2) An arbitration agreement on legal disputes concerning a tenancy agreement for residential property in Germany shall be ineffective. This does not apply in the case of premises of the type specified in § 549 (2) nos. 1 to 3 of the German Civil Code.

(3) Legal regulations outside this book, according to which disputes may not or only under certain conditions be subjected to arbitration proceedings, remain unaffected.

It may be noted that Sec. 1030 (1) ZPO only requires a "proprietary" claim, which is broader than the scope of arbitral matters suggested by the Model Law, which includes "commercial" disputes only (cf. Art. 1 (1) Model Law). In addition to certain rather specific matters that are being considered as non-arbitrable, such as certain patent-related disputes,[47] it may reasonably be assumed that the question of arbitrability of corporate disputes in Germany has the highest practical relevance. In this regard, the Federal Court of Justice held in 1996 that shareholder disputes concerning the validity of shareholder resolutions were not arbitrable (Schiedsfähigkeit I, or Arbitrability I decision).

As such arbitral awards had an effect toward all shareholders of the corporation (being of erga omnes effect in contrast to the general inter parties effect of other arbitral awards), the procedural rights of the shareholders not involved in the arbitration proceedings would be prejudiced:

> Objections to arbitrability of such disputes arise from the fact that decisions rendered in accordance with Sec. 258 (1), 249 (1) German Stock Corporation Act, combined with the applicable procedural provision Sec. 325 (1) German Code of Civil Procedure, take legal effect for and against all shareholders and corporate bodies, even if they did not participate in the proceedings as a party. This extension of legal validity is intended to provide the corporation with a quick and reliable resolution of the dispute. It is based on a specific corporate law provision that cannot be removed from the context of the procedural rules that supplement it and that cannot be transferred to a private arbitral tribunal.[48]

In 2009 the Federal Court of Justice gave up this general non-arbitrability doctrine for shareholder disputes (Schiedsfähigkeit II, or Arbitrability II decision), addressing and partly alleviating the previously expressed worries with the following reasoning:

> The matter of the arbitrability of disputes concerning the invalidity of shareholder resolutions under the law of limited liability companies ... is not a matter to be resolved solely by the legislator. It can also be solved privately and autonomously by the shareholders involved – i.e. primarily by a provision in the articles of association, possibly also on the basis of an agreement reached ad hoc.
>
> For just as the shareholders may – by a unilateral agreement – withdraw or annul a resolution previously passed by a majority decision in accordance with the articles of association, they can also, by mutual agreement and subject to the previously stipulated [procedural] prerequisites of comparability, grant an arbitral tribunal the power to review the resolution in accordance with the standards of objective company law and, if necessary, to declare it null and void with the effects resulting from Sec. 248, 249 German Stock Corporation Act. It is decisive that this task is completed prior to the beginning of arbitral proceedings and that the above-mentioned procedural guarantees demanded in the decision of the Senate with the judgment of 29 March 1996 ('Arbitrability I'), shall be guaranteed by means of an according contractual agreement.[49]

However, in order to safeguard the procedural rights of all shareholders, it stipulated minimum requirements which must be met to allow for the arbitrability of shareholder disputes:

---

[47] *Cf.* W. Voit, *Sec. 1030*, in ZIVILPROZESSORDNUNG para. 3 (H.-J. Musielak & W. Voit eds., 16th ed. 2019).
[48] Federal Court of Justice (BGH), judgment dating Mar. 29, 1996, case no. II ZR 124/95, NJW 1996, 1753.
[49] Federal Court of Justice (BGH), judgment dating Apr. 6, 2009 – II ZR 255/08, NJW 2009, 1962, 1964.

However, an arbitration clause that provides for arbitration proceedings also for disputes regarding the validity of shareholder resolutions must meet the standards of Sec. 138 I of the German Civil Code: ...

Because of its essential significance for the existence of the legal system, legal protection may – at most – be waived by party agreement in individual concrete cases and forms, but not in its substance. If the agreement of an arbitration clause leads to a disadvantage of a party – here understood in the broad sense of being affected by the legally binding effect of an arbitral award – or to the withdrawal of the necessary legal protection, the arbitration agreement is incompatible with public policy standards and is therefore null and void.

Accordingly, as the court of appeal has correctly recognised, the validity of an arbitration clause governing disputes over defects in resolutions – measured against the standard of Sec. 138 of the German Civil Code – requires the fulfilment of the following minimum requirements ... :

The arbitration agreement must have been agreed to by all shareholders either in the articles of association or separately; all shareholders and the corporate bodies must be informed about the arbitral proceedings in due course and must, therefore, be able to join the proceedings as third parties; unless the arbitrators are appointed by a neutral institution, all shareholders must be able to participate in the selection and appointment of the arbitrators; and all disputes concerning a certain shareholder's resolution must be decided by the same arbitral tribunal.[50]

Accordingly, shareholder disputes generally became arbitrable in 2009, though specific prerequisites must be met to allow for arbitral proceedings in such matters.

While these two decisions both concerned German limited liability companies (Gesellschaft mit beschränkter Haftung, GmbH), the Federal Court of Justice recently held that the same principles may also apply to limited partnerships (most notably the German Kommanditgesellschaft, KG), "provided that no deviations compared to corporations are required" (Schiedsfähigkeit III, or Arbitrability III decision).[51]

It should furthermore be noted that no decisions have been rendered yet regarding the arbitrability of disputes over shareholder resolutions in stock corporations. In this context, regard must be had to Sec. 246 (3) German Stock Corporation Act, which constitutes mandatory law and stipulates the exclusive jurisdiction of the national courts for such disputes.

To ensure the arbitrability of shareholder disputes in corporations and limited partnerships, both the arbitration agreement as well as the applicable procedural rules must, therefore, meet the Federal Court of Justice's minimum standards. For this purpose, the DIS offers Supplementary Rules for Corporate Disputes and a specific model arbitration clause for articles of association.[52]

4 CONCLUSION

Arbitration in Germany is shaped both by the closeness of its arbitration law to the Model Law and, where applicable, by the 2018 DIS Arbitration Rules. These new rules, striving to keep Germany arbitration friendly, focus on efficiency and on striking a balance between international and domestic expectations. And while German Arbitration Law, as contained in chapter 10 of the German Code of Civil Procedure, is also subject to ongoing discussions about

---

[50] Id.
[51] Federal Court of Justice (BGH), decision dating Apr. 6, 2017, case no. I ZB 23/16, NJW-RR 2017, 876, 878.
[52] DIS *Musterklausel für den Gesellschaftsvertrag für Schiedsverfahren nach den Ergänzenden Regeln für gesellschaftsrechtliche Streitigkeiten 2018* and Annex 5 to the 2018 DIS Arbitration Rules, *Supplementary Rules for Corporate Disputes*.

its revision, no major amendments are to be expected, and one may safely assume that the German legislator has no intentions to change Germany's status as a Model Law country.

Accordingly, the legal framework for arbitration in Germany is very much in line with international expectations and best practices, and the provisions in regard to the independence and impartiality of arbitrators provide an well-practiced framework to safeguard procedural fairness in arbitration proceedings, stipulating disclosure duties for arbitrators, on the one hand, as well as requiring an objective threshold to be met as regards the circumstances that may give rise to justifiable doubts that warrant a challenge of the arbitrator. When applying these legal standards to individual cases one may safely assume that the ever-present cases of (actual or alleged) previous professional and personal relationships between an arbitrator and one of the parties will account for the majority of cases. In addition, the matter of previous expert statements or (legal) opinions expressed by an arbitrator have recently (again) been subject to legal discussion. And while the general opinion seems to be that abstract opinions (being unrelated to the individual arbitration case) may not give rise to reasonable doubts, this issue appears not to be fully settled yet, as it is subject to discussion, and it remains to be seen whether recent decisions relating to bias of expert witnesses may also be applied to arbitrators and judges in the future. In regard to the conduct of arbitrators during the proceedings, arbitral tribunals are granted a wide discretion and the threshold for challenging arbitrators for procedural conduct tends to be high. At the same time, awards rendered under participation of a successfully challenged arbitrator suffer from an infringement of procedural fairness and are thus likely to be annulled. In regard to arbitration proceedings under the 2018 DIS Arbitration Rules, it may be noted that challenging procedures deviate from the common procedure, which is that tribunals themselves decide on challenges to arbitrators. Instead, the institution refers these matters to the Arbitral Council of the DIS.

Following an arbitration-friendly approach, German courts generally apply a broad interpretation to standard arbitration agreements to include within their scope a multitude of possible claims. The subjective scope of arbitration agreements, on the other hand, is shaped foremost by party autonomy and privity, and arbitration agreements are extended to those parties only who agreed to it. As part of discussions around reforms of the German Arbitration Law, this matter is subject to discussion, and some call for a formal extension of the scope to facilitate multi-company disputes and a softening of the writing requirement – not with the idea of agreeing orally on arbitration in the future but rather to be able to extend arbitration agreements to parties who perform under contracts containing written arbitration agreements without formally signing such agreements.

In regard to arbitrability, German arbitration law merely requires a "proprietary" claim. One of the most notable lines of jurisprudence in this regard concerns the arbitrability of corporate disputes in light of the binding effect of such arbitral awards toward all shareholders: the trilogy of Schiedsfähigkeit/Arbitrability decisions by the Federal Supreme Court. Over the years, the court has adopted a more liberal approach to this question and now allows for arbitrability of shareholder disputes under certain conditions at least in relation to German limited liability companies (GmbH). However, unless arbitration clauses meet specific standards that safeguard the procedural participation rights of the further shareholders, such clauses will be considered invalid.

16

Judicial Control of Arbitral Awards in Italy

Marta Infantino

1 INTRODUCTION

Since antiquity, arbitration has been well known in the Italian peninsula.[1] Basic rules of arbitration are today spelled out in the Italian civil procedure code (hereinafter CCP). The code was enacted in 1940, but has, since then, undergone radical changes, including a comprehensive reform in 2006.[2] Despite the fact that current rules are largely in line with those of other countries and with international legal standards, Italy is generally perceived, by insiders and outsiders alike, as a nonfriendly arbitration country.[3]

In the following pages, we are going to delve into the historical and current general features of Italian arbitration law (Sections 2–3) and investigate the approach of Italian judges toward arbitral proceedings and awards. We will focus first on the way in which arbitration agreements are construed by courts (Section 4) and then move to courts' approaches to parties' requests for vacating Italian arbitral awards (Section 5) and for recognizing/enforcing foreign arbitral awards (Section 6). As this survey will make clear, Italy's bad reputation in the field is largely a remnant of the most recent past and is nowadays only partially deserved (Section 7).

2 NARRATIVES AND NUMBERS

In spite of the presence of a substantial body of highly regarded and world-renowned arbitration specialists, today's Italian market for arbitration is predominantly domestic and marked by the

---

[1] Guido Alpa, *Arbitration and ADR Reforms in Italy*, 29 EUROPEAN BUSINESS LAW REVIEW 313, 314, n. 1 (2018).
[2] For a general presentation, in English, of Italian arbitration rules, *cf.* Mauro Rubino-Sammartano, *Italy*, in GETTING THE DEAL THROUGH: ARBITRATION 2018 176–184 (Gerhard Wegen & Stephan Wilske eds., 13th ed. 2018); Micael Montanari & Martina Lucenti, *International Arbitration 2018. Italy* ICLG (2018), https://iclg.com/practice-areas/international-arbitration-laws-and-regulations/italy#chaptercontent10; Tony Cole, Pietro Ortolani, & Barbara Warwas, *Arbitration in Southern Europe: Insights from a Large-Scale Empirical Study*, 26 AMERICAN REVIEW OF INTERNATIONAL ARBITRATION 187, 218–233 (2015); Lynn Abell, *Disarming the Italian Torpedo: The 2006 Italian Arbitration Law Reforms as a Small Step toward Resolving the West Tankers Dilemma*, 24 AMERICAN REVIEW OF INTERNATIONAL ARBITRATION 335–359 (2013).
[3] *Cf.* Cole, Ortolani, & Warwas, *supra* note 2, at 224; Stefano Azzali, *Does the Seat of Arbitration Still Matter? Can Italy Be a "Good" Place for Arbitration?*, NYU LAW, TRANSNATIONAL NOTES (Jan. 7, 2013), https://blogs.law.nyu.edu/transnational/2013/01/does-the-seat-of-arbitration-still-matter-can-italy-be-a-good-place-for-arbitration/; Abell, *supra* note 2, at 335–359.

tendency to resort to ad hoc, rather than institutional arbitration.[4] Many structural, cultural, and historical reasons explain these features. The original rules contained in the CCP of 1940 were generally "unfavorable to arbitration."[5] The CCP made arbitral justice strictly dependent upon the state's justice, the best illustration being the rule according to which arbitral awards were binding upon parties only after they were ratified by Italian courts.[6] Italian practice thus developed a strong preference for the so-called *irrituale* arbitration, that is, a sort of contractual mediation whose outcome was an award binding for parties only, but whose proceedings were not constrained by judicial control.[7]

Through the years, and especially in the 1980s and 1990s, many statutory reforms were carried out to reverse the anti-arbitration attitude,[8] albeit with limited effects. Still, in the first decade of the 2000s, the Italian Supreme Court was filling the statutory gaps with a series of opinions that maintained a strong anti-deferential attitude toward arbitral justice. For instance, in the silence of the code on the matter, the Court of Cassation held in a 2000 case that, even if an arbitral panel was already seized, ordinary judges were not deprived of the power to decide on the validity of the arbitration clause.[9] According to this rule, parties might have ended up "subjected to two simultaneous proceedings, resulting in a colossal waste of resources."[10] In the same year, the Court of Cassation truncated a long debate by holding that a decision, on whether judges (or arbitrators) were competent to hear a dispute, was one of merit rather than procedure, and therefore it had to be challenged through an ordinary appeal (before the appeals court) rather than through the (much faster) appeal on jurisdictional ground before the Court of Cassation itself.[11] In practice, "parties wishing to challenge an ordinary judge's competence were ... forced to initiate an appeal on the merits, only to become hopelessly quagmired in all

---

[4] See the results of the opinion-based survey published in 2015 by Cole, Ortolani, & Warwas, *supra* note 2, at 219–222, as well as the statistics offered by Vincenza Bonsignore, *La ricerca ISDACI sulla diffusione della giustizia alternativa in Italia nel 2016*, in Decimo rapporto sulla diffusione della giustizia alternativa in Italia 7, 26–80 (Istituto Scientifico per l'Arbitrato, la Mediazione e il Diritto Commerciale ed., 2018), www.camera-arbitrale.it/upload/documenti/centro%20studi%20pubblicazioni/10-decimo-rapporto-giustizia-alternativa.pdf; Filippo Danovi, Riflessioni ed esperienze sull'arbitrato 149–164 (2018). *See also* Pietro Fogari, *The Strange Case of Italy and Its Distrust of International Arbitration* Kluwer Arbitration Blog (Dec. 18, 2015), arbitrationblog.kluwerarbitration.com/2015/12/18/the-strange-case-of-italy-and-its-distrust-of-international-arbitration/.

[5] Emmanuel Gaillard & John Savage, Fouchard, Gaillard, Goldman on International Commercial Arbitration 78 (1999).

[6] Article 825(3) CCP, original version ("Arbitral awards are equated to judgments after the approval of the tribunal"); for a commentary of this rule and its historical evolution, *see* Giovanni Bonato, La natura e gli effetti del lodo arbitrale. Studio di diritto italiano e comparato 12–65 (2012), www.hal-univ-paris10.archives-ouvertes.fr/hal-01503120/document. Another feature of the original rules in the CCP was the protection on the "national" market for arbitration: according to art. 812(1) CCP, original version, "arbitrators should be Italian citizens."

[7] Giorgio Bernini, *Domestic and International Arbitration in Italy after the Legislative Reform*, 5 Pace Law Review 543, 544–547 (1985).

[8] *See* in particular law of Feb. 9, 1983, no. 28, and law of Jan. 5, 1994, no. 25 (reforming the Code of Civil Procedure and repealing the provision that arbitrators should be Italian citizens); *see also* law of Nov. 18, 1998, no. 145 (allowing resort to arbitration in the sector of government contracts).

[9] Court of Cassation, Labor Panel, Aug. 30, 2000, no. 11404 (2001) *Giustizia Civile* 2185. The relevant rule in the CCP code was art. 819-bis CCP, which at that time only provided that "the competence of the arbitrators is not excluded by the connection between the controversy referred to them and a cause pending before the judge." For the current rule, *see* note 18.

[10] Abell, *supra* note 2, at 347. As the author notes, this position was in stark contrast to the approach adopted by UNCITRAL Model Law Article 8, which provides for a highly deferential standard wherein courts stay proceedings and refer parties immediately to arbitration unless they find the agreement is "null and void, inoperative or incapable of being performed."

[11] *Cf.* Court of Cassation, Plenary, Aug. 3, 2000, no. 527 (2001) *Foro Italiano* I, 839 (for national arbitration); Court of Cassation, Plenary, Apr. 15, 2003, no. 6349 (2004) *Rivista dell'arbitrato* 39 (for international arbitration). For the current rule, *see* note 19.

three levels of the Italian court system for years."[12] Given Italy's reputation as a country in which civil justice is slow, the efforts of the Italian courts to maintain this grasp on private arbitration has long contributed to strengthening outsiders' (and even insiders') idea of Italy as a non-appropriate venue for arbitrating disputes.[13]

Much of the rules just mentioned were overturned by the many statutory reforms carried out in the early 2000s. Such reforms aimed to provide stronger support for arbitration in order both to relieve courts from their backlog and to comply with international standards, such as those enshrined in the yearly Doing Business Reports by the World Bank.[14] In particular, the legislative decree no. 40/2006 and the law decree no. 132/2014 heavily reshaped arbitration and its relationship with judicial proceedings[15] while other statutes regulated arbitration procedures in a number of sectors – from public procurement to sport and corporate disputes and to disputes between financial and banking institutions and their clients.[16]

For our purposes, the most important reform was the one carried out by the legislative decree no. 40/2006. The reform undertook a comprehensive restyling of the CCP, clarifying, among other things, that arbitral awards have the same effects as judgments,[17] that parties cannot bring to ordinary courts a challenge on the validity or efficacy of an arbitral agreement if an arbitral tribunal is already seized of the issue,[18] and that state judges' opinions about their own competence in relation to an arbitration agreement should be challenged as decisions on jurisdiction (rather than as decisions on merit).[19] The same reform also abolished the distinction between national and international arbitration and overturned the previous rule, according to which

---

[12] Abell, *supra* note 2, at 345.

[13] *Cf.* Jan Paulsson, *International Arbitration Is Not Arbitration*, 2 STOCKHOLM INTERNATIONAL ARBITRATION REVIEW 1, 3 (2008) ("[A]ll a clever and resourceful defendant needs to do is file a suit in, for example, Italy, and it can be fairly certain nothing will happen for a decade"); Jürgen Basedow, *EU Law in Chinese International Commercial Arbitration*, in CHINA AND INTERNATIONAL COMMERCIAL DISPUTE RESOLUTION 37, 40–41 (Qiao Liu, Wenhua Shan, & Xiang Ren eds., 2016) ("Italian courts have ... become attractive venues for private parties who simply want to delay either arbitral proceedings or judicial proceedings in other Member States"); Abell, *supra* note 2, at 335 ("Italian courts' refusals to immediately defer to the arbitrators' determination of competence and the lack of an efficient mechanism for referring parties back to arbitration have also contributed to Italy's reputation as a torpedo jurisdiction with respect to arbitration in particular"); Cole, Ortolani, & Warwas, *supra* note 2, at 219 ("Arbitration in Italy has developed in the context of a famously slow Italian court system, which has not only resulted in what anecdotal evidence indicates is a high rate of ad hoc arbitration, but has also to a significant degree prevented Italy from becoming a major arbitral center ... Concerns about the delays ... have often deterred foreign parties from agreeing to arbitrate in Italy, lest the arbitration be delayed by the need to seek court assistance").

[14] Through its Doing Business Reports, the World Bank has measured since 2003 the business friendliness of the world's legal systems. One of the criteria is the "alternative dispute resolution index," which is based, inter alia, upon the efficacy of arbitration in commercial disputes. *See* www.doingbusiness.org/en/methodology/enforcing-contracts.

[15] Legislative decree of Feb. 2, 2006, no. 40 (reforming the Code of Civil Procedure); law decree of Sept. 12, 2014, no. 132, later converted into law of Nov. 10, 2014, no. 162 (introducing a new mechanism for parties to transfer a dispute before a state court to arbitration).

[16] *See* the statutes mentioned in Section 3. It should be noted that reforms favoring arbitration were part and parcel of a major trend that emphasized the significance of extra-judicial justice; *see also* the legislative decree of Mar. 4, 2010, no. 28 (making mediation a condition precedent for trial in certain civil and commercial matters) and the legislative decree of Aug. 6, 2015, no. 130 (establishing out-of-court procedures for the settlement of disputes between consumers and traders resident and established in the European Union).

[17] Article 824-bis CCP, current version: "the award shall have the same effects as a judgment rendered by the judicial authority." The Court of Cassation then reversed its previous case law (*supra* note 11) and asserted in 2013 that arbitral awards have a jurisdictional nature: *see* Court of Cassation, Oct. 25, 2013, no. 24153 (2014) XXXIX *Yearbook of Commercial Arbitration* 424–426.

[18] Article 819-ter (3) CCP, current version: "If the arbitral proceedings are already pending, questions relating to the invalidity or inefficacy of the arbitral agreement cannot be posed to the ordinary judge."

[19] Article 819-ter (1) CCP, current version: "The judgment by which a judge affirms or denies her own competence in relation to an arbitral agreement can be appealed in the forms provided by articles 42 and 43 of the same Code."

arbitral awards were always challengeable on the merits.[20] Despite a few criticisms (most importantly, for the refusal to grant arbitrators the power to issue interim measures),[21] the reform was generally praised, inside and outside Italy, as a major step toward the development of a more arbitration-prone culture and practice.

The statutory changes, combined with a growing judicial backlog, which made many, including judges, look to arbitration as a remedy to the backlog of cases clogging courts, have gradually eroded courts' hostility and suspicion towards arbitration.[22] Yet, the openness of the Italian legal system toward arbitration remains questioned. Italy's many arbitral institutions are relatively young, and few of them have significant experience in administering arbitrations and sizable caseloads (the main exception being the Chamber of Arbitration of Milan, established in 1985 as a branch of the local Chamber of Commerce and operative since 1986).[23] Most of domestic arbitrations are handled through ad hoc (and often *irrituali*) arbitral procedures, which tend to be slower and more expensive than average arbitration at the European level.[24] Even in commercial settings, arbitration remains a minor dispute resolution mechanism.[25] This might be due to several factors. On the one hand, Italian (mostly domestic and judicial oriented) university education has historically neglected arbitration law in law schools' curricula.[26] On the other hand, the Italian legal market is saturated and divided between a few elite lawyers, fluent in English and endowed with postgraduate degrees and an international clientele, and myriad unspecialized lawyers who work outside the country's financial and economic hubs, and who tend to favor litigation over arbitration.[27] Finally, as a (masterfully conducted) 2015 perception survey about arbitration recently argued, there is a "lack of a widespread arbitration culture, not only amongst legal practitioners but also amongst business people."[28]

---

[20] Article 829(2) CCP, current version: "An appeal on a point of law is allowed only if expressly set out by the parties in the arbitration agreement or by the law."

[21] Art. 818 CCP, current version: "The arbitrators cannot issue sequestration orders or other types of intermediary measures, except as otherwise provided for by law." The rule clearly deviates from UNCITRAL Arbitration Rules' Article 26 (the other major deviation being the provision that, contrary to art. 16 of the UNCITRAL Arbitration Rules, arbitrators are liable for their misconduct during proceedings under art. 813-ter CCP, current version). For a critical comment on the choice, *cf.* Rubino-Sammartano, *supra* note 2, at no. 4.

[22] *See* for instance the decision Court of Cassation, Oct. 25, 2013, no. 24153, *supra* note 17.

[23] Cole, Ortolani, & Warwas, *supra* note 2, at 223. There is a considerable literature in English on the CAM: *cf.* Stefano Azzali, *Arbitration in Italy: Features of the Milan Chamber of Arbitration, in* INTERNATIONAL COMMERCIAL ARBITRATION. DIFFERENT FORMS AND THEIR FEATURES 188–203 (Giuditta Cordero-Moss ed., 2013); THE CHAMBER OF ARBITRATION OF MILAN RULES: A COMMENTARY (Ugo Draetta & Riccardo Luzzato eds., 2012); Benedetta Coppo, *The 2010 Revision of the Arbitration Rules of the Chamber of Arbitration in Milan*, 14 VINDOBONA JOURNAL OF INTERNATIONAL COMMERCIAL LAW & ARBITRATION 283–296 (2010); Teresa Giovannini & Valentina Renna, *The Italian Experience of Arbitration and the Arbitration Rules of the Chamber of Arbitration of Milan: A Parallel View*, 14 VINDOBONA JOURNAL OF INTERNATIONAL COMMERCIAL LAW & ARBITRATION 297–313 (2010); Michelangelo Cicogna, *Milan Chamber of Arbitration, in* INSTITUTIONAL ARBITRATION: TASKS AND POWERS OF DIFFERENT ARBITRATION INSTITUTIONS 169–190 (Pascale Gola, Claudia Gotz Staehelin, & Karin Graf eds., 2009).

[24] Cole, Ortolani, & Warwas, *supra* note 2, at, respectively 220 and 222. Another feature of Italian arbitration practice is the "inquisitorial" approach of Italian arbitrators, who tend to be more interventionists in the procedure than their European colleagues, directly examining witnesses, maintaining a strictly control over the production of evidence, and appointing their own experts alongside parties' one. *Cf. id.* at 229; Rubino-Sammartano,*supra* note 2, at no. 49.

[25] Cole, Ortolani, & Warwas, *supra* note 2, at 231.

[26] *See* MAURO BUSSANI, IL DIRITTO DELL'OCCIDENTE. GEOPOLITICA DELLE REGOLE GLOBALI 23, 220 (2010).

[27] *See* PAOLO BUONANNO & MATTEO M. GALIZZI, ADVOCATUS, ET NON LATRO? TESTING THE SUPPLIER-INDUCED-DEMAND HYPOTHESIS FOR ITALIAN COURTS OF JUSTICE (Fondazione Eni Enrico Mattei Working Papers no. 441/2010, May 2010), www.services.bepress.com/feem/paper441; BRUNO NASCIMBENE, THE LEGAL PROFESSION IN THE EUROPEAN UNION 144 (2009); *see also* Marta Infantino, *The Italian Legal Recipe: Basic Ingredients and the Bustle of Time*, 6 JOURNAL OF COMPARATIVE LAW 70, 82–83 (2011).

[28] Cole, Ortolani, & Warwas, *supra* note 2, at 231.

Whatever the reasons, the undeniable result is that Italy is still viewed – both by outsiders and insiders – as a relatively unpopular seat of arbitration. According to the already mentioned opinion-based survey, "only 2.46% of non-Italian respondents listed Italy as one of their five preferred seats for an international arbitration" while "when asked to recommend five States, from those included in the Study, as a seat for an international arbitration, only 71.79% of Italian respondents recommended Italy, making Italy the fourth most preferred State even amongst Italian respondents."[29] Perceptions, unfortunately, are confirmed by practice. According to the last edition of the report on ADR practice (published in 2018 and reporting the results of a 2016 survey), the total number of requests for starting an institutional arbitration in Italy (statistics for ad hoc arbitrations being not available) was equal, in 2016, to 708.[30] Approximately 97 percent of these proceedings were domestic,[31] and their average value was equal to €184.234.[32] In 2016, the most active institutional arbitral institution was the Arbitral Tribunal of the Centro Studi Diritto Condominiale (CESCOND), a private chamber for hearing condominium litigation (with 165 new claims lodged), followed by Italy's most active international arbitration center, the Chamber of Arbitration in Milan (CAM) (with 134 new claims lodged).[33] The number of applications lodged before the CAM did not rise in the following year. According to the chamber's last report, the CAM registered in 2017 only 131 new claims, most of which were promoted by or against Italian-based parties.[34]

3 SPECIAL REGIMES

As mentioned, in the last twenty years the legislature has taken steps to favor arbitration over ordinary justice. In addition to the general reforms already mentioned, several other laws allowed parties to submit to arbitration issues that were previously thought to be non-arbitrable and established new public and private bodies to manage arbitration proceedings, creating a number of special arbitral procedures. Such special arbitration regimes are in principle governed by the general law on arbitration as set out in the CCP, although they also include rules deviating from the general ones. The approach can be criticized on the ground that the multiplication of derogatory regimes affects the unity of arbitration law and creates confusion.

For instance, in 1998, a statute clarified that disputes arising out of government contracts could be submitted to arbitration.[35] The rule is today enshrined in art. 209(1) of the legislative decree no. 50/2016 (the so-called code of public contracts), according to which "disputes ... arising out from the performance of public contracts ... can be arbitrated."[36] Disputes are administered under the rules of the CCP by a special arbitration chamber established under

---

[29] *Id.* at 224.
[30] Bonsignore, *supra* note 4, at 47.
[31] *Id.* at 69 (according to the same report, all requests for international arbitration were brought before local Chambers of Commerce, and in particular before the Chamber of Arbitration of Milan).
[32] *Id.* at 70.
[33] *Id.* at 68.
[34] *See* Camera Arbitrale di Milano, *Arbitrato CAM 2017 Statistiche analitiche*, CAMERA ARBITRALE DI MILANO (2018), www.camera-arbitrale.it/upload/documenti/statistiche/statistiche-arbitrato-2017.pdf (noting that, of the 345 parties to the new claims, 90.4 percent were based in Italy).
[35] *See* law Nov. 18, 1998, no. 145, art. 10.
[36] By contrast, disputes arising out from the tendering procedure are governed by administrative law and are under the exclusive competence of administrative courts: *see* art. 133(1) of law of July 2, 2010, no. 104 (the so-called Code of Administrative Procedure); *see also* Alberto Massera, *Italie*, *in* DROIT COMPARÉ DES CONTRATS PUBLICS 715–740 (Rozen Noguellou & Ulrich Stelkens eds., 2010).

the Autorità Nazionale Anti Corruzione.[37]. Arbitral awards rendered by the special arbitration chamber, differently from ordinary awards, can always be challenged on the merit.[38]

A law of 2003 clearly stated that disputes brought by sport federations and their members about the application and compliance with lex sportiva, including on disciplinary sanctions, are heard by the arbitration bodies of the Comitato Nazionale Olimpico Italiano (CONI) (Italy's authority for the sport system). The decisions rendered by the arbitration bodies of the CONI are binding for sport federations and their members and are largely shielded from judicial review.[39] Arbitration proceedings are governed by procedural rules determined by CONI itself.[40] In the same year, a general reform of company law established that unlisted companies' articles of incorporation and bylaws might provide that disputes arising among the company's members, or between the company and any of its members, should be settled by arbitration.[41] Intracompany arbitration is governed by the CCP, except for a few derogatory rules: for instance, arbitral awards rendered on the validity of decisions made in shareholders' meetings can always be challenged on the merit, no matter what a company's articles of incorporation or bylaws provides.[42]

In 2005, the government introduced special procedures for arbitrating disputes between financial and banking institutions and their clients.[43] As a result, a special arbitration procedure for hearing contractual disputes brought by customers against financial institutions was established in 2007 before the Commissione Nazionale per le Società e la Borsa (CONSOB) (the regulatory body for Italian stock exchange).[44] In 2009 a similar procedure applying to contractual disputes between banks and their customers was set up before the Bank of Italy.[45] While under these regimes, bank customers remain free to pursue their claims in arbitration or before ordinary courts. Financial institutions and banks are obliged to adhere to the special dispute resolution system and to inform their clients about their right to resort to arbitration.[46] Arbitral proceedings before CONSOB's and Bank of Italy's arbitral bodies are governed by detailed rules enacted by the CONSOB and the Bank of Italy themselves.[47] The arbitral panel's decision is binding upon the respondent financial and banking institution and is enforced through a set

---

[37] See art. 209(10) of the legislative decree no. 50/2016.

[38] Id. at art. 209(7).

[39] See law decree of Aug. 19, 2003, no. 220, converted into law of Oct. 17, 2003, no. 280. In the following year, the field underwent significant changes. See now CONI's Justice Code, June 11, 2014, www.coni.it/it/rdds/normativa/sportiva.html.

[40] See CONI's Justice Code, supra note 39.

[41] See arts. 34–36 of the legislative decree of Jan. 17, 2003, no. 5. See Diego Corapi, *Arbitration and Company Law in Italy*, 12 EUROPEAN COMPANY LAW 154–159 (2015); Valerio Sangiovanni, *Current Development: Some Critical Observations on the Italian Regulation of Company Arbitration* 17 AMERICAN REVIEW OF INTERNATIONAL ARBITRATION 281–291' (2006).

[42] See art. 36(1), legislative decree of Jan. 17, 2003, no. 5. On this rule, cf. Silvia Turatto, *Problemi di diritto intertemporale relativi all'impugnazione del lodo per violazione delle regole di diritto*, 2018 RIVISTA TRIMESTRALE DI DIRITTO E PROCEDURA CIVILE 286–308 (2018); Alpa, supra note 1, at 318–319. The rule survived untouched the 2006 reform of the general arbitration law: Court of Cassation, May 9, 2016, no. 9285 (2016) 40 Guida al diritto 60.

[43] Law of Dec. 28, 2005, no. 207.

[44] See Legislative decree of Oct. 8, 2007, no. 179, establishing CONSOB's Chamber of Arbitration. In 2016 the chamber's functions were transferred to a new CONSOB's body, the Arbitro per le Controversie Finanziarie: see the legislative decree of Aug. 6, 2015, no. 130, and CONSOB Regulation May 8, 2016, no. 19602. For a commentary, see Nicola Soldati, *L'arbitro per le controversie finanziarie presso la CONSOB (ACF)*, 2016 Contratti 1056–1064 (2016).

[45] See art. 128-bis of the law of Sept. 1, 1993, no. 385, and Bank of Italy, regulation of Nov. 2, 2016, www.bancaditalia.it/compiti/vigilanza/normativa/archivio-norme/disposizioni/disposizioni/disp_mod_ABF_021116.pdf, establishing the Bank of Italy's Arbitro Bancario Finanziario.

[46] Cf. art. 3, CONSOB Regulation of May 8. 2016, no. 19602 (for the Arbitro per le Controversie Finanziarie) and sections II and IV of the Regulation of the Bank of Italy of Nov. 2, 2016 (for the Arbitro Bancario Finanziario).

[47] Cf. CONSOB regulation no. 19602/2016 and Regulation of the Bank of Italy of Nov. 2, 2016.

of highly effective reputational sanctions. Yet, similarly to mediation, the decision never acquires the authority of res judicata.[48]

As this summary shows, Italian special arbitration regimes are highly fragmented, enjoying different degrees of autonomy vis-à-vis the civil justice system and general rules on arbitration. What should be further noted is that the success of such special regimes has been far from uniform. While in some sectors (e.g., public procurement) the flight to institutional arbitration has experienced a slow start,[49] in others (e.g., banking contracts) it immediately skyrocketed.[50] The next sections will focus on general rules only, unless special rules warrant attention. We will first deal with rules determining the scope of arbitrable disputes (Section 4) and then move to rules on vacating and enforcing arbitral awards (Sections 5–6, respectively).

4 THE SCOPE OF ARBITRATION

The general rule determining the scope of arbitrability under Italian law is set out by art. 806(1) CCP, according to which "parties may submit to arbitration any civil dispute that is not referring to entitlements they cannot freely dispose of, except when otherwise provided by law." In other words, everything can be arbitrated except for private matters, which under Italian law cannot be freely disposed of by the disputing parties, and for matters in which recourse to arbitration is forbidden in whole in or part by law.

The former category includes issues of citizenship, marriage, parenthood, nationality, and fundamental rights.[51] The latter category includes employment disputes,[52] public contracts disputes in which the issue at stake concerns the tendering procedure,[53] company disputes in which participation of state prosecutors is mandatory,[54] and disputes concerning debts from bankruptcy.[55] Nonprivate matters, such as issues relating to criminal offences and tax law, are held by scholars and courts to be non-arbitrable.[56] According to Italian case law, the non-amenability to arbitration might be subsequent to the arbitral agreement: in a well-known case

---

[48] See arts. 15–16, CONSOB Regulation no. 19602/2016 (for the Arbitro per le Controversie Finanziarie) and sec. VI of the Regulation of the Bank of Italy of Nov. 2, 2016 (for the Arbitro Bancario Finanziario). *See also* Constitutional Court, July 21, 2011, no. 218 (2011) *Foro Italiano* 2906 (specifying that the Arbitro per le Controversie Finanziarie is not, and cannot be equated to, a judicial authority).

[49] According to the latest data available, in 2016 only seven requests for arbitration were lodged before the competent authority (Bonsignore, *supra* note 4, at 67–68).

[50] In 2017 the Arbitro Bancario Finanziario received 30,644 requests for arbitration: *see* Bank of Italy, *Relazione sull'attività dell'Arbitro Bancario Finanziario. Appendice 2017* (June 2, 2018), www.arbitrobancariofinanziario.it/abf/relazione-annuale/versione-italiana/Appendice_ABF_2017.pdf.

[51] ELENA GABELLINI, L'AZIONE ARBITRALE. CONTRIBUTO ALLO STUDIO DELL'ARBITRABILITÀ DEI DIRITTI 82–84, 157–232 (2018); ELENA ZUCCONI GALLI FONSECA, DIRITTO DELL'ARBITRATO 82–83, 92, 119–120 (2016); Elena Zucconi Galli Fonseca, *Art. 806 – Controversie arbitrabili, in* ARBITRATO 1, 26–53 (Federico Carpi ed., 3d ed. 2016).

[52] Employment disputes might be subject to arbitration only if this is provided by the sectoral collective agreement: *see* art. 806(2) CCP; for a commentary, *see* GABELLINI, *supra* note 51, at 279–325.

[53] Such disputes fall under the exclusive competence of administrative tribunals: *see* art. 133(1) of law no. 104/2010.

[54] For instance, this is the case of disputes regarding the revocation of a company's liquidator under art. 2487(4) of the Civil Code: art. 34(5), legislative decree no. 5/2003; *see also* GABELLINI, *supra* note 51, at 327–375.

[55] According to the case-law, bankruptcy disputes are attracted by the exclusive jurisdiction of bankruptcy tribunals: Court of Cassation, Plenary, July 21, 2015, no. 15200 (2015) *Giurisprudenza italiana* 2445; *cf.* GABELLINI, *supra* note 51, at 455–472. Antitrust matters, by contrast, are arbitrable (*see* Court of Cassation, Aug. 21, 1996, no. 7733 (1996) *Giustizia civile massimario* 1207; Milan Appeals Court, Sept. 13, 2002 (2003) *Diritto industriale* 346), and so are tort disputes (*see* art. 808-bis CCP: "parties might agree to submit to arbitrate one or more possible future non-contractual disputes, provided that they are properly identified").

[56] *See* the references cited by Aldo Frignani, *Interpretation and Application of the New York Convention in Italy, in* RECOGNITION AND ENFORCEMENT OF ARBITRAL AWARDS. THE INTERPRETATION AND APPLICATION OF THE NEW YORK CONVENTION BY NATIONAL COURTS 561 at 579 (George A. Bermann ed., 2017).

in which the performance of an international contract of sale of goods was frustrated by the adoption of an international embargo, the Genoa Appeals Court deemed that the embargo deprived the parties of the right to arbitrate the disputes arising out of the contract, notwithstanding that the latter provided for dispute resolution to be administered by the ICC in Paris.[57]

Collective or class disputes are deemed not to be amenable to arbitration.[58] Three main reasons underlie this conclusion. First, the history of Italian collective actions, even before ordinary courts, has only recently started and has so far not been particularly successful. The first opt-in relating to collective consumers action was introduced by law in 2007, yet with such stringent requirements that since then very few collective complaints have been lodged before courts.[59] Second, the CCP provides that multiparty arbitration proceedings are possible only if they arise out of the same arbitration agreement and all the parties had an equal opportunity to appoint the arbitrators – two requirements that very rarely, if ever, can be met in class arbitration.[60] Third, it should be kept in mind that arbitration clauses (whether collective or not) inserted in business-to-consumer contracts are presumed to be unconscionable.[61] This statistically reduces the chances that parties agree upon collective arbitration.

One should further coordinate the rules on arbitrable disputes with the statutory provisions defining the size and form of arbitration clauses. According to art. 807(1) CCP, arbitration clauses must be made in writing.[62] Arbitration clauses might be the object of an autonomous agreement or be incorporated in a contract;[63] in the latter's case, art. 808(2) CCP specifies that "the validity of the arbitration clause should be assessed independently from the underlying contract" – that is,

---

[57] Genoa Appeals Court, May 7, 1994 (1996) XXI *Yearbook of Commercial Arbitration* 594. In this case, the Republic of Iraq entered into contracts with two Italian shipbuilders for the supply of corvettes. A clause in the contracts provided for arbitration in Paris before the ICC. Before most corvettes were delivered, Italy (in compliance with a UN Security Council's resolution and with EU law) issued embargo legislation against Iraq restricting weapons trade with Iraq. The Italian parties commenced proceedings against Iraq before the court of first instance of Genoa, seeking termination and damages. Iraq objected to the court's jurisdiction and claimed that the dispute should be referred to arbitration. The Italian parties claimed that dispute on the effect of the embargo concerned issues that could not be submitted to arbitration. The Genoa court of first instance denied its jurisdiction, but the court of appeals reversed the decision, arguing that the embargo legislation had rendered the arbitral clause, originally valid, null and void.

[58] Gabriele Crespi Reghizzi & Matteo Dragoni, *Class Actions and Arbitration Procedures – Italy*, in CLASS ARBITRATION IN THE EUROPEAN UNION 115, 117, 134–135 (Philip Billiet ed., 2015).

[59] The law of Dec. 24, 2007, no. 244 introduced a new art. 140-bis on collective action in the legislative decree of Sept. 6, 2005, no. 206, the so-called Consumers Code; in 2019, a new reform slightly loosened the requirements of the action and moved it from art. 140-bis of the Consumers Code (now abolished) to art. 840-bis and ff. in the CCP. Equally unsuccessful has so far been the introduction by the legislative decree of Dec. 20, 2009, no. 198 of a class-like action against the state for performance of public services (*see* Crespi Reghizzi and Dragoni, *supra* note 58, at 124–125).

[60] Art. 816-quater (1) CCP:

> If more than two parties are bound by the same arbitration agreement, each of them may summon all or some of the other parties in the same arbitration, provided that [i] the agreement to arbitrate defers the power to appoint the arbitrators to a third party, [ii] the arbitrators are appointed with the consent of all parties, or [iii] if, after the first party has appointed its own arbitrator, the others have jointly appointed an equal number of arbitrators, or have deferred such appointment to a third party.

[61] Art. 33(2), letter (t) of the legislative decree of Sept. 6, 2005, no. 206: "The following terms are presumed prima facie unconscionable: any term whose object or effect is . . . (t) to establish derogation to the jurisdiction of ordinary courts to the detriment of consumers."

[62] This includes, according to the Court of Cassation, agreements entered upon through telefax: Court of Cassation, June 14, 2007, no. 13916 (2008) *Giustizia Civile* I, 1767.

[63] Art. 808(1) CCP so provides. If the agreement entered upon by the parties contains a reference to general terms and conditions with an arbitration clause, parties are deemed to have agree upon arbitration: Court of Cassation, June 16, 2011, no. 13231 (2012) *Rivista dell'Arbitrato* 835. By contrast, the arbitral clause contained in a contract cannot be extended, in the absence of any reference, to other contracts between the same parties, even if these contracts are connected to the first one: in other words, the arbitration clause of the main contract does not extend to other, albeit related, contracts (Court of Cassation, July 28, 1998, no. 7398 (1999) *Rivista di diritto internazionale privato e processuale* 319).

the invalidity of the contract does not automatically extend to the arbitration clause.[64] Art. 808-quater CCP adds that "[i]n case of doubt, the arbitration clause should be interpreted as applying to all disputes arising out from the contract or from the relationship to which it refers."[65] The rule, however, is cautiously interpreted by courts. The underlying argument for this approach is that, since arbitration is derogatory to ordinary jurisdiction, the scope of the clause should be construed narrowly. This means, for instance, that, when the arbitration clause included in a service contract mentions only disputes "arising out from the interpretation of the contract," the clause does not apply to claims for breach against the nonperforming party.[66] Similarly, the clause providing for arbitration of "all disputes arising out from the contract" does not cover neither tort claim brought by a customer against his contractor for the damages arising out of the defects of the work,[67] nor the claim for unfair competition and precontractual liability brought by an airline company against another one, after the latter refused to pursue negotiations for a merger of the two companies.[68]

5 VACATING ARBITRAL AWARDS

Only Italian arbitral awards can be challenged before Italian courts. Italian arbitral awards are defined as those rendered within proceedings whose venue is within the territory of the Italian Republic, no matter whether the arbitration was domestic or international.[69] The challenge might take one of the following three forms: a request for setting the award aside (regulated by art. 829 CCP), a request for revoking the award, and a third-party opposition to the award (which are both governed by art. 831 CCP).[70] Requests for revocation and third-party opposition are of unusual application. The former presupposes that the party seeking revocation gives evidence of the malicious behavior of either the other party or of the arbitrators,[71] while the latter allows a third party to the dispute to oppose an award jeopardizing his or her rights.[72]

---

[64] Rubino-Sammartano, *supra* note 2, at no. 10.
[65] The CCP devotes to the interpretation of arbitration clauses a few rules which are meant to complement the ordinary criteria for contractual interpretation, as set out by articles 1362–1371 of the Civil Code. For instance, art. 808-ter CCP states that, if the arbitration does not "expressly state in writing" that the parties wish to resort to an *irrituale* arbitration, there is a presumption that the clause refers to ordinary arbitration.
[66] Court of Cassation, Jan. 18. 2017, no. 1213 (2017) 17 *Guida al diritto* 62. Yet, an arbitration clause referring to "disputes arising out from the interpretation, conclusion, and termination of the contract" also covers disputes about contractual breaches: Court of Cassation, Sept. 10, 2012, no. 15068 (2012) *Giustizia civile massimario* 1101.
[67] Court of Cassation, Feb. 15, 2017, no. 4035 (2017) *Foro Italiano – Repertorio*, entry 'Arbitrato', no. 39; similarly, *see* Court of Cassation, Feb. 3, 2012, no. 1674 (2014) *Rivista dell'Arbitrato* 589.
[68] Court of Cassation, Oct. 13, 2016, no. 20673 (2017) *Rivista dell'Arbitrato* 87.
[69] *See* art. 816(1) CCP: "[p]arties determine the seat of arbitration within the territory of the Italian Republic. Otherwise the seat is determined by arbitrators." For a commentary of this provision, *cf.* ZUCCONI GALLI FONSECA, *supra* note 51, at 64–65; CLAUDIO CONSOLO, LE IMPUGNAZIONI DELLE SENTENZE E DEI LODI 535 (3d ed. 2012). Italy thus follows a monistic approach, providing rules that apply equally to domestic and international arbitration.
[70] For arbitral awards stemming from an *irrituale* arbitration, a further remedy is provided by art. 808-ter (2) CCP, according to which the award might be declared null and void by an ordinary court under the conditions set out by the provision.
[71] Under art. 831(1) CCP, revocation is possible if the party requesting it proves either one of the following facts: (1) the other party acted with willful misconduct against the first party; (2) the award was based on false evidence, provided that the falsity was established after the award was given; (3) after the award was given, the first party discovered decisive documents that could have not been filed in the proceedings due to force majeure or willful misconduct of the other party; and (4) the arbitrators acted with willful misconduct against the first party, provided that the misconduct is ascertained by a final judgment. The request for revocation should be lodged before the court of appeals in whose district the arbitration had its seat: art. 831(3) CCP.
[72] A request for third-party opposition is lodged before the court of appeals in whose district the arbitration had its seat, and is governed by art. 831(3) CCP. It is not yet agreed whether the court decision on this opposition produces effects

The ground that is by far the most common for vacating domestic arbitral awards is the one set out by art. 829 of the CCP, which was entirely rewritten by the 2006 general reform of arbitration. According to art. 829 CCP:

> (1) Notwithstanding any previous waiver, a recourse for setting aside may be filed if:
> (1) the arbitration clause is null and void ... ;
> (2) the arbitrators were not appointed according to the rules set out by the law or by the parties, provided that this ground for setting aside was raised during the proceedings;
> (3) the award was rendered by a person who could not be appointed as arbitrator according to art. 812 CCP;
> (4) the award exceeded the limits of the arbitration clause ... ;
> (5) the award does not comply with the requirements set forth by art. 823, nos. (5), (6), (7) [i.e., it does not state the reasoning underlying the decision, does not contain the decision itself, or it was not signed by the arbitrators];
> (6) the award was rendered after the expiry of the time-limit set out by the parties or by the law;
> (7) during the proceedings, the formalities prescribed by the parties for the validity of the proceedings were not complied with, and the nullity was not cured;
> (8) the award is contrary to a previous award or to a previous judgment having the force of res judicata between the parties which is no longer subject to recourse, provided that such an award or judgment was submitted in the proceedings;
> (9) the principle of due process was not complied with in the proceedings;
> (10) the award does not rule on the merit of the case;
> (11) the award is contradictory;
> (12) the award does not settle all the claims raised by the parties as required by the arbitration clause.
>
> (2) The party that caused a ground for setting aside, renounced to invoke it, or did not raise a violation of a procedural rule at the first opportunity she had, is precluded from filing a recourse for setting aside the award on such grounds.
>
> (3) Parties can file a recourse for setting aside an award on the ground of the mistaken application of the law only if this ground for recourse is expressly provided by the law or by the arbitration clause. Under any circumstances, parties can always file a recourse for setting aside awards which are contrary to public policy.
>
> (4) Parties can always file a recourse for setting aside an award on the ground of the mistaken application of the law (1) in employment disputes; (2) if the mistaken application of the law concerns matters which the parties could not submit to arbitration.[73]

The provision should be further complemented by art. 817(2) and (3) CCP, which, in the relevant part, provides several different provisions:

---

only on the requesting third party or also on the parties to the arbitral proceedings: Rubino-Sammartano, *supra* note 2, at no. 43.

[73] The special arbitration regimes mentioned in Section 3 sometimes provide for additional or different grounds for setting aside arbitral awards. For instance, arbitration clauses in unlisted companies' bylaws must require that all arbitrators are appointed by a third party who is unrelated to the company; otherwise the clause is null and void and the arbitral award rendered upon it might be set aside (art. 34(2) of the legislative decree no. 5/2003). An arbitral award rendered in the field of public procurement is null and void if arbitrators were not selected according to the rules set forth by the Code of Public Contracts (art. 209(7) of the legislative decree no. 50/2016). Further, arbitral awards rendered on the validity of decisions of shareholders' meetings and on public contracts can always be challenged on the merit, no matter what a company's deed of incorporation, bylaws, or public contracts provide: *see* art. 36(1) of the legislative decree no. 5/2003 and art. 209(7) of the legislative decree no. 50/2016.

(2) ... The party who claims that arbitrators are not competent because of the inexistence, nullity, or ineffectiveness of the arbitral clause, but did not raise such objection at the first opportunity she had, is precluded from filing a recourse for setting aside the award on the ground of arbitrator's incompetence, except in the case in which the dispute could not be submitted to arbitration at all.

(3) The party who claims that other parties' submissions went beyond the scope of the arbitration agreement but did not raise the objection during the arbitral proceedings, is precluded from filing a recourse for setting the award aside on this ground.

On the procedural side, recourses for setting aside an arbitral award should be brought before the court of appeals in whose district the arbitration had its seat (arts. 828(1) and 830(1) CCP). The recourse must be proposed within ninety days from the service of the award by the winning party on the losing party, or within one year from the date of the last signature on the award if the notice of the award has not been served by the winning party (see art. 828(1) and (2) CCP).[74]

If the court of appeals upholds the plaintiff's request, it declares the award null and void. When the court of appeals sets aside an award for reasons mentioned by art. 829(1), nos. (5), (6), (7), (8), (9), (11), and (12), and by art. 829(3) and (4), it also decides the merit of the case (art. 830(2) CCP).[75] In all the other cases, the dispute should be resubmitted by the parties to arbitration, as provided by the original arbitration clause.[76] Whatever the outcome of the set-aside recourse, parties might challenge the appeals court's decision before the Supreme Court of Cassation but only on the basis of a mistaken application of the law by the court of appeals.[77] This means that, differently from what happens in other jurisdictions, the finality of the award is conditioned upon a dual possibility of appeal: one before the court of appeals on the ground of invalidity, and another one before the Supreme Court on the correctness of the court of appeals' decision.[78]

As the beginning of art. 829(1) CCP makes clear, the grounds for setting aside an arbitral award are determined by the law and cannot be excluded by the parties, their waiver in this regard being null and void. Further, it is generally understood that the list of grounds for challenging an award set forth by art. 829 CCP is exhaustive, and that parties cannot expand it at their will.[79] However, parties have some margin to maneuver. First, they are free to overturn the rule (set forth by art. 829(3) CCP) about the challenge nature of an award before the court of appeal for mistaken application of the law.[80] Second, there is no doubt that parties can waive their right to file a recourse for setting aside the award after the latter has been issued. Third, even before the award is issued, parties can explicitly or implicitly waive their right to file a recourse by failing to promptly react to a defect affecting the regularity of arbitral proceedings, if the defect is one of those that can be remedied by a party's inaction.[81]

---

[74] Pending the appeal, the award is fully enforceable; however, the party wishing to challenge the award may apply to the competent court of appeals and seek a stay of the enforceability of the award, provided that her request is based on serious grounds and the enforcement would cause irreparable harm to him or her: see art. 830(4) CCP.

[75] Unless the arbitration clause provides otherwise: art. 830(2) CCP. The same provision further specifies that, if one of the parties was residing abroad at the time in which the arbitration clause was entered into, the court of appeals does not rule on the merit unless the arbitration clause expressly allows it to do so.

[76] Unless, of course, the award is set aside because of the invalidity of the arbitration clause: art. 830(3) CCP.

[77] Montanari & Lucenti, *supra* note 2, at no. 10.4.

[78] Alpa, *supra* note 1, at 317–318 (who suggests to erase the phase before the court of appeals).

[79] Montanari & Lucenti, *supra* note 2, at nos. 10.2 and 10.3.

[80] Art. 829(3) CCP so provides.

[81] See in particular art. 817(2) and (3) CCP, mentioned earlier in this section.

In this regard, it should be clarified that grounds for setting aside an award under Italian law can be divided into two main groups. On the one hand, there are defects that directly affect the regularity of arbitral proceedings (see art. 829(1) CCP, nos. (1), (2), (3), (6), (7), (8), (9)); on the other hand, there are defects that directly affect per se the arbitral award (see art. 829(1) CCP, nos. (4), (5), (10), (11), (12), plus art. 829(3) CCP on mistaken application of law and violation of public policy). The latter category of defects can obviously be denounced only after the rendering of the award, with the result that parties cannot waive their right to challenge the award on those grounds before the award is issued. By contrast, defects directly affecting the regularity of arbitral proceedings should in principle be promptly raised by the interested party, who would otherwise be deemed to have waived her right to set aside the award.[82] There are a few exceptions to this rule, though. Some defects affecting the regularity of arbitral proceedings are deemed to be so serious that a party is allowed to file a recourse for setting aside the award even if that party did not raise the relevant objection during the arbitral proceeding: this is so for the grounds of invalidity mentioned by art. 829(1) CCP, nos. (3) and (9), plus for the case in which the dispute could not be submitted to arbitration at all (art. 829(4) CCP).

In practice, not all grounds for setting aside an award are equally popular. Before the 2006 reform overturned the rule that arbitral awards could always be vacated for mistaken application of the law, this was by far the most common challenge raised against the award. Given that the reform only applied to arbitral awards rendered in proceedings commenced after March 2, 2006 (that is, after the date in which the reform entered into force),[83] many of the post-2006 recourses for setting aside awards were – better to say: are – still based on the old principle. At the other end of the spectrum, attacking an award for "public policy" reasons is extremely uncommon, in spite of the substantial literature that that has investigated the meaning and the role of "public policy" in arbitral disputes.[84]

As art. 829(1) CCP makes clear, arbitrators' lack of independence and neutrality or misconduct during the arbitral proceedings is not per se a ground for setting the award aside. This does not mean, however, that an arbitrator's lack of independence and neutrality or misbehavior does not matter. According to art. 815 CCP, a party might object to the appointment of an arbitrator who is does not meet the requirements set out by the parties and by the same article. More in detail, art. 815 CCP provides the following provisions:

(1) A party may make an objection to an arbitrator if:
   (1) the arbitrator does not meet the requirements set out by the parties;
   (2) the arbitrator, or a corporation, legal entity or association of which she is a director, has an interest in the dispute;

---

[82] This is provided by art. 829(1) CCP, nos. (1), (2), (6), (7), (8), and by art. 817(2) and (3) CCP.
[83] Art. 27 of the legislative decree no. 40/2006. In 2016, the Plenary of the Supreme Court of Cassation held that art. 27 of the legislative decree no. 40/2006 should be construed as allowing the setting aside of awards for mistaken application of the law whenever the parties entered in the arbitration agreement before March 2, 2006, no matter whether the arbitral proceedings were commenced after that date: Court of Cassation, Plenary, May 9, 2016, no. 9341 (2016) 37 Guida al diritto 48; Court of Cassation, Plenary, May 9, 2016, no. 9284 (2016) 40 Guida al diritto 61. For a summary of the problems raised by intertemporal law in this regard, see Turatto, supra note 42, at 286–308.
[84] Italian scholarship's position on the issue is that the "public policy" that matters is the one of the jurisdiction whose substantive law governs the dispute. If the latter is a foreign law, then the notion of public policy must be construed narrowly, that is, with reference to international public policy; if the applicable substantive law is Italian law, then public policy must be construed with reference to national public policy, the boundaries of which are determined by the fundamental principles of Italian law enshrined in the Italian Constitution and the European Convention on Human Rights. See, for all, ELENA MARINUCCI, L'IMPUGNAZIONE DEL LODO ARBITRALE DOPO LA RIFORMA. MOTIVI ED ESITO 273-287 (2009).

(3) the arbitrator, or her spouse, is a relative up to the fourth degree of, lives with or has regular meals with a party, a party's agent or any of the party's counsels;

(4) her spouse has a pending litigation or a serious hostility towards one of the parties, a party's agent or one of the party's counsels;

(5) she is employed by or regularly advises as consultant or renders services to one of the parties, or to the person or body that controls one of the parties, or to a company controlled by one of the parties; or has another financial or associative relationship with any of the parties that affects her independence; or is the guardian or receiver of one of the parties;

(6) she gave advice or assistance to one of the parties in a previous phase of the dispute or has acted as a witness in it.

(2) A party cannot make an objection to the arbitrator she previously appointed unless she came to know the reasons underlying the objection after the appointment was made.

(3) A party shall make the objection to an arbitrator ... within ten days from the date in which the appointment was communicated to her or she had knowledge of the reasons underlying the objection.[85]

If the objection is (well-grounded, yet) unsuccessful, the same party might then file a recourse against the arbitral award rendered with the participation of the objected arbitrator under the heading of art. 829(1) CCP, no. (2) (that is, for violation of the rules concerning the constitution of the arbitral tribunal)[86] or no. (9) (that is, for violation of the due process clause).[87] In practice, however, such requests have been in the past rarely been upheld.[88] Perhaps the trend is now reversing, as shown by a widely commented decision of the Court of Cassation in 2017, in which the court confirmed the decision of the arbitral tribunal of Milan to disqualify the president of an arbitral tribunal, who, after being accused by one party of having accepted a bribe from the other party, sued the accusing party for defamation.[89]

A similar reasoning might be applied to arbitrators' misconduct during proceedings. While arbitrators' misconduct during proceedings is not per se mentioned by art. 829(1) CCP as one of the criteria for setting aside an arbitral award, there is little doubt that misconduct resulting in a violation of due process might give rise to a party's right to file recourse against the award on the

---

[85] The list provided by art. 815 CCP does not entirely coincide with international guidelines, such as, for instance, with the IBA Guidelines on Conflicts of Interest in International Arbitration (see www.ibanet.org/publications/publications_iba_guides_and_free_materials.aspx). The latter are however applied by Italian arbitral institutions and most prominently by the Chamber of Arbitration of Milan: see Rubino-Sammartano, supra note 2, at no. 18; Rinaldo Sali, Art. 18. Statement of Independence and confirmation of arbitrators, in THE CHAMBER OF ARBITRATION OF MILAN RULES 239, 263–264 (Ugo Draetta & Riccardo Luzzato eds., 2012).

[86] Court of Cassation, Nov. 15, 2010, no. 23056 (2010) Rivista dell'Arbitrato 675; see also ZUCCONI GALLI FONSECA, supra note 51, at 199–200; Zucconi Galli Fonseca, supra note 51, at 879–881.

[87] Francesco Carpi, L'indipendenza e l'imparzialità dell'arbitro. La sua responsabilità, 72 RIVISTA TRIMESTRALE DI DIRITTO E PROCEDURA CIVILE 239–245 (2018); ZUCCONI GALLI FONSECA, supra note 51, at 184; Zucconi Galli Fonseca, supra note 51, at 881.

[88] Court of Cassation, Oct. 13, 2015, no. 20558, at dejure.it (confirming the decision of the Rome appeals court's decision not to set aside an arbitral award on the ground that one of the arbitrators was working in the same law firm of the counsel of one of the parties); Court of Cassation, Nov. 15, 2010, no. 23056 (2010) Rivista dell'Arbitrato 675 (the court confirmed the decision of the Rome appeals court not to set aside the arbitral award rendered by an arbitrator who had in the past been the CEO of one the litigant companies); Court of Cassation, Aug. 28, 2004, no. 17192 (2005) Giustizia Civile I, 3049 (the court confirmed the decision of the appeals court of Rome not to set aside the arbitral award rendered by an arbitrator who was working in the same law firm of the counsel of one of the parties).

[89] Court of Cassation, Aug. 31, 2017, no. 20615 (2018) Rivista di Diritto Processuale 571.

ground of art. 829(1) CCP, no. 9.[90] However, to my knowledge, there is yet no case law on this issue.

In terms of frequency, it has been calculated that, in the last decade, more or less, 450 to 500 recourses against arbitral awards were registered each year before Italian courts of appeals.[91] It is commonly held that appellate courts rarely uphold challenges against arbitral awards.[92] For instance, according to an inquiry carried out in the four most active appeals courts (Milan, Turin, Brescia, and Florence), awards were vacated on average only in 4 percent of the cases.[93] However, on the basis of a review I carried out on the fifty-one decisions issued by the Supreme Court upon recourses against appellate decisions on challenges in the last five years (from January 2014 to December 2018), the numbers were quite different.

All the decisions concerned domestic arbitral awards in the survey highlighted that, of the fifty-one cases on challenges against arbitral awards which arrived at the Supreme Court between 2014 and 2018, appellate courts at the trial level had confirmed the award in forty cases, while they had upheld the challenge and annulled the award in eleven cases[94] – which means a ratio of one award overturned every four upheld. From the survey, it also emerged that the grounds for setting-aside requests most commonly relied upon by the parties before appellate courts were the following: (1) defects in the arbitral awards reasoning under art. 829(1) CCP, no. (5); (2) an award exceeding the scope of the arbitration clause under art. 829(1) CCP, no. (4); (3) the invalidity of the arbitration clause under art. 829(1) CCP, no. (1); and (4) probably as a legacy of the older rule on the challengeable nature of awards on merit grounds (which was allowed under the pre-2006 arbitration rules), violation of law under art. 829(3) CCP.[95]

Moving to the Court of Cassation, the overview shows that, in the last five years, the Supreme Court had issued on average ten decisions a year on recourses against appellate decisions on challenges.[96] What emerges from reviewing such decisions is that the Supreme Court is nondeferential to both appellate courts and arbitral tribunals. While the Court of Cassation confirmed the decision of the courts of appeals in thirty-eight cases, it reversed appellate judgments in thirteen cases. The final result was that, of the fifty-one arbitral awards whose vacation proceedings arrived at the Supreme Court between 2014 and 2018, thirty-one arbitral awards became final, while twenty proceedings for setting the award aside were either upheld or reopened.

When confronted with data from other jurisdictions, this picture shows that Italy still is a country in which arbitral awards are likely, more than elsewhere, to be challenged before the

---

[90] Carpi, *supra* note 87, at 239–245.
[91] Antonio Briguglio, *Il controllo giudiziale del lodo: male necessario, perno essenziale di ogni indagine comparatistica sull'arbitrato, e chiave di volta della collocazione dell'arbitrato nel sistema e nella concreta esperienza*, 2016 RIVISTA DELL'ARBITRATO 423, 424 (2016).
[92] Montanari & Lucenti, *supra* note 2, at no. 1.3.
[93] Briguglio, *supra* note 91, at 424. *See also* Cole, Ortolani, & Warwas, *supra* note 2, at 228 (noting that "there is evidence that at least in Milan, the leading arbitration jurisdiction in Italy, such applications are indeed rarely granted").
[94] I have the statistical survey on file. Some appellate courts are clearly hearing more arbitration cases than others. Of the fifty-one cases arrived at the Supreme Court in the concerned period, eight were from the Milan court of appeals, six from the Florence court of appeals, five from the Naples and Rome courts of appeals respectively, and four from the Ancona court of appeals.
[95] Consistently with this result, a European-wide survey published in 2015 found that challenges to the validity of arbitration agreements are more common in domestic arbitration in Italy than elsewhere: while on average 41.94 percent of respondents had not experienced such a challenge in the preceding five years, this was true of only 22.86 percent of Italian respondents: *see* Cole, Ortolani, & Warwas, *supra* note 2, at 227.
[96] In particular, the court ruled on the issue fourteen times in 2014, thirteen in 2015, six in 2016, six in 2017, and twelve in 2018.

courts.[97] Of course, the existence of annulment applications does not mean that annulment is granted. Maybe the willingness of parties to challenge awards is only a remnant of the historical anti-deferential posture of Italian courts toward arbitration; maybe it is a much more deeply ingrained and a long-term consequence of the far-too-high number of lawyers practicing between Lampedusa and the Alps. Whatever the causes, the rate of challenges brought against arbitral awards evidences that the system is not yet working at its best.

6 ENFORCEMENT OF ARBITRAL AWARDS

When it comes to enforcement, Italian arbitration law provides for separate procedures for enforcing domestic and foreign arbitration awards. Rules for the enforcement of domestic awards are set out in art. 825 CCP while rules for the enforcement of international awards are set out in arts. 839 and 830 CCP. To enforce a domestic award, a party must file a request for exequatur before the tribunal (that is, the court of first instance) of the district in which the arbitration had its seat. The tribunal is only bound to check the formal regularity of the award, i.e., that the award is in writing, decided, and signed by the majority of the arbitrators.[98] The decision might be appealed before the appeals court[99] (and then further challenged before the Court of Cassation but only for mistaken application of law).

More complex is the procedure for the enforcement of foreign awards, which are decisions rendered by arbitral tribunals whose seat was outside the national territory.[100] The procedure is largely in conformity with the 1969 New York Convention on the Recognition and Enforcement of Foreign Arbitral Awards, which Italy ratified without reservations or declarations. The party wishing to enforce a foreign award must file in an application with the court of appeals of the place in which the other party is domiciled.[101] According to art. 839(4) CCP, "the President of the appeals court checks the formal regularity of the application and the attached documents, and then issues an order which renders the award enforceable in Italy, unless: (1) the dispute was not arbitrable according to Italian law, or (2) the award is in contrast with public policy." A party might challenge the decision of the president of the court of appeals before the court of appeals itself within thirty days from the date in which the order is communicated.[102] The court of appeals might then refuse recognition and/or the enforceability of the award for the reasons

---

[97] Cole, Ortolani, & Warwas, *supra* note 2, at 228.

[98] *See* art. 825(1) CCP:

> the party seeking to enforce a domestic award in the territory of the Republic must file an application before the tribunal of the district in which the arbitration had its seat, attaching the original award or a certified copy, and the original or a certified copy of the arbitration agreement. The tribunal checks the formal regularity of the award, and issues an order which renders the award enforceable.

[99] *See* art. 825(3) CCP: "A party can file a recourse against the tribunal's order denying or upholding the unenforceability of the award before the court of appeals within 30 days from the date in which the tribunal's order is communicated."

[100] This is the standard way of reading art. 816 CCP. *See* Frignani, *supra* note 56, at 562 (specifying that foreign awards are "also awards made in the territory of the requested State but which are not considered as domestic in that State, as well as those made in the context of a dispute between two Italian nationals"); Paolo Biavati, *Arbitrato internazionale*, in ARBITRATI SPECIALI 577, 584–585 (Federico Carpi ed., 2d ed. 2016).

[101] If the other party is domiciled abroad, the court of appeals of Rome is competent: *see* art. 839(1) CCP. Art. 839(2) and (3) CCP adds that the applicant must file the original version of the award or a certified copy, a certified translation if the award was not rendered in Italian, and the arbitration agreement. These conditions are held to be purely procedural; therefore, if a court dismisses the petition for the lack of one of these conditions, the party is not prevented from filing a new petition: Court of Cassation, May 4, 1998, no. 441 (1999) *Rivista di Diritto Internazionale Privato e Processuale* 277.

[102] Art. 840(1) CCP.

set out in Article V of the New York convention. More in detail, art. 840(3) and (5) provides as follows:

(3) Recognition and enforcement of the foreign award are refused by the appeals court if the party against whom the award is invoked furnishes proof that:

(1) the parties to the agreement were, under the law applicable to them, under some incapacity, or the said agreement is not valid under the law to which the parties have subjected it or, failing any indication thereon, under the law of the country where the award was made; or

(2) the party against whom the award is invoked was not given proper notice of the appointment of the arbitrator or of the arbitration proceedings or was otherwise unable to present her case; or

(3) the award deals with a dispute not contemplated by, or exceeding the scope of, the arbitration agreement; nevertheless, if the decisions on matters submitted to arbitration can be separated from those not so submitted, that part of the award which contains decisions on matters submitted to arbitration may be recognized and enforced; or

(4) the composition of the arbitral authority or the arbitral proceeding was not in accordance with the agreement of the parties, or, failing such agreement, was not in accordance with the law of the country where the arbitration took place; or

(5) the award has not yet become binding on the parties, or has been set aside or suspended by a competent authority of the country in which, or under the law of which, that award was made . . . .

(5) Recognition and enforcement of an arbitral award are also refused if the court of appeals finds that:

(1) the subject matter of the dispute could not be arbitrated under Italian law; or
(2) the award is contrary to public policy.

Art. 840(6) CCP makes it clear that the CCP's rules on this point are "without prejudice to the international conventions of which Italy is a signatory." This means that, in case of conflict or doubt, the conditions set out in the New York Convention take priority over domestic rules.[103] The same applies to the other international treaties to which Italy is part, such as, for instance, the 1927 Geneva Convention on the Execution of Foreign Arbitral Awards, the 1961 European Convention on International Commercial Arbitration, and the 1965 ICSID Convention on the Settlement of Investment Disputes between States and Nationals of Other States. In particular, under the latter convention, ICSID investment arbitral awards are automatically recognized and enforced in Italy as if they were a domestic final judgment.[104]

Leaving aside special arbitration regimes, what should be stressed with regard to the approach of Italian courts to foreign arbitral awards is the following. In this field, differently from what happens at the domestic level, Italian courts have generally proved deferential toward foreign awards and sensitive to the need of favoring their circulation.[105] Since the ratification of the

---

[103] Frignani, *supra* note 56, at 561.
[104] Art. 54(3) ICSID Convention, on which *see* Marta Infantino, *International Arbitral Awards' Reasons: Surveying the State-of-the-Art in Commercial and Investment International Dispute Settlements*, 5 JOURNAL OF INTERNATIONAL DISPUTE SETTLEMENT 175, 190–191 (2014). Italy is a party to 103 bilateral investment treaties that provide for investor-state arbitration: Rubino-Sammartano, *supra* note 2, at no. 2 (also providing a list of the pending ICSID cases in which Italy is currently involved). From 1998 to 2015, Italy was also a party to the Energy Charter Treaty; investments made before Italy's withdrawal in 2015 will still be governed by the Treaty for the twenty years after the withdrawal.
[105] Montanari & Lucenti, *supra* note 2, at no. 11.5; Frignani, *supra* note 56, at 570–581 (also for a thoroughly assessment of Italian case-law on this point); Rubino-Sammartano, *supra* note 2, at no. 46 (who notes "Italian courts are generally

New York Convention, very few challenges to the recognition and enforcement of a foreign award have been accepted. The majority of the very few cases, in which foreign arbitral awards were denied either recognition or enforcement, were cases where the award was deeply flawed, either because of the improper composition of the arbitral tribunal or because of the arbitrators' noncompliance with the arbitral procedure under art. V(1)(d) of the New York Convention, and now art. 840(3) CCP, no. (4). For instance, exequatur was denied in a case in which the award was issued by a panel of two arbitrators, when the arbitration agreement provided for a three-arbitrator tribunal.[106] Exequatur was also denied in cases in which arbitrators did not state the grounds for their decision, although the parties had explicitly asked for a reasoned award with grounds,[107] and in which the arbitrators, despite the obligation to decide according to the law, settled the dispute as amiable compositors.[108] In a dispute concerning a sale contract between a Chinese party and an Italian party, in which the arbitration clause provided that if a dispute were commenced by the Chinese party, arbitration would have been before the CIETAC, and if a dispute were commenced by the Italian party, the arbitration would have been before the Stockholm Arbitration Center, exequatur was denied to an award issued by a CIETAC arbitral tribunal that was instituted by the Chinese party after the Italian party had commenced arbitral proceedings in Stockholm.[109]

The denial of recognition or enforcement on other grounds has been even rarer.[110] In one case, the Court of Cassation quashed a decision of the Milan court of appeals that had recognized an award rendered by an Austrian arbitral tribunal for violation of art. V(1)(b) of the New York Convention (and now art. 840(3) CCP, no. (2)). According to the Court of Cassation, the arbitral award could not be recognized because, when the arbitration proceedings were started (in late July), the Italian defendant was given only two weeks to appoint her arbitrator and three weeks to first appear before the arbitral tribunal, with both deadlines falling within the month of August – that is, the month in which most Italian law firms, including those that can provide services in German (which was the language of the arbitration), are closed.[111] It has been held that, in the case of a party's challenge to the recognition or enforcement of a foreign class arbitration award in an opt-out action, on grounds of procedural unfairness and lack of opportunity to present her case, Italian courts would most likely deny recognition or enforcement,[112] but to date there is no case law on the issue.

The impression that one gets from reviewing the case law on recognition and enforcement of foreign arbitral awards is apparently confirmed by statistics. Data collected by the court of appeals of Milan show that out of thirty-eight requests regarding the recognition of foreign awards in Italy that have been filed before that court from 2005 to 2012 the court granted the

---

definitely in favour of enforcing foreign awards. Recognition or enforcement is refused if the award has been set aside or stayed by a competent authority of the state where the award was made").

[106] Florence Appeals Court, Apr. 13, 1978 (1979) *Yearbook of Commercial Arbitration* 294 (1979).

[107] Court of Cassation, Feb. 8, 1982, no. 722 (1982) *Foro Italiano* I, 2285.

[108] Court of Cassation, Feb. 19, 2000, no. 1905 (2000) *Corriere Giuridico* 149.

[109] Court of Cassation, Feb, 7, 2001, no. 1732 (2001) *Rivista di Diritto Internazionale Privato e Processuale* 443.

[110] Frignani, *supra* note 56, at 579–581 (noting that, although parties often raise the issue of violation of public policy under art. V(2)(b) of the New York Convention, and now art. 840(5) CCP, no. (2), such requests are routinely rejected).

[111] Court of Cassation, Apr. 3, 1987, no. 3221 (1988) *Rivista di Diritto Internazionale Privato e Processuale* 714.

[112] Crespi Reghizzi & Dragoni, *supra* note 58, at 135 (who additionally note that "class arbitration is inherently procedural, and Italian courts could easily deny the enforcement of a class award also on the basis of procedural irregularities, availing itself of the (procedural) public policy exception": *id.* at. 136).

request thirty-five times and rejected only three requests: one for non-arbitrability of the subject matter and the other two for lack of formal requirements.[113]

Once again, a quite different picture emerges from the statistical review of the judgments issued by the Supreme Court on the issue in the last five years – that is, between January 2014 and December 2018. The survey shows that, in this period, only four challenges were brought before the Court of Cassation against appellate courts' decisions on recognition and/or enforcement of foreign arbitral awards. In two cases, the appeals courts had upheld the request for enforcement, while in the other two cases they rejected it. The survey also confirmed that the Supreme Court is not deferential to (foreign) arbitral awards: the court granted the foreign awards enforceability in one case[114] but denied it in the other three cases. In one instance, the court based its decision upon the fact that the appeals court had not verified whether the defendant, against whom the enforcement was sought, was actually a party of the arbitration, under which the award was rendered.[115] In the second case, enforceability was denied under art. 840(3) CCP, no. 1 because the arbitration clause, under which the proceedings were commenced, had not been signed by a party to the dispute.[116] Finally, in the third case, the court denied enforcement, under art. 840(3) CCP no. (5), because the award had been in the meantime annulled in the very country in which it was issued.[117]

7 CONCLUSION

As this survey shows, Italy's current arbitration rules are very much in line with those in force in other countries and with international standards. The recurrent (self-) narrative of Italy being a nonfriendly arbitration country is largely due to the inertia of its historical reputation. This is not to deny that some of the contextual features, which have actually shaped that reputation through time, are still traceable in the system. The domestic-mindedness of legal education and practice, high litigation rates, a far too high ratio of (domestically trained) lawyers to population, courts' activism in reviewing arbitral awards, and the lengthiness of judicial trials, are undoubtedly plaguing Italian ordinary and arbitral settlement of disputes.

Yet, there are also many signals – e.g., statutory reforms favoring ADRs, the multiplication of special arbitral regimes, the judicial revirements recognizing the autonomy of arbitral justice, the success of the arbitral services at the Milan Chamber of Arbitration, which indicate that the wind is changing. If so far the wind has not been blowing strongly enough to overturn (self-) narratives about the Italian distrust in arbitration, it might simply be because a pro-arbitration reputation cannot be established overnight. We will wait and see.

---

[113] Azzali, *supra* note 3.
[114] *Cf.* Court of Cassation, Aug. 19, 2015, no. 16901 (2016) *Rivista dell'Arbitrato* 125.
[115] Court of Cassation, Mar. 12, 2018, no. 5895, at dejure.
[116] Court of Cassation, Sept. 19, 2017, no. 21655, at dejure.
[117] Court of Cassation, Sept. 7, 2015, no. 17712, at dejure.

17

Judicial Control of Arbitral Awards in Nigeria

Tunde Ogunseitan and Nathalie M-P Potin

1 INTRODUCTION

Nigeria[1] has a mixed legal system consisting of common law, sharia law,[2] and customary law.[3] At the pinnacle of these laws is the 1999 Constitution.[4] The judiciary powers are vested in courts established by the constitution.[5] Arbitration in Nigeria is governed by the federal statute Arbitration & Conciliation Act 1988 (ACA),[6] which incorporates the 1985 UNCITRAL Model Law on International Commercial Arbitration (UNCITRAL Model Law), with some minor modifications. Nigeria is a federal system where several states have enacted their own arbitration legislation. One example of this is the Lagos State Arbitration Law of 2009 (LSAL).[7] It applies to all arbitration proceedings in the state of Lagos that are not specifically governed by any other law. As compared to the federal statute, the Lagos Arbitration Act is more modern, having been adopted in 2009.

Owing to this dual structure, the federal and state courts have overriding jurisdiction over arbitration matters. Both state and federal high courts can exercise supervisory jurisdiction over arbitral proceedings under ACA.[8] The dual judicial structures raise questions on the finality of the decision of the high court of each of its thirty-six states. This is fundamentally tied to the extent to which a court can intervene in arbitral proceedings. This power to intercede is set out

---

[1] Nigeria is a federation of thirty-six states and a Federal Capital Territory. The National Assembly as well as each of the state legislatures can enact the laws pertaining to arbitration to the extent it aids to the development of commerce. In the event of any inconsistencies between state and federal law, section 4(5) of the 1999 Constitution provides that "If any Law enacted by the House of Assembly of a State is inconsistent with any law validly made by the National Assembly, the law made by the National Assembly shall prevail, and that other Law shall, to the extent of the inconsistency, be void."

[2] Islamic law, just like most other laws, recognizes the need and importance of arbitration. Quranic basis for arbitration is found in 4:35 and 49:9 among others. See B. A. Bukar & M. A. Adamu, *Legal Framework for the Resolution of International Commercial Disputes – An Examination of Nigeria's Arbitration Law*, 16 JOURNAL OF INTERNATIONAL ARBITRATION 47–53, 48 (1999).

[3] A. OBILADE, THE NIGERIAN LEGAL SYSTEM 55, 56 (1979).

[4] The Constitution of the Federal Republic of Nigeria 1999 section 1(1).

[5] The Constitution of the Federal Republic of Nigeria 1999 section 6. The Federal High Court and High Court of the Federal Capital territory and the High Courts of States are bestowed with jurisdiction on domestic and international arbitration matters. Onward appeals from those courts will go to the Court of Appeal and the Supreme Court.

[6] Chapter A18, Laws of the Federation of Nigeria.

[7] In its legal system, Nigeria sometimes operates a plurality of laws. It is seen through the lens of covering the field see section 4(5) of the Constitution of the Federal Republic of Nigeria 1999. In addition see Compagnie Générale de Géophysique v. Etuk (2004) 1 *Nigerian Weekly Law Reports* [hereinafter NWLR] (Part 853) 20.

[8] Magbagbeola v. Sanni (2005) 11 NWLR (Part 936) 253.

in section 34 of the ACA[9] and sections 6(3)[10] and 21(1)[11] of the LSAL.[12] The *court* under the ACA could either be the "High Court of State, High Court of FCT or Federal High Court."[13] The Supreme Court clarified this point in the case of *Skye Bank* v. *Iwu*[14] while determining whether the National Industrial Court has finality in labor law matters. Eko, JSC held that the statutory provision in ACA cannot override the constitutional provisions. He added that the intention of the constitution is not to give finality to the decision of the Court of First Instance and that the right to appeal was a constitutional mandate.

The relationship that exists between the national courts and arbitration has been termed as "forced cohabitation"[15] and is not a true partnership. One of the fundamentals of arbitration is the resolution of commenced disputes without the courts. It is clear that arbitration cannot function effectively on its own without the tacit support of the national courts.[16] Courts have multifaceted roles to play in the life span of any arbitration. Parties who choose to incorporate arbitration agreements into their contracts would consider the neutrality and impartiality of the local legal system, national arbitration law and the track record of enforcing agreements to arbitrate. Therefore it is essential for the courts to take a pro-arbitration approach.

The role of the courts is paramount during the proceedings, but courts also assume a fundamental role after an award is issued and becomes enforceable. Upon application of any party and by leave of the court, an award can be enforced by the court.[17] The duality of the Nigerian Federal system appears to allow the potential enforcer of an award the opportunity to choose under which regime to enforce his or her award. This dual approach has benefits such as flexibility but might also raise issues of finality.

We will attempt to briefly review the court's general role in arbitration proceedings in Nigeria. The legal precedents in Nigeria highlight the various powers which may be exercised by the

---

[9] Section 34 of the ACA provides that: "A court shall not intervene in any matter governed by this Act except where so provided in this Act."

[10] Section 6(3): "Where a Court makes an order of stay of proceedings under subsection (l) of this Section, the Court may, for the purpose of preserving the rights of parties, make such interim or supplementary orders as may be necessary."

Section 6(1): "A Court before which an action is brought in a matter subject to an Arbitration Agreement shall, if a party so requests, not later than when submitting the first statement on the substance of the dispute stay proceedings so long as they concern that matter."

[11] Section 21(1): "The Court shall have the power to issue interim measures for the purposes of and in relation to arbitration proceedings as it has for the purpose of and in relation to proceedings in the Courts and shall exercise that power in accordance with the rules set out in the Schedule to this Law."

[12] Statoil Nigeria v. Nigerian National Petroleum Corp (2013) 14 NWLR (Part 1373) 1, www.mondaq.com/Nigeria/x/669322/Arbitration+DisputeResolution/International+Arbitration+2017+Third+Edition. In this matter the Court of Appeal decided to discharge injunctions that purported to restrain pending arbitrations.

[13] See Section 57(1) of ACA; Magbagbeola v. Sanni (2002) 4 NWLR (Part 756) 193 at 206, paras. A-B, where it was held that *court* means the High Court of a state, the High Court of the Federal Capital Territory, Abuja, or the Federal High Court. *See also* Federal High Court (Civil Procedure) Rules 2000, Order 20 Rule 17(1).

[14] (2017) Law Pavilion Electronic Law Report [hereinafter LPELR] 42595 (SC).

[15] A. TWEEDDALE & K. TWEEDDALE, ARBITRATION OF COMMERCIAL DISPUTE: INTERNATIONAL AND ENGLISH LAW AND PRACTICE (2005).

[16] C. A. Mordi, *An Analysis of National Courts Involvement in International Commercial Arbitration; Can International Commercial Arbitration Be Effective without National Courts?*, 6 OPEN JOURNAL OF POLITICAL SCIENCE 95–104 (2016), http://dx.doi.org/10.4236/ojps.2016.62009.

[17] ACA 1988 section 51(1): "An arbitral award shall, irrespective of the country in which it is made, be recognised as binding and subject to this section 32 of this Act, shall, upon application in writing to the court, be enforced by the court"; and LSAL 2009 section 56(1): "An arbitral award shall, irrespective of the jurisdiction or territory in which it is made, be recognized as binding, and subject to this Section and Section 58 of this Law, shall upon application in writing to the Court by a party, be enforced by the Court."

different courts in Nigeria. While the precedents have been largely positive, some particular judgments have left commentators unsure about the extent of their application.[18]

2 ROLE OF COURT BEFORE COMMENCEMENT OF ARBITRATION

2.1 Arbitration Agreement

At the federal level, unless a contrary intention is expressed in the agreement, an arbitration agreement remains irrevocable, except by agreement of parties or by leave of the court or judge.[19] Parties to an arbitration agreement cannot contract to oust the jurisdiction of the courts in any dispute that may arise between them. An arbitral clause ousting a court's jurisdiction will be invalid as contrary to public policy and the constitution.[20] Despite such clear precedents, sometimes parties will approach the courts early on in the arbitral process if they do not wish to participate in arbitration. The role of the courts in assisting the process of arbitration is in upholding the integrity of agreements to arbitrate and exercising powers to stay cases brought before them in order to give effect to a binding agreement to arbitrate.[21] In such situations, the courts will enforce arbitration agreements that are validly made.[22]

The Nigerian courts at federal and state level have specified that the parties cannot by contract oust the jurisdiction of the court, but any person may covenant that no right shall accrue until a third person has decided on any difference that may arise between himself and the other party to the covenant.[23] Where it is expressly, directly and unequivocally agreed upon between the parties that there shall be no right of action whatsoever until the arbitrators have decided, it is a bar to the action that there had been no such arbitration.[24] Therefore, while parties cannot by contract oust the jurisdiction of the courts, they can agree that no right of action shall accrue in respect of any differences that may arise between them until such differences have been adjudicated upon by an arbitrator.

2.1.1 Doctrine of Separability

The doctrine is well established in Nigerian law. In *Celtel Nigeria BV v. Econet Wireless Limited & Ors.*,[25] the Nigerian Court of Appeal stated that:

> Arbitral proceedings are therefore treated with a broad liberal/open mind leaning on the side of dynamism, commercial sense, latitude, and commonsense. In other words, suffice it to say that the object of [the] arbitral tribunal is to ensure that at the end of the day the arbitrators reached a practical, sensible, just and fair decision on the face of it.

---

[18] See the recent judgment in Global Gas and Refinery Limited and Shell Petroleum Development Company LD/1910/2017 (unpublished).

[19] Section 2 the ACA has been watered down by the LSAL. Section 4 of the LSAL has a similar provision to the ACA but has deleted the reference to local courts or a judge.

[20] See Compagnie Miniereet Metallurigioue v. Hereon, *Mid-Western State of Nigeria Law Reports* [hereinafter MSNLR] 169, 175–176 (1970); Owena Bank v. Vita Construction Ltd (2006) 5 *Commercial Law Reports Nigeria* [hereinafter CLRN] (CA).

[21] S. D. UNDERHILL, DO STATE COURTS REALLY HAVE A USEFUL ROLE TO PLAY IN INTERNATIONAL ARBITRATION? (2003).

[22] B. Markham, *The Essential Judge: The Role of the Courts in a System of National and International Commercial Arbitration*, 22 ARBITRATION INTERNATIONAL 73, 74 (2006).

[23] SCOA Nigeria Ltd v. Sterling Bank Plc (2016) LPELR-40566 (CA).

[24] See A.I.D.C v. Nigeria L. N.G Ltd (2000) 4 NWLR (Part 653) 494 (SC); City Engineering Nigeria Ltd v. Federal Housing Authority (1997) 9 NWLR (Part 520) 22A (SC).

[25] CA/895/2012 (unreported) delivered on Feb. 13, 2014, Ikyegh, JCA in defining arbitration held at page 55.

Section 12 (2) of the ACA[26] and section 19(2) of the LSAL indicate that an arbitration clause in an agreement is a separate agreement and that disputes arising under the agreement must be settled by a tribunal of their own choice.[27] These statutes reinforce at the federal level the Supreme Court's ruling in NNPC v. *Klifco Nigeria Limited*,[28] where the court ruled that the arbitration agreement survived a novation, and since the party did not raise the jurisdictional plea before the tribunal, it could not do so before the court for the first time.[29] This position is also reflected at the state level, and in *Frontier Oil Limited* v. *Mai Epo Manu Oil Nigeria Limited*[30] the High Court of Lagos State affirmed that courts of law have inherent jurisdiction to decide disputes between parties, but where the parties by their own agreement opt for arbitration the courts will always respect such agreements and decline jurisdiction.[31]

2.1.2 *Arbitrability and Public Policy*

There are exceptions to the general approach. A primary exception is public policy. For example, the arbitrability of issues of government revenue is less clear.[32] In the *Federal Inland Revenue* case, the court held that a case involving Federal Inland Revenue Service is not arbitrable because collecting government revenue is a function carried out solely by the Federal Inland Revenue Service.[33] However, in the *Statoil* case, the court held that, although the dispute may be related to taxation matters, if the parties agree to refer it to arbitration, then the arbitral tribunal has jurisdiction.[34]

2.2 *Stay of Proceedings*

Sections 4 and 5 of the ACA give courts the power to grant a stay of proceedings in respect of matters brought before it which are the subject of an arbitration agreement. Section 4 of the ACA empowers the court before which an action, which is the subject matter of an arbitration, is brought to order a stay of proceedings and refers the parties to arbitration upon request by any party to the arbitration agreement.

Section 5 of the ACA,[35] while also empowering the courts to grant stay of proceedings, confers discretion on a court to stay proceedings in favor of arbitration subject to three conditions: (1) the

---

[26] The section provides: "For purposes of subsection (1) of this section, an arbitration clause which forms part of a contract shall be treated as an agreement independent of the other terms of the contract and a decision by the arbitral tribunal that the contract is null and void shall not entail ipso jure the validity of the arbitration clause."

[27] Rean v. Benthworth, Fin. 1 *Appellate Courts Landmark Cases* [hereinafter ACLC] 419.

[28] (2011) 10 NWLR (Part 1255) 209.

[29] Section 12(2) Act; Section 19(2) of the LSAL. In the Section 19(2) of the LSAL, the expression 'null and void' in Section 12(2) of the Federal Arbitration Act has been replaced with the words 'invalid, non existent or ineffective', while 'ipso jure' is replaced with 'shall not invalidate the arbitration clause'.

[30] (2005) 2 CLRN 148.

[31] Quoting Obi Obembe v. Wemabod Estates Ltd (1977) 5 *Supreme Court Reports* [hereinafter SC] 131.

[32] The following subject matters were held to be non-arbitrable in Nigeria: tax disputes, in light of section 251 of the constitution that vests exclusive jurisdiction over revenue to Federal High Court; actions in rem determining title to property and rights of parties; trade disputes, since the Trade Disputes Act states that such disputes are resolved by conciliation and arbitration as provided by the Act and not under ACA; intellectual property matters, that are reserved for Federal High Court under section 35(a) ACA; fraud, because it was held to be correct for a party alleging fraud to seek leave of the court to revoke the arbitration agreement to ensure that arbitrators are not given powers to arbitrate on the issues of fraud; winding up of a company or bankruptcy; and disputes arising out of illegal contracts such as prostitution and slavery.

[33] Federal Inland Revenue Service v. Nigerian National Petroleum Corporation & 2 Ors. – Suit No. FHC/CS/774/2011, www.mondaq.com/Nigeria/x/669322/Arbitration+Dispute+Resolution/International+Arbitration+2017+Third+Edition.

[34] Statoil (Nig) Ltd v. Nigerian National Petroleum Corporation (2013) 14 NWLR (Part 1373) 1.

[35] The section provides as follows:

application must be made in a timely manner in that the applicant must not submit to the court's substantive jurisdiction to determine the dispute, (2) it must be appropriate in the circumstances to refer the dispute to arbitration, and (3) the applicant must be ready and willing to do everything necessary for the proper conduct of the arbitration.

Section 5 of the ACA adds that the party applying for a stay should do so at any time after an appearance but before delivering any pleadings or taking any other steps in the proceedings and importing the element of discretion on the courts. Orojo and Ajomo in discussing the two sections, which they described as incompatible, stated that section 4 of the ACA is taken from the UNCITRAL Model Law designed to regulate international commercial arbitration, while section 5 was taken from the repealed Arbitration Act of 1914 meant to regulate domestic arbitration.[36] It has been argued that section 4 of the ACA is wider than section 5 of the ACA and could be used in all cases envisaged by section 5 of the ACA and that section 4 of the ACA can be used for both domestic and international arbitration.[37] Commentators believe that, when put in their historical perspective, sections 4 and 5 of the ACA govern distinct circumstances. Section 4 of the ACA implements Nigeria's international obligation under the New York Convention and applies the required mandatory stay standard to court proceedings brought in violation of an international arbitration agreement. Section 5 of the ACA, on the other hand, is the reenactment of a provision that existed prior to Nigeria's ratification of the New York Convention and should, therefore, continue to be applied only in the domestic context.

It has also been argued that another reason why section 4 is preferred is that the grant of stay under section 5 of the ACA is not automatic as the grant is subject to the conditions set out in the section, which is discretionary.[38] It is, however, advised that sections 4 and 5 of the ACA should be read together in all cases pending the amendment of the ACA.[39]

The Lagos State Arbitration Law removes this inconsistency with only one requirement – it mandates the court to stay proceedings once the request by an applicant is made not later than when submitting its first statement on the substance of the dispute.[40] The court may, however, not order a stay of proceedings or order a referral where the defendant has taken any other steps in the litigation proceedings other than entering appearance.[41]

---

(1) If any party to an arbitration agreement commences any action in any court with respect to any matter which is the subject of an arbitration agreement any party to the arbitration agreement may, at any time after appearance and before delivering any pleadings or taking any other steps in the proceedings, apply to the court to stay the proceedings.

(2) A court to which an application is made under subsection (1) of this section may, if it is satisfied that:

    (a) there is no sufficient reason why the matter should not be referred to arbitration in accordance with the arbitration agreement; and

    (b) the applicant was at the time when the action was commenced and still remains ready and willing to do all things necessary to the proper conduct of the arbitration, make an order staying the proceedings.

[36] O. OROJO & A. AJOMO, LAW AND PRACTICE OF ARBITRATION AND CONCILIATION IN NIGERIA 320 (1999).
[37] J. Yakubu, *The Interplay of Adjudicatory Function between the Arbitral Tribunals and the Courts with Respect to Arbitral Proceedings*, in CONTEMPORARY ISSUES IN NIGERIAN LAW. ESSAYS IN HONOUR OF HON. JUSTICE, UMARU FARUK ABDULLAHI, CON 196 (S. Kanam & A. Madaki eds., 2006).
[38] G. Nwakoby, *The Courts and the Arbitral Process in Nigeria* 4 UNIZIK LAW JOURNAL 27 (2004).
[39] *Id.*
[40] Section 6(2) of the LSAL.
[41] Section 6(2) LSAL; *see also* M.V. Lupex v. NOC & S Ltd (2003) 15 NWLR (Part 844) 469.

3 ROLE OF JUDICIARY DURING ARBITRATION

Once the arbitral proceedings are commenced, the Nigerian courts play an important role in eliminating the obstacles hindering its progress. Even though the arbitral tribunals have the freedom to settle the issues submitted thereto, the following issues require the courts' interference.

3.1 Procedural Irregularities and Arbitrator Misconduct during the Proceedings

The supervisory power of the Nigerian courts to deal with issues of procedural irregularity is limited, and parties are generally required to raise any such issues with the arbitral tribunal directly. It is only when the arbitral tribunal fails to deal with these issues or does not adequately deal with them that the Nigerian courts may decide the same.[42]

Arbitrator misconduct is the ground for having an award set aside[43] but not a ground for refusing recognition and enforcement of awards. Misconduct is not defined and is difficult to prove. The Nigerian courts have sought to narrow the definition of misconduct and in *Baker Marina Nig. Ltd. v. Danos & Curole Cont. Inc.*,[44] the court indicated that failure on the part of an arbitrator to comply with the terms of an arbitration agreement will amount to misconduct. The court, in this case, went further to find that it can never be misconduct on the part of an arbitrator to come to an erroneous decision even if his or her error is one of fact or law and whether or not his or her findings of fact are supported by evidence.

The Supreme Court in *Kano State Urban Development Board v. Fanz Construction Co. Ltd.*[45] listed some situations that may constitute misconduct as a ground for setting aside an arbitral award where:

a. there is irregularity in the proceedings, as, for example where the arbitrator failed to give the parties notice of the time and place of the meeting;
b. the agreement required the evidence to be taken orally, and the arbitrator received affidavits;
c. the arbitrator refused to hear the evidence of a material witness;
d. the examination of witnesses was taken out of the parties' hands;
e. the arbitrator failed to have foreign documents translated;
f. the reference being to two or more arbitrators and they did not act together;
g. the arbitrator, after hearing evidence from both parties, received further evidence from one without informing or hearing the other;
h. the arbitrator attended the deliberations of the appeal board reviewing his award; or
i. the arbitrator failed to act fairly towards both parties.

In a later case, the Supreme Court in *A. Savoia Ltd v. A.O. Sonubi*[46] held that misconduct denotes the following: (1) where the arbitrator fails to comply with the terms, express or implied, of the arbitration agreement; (2) where, even if the arbitrator complied with the terms of the arbitration agreement, the arbitrator makes an award which on grounds of public policy ought not to be enforced; (3) where the arbitrator has been bribed or corrupted; (4) technical misconduct, such as where the arbitrator makes a mistake as to the scope of the authority

---

[42] Section 33 the ACA and section 58 of the LSAL.
[43] Section 30 of the ACA.
[44] (2001) 7 NWLR (Part 712) at 352. The earlier case of Baker Marine Nig. Ltd. v. Chevron Nig. Ltd. (2000) 12 NWLR (Part 681) at 393 was referred to.
[45] (1990) NWLR (Part 142) 1.
[46] A. Savoia Ltd v. A.O. Sonubi (2000) 12 NWLR (Part 682) 53.

conferred by the agreement of reference (this, however, does not mean that every irregularity of procedure amounts to misconduct); (5) where the arbitrator or umpire fails to decide all the matters which were referred to him or her; (6) where the arbitrator or umpire has breached the rules of natural justice; and (7) if the arbitrator or umpire has failed to act fairly toward both parties as, for example, by hearing one party but refusing to hear the other or by deciding the case on a point not put by the parties.

Despite this seemingly wide approach to misconduct, in *A. Savoia Ltd v. A.O. Sonubi*, it was argued that the arbitrator misconducted himself by receiving and deciding upon inadmissible evidence (for reasons of it being inconsistent and unwarranted), by applying different yardsticks of justice and by relying on his own expertise as opposed to the evidence before him. The court disagreed and dismissed all subsequent appeals. In another narrow construction of what constitutes misconduct it was decided that an error of law on the face of the award by the tribunal will bind the parties whether it is right or wrong unless there is a clear violation of the principles of law contained in the award.[47]

As a matter of policy, it has been argued that *misconduct* should be removed from the ACA and the state laws as the ground for setting awards aside. This is because of the large number of cases being brought on spurious grounds under the label of misconduct, which, as a common law concept, leaves a lot of room for various interpretations.[48] Other commentators are also of the view that the concept of misconduct has been abused under the ACA and recommended to change the language in the ACA and state laws to something more specific, such as justifiable doubts as to arbitrator impartiality, lack of qualifications, etc.[49] However, others say that it is doubtful that different statutory language will change practice since the English concept of error on the face of the award is often the one that has been abused.[50]

3.2. Determining Arbitrator Bias and Parameters of Conflict of Interest

Arbitrators have a duty to disclose any circumstances likely to give rise to any justifiable doubts as to their impartiality or independence,[51] and an arbitrator may be challenged if such justifiable doubts are found to exist.[52] Parties are free to agree on the procedure to be followed in challenging arbitrators' independence and impartiality, which limits the role courts play in the process.[53] There are no separate rules on conflict of interest aside from IBA Guidelines.[54] Very limited information is available on reception of the Conflicts of Interest Guidelines in Nigeria. In the recent case of Global Gas and Refinery Limited v Shell Petroleum Development Company, the Guidelines were not considered at all when the High Court in Lagos State decided to set aside an ICC award for lack of disclosure by an arbitrator.[55]

---

[47] Arbico Nig Ltd v. N.M.T. Ltd (2002) 15 NWLR (Part 789) 466.
[48] E. Onyema, *Enforcement of Arbitral Awards in Sub-Saharan Africa*, 26 ARBITRATION INTERNATIONAL 115–138 (2010); *cf.* www.globalarbitrationreview.com/print_article/gar/chapter/1036953/nigeria?print=truec.
[49] A. A. Olawoyin, *Charting New Waters with Familiar Landmarks*, 26 JOURNAL OF INTERNATIONAL ARBITRATION 373–404 (2009).
[50] *Id.*
[51] Section 8(1) of the ACA.
[52] Section 8(3) of the ACA.
[53] A. Adekoya & E. David, *Nigeria: Arbitration Guide IBA Arbitration Committee*, AELEX, www.aelex.com/wp-content/uploads/2017/12/Nigeria-Arbitration.pdf.
[54] *Id.*
[55] Global Gas and Refinery Limited and Shell Petroleum Development Company LD/1910/2017 (unpublished). This judgement has been heavily criticized by the arbitration community in Nigeria and there is likely to be an appeal to the Court of Appeal.

4 ROLE OF COURT AFTER ARBITRATION: RECOGNITION OF AWARDS AND REQUIREMENTS FOR ENFORCEABILITY

Nigeria ratified the Convention on the Recognition and Enforcement of Foreign Arbitral Awards (the New York Convention) in Schedule 2 of ACA. The New York Convention applies only to awards made in contracting states that have reciprocal legislation recognizing Nigerian awards.[56] Nigerian law does not require awards to be registered,[57] but an enforcing party has to be aware of the window in which an award must be enforced in Nigeria.[58]

The limitation period for enforcement of arbitral awards depends on the state where an award is sought to be enforced.[59] For example, section 8(1) of the Limitation Law of Lagos State states that an action to enforce an arbitration award shall not be brought after the expiration of six years from the date on which the cause of action accrued. In this context, the cause of action accrues after the losing party refused to enforce the award. However, since the meaning of "cause of action" in this context is not settled, the law in Lagos State currently appears to be that the limitation period for enforcement of arbitral awards starts running from the date the cause of action that resulted in the award arose.[60] It remains unclear whether this principle applies to the whole country or only Lagos State since the court referred to section 63 of the Limitation Law of Lagos State.[61] This position has been criticized on the basis that the parties are effectively denied an enforceable award if there is simply an extensive delay. If compared to another common law system, English courts have for example interpreted a similar provision to mean that the cause of action arises when the losing party fails to honor the award.[62]

The award may, by leave of court, be enforced in the same manner as a judgment or order of the court.[63] The applicant does not need a separate application to apply for leave to enforce and the order for enforcement of an arbitral award.[64] The application for leave to enforce an arbitral award would be made to the High Court of a state, the High Court of the Federal Capital Territory, Abuja or the Federal High Court.[65]

Order 39 Rule 4 of the High Court of Lagos State (Civil Procedure) Rules 2012 requires the application for leave to enforce an arbitral award to be on notice to the other side. However, in the Federal High Court, Order 52 Rule 16 of the Federal High Court Civil Procedure Rules

---

[56] Section 51(1) of ACA states that an arbitral award shall, irrespective of the country in which it was made, be recognized as binding and be enforced by the court. To apply for enforcement, a party needs to supply the original award and original arbitration agreement (section 51(2) ACA). The enforcing party also needs to seek leave of the court. The Court of Appeal ruled that leave can be obtained ex parte but this view has been criticized because it makes a person's assets vulnerable to attachment without an opportunity to object to enforcement: Mercantile Group (Europe) A.G. v. Aiyela and others, CA/L/348/92, July 1, 1996; *cf.* Sons Ltd. and another v. BIL. Construction Ltd (1999) 12 NWLR (Part 630), supporting the same position. See also section 56 of the LSAL.

[57] A. Adebayo, *Limitation Period for the Enforcement of Arbitral Awards in Nigeria*, 22 ARBITRATION INTERNATIONAL 613–626 (2006).

[58] See City Engineering v Nigeria Ltd v FHA [1997] 9 NWLR Part 520, 224.

[59] Id.

[60] Murmansk Steve Steamship v. Kano Oil Millers Ltd (1974–1975) 9 *Nigerian Supreme Court Cases* [hereinafter NSCC] 590; City Engineering Nig. Ltd v. Federal Housing Authority (1997) 9 NWLR (Part 520), cited in A. G. Abaralegbe, *Challenges in Enforcement of Arbitral Awards in Capital-Importing States*, 23 JOURNAL OF INTERNATIONAL ARBITRATION 401–426 (2006) and Adebayo, *supra* note 57, at 613–626.

[61] Abaralegbe, *supra* note 60, at 401–426.

[62] Id.; *cf.* Adebayo, *supra* note 57, at 613–626.

[63] Section 31(3) of the ACA.

[64] Tulip (Nigeria) Limited v. Noleggioe Transport Maritime S.A.S. (2011) 4 NWLR (Part 1237) 254.

[65] Sections 31(3) and 57 of the ACA.

2009 provides that the application for enforcement of an arbitral agreement can be made ex parte, but the court hearing the application may order it to be made on notice. Since section 32 of the ACA provides that any of the parties to an arbitration agreement may request the court to refuse recognition or enforcement of the award, it would seem that the other party must be notified of the application before a decision is made.

4.1 Grounds for Refusal to Enforce

Where the other party against whom enforcement is sought establishes valid grounds for setting aside the award, the application for enforcement would be refused by the court. Any decision reached by the court in relation to the application to enforce can be appealed. If leave for enforcement is granted, the losing party could appeal to the Court of Appeal to set aside the order granting leave. As an alternative, the losing party may, within three months from the date of the award or three months from the date the request for an additional award is disposed of by the arbitral tribunal, apply to the court requesting the court to set aside the award.[66] The losing party may also request the court to set aside the award on the ground that the award was improperly procured.[67]

The grounds for refusing to enforce an arbitral award are not limited to violation of rules of public policy. Pursuant to section 52(2)(a) of the ACA and section 57(2) of the LSAL, which apply to international arbitration, enforcement of an award may be refused if the party against whom it is invoked furnishes the court with proof that:

(i) a party to the arbitration agreement was under some incapacity; or
(ii) the arbitration agreement is not valid under the law which the parties have indicated should be applied, or failing such indication, that the arbitration agreement is not valid under the law of the country where the award was made; or
(iii) [the party] was not given proper notice of the appointment of an arbitrator or of the arbitral proceedings or was otherwise not able to present [its] case; or
(iv) the award deals with a dispute not contemplated by or not falling within the terms of the submission to arbitration; or
(v) the award contains decisions on matters which are beyond the scope of submission to arbitration, so however that, if the decisions on matters submitted to arbitration can be separated from those not submitted, only that part of the award which contains decisions on matters submitted to arbitration may be recognised and enforced; or
(vi) the composition of the arbitral tribunal, or the arbitral procedure, was not in accordance with the agreement of the parties; or
(vii) there is no agreement between the parties under sub-paragraph (vi) of this paragraph, that the composition of the arbitral tribunal, or the arbitral procedure, was not in accordance with the law of the country where the arbitration took place; or
(viii) the award has not yet become binding on the parties or has been set aside or suspended by a court of the country in which, or under the law of which, the award was made.

In addition, enforcement will be refused pursuant to section 52(2)(b) of the ACA and section 57(2) of the LSAL if the court finds that the subject matter of the dispute is not capable of settlement by arbitration under the laws of Nigeria or that the recognition or enforcement of the award is

---

[66] Section 29 of the ACA and section 55 of the LSAL.
[67] Section 30 of the ACA.

against public policy of Nigeria.[68] That part of the ACA that deals with domestic arbitration states that enforcement of an award may be refused by the court where it is shown that the arbitrator misconducted himself, the arbitral tribunal lacked jurisdiction or the arbitral award was improperly procured.[69] Due to the fact that the part of the ACA that is specific to international arbitration is additional to the provisions that relate to domestic arbitration, it is believed that the grounds set out in sections 29 and 30 of the ACA will also apply to international arbitration.

A party aggrieved by the decision of the court on enforcement may appeal to the Court of Appeal.[70] Proceedings for recognition and enforcement can be stayed pending an application to set aside the award.[71] Enforcement proceedings can be stayed on the grounds of forum non-conveniens.[72] The court may sometimes require security from the party requesting a stay of enforcement proceedings.[73] In *Toepher of New York v. Edokpolor*,[74] the Supreme Court of Nigeria held that a foreign award could be enforced in Nigeria by suing upon the award. To succeed in the action, the plaintiff must prove the existence of the arbitration agreement, the proper conduct of the arbitration in accordance with the agreement and the validity of the award. The defendant may, however, resist the enforcement of the award by challenging the conduct of the arbitration or the jurisdiction of the arbitral tribunal. Where a party intends to bring such an action in the Federal Capital Territory, Abuja, the action may be commenced under the undefended list summary procedure. Similarly, where a party intends to bring the action in Lagos, the action may be commenced under the summary judgment procedure. It has been widely reported that this procedure could take about a year or more to conclude, depending on the circumstances of the case.

4.2 Enforcement of Domestic Arbitral Awards

An arbitral award is recognized as binding. A party may upon application in writing to the court, obtain a leave of the court to have the award enforced in the same manner as a judgment or order to the same effect.[75] In the case of *Raz Pal Gozi Cons. v. FCDA*[76] the Supreme Court made it clear that the court cannot convert the arbitration award to its own judgment. The court went further to explain that the role of the High Court in an arbitral award is merely to enforce it when the award is not challenged.[77] An award may, by leave of the court or a judge, be enforced in the same manner as a judgment or order to the same effect.[78] The party relying on the award,

---

[68] Section 52(2)(b) of the LSAL has been modified by deleting the reference to the award being against 'the public policy of Nigeria' as a ground for setting aside. The Lagos State Arbitration Law has deleted 'of Nigeria' and only refers to the award being against public policy.

[69] Sections 29 and 30 of the ACA.

[70] Section 241 Constitution of the Federal Republic of Nigeria, 1999.

[71] Shell Trustees (Nig.) Ltd v. Imani & Sons Ltd (2000) 6 NWLR (Part 662) 639.

[72] Supreme Court, M. V. Lupex v. Nigerian Overseas Chartering and Shipping Ltd (2003) 15 NWLR (Part 844) 469 (although it relates to the enforcement of an arbitration agreement, the same principles will apply to the enforcement of foreign arbitral awards); *see also* Arbitration and Conciliation Act 1988 (CAP. A18 Laws of the Federation of Nigeria 2004), section 52.

[73] Union Bank of Nigeria Limited v. Odusote Bookstores Ltd (1994) 3 NWLR (Part 331) 129 at 150, para. F, where the Supreme Court held that a judgment creditor is entitled to the fruit of his judgment, therefore a stay of money judgment will be refused in the absence of the provision of security. This will also be the mood of the court in an application for the stay of recognition and enforcement proceedings.

[74] (1965) 1 *All Nigeria Law Reports* [hereinafter All NLR] 292.

[75] Section 31 (1) & (3) of the ACA.

[76] (2001) 10 NWLR (Part 722) 559.

[77] *See* Belgore JSC, at 572.

[78] See *supra* note 56.

while applying in writing to the court for its enforcement, is required to provide the duly authenticated original award or duly certified copy thereof and the original arbitration agreement or a duly certified copy thereof.[79]

4.3 Enforcement of International Awards

The purpose of the New York Convention is to ensure that courts enforce agreements to arbitrate and to facilitate the recognition and enforcement in a State of arbitral awards made in another state or otherwise constituting nondomestic awards.[80] The New York Convention as noted earlier was domesticated into the Laws of Nigeria and forms the Second Schedule of the ACA. Section 54 of the ACA states as follows:

> (1) Without prejudice to section 51 and 52 of this Act, where the recognition and enforcement of any award arising out of an international commercial arbitration are sought, the Convention on the Recognition and Enforcement of Foreign Awards (hereafter referred to as "the Convention") set out in the Second Schedule to this Act shall apply to any award made in Nigeria or in any contracting state:
>
>> (a) Provided that such contracting state has reciprocal legislation recognising the enforcement of arbitral awards made in Nigeria in accordance with the provisions of the Convention;
>> (b) The Convention shall apply only to differences arising out of legal relationship which is contractual.

By virtue of the provisions of section 51 of ACA, an arbitral award is recognized as binding irrespective of the country in which it is made subject to section 32 of the ACA. The party wishing to enforce the award is to apply to the court in writing and to supply the following documents:

> (a) the duly authenticated original award or a duly certified copy thereof; (b) the original arbitration agreement or a duly certified copy thereof; and (c) where the award or arbitration agreement is not made in the English language, a duly certified translation thereof into the English language.

It is clear that in Nigeria, international arbitration is governed partly by the ACA and the New York Convention.

4.3.1 Setting Aside of Award

Arbitrators have jurisdiction to decide only what has been submitted to them by the parties for determination. If they decide something else, they will be acting outside their authority, and, consequently, the whole of the arbitration proceeding, including the award, will be null and void.[81] A party who is aggrieved by an arbitral award may within three months from the date of the award or if it is a case where there was a request for an interpretation, correction or additional award, from the date the request is disposed of by the arbitral tribunal, request the Federal or State court to set aside the award upon proof that the award contains decisions on matters that are beyond the scope of the submission to arbitration.[82] It is important that the arbitral agreement or submission should be drafted so that it is apparent what types of disputes are to be referred

---

[79] Section 31 (2) (a) & (b) of the ACA.
[80] R. GOODE, H. KRONKE, & E. MCKENDRICK, TRANSNATIONAL COMMERCIAL LAW 636 (2007).
[81] Kano State Urban Development Board v. Fanz Construction Co. Ltd. (1990) NWLR (Part 142) 1 at 34.
[82] Sections 29 & 30 of the ACA.

to arbitration since the authority of the arbitral tribunal is derived from the nature of the reference, and, where the arbitral tribunal exceeds this authority, the proceedings may be set aside.[83]

4.3.2 *Procedure*

In making an order to set aside an arbitral award, the federal or state court will not entertain the merits of the dispute. The federal or state court may not set aside an award simply because of misinterpretation or violation of rules of law evidenced in the arbitral award unless the error could be viewed as misconduct on the part of the arbitrator. Nigerian courts have held that an award that is based on an error of law or that is not justified by the evidence submitted to the arbitrator will not be set aside.[84] The violation of the rules of public policy does not always constitute a ground for setting aside an arbitral award. This is because section 48(b) of the ACA gives a court the discretion to determine whether to set the award aside or not. The ACA does not give permission to the parties to exclude any of the grounds for setting aside. The application to set aside an award may not always be brought as an action for setting aside. It could be brought in an action on the merits of the dispute that had already been initiated but was stayed pending the arbitration. In the absence of an existing action, the applicant may institute a fresh action and seek declarations that the award should be set aside.[85]

The application to set aside an arbitration award must be made within three months from the date of the award or, if an additional award has been requested, within three months from the date such request for an additional award is disposed of by the arbitrators.[86] There is no special form prescribed by the ACA for the action to set aside an arbitral award. However, the Arbitration Applications Rules 2009 made under the LSAL provide that applications seeking recourse against an award shall be made by originating motion. Rather than set aside an award, the federal or state court before which the application to set aside is brought may at the request of a party suspend proceedings for such period as it may determine to afford the arbitral tribunal the opportunity to resume proceedings or take actions to eliminate the grounds for setting aside of the award.[87] Any lower Nigerian court's decision on the enforcement of a foreign award is subject to appeal.

4.3.3 *Grounds to Set Aside Award*

The court may set aside an award if it finds that the subject matter of the dispute is not capable of settlement by arbitration under the laws of Nigeria or the award is against the public policy of Nigeria.[88] The evidentiary standard for setting aside awards in Nigeria is high. Courts tend to give "priority to the upholding of Arbitral Awards" and there is only a "narrow compass" where courts can override this policy.[89] Courts "have to show reluctance" to give effect to parties' choice of arbitration over court proceedings.[90] Awards will not be set aside unless there is something "radically wrong and vicious in the proceedings."[91]

---

[83] P. O. Idornigie, *Relationship between Arbitral and Court Proceedings in Nigeria*, 19 JOURNAL OF INTERNATIONAL ARBITRATION 443–459 (2002).
[84] *Revenue Mobilization, Allocation & Fiscal Commission v. Units Environmental Sciences Limited* (2010) LPELR-9205(CA).
[85] Order 52 Rule 15(h) of the Federal High Court (Civil Procedure) Rules, 2009.
[86] Section 29(1) of the ACA.
[87] Section 29(3) of the ACA.
[88] Section 48(b)(i) of the ACA.
[89] Guinness Nigeria Plc. v. NIBOL Properties Ltd (2015) 5 CLRN 65.
[90] Arbico Nigeria Limited v. Nigeria Machine Tools Limited (2002) 15 NWLR (Part 789) 466.
[91] Ebokan v. Ekwenibe & Sons Trading Co. (2001) 2 NWLR (Part 696) 32 (CA) at 43.

Arbitral proceedings are traditionally an alternative to litigation and parties resort to arbitration because of the problems associated with litigation. If parties embrace the doctrine of party autonomy and accept the arbitral proceedings, the courts will have no role to play in this regard.[92] However, the remedy open to an aggrieved party is to try to set aside the award under sections 29, 30 or 48 of the ACA on any of the grounds provided in those sections or to resist recognition and enforcement of the award[93]. According to section 29 of the ACA, arbitral awards may be set aside by the court on the ground that the award contains decisions that are beyond the scope of the arbitration agreement. If matters submitted to arbitration can be separated from those not submitted to arbitration, only that part of the award that contains decisions on matters not submitted to arbitration may be set aside by court. A domestic arbitral award may be set aside where the arbitrator is seen to have misconducted himself or where the arbitral proceedings, or award, haves been improperly procured.[94]

Section 48 of the ACA sets out the grounds on which international arbitral awards made in Nigeria may be set aside:

(a) If the party making the application furnishes proof that:
   (i) a party to the arbitration agreement was under some incapacity; or
   (ii) the arbitration agreement is not valid under the law which the parties have indicated should be applied, or failing such indication, that the arbitration agreement is not valid under the laws of Nigeria; or
   (iii) he was not given proper notice of the appointment of an arbitrator or of the arbitral proceedings or was otherwise not able to present his case; or
   (iv) the award deals with a dispute not contemplated by or not falling within the terms of the submission to arbitration; or
   (v) the award contains decisions on matters which are beyond the scope of the submission to arbitration, so however that if the decisions on matters submitted to arbitration can be separated from those not submitted, only that part of the award which contains decisions on matters not submitted to arbitration may be set aside; or
   (vi) the composition of the arbitral tribunal, or the arbitral procedure, was not in accordance with the agreement of the parties, unless such agreement was in conflict with a provision of this Act from which the parties cannot derogate; or
   (vii) that there was no agreement between the parties under subparagraph (vi) of this paragraph, that the composition of the arbitral tribunal or the arbitral procedure was not in accordance with this Act; or

(b) If the Court finds that:
   (i) the subject matter of the dispute is not capable of settlement by arbitration under the laws of Nigeria; or
   (ii) the award is against public policy of Nigeria.

Section 29 of the ACA sets down situations where a court may set aside an award. A party who is aggrieved by an arbitral award may apply to have it set aside within three months from the date of the award. In the case of *Araka* v. *Ejegwu*,[95] the respondent who was aggrieved with the award, waited seven months before applying to have it set aside. The court held on this ground

---

[92] Idornigie, *supra* note 83.
[93] A. Okekeifere, *International Commercial Arbitration and the UNCITRAL Model Law under Written Federal Constitutions Necessity versus Constitutionality in the Nigerian Legal Framework*, 16 JOURNAL OF INTERNATIONAL ARBITRATION 49–71, 52 (1999).
[94] Section 30 of the ACA.
[95] (1999) 2 NWLR (Part 589) 107.

that the appeal was clearly incompetent and the statute barred because it was filed outside the time window, which was not extended by the arbitral tribunal. It, therefore, struck out the appeal.[96] The federal or state court to which the application is made may set aside the arbitral award if the party making the application furnishes proof that the award contains decisions on matters that are beyond the scope of the submission to arbitration. Where the decisions on matters submitted to arbitration can be separated from those not submitted, only that part of the award which contains decisions on matters not submitted may be set aside.[97] When an award is set aside, in whole or in part, the effect is that it deprives the award or part of it of any legal effect and therefore becomes unenforceable.[98] By virtue of section 30 of ACA, the court may set aside an award where an arbitrator has misconducted himself, or where the arbitral proceedings or award was improperly procured.

4.3.4 Setting Aside an International Arbitral Award

The court may set aside an arbitral award in an international commercial arbitration according to the above-mentioned section 48 of the ACA. Under section 52 of the ACA, the court where recognition or enforcement of an award is sought or where application for refusal of recognition or enforcement thereof is brought may, irrespective of the country in which the award is made, refuse to recognize or enforce any award. The conditions for refusal of recognition of the award are the same as stated under section 48 except for the addition of subsection (viii) which states: "that the award has not yet become binding on the parties or has been set aside or suspended by a court in which, or under the law of which, the award was made."

Besides these situations where the party has to prove to the court, the court may also set aside an award where it finds that the subject matter of the dispute is not capable of settlement by arbitration under laws of Nigeria or that the award is against public policy of Nigeria.[99] Similarly, articles 34(2)(b)(i) and (ii) of the UNCITRAL Model Law provide that an arbitral award may be set aside if the subject matter of the dispute is not capable of settlement by arbitration under the law of the state or the award is in conflict with the public policy of the state.[100] As seen, one of the grounds for setting aside is when the award is against public policy, for instance, if it encourages slavery or the slave trade in any form or if one of the parties was denied a fair hearing. Thus, on grounds of public policy, certain matters may not be arbitrable. Generally, however, maritime, insurance, commodity contracts, engineering contracts, rent review clauses in commercial leases, partnership agreements, manufacturing, computer applications, imports and exports, general trading and process industry disputes are arbitrable.[101]

4.3.5 Public Policy Ground

Public policy is not defined in ACA, but the general understanding of the concept in Nigeria is aligned with that of the international community.[102] Public policy means a violation of general

---

[96] *See also* the decision of the Supreme Court in Bill Construction Co. Ltd. v. Imani & Sons Ltd. (2006) 19 NWLR (Part 1013) 1, where the court held that there was no infraction of the respondent's right to fair hearing, since his notice of preliminary objection was filed outside the three months prescribed by the ACA.
[97] Section 29(2) of the ACA.
[98] Idornigie, *supra* note 83.
[99] Section 52 (2) (b) (i) & (ii).
[100] *See* P. O. Idornigie, *The Principle of Arbitrability in Nigeria Revisited*, 21 JOURNAL OF INTERNATIONAL ARBITRATION 279–288, 280 (2004).
[101] *Id.*
[102] A. I. Okekeifere, *The Enforcement and Challenge of Foreign Arbitral Awards in Nigeria*, 14 JOURNAL OF INTERNATIONAL ARBITRATION 223–242 (1997).

principles of morality and justice (i.e., awards arising out of prostitution, gambling, slavery, slave trade), violation of domestic public policy, fraud on the law of Nigeria or another country (i.e., illegal contract), and violation of foreign mandatory law (i.e., international public policy).[103] Denying a party a fair hearing is also against Nigeria's public policy.[104]

Public policy considerations are likely to widen or reduce the scope. Indeed, the combined effects of sections 35, 48(b) (ii) and 52(2) (b) (ii) of the ACA support this view. Similarly, in Article 34(2) (b) (ii) of the UNCITRAL Model Law, reference is also made to public policy.[105] The issue of scope is quite different from arbitrability. Paul Idornigie aligns with Sutton, Kendall and Gill to caution that the question of whether particular disputes can be referred to arbitration should not be confused with the question of what disputes fall within the terms of a particular arbitration agreement, that is, the scope of the arbitration agreement.[106]

4.4 How Far Can the Court Intervene?

The court's intervention is limited by virtue of section 34 of the ACA. In regard to the matters governed by ACA, the court's role is limited to the extent provided for in the Act. In *Statoil Nigeria Limited v. Nigerian National Petroleum Corporation*,[107] in a unanimous decision, the Court of Appeal held that a court cannot issue injunctions to restrain arbitral proceedings. The court cited section 34 to state where there is no provision to interfere, the court must not interfere. The Court of Appeal affirmed the Statoil decision in *Nigerian Agip Exploration Limited v. Nigerian National Petroleum Corporation*.[108] The Statoil and NAE decisions have been celebrated as reinforcing the position that domestic courts should not intervene where parties have consented to arbitral proceedings, except to the extent that such intervention is expressly permitted by the ACA.

In *Shell Petroleum Development Company of Nigeria v. Crestar Integrated Natural Resources Limited*,[109] the applicant (Crestar) sought an interlocutory injunction from the Court of Appeal to restrain (among others) SPDC from continuing with an ICC arbitration between the parties, seated in London. SPDC relied on the Statoil and NAE decisions in inviting the court to dismiss the application. The Court of Appeal considered it necessary to clarify that section 34 of the ACA is only applicable to matters "governed by the Act" so that if it is found in any proceeding, that the particular facts and circumstances do not come within the purview of the Act, the provisions of section 34 of the ACA cannot apply with full force. The court found that the ACA only applied to "domestic" arbitral proceedings seated in Nigeria. For that reason, it considered that a court's jurisdiction to restrain foreign arbitral proceedings is not a matter that is governed by the ACA. Relying on section 15 of the Court of Appeal Act, the court found that it had jurisdiction to grant the injunction and further found that it was appropriate to grant the said injunction in the circumstances.

Some authors are of the opinion that the court's interpretation of section 34 was correct. However, serious concerns exist as to the application of section 34 and the wider effect of the court's decision. Paul Idornigie and Isaiah Bozimo, in their article analyzing the case, state it

---

[103] *Id.*
[104] *Id.*
[105] Idornigie, *supra* note 100, at 286.
[106] *Id.*
[107] (2013) 14 NWLR (Part 1373) 1.
[108] (2014) 6 CLRN 150.
[109] Appeal No. CA/L/331M/2015.

appears that the Court of Appeal has inadvertently declared the ACA to be inapplicable to international arbitration, even if seated in Nigeria. They call this interpretation to be incorrect because part III of the ACA expressly makes additional provisions relating to international commercial arbitration. It also seems that the decision has created two regimes. As it concerns domestic arbitration, the courts do not have jurisdiction to issue anti-arbitration injunctions. However, in international arbitration, the jurisdiction remains intact. The Court of Appeal interfered with the arbitral tribunal's power to determine its jurisdiction. The doctrine of competence–competence is one of the cornerstones of international commercial arbitration. The injunction was sought on the premise that the arbitration agreement was null and void. The arbitral tribunal did not have the opportunity to decide this question.[110]

In *Guinness Nigeria Plc.* v. *NIBOL Properties Ltd.*,[111] Guinness issued proceedings to set aside a final award made pursuant to arbitral proceedings between the parties. NIBOL commenced separate proceedings to enforce the final award. Both applications were consolidated. The High Court of Lagos State made several "arbitration-friendly" pronouncements and held that there is a live judicial policy of ascribing priority to the upholding of arbitral awards by the regular courts. There is a narrow compass that attracts the courts to override this policy by setting aside an award.

The court proceeded to refer to the following decisions of the Court of Appeal, in *Aye-Fenus Ent. Ltd.* v. *Saipem Nig. Ltd.*,[112] where the court found that the parties to a transaction choose their arbitrator for better or for worse to be the judge both as to the decisions of law and decisions of fact in dispute between them. Thus, none of them can, when the award is prima facie good, object to its decision upon the law or the facts simply because the award is not in his favor. In *Arbico Nigeria Limited* v. *Nigeria Machine Tools Limited*,[113] it was held that the court in spite of its wide power has to bear in mind that the parties have provided in their agreement to have their dispute or difference referred to arbitration as against the regular courts. It has to show reluctance to interfere with the arbitrator's jurisdiction as the sole judge of the law and facts unless it is compelled to do so. In *Baker Marine Nigeria Limited* v. *Chevron Nigeria Limited*,[114] the lower court was not sitting as an appellate court over the award of the arbitrators.[115]

Section 12 of the ACA empowers the arbitral tribunal to decide on its own jurisdiction which shall form an award to be enforced. A party who is aggrieved by the ruling of the arbitral tribunal on its jurisdiction (whether the tribunal found that it had jurisdiction or not) may within three months from the date of the ruling apply to the court to set aside the ruling. The aggrieved party does not have to wait till the final award before challenging the ruling of the arbitral tribunal on its jurisdiction.

It is doubtful whether the issue of the arbitrators' jurisdiction could be submitted to court before the arbitral proceedings commence or before the arbitrators have ruled on their jurisdiction. This is because according to section 34 of the ACA, a court shall not intervene in any matter governing the Act, except, where so provided by the ACA. There is no provision in the ACA that gives the court power to interfere in an arbitrator's jurisdiction.

That a court has been approached for a decision does not mean the arbitrators must suspend the arbitral proceedings until the court decides. In any event, except as provided by the Act, the

---

[110] P. O. Idornigie & I. Bozimo, *Attitude of Nigerian Courts towards Arbitration*, in Rethinking the Role of African National Courts in Arbitration 255 (E. Onyema ed., 2018).
[111] (2015) 5 CLRN 65.
[112] (2009) 2 NWLR (Part 1126) 483.
[113] (2002)15 NWLR (Part 789) 1.
[114] (2000) 12 NWLR (Part 681) 391.
[115] *See also* Bellview Airlines Limited v. Aluminium City Ltd (2005) 7 CLRN 143.

court does not have the power to interfere in the arbitral process. Nigerian law vests the authority with an arbitral tribunal to decide on its jurisdiction; however, this does not deprive the courts of examining, with the full scope of judicial review, whether an arbitration agreement is contrary to public policy, null and void or ineffective.[116]

The law has created inconsistency in the interpretation of the section while seeking to strike a balance between the ambit of authority over jurisdiction between the court and the tribunal. This is illustrated under section 12(1) of the ACA, which provides that an arbitral tribunal shall be competent to rule on any question or objection to its jurisdiction with respect to the existence or validity of an arbitration agreement. Sections 4 and 5 of the ACA also provide that the court, before whom a matter subject to arbitration is brought, shall stay proceedings and refer the parties to arbitration, respectively. Also, section 34, which is similar to Article 5 of the UNCITRAL Model Law, prohibits the court's intervention in arbitration matters except in situations expressly provided by the Act.[117]

4.5 Delay to Decide Annulment

Given the principle that an award may not be enforced if an annulment (or setting aside) proceeding in relation to the award is ongoing, would a super-lengthy or interminable annulment proceeding be considered a form of subtle control of the award? A classic example is the long-running *IPCO* v. *NNPC* annulment proceedings before the Nigerian court (thirteen years), during which period the award could not be enforced by the English court. There are lots of cases like that which are often deliberately locked up in the Nigerian judicial system.

5 CONCLUSION

The objective of this chapter has been to provide a shortcut in a complex maze of Nigerian law. It would appear from the case law and the ACA that the judicial intervention in awards is limited. The Nigerian courts have continually affirmed that they will consider the prosperity of an award and have made positive decisions to that effect. Their position is surely a boon to litigants who want a quick resolution once they have gone through the hassle of arbitration and want to seek the fruits of that arbitration. However, the courts will have to also improve their efficiency in getting these fruits to the successful litigant. The Nigerian judiciary should give arbitration cases prompt hearing in order to maintain the essence of the process. Perhaps the solution to boost efficiency might be to ensure specialization in the field by certain members of the bench and dedicating specific federal and states courts to deal exclusively with matter arising out of domestic and international arbitration.

---

[116] In KSUDB v. FANZ Construction Ltd (1990) 4 NWLR (Part 142) 1 at 32–33, it was held that disputes such as indictment for an offense of a public nature, disputes arising out of illegal contracts and void agreements, disputes leading to a change of status, disputes that may result in the arbitral panel giving decision in rem (that is, on rights exercisable against the world), disputes where a party already admits liability but only fails act, and disputes where the causes of action no longer exist, are not arbitrable on account of public policy.

[117] J. O. Olorunfemi, *The Effect of Arbitration Agreement on the Jurisdiction of the Court in Nigeria*, 2 NIGERIA JOURNAL OF PUBLIC LAW 310, 315 (2009); M. M. Akanbi, *Examining the Effect of Section 34 of the Arbitration and Conciliation Act of 1988 on the Jurisdiction of Courts in Nigeria*, 2 NIGERIA JOURNAL OF PUBLIC LAW 298, 299 (2009); E. O. Ezike, *The Validity of Section 34 of the Nigerian Arbitration and Conciliation Act*, 8 THE NIGERIA JURIDICAL REVIEW 142,151 (2000–2001); N. Ikeyi, *The Courts and the Arbitral Process in Nigeria*, 6 ARBITRATION AND DISPUTE RESOLUTION JOURNAL 369 (1997); A. Azouzu, *The Arbitration and Conciliation Decree (Cap. 19) as a Legal Framework for Institutional Arbitration: Strengths and Pitfalls*, 2 LAWYERS' BI-ANNUAL 1 (1995). See also the case of Statoil v. Nigeria Ltd v. Nigerian National Petroleum Corporation (2013) NWLR (Part 1373) 1 at 28, 29.

18

Judicial Control of Arbitral Awards in Poland

Jerzy Pisuliński and Piotr Tereszkiewicz

1 INTRODUCTION

Domestic and international arbitration in Poland is regulated by provisions in the Code of Civil Procedure (CCP), Part Five titled "Arbitration Court."[1] Part Five entered into force in October 2005 and modernized the Polish legal framework for arbitration. The CCP largely implement provisions of the UNCITRAL Model Law on International Commercial Arbitration (UNCITRAL Model Law).[2] There are, however, certain divergences that will be discussed in this chapter. Most recently, certain provisions of Part Five were amended in July 2019, with a view to promoting arbitration as a preferred means of dispute resolution.[3]

Poland has been a party to the New York Convention since 1962 and the European Convention on International Commercial Arbitration since 1964. Poland is also a party to the Geneva Protocol on Arbitration Clauses of 1923. By contrast, Poland has refrained from signing the Convention on the Settlement of Investment Disputes between countries and nationals of other countries (Washington Convention). Further, Poland is party to numerous bilateral investment treaties (Algeria, Bosnia and Herzegovina, Croatia, Iraq, Macedonia, Montenegro, Morocco, Serbia, Slovenia, Syria and Turkey), with provisions relating to the recognition and enforcement of the arbitral awards.

2 ARBITRABILITY OF DISPUTES

The catalog of arbitrable disputes has been gradually expanding under Polish law, partially due to 2005 reforms, which included Article 1157 CCP, which provides for the arbitrability of asset-related disputes and disputes relating to non-monetary disputes (except disputes over maintenance and alimony). The Supreme Court has reasoned that arbitrability hinges on the abstract legal power of the parties to decide on their rights arising out of their

---

[1] Code of Civil Procedure [*Kodeks postępowania cywilnego*] of Nov. 17, 1964, consolidated text by Dziennik Ustaw (Journal of Laws) of 2019, item 1460 with subsequent amendments.
[2] United Nations document A/40117, annex I, as adopted by the UN Commission on International Trade Law on June 21, 1985.
[3] Law of July 31, 2019 on amendments to certain statutes aiming to reduce regulatory burden [Ustawa z dnia 31 lipca 2019 r. o zmianie niektórych ustaw w celu ograniczenia obciążeń regulacyjnych], Dziennik Ustaw (Journal of Laws) of 2019, item 1495.

relationship.[4] The 2019 amendments reinforced this view with respect to mandating the arbitrability of disputes with few exceptions. Further, the reform of 2019 extended the arbitrability of disputes in the domain of business associations. Before the reform of 2019, arbitrability in this area was unsettled as to whether Article 1163 §1 CCP was a lex specialis in relation to Article 1157 CCP. In its resolution of May 7, 2009,[5] the Supreme Court held that an arbitration clause in the statute of a commercial company concerning disputes arising from company relationships does not allow for its dissolution at a general meeting of the company.[6] This was changed by an amendment to the CCP. According the new Article 1163 § 1 CCP, an arbitration agreement contained in the statute of a commercial company concerning disputes resulting from the legal relationship of a company binds the company, its shareholders or partners, and the companies' bodies and members of these bodies. Finally, it should be noted that labor law cases, as well as consumer law disputes, are arbitrable, but only if a written agreement to arbitrate is entered into after the dispute begins under Article 1164 CCP.[7]

2.1 Equality of the Parties to an Arbitration Agreement

Article 1161 § 2 CCP imposes a general prohibition against any arbitration agreement that violates the principle of the equality of the parties. In particular, this provision prohibits arbitration agreements under which only one party is entitled to bring a claim before an arbitral tribunal. This provision has been interpreted in a number of judicial decisions. Most importantly, it has been held that the equality of the parties should be understood with a view to the content of the arbitration agreement rather than the organization of the arbitration tribunal.[8] In order to determine whether an arbitration agreement lacks legal effect due to the principle of the equality, the entire procedure of appointment of arbitrators must be evaluated, including the measures applicable in case of justified doubts as to the impartiality of the arbitrator.[9] According to the Supreme Court, the principle of the equality of the parties may be infringed where one party is empowered to select the rules of procedure of an arbitration tribunal.[10]

---

[4] Supreme Court of June 18, 2010, case V CSK 434/09, Lex (Database) no. 738365; L. Sokołowska, *Zmiana kryterium zdatności arbitrażowej w prawie polskim z perspektywy prawnoporównawczej* (The Reform of Rules on Arbitrability of Disputes in Polish Law from a Comparative Perspective), 1 ADR 57–64 (2019).

[5] Case (III CZP 13/09), Orzecznictwo Sądu Najwyższego Izba Cywilna (OSNC) (Rulings of the Supreme Court Civil Chamber) 2010, no. 1, item 9.

[6] This question was discussed in the scholarship. See more A. Szumański, *Dopuszczalność kognicji sądu polubownego w sporach o zaskarżanie uchwał zgromadzeń spółek kapitałowych* (Admissibility of Jurisdiction of Arbitration Court in the Disputes Regarding Claims against Resolutions of Corporate Meeting of Commercial Companies), in ROZPRAWY PRAWNICZE. KSIĘGA PAMIĄTKOWA PROF. M. PAZDANA (Legal Treaties. Liber Amicorum Maksymilian Pazdan) 540–567 (L. Ogiegło, W. Popiołek, & M. Szpunar eds., 2005); R. Kos, *Zdatność arbitrażowa sporów o ważność uchwał spółek kapitałowych* (Arbitrability of Disputes Pertaining to Validity of Corporate Resolutions), 3 PRZEGLĄD PRAWA HANDLOWEGO 28–36 (2014); W. Jurcewicz & C. Wiśniewski, *Zdatność arbitrażowa sporów korporacyjnych - perspektywa polska* (Arbitrability of Corporate Disputes. The Polish Perspective), 10 PRZEGLĄD PRAWA HANDLOWEGO 4–11 (2015).

[7] Consumer law disputes mean disputes resulting from legal relationships between traders (business parties) and consumers; for more on arbitrability of consumer disputes, *see* A. Budniak-Rogala, *Zapis na sąd polubowny z udziałem konsumenta – uwagi na tle regulacji z art. 1164[1] KPC* (Arbitration Agreement with a Consumer – Remarks on the Regulation of Article 1164[1] CCP), 1 & 2 ADR 5–14 & 5–24 (2017).

[8] Supreme Court of Oct. 19, 2012, case V CSK 503/11, Lex no. 1254742. In this judgment the SN considered whether a fact that one party is a member of the organization, which established an arbitration tribunal may have an impact on the process of selection of arbitrators and whether it may infringe on the equality of the parties.

[9] Court of Appeal in Katowice of Jan. 16, 2013, case V ACz 1106/12, Lex no. 1267291.

[10] *Supra* note 8.

2.2 Law Applicable to an Arbitration Agreement

The question of governing law over the arbitration agreements is comprehensively dealt with by the Polish Act on Private International Law of 2011 (PIL).[11] In principle, an arbitration agreement is governed by the law chosen by the parties (Art. 39. 1 PIL Act). When the law applicable to the contract has not been chosen by the parties, the arbitration agreement is governed by the law of the country in which the arbitration proceedings take place in accordance with the parties' agreement. If no venue of arbitration is provided for in the arbitration agreement, then arbitration agreement is governed by the law applicable to the legal relationship which the dispute concerns. The arbitration agreement is valid under the law of the law of the country in which arbitration proceedings take place or the arbitral tribunal renders its judgment (Art. 39. 2 PIL Act). Further, the PIL provides that formal requirements of an arbitration agreement are subject to the law of the country in which the arbitral proceedings take place. It is sufficient, however, to fulfill the formal requirements of the law of the country, which governs the arbitration agreement (Art. 40 PIL Act).

3 NATURE AND FORMAL REQUIREMENTS OF AN ARBITRATION AGREEMENT

The CCP lays down the basic formal requirements as to the validity of the arbitration agreement. First, the arbitration agreement must be concluded in writing (Article 1162 § 1 CCP). According to Article 1162 § 2 CCP, this requirement is satisfied when the arbitration agreement is contained in an exchange of documents or statements between the parties by means of communication that provides a retrieval record of the agreement or when the written contract refers to a document containing an arbitration clause (incorporation by reference). This provision does not apply to labor disputes and disputes involving consumers, where the requirement of the written form is strictly construed (Article 1164 CCP). Furthermore, as discussed in the following, an arbitration agreement may be incorporated in the statute of an association or a company (Article 1163 CCP). It is worthwhile to note that a power of attorney includes the power to enter into binding arbitration agreements in certain situations. According to Article 1167 CCP, a power of attorney to perform a legal act granted by a business party includes the authorization to agree to an arbitration clause, unless the power of attorney indicates otherwise.[12]

3.1 Legal Nature of the Arbitration Agreement

It has long been recognized in the Polish legal system that an arbitration agreement contained in an underlying agreement or contract is legally autonomous.[13] Pursuant to Article 1180 § 1 CCP, invalidity or expiration of the underlying agreement does not result in the invalidity or expiration

---

[11] Act of Feb. 4, 2011 Private International Law [*Prawo prywatne międzynarodowe*], consolidated text.: Dziennik Ustaw (Journal of Laws) 2015, item 1792; for more on the law applicable to arbitration agreement *see* J. Poczobut, *Umowa o arbitraż w polskim prawie prywatnym międzynarodowym – z uwagami porównawczymi* (Arbitration Agreement in Polish Private International Law from a Comparative Perspective), *in* SYSTEM PRAWA PRYWATNEGO (System of Private Law), 20B: PRAWO PRYWATNE MIEDZYNARODOWE (Private International Law) 659 et seq (Z. Radwański ed., 2015).

[12] For more on scholarly interpretations regarding this provision, *see* G. Żmij, Zapis na sąd polubowny (The Arbitration Clause), *in* DIAGNOZA ARBITRAŻU. FUNKCJONOWANIE PRAWA O ARBITRAŻU I KIERUNKI POSTULOWANYCH ZMIAN (Assessment of Arbitration: The Current State of Arbitration and Recommendations for Future Changes) 106–107 (B. Gessel-Kalinowska vel Kalisz ed., 2014).

[13] *See* T. ERECINSKI & K. WEITZ, SĄD ARBITRAŻOWY (*Arbitration Court*) 87–89 (2008); M. Tomaszewski, *Umowa o arbitraż* (Arbitration Agreement), in SYSTEM PRAWA HANDLOWEGO (*System of Commercial Law*), 8: ARBITRAŻ

of the arbitration agreement.[14] This closely follows the provision of Article 16 (1) of UNCITRAL Model Law. While the arbitration agreement may be a single clause of an underlying contract, it is not a clause of a common obligatory contract (pl. *umowa zobowiązująca*), meaning its legal effect is subject to an autonomous evaluation.[15] The Supreme Court regards an arbitration agreement as a sui generis agreement, involving characteristics of both contract law and a procedural agreement. In any case, the arbitration agreement is subject to rules and principles of private law, including the rules on nullity and defects of consent.[16] However, this principle is limited under Polish law. There are cases in which the same reasons that are responsible for the nullity of the underlying agreement may also cause the nullity of the arbitration agreement (such as, lack of legal capacity by one or more parties, defects of consent).

3.2 *Content of Arbitration Agreement*

It must be underscored that the arbitration agreement has to be specific as to the role of the arbitration tribunal. If a clause in the agreement provides that the role of an arbitration tribunal is to undertake mediation between the parties with a view to them reaching a settlement, such a clause cannot be considered an arbitration clause.[17] Article 1161 § 1 CCP requires that parties to an arbitration agreement must determine "at least the matter of the dispute or the legal relationship from which the dispute arose or could potentially arise" so that it is possible to conclude that future disputes will be subject to arbitration. More specifically, in one approach found in Polish case law concerning the requirements for the creation of an arbitration agreement, the court needs only to determine a legal relationship from which a dispute may emerge. A more rigorous approach recognized by some courts makes it necessary for the court to determine whether a specific dispute arises out of the legal relationship[18] or, as it is alternatively stated, the legal relationship from which the dispute is submitted to arbitration ought to be sufficiently specific and individualized.[19] It appears that the liberal approach is prevailing in arbitration practice. In any case, it is not presumed that all disputes come within scope of an arbitration clause without specifying a legal relationship from which they may result.[20] For instance, an arbitration clause relating to "the relationship resulting from the execution of a contract might not be sufficiently precise, since it leaves too big a margin of appreciation in interpreting the scope of the arbitration clause."[21] There may also be other provisions that limit the scope of the arbitration clause. For example, the parties may agree on carve-outs that require certain disputes to be litigated, and the remaining types of disputes to be arbitrated.[22] Also, arbitration agreements may be time limited, meaning they lose their binding effect after a certain period of time has elapsed.[23]

HANDLOWY (*Commercial Arbitration*) 340–345 (A. Szumański ed., 2015); A. W. WISNIEWSKI, MIĘDZYNARODOWY ARBITRAŻ HANDLOWY W POLSCE (International Commercial Arbitration in Poland) 302–306 (2011).

[14] Supreme Court of Dec. 15, 2000, case I CKN 1131/00, OSNC 2001, no. 7-8, item 107.
[15] Supreme Court of Mar. 2, 2017, case V CSK 392/16, Lex no. 2273374.
[16] Supreme Court of Apr. 13, 2005, case V CK 532/04, Lex no.1111037; Supreme Court of Jan. 7, 2009, case II CSK 397/08, Lex no. 523608; Supreme Court of Oct. 24, 2012, case III CSK 35/12, Lex no. 1232776.
[17] Supreme Court of Oct. 11, 2001 r., case IV CKN 139/01, Lex no. 53085.
[18] Supreme Court of Nov. 7, 2013 r., case V CSK 545/12, Lex no. 1422127.
[19] *Id.*
[20] In particular, Supreme Court of Dec. 10, 2003, case V CK 27/03, Lex no. 602085; *supra* note 18.
[21] Supreme Court of Apr. 4, 2012, case I CSK 354/11, Lex no. 1164720.
[22] Supreme Court of Nov. 16, 2016, case I CSK 780/15, Lex no. 2195669.
[23] Court of Appeal in Warsaw of June 18, 2015, case I ACa 1822/14, Lex no. 1771043.

The question of interpretation of an arbitration agreement has been subject to several Supreme Court judgments. The leading case ruled that an arbitration agreement should be interpreted neither restrictively nor extensively with a view to upholding the jurisdiction of the arbitration tribunal. The interpretation of an arbitration agreement should ensure that the common intention of the parties is established and respected.[24] In line with the established jurisprudence of the Supreme Court, the interpretation of an arbitration agreement is subject to the general provision of Article 65 Civil Code (*kodeks cywilny*),[25] which deals with the interpretation of declarations of will (legal acts).[26] Some legal scholars emphasize that the jurisprudence of the Supreme Court continues to perceive an arbitration agreement as a divergence from a constitutionally guaranteed right to bring a claim in court, which justifies a tendency toward a restrictive interpretation of the scope of arbitration agreements.[27] This implies that at present Polish law does recognize a pro-arbitration presumption in the interpretation of arbitration agreements.

3.3 Arbitration Agreement and Third Parties

The arbitration agreement may be incorporated into the articles of association of a commercial company and in such case, it binds partners or shareholders (Art. 1163 §1 CCP) to arbitrate their disputes. This rule applies, by virtue of Art. 1163 §3 CCP, to other cooperative legal forms recognized under Polish law, such as cooperatives (*spółdzielnie*) and associations (*stowarzyszenia*). Further, the arbitration may bind third parties. For instance, in case of an assignment of an obligation in a contract, the arbitration agreement binds the assignee, as an assignment of an obligation is not considered a reason for extinguishing the arbitration agreement.[28] In one Supreme Court decision, it was held that an arbitration agreement concluded by one of debtors (who are jointly and severally liable) with another party does not bind remaining co-debtors despite their joint and several liability to the other party.[29] Finally, it should be noted that an arbitration agreement concluded by a commercial partnership does not bind its partners that are personally liable for partnership obligations, unless they have explicitly accepted the arbitration agreement. Similarly, an arbitration agreement contained in a contract, following which a bill of exchange is to be issued, does not extend to a dispute regarding the rights against the issuer of the bill of exchange.[30]

3.4 Legal Effects of an Arbitration Agreement

First, a lack of an arbitration agreement is a ground for setting aside an arbitral award or refusing its recognition or enforcement by national courts. This is clearly expressed in both Article V 1 (a) and (c) of the New York Convention, as well as in Article 1206 § 1 point 1 and 3, Article 1215 § 2 point 1 and 3 of the CCP. The CCP contains a catalog of provisions regarding the procedure for establishing whether an arbitral tribunal has jurisdiction to decide a given dispute.

---

[24] *Supra* note 22.
[25] Ustawa z 23 kwietnia 1964 r. (Act of 23 April 1964), consolidated text Dziennik Ustawa (Journal of Laws) 2019, item 1145 with amendments.
[26] Supreme Court of Mar. 1, 2000, case I CKN 1311/98, Lex no. 138641; Supreme Court of Dec. 13, 2006, II CSK 289/06, Lex no. 488987.
[27] Żmij, *supra* note 12, at 152. Recently, a more liberal position was taken by the Supreme Court, *supra* note 22.
[28] Supreme Court of Sept. 3 Supreme Court 1998, I CKN 822/97, case Lex no. 34448.
[29] Supreme Court of July 13, 2011, case III CZP 36/11, OSNC 2012, no. 3, item 31.
[30] Supreme Court of Dec. 16, 2010, case I CSK 112/10, OSN 2011, no. 9, item 102. The decision is best justified in the light of legal independence of the obligation arising out of a negotiable instrument from the underlying contract.

Article 1180 § 1 CCP provides that the arbitral tribunal may rule on its own jurisdiction, including the existence, validity, effectiveness, and scope of the arbitration agreement. The ruling on the arbitral tribunal's jurisdiction may be contained in the final award or in a separate decision (cf. Article 1180 § 3 CCP). If the tribunal issues a separate decision upholding its jurisdiction, then either party may seek a ruling from a court within two weeks of receipt of the decision. If a party fails to make a timely appeal, then it will be barred from claiming a lack of validity of the arbitration agreement or the arbitral tribunal's ruling on its scope.[31] Most importantly, initiation of a proceeding before a court does not stay the hearing of the case before the arbitral tribunal.

A decision by an arbitral tribunal that declines jurisdiction over a dispute due to a lack of a valid arbitration agreement is not reviewable by a court.[32] Further, an arbitral tribunal is not bound by a court decision on the basis of Article 1165 § 1 CCP, whereby a court must reject a party's petition to initiate court proceedings where there is a valid and effective arbitration agreement. Also, an arbitral tribunal may still consider an arbitration agreement to be ineffective, despite a court ruling that it is an enforceable agreement. Nevertheless, the final judgment of the court finding that the arbitral tribunal lacks jurisdiction is binding on the arbitral tribunal. This represents a narrow view of the kompetenz–kompetenz doctrine and differs from the position adopted in the UNCITRAL Model Law.[33] Finally, it must be noted that Article 1165 § 3 CCP expressly states that initiating a court proceeding does not prevent the arbitration tribunal from hearing the case. This means that one party may sue for payment before a court, while the other party demands the contract be declared void by an arbitral tribunal. Thus, parties do not waive their right to arbitrate when they participate in court proceedings.

4 ARBITRAL PROCEEDINGS

4.1 Substantive Law Governing the Merits of the Dispute

Pursuant to Article 1194 § 1CCP, an arbitral tribunal shall resolve the dispute in accordance with the law applicable to the transaction but may rely instead on general principles of law or the rules of equity if expressly authorized by the parties. In particular, the parties may include a reference to an international model law, such as the Principles of European Contract Law (PECL) or Unidroit Principles on International Commercial Contracts (PICC).[34] However, rendering a decision solely based on the lex mercatoria is not authorized under Article 1194 CCP.[35] Another important limitation on arbitral discretion relates to disputes involving consumers, where Article 1194 § 3 CCP prohibits the use of general principles of law or the rules of equity if their application deprives a consumer of a protection afforded to him or her by mandatory provisions of law, such as consumer protection laws. In the event the parties do not

---

[31] Court of Appeal in Warsaw of Aug. 23, 2012, case I ACa 46/11, Lex no. 1220679.
[32] Supreme Court of 28 Jan. 2011, case I CSK 231/10, Lex no. 784175.
[33] R. Sikorski, Zagadnienia ogólne (General Issues), in DIAGNOZA ARBITRAŻU. FUNKCJONOWANIE PRAWA O ARBITRAŻU I KIERUNKI POSTULOWANYCH ZMIAN (Assessment of Arbitration: The Current State of Arbitration and Recommendations for Future Changes) 259 (B. Gessel-Kalinowska vel Kalisz ed., 2014).
[34] M. PAZDAN, PRAWO PRYWATNE MIĘDZYNARODOWE (Private International Law) 398 (2017).
[35] Ł. Błaszczak, Postępowanie przed sądem polubownym. Wyrok (Arbitral Proceedings. Award), in DIAGNOZA ARBITRAŻU. FUNKCJONOWANIE PRAWA O ARBITRAŻU I KIERUNKI POSTULOWANYCH ZMIAN (Assessment of Arbitration: The Current State of Arbitration and Recommendations for Future Changes) 305 (B. Gessel-Kalinowska vel Kalisz ed., 2014).

agree on the applicable law, the tribunal determines the applicable law in accordance with the conflicts of law rules.

4.2 Selection of Arbitrators and the Composition of the Arbitral Tribunal

The CCP contains a catalog of provisions dealing with the selection of arbitrators. Most importantly, parties are granted freedom to determine the composition of the arbitral tribunal and to select arbitrators (Article 1169 § 1 and Article 1171 § 1 CCP). Parties are free to indicate the number of arbitrators in the arbitration agreement. However, an agreement that grants one of the parties more rights in appointing the arbitral tribunal does not have legal effect according to Article 1169 § 3 CCP. Should the number of arbitrators not be determined contractually, the default rule of Article 1169 § 2 CCP provides that the arbitral tribunal shall be composed of three arbitrators. If a named arbitrator in the arbitration agreement refuses to be an arbitrator, the arbitration agreement will be invalidated, unless the parties decide otherwise (Article 1168 § 1 CCP). The arbitration agreement also loses legal effect in cases where the appointed tribunal refuses to act, fails to schedule a hearing (Article 1168 § 2 CCP) or when the arbitrators fail to reach a unanimous (if required) or majority decision (Article 1195 § 4 CCP). The parties may at any time agree on the termination of the mandate of the arbitrators by submitting a joint written declaration (Article 1177 § 2 CCP).[36]

If the parties' agreement does not state a method of appointing arbitrators, Article 1171 CCP provides detailed rules on appointing arbitrators. Under these rules, each party appoints an equal number of arbitrators who then appoint the presiding arbitrator or, if the dispute is to be resolved by a sole arbitrator, they together appoint the sole arbitrator. If one of the parties fails to act in accordance with the agreed upon procedure, the other party may request the court to make the relevant appointment. Pursuant to Article 1170 § 1 CCP, any natural person of any citizenship with full capacity to perform legal acts, may serve as an arbitrator.[37] However, in contrast to UNCITRAL Model Law, an active judge cannot serve as an arbitrator (Article 1170 § 2 CCP). This prohibition does not extend to retired judges. Parties to an arbitration proceeding are not required to have legal representation.

4.3 Impartiality of Arbitrators

The question of the impartiality and independence of arbitrators is dealt with under CCP, which follows the rules found in the UNICTRAL Model Law. A person appointed as an arbitrator is required to immediately disclose to the parties any circumstances that could raise doubts as to the arbitrator's impartiality or independence (Article 1174 § 1 CCP).[38] The parties are not allowed to waive the disclosure requirements of Article 1174 CCP.[39] Grounds for challenging an arbitrator that are listed in Article 1174 § 2 CCP follow Article 12 (2) UNCITRAL Model Law.[40] An arbitrator may be challenged in the event that circumstances raise justifiable

---

[36] A. Szumański, Arbitrzy i zespół orzekający (Arbitrators and Panels), in SYSTEM PRAWA HANDLOWEGO (System of Commercial Law), 8: ARBITRAŻ HANDLOWY (Commercial Arbitration) 447 (A. Szumański ed., 2015)

[37] There is no requirement that an arbitrator should be a Polish citizen, Ł. BŁASZCZAK & M. LUDWIK, SĄDOWNICTWO POLUBOWNE (ARBITRAŻ) (Arbitration court) 233 (2007).

[38] For more about a declaration of impartiality or independence see M. ASŁANOWICZ, POZYCJA PRAWNA ARBITRA W ARBITRAŻU HANDLOWYM (A Legal Position of Arbitrator in the Commercial Arbitration) 134–149 (2015); Szumański, supra note 36, at 432–435.

[39] ERECIŃSKI & WEITZ, supra note 13, at 197.

[40] Szumański, supra note 36, at 440.

doubts as to the arbitrator's impartiality or independence or it becomes apparent that the arbitrator does not possess the qualifications prescribed by the agreement of the parties. The party may challenge its appointed arbitrator only upon grounds that became known to the party after the appointment (Article 1174 § 2 CCP). Further, the CCP's challenge procedure is an adoption of Article 13 UNCITRAL Model Law. Unfortunately, the CCP fails to provide examples or guidance regarding situations that raise doubts as to arbitrator's impartiality or independence. An alternative source of guidance is the Guidelines of the International Bar Association on Conflicts of Interest in International Arbitration,[41] unless the rules to be applied are those of a permanent arbitration court or the arbitration agreement designates rules for making this determination. The Supreme Court has emphasized that the provisions of CCP do not preclude arbitrator ex lege as is the case with judges, circumstances that could raise doubts as to the impartiality of an arbitrator include grounds for excluding a judge as defined in Articles 48 and 49 CCP.[42] The Supreme Court reasoned that when a party makes a request to exclude an arbitrator and its request is rejected by the arbitral tribunal or association, a party may a claim to set aside the arbitral award. When the party did not demand an exclusion of an arbitrator, then there is no legal basis for setting the award aside based on lack of impartiality or independence.[43] From the party's perspective, it is important to note that a court decision on the party's challenge of an arbitrator may be appealed on the basis of the provision of Article 394 § 1 point 10 CCP.[44]

According to the Supreme Court, a court decision on the party's challenge of an arbitrator is subject to an interlocutory appeal on the basis of Article 394 § 1 point 10 CCP. The Supreme Court rejected the view that allowing an interlocutory appeal contributes to unnecessarily prolongation of arbitration proceedings. An arbitral court may stay its proceedings until a court decides on the matter in question.[45] The position of the Supreme Court has been critiqued in legal scholarship on the account that the CCP regards an arbitral award or tribunal decision on a challenge as conclusive and rejects the Supreme Court's application of judicial rules by analogy to arbitrators.[46]

4.4 Proceedings before the Arbitral Tribunal

Under Polish law, arbitral tribunals are not obligated to follow CCP provisions directed at judicial proceedings.[47] Unless the parties have agreed otherwise, the arbitral tribunal may conduct the proceedings in the manner it deems appropriate (Article 1184 CCP). It should be emphasized that the arbitral tribunal is required to ensure that the parties are afforded the same procedural rights, the right to be heard, and the right to submit statements and evidence. According to Article 1183 CCP, the parties must be treated equally in the arbitration proceedings. Conducting an arbitration proceeding without material evidence offered by a party would be a violation of Art. 1183 CCP.[48] While the state court does not control whether the assessment made by the arbitral tribunal is correct, an award based on a selective, unreliable assessment of

---

[41] Guidelines (2014 version).
[42] Supreme Court of Sept. 8, 2011, case III CZP 41/11, Lex no. 898218.
[43] See Supreme Court of Sept. 24, 1999, case I CKN 141/98, OSNC 2000, no. 4, item 65; *supra* note 42.
[44] See *supra* note 42.
[45] *Id.*
[46] M. Wójcik, *Uwagi ogólne do art.* 394 (General Comments to Article 394), *in* KODEKS POSTEPOWANIA CYWILNEGO. KOMENTARZ (Code of Civil Procedure. A Commentary) 1442 (A. Jakubecki ed., 2010).
[47] Supreme Court of Nov. 26, 2008, case III CSK 163/08, Lex no. 479315.
[48] Court of Appeal in Warsaw of Jan. 25, 2013, case I ACa 374/12, Lex no. 1286655.

evidence violates the rule of law and thus violates the basic principles of the legal order of the Republic of Poland (public policy).

According to the CCP, oral hearings are not obligatory. Unless otherwise agreed by the parties, the arbitral tribunal decides whether to conduct a hearing to allow the parties to make statements and submit evidence or whether the proceedings will be conducted on the basis of written submissions (documents and other letters). If the parties have not agreed that the proceedings will be conducted without a hearing, the arbitral tribunal shall be obliged to conduct a hearing upon a request of one of the parties (cf. Article 1189 § 1 CCP).

Under the CCP, there are no specific restrictions as to who may serve as a witness. Witnesses are not required to give testimony under oath in an arbitral proceeding and the arbitral tribunal cannot apply coercive measures to obtain evidence (Article 1191 § 1 CCP). Nevertheless, the arbitral tribunal may request the assistance of a court in obtaining witness testimony and to support other actions, which the arbitral tribunal is not authorized to undertake by itself (cf. Article 1192 CCP). Finally, it should be noted that Article 1191 § 2 CCP allows arbitral tribunals to appoint experts, order the parties to provide experts with relevant information, enable experts to access documents, or to inspect property (unless the parties have agreed otherwise).

4.5 Arbitral Award

In accordance with 1197 § 1 CCP, the arbitration award must be in writing and signed by the arbitrators and must be in a written form.[49] The fact that an award has been orally communicated is not relevant in this respect. If there are three or more arbitrators in a given case, it is sufficient that a majority sign the award and indicate the reasons for the other arbitrators not signing (cf. Art. 1197 § 1 CCP). An arbitral award that has not been signed is considered to be "nonexistent" and does not have legal force under the CCP.[50] Furthermore, f the rules of 1197 § 2 and 3 CCP require the award to designate the parties and arbitrators, the arbitration agreement or other grounds for jurisdiction, the date of the award, the place the award is issued, and the reasons for the decision (justification). However, the failure to enunciate the reasons for the decision does not prevent the arbitral award from having legal effect.[51]

Pursuant to Article 1195 § 2 CCP, an arbitrator who voted against the opinion of the majority of arbitrators may indicate, next to the arbitrator's signature, that he or she was of a dissenting opinion. A justification of the dissenting opinion must be submitted within two weeks from the date of preparation of the reasons for the award and attached to the case files (Article 1195 § 3 CCP). It is broadly recognized that arbitral tribunals may grant any kind of remedy or relief available under substantive law, as long as it does not violate public policy. The CCP does not expressly clarify that interim and partial awards are possible, but the prevailing view is that arbitral tribunals may issue such awards.[52] Interim and partials awards are enforceable if they fulfill the conditions of enforcement.

---

[49] Ł. BŁASZCZAK, WYROK SĄDU POLUBOWNEGO W POSTĘPOWANIU CYWILNYM (Proceedings before an Arbitral Tribunal: Arbitral Award) 188 (2010); ERECINSKI & WEITZ, supra note 13, at 332.

[50] BŁASZCZAK, supra note 49, at 188; M. Łaszczuk & J. Szpara, Postępowania postarbitrażowe (Post-arbitration Proceedings), in SYSTEM PRAWA HANDLOWEGO (System of Commercial Law), 8: ARBITRAŻ HANDLOWY 575 (Commercial Arbitration) (A. Szumański ed., 2010).

[51] Łaszczuk & Szpara, supra note 50 (considering the reasons for the decision [justification] an obligatory but not a constitutive element of an arbitral award under CCP).

[52] See G. Żmij, Środki tymczasowe i zabezpieczające w międzynarodowym arbitrażu handlowym (Interim Measures in the International Commercial Arbitration), in ROZPRAWY PRAWNICZE. KSIĘGA PAMIĄTKOWA M. PAZDANA (Legal Treaties. Liber Amicorum Maksymilian Pazdan) 557 (L. Ogiegło, W. Popiołek, & M. Szpunar eds., 2005).

4.6 Requirements of Enforceability of Arbitral Awards

The provisions of CCP list the requirements of recognition and enforceability of arbitral awards in Poland. As a principle, arbitration awards or settlements before an arbitration tribunal have the same legal force as a court judgment or a settlement concluded before a court after the awards recognition by a Polish court (Article 1212 § 1 CCP). This applies to both domestic and foreign arbitral awards. The CCP states that the act of recognition or declaration of enforceability by a national court grants arbitral awards the same legal force as is attributed to national court judgments.[53] The Polish legislature rejected the model of "automatic" ipso iure recognition of an arbitral award. Pursuant to Article 1213 CCP, courts recognize arbitral awards and declare them enforceable at the request of the party.[54]

5 SETTING ASIDE AN ARBITRAL AWARD

Recourse to a national court against an arbitral award issued in the Republic of Poland may be made only by an application for setting aside in accordance with the provisions of the CCP. According to the prevailing view, the right to initiate proceedings to set aside an arbitral award cannot be contractually excluded.[55] CCP provisions differentiate between domestic and foreign arbitral awards. A foreign arbitral award may be refused enforcement only under the provisions of the CCP or under the New York Convention if the award was issued in a signatory state. By contrast, a domestic arbitral award may be challenged before a national court within two months from service of the award on the party (Article 1208 § 1 CCP). The provision of Article 1208 § 2 CCP extends the period in exceptional cases. Exceptional cases include when it is alleged that the award was obtained by means of a crime or on the basis of a forged document, or when the award constitute a res judicata, the period to file an application to set aside the award runs from the date on which the party learned of the ground for the application, but may not exceed five years from the service of the award.

A national court judgment rendered following the application for setting aside an arbitral award is not subject to an ordinary appeal but may be appealed to the Supreme Court. A national court may not remand an award to the arbitral tribunal. Nevertheless, in cases of interlocutory appeals, Article 1209 § 1 CCP authorizes the court to stay the set aside proceedings upon a motion of one of the parties. The objective of this measure is to enable the arbitral tribunal to resume the proceedings in order to eliminate the basis (the reason) for setting aside the arbitral award. In the course of such proceedings, the arbitration tribunal shall undertake actions mandated by the court.

The grounds for setting aside an arbitral award found in Article 1206 § 1 CPC closely resemble the provisions of Article V of the New York Convention and Article 34 (2) of UNCITRAL Model Law, including

---

[53] BŁASZCZAK, supra note 49, at 403–405.
[54] The requesting party shall attach the original or a certified copy of the award or the settlement as well as the original or certified copy of the arbitration agreement, cf. Article 1213 § 1 CCP.
[55] ERECINSKI & WEITZ, supra note 13, at 390. M. Zachariasiewicz, Postępowania post-arbitrażowe: skarga o uchylenie orzeczenia sądu polubownego oraz uznawanie i wykonywanie orzeczeń arbitrażowych (Post-arbitration Proceedings: Petition to Set Aside an Arbitral Award and Recognition and Enforcement of Arbitral Awards), in DIAGNOZA ARBITRAŻU. FUNKCJONOWANIE PRAWA O ARBITRAŻU I KIERUNKI POSTULOWANYCH ZMIAN (Assessment of Arbitration: The Current State of Arbitration and Recommendations for Future Changes) 426 (B. Gessel-Kalinowska vel Kalisz ed., 2014), considers the prevailing view debatable.

(1) There was no arbitration agreement, the arbitration agreement was null and void, or the arbitration agreement became invalid in accordance with the law applicable thereto. In this respect it must be emphasized that a court adjudicating in a proceeding to set aside an arbitral award may not *ex officio* invoke this ground for setting aside an arbitral award, the ground must be stated in the party's petition for setting aside an arbitral award.[56]
(2) The party making the application was not given proper notice of the appointment of an arbitrator or of the arbitral proceedings or was otherwise unable to present his case.
(3) The award deals with a dispute not contemplated by or not falling within the terms of the submission to arbitration or contains decisions on matters beyond the scope of the submission to arbitration; if decisions on matters submitted to arbitration can be separated from those not so submitted, only that part of the award that contains decisions on matters not submitted to arbitration may be set aside. Furthermore, a party that during the arbitration proceedings did not object to claims falling outside of the scope of the arbitration agreement may not invoke those circumstances when applying for the arbitral award to be set aside.[57]
(4) The composition of the arbitral tribunal or the basic rules of the arbitral procedure was contrary to that agreed by the parties or to the provisions of law.
(5) The award was criminally obtained, or it was based on counterfeit documents.
(6) A final and binding judgment has already been issued in the same case between the same parties (res judicata). It is controversial whether this applies only to judgments of national courts or also includes arbitral awards that were recognized or declared enforceable by national courts.[58]

It is worthwhile to note that the catalog of grounds for setting aside an arbitral award listed under the CCP provisions is broader than those found in UNCITRAL Model Law. In particular, the grounds for setting aside an award listed in Article 1206 §1 points 5 and 6 CCP are more specific than the UNICTRAL Model Law, in which such circumstances would be taken into account under the public policy clause pursuant to Article 34(1)(b)(ii).[59]

Pursuant to Article 1206 §2 CCP, an arbitral award is also set aside if the court finds the subject matter of the dispute is not capable of settlement by arbitration under Polish law or the award is in conflict with the basic principles of the Polish legal order (public policy). According to the Supreme Court, the assessment as to whether the arbitral award is in conflict with basic principles of the legal order relates to the content of the award rather than procedural irregularities of the arbitration proceedings. It follows that an arbitrator's failure to disclose a link to a party relates to the content of the award.[60] Finally, an award is set aside if it deprives a consumer of protections afforded by mandatory provisions of law or when the choice of law clause in the contract deprives a party of protections afforded by mandatory provisions of law that would have been applicable but for the choice of law.

---

[56] Supreme Court of Mar. 27, 2013, case V CSK 222/12, Lex no. 1331378.
[57] *Supra* note 31.
[58] According to the prevailing view, this ground applies only to judgments of state courts, *see* K. Weitz, *Uchylenie wyroku sądu polubownego z powodu prawomocnego wyroku sądu (art. 1206 §1 pkt 6 k.p.c.)* (Setting Aside an Arbitral Award Due to a Final Court Judgment), *in* KSIĘGA PAMIĄTKOWA 60-LECIA SĄDU ARBITRAŻOWEGO (The 60th Anniversary of the Court of Arbitration) 699–700 (J. Okolski ed., 2010).
[59] Zachariasiewicz, *supra* note 55, at 505.
[60] Supreme Court of Sept. 9, 2011, case I CSK 535/2009, Biuletyn Sądu Najwyższego (Bulletin of the Supreme Court) 2011, no. 10, p. 6.

Separate provisions of Article 1215 CCP deal with the recognition and enforcement of judgments and settlements by foreign arbitration tribunals. In such cases, a party must approach a Polish court to have an award recognized or enforced, since a court hearing is required by Article 1215 § 1 CCP. The grounds for refusing to recognize or enforce an award are largely the same as in domestic cases. In particular, Article 1215 § 2 CCP allows a court the ability to refuse to recognize or enforce a foreign arbitral award on the grounds that (1) there was no valid agreement to arbitrate or an agreement to arbitrate became invalid; (2) there was procedural unfairness, in particular when a party was unable to present his or her case; (3) the award deals with a dispute not contemplated by or not falling within the terms of the submission to arbitration; (4) the composition of the arbitral tribunal or the basic rules of the arbitral procedure were contrary to that agreed upon by the parties or as provided by the law of the country in which it was rendered; and (5) the award was set aside by a court of the country in which, or under the law of which it was rendered.

There have been only a few Supreme Court judgments dealing with the issue of recognition and enforcement of foreign arbitral awards.[61] In an important judgment, the Supreme Court held that if a party did not raise a plea that a foreign arbitral tribunal had no jurisdiction over a dispute, it may not invoke a lack of an arbitration clause or its nullity in the judicial proceeding related to the recognition and enforcement of an arbitral award.[62] Undoubtedly, this does not apply to a party who failed to raise such a plea, since this party did not participate in the arbitration at all.[63]

5.1 Limits of Judicial Review of Arbitral Awards

As a matter of principle, a state court may not review the substance of the arbitral award under Polish law. Moreover, Polish law does not provide for an appeal from an arbitration award to a national court. Nevertheless, the parties may agree that the proceeding before the arbitral tribunal includes more than one instance. According to the Supreme Court,[64] if the parties agreed that the proceeding before the arbitral tribunal should include more than one instance, then the rules of arbitration proceedings apply equally to the appellate arbitration proceedings.

The Supreme Court has held that a court may not question whether an arbitral tribunal correctly interpreted or applied provisions of substantive law. An exception to this rule is allowed when an incorrect application of law would deprive a party its consumer rights.[65] In the context of judicial control, a court is not to be considered a higher instance tribunal, reviewing the merits of the arbitral award.[66] More specifically, the court does not assess whether the arbitral award has

---

[61] See G. Sikorski, *Odmowa nadania klauzuli wykonalności wyrokowi polubownego sądu zagranicznego z powodu sprzeczności z zasadami porządku prawnego* (The Refusing of Issue an Enforceability Clause to a Foreign Arbitral Award because of Violations of Public Policy), 2 PRZEGLĄD SADOWY 30–39 (2009); T. Ereciński, *Uznanie i stwierdzenie wykonalności wyroku sądu polubownego lub ugody przed nim zawartej* (Recognition and Enforcement of an Arbitral Award or of the Settlement Concluded before It), *in* VI KODEKS POSTĘPOWANIA CYWILNEGO. KOMENTARZ (Code of Civil Procedure. Commentary) 1023–1032 (T. Ereciński ed., 2017); M. ASŁANOWICZ, SĄD POLUBOWNY (ARBITRAŻOWY), KOMENTARZ DO ART. 1154–1217 KPC (Arbitration Court. Commentary to Article 1154–1217 Code of Civil Procedure) 177–180 (2017).
[62] Supreme Court of Sept. 13. 2011, case V CSK 323/11, OSNC 2013, no. 4, item 52.
[63] ERECINSKI & WEITZ, *supra* note 13, at 241–242.
[64] Supreme Court of Mar. 20, 2015, case II CSK 352/14, OSNC 2016, no. 5, item 63.
[65] See for instance Supreme Court of Dec. 21, 2004, case I CK 405/04, Lex no. 500191; Supreme Court of Jan. 7, 2009, *supra* note 16, where it was held that an allegation that substantive law was violated is not sufficient for setting aside an arbitral award.
[66] Supreme Court of Mar. 9, 2012, case I CSK 312/11, https://www.saos.org.pl/judgments/97419.

been rendered in conformity with provisions of procedural and substantive law provided that the arbitral award does not violate public policy.[67] The criterion for substantive control of arbitral awards is whether public policy has been infringed upon.[68] Incorrect or wrong interpretation of substantive law by an arbitral tribunal is not sufficient to constitute a ground for setting aside an arbitral award.[69] Furthermore, state courts are not allowed to examine whether the factual circumstances of a dispute were correctly established, neither are courts allowed to undertake additional inquiries as to factual circumstances.[70] Nevertheless, an arbitral award that is manifestly inconsistent with the underlying facts of the dispute may be considered contrary to public policy.[71] According to a scholarly view, a court ought to undertake factual inquiries where there is a prima facie case that public policy has been infringed upon.[72]

5.2 Substantive Violations of Public Policy

The Polish courts use the public policy exception to the enforceability of arbitral awards when awards infringe on the public order, that is, the main principles of the organization of the state and the principles of the socioeconomic order. These fundamental principles include rights defined in the Polish Constitution[73] and the fundamental principles of the various fields of law.[74] Specific areas where the public policy exception has been invoked include arbitral awards that are deemed punitive in nature. An arbitral decision, which awards damages that significantly exceed the loss sustained, may be considered a violation of public policy.[75] In this vein, the Supreme Court held that if no loss was sustained, the award of damages constitutes a violation of fundamental principles.[76] Similarly, damages for nonperformance of an obligation cannot be set arbitrarily, but must reflect the actual damage sustained.[77] Other examples include awards that infringe on Civil Code provisions dealing with prescription of claims[78] and awards that result from an incorrect interpretation of provisions on tenders subject to public procurement law.[79]

---

[67] *Supra* note 65.
[68] M. Pilich, *Klauzula porządku publicznego w postępowaniu o uznanie i wykonanie zagranicznego orzeczenia arbitrażowego* (The Public Policy in the Procedure of Recognition and Enforcement of a Foreign Arbitral Award), 1 KWARTALNIK PRAWA PRYWATNEGO 179 (2003); M. Zachariasiewicz, *Klauzula porządku publicznego jako podstawa odmowy uznania lub wykonania orzeczenia sądu polubownego w polskim prawie arbitrażowym na tle prawnoporównawczym* (The Public Policy Control as Ground for Refusing the Recognition or Enforcement of an Arbitral Award under Polish Arbitration Law from Comparative Perspective), 6 PROBLEMY PRAWA PRYWATNEGO MIĘDZYNARODOWEGO 61, 94 (2010).
[69] Supreme Court of Apr. 28, 2000, case II CKN 267/00, OSNC 2000, no. 11, item. 203.
[70] For instance, Court of Appeals in Katowice of Oct. 25, 2005, case I ACa 1174/05, Lex no. 196062.
[71] Originally held by Supreme Court of Feb. 15, 1964, case I CR 123/63, OSNC 1965, no. 4, item 61; confirmed by Supreme Court of Sept. 26, 2003, IV CK 17/02, Lex no. 278683.
[72] Zachariasiewicz, *supra* note 68, at 96 (draws from the ILA Recommendation).
[73] Constitution of the Republic of Poland of Apr. 2, 1997, Dziennik Ustaw (Journal of Law) 1997, No. 78 item 483.
[74] Zachariasiewicz, *supra* note 68, at 108.
[75] A. Wiśniewski, *Klauzula porządku publicznego jako podstawa uchylenia wyroku sądu arbitrażowego* (The Public Policy as Ground for Setting Aside an Arbitral Award), 2 ADR 127 (2009); Zachariasiewicz, *supra* note 68, at 103.
[76] Supreme Court of June 11, 2008, case V CSK 8/08, Monitor Prawniczy 2008, no.14, p. 734.
[77] Supreme Court of Oct. 10, 2006, case II CSK 123/06, Lex no. 398393.
[78] This position was adopted as early as 1973 and confirmed by the decision of the Supreme Court of Dec. 21, 1973, case I CR 663/73, Orzecznictwo Sądów Polskich (OSP) (Jurisprudence of Polish Courts) 1975, no. 1, Item. 4; Court of Appeals in Katowice of Oct. 18, 2004, case I ACa 565/04, Lex no. 147145.
[79] Court of Appeals in Warsaw of May 29, 2000, case I ACa 65/00, Orzecznictwo Sądów Apelacyjnych (OSA) (Jurisprudence of the Appellate Courts) 2001, no. 2, item 1.

5.3 Procedural Violations of Public Policy

Supreme Court judgments and scholarship have advocated the use of the public policy exception in cases involving procedural irregularities during arbitral proceedings.[80] According to the Supreme Court, the right to an impartial and independent hearing before a tribunal constitutes one of the basic principles of the Polish legal order.[81] Thus, the courts are entrusted to determine whether an arbitral award was rendered in conformity with the fundamental principles of procedural law. Also, the res judicata principle requires voiding judgments or arbitration awards in disputes previously resolved in final, conclusive, and binding decisions.[82]

The Polish courts have rendered ruling on other procedural issues. A violation of the principle of the equality of the parties may provide a reason to set aside an arbitral award when a party is deprived of a possibility to present its case altogether.[83] In assessing whether a party has been deprived of the possibility to present its case, a court is obligated to comprehensively examine the arbitral proceedings, but not the substance of the arbitral award.[84] "Deprived of a possibility" to present a case requires more than incorrect evaluation of evidence by the arbitral tribunal[85] or a lack of a reasoned award (finding of facts and rationales for the award) to constitute a violation of public policy.[86] Still, an arbitral award based on selective evidence and neglect of evidence violates the rule of law and is in conflict with the basic principles of the Polish legal order.[87]

6 CONCLUSION

This chapter shows that the provisions of the Polish Code of Civil Procedure provide for a comprehensive and modern regulation of arbitral proceedings. Still, arbitration in Poland has a much shorter history than in most Western jurisdictions. This is a reason why a number of issues important to arbitration practice has not yet been fully determined by the Supreme Court. At the same time, it must be emphasized that more and more courts have rendered decisions that provide interpretations of open-ended standards contained in the CCP. This growing jurisprudence should help create a set of comprehensive and predictable rules on arbitration in the near future. For the time being international model laws and sector standards play a fundamental role as a frame of reference for Polish arbitration practice and have established rules and practices complementing the CCP.

---

[80] As noted in Article V.1(b) & (d) of the New York Convention.
[81] *Supra* note 60.
[82] Court of Appeals in Szczecin of Mar. 21, 2013, case I ACa 855/12, Lex no. 1344234.
[83] *See* Supreme Court of Dec. 13, 2006, *supra* note 26; Zachariasiewicz, *supra* note 68, at 108.
[84] Supreme Court of May 11, 2007, case I CSK 82/2007, OSNC 2008. No. 6, item 64.
[85] Supreme Court of Mar. 6, 2008, case I CSK 445/07, Lex no. 445285; Court of Appeals in Warsaw of Feb. 20, 2017, case VI ACa 871/16, Lex no. 2307616.
[86] *See* Pilich, *supra* note 68, at 176; ERECINSKI & WEITZ, *supra* note 13, at 372.
[87] *Supra* note 48.

19

Judicial Control of Arbitral Awards in Russia

Dmitry Dozhdev

1 INTRODUCTION: STRUCTURE OF ARBITRATION LAW IN RUSSIA

The USSR was one of the first states to ratify the New York Convention on the recognition and enforcement of foreign arbitral awards.[1] The Soviet organizations complied with the foreign arbitral awards by strictly following the rules of contract and procedural discipline appropriate to a centralized economy. With the demise of Soviet Union, the need for procedural means of the recognition and enforcement of foreign arbitral awards in the national procedural law arose. A 1988 Decree of the Presidium of the USSR Supreme Soviet[2] officially implemented provisions of the New York Convention into national law. In 1993, the Russian Federation adopted International Commercial Arbitration Law (hereinafter ICAL) based on the UNCITRAL Model Law of 1985.[3] The ICAL granted competence to arbitration associations over disputes between companies with foreign participation and those disputes between such companies and Russian companies.[4] The disputes between Russian companies were not subject to the New York Convention. This was addressed by the enactment of the 2002 Russian Federation Commercial Procedure Code (CPC) on arbitral tribunals, which established a legal framework for domestic arbitration that followed international rules on the recognition and enforcement of arbitral awards.[5] With the adoption of the CPC, the Russian system of international and domestic arbitration was made comprehensive.[6]

Amendments to the UNCITRAL Model Law required revision of Russian arbitration law. In 2012, the Russian president called for further development of arbitration in Russia. The presidential mandate[7] ordered the drafting of necessary amendments to the Russian arbitration system in collaboration with the Russian Chamber of Commerce and the Russian Union of

---

[1] UN Treaty Series, vol. 330, No. 4739.
[2] Decree of the Presidium of the USSR Supreme Soviet, No. 9131-XI (June 21, 1988).
[3] International Commercial Arbitration Law, No. 5228-1 (Dec. 11, 1985). The preamble to the Law (as edited by the Federal Law of Dec. 29, 2015, No. 409, in force since Sept. 1, 2016) specially indicates the relevance of the arbitration as a widely applied means of solving the disputes in the sphere of the international commerce and the need of complex and uniform regulation of the procedural issues of arbitration at the end of the law and states that the law is based on the international treaties of the Russian Federation and the 1985 UNCITRAL Model Law "On the international commercial arbitration" (with the amendments adopted in 2006).
[4] ICAL, Article 1 (2).
[5] Russian Federation No. 102 (July 24, 2002).
[6] On the structure of the Russian arbitration law in English, see R. KHODYKIN, ARBITRATION LAW IN RUSSIA: PRACTICE AND PROCEDURE (2013).
[7] Mandate of the president of Dec. 22, 2012, No. Pr-341.

Businessmen.[8] On December 1, 2016, a new federal law on arbitration entered into force.[9] Federal Law No. 382 supports the formation of arbitral tribunals, the production of evidence, and the recognition and enforcement of foreign arbitral awards in the Russian Federation[10] and envisages new rules of recognition that do not require enforcement, such as declaratory awards.

The new arbitration law authorized the creation of new international arbitration institutions besides the International Commercial Arbitration Court (ICAC) at the Russian Federation Chamber of Commerce,[11] which has been in existence since 1932. A new permanent arbitration institution – the Russian Arbitration Center attached to the nongovernmental Russian Institute of Modern Arbitration – was created in 2017 and hears domestic arbitration cases.[12] The 2018 Caseload Report[13] showed that the number of cases heard by the new arbitration institution exceeded 250. It is expected that other permanent arbitration institutions will appear shortly.

2 STATE COURTS AND ARBITRATION: ISSUES OF ASSISTANCE AND CONTROL

Article 5 of the ICAL limits the interference of national courts into the issues regulated by arbitration law. National courts rarely intervene into arbitration disputes other than to assist the proceedings. This noninterventionist approach reflects the pro-arbitration bias established in Russian law. The ICAL provides five areas suitable for judicial intervention,[14] all of them oriented to support, rather than to control, the arbitration procedure: courts can (1) take interim measures,[15] (2) determine the competence of arbitral tribunal to decide its own jurisdiction, (3) determine the validity of the arbitration clause,[16] (4) set aside or vacate arbitral awards,[17] and (5) recognize and enforce the arbitral award in the event that the parties do not voluntarily comply.[18] These issues are reviewed in the following sections.

---

[8] Mandate of the president of Dec. 27, 2013, No. Pr-2086
[9] Russian Federation Law No. 382. The law was accompanied by further amendments in the respective legislation (Federal Law of Dec. 29, 2015, No. 409). Minor amendments to the ICAL have been later made by the federal law of Dec. 25, 2018, No. 485, www.pravo.gov.ru, 25.12.2018 and No. 0001201812250104. Both Acts were enacted on Sept. 1, 2016. Previously, prominent specialists considered the absence of special procedure of recognition of declaratory awards as lacuna of the Russian law: N. I. Marysheva, *Issues of Codification of Norms of the International Civil Procedure in Russia*, 6 JOURNAL OF RUSSIAN LAW, 47–58, 56 (2004).
[10] Federal Law No. 382 increases availability of arbitration by favoring the creation of new permanent (nongovernmental) arbitration tribunals attached to the NCO (Article 44 (1)) and allows international arbitration tribunals to hear cases in Russia.
[11] See http://mkas.tpprf.ru. The ICAC has thirteen offices quartered in various regions of Russia, which heard 363 cases in 2017 and 454 in 2018. Since 2017 statistics include domestic cases. As for the international cases, the statistical data available before 2017 (found at http://mkas.tpprf.ru/ru/Stat/page.php) show figures that are in line with those of LCIA: 274 heard in 2013, 314 in 2014, 317 in 2015, and 271 in 2016.
[12] See https://centerarbitr.ru. Since domestic and international arbitration are viewed as separate institutions (domestic arbitration is governed by the Federal Law No. 382, while international arbitration carried out in Russia is referred to ICAL), the recognition and enforcement of arbitral awards is treated in separate sections of the RF Commercial Procedure Code (CPC): Chapter 30 deals with the enforcement of domestic arbitral awards; Chapter 31 deals with the recognition and enforcement of foreign arbitral awards (as well as foreign court judgments).
[13] See https://centerarbitr.ru/en/2018/04/16/caseloadeng.
[14] Survey of the court practice of dealing with cases connected to the functions of assistance and control via arbitration and the international commercial tribunals, approved by the Presidium of the Russian Federation Highest Court on Dec. 26, 2018 (the text can be found at http://www.vsrf.ru/documents/all/27518/?fbclid=IwAR08fv2uAuMif0JUw-S5UegnCO3lAoutJsDsZ5v7JhUG7WleFglo4DqIU8Q), operates under the terms "support and control."
[15] ICAL Article 9.
[16] ICAL, Article 8 and Article 148 (1) CPC.
[17] ICAL, Article 34.
[18] Article 35 ICAL, Article 36 and CPC, Chapter 31.

2.1 Interim Measures

ICAL Article 9 states that the application of a party for interim measures does not affect the authority of the arbitral tribunal to decide on the merits of the case. Articles 90, 92, 94, and 99 of the CPC determine when interim measures should be given. According to the Article 90, a party applying for the interim measures must prove that without such measures it would be difficult to enforce the arbitral award ("judicial acts"). The Russian state courts are rather conservative in assessing the perspectives of enforcement of "judicial acts" and usually refuse to grant interim measures in international arbitration.[19] The reluctance of the courts to provide interim measures is due to the rigorous requirements asserted by the Statement of the Plenum of the Russian Highest Commercial Court (Highest Court) on the application of interim measures by courts.[20] Point 10 of the statement demands that the court assess whether the interim measure applied for "is connected to the matter of the case, if it is commercial [in nature], and how it would secure the realization of the ends of the interim measures taking into account the grounds envisaged by the Article 90 (2) Russian Commercial Procedure Code." Article 92 (5) of the CPC enumerates formal requirements for the application for interim measures, including the need for "an authenticated [copy] by the president of the permanent arbitration tribunal of the claim" and requires party applying for interim measures to provide evidence that the claim has been by the tribunal.[21]

In 2016 Russian Law amended the ICAL to conform to the new edition of the UNCITRAL Model Law.[22] Regarding the powers of the tribunal to order interim measures, the ICAL briefly states that the tribunal can take interim measures it finds to be appropriate. However, the ICAL does not provide conditions for granting interim measures as given by Article 17.[23] It does not mention the likelihood of harm in case the measures are not ordered or the reasonable possibility that the requesting party would succeed on the merits of the claim. The regulations advanced by the ICAL in its new edition are more liberal and pro-arbitration oriented.

2.2 Competence–Competence Principle

The autonomy, also referred to as severability, of the arbitration clause or agreement means that its validity does not depend upon the validity of the contract and implies that it is the arbitration tribunal that initially decides on the validity of the arbitration clause (and the contract) and its competence to decide the case. The autonomy of the arbitration agreement and competence–competence principle are mutually supportive of each other.[24]

The competence–competence principle under Article 16 (1) of the ICAL allows the arbitration tribunal to decide on its own competence as well as on any challenge to the existence or validity of the arbitration agreement. Previously (1970s and 1980s), the courts relied on the presumption that orders of arbitration tribunals are less compulsory in nature those of the courts.

---

[19] J. A. Panarjina, *Application of Interim Measures by the Russian State Courts in Relation to the International Arbitration Procedure* [in Russian], 1 TRIBUNE OF THE INTERNATIONAL COMMERCIAL ARBITRATION, 85 (2011).

[20] No. 55 (Oct. 12, 2006). *See* B. R. KARABELNIKOV, INTERNATIONAL COMMERCIAL ARBITRATION 46–47 (2012).

[21] The 2006 amendments to the UNCITRAL Model Law in reference to the issue of interim measures by recognizing the competence of the arbitrators to secure the status quo between the parties.

[22] Russian Federation Law No. 409 (Dec. 29, 2015; entered in force on Sept. 1, 2016).

[23] For a critique of Article 17, *see*, GARY B. BORN, INTERNATIONAL COMMERCIAL ARBITRATION 2466 (2d ed. 2014).

[24] EMMANUEL GAILLARD, JOHN SAVAGE, FOUCHARD, GAILLARD, GOLDMAN ON INTERNATIONAL COMMERCIAL ARBITRATION 214 (1999).

The Russian courts have more recently have shown more respect to the sanctity of the arbitration process and arbitration clauses.[25]

In a seminal decision of the High Commercial Court,[26] the court stated that the competence of the arbitration can be discussed according to Article 235 of the CPL by which any party to an arbitration may demand that a court vacate a decision of the arbitration tribunal that is not final or to question its competence.[27] But the court will determine competence only after the arbitration tribunal first makes a decision on its own competence. In other words, the Highest Commercial Court recognized that according to the Russian law it is impossible to challenge the arbitration clause without a preliminary decision of the arbitration tribunal on its own competence. The arbitral tribunal can issue a statement on its own competence either as a preliminary decision or within the decision on the merits of the case. If the decision on competence is issued as a preliminary matter, each party may challenge the tribunal's determination in court within one month of the decision and seek an annulment.[28] A court challenge does not stop the arbitration proceeding or the issuance of an award.

2.3 Courts' Referring Parties to Arbitration

If a party to the arbitration agreement requests that a court refer the dispute to arbitration, the court must comply. However, the request must be made prior to a decision on the merits. Otherwise, the party will be presumed to have waived its right to arbitrate. Furthermore, the request must be based on the arbitration agreement, be arbitrable, and not involve domestic affairs[29] and the arbitration agreement must be valid, operative, and enforceable.[30] These conditions were confirmed by Information Letter of the Highest Commercial Court. The policy of protecting foreign investors by the commercial courts is found in Point 19 of the Statement of the Plenum of the Highest Court of June 27, 2017, on dealing with economic disputes involving a foreign party. The statement requires courts to stop hearings; however, it does not oblige the court to refer the parties to the arbitration, but simply requires it to suspend the court procedure ("to leave the claim without dealing").[31]

In practice, Russian courts go further by supporting the enforcement of arbitration clauses. In one famous case,[32] the public prosecutor of the Kaliningrad region brought a claim seeking to invalidate a loan contract with a foreign bank. The claim was suspended based upon the validity of the arbitration clause in the contract. Moreover, the Federal Commercial Court of the Northwestern region obliged the public prosecutor to comply with the arbitration clause.[33] This

---

[25] No. 58 (Jan. 19 2001). See KARABELNIKOV, supra note 20, at 82.
[26] Decision of Apr. 1, 2009. It was issued under the category of "statement," an act binding on the lower courts.
[27] ICAL, Article 16 (3).
[28] Federal Law No. 382, Article 16 (3) and CPC, Article 235.
[29] If the arbitration agreement implies that the dispute should be heard by an international arbitration, it should first be determined whether the award would be issued abroad or should be considered "international" – i.e., contains some foreign element. These conditions should be met to ensure the arbitration agreement falls within the New York Convention 1958 provisions. B. R. KARABELNIKOV, ENFORCEMENT AND VACATION OF THE AWARDS OF THE INTERNATIONAL COMMERCIAL ARBITRATIONS. A COMMENT ON THE NEW YORK CONVENTION 1958 AND CHAPTERS 30 AND 31 OF THE RF COMMERCIAL PROCEDURE CODE 2002 29 (3d ed. 2008), p..
[30] These conditions for a demand for referral to arbitration are based on the Article II (1) and (3) of the New York Convention 1958; ICAL Articles 8 (1); Federal Law No. 382, Article 8 (1); CPC, Article 148 (1)(5).
[31] KARABELNIKOV, supra note 20, at 53–54.
[32] V. V. Jarkov, The Claim of the Public Prosecutor and the Arbitration Clause in a Contract [in Russian], 3, INTERNATIONAL COMMERCIAL ARBITRATION 51, 58 (2006).
[33] Statement of the Federal Commercial Court of the Northwest District (Sept. 23, 2005) No. A21-2499/03-C1.

rationale is also used when there is no arbitration clause but the parties subsequently agree to submit the dispute to arbitration.[34] This provision of the law clearly demonstrates pro-arbitration bias. The Commercial Court of Moscow in a recent case stated that:

> If a party before the court ... declares to the court that there exists a valid arbitration agreement between the parties and the dispute is within the scope of the arbitration clause, the court acting in accordance with the Article 148 (1)(5) the Russian Federation Commercial Procedure Code should indicate to the parties that the dispute should be treated by the arbitration tribunal determined by the parties.[35]

On the other hand, if a party does not disclose the existence of an arbitration agreement before the court begins hearings on the merits, the party is considered to have waived its right to arbitrate.[36] In assessing the grounds of a party's right to arbitrate, the court, in accordance with the Article II (3) of the New York Convention, determines if the arbitration agreement is not "null and void, inoperative or incapable of being performed." This wording is reproduced in the Article 148(1)-(5) of the CPC: "under condition that the arbitration agreement is not invalid, has not lost its force or cannot be enforced."

In assessing the validity and enforceability of an arbitration agreement priority is given to the intention of the parties to refer the dispute to an arbitration body. The courts assume this is the case when the parties have defined the place of the hearing, chosen a permanent arbitration institution, or defined the formation of the arbitral tribunal as well as state that the agreement was valid at the time the arbitral award was issued.[37] However, Law No. 382 states that lacking an agreement on the composition of the tribunal, the arbitrators may be nominated by the court ("competent authority") on the application of a party (Article 11). The courts should also assist in the gathering of evidence (Article 30).[38]

3 SCOPE OF ARBITRATION

Russian arbitration law provides a clear and well-structured test on the arbitrability of disputes. Every dispute of a commercial nature can be referred to arbitration, unless the law specifically states that some disputes are not arbitrable. Every dispute involving a foreign party or with a foreign aspect can be referred to international commercial arbitration. Article 11(1) of the Civil Code of the Russian Federation (Russian CC) establishes that "Protection of violated or disputed civil law rights shall be conducted, in accordance with the jurisdiction over cases established by procedural legislation, by a court, commercial court or arbitration."

---

[34] CPC, Article 148 (1)(6).
[35] Statement of the Commercial Court of the Moscow District (May 3, 2018) No. A40–93716/2017.
[36] CPC, Article 148 (1)(5). *See also*, Statement of the Economy Collegium of the Highest Court No. 306-EC15–13927 of Feb. 8, 2016, and supported by the seminal survey of the Plenum of the Highest Court of June 27, 2017 (dealing the economic disputes arising from the relationships with a foreign element by the commercial courts), No. 23, Point 18.
[37] Statement of the Commercial Court of the Northwest District (June 8, 2016) No. F07–3384/2016 on Case No. A56–50929/2015; Statement of the Commercial Court of the Moscow District (Feb. 2, 2017) No. F05–707/2017 on Case No. A40–154787/2016; Statement of the Eleventh Commercial Court of Appeal (Samara city) (Feb. 26, 2019) No. A55–29953/2018.
[38] Article 30. Support of the court in gathering evidence:

> In the terms of the arbitration administered by the permanent arbitration institution, the arbitral tribunal or a party, with the consent of the arbitral tribunal, can apply to the court asking for assistance gathering of the evidence. The court approves the application or refuses to comply with it on the grounds envisaged by the procedural statute law of the Russian Federation.

Article 1(2) of the ICAL advances a general principle that "disputes resulting from contractual and other civil law relationships arising in the course of foreign trade and other forms of international economic relations, provided that the place of business of at least one of the parties is situated abroad" may be referred to international commercial arbitration on the agreement of the parties.[39] Article 1(4) of the provides: "This Law shall not affect any other law of the Russian Federation by virtue of which certain disputes may not be submitted to arbitration or may be submitted to arbitration only according to provisions other than those of this Law." According to the Federal Law No. 102, Article 1(2) any dispute arising from civil law relationships can be referred to the arbitration, unless another federal law provides to the contrary.[40] The same norm is present in Federal Law No. 382 (Article 1(3)). These provisions are inspired by the idea of autonomy of the parties, the right to arbitrate being understood as a constitutional liberty.

One issue persisted about whether the rules on exclusive jurisdiction of the commercial courts exempted certain disputes from arbitration. Private law disputes are divided between the jurisdiction of the courts of general jurisdiction and the commercial courts. The division of jurisdiction lead to establishing the "exclusive competence" of the commercial courts in the areas involving the rights in immovable property and other assets, such as, stocks and shares, which require public registration, as well as claims relating to intellectual property and related disputes.[41]

Russian commercial courts have interpreted this "exclusivity" regulation as broadly relating to arbitrations in general. A series of awards have been questioned and not executed due to the uncertainty over the issue of "exclusivity" of the commercial courts. The court practice of not enforcing arbitral has been opposed by the Russian Constitutional Court. In its seminal Statement No. 10-P of May 26, 2011 (binding on the lower courts according to Article 79 of the Constitution), the Constitutional Court interpreted Article 248 (exclusive jurisdiction of commercial courts) as applicable to courts of general jurisdiction and held that limitations imposed on the jurisdiction of some state courts does not affect the objective scope of arbitration under Russian arbitration law.[42] Another longstanding issue was the arbitrability of corporate

---

[39] If both parties are residents of Russia, the Russian court would invalidate the arbitration clause that refers the disputes to the international arbitration. *See, e.g.*, Statement of the Seventeenth Commercial Appellate Court (Perm) of Nov. 22, 2018 No. 17АП-17735/2018-ГК on the case No. А60-27607/2018.

[40] At present, there exists only one law in the Russian Federation, Federal Law No. 127 of Oct. 26, 2002, on insolvency (bankruptcy) that requires all claims against the bankrupt should be brought within the insolvency procedure (Article 126 and Article 63 (1)). Article 33 (3) of Federal Law No. 127 directly prohibits the referral bankruptcy disputes to arbitration. *See also*, Statement No. 35 of the Presidium of the Highest Commercial Court of June 22, 2012, (Point 27) (bankruptcy disputes are exempted from arbitration).

[41] CPC Article 248(1)) provides that the exclusive jurisdiction of commercial courts of the Russian Federation in cases involving foreign parties belong the cases on:

(1) disputes regarding state-owned assets of the Russian Federation, including disputes relating to the privatization of state property and expropriation of property for public purposes;
(2) disputes regarding real property, or the titles to it, if such property is located in the Russian Federation;
(3) disputes related to the registration or issuance of patents and the registration and issuance of certificates for trademarks, industrial designs, utility models or registration of other rights to intellectual property that require registration or issuance of a patent or a certificate in the Russian Federation;
(4) disputes to invalidate entries in public registers (inventories), filed by the competent authorities of the Russian Federation, leading such a register (inventory);
(5) disputes relating to the establishment, liquidation or registration in the Russian Federation legal entities and individual entrepreneurs, as well as challenging the decisions of these entities.

[42] B. Karabelnikov & D. Pellew, *Enforcement of International Arbitral Awards in Russia – Still a Mixed Picture*, 19 ICC COURT BULLETIN 65–85, 71 (2008); KARABELNIKOV, *supra* note 20, at 152–160.

disputes. This issue was resolved by Federal Law No. 531 of Dec. 27, 2018,[43] which introduced a new Article 7.1 into Federal Law No. 382 that stated that the arbitration agreement of the parties is the only requirement needed to refer corporate disputes to arbitration.

Presently the only relevant limitation to the objective scope of arbitration of disputes in Russia relies in the distinction of private and public relationships. The respect afforded party autonomy to choose the tribunal does not prevent the state from referring the disputes with public aspects to the state courts. The statute law cited provides that only disputes arising from private relationships can be settled by arbitration. A survey of the court practice of referring the cases connected to the functions of assistance and control to arbitration and to international commercial tribunals 2018 (Point 16) specially emphasizes this criterion and affirms that the exhaustive list of disputes exempted from arbitration provided at Article 33 (2)(1-8) ICAL guarantees adequate balance of public and private interests in the system of protection of rights (Ruling of the Russian Constitutional Court of Feb. 5, 2015, No. 233-O). The survey accumulates several examples of the application of the private/public criterion by the courts. Thus, the federal law of July 18, 2011, on the purchase of goods, works, and services by legal persons of a special kind, No. 223, refers to the private person and implied private nature of the respective relationships. The relationships regulated by the Federal Law No. 223 are not exempted from arbitration. Upholding the decision of lower court, the Federal Commercial Court of the Moscow District in its statement of May 3, 2018, No. A40–93716/2017, indicated that the dispute arising from the concession agreement is a dispute between private parties and does not affect public interests.

On the other hand (Point 15 of the 2018 survey), the disputes arising from the relationships regulated by the Russian legislation on the public contracting system (by the federal law of July 21, 2005, on placing orders for contracting goods, works, and services for public and municipal needs No. 94), in particular, were replaced by the federal law of April 5, 2013, on the contractual system in the sphere of the purchase of goods, works, and services for public and municipal needs (No. 44) and are exempt from arbitration (Article 13 (8) of Federal Law No. 409).

The 2018 survey stresses that disputes arising from public relationships cannot be settled by arbitration (Point 13). In one case a municipality mortgaged municipal land to secure a loan. The bank demanded at the court of primary instance to enforce an arbitral award directed at seizure of the land, and the court ordered a writ of execution. The court of appeal, however, overruled the order, indicating the public nature of the land remaining in the municipal property. Upholding this decision the Russian Highest Court advanced a remarkable reasoning according to which the confidential character of arbitration is incompatible with wide public interest to the municipal property and strict public control thereof. Another ground to refuse recognition of the arbitral award was that seizure of the municipal property equated to its tacit privatization, while the Article 33 (2)(5) ICAL envisages direct exemption of the cases dealing with privatization of state and municipal property from the scope of arbitration.

4 VACATING ARBITRAL AWARDS ISSUED IN RUSSIA

Arbitral awards can be challenged in court under Article 230 (1) of the CPC.[44] A party opposing the award must file recourse for setting aside the award under Article 34 (1) of the ICAL. The party opposing the award must comply with a set of conditions stated in Article 34 (2) of the

---

[43] *See* https://www.eg-online.ru/document/law/392982.

[44] When Article 230 (5) admits that in the cases envisaged by the international treaty of the Russian Federation the foreign arbitral award made under the Russian law can be vacated by the Russian court, the reference is evidently made to the Article V (1)(e) New York Convention, which provides for setting aside the award by the competent authority of the country "in which, or *under the law of which*, that award was made" (emphasis added). This unhappy

ICAL. The following two sections examine when parties are barred from challenging an award and the grounds for vacating domestic awards.

4.1 Refusal from Challenging the Award

There exists a controversy regarding the proper meaning of the Article 34 of the UNCITRAL Model Law: whether a party is barred from challenging an award in court (parties have agreed that the arbitral award would be final and binding). Only a limited number of countries recognize the power of the parties to exclude by agreement any form of judicial control over an arbitral award.[45] For example, under French law[46] parties may decide in their arbitration agreement that the award cannot be set aside.[47] Russia also allows for the exclusion of a right to appeal to a court to set aside an award when there is a previous agreement by the parties that bars such appeals.[48] Such clauses exclude all rights to apply to the court for setting aside the award. This rule applies only to international disputes[49] and does not apply to ad hoc arbitration.

Nonetheless, an award may be set aside if viewed as a violation of public order. An appeal on the ground that the arbitral tribunal violated the scope of the arbitration agreement has been considered in cases where the parties agreed on the finality of the award,[50] but Russian also precludes appeals on this ground. However, there is a debate on whether the public order exception can be more expansively applied. A balance must be struck between the parties' autonomy and the requirements of justice. Excluding consumers and parties in a weaker negotiating position, the courts are inclined to honor the parties' agreement not to appeal in B2B contracts (between commercially sophisticated parties).[51]

4.2 Grounds for Vacation of Arbitral Awards

The grounds for vacating arbitral awards are provided in ICAL Article 34(2) and CPC Article 233(2):

(1) One of the parties to the arbitration agreement lacked legal capacity or the agreement is invalid under the law to which the parties have subordinated the agreement, or – if they did not – under the law of the Russian Federation;

---

wording refers to the procedural law and, thus, provides no base for challenging the awards when Russian substantial law was applied. See on this problem: KARABELNIKOV, *supra* note 20, at 261–267.

[45] R. Khodykin, *National Court Review of Arbitral Awards: Where Do We Go from Here?*, in THE EVOLUTION AND FUTURE OF INTERNATIONAL ARBITRATION 269–285 (S. Brekoulakis, J. D. M. Lew, & L. Mistelis eds., 2016).

[46] Décret No. 2011-48 of Jan. 13, 2011, portant réforme de l'arbitrage (May 1, 2011).

[47] J. Kirby, *Finality and Arbitral Rules: Saying an Award Is Final Does Not Necessarily Make It So*, 29 JOURNAL OF INTERNATIONAL ARBITRATION, 119–128, 127 (2012).

[48] Federal Law of Dec. 29, 2015, on arbitration in the Russian Federation No. 382, Article 40: Challenging the arbitration award

In the arbitration agreement previewing administration of the arbitration by the permanent arbitration body the parties can directly preview, that the arbitral award is final for them. The final arbitral award cannot be vacated. In the arbitration agreement does not preview that the arbitral award is final, such award can be vacated on the grounds envisaged by the procedural statute law of the Russian Federation.

See also, ICAL, Article 34 (1).

[49] A. A. Jagelnitsky & O. D. Petrol, *Agreements on Exclusion of the Right to Appeal the International Arbitration Awards* [in Russian], 2 NEW HORIZONS OF THE INTERNATIONAL ARBITRATION 269–278 (2014).

[50] D. Pellew, *Some Observations on the Current Proposed Reforms to Russian Arbitration Law*, 2 NEW HORIZONS OF THE INTERNATIONAL ARBITRATION 61–78, 67–68 (2014).

[51] R. Khodykin, *Setting Aside Arbitral Awards and Parties Autonomy: Discussing Where to Draw the Line* [in Russian], 5 NEW HORIZONS OF THE INTERNATIONAL ARBITRATION 184–198 (2019).

(2) A party was not duly notified of the arbitration hearings, including the time and place of the hearings, or was [otherwise precluded from] advancing its position;
(3) The award issued was not contemplated by the arbitration agreement, not falling under its conditions or exceeding its scope. If the provisions of the award can be detached from those that do not fall under agreement, only part of the award that does not comply with the scope of the arbitration agreement can be vacated;
(4) Composition of the arbitral tribunal or the arbitral proceeding was not in accordance with the agreement of the parties or with the federal law.

Alternatively, the arbitral award can be set aside, if the court establishes that the subject matter of the dispute cannot be subjected to arbitration according to federal law or if it would be contrary to the public order of the Russian Federation.

Russian arbitration law requires that any appeal be filed within three months from the date the opposing party received the award.[52] If the court finds no grounds for vacating the award it should provide no assessment on the merits of the case. This approach is supported by Survey No. 96 of the Presidium of the Highest Commercial Court of (December 22, 2005) at Point 12 (recognition and enforcement of foreign judgments, vacating arbitral awards and granting writs of execution of arbitral awards).[53] Federal Law No. 409 of September 1, 2016, revised ICAL Article 34 (4) to permit courts to suspend judicial procedures in order to allow for the resumption of arbitration hearings. Alternatively, the court may also preempt the arbitration hearings by ordering respective interim measures and oblige the respondent to provide proper security.[54]

5 RECOGNITION AND ENFORCEMENT OF FOREIGN ARBITRAL AWARDS

This section examines the mechanism for enforcing foreign arbitral awards and the grounds for not enforcing such awards. It then discusses the scope of the public policy exception as a ground for vacating awards.

5.1 Recognition and Enforcement of Foreign Arbitral Awards and Grounds for Refusal

In accordance with the New York Convention, the arbitral awards issued abroad are binding on the parties and enforceable in the Russian Federation.[55] Russian arbitration law recognizes limited grounds for refusal of recognition of foreign arbitral awards. CPC Article 241 (1) treats the recognition and enforcement of foreign arbitral awards as nearly absolute.[56] In the case of the

---

[52] ICAL, Article 34 (3); CPC, Article 230 (3).
[53] Survey of the court practice of referring the cases connected to the functions of support and control to arbitration and to international commercial tribunals, approved by the Presidium of the Highest Court on Dec. 26, 2018. Court practice has been consistent with this principle. See, Moscow Commercial Court Ruling of Aug. 14, 2019, No. A40-130614/19-141-1129: refused to vacate an arbitral award based on ICAC of Feb. 21, 2019, No. M-142/2018, indicating that provisions of the ICAL (Article 34) and of the CPC (Article 233) imply that the court dealing with a challenge should limit itself to establishing the presence or absence of grounds for setting the award aside. See also, Survey 2018 (Point 18) in support of these limitations, referencing Article 46 (1) of Federal Law No. 102 as well as to the Codes of Civil Procedure, Article 420 and CPC, Article 232 (4).
[54] ICAL, Article 36 (2).
[55] CPC, Article 16 (4).
[56] Article 241, recognition and enforcement of the foreign court judgments and foreign arbitral awards:

1. Foreign court judgments issued on the disputes arising in the course of entrepreneurial or other economic activities, arbitral awards and international commercial arbitration awards issued in the territory of foreign states on disputes arising in the course of entrepreneurial or other economic activities should be recognized and enforced in the Russian Federation by commercial courts, if recognition and enforcement of such judgments and awards is previewed by the international treaty of the Russian Federation.

arbitral awards such treaty would be the New York Convention 1958. Since the enactment of the ICAL, the Russian courts have willingly issued writs of execution of foreign arbitral awards.

The policy is that arbitral awards should be promptly executed unless a time period for execution is provided in the award itself. A party simply applies to a Russian court for a writ of execution according to Russian procedural law.[57] The court then determines whether the grounds for refusal of recognition are present or not[58] but is prohibited from reexamining the case on the merits.[59] The limited grounds for nonenforcement of arbitral awards are provided in CPC Article 244: (1) the award did not enter into force under the law of the country that was the seat of the arbitral proceeding; (2) the challenging party was not given timely and proper notice about the time and place of the hearings or was otherwise unable to present its case to the tribunal; (3) the case was not arbitrable since exclusive jurisdiction over the dispute rested with the Russian courts; (4) there is a valid court judgment in the Russian Federation resolving a dispute between the same parties on the same subject and on the same grounds; (5) the court of the Russian Federation has opened a procedure on the case between the same parties on the same subject and on the same grounds, prior to the initiation of the arbitral proceedings, or a court of the Russian Federation previously accepted an application on the dispute between the same parties on the same subject and on the same grounds; (6) the statute of limitations has expired for bringing the arbitral action; and (7) the enforcement of a foreign judgment would be contrary to the public policy of the Russian Federation. ICAL Article 36 (1) lists similar grounds for vacating arbitral awards, including[60] the non-arbitrability of the dispute and the public policy exception (ex officio). The next section explores the public policy ground (popularly known as the public policy exception) for the vacation or nonenforcement of a foreign arbitral award.

5.2 Public Policy Exception

The public policy exception, which allows a competent court to deny recognition and enforcement of an international arbitral award, is recognized in Article V (2)(b) of the New York Convention and replicated in Russian law in CPC Article 244 (1)(7) and ICAL Article 36 (1).[61] The heightened standard of proof and its placement on the party opposing recognition and enforcement of the arbitral award are compatible with the pro-enforcement bias of the New York Convention and the restrictive use the exception in Russian court practice.

In general, the Russian courts refuse to review the merits of arbitral cases on the ground of an alleged violation of public policy. The wording of the Article V (2)(b) of the New York Convention that recognition of a foreign arbitral award may be denied if the court finds that the recognition and enforcement would be contrary to the public policy of the forum state.[62] In contrast to Article V (1), which directly indicates that the violation is to be assessed at the "request of the party against whom it is invoked" as ground of refusal. Russian courts have not followed he trend of reviewing the merits of the award sua sponte. The notion of public policy has been narrowly construed by the Highest Court as referring to "the foundations of societal regime of

---

[57] Federal Law No. 382, Article 41.
[58] CPC, Article 243 (3).
[59] CPC, Article 243 (4); Federal Law No. 382, Article 42.
[60] See also, ICAL, Article 34 (2).
[61] The public policy exception is widely recognized to be of exceptional nature. See N. BLACKABY, C. PARTASIDES, A. REDFERN, & M. HUNTER, REDFERN & HUNTER ON INTERNATIONAL ARBITRATION para. 11–103 (6th ed. 2015).
[62] GUIDE ON THE CONVENTION ON THE RECOGNITION AND ENFORCEMENT OF FOREIGN ARBITRAL AWARDS. NEW YORK, 1958. UNCITRAL SECRETARIAT 273 (Emmanuel Gaillard & George A. Bermann eds., 2017).

the Russian state" and where the application of foreign law would be incompatible with Russian legal consciousness.[63]

Information letter of the Presidium of the Highest Commercial Court of December 22, 2005, states that the "public policy of the Russian Federation implies good faith and equality of the parties, entering private relationships, and equivalence of the remedies of civil law liability to the degree of fault of the breach."[64] This view subordinates the notion of public policy to the general principles of civil law and was correctly criticized.[65] The Russian courts in the following years demonstrated adequate understanding of the public policy exception by narrowly interpreting it to refer to the most fundamental principles of the economic, political, and legal systems of the state. More specifically, court practice has limited the exception to consequences that affect the constitutional rights and liberties of Russian citizens and the security of the state.[66]

Meanwhile, some courts announced their own definition of public policy. The Federal Commercial Court of the North-Western district has stated that public policy "includes not only basic moral and religious principles, economic and cultural traditions that formed Russian civil society, but the founding principles of Russian law as well."[67] Such creativity of the courts apparently contradicts the constitutional foundations of Russian law.[68] In overruling the statement of the North-West Court, the Highest Commercial Court again stressed that courts are not authorized to review foreign arbitral awards on the merits of the case.[69]

The presidium of the Highest Commercial Court issued an information letter on February 26, 2013 relating to application of the public policy exception by commercial courts.[70] The court made clear that in assessing the enforceability of foreign arbitral awards and in considering the public policy exception courts should not review the merits of the case.

The presidium held that the public policy exception only referred to "fundamental and universal legal principles having highest mandatory nature, universality, particular social and public relevance, and forming the basis of the economic, political and legal system of the State."[71] Among the principles it enumerated is the prohibition of actions directly forbidden by mandatory rules of Russian law, which include detriment to the "sovereignty or security of the State, infringe the interests of large social groups, violate the constitutional rights and liberties of private persons." This more precise definition is aligned with the pro-arbitration policy of the Russian Federation. The information letter also provided guidance including that (1) the public policy assessment should not amount to review or revision of the merits of the case, (2) the public policy exception may be applied by the court ex officio, (3) the burden of proof lies

---

[63] Ruling of the civil cases collegium of the RF Highest Court of Sept. 25, 1998 (1999) Bulletin of the RF Highest Court, 3, p. 13.

[64] No. 96 at Point 29.

[65] KARABELNIKOV & PELLEW, supra note 42, at 71.

[66] E.g., Statement of the FCC Eastern-Siberian district of Jan. 22, 2007, No. A51–5134/06-F02–7285/06-C2. Numerous examples of such developed interpretation of public policy can be found at KARABELNIKOV, supra note 20, at 397.

[67] Statement of the FCC North-West district of Apr. 24, 2009, No. A56–60007/2008; statement of the FCC North-West district of Sept. 18, 2009, No. A21–802/2009; statement of the FCC North-West district of Mar. 6, 2012, No. A56–49603/2011.

[68] Convincing critics at P. De Vareilles-Sommières & I. V. Getman-Pavlova, *Violation of "Super-Mandatory" Rules as Ground for Refusal of Recognition and Enforcement of Foreign Arbitral Awards (Court Practice of France and Russia)*, 1 LAW. JOURNAL OF HIGH SCHOOL OF ECONOMICS 22–42, 38 (2015).

[69] Statement of the Highest Commercial Court of Sept. 13, 2011, No. 9899/09.

[70] Information Letter No. 156. In English, a clear exposition and assessment of the Information Letter No. 156 can be found at Anton Asoskov & Alyona Kucher, *Are Russian Courts Able to Keep Control over the Unruly Horse? The Long-Awaited Guidance of the Russia's Highest Commercial Court on the Concept of Public Policy*, 30 JOURNAL OF INTERNATIONAL ARBITRATION 581–589 (2013).

[71] The definition is quoted at The UNCITRAL Secretariat Guide on the New York Convention, p. 259.

on the party opposing the recognition and enforcement, (4) the public policy exception does not substitute for special grounds for refusal of recognition and enforcement, and (5) foreign arbitral awards do not violate the public order of the Russian Federation on the sole ground that the applied norms represented by the foreign law do not correspond to the law of the Russian Federation.

The related survey of Information Letter 156 collected precedential examples of applications of the public policy exception to provide recommendations to the lower courts. For example, the fact that the goods at the center of a dispute where not certified, as required by Russian law, did not amount to a violation of public policy, especially since the seller was not obliged to provide such a certification under the contract.[72] In another case, a foreign company did not obtain approval of the large-scale transaction as required under Russian law. Again, the information letter stated that the lack of approval did not constitute a violation of public policy, since it was not required by the corporate law to which the foreign company was subjected. The court reasoned that not obtaining the approval affected the rights of the shareholders of the company but not the rights of the counterparty to the transaction.[73]

Furthermore, a party who is not duly informed of the time and place of the arbitration should mount a challenge under Article V (1) and not use the public policy exception.[74] However, the claim of procedural irregularities (lack of due process) is often conflated with the public policy exception. The request for vacation or nonenforcement of an award based procedural irregularities amounts to a violation of public policy. For example, the lack of impartiality of arbitrators has been viewed by Russian courts as contrary to public policy.

In recent years, there has been a trend toward the abuse of the public policy exception by the courts, even in the presence of special grounds for refusal. One recent example of unnecessary duplication of grounds was illustrated in a 2019 ruling of the Economic Collegium of the Highest Court.[75] The High Court affirmed the ruling of the Commercial Court of Moscow City of November 23, 2018, and the statement of the Commercial Court of Moscow District of February 26, 2019. The Highest Court indicated that an award of the London Court of International Arbitration (LCIA), despite the existence of ongoing arbitral proceedings, would violate the public policy of the Russian Federation. This was unnecessary because the award could have been vacated under the separate ground found in Article V (1) (e).[76] The public policy exception should be assessed by the court ex officio. The burden of proof lies on the party opposing the recognition of the award. The high standard of proof implies the presentation of evidence, and this becomes, thus, possible even at the level of appeal.

The Highest Courts have repeatedly stated that not every mandatory rule fits within the category of the public policy of the Russian Federation. The issue of domestic mandatory rules forms part of public policy of the forum state,[77] butthe rules or laws are considered only to be supermandatory rules[78] (rules that cannot be overridden by any international treaty or choice of the law). The courts have stated that a mere contradiction between an award and provisions of

---

[72] Information Letter No. 156, Point 3.
[73] *Id.* at Point 8.
[74] *Id.* at Point 4. See also, UNCITRAL Secretariat Guide on the New York Convention, p. 270.
[75] No. 305-EC19–7556 (June 10, 2019).
[76] LCIA No. 163281 (TRK Holding Ltd) (Aug. 3, 2018). The Highest Court made reference to the Article 31 ICAL on the form of the award available to the parties, while the reference to the Article 36 (1) (reproducing Article 36 (1)(a) UNICITRAL Model Law) corresponding to the Article V (1) New York Convention 1958 would be more appropriate.
[77] Luke Villiers, *Breaking in the "Unruly Horse": The Status of Mandatory Rules of Law as a Public Policy Basis for the Non-Enforcement of Arbitral Awards*, 18 AUSTRALIAN INTERNATIONAL LAW JOURNAL, 155–180, 158 (2011).
[78] Russian CC, Article 1192.

the Russian law does not by itself constitute a violation of public policy amounting to a ground for denial of recognition and enforcement of a foreign arbitral award. This restrictive interpretation of public policy respects the pro-enforcement of arbitral awards inspired by the New York Convention.

The terms *mandatory* and *supermandatory* need clarification because the Russian CC does not make such a distinction, simply stating the "application of mandatory rules."[79] It reasons that only selected rules rise to the level of public policy and are of specific character to gain specific relevance in protecting the rights and interests of the parties. The Russian courts have indicated that the term *mandatory*, as used in Article 1192, is misleading and causes confusion over distinguishing mandatory rules and mandatory rules of exceptional character (not excludable by choice of law). The term *supermandatory rules* has been advanced by a prominent Russian scholar[80] and has been widely recognized. The concept of "overriding mandatory rules" was first applied in the Rome Convention on the Law Applicable to Contractual Obligations 1980[81] and was reproduced in the Article 1192 of the Russian CC.

The Russian CC of 2013 changed the wording of Article 1192 with the term *rules of immediate application*. The wording "rules of immediate application" speaks to the recent Statement No. 24 of the Plenum of the Highest Court of July 9, 2019, on application of rules of the international private law by the courts of the Russian Federation,[82] with the reference to Article 1192 of the Russian CC. Statement No. 24 underlines that not every mandatory rule is rule of immediate application.[83] It states that a "[m]andatory rule has special relevance and falls under rules of immediate application, if its main objective rests in the protection of public interest, connected with the basis of economic, political or legal system of the State."[84] The special mandatory rules regime demands that the court apply such rules ex officio, if it concerns the relationship in dispute.[85] This interpretation appeals to the notion of "public interest," instead of private "rights and legally protected interests" as it is indicated in Article 1192. However, the statement clearly distinguishes the sphere of rules of immediate application from that of public policy and devotes to the latter a separate section.[86] The Highest Court has followed the distinction in the Russian CC where issues of public policy are treated separately from supermandatory rules.[87]

---

[79] *Id.*

[80] O. N. Sadikov, *Mandatory Rules in the International Private Law* [in Russian], 2 MOSCOW JOURNAL OF INTERNATIONAL LAW 71–81 (1992).

[81] EEC's Rome Convention on the Law Applicable to Contractual Obligations of June 19, 1980) OJ L266. The terminology present in Rome Convention 1980 found further application in the Regulation (EC) No. 593/2008 of the European Parliament and of the Council of June 17, 2008, on the law applicable to contractual obligations (Rome I), where the term "overriding mandatory provisions" (Article 9 (1)) is used. The Regulation (EC) No. 593/2008 of the European Parliament and of the Council of June 17, 2008, on the law applicable to contractual obligations (Rome I), Article 9 overriding mandatory provisions: "Overriding mandatory provisions are provisions the respect for which is regarded as crucial by a country for safeguarding its public interests, such as its political, social or economic organisation, to such an extent that they are applicable to any situation falling within their scope, irrespective of the law otherwise applicable to the contract under this Regulation."

[82] Statement of the Plenum of the Highest Court of July 9, 2019, on application of rules of the international private law by the courts of the Russian Federation No. 24 Russian Newspaper, Federal Issue, No. 154 (7912).

[83] *See* Russian CC, Article 422.

[84] Statement, *supra* note 82, at Point 10.

[85] *Id.* at Point 11.

[86] *Id.* at Point 12.

[87] Article 1193 RF Civil Code:

> The rule of the foreign law applicable according to the provisions of the present Section [i.e., Choice of Law – Section VI. Private International Law] should not be applied in the exceptional cases, when the consequences

The notion of rule of immediate application belongs to the realm of conflict of laws and makes part of the process of assessing applicable law, a determination of public policy in deciding the enforceability of foreign arbitral awards. The use of the public policy exception subordinates parties' autonomy to the general and indispensable principles of a national legal system. Still the area of overriding rules as distinct from public policies is somewhat unsettled. The concept of overriding rules is much narrower than that of public policy that has been narrowly construed by the Russian courts.[88]

Statement No. 24 also recognizes the courts' authority to take into consideration foreign overriding rules where the arbitral dispute directly implicates the rules of a foreign country. In assessing the consequences of application of such rules the court must decide whether the foreign rules' objectives and nature contradict Russian public policy (affect sovereignty or security of the Russian Federation, violate constitutional rights and liberties of Russian physical or legal persons). The statement stresses the exceptional character of the public policy exception which contradicts the chosen law of the dispute selected by the disputants.

6 CONCLUSION

This review of the Russian arbitration system reveals the intimate relation between the state courts and arbitration. Arbitration as a means of dispute resolution is supported by a pro-arbitration ideology embodied in federal statutory law, backed by statements of the highest courts, surveys of the court practice, and seminal decisions. On the other hand, the lower courts continue to oppose the alternative dispute resolution system, especially in regard to international commercial arbitration.

The reluctance of the Russian state courts to recognize foreign arbitration competence is mitigated by general recognition of the competence–competence principle in Russia. The enforcement of foreign arbitral awards is compulsory. Nonetheless, the lower courts continue to abuse the public policy exception to not enforce foreign arbitral awards. Recent reform of domestic arbitration is expected to further enlarge the scope of arbitration, to promote international arbitration in Russia, and to facilitate the recognition and enforcement of foreign arbitral awards.

---

of its application are apparently contrary to the basis of legal order (public policy) of the Russian Federation. In such case, if needed, the respective rule of Russian law should be applied.

The refusal of application of the rule of foreign law cannot be based only on the difference of legal, political, or economic system of the respective foreign state from the legal, political, or economic system of the Russian Federation.

[88] Statement of July 9, 2019, No. 24 recognizes the special nature of mandatory rules that relater to objects of private rights, the limitations on the acquisition of land plots or shares in some companies by foreigners, and circumstances precluding conclusion of marriage by a foreigner on the territory of the Russian Federation.

20

Judicial Control of Arbitral Awards in Spain

Teresa Rodríguez de las Heras Ballell

1 SPANISH ARBITRATION ACT IN CONTEXT[1]

1.1 Evolution and Main Features

Arbitration enjoys a long tradition in Spain.[2] It has been consistently recognized by and promoted throughout historical laws[3] as an alternative method for dispute resolution. The recognition of arbitration in legal texts can be traced to Spanish medieval law.[4] *Breviario de Alarico*, or *Lex Romana Visigothorum*,[5] promulgated on February 2, 506, and *Liber Iudiciorum*,[6] among others, acknowledged that the value of arbitration was definitively enshrined in the fundamental *Siete Partidas*.[7] Since then, a series of famous arbitral awards – *Compromiso de Caspe* 1321 and 1363 (the Covenant of Caspe), *Sentencia Arbitral de Guadalupe* 1486 (the Arbitral Award of Guadalupe) – and regal laws in Castile fostered the institution by ordering the enforcement of commitments agreed by the parties (*Ordenanza de Madrid* of 1502). These legal and arbitral decisions paved the way to the incorporation of the institution of arbitration into the *Novísima Recopilación* (1804).[8] The resort to arbitration for solving disputes among merchants

---

[1] The following acronyms referring to judgments of Spanish courts are used in the chapter: STC (decision of Spanish Constitutional Court); STS (decision of the Spanish Supreme Court); STSJ (decision of High Court of Justice); SAP (decision of Provincial Court). For search purposes, judgments are identified according to the Spanish rules and in relation to the different available databases for case law. To that end, location number and reference are added with the following codes: AC, RAJ or RJ, REC, ECLI or LALEY.

[2] ANTONIO MERCHÁN ÁLVAREZ, EL ARBITRAJE. ESTUDIO HISTÓRICO-JURÍDICO (1981).

[3] ANTONIO FERNÁNDEZ DE BUJÁN, JURISDICCIÓN Y ARBITRAJE EN DERECHO ROMANO (2006); GABRIEL BUIGUES OLIVER, LA SOLUCIÓN AMISTOSA DE LOS CONFLICTOS EN DERECHO ROMANO: EL ARBITER EX COMPROMISSO (1990).

[4] RAFAEL ALTAMIRA, SPAIN: SOURCES AND DEVELOPMENT OF LAW (Carlos Petit ed. & comm., 2017); RAMÓN MENÉNDEZ PIDAL, HISTORIA DE ESPAÑA (1964).

[5] A compilation of post-classical vulgar Roman law elaborated during the reign of Alarico II (484–507 B.C.E.).

[6] Divided in twelve books and fifty-four chapters, *Liber Iudiciorum* contained a unitary legal regime for civil, criminal and ecclesiastical matters promulgated by Recesvinto in 654 B.C.E. The text is in www.boe.es/biblioteca_juridica/publicacion.php?id=PUB-LH-2015-2&tipo=L&modo=2.

[7] *Las Siete Partidas* are a body of rules drafted by the crown of Castile under the reign of Alfonso X, a.k.a. "The Wise," with the aim of achieving legal uniformity for the kingdom. It is deemed one of the most important contributions to the history of law and a "humanist encyclopedia," as it tackled philosophical, moral, and theological issues with a Greco-Latin approach. It is written in Castilian Spanish and constitutes an instrument of ordinary law based on Justinian Roman Law, Canonical Law, and Feudal Law. The text is in www.boe.es/biblioteca_juridica/publicacion.php?id=PUB-LH-2011-60&tipo=L&modo=2.

[8] The *Novísima Recopilación* of the laws of Spain is a compilation of 4,044 laws in 340 chapters and twelve books published in 1805. The facsimile is in www.boe.es/publicaciones/biblioteca_juridica/publicacion.php?id=PUB-LH-1993-63_NOV%C3%8DSIMA_RECOPILACI%C3%93N_DE_LAS_LEYES_DE_ESPA%C3%91A&tipo=L&modo=1.

and guilds, as a response to their aversion to ordinary courts, gave a lot of impetus to arbitration during that period.

The most relevant landmark of the legal presence and recognition of arbitration in the Spanish historical legal system is the enshrining of arbitration in the liberal Constitution of 1812[9] as a fundamental right. Under its liberalism tenets, the Constitution of 1812 provided for the right of parties to settle their disputes by arbitration and the equalization of the legal value of arbitral awards and court decisions.[10]

The constitutional enshrinement of arbitration in the liberal Constitution of 1812 represented a crucial milestone in the shaping of the arbitral institution in the Spanish legal system. Nevertheless, the nineteenth-century liberalism inspiring the Constitution of Cádiz led to a scattered threefold legal treatment of arbitration that in practice hampered its development and growth. The legal regime for arbitration was divided into three texts. First, commercial arbitration was contained in the provisions of the Commercial Code of 1829 (by Sainz de Andino); second, the validity and enforceability of arbitration clause was regulated by the provisions of the draft Civil Code of 1851 and the Civil Code of 1889 (by García Goyena) as a contract; third, procedural aspects of arbitration and a complex system of appeals were included in the Civil Procedural Act of 1881.

That tripartite regulation of arbitration harmed the consolidation of arbitration and its expansion stalled. The Arbitration Act of 1953[11] did not unblock that unfavorable situation. On the contrary, it adopted a highly restrictive and strongly formalist trend that stifled arbitration. Finally, the post-Constitution (Constitution of 1978) Arbitration Act of 1988[12] reversed that deceleration process and aimed to modernize the institution and align again the Spanish legal system with international practices and comparative law. In 1977, Spain had ratified the New York Convention,[13] which entered into force on August 10, 1977.

The definitive completion of the modernization cycle is undertaken by the enactment of the current Spanish Arbitration Act in 2003[14] (hereinafter LA). The LA, based on the UNCITRAL Model Law and aligned with international principles, succeeded in setting a modern legal framework for arbitration that has enabled a very positive evolution and sound consolidation of arbitration in Spain over almost two decades. Subsequent amendments of the LA made in 2011 and 2015[15] have also entailed significant improvements, such as the explicit recognition of the arbitrability of intra-corporate disputes.[16]

With a longstanding tradition and a few setbacks in history, arbitration has today in Spain a sound, modern, reliable, and arbitration-friendly legal system.[17]

---

[9] The Spanish constitution of the Spanish monarchy, popularly called Constitution of Cádiz, was promulgated by the Spanish Parliament, exceptionally convened in Cádiz, on Mar. 19, 1812. It is considered a fundamental historical landmark for the Spanish legal system as it was the first constitution enacted in Spain and one of the most liberal constitutions of its time.

[10] Antonio Merchán Álvarez, *La jurisdicción arbitral en la Constitución de Cádiz*, 15 HISTORIA. INSTITUTIONES. DOCUMENTOS 127–144 (1988).

[11] Law of Dec. 22, 1953, on Arbitration of Private Law, published in Official Bulletin (BOE) number 358, of Dec. 24, 1953.

[12] Law 36/1988, of Dec. 5, on arbitration, published in Official Bulletin (BOE) number 293, of Dec. 7, 1988.

[13] Convention on the Recognition and Enforcement of Foreign Arbitral Awards (New York, 1958).

[14] Law 60/2003, of Dec. 23, on arbitration, published in Official Bulletin (BOE) number 309, of Dec. 26, 2003.

[15] Law 42/2015, of Oct. 5, of reform of the Civil Procedural Law 1/2000, published in Official Bulletin (BOE) number 239, Oct. 6, 2015. This reform law amended only paragraph 1 of Article 11 LA.

[16] José Fernando Merino Merchán, *Configuración del arbitraje intrasocietario en la Ley 11/2011*, 52 EL NOTARIO DEL SIGLO XXI 1–4 (2013).

[17] A system that preserves its Roman law and Greco-Latin roots, as unveiled and stressed in ANTONIO FERNÁNDEZ DE BUJÁN, LA DEUDA HISTÓRICA DEL ARBITRAJE MODERNO. CONCORDANCIAS ENTRE LA LEY 60/2003, DE ARBITRAJE Y EL

1.2 Numbers and Statistics: Arbitration in Spain

Arbitration, together with other alternative dispute resolution mechanisms such as mediation and conciliation, is preferred by parties to settle their conflicts almost as much as judicial adjudication. A recent survey on the arbitration in Spain[18] reveals than 47 percent of interviewed parties prefer arbitration as the primary and sole mechanism (27 percent) or in combination with other alternative dispute resolution mechanisms (20 percent). Although these data prove that arbitration is firmly established in Spain as a dispute resolution method, the choice of court adjudication is still prevailing (53 percent).

Furthermore, the resort to arbitration has not yet pervaded the entire business market as the predominant use is concentrated in certain sectors and business areas. As a matter of fact, the primary users of arbitration are big companies – with turnover higher than €5,000 million. Nevertheless, the preference for the arbitration as the ideal dispute resolution mechanism significantly raises in case of international disputes (89 percent).

In general terms, the rapidity in the settling of disputes and the expertise and specialized knowledge of arbitrators are perceived as the most positive advantages of arbitration compared to court adjudication. However, the cost of the arbitration proceedings and the lack of case law are deemed as the most deterring disadvantages. Such a perception confirms, indeed, the mainstream concern that the cost is a critical point in the expansion and the success of arbitration, both at a domestic level and at an international one.

After nearly a decade and a half of application, the LA has meant an undisputable advance for the development and the quality of arbitration in Spain. Quantitative data, in terms of the number of arbitral proceedings, as well as qualitative aspects enshrined in the LA – unitary model, anti-formalism, recognition of foreign arbitral awards, etc. – demonstrated the achievements of the LA. Within a broader modernization program of the justice administration, that would include a law on mediation of commercial and civil disputes, the need to enhance the effectiveness and amend those aspects of the LA, which practice had left room for improvement, was considered. Hence, the most recent amendment of the LA was undertaken in 2011. The Organic Law 11/2011, of May 20, on the reform of Arbitration Act and the regulation of the institutional arbitration in the State Public Administration,[19] is published in the Official Bulletin concurrently with the Organic Law 5/2011, which complements the former with the required amendments on the judiciary legal framework (Ley 6/1985 del Poder Judicial). The simultaneous reform in the judicial and the arbitral legal regimes is explained by the need to regulate the judicial assistance and control of arbitration. Hence, the most significant changes undertaken in 2011 were related to the jurisdiction of the High Courts of Justice (Tribunales Superiores de Justicia) for the judicial appointment and removal of arbitrators, the annulment of arbitral awards, and the recognition of foreign arbitral awards. Such fundamental changes, in conjunction with other miscellaneous amendments to provisions related to procedures, awards, or arbitrators were aimed to strengthen arbitrators' capacity and responsibility, avoid conflicts of interest, reinforce the independence and transparency of arbitral institutions, and thereby enhance the attractiveness of Spain as a venue

---

DERECHO ARBITRAL GRIEGO Y ROMANO (2017), where the author draws the concordances between the current Spanish Arbitration Act of 2003 and the arbitration rules in Greco and Roman Laws.

[18] *Primer Estudio de Arbitraje en España*, ROCA JUNYENT (2018), http://www.rocajunyent.com/content/uploads/informe_rocajunyent_digital.pdf.

[19] Law 5/2011, of May 20, modifying the Organic Law on Judicial Power and Law 11/2011, of May 20, modifying the law on the regulation of the institutional arbitration in the State Public Administration.

for international arbitration. Subsequently, only minor amendments have been made by the Law 42/2015, of October 5, 2015, that reforms the Civil Procedural Law.

1.3 Essence of Arbitration: Constitutionality and Sphere of Arbitrability

The Spanish Constitutional Court (hereinafter, TC) has repeatedly confirmed – decision numbers 43/1988, 233/1988, 15/1989, 288/1993, and 174/1995 – the compatibility of arbitration with the right of access to justice as enshrined in Article 24 of Spanish Constitution of 1978.[20] Against the arguments argued by those voices,[21] which question the constitutionality of arbitration as a waiver of access to justice, the TC upholds that a party's autonomy constitutes the legal ground for affirming the constitutionality of arbitration. That approach captures the classical motto *ubi partes sunt concordes nihil adjudicem* (when both parties are in agreement, a judge is not needed).[22] The freedom of the parties to decide to solve their conflicts does not lessen the constitutional right to access justice. On the contrary, it is based on the freedom of the parties as a superior value of the legal system as per Article 1.1 of the Spanish Constitution of 1978.

Even the constitutionality of a legal provision presuming an agreement to settle by arbitration, unless otherwise agreed by the parties, in certain disputes related to ground transportation has been confirmed by the TC in its decision number 352/2006, of December 14, 2006.[23] The TC upheld the constitutionality of the controversial provision (Article 38.1 Law 16/1987 on Ground Transportation),[24] according to which parties are entitled to decide to settle their disputes by arbitration and such an agreement is presumed to exist where the amount of the dispute does not exceed €15,000. The legal presumption applies unless any of the parties expressly manifest the objection to be subject to arbitration before the initiation of the transportation activity. The TC held that the right of any of the parties to express opposition to the *ope legis* presumption any time before the start of the activity is sufficient to avoid an unjustified violation of the right to access to justice as enshrined in Article 24 of the Spanish Constitution. Hence, a legal presumption for the resolution of disputes by arbitration in a specific sector (ground transportation) and under a certain amount (€15,000) is not disproportionate and is in conformity with the Constitution.

Upon the recognition of the total constitutionality of arbitration, the debate has subsequently diverted to a different discussion.[25] Should arbitration be admissible in conflicts related to acts adopted by Public Administration and in Public Law? Unlike other jurisdictions, in the Spanish legal system, a total ban of arbitration ratione personae does not exist, preventing the state and the public authorities from resorting to arbitration in an absolute manner. On the contrary, the historical prohibition[26] has been initially restricted to certain matters (ratione materiae) related

---

[20] José Manuel Bandrés Sánchez-Cruzat, EL DERECHO FUNDAMENTAL AL PROCESO DEBIDO Y EL TRIBUNAL CONSTITUCIONAL (1992).
[21] Juan Carlos Calvo Corbella, *La solución de conflictos mediante el arbitraje y la tutela judicial de derechos*, in I LOS DERECHOS FUNDAMENTALES Y LIBERTADES PÚBLICAS 43–72, 59 & ff (1993).
[22] Ana Fernández Pérez, EL ARBITRAJE ENTRE LA AUTONOMÍA DE LA VOLUNTAD DE LAS PARTES Y EL CONTROL JUDICIAL 247 (2017).
[23] Published in the Official Bulletin (BOE) number 14, Jan. 16, 2007.
[24] Law 16/1987, of July 30, on the Organization of Ground Transportation, published in Official Bulletin (BOE) number 182, July 31, 1987.
[25] José Fernando Merino Merchán, *El arbitraje y el derecho público español. Una propuesta legislativa*, in UNA PROPUESTA PARA LA INTRODUCCIÓN EN NUESTRO SISTEMA ADMINISTRATIVO Y TRIBUTARIO DE MEDIDAS ALTERNATIVAS DE RESOLUCIÓN DE CONFLICTO (ADR) 89–106 (Pablo Chico de la Cámara ed., 2017).
[26] Royal Decree of Bravo Murillo of Feb. 27, 1852, radically excluded from arbitration any dispute concerning rights or assets of the Treasury.

to public-sector activities. That restrictive approach was progressively moderated in a series of legislation enacted throughout the twentieth century. The softening trend toward a more permissive response culminated in 2011, with the express legal recognition that public entities and bodies performing functions in the public sector, provided that they do not have the character of public administration, are entitled to solve disputes by arbitration in conformity with the current LA.

In the consolidation of this expanding trend, LA took a significant step forward. Article 2.2 LA acknowledges the possibility that in international arbitration – noting that the Spanish LA has followed a monist approach as it applies to both domestic and international arbitration – one of the parties may be a state or an enterprise or organization controlled by a state. In those cases, the Preamble of the LA declares that "the State shall be treated as a private party." The state or governmental bodies are not entitled to claim either sovereign immunity or immunity from enforcement of an award by invoking legal prerogatives. Thus, the Spanish LA is unequivocally aligned with the UNCITRAL Model Law and the New York Convention.[27]

Preceding the earlier-referred provision (Article 2.2), the first paragraph of Article 2 encapsulates the policy decision defining the scope and importance given to arbitration as an alternative method for dispute resolution. With a generously opened declaration[28] – "all disputes relating to matters that may be freely disposed of at law can be settled by arbitration"[29] – LA amply demarcates the sphere of "arbitrability" under the abstract notion of "freely disposable" matters. That entails that there is no list of excluded matters in the LA; therefore, a specific legal basis for an exception should be found and proven in each case. Thus, Article 2.1 decisively conveys a general principle in favor of arbitration. Not only is arbitrability relevant in a positive scoping exercise but also the lack of arbitrability is critical as a limitation to the validity of arbitral awards, the legal grounds for setting them aside, and to the recognition and enforcement of those awards.

In absence of a list of excluded matters and in the face of such a general declaration, "exceptions to arbitrability are in decline."[30] The proliferation of special arbitration in a number of sectors – consumer arbitration, transport, intellectual property, trademarks and industrial designs, leasing, telecommunications, sport, employment – has attracted to the realm of arbitration multiple disputes. Although in such cases, the LA, as the general law, applies only on a subsidiary basis (Article 1.3 LA), except for employment arbitration that is subject to its own law and not the LA.

2 ANNULMENT OF ARBITRAL AWARDS: PERIMETER AND GROUNDS

Title VII of the LA contains the rules on setting aside and reviewing arbitral awards. In conformity with Article 34 (Chapter VII) of the UNCITRAL Model Law and based on the Geneva Convention on International Commercial Arbitration of 1961 (Article IX), signed by

---

[27] Carlos González-Bueno, *Article 2 Matters Subject to Arbitration*, in THE SPANISH ARBITRATION ACT. A COMMENTARY 17–21 (Carlos González-Bueno ed., 2016).
[28] *Id.* at 17.
[29] Original version in Spanish, Article 2.1 LA: "Son susceptibles de arbitraje las controversias sobre materias de libre disposición conforme a derecho."
[30] González-Bueno, *supra* note 27, at 19.

Spain in 1961 and subsequently ratified in 1975, Article 40 LA states that recourse against arbitral awards may be made only by an application for setting aside in accordance with the provisions of Title VII of the LA. In addition, although arbitral awards constitute res judicata, under exceptional circumstances and exclusively on the grounds provided for the review of final court decisions in the Civil Procedural Law (Article 510 LEC), arbitral awards may be reviewed.

2.1 Grounds for Setting Aside Arbitral Awards

Article 40 LA sets out the grounds for setting aside an arbitral award that mirrors the six grounds for setting aside provided for by Article 34(2) UNCITRAL Model Law. In accordance with Article 40(1) LA, an arbitral award may be set aside only if the applicant alleges and furnishes proof: (a) that the arbitration agreement does not exist or is not valid; (b) that the applicant was not given proper notice of the appointment of an arbitrator or of the arbitral proceedings or was otherwise unable to present his case; (c) that the award contains decisions on questions not submitted to arbitration; (d) that the appointment of the arbitrators or the arbitral procedure was not in accordance with the agreement of the parties, unless such agreement was in conflict with an imperative provision of this act, or, failing such agreement, the agreement was not in accordance with this act; (e) that the subject matter of the dispute is not apt for settlement by arbitration; and (f) that the award is in conflict with public policy.

Unlike Article 34 of the UNCITRAL Model Law, the LA does provide that the court may appreciate and determine the existence of not only the circumstances laid down under letters (e) and (f) (non-arbitrability and conflict with public policy), as the UNCITRAL Model Law does, but also the fact that "the party making the application was not given proper notice of the appointment of an arbitrator or of the arbitral proceedings or was otherwise unable to present his case" (letter b). In such cases, the court may act on its own initiative or upon the request of the public prosecutor in connection with those interests which fall under the latter's protection.

A first assessment of the legal regime for annulment of arbitral awards in the Spanish system based on the mere comparison of the legal provisions with the UNCITRAL Model Law's ones produces a positive and favorable outcome. The Spanish law on arbitration is entirely aligned with the international principles on setting aside arbitral awards. First, as the Spanish Constitutional Court held in the decision 288/1993, of October 4, arbitration is recognized as a "jurisdictional equivalent," insofar as parties can attain effects equal to those produced by courts, a decision settling a dispute with res judicata effect. Second, the recourses against arbitral awards are then limited to annulment in specific circumstances. Third, the grounds for setting aside arbitral awards do fully mirror the ones provided for by the UNCITRAL Model Law. No deviation or significant change from the international patterns in that regard exist. Finally, any attempt to use annulment as an appeal recourse to review the merits of the case or attack an award simply for the disagreement of the parties with the decision is rejected and fails (see Spanish Supreme Court judgment of February 21, 2006).

Yet, the analysis of the case law and the observation of judicial praxis do also confirm the afore statement. The line of reasoning consolidated by Spanish case law on annulment of arbitral awards and recognition of foreign arbitral awards reveals an adequate understanding and application of international principles. As a basic consideration, it can be affirmed that setting aside of arbitral awards on the specific grounds as provided for by the law is correctly applied and construed within its limited scope and in perfect consistency with international trends and the interpretative background. As the Spanish Constitutional Court held in several decisions, the use of annulment to review how the merits of the case were judged would denaturalize the institution of arbitration as a legitimate alternative dispute resolution mechanism.[31]

Not surprisingly, the number of applications for setting aside arbitral awards is statistically low. Although there is no continuity in the available data that would allow drawing a consistent statistical trend, according to the data provided by the Court of Arbitration of Madrid[32] in 2018, no arbitral award was annulled of the 111 cases managed with an aggregated value of €1,100 million. Qualitative data do also confirm the same perception. According to the afore-referred survey on the arbitration in Spain, 74 percent of the respondents had not been involved in annulment proceedings in the previous annual period and 26 percent had been immersed in one to five proceedings in the same period. The perception of the success of the application for setting aside an arbitral award is majorly low. More than 90 percent of the surveyed companies estimate the rate of success in less than 10 percent. Among the grounds for setting aside, public policy (50 percent) and infringement of procedural rules (37 percent) are the most frequently alleged as per the survey on arbitration in Spain.[33]

2.2 Interpretation and Application by Courts

The following discussion is focused on three selected grounds for setting aside arbitral awards as per Article 41 LA and in line with judicial interpretation. Section 3 is entirely devoted to the analysis of public order as grounds for setting aside.

2.2.1 Arbitration Agreement

Article 41.1.a) LA states that the arbitral award can be set aside if the applicant party alleges and provides that "the arbitration agreement does not exist or is not valid." It leads to several scenarios from the total inexistence of an arbitration agreement and invalidity cases, to issues related to the scope of the arbitration agreement, and the inclusion of the clause in adhesion contracts. The following sections review the requirements to create an enforceable arbitration agreement.

2.2.1.1 EXISTENCE OF A CLEAR, UNEQUIVOCAL, AND OBSERVABLE CONSENT The key element to declare a valid arbitration agreement is the existence of a clear, unequivocal, and observable consent of the parties to settle the dispute by arbitration.[34] Concurrently, it entails an unequivocal, but not necessarily express, waiver to ordinary courts. Article 9 LA has lessened the formalities for a valid arbitration agreement. But the consent of the parties must be always unequivocal and accredited. Court decisions reaffirm the prevailing value of consent over any "ritual form" or special formality that is not required for an arbitration agreement to be valid.[35] Accordingly, extremely condensed formulae such as "ag/arb Londres" in an email suffices to express unequivocal consent.[36] Only in cases where arbitration clauses are so confusing[37] or

---

[31] Spanish Constitutional Court decisions 174/1995 of Nov. 23, 1995 (LA LEY 651/1996) (ECLI STC:1995:174); and 75/1996 of Apr. 30, 1996 (LA LEY 5506/1996) (ECLI: ES TC: 1996:75).
[32] *Factsheet 2018*, MADRID COURT OF ARBITRATION, arbitramadrid.com/web/guest/estadisticas-2017.
[33] *Supra* note 18.
[34] *See* STS Feb. 6, 2003 (RJ 850/2003); Feb. 11, 2010 (ECLI:ES:TS:2010:1669); June 27, 2017 (ECLI:ES:TS:2017:2500).
[35] *See* STS Feb. 6, 2003 (RAJ 2003/805).
[36] Auto TSJ of Andalucía of Oct. 28, 2014, ECLI:ES:TSJAND:2014:161A; Auto TSJ of Cataluña of May 6, 2016, ECLI: TSJCAT:2016:208A.
[37] Auto AP of Tarragona Jan. 25. 2017, ECLI:ES:APT:2017:152ª declares null a clause stating that parties decide to settle their disputes by arbitration "at the Courts of Madrid."

contradictory[38] that no agreement to settle by arbitration can be accredited, courts have declared the arbitration clause invalid or inexistent.

2.2.1.2 VALIDITY OF HYBRID CLAUSES Case law on the validity of "hybrid, optional, or split dispute resolution clauses" has been, however, erratic.[39] Hybrid clauses[40] entitle any of the parties (in the case of symmetric clauses) acting as the claimant, or one of the parties (in the case of asymmetric clauses) to choose between arbitration or ordinary jurisdiction, or among different jurisdictions, to settle the dispute. The Supreme Court held in certain cases[41] that the concurrence of an arbitration agreement with a choice-of-court agreement does not annul both, as it must be interpreted as the decision of the parties to resort to those courts where the arbitration agreement does not apply or when they voluntarily renounce arbitration; in other cases,[42] the same Supreme Court states that the choice of forum undermines the existence of a real unequivocal will of the parties to settle by arbitration. Nonetheless, the rigorous interpretation of the traditional requirement of "unequivocal choice" for the validity of an arbitration clause has been progressively attenuated. Consequently, optional, hybrid, or multitiered clauses would not be afflicted by an inherent contradiction. Hence, an increasing jurisprudential line admitting the validity of hybrid clauses – drafted as symmetric clauses – is gaining consistency.[43] The validity of asymmetric hybrid clauses is (in absence of clear judicial decisions) more uncertain.[44]

2.2.1.3 RULES OF INTERPRETATION AND THE SCOPE OF THE ARBITRATION AGREEMENT Arbitration agreements, either drafted as an individual clause in a contract or as an entire agreement, are made equivalent by the Spanish Supreme Court to any other legal transaction.[45] Accordingly, arbitration agreements must be interpreted in accordance with general rules of contract interpretation as laid down in the Civil Code.[46] Interpretation is critical for demarcating the scope of the arbitration agreement. In delineating the material scope of arbitration clauses, the analysis of the Supreme Court decision 409/2017 of June 27, 2017,[47] provides substantial reasoning and illustrative insights. In the factual scenario, two relevant issues were interwoven. First, the fact that the arbitration clause was included in a standard form contract that was a master agreement for future financial transactions between the parties. Second, the drafting of the clause[48] referred to "any and all conflicts arising from the contract, its interpretation, its

---

[38] SAP Madrid of Apr. 2, 2004, JUR 2004\248159 declares null a clause stating an appeal of the arbitral award before ordinary courts as it contradicts the basis of arbitration.
[39] STS of Feb. 11, 2010, ECLI:ES:TS:2010:1669.
[40] The category of hybrid clauses may also include the multitiered or multistep clauses where the optional scheme is established in relation to diverse alternative dispute resolution methods (mediation, negotiation, arbitration).
[41] STS of July 10, 2007, ECLI:ES:TS:2007:4828. Lower courts have also upheld the admissibility of hybrid clauses such as the Provincial Court (AP) of Madrid in its order (Auto) of Oct. 18, 2013 (LA LEY 172387/2013).
[42] STS of Feb. 11, 2010, ECLI:ES:TS:2010:1669.
[43] MIGUEL Á FERNÁNDEZ-BALLESTEROS, AVENENCIA O ADR. NEGOCIACIÓN, MEDIACIÓN, PERITAJES, CONCILIACIÓN, PACTOS Y TRANSACCIONES (2014). See for instance STS July 10, 2007 (LA LEY 72190/2007); STS Jan. 12, 2009 (LA LEY 1908/2009).
[44] Álvaro López de Argumedo Piñeiro & C. Balmaseda, La controvertida validez de las cláusulas híbridas y asimétricas en Europa a propósito del auto de 18 de octubre de 2013 de la Audiencia Provincial de Madrid, 8258 DIARIO LA LEY (2014).
[45] Miguel Gómez Jene, El Convenio Arbitral: Statu Quo, 2 CUADERNOS DE DERECHO TRANSNACIONAL 7–38(2017).
[46] STS May 27, 2007 (REC 2613/2000).
[47] For a commentary, see Ana Isabel Blanco García & Pablo Quinzá Redondo, Control judicial de la validez del convenio arbitral en un contrato de adhesión: Sentencia núm. 409/2017 de 27 de junio del Tribunal Supremo, 10 CUADERNOS DE DERECHO TRANSNACIONAL 544–550 (2018).
[48] In the original version in Spanish: "toda controversia o conflicto que se derive del presente contrato, su interpretación, cumplimiento y ejecución se someterá a arbitraje."

performance and its execution." As per Article 9.2 LA, "if the arbitration agreement is included in an adhesion contract, its validity and its interpretation shall be governed by the rules applicable to those contracts." To that end, Spanish Law on Standard Terms 7/1998[49] provides for specific interpretation rules.[50] Notably, the maxim *interpretatio contra proferentem* whereby the clause is construed against the party who has drafted it (*stipulatorem* or *proferentem*).

Parties had entered into two derivative contracts (swaps), concluded in execution of a Framework Agreement for Financial Transactions (CMOF in Spanish) previously signed by the parties – the client and the bank. The arbitration clause at stake was included in the CMOF that it is a contract of adhesion. The client exercised an action before the ordinary court, instead of arbitration, to have the two derivative contracts declared null on the grounds of an invalidating mistake due to lack of precontractual information provided by the bank. The bank based its position on two main allegations. On the one hand, on the basis of the "elastic or expansive effect" of arbitration clauses, as elaborated and defended by part of the jurisprudential doctrine,[51] the scope of the arbitration clause should be expanded to cover nullity and invalidity, although the wording of the clause refers only to interpretation, performance, and execution. On the other hand, the arbitration clause included in the CMOF applies to the two derivative contracts, as they have been concluded in execution of the Framework Agreement. Yet, as the arbitration clause expressly refers to conflicts related to "execution" of the Framework Agreement, any disputes arising from the derivate contracts would be covered by the clause, insofar as both contracts have been concluded "in execution of the CMOF."

Surprisingly, the Supreme Court rejected both arguments and reversed the reasoning. First, insofar as the arbitration clause is included in an adhesion contract, the interpretation rule *contra proferentem* is applicable. Accordingly, the Supreme Court understood that the arbitration clause should be construed restrictively for the benefit of the client. Such a restrictive interpretation entailed not to apply the "elastic effect" of the arbitration clause. Therefore, the Supreme Court upheld that the arbitration clause included in the CMOF did not cover the nullity of the agreement as it was not expressly mentioned in the clause. Second, the Supreme Court held that the CMOF and the derivative contracts are "differentiated transactional units." Hence, the arbitration clause included in the CMOF does not naturally extend over disputes arising from the derivative contracts concluded in its execution.[52] As per the Supreme Court, specific arbitration clauses should have been agreed upon for each derivative contract and included therein accordingly.

The restrictive decision of the Supreme Court surprises because court decisions and legal provisions are clear in stating the validity of an arbitration clause included in adhesion contracts,

---

[49] Law 7/1998, of Apr. 13, on Standard Terms (Contracts of Adhesion), published in Official Bulletin (BOE), Apr. 14, 1998.
[50] Jesús Alfaro Águila-Real, *La interpretación de las condiciones generales de los contratos*, 7–61 REVISTA DE DERECHO MERCANTIL 183–184 (1987); JESÚS ALFARO ÁGUILA-REAL, LAS CONDICIONES GENERALES DE LA CONTRATACIÓN (1991); COMENTARIOS A LA LEY SOBRE CONDICIONES GENERALES DE LA CONTRATACIÓN (Ignacio Arroyo Martínez & Jorge Miquel Rodríguez coords., 1999); RODRIGO BERCOVITZ RODRÍGUEZ-CANO, COMENTARIO A LA LEY DE CONDICIONES GENERALES DE LA CONTRATACIÓN (1999); FEDERICO DE CASTRO Y BRAVO, LAS CONDICIONES GENERALES DE LOS CONTRATOS Y LA EFICACIA DE LAS LEYES (1987); JAVIER PAGADOR LÓPEZ, CONDICIONES GENERALES Y CLÁUSULAS CONTRACTUALES PREDISPUESTAS. LA LEY DE CONDICIONES GENERALES DE LA CONTRATACIÓN (1999); EDUARDO POLO, PROTECCIÓN DEL CONTRATANTE DÉBIL Y LAS CONDICIONES GENERALES DE LOS CONTRATOS (1990).
[51] Among others, STS 741/2007, July 2, 2007 (LA LEY 72193/2007).
[52] An approach that is not shared by some scholars and practitioners – Francisco G. Prol Pérez, *La validez de la cláusula arbitral en una operación de SWAP derivada de un contrato marco de operaciones financieras (CMOF)*, 9070, DIARIO LA LEY, SECCIÓN TRIBUNA (Oct. 27, 2017), 1–9 – nor by lower courts such as Provincial Court of Barcelona decision of May 16, 2017.

which the decision 409/2017 does certainly not deny. Besides, case law of the Supreme Court and lower courts[53] is also conclusive in the expansive interpretation of arbitration clauses under the principle of "elastic or expansive effect." Therefore, it is disconcerting that the Supreme Court adopts a restrictive interpretation and, above all, assumes that the arbitration clause is "obscure" for the purposes of applying the interpretation rules for standard contract terms.

Notwithstanding the relevance of the afore-discussed Supreme Court decision, it seems a deviation from the general jurisprudential line favorable to recognize the "elastic effect" of the arbitration agreement. That might be understood as a circumstantial reaction to counter the pernicious effects of certain banking practices and financial transactions in a post-crisis context. Should that contextualized analysis be acceptable, it would be aligned with the excessive resort to public policy as grounds for setting aside arbitral awards as it is expounded in the following.

2.2.2 Impartiality and Independence of Arbitrators

The impartiality and independence of arbitrators are crucial. In practice, delimiting the circumstances raising reasonable doubts on such independence and impartiality is, however, intricate. In addition to the legal measures established by the legislation, rules adopted by IBA, ICC, and other arbitration institutions provide helpful guidance. In Spain, the Club Español del Arbitraje[54] has issued valuable recommendations, as well as best practices adopted by Arbitration Institutions. The requirement of availability along with independence and impartiality is becoming frequent and widespread among Spanish arbitration institutions.

2.2.3 Procedural Irregularities

Views on which procedural irregularities amount to setting aside the arbitral award differ between legal literature and courts' decisions. Some authors advocate for a lax interpretation of procedural irregularities as grounds for annulment. Although any minor irregularity in the procedure is not enough to set aside the award; however, if the irregularities have certain significance,[55] there is no need to prove that they have caused one of the parties to be defenseless or deprived them of a right of defense.[56] Accordingly, substantial procedural irregularities, even if they have not implied a situation of defenseless for the parties, would constitute grounds for setting aside the award. On the contrary, the Superior Court of Justice of Madrid in its judgment of July 8, 2013, adopts a much more stringent approach.[57] Procedural irregularities to set aside an arbitral award are those that cause defenselessness or deprive the parties of their right of defense in the arbitration proceedings. Thus, in absence of defenselessness, procedural irregularities become irrelevant for the purposes of the annulment of the arbitral award. The legal basis for such a position is arguable. The fact that the case was related to an arbitration in equity, the parties had agreed to the procedural rules with the arbitrator, and the arbitrator was, by decision of the parties, a layperson in law – he was an engineer – can explain the court's efforts to lessen

---

[53] Provincial Court decision (SAP) of Madrid, Dec. 23, 2004; and SAP of Ciudad Real, June 30, 2017.
[54] *Código de Buenas Prácticas Arbitrales del Club Español del Arbitraje*, CLUB ESPAÑOL DEL ARBITRAJE (2019), https://www.clubarbitraje.com/.
[55] Lower courts have also insisted on the need that procedural irregularities are relevant and of substantial significance, according to the Provincial Court of Madrid in its judgment of July 29, 2005, AC 2005, 1547.
[56] MIGUEL L. LACRUZ MANTECÓN, LA IMPUGNACIÓN DEL ARBITRAJE 232 (2011); Juan Cadarso Palau, *Artículo 41 Motivos*, in COMENTARIOS A LA NUEVA LEY DE ARBITRAJE DE 60/2003 DE 23 DE DICIEMBRE 570 (Julio González Soria coord., 2011).
[57] Fernando Bedoya & Rocío Bonet, *Irregularidades del proceso arbitral insuficientes para motivar la anulación de un laudo*, 22 REVISTA DEL CLUB ESPAÑOL DE ARBITRAJE 165–180 (2015).

the procedural formalities and its disregard of their invalidating effect on the final award.[58] The particularities of the context surrounding the case invite the review of other judgments.

The High Court of Justice (TSJ) of Madrid[59] held that an arbitral award issued by a two-arbitrator tribunal, due to the resignation of the third arbitrator without being replaced, was null and void. The court set aside the arbitral award on grounds of procedural irregularities that implied a transgression of public order. A belated issuing of the arbitral award has been treated diversely. Lower courts have mostly held that the failure to issue the award within the stipulated deadline without objection of the parties in the prescribed period does not amount to a setting aside of the arbitral award – High Court of Valencia, in its judgment of May 25, 2009 (STSJ); or High Court of Madrid, in its judgment of December 23, 2009 (STSJ). That breach was not considered sufficient to annul the award, even if it might give rise to arbitrators' liability. Contrarily, the High Court of Barcelona in its judgment of February 10, 2010 (STSJ) held that a belated award contradicts the principle of legal certainty and celerity of arbitration and, in that extent, suffices to set aside the arbitral award. Yet, annulment of awards on grounds that the arbitral award was not sufficiently reasoned (Article 37 LA, unless it is issued in the terms agreed upon by the parties in accordance with the preceding paragraph of the article) is infrequent. Courts have held that mentioning the essential legal standards,[60] even briefly,[61] on which the decision is based, suffices.[62] The use of the public policy exception to indirectly tackle insufficiently reasoned awards[63] is a risky route to be taken that might lead toward a substantial judicial control over the decision of the arbitrator. Different scenarios are possible from mistaken reasoning to total incoherent award or full arbitrary decision.[64] The resort to the public policy exception for setting aside the arbitral award should be very carefully accepted in such cases in order to avoid excessive judicial control.

2.3 Waiver of the Action for Setting Aside the Arbitral Award

In setting the balance between private autonomy, as the fundamental pillar of arbitration, and judicial control, as the expression of public interests, the possibility of parties' waiver of any recourse against the award is highly controversial. Some domestic arbitration models have embraced this policy option and have acknowledged the right of the parties to exclude any form of recourse against the arbitral award.[65] UNCITRAL Arbitration Rules, upon the revision of 2010, even include a model arbitration clause for contracts with a possible waiver statement: "The parties hereby waive their right to any form of recourse against an award to any court or other competent authority, insofar as such waiver can validly be made under the applicable law."

---

[58] The procedural irregularities alleged by the party seeking the annulment were the following: failure to issue the arbitral award within the stipulated period, a belated notification of the arbitral award to the parties, unilateral modification of the award by the arbitration in order to readjust the calculation formula of the arbitrator's fees, ulterior modifications of the award not in conformity with neither the agreement of the parties not the legal provisions applicable by default.

[59] High Court of Justice (TSJ) of Madrid, Feb. 9, 2016, AC 2016, 532.

[60] José Carlos Fernández Rozas, *Motivación del laudo arbitral en equidad (STSJ Galicia CP 1.ª n.º 18/2012, de 2 de mayo)*, IV ARBITRAJE. REVISTA DE ARBITRAJE COMERCIAL Y DE INVERSIONES 455–467 (2013).

[61] STSJ Madrid of Apr. 4, 2017 (AC 2017\559).

[62] Pedro A. De Miguel Asensio, *Iura Novit Curia and Commercial Arbitration in Spain*, in IURA NOVIT CURIA IN INTERNATIONAL ARBITRATION 319–354 (Franco Ferrari & Giuditta Cordero-Moss eds., 2018).

[63] STSJ Madrid of Oct. 24, 2017 (ECLI: ES:TSJM:2017:11067).

[64] MARÍA JOSÉ MENÉNDEZ ARIAS & JOSÉ CARLOS FERNÁNDEZ ROZAS, MOTIVACIÓN DEL LAUDO ARBITRAL (2018).

[65] Klaus Peter Berger, *The Modern Trend towards Exclusion of Recourse against Transnational Arbitral Awards: A European Perspective*, 12 FORDHAM INTERNATIONAL LAW JOURNAL 605–657 (1988).

In the Spanish legal system, views contrary to the admissibility of an anticipated waiver prevail. Naturally, parties can decide not to exercise the action by simply letting the prescribed period pass (Article 41.4 LA). But an advance waiver raises very different concerns. The waiver of a right cannot be detrimental to public order, public interest or third parties' rights. Judicial control[66] over arbitral award is deemed essential for the arbitral institution. Therefore, the right to access to justice for those who have decided to settle their disputes by arbitration is embodied in the judicial control over the award in very limited and specific cases. Accordingly, an arbitration clause waiving the right to recourse would be not valid as it conflicts with constitutional values and rights. The extensive freedom of parties to agree on arbitration as an alternative method for dispute resolution encounters these limits on the basis of public-order considerations.

3 PUBLIC POLICY AS GROUNDS FOR SETTING ASIDE: USE AND ABUSE

The exception of public policy is the most problematic as the contours of the concept and the limits of the scope as grounds for setting aside is rather indefinite and blurred.

3.1 Concept and Scope of Public Policy: Exception in Arbitration

Scholars distinguish between procedural public policy and material public policy. On the one hand, the procedural public policy encompasses the rules of "due process." Case law shapes in more detail the procedural public policy as comprising "constitutional rules regarding attendance, audience, reciprocity and the right to produce evidence" (judgment issued on January 7, 2010, by the High Court of Valencia (STSJ)), or any dimension of the right to access to justice so as enshrined in the Article 24 of the Spanish Constitution of 1978 such as the right of defense, the prohibition of denial of defense, the right to due process with every legal guarantee, the right to request and provide evidence, the right to appeal, and the right to receive a decision based on the merits of the case (High Court of Madrid decision of May 12, 2008). Furthermore, the procedural public policy is also violated when a decision is adopted on unreasonable or arbitrary grounds.

On the other hand, the material public policy describes the set of political, economic, and social principles that conform to the foundational values of a state at a specific time. Accordingly, the duty to act in good faith, the banning of abuse of rights, or the nondiscrimination right are part of the material public policy. The Constitutional Court[67] has also confirmed the interpretation that the public policy describes the set of political, moral, economic, and legal principles, both public and private, that are absolutely instrumental to preserve a society at a specific time. The application of the exception of public policy in relation to an arbitral award is twofold: annulment of domestic arbitral awards and recognition and enforcement of foreign arbitral awards.

Furthermore, public policy is also related to mandatory rules, as the public policy delimits the principles, fundamental rights, and general provisions that cannot be derogated by parties' agreement. Nevertheless, if a violation of the public policy does always imply the infringement

---

[66] José Luis González-Montes Sánchez, El control judicial del arbitraje (2008); José Luis González-Montes Sánchez, La asistencia judicial al arbitraje (2009); Carmen Senés Motilla, La intervención judicial en el arbitraje (2007).

[67] Judgments 15/1987 of Feb. 11 (LA LEY 85965-NS/0000), 116/1988 of June 20 (LA LEY 1142/1988) and 54/1989 of Feb. 23 (LA LEY 620/1989).

of mandatory provisions, the mere violation of any mandatory provision does not necessarily entail a violation of public policy – High Court of Madrid decision of April 21, 2015 (LA LEY 55248/2015).

Since the enactment of the LA, lower courts' decisions (*Audiencias Provinciales*, AP) have also consistently pronounced on the concept of public policy as grounds for setting aside arbitral awards within three coordinates:

- First, public policy cannot be used as an "escape clause" to trigger judicial control over the fairness of the arbitrators' decision where it is not against public policy;
- Second, the annulment action cannot be used as an appeal recourse. Therefore, a competent court to hear the application for setting aside must be constrained to the grounds for setting aside arbitral awards provided for by the law;
- Third, the annulment cannot entail a review of the legal reasoning of the arbitral tribunal, but it must be exclusively focused on in procedendo irregularities.

Within the aforementioned coordinates Provincial Courts (AP) have annulled arbitral awards on the grounds of public policy where the principles of contradiction and the right to allege and practice evidence were not respected,[68] the right of defense of a third party affected by the arbitral award was ignored,[69] or the evidence was obtained in violation of fundamental rights.[70]

Upon the reform of the LA in 2011, the jurisdiction to annul arbitral awards was transferred from the *Audiencias Provinciales* to the *Tribunales Superiores de Justicia* (High Courts, TSJ). Since then, arbitral awards have been set aside on the grounds of, among others, lack of impartiality of the arbitrator,[71] lack of motivation of the arbitral award,[72] and infringement of the right to propose and practice evidence in the arbitral proceeding.[73]

3.2 Notion of "Economic Public Policy" as an Inflexion Point: Extent, Relevance, and Prospects

Nonetheless, such a favorable attitude toward arbitration and the respect to arbitral awards' effectiveness, the escalation of disputes related to the sale of interest rate swap-agreements by financial institutions settled by arbitration in the after-crisis scenario has triggered a succession of rulings setting aside arbitral awards on the grounds of breach of "economic public policy." Such a deviation in the stable trend followed by case law in prudently interpreting the public policy as grounds for setting aside arbitral award was initiated by the controversial decision of the TSJ of Madrid (Sala Civil) of January 28, 2015.[74] A series of subsequent decisions issued by the same court on facts that were almost identical followed.[75] The trigger of such a controversial tendency shift was an expansive interpretation of the notion of public policy to include the idea of

---

[68] SAP Madrid of Nov. 25 2008 (LA LEY 307358/2008), SAP Barcelona of Mar. 11 2009 (LA LEY 174213/2009).
[69] SAP Barcelona of May 28, 2008 (LA LEY 105146/2008), SAP Valladolid of Apr. 8, 2013 (LA LEY 60214/2013).
[70] SAP Alicante of June 15, 2011 (LA LEY 174356/2011); SAP Barcelona of Mar. 11, 2009 (LA LEY 174213/2009); SAP Vizcaya of Feb. 12, 2009 (LA LEY 118650/2009).
[71] STSJ Madrid of Jan. 10, 2017 (LA LEY 1866/2017); STSJ Madrid of Feb. 21, 2017 (LA LEY 23430/2017); STSJ Madrid of Nov. 4, 2016 (LA LEY 186560/2016); STSJ Cataluña of May 10, 2012 (LA LEY 100360/2012); STSJ Madrid of Jan. 13, 2015 (LA LEY 2855/2015).
[72] STSJ Madrid of Feb. 3, 2015 (LA LEY 95630/2015), of Dec. 7, 2015 (LA LEY 201845/2015); STSJ Galicia of May 2, 2012 (LA LEY 78304/2012).
[73] STSJ Madrid of Mar. 6, 2017 (LA LEY 31111/2017), of Jan. 18, 2017 (LA LEY 8877/2017).
[74] STSJ of Madrid (Sala Civil) of Jan. 28, 2015 (LA LEY 13315/2015).
[75] STSJ of Madrid of Apr. 6, 2015 (LA LEY 39614/2015), of Apr. 14, 2015 (LA LEY 55247/2015), of Oct. 23, 2015 (LA LEY 186223/2015), of Nov. 17, 2015 (LA LEY 196474/2015).

"economic public policy." With this expansion, the court tries to add other principles and basic rules whose observance is inexcusable in cases that deserve special protection. Specifically, the general principle of good faith in contracting is enunciated as the primary content of the notion of economic public policy. The court held that the duty to act in good faith is a fundamental principle in contracting and dealing in case of disequilibrium between parties, imbalance, or asymmetry.

This inflexion point in the moderate trend of judicial treatment of annulment of arbitral awards arouses some concerns about excessive use and inadequate interpretation of the concept of "public order" in the application for setting aside that might lead to an indirect discreet revision of the merits of the case at a judicial instance.

The dissenting vote issued by the president of the court (TSJ Madrid) reflects the underlying controversy and provides sound reasoning against the majority decision. The president disagrees with a decision that exceeds the scope and the functions of the annulment action. A reexamination of the merits of the case is not allowed in the setting aside of an arbitral award. In particular, the decision on the applicable law, its interpretation, and application to the facts are entrusted to the arbitral tribunal by agreement of the parties. Judicial control is excluded therefrom. Furthermore, the president alerts judges about the excessive use of the public policy exception that would entail de facto a contra legem expansion of the scope of power legally attributed to the judicial control over the arbitral awards. Finally, the president stresses in his dissenting vote that, even if an arbitral award is deemed wrong, inadequate, or contrary to the case law, it is not sufficient to allege the infringement of the public policy. Only irrational, arbitrary, or illogical decisions would deprive parties of access to justice. Otherwise, the court can disagree with the decision adopted by the arbitral tribunal, but it is not empowered to annul the arbitral award on the grounds of the public policy exception.

The extent and the practical relevance of this trend shift based on an expanding interpretation of the public policy exception to cover the "economic public policy" seem, however, limited to rather specific social and economic circumstances: a post-crisis scenario where the proliferation of cases against financial entities on the basis of lack of consent in imbalanced swaps agreements where the court finds an asymmetry of bargaining power, information, and risk-taking capacity. Beyond these factual limits, the interpretation line preserves the consistency and alignment with international principles.

4 RECOGNITION AND ENFORCEMENT OF FOREIGN ARBITRAL AWARDS

The last chapter of LA, devoted to exequatur[76] of foreign arbitral awards, includes only one article providing for rules applicable to foreign awards preceded by a legal definition thereof. As per Article 46.1 LA, a foreign arbitral award is considered to be an award that has been issued outside of the Spanish national territory. Upon the definition of the conceptual contour, the following paragraph does simply confirm that the exequatur of such foreign arbitral awards shall be governed by the New York Convention, without prejudice to the provisions of other more favorable international conventions likely to be applicable thereto.

---

[76] An analysis of procedural aspects of the proceedings for the recognition and the enforcement of foreign awards in María José Menéndez Arias, Jesús Almoguera & Antonio Góngora, Reconocimiento de laudos extranjeros en España: algunas consideraciones procedimentales y de competencia tras la Ley de Cooperación Jurídica Internacional en Materia Civil a la luz de la más reciente jurisprudencia (2018).

Insofar as Spain has ratified the New York Convention without reservations, all formalities (Article IV New York Convention)[77] and grounds (Article V New York Convention) to refuse the recognition and enforcement of the award, both at the request of the party against whom it is invoked and ex officio by the competent authority in the country where recognition and enforcement is sought, apply. Upon the proving or the finding of any of the listed grounds, the court may refuse the recognition and enforcement, but it is not bound to mandatorily deny the sought enforcement.

Grounds for denying the recognition and the enforcement of foreign award as per the referral of Article 46 LA to the Article V New York Convention amply mirror the grounds for setting aside an arbitral award in conformity with Article 41 LA. With only a few particularities arising from the fact that in the former case the award to be enforced has been made in the territory of a state other than the state where the enforcement is sought (essentially, letter e) of paragraph 1 or letter a) of paragraph 2 of Article V New York Convention), previous comments on Article 41 LA can be reproduced here.

5 ASSESSMENT AND EXPECTATIONS

The longstanding tradition of arbitration in Spanish laws and the alignment with international practices and standards of the most recent legislation have laid the foundations for the consolidation today of a modern, reliable, sound, and arbitration-friendly model. The trend shift that meant the enactment of the Arbitration Act of 1953, in practice an anti-arbitration law, in the context of an economic autarchy was overcome with the succeeding law of 1988 and finally reversed with the current legislation of 2003 (LA). The judicial resistance to arbitration, typical of that political regime, has subsided. Spain has ratified the most relevant international instruments on arbitration and aligned its legal solutions and practices with modern standards of international arbitrations. The arbitration-friendly culture has been cultivated and enhanced at universities with modernized syllabi including arbitration courses and the systematic application of experiential learning methodologies with moot courts and mock trials. Arbitration institutions for administering arbitration proceedings have been created and actively promote arbitration in Spain. Yet, both legal provisions and case law on the annulment of arbitral awards and recognition and enforcement of foreign awards consistently reveal an adequate understanding and application of international principles and are fully in conformity with international conventions.

In such a favorable context and under such circumstances conducive to arbitration, any deviation in the positive trends attracts attention and deserves close analysis. Therefore, previous sections have been devoted to assessing the impact of an emerging judicial line encouraging an extensive interpretation of the concept of "public policy exception" as grounds for setting aside arbitral awards. Under that reasoning, the concept of public policy is enlarged to cover the "economic public policy." Clearly, such an interpretative game arguably leads to an abusive use of the public policy exception for the annulment of arbitral awards and, consequently, might jeopardize the consistent and contained judicial practice, in terms of understanding, interpreting, and applying the grounds for setting aside and objecting to the recognition and enforcement of foreign arbitral awards. Even so, a contextualized assessment of court decisions under scrutiny reveals a much less dramatic image. Regardless of the opinion that this judicial line may merit,

---

[77] STS 5427/2000, of Sept. 28, 2004, denied the recognition of the foreign award as the party applying for recognition and enforcement failed to supply either the duly authenticated original award or a duly certified copy thereof without justification or proof of events that might prevent it from furnishing the required documents.

it seems that decisions are limited to rather specific social and economic circumstances in an after-crisis scenario and are related to highly similar fact accounts – asymmetry of bargaining power, information, and risk-taking capacity between financial entities and clients. Beyond these specific circumstances, the interpretative line of courts in annulment cases proves to preserve its consistency and its alignment with international principles. All these factors stir positive expectations and promising prospects for arbitration.

The analysis of these cases as an anomaly in the framework of an arbitration-friendly model invites two further thoughts. First, there is the relevance of judicial interpretation on the legal grounds for setting aside arbitral awards. Although it is a quite obvious consideration, in practice, it becomes a crucial remark. Clear, unambiguous, and internationally harmonized legal provisions setting the grounds for annulment and admissible objections to recognition and enforcement of arbitral awards are primary. But a contained, predictable, and consistent application and construction by courts is key to ensure the effet utile of legal provisions. Second, the public policy exception is a concept of imprecise perimeter and vague substance. These are the natural contours of an indeterminate legal concept. The merit of the notion lies indeed in that malleability. Thus, an excessive use of the public policy exception as a last resort is inadvisable, as it forces the reasonable limits of the concept. In elaborating a common understanding of the core, main features, and impassable limits of the public policy exception, scholars, practitioners, legislators, and courts must contribute.

21

Judicial Control of Arbitral Awards in Switzerland

*Phillip Landolt**

1 GENERAL COMMENTS ON INTERNATIONAL ARBITRATION LAW IN SWITZERLAND

Switzerland has long been a New York Convention (NY Convention)[1] state. Although Switzerland's arbitration law is not based on the UNCITRAL Model Law (Model Law), it does by and large conform to the fundamental principles of the Model Law as amended in 2006, in particular in relation to the interpretation of arbitration agreements, and the vacation and enforcement of international arbitration awards.

Swiss law distinguishes between international arbitration and domestic arbitration. This proceeds from article 176 of Switzerland's arbitration statute, Chapter 12 of the Swiss Private International Law Act[2] (PIL), which defines the scope of international arbitration as arbitrations with their seat in Switzerland and in which, at the time of the conclusion of the arbitration agreement,[3] at least one of the parties had neither its domicile nor its habitual residence in Switzerland. Domicile for registered corporate entities is treated as the place of formal registration.[4] For registered corporate entities, habitual residence does not apply. No other provision in Swiss international arbitration law is more stringent than those under the NY Convention.[5]

If, within the meaning of article 176 of the PIL, an arbitration is a Swiss international arbitration then the arbitration provisions of the PIL will apply. If the arbitration is seated in Switzerland, but it is not an international arbitration within the meaning of that article, then the arbitration provisions of the Swiss civil procedure code (CPC) will apply, namely part three of that code. The one exception is that, even if the requirements under article 176 of the PIL are satisfied for an arbitration to be international, by paragraph 2 of that article the parties may by

---

* The author wishes to acknowledge and thank Ms. Lucille Piguet for her valuable assistance in researching and the initial drafting of parts of this chapter.
[1] New York Convention as transposed into Swiss law: RS 0277.12 (approved by the Federal Assembly on Mar. 2, 1965; date of signature Dec. 29, 1958; date of ratification June 1, 1965; date of entry into force Aug. 30, 1965).
[2] All references to the PIL and any other Swiss statutes are in unofficial English translation.
[3] Although Art. 176 of the PIL expressly indicates that it is the situation at the time of the entering into of the arbitration agreement that is decisive, a degree of uncertainty about the relevant timing does exist under Swiss law. Nonetheless, under a draft bill published by the Swiss Federal Council on Oct. 24, 2018, seeking to reform Swiss international arbitration law this uncertainty is decisively resolved in favor of the express wording of the PIL.
[4] Art. 21 of the PIL, applied to arbitration by analogy.
[5] Notably the formal requirements for the recognition of an arbitration agreement in Art. 178(1) of the PIL are less stringent than those in Article II (1) and II(2) of the NY Convention.

"express declaration" exclude the application of the arbitration provisions of the PIL, in which case those under part three of the CPC will apply.

This country report will confine itself to Swiss international arbitration. Chapter 12 of the PIL was intended as a complete code for Swiss international arbitration. Nonetheless, since its adoption in 1989 various matters under it needing clarification have arisen, and the Swiss Supreme Court has done so in a number of cases over the years. There is currently a legislative reform of Swiss international arbitration afoot, expected to come into force in 2020. This reform is proceeding on the basis that Swiss international arbitration law has been a success and only a limited number of minor adjustments to it are necessary. One of the types of adjustments is to include in the statute provision on the various items identified as in need of clarification to ensure it is a complete code.

One of the prominent features of Swiss international arbitration law is that it is ordained to support and promote arbitration as a dispute settlement mechanism. One sees this feature certainly in the way arbitration agreements are construed and also in the high degree of finality which international arbitration agreements enjoy in Switzerland in both law and actual practice. Challenges to Swiss international arbitration awards lie exclusively to the Swiss Supreme Court (article 191 PIL). This promotes finality both in that there is only one stage of challenge and in that the Swiss Supreme Court is institutionally and legally constituted only to intervene in particularly grievous cases. Statistically, between 1989 and 2017 there have been 438 decisions of the Swiss court on the merits in cases challenging international arbitration awards. Of these, only 33 have succeeded, even partially, that is 7.53 percent.[6]

2 JUDICIAL INTERPRETATION OF SCOPE OF ARBITRATION CLAUSES

Article 178(2) of the PIL governs most matters relating to the scope of Swiss international arbitration agreements. This comprises, for the most part, temporal, personal ,and substantive scope, and therefore notably which parties and subject matter are included in the arbitration agreement. The wording of article 178(2) of the PIL does not, however, suggest that it is the provision governing the scope of arbitration agreements and almost exclusively so. It states: "Furthermore, an arbitration agreement is valid if it conforms either to the law chosen by the parties or to the law governing the subject-matter of the dispute, in particular the main contract, or to Swiss law." On its face, one sees that the provision is mainly concerned with, first, the substantive validity of arbitration clauses and, secondly, dictating what law applies to determine such substantive validity in an arbitration-friendly manner.[7] Substantive validity is essentially the question of whether there has been at all a valid agreement on arbitration and not yet on what particular matters and between whom.

It is, of course, a related but further step to deal with questions of the scope of any such substantively valid agreement to arbitrate, but in the virtual absence of any other provision in the PIL it is article 178(2) of the PIL which is used to answer these questions, and it does so in the same

---

[6] F. Dasser & P. Wójtowicz, *Challenges of Swiss Arbitral Awards – Updated Statistical Data as of 2017* 36 ASA BULLETIN [hereinafter ASA BULL.], 276–294 (2018).

[7] B. BERGER & F. KELLERHALLS, INTERNATIONAL AND DOMESTIC ARBITRATION IN SWITZERLAND 131, para 395 (3d ed. 2015) ("The rule *in favorem validitatis* implicates that it is in all cases the most favourable law among those listed in PIL, Art. 178(2) that determines the validity of the arbitration agreement"); P.-Y. Tschanz, *Commentary on Art. 178 PILA, in* COMMENTAIRE ROMAND LDIP 1538, 178 N 72 (A. Bucher ed., 2011) ("*Ce critère est celui du résultat le plus favorable à la validité de la convention d'arbitrage (favor validitatis)*") (This criterion is that of the result which is most favorable to the validity of the arbitration agreement (favor validitatis)).

pro-arbitration manner as it does in respect of its treatment of substantive validity – there is arbitral jurisdiction if permitted under any of (1) the law chosen by the parties to govern the arbitration agreement, (2) the law chosen by them to govern their main contract, or (3) Swiss law. It is very rare in practice for parties to choose a law specifically applicable to their arbitration agreement and even rarer for them to choose any such law at variance to what they have chosen for their main contract in general. Therefore, the doctrine of separability of arbitration agreements[8] notwithstanding, in practice the more arbitration-friendly outcome of any scope enquiry as between the chosen law of the contract and Swiss law will prevail. Given Swiss contract law's flexible and liberal character, it will in practice usually be Swiss law which, of the two, proves more inclusive in terms of subject matter and persons bound. Therefore, it is usually the more arbitration-friendly of the two, and the one that is ultimately applied. In the case law, one rarely sees interpreting the scope of arbitration agreements under article 178(2) of the PIL any law applied but Swiss law, but that may as much be an emanation of Swiss courts being principally kitted out with the "hammer" of Swiss law and therefore seeing every problem as a nail!

Interpretation of arbitration clauses to ascertain their scope in terms of subject matter depends, under Swiss law, for the most part upon the general principles of contractual interpretation set out in article 18 of the Swiss Code of Obligations (CO). In accordance with article 18 CO, an arbitration agreement is first interpreted with a view to ascertaining the real common intention of the parties. If that fails, for example, because the parties did not, in fact, have a discernible real common intention, as a second step, the interpretation proceeds in accordance with the principle of confidence, that is, with the meaning that objectively should be ascribed to the expressions used by each party. The words that the parties used, as well as all the surrounding circumstances at the time of contracting, are evaluated so as to determine this objective meaning.

In relation to this second-stage analysis, Swiss law applies certain presumptions specific to the interpretation of arbitration clauses. One of these is that once an arbitration clause is accepted as valid in relation to any one matter or matters in dispute, there is a presumption that it has a broad material scope, with a view to the efficacy of arbitration and in particular to avoid the inefficacy of dispersing among different fora disputes arising from the same factual matrix. Once it has been established that the parties have agreed on arbitration and thereby waived their constitutional right of access to the ordinary courts, it is presumed that they intended to vest the arbitral tribunal with comprehensive jurisdiction over the differences in respect of the defined legal relationship to which the arbitration agreement refers.[9]

---

[8] Both this separability doctrine as formulated in Swiss international arbitration law (Art. 176(3) PIL) and that in Article 16(1) of the Model Law would appear, however, not to extend to the question of whether the law applying to the contract cannot without more be taken to apply to an arbitration agreement within it.

[9] See BERGER & KELLERHALLS, *supra* note 7, at 162–163, para. 484, as well as at 164–165, paras. 489–490, and the decisions of the Swiss Supreme Court cited there:

> 489. Once it has been established that the parties intended to derogate from the jurisdiction of the courts, the Swiss Federal Tribunal no longer applies a restrictive interpretation. To the contrary, it states that in such a case one should take into account the parties' common intention to have the difference decided by an arbitral tribunal. Therefore, it shall be assumed that the parties, if they have indeed concluded an arbitration agreement, wish the tribunal to have broad jurisdiction.
>
> 490. A 'broad jurisdiction' means that a liberal or 'pro-arbitration' approach with regard to the scope and content of an arbitration agreement shall apply. This entails, first of all, that the arbitration agreement, even if combined with the main contract in a single document, has its own autonomous fate, unless otherwise agreed by the parties. In cases of doubt, the parties shall thus be considered as having intended not only to submit disputes arising from the performance of the main contract to arbitration, but also differences in relation to the formation, validity, invalidity and termination thereof. Moreover, the liberal or 'pro-arbitration' approach

It might legitimately be contended that this is not just a practical result of making arbitration a viable alternative to state court litigation but also an expression of a general presumption of subject matter inclusiveness in article V(1)(c) of the NY Convention where the burden of proving the arbitration agreement is of narrower scope is on the party challenging it. The parts outside of the substantive scope of the agreement may be severed, and those within saved for arbitration.

Swiss law, by contrast, contains no presumption of inclusiveness of persons, but there are various doctrines under Swiss law to include nonsignatories, notably where the party seeking to escape the arbitration has involved itself in the performance of the contract subject to the arbitration.[10]

Also, Swiss law leans in favor of efficiency of arbitration and, therefore, its viability as a dispute settlement mechanism, in that substantially similar arbitration clauses in two or more contracts are interpreted as one arbitration clause over all claims of all parties to all contracts. Also, article 112(2) CO is quite generous (by comparative law standards, in particular, vis-à-vis English law under the Contracts (Rights of Third Parties) Act 1999) in accepting actions for nonparties to a contract, and Swiss law treats such third parties as benefiting from any arbitration provision in the contract.

The scope of an arbitration agreement as limited in time is in practice of lesser importance than substantive and personal scope. Nonetheless, two questions in relation to scope in time that do arise in practice are in relation to (1) arbitrations started without prior satisfaction of preconditions, such as a requirement to mediate, and (2) arbitrations concluded after an agreed period for the award has expired. In a 2016 decision,[11] the Swiss Supreme Court provided clarity on what pre-arbitration requirements must be complied with and the consequences of a failure to do so. On the facts there, prior to arbitration there was a requirement for a party to make a conciliation attempt under the 2001 ICC Alternative Dispute Resolution Rules (ICC ADR Rules). When the dispute arose the claimant duly filed its request for conciliation under those rules, and there were written exchanges, and even a conciliator was appointed. But when complications arose in the setting of a conference to discuss procedure, the claimant stopped the conciliation and initiated the arbitration. The Swiss Supreme Court found that the claimant had not complied with the pre-arbitration requirements since article 5(1) of the ICC ADR Rules requires at minimum before withdrawing the conciliation that at least one discussion had taken place between the conciliator and the parties and that this on the facts had not occurred. The Swiss Supreme Court stated that the consequence of this failure to comply with a clear pre-arbitration requirement was that the arbitration was suspended until the claimant had satisfied the requirement.

On the subject of requirements to render the award within a certain time, the Swiss Supreme Court distinguishes between, on the one hand, express specific agreements between the parties on time periods and a tribunal's unexcused failure to observe them in rendering the award, and, on the other, time periods within arbitration rules where there is some excuse for the lateness of the award. Therefore in ATF 140 III, the Swiss Supreme Court held that the arbitrator had lost jurisdiction ratione temporis by failing without excuse, subsequent to repeated reminders, to render the award within a period of time expressly agreed between him and the

> means – without any indication to the contrary – that the parties shall be deemed to have agreed that the arbitral tribunal's jurisdiction not only covers contractual claims ... but also extends to claims arising from *culpa in contrahendo* or liability based on trust ... and other extra-contractual claims.
>
> Id. at 164–165.

[10] See most recently, Decision of the Swiss Supreme Court 4A_459/2016 of Jan. 19, 2019, at consid. 2.1.

[11] Decision of the Swiss Supreme Court 4A_628/2015, Mar. 16, 2016.

parties. But in a decision of January 11, 2017,[12] the Swiss Supreme Court declined to hold that the tribunal had lost jurisdiction for its failure to meet the six-month time limit under the expedited procedure in article 42 of the Swiss Rules of International Arbitration.

It is important to note that although Swiss international arbitration law treats arbitration agreements in a pro-arbitration manner, in particular with a view to vindicating the parties' presumed intention of one-stop dispute resolution, the court's review of arbitrators' decisions on jurisdiction is an exacting one. Whereas in regard to all other bases of setting aside an arbitral award, the only remedy is the nullification (partial or complete) of the award;[13] with regard to jurisdiction challenges, the court is empowered to substitute its own decision.[14] Moreover, the Supreme Court affords no deference to the arbitral tribunal's legal treatment of its jurisdiction but rather freely assesses legal questions on jurisdiction and preliminary questions. Although the Supreme Court will not supply legal arguments for parties challenging arbitral jurisdiction,[15] the Supreme Court is not bound by the parties' and the tribunal's legal reasoning providing the facts have been sufficiently established to support the reasoning supplied by the Supreme Court.[16] As regards jurisdiction, the Supreme Court is nonetheless bound by the facts found by the arbitral tribunal.[17]

In a recent case,[18] the Swiss Supreme Court rejected the arbitral tribunal's decision that it had jurisdiction over a natural person in connection with his founding of a legal person (a limited company under Turkish law) which was subject to the arbitration agreement. The arbitral tribunal had found on the facts that the natural person had entered into an agreement for and on behalf of that legal person which at that time had not yet been registered. Under article 645 CO, a person who enters into obligations on behalf of a legal person not yet registered is liable in respect of those obligations unless the legal person assumes the obligation within three months of its registration. The arbitral tribunal found that the legal person once registered had not assumed the obligation, with the result that the person who entered into the obligations on its behalf was liable. The arbitral tribunal found moreover that, as a matter of law, the person who acted on behalf of the not-yet-registered company was a certain natural person, and on that basis that natural person was subject to the arbitration agreement in the obligation. No party had ever raised the possibility that the person who acted was anyone other than the natural person acting in his or her personal capacity, and the arbitral tribunal's decision was based on the acceptance that it was the natural person in his or her own capacity who had so acted. The complainant before the Supreme Court argued unsuccessfully that the natural person had no personal liability based on a supposed ratification by conduct. For the Supreme Court, however, once the complainant has raised the plea contesting personal liability the Supreme Court is entitled to apply the law ex officio to examine if there was some other legal basis to deny such personal responsibility. In this case, the Supreme Court did, in fact, conclude that no personal liability existed and that, therefore, the arbitral tribunal had wrongly found that it had jurisdiction over that natural person. The Supreme Court's approach was to find that the natural person had acted in his capacity as a representative of another incorporated entity, this one registered,

---

[12] Decision of the Swiss Supreme Court 4A_188/2016.
[13] This is by operation of article 77(2) of the Supreme Court Act (SCA) read in conjunction with article 107(2) SCA.
[14] ATF 136 III 605, consid. 3.3.4, ATF 117 II 94, consid. 4, decision 4A_394/2017.
[15] 4A_7/2019, consid. 2, 4A_378/2015, consid. 3.1, ATF 128 III 50, consid. 1c).
[16] B. CORBOZ, COMMENTAIRE DE LA LTF 77 N 86, 106 N 36 (2d ed. 2014); ATF 142 III 239, consid. 3.1; ATF 140 III 86, consid. 2.
[17] ATF 142 III 239, consid. 3.1; ATF 140 III 477, consid 3.1.
[18] 4A_473/2018.

and that it was this other corporate entity, which by article 645 CO was liable, and not the natural person himself. In coming to this conclusion, the Supreme Court based itself on what might be considered the rather slender evidential foundation that the counterparty originally intended to contract with this other legal person but later contracted with the company as yet unregistered.

This case stands as evidence for the degree to which the Supreme Court considers itself unconstrained, as far as legal questions are concerned, in reviewing arbitrators' treatments of their own jurisdiction. Indeed, statistically, by far the highest success rate for all grounds of challenge is an error in jurisdiction. About 11.3 percent of challenges on this basis between 1989 and 2017 succeeded (in whole or in part), compared to the next most successful basis, procedural violations, at 5.5 percent.[19]

3 REQUIREMENTS FOR ENFORCEABILITY OF AWARDS

By article 190(1) of the PIL, Swiss international arbitration awards are enforceable as of the time of receipt by any party against whom it is being enforced. The award may be validly sent by any agreed means, and, in the absence of agreement, even notification by email is sufficient.[20] Article 193(2) of the PIL provides that upon application by a party the court will certify the enforceability of an award. The court to which application must be made is the general first instance court of the Swiss canton where the seat of the arbitration was. Thus, for Geneva, the court having jurisdiction is the Court of First Instance. The procedure is a fairly simple and swift one. Aside from paying the modest court fees, one also must pay the ad valorem stamp duty. The certification procedure includes a stage where the court consults the Geneva tax office for the ascertainment of the amount of the tax payable. Unfortunately, this can take several weeks. Court certification of the enforceability of an arbitration award is not constitutive of enforceability as a matter of Swiss law but only evidence of it. It is a violation of article IV of the NY Convention for an enforcing court to require certification of enforceability of the award at the State of the seat. It is probably also a violation of article III of the NY Convention to require so.

To be enforceable in Switzerland, a Swiss international arbitration award must comply with the requirements of article 189 of the PIL. This means that the award must comply with any decision-making procedure (providing all members of the tribunal have had an opportunity to participate in the deliberations and decide[21]) and requirements of form agreed by the parties. Failing any such agreement, the award is that agreed by the majority of the members of the tribunal or, in the absence of a majority, by the president alone, and it must be in writing, supported by reasons, dated and signed. The parties may validly dispense with the requirement of writing for the arbitral award, such that an oral award will be treated as enforceable. But such agreement is rarely found, as it risks attracting serious difficulties of enforcement.[22] The signature of all arbitrators is required in principle, but not if for legitimate reasons an arbitrator (who is not the president) is not able to sign. It was generally thought that it was always required that at least the president sign the award,[23] but the Swiss Supreme Court held that an award

---

[19] Dasser & Wójtowicz, *supra* note 6, at 280.
[20] Decision of the Swiss Supreme Court 4P.273/1999, at consid. 5b.
[21] Decision of the Swiss Supreme Court 4P.115/2003 at consid. 3.2.
[22] M. Molina, *Chapter 2, Part II: Commentary on Chapter 12 PILS, Article 189 [Arbitral Award]*, in ARBITRATION IN SWITZERLAND: THE PRACTITIONER'S GUIDE 255, NN 46–47 (M. Arroyo ed., 2d ed. 2013).
[23] *Id.* at 260, N 61.

cannot be annulled even if the president did not sign it if it is proven that he or she took part in the deliberations.[24]

Not just in relation to the form of the award, but more generally concerning the enforceability of an award, (as far as Swiss law is concerned) the principle of party autonomy prevails. The parties may thus not only waive what otherwise would be required of an arbitration award for enforceability, but they may also add requirements for example to ensure the efficiency of the award's enforcement and to evidence the sufficiency of the proceedings. Among the possible requirements proposed by legal commentators[25] are these: the names of parties, the seat of the arbitral tribunal, the prayers for relief, the history of the procedure, and a recitation of the relevant facts.

The PIL does not distinguish between the enforcement of NY Convention awards and the enforcement of foreign awards not subject to the NY Convention.[26] Article 194 of the PIL simply provides that "the recognition and enforcement of a foreign arbitral award are governed by the New York Convention of June 10, 1958, on the Recognition and Enforcement of Foreign Arbitral Awards." So all "foreign arbitral awards" are subject to the NY Convention as far as enforcement in Switzerland is concerned.

Article IV NY Convention sets forth formal requirements to apply for the enforceability of an award. According to article IV(1) NY Convention, the party requiring recognition and enforcement must provide for the original award (or certified copy) and the original arbitration agreement (or certified copy).[27] In accordance with article IV(2) NY Convention, a translation of the award and the arbitration agreement must be submitted in a Swiss Federal official language (German, French, or Italian). Subject to party agreement in derogation, the award must be legally signed by the arbitrators, which Swiss embassies and consulates can certify.[28]

Swiss courts require that copies and translation certifications must comply with the law of the State in which the procedure was conducted; although the NY Convention itself does not indicate the applicable law on this matter.[29] Swiss courts will ask for no other documents and will not be restrictive on these matters. Swiss courts are increasingly flexible in the application of article IV NY Convention.[30] Indeed, certain Swiss cantonal courts do not require translation in certain circumstances and will not even review formal requirements if they are not raised by the defending party. They have also admitted documents in satisfaction of formal requirements submitted after the initiation of enforcement proceedings.[31]

In Switzerland, enforcement proceedings of foreign arbitral awards differ according to whether the relief in the award is monetary or non-monetary and whether or not the debtor is domiciled in Switzerland. The enforcement of monetary awards proceeds under the Swiss Debt Enforcement and Bankruptcy Act (DEBA).[32] In outline, under article 67 DEBA the award creditor requests the debt enforcement office at the Swiss domicile of the award debtor to send

---

[24] Decision of the Swiss Supreme Court 4P.154/2005 consid. 3. *See also* Molina, *supra* note 22, at 260, N 61.
[25] Molina, *supra* note 22, at 261, N 65.
[26] The Federal Council withdrew its reciprocity reservation by Federal Decision dated Dec. 17, 1992 (RO 1993, 2434; RO 1993, 2439).
[27] E. GEISINGER & N. VOSER, INTERNATIONAL ARBITRATION IN SWITZERLAND: A HANDBOOK FOR PRACTITIONERS 210 (2d ed. 2013).
[28] *Id.*
[29] *Id.*
[30] *Id.*
[31] *Id.* at 211.
[32] D. GIRSBERGER & N. VOSER, INTERNATIONAL ARBITRATION: COMPARATIVE AND SWISS PERSPECTIVES 457 (3d ed. 2016). *See also* GEISINGER & VOSER, *supra* note 27, at 203–205.

the latter a request for the payment. The debt enforcement office does so under 69 DEBA. If the debtor objects to the payment order within ten days, the court will examine the enforceability of the award pursuant to articles IV and V NY Convention in summary proceedings. In these summary proceedings, the court will limit itself to consideration of any validly invoked and ex officio NY Convention grounds to refuse the debt enforcement. Subject to any appeal to the canton's higher court and then in some limited circumstances to the Swiss Supreme Court, if the court finds that there are none, the procedure for the seizure of the debtor's assets may begin.

The court will consider the enforceability of the award as a matter incidental to the request for monetary relief and will not order enforcement in its decision unless the creditor has expressly applied for such relief. Therefore, where there is in addition non-monetary relief in an award requiring enforcement it is important to include in the application to the court in the debt proceedings a separate and express request for enforcement of the award. It may also be advantageous to obtain the freezing of the debtor's assets as preliminary relief. The circumstances where a freezing order is available are enunciated in article 271 DEBA. The Swiss Supreme Court held that an NY Convention foreign arbitration award satisfies the ground in article 271(6) DEBA, i.e., it is prima facie a document justifying the final removal of opposition to debt enforcement (*titre de mainlevée définitive*).[33] The Swiss Supreme Court's reasoning in this case admits that any foreign arbitral award enforceable in Switzerland under article 194 PIL satisfies this requirement (and not just NY Convention awards).

Where the award debtor is not domiciled in Switzerland, subject to some exceptions, it will usually be necessary first to obtain a freezing order, in order under article 52 DEBA to create the jurisdiction of the debt enforcement office (at the place of the assets subject to the freezing order). Non-monetary awards are enforced in Switzerland in summary proceedings under articles 335 to 346 CPC.[34] In outline, there are two steps. First, the court assesses compliance with articles IV and V NY Convention. If such compliance is ascertained, then the award is enforced by means of the coercive measures under article 343(1) CPC (e.g., fines for noncompliance).

4 BIAS OF ARBITRATORS

Article 180(c) of the PIL provides that an arbitrator may be challenged if justifiable doubts as to his or her independence exist. The German, French, and Italian equivalents of "justifiable doubts" (*berechtigte Zweifel, douter légitimement*, and *dubitare legittimamente*) make clear that not just any doubts will suffice to remove an arbitrator for bias. The case law of the Swiss Supreme Court has in fact specified that not only is the test for bias an objective one (and not merely bias in the subjective eyes of a party) but there must be cogent proof of such bias.

Although article 180(1)(c) of the PIL refers only to the independence of an arbitrator, it is interpreted to include a requirement of impartiality; inasmuch as any distinction may be taken between the two concepts. This reflects constitutional guarantees of an impartial and independent tribunal of article 30(1) of the Swiss Federal Constitution. In the result, in Swiss international arbitration, arbitrators must be free of specific objective indications giving rise to serious doubts that they are not positioned to deal with the case based on merits considerations alone.[35] So the test is substantially that in article 12(2) of the Model Law, an objective one, and the standard of

---

[33] 5A_355/2012.
[34] GIRSBERGER & VOSER, *supra* note 32, at 458. *See also* GEISINGER & VOSER, *supra* note 27, at 205–206.
[35] ATF 118 II 359 at consid. 3c.

proof is a fairly high one. The Swiss Supreme Court is restrictive in recognizing a violation of article 180 PIL.[36] However, according to the Swiss Supreme Court,[37] an arbitrator must be sufficiently independent and impartial to the same level of national judges. Since this requirement extends from constitutional principles, the assessment must be conducted in accordance with the Constitution.[38]

In applying the Swiss constitutional test for bias in the arbitration context the Swiss Supreme Court often refers to the IBA Guidelines on Conflicts of Interest in International Arbitration[39] since they are of specific application in the arbitration context. The Swiss Supreme Court has described the IBA Guidelines as "useful" and "susceptible to contributing to the harmonization and unification of standards governing conflicts of interest in international arbitration."[40] It certainly does not consider them binding although no case has arisen where the Parties have specifically adopted the IBA Guidelines as rules (not just guidelines) for their arbitration. Furthermore, the Swiss Supreme Court takes into account the practical fact of the existence of large international law firms and international networks of law firms. It has held that a particular lawyer acting in an arbitration, whether as an arbitrator or as counsel, is not necessarily synonymous with his or her law firm or network of law firms for the purposes of conflict analysis.[41] The Swiss Supreme Court has stated and emphasized that the particular circumstances of the instant case must be assessed. In this way, the fact that different law firms in their marketing emphasize their network and its advantages for their clients, but that such law firms within the network are in fact financially independent has been found not to constitute a conflict of interest.[42] The fact that there is no sharing of profits also convinced the court of the absence of a conflict of interest.[43]

There is a lack of independence under Swiss arbitration law if there is a personal tie of sufficient importance between an arbitrator and a party or its counsel.[44] There is a lack of impartiality where an arbitrator has in the past publicly associated herself with a position in relation to a sufficiently important legal issue in the arbitration.[45] In assessing challenges to arbitrators for bias, the Swiss courts require that an application will first have been made to any arbitration institution notably pursuant to a set of arbitration rules. A failure to have acted first and in a timely manner in accordance with such rules will generally be treated as a waiver of the particular facts of bias.

Challenges to arbitral awards on the basis of arbitrators' bias are made under article 190(2) (a) of the PIL, which refers to the tribunal being improperly constituted. It will not be a surprise that the Swiss bias challenge is conceptualized as a species of improper constitution of the tribunal, as the basis under the NY Convention for refusing to enforce an arbitration award tainted by bias, that, in Art. V(1)(d), is also described as a complaint in relation to the composition of the arbitral tribunal. Since Art. Art. V(1)(d) of the NY Convention refers to the requirements of

---

[36] M. Orelli, *Chapter 2, Part II: Commentary on Chapter 12 PILS, Article 180 [Challenge of an Arbitrator]*, in ARBITRATION IN SWITZERLAND: THE PRACTITIONER'S GUIDE 118, NN 12 (M. Arroyo ed., 2d ed. 2013).
[37] ATF 142 III 521.
[38] *Id. See* F. Robert-Tissot, *Arbitrage – Chronique de jurisprudence du Tribunal fédéral en matière d'arbitrage international et internes (1er mars 2016 au 28 février 2018)*, JUSLETTER, Dec. 3, 2018, p. 5.
[39] *See* Robert-Tissot, *supra* note 38.
[40] ATF 142 III 521 consid. 3.1.2 (free translation).
[41] *Id.* at 3.3.1.1.
[42] *Id.* at 3.3.1.2.
[43] *Id.* at 3.2.2.
[44] ATF 92 I 271 and ATF 111 Ia 72 at consid. 2a.
[45] ATF 133 I 89 at consid. 3.4.

the place of arbitration to the constitution of the tribunal, and article 194 of the PIL, as we have seen, refers to the NY Convention for enforcement of foreign arbitration awards, enforcement may be denied on the basis of arbitrators' bias (article 190(2)(a) PIL) on the same basis as bias challenges to arbitrators (article 180(c) PIL).

5 PROCEDURAL IRREGULARITIES AND ARBITRATORS' MISCONDUCT DURING PROCEEDINGS

A violation of due process (the right to be heard) is a ground to set aside the award under article 190(2)(d). It is equally a ground to refuse to enforce the arbitral award in Switzerland (article V (1) let. b NY Convention read in conjunction with article 194 PIL).[46] Even though the NY Convention only mentions due notice to the defending party or otherwise not being able to present a case, Swiss courts treat this provision as including all aspects of mandatory procedural rights (enunciated in article 182(3) PIL; see later in the chapter).[47]

In Swiss international arbitration, there is, at least conceptually, the same constitutional right to a fair procedure as that before Swiss State court judges. But in practice, the protections in arbitration are less stringent than before the Swiss courts. This results from the acceptance of a greater degree of procedural flexibility in international arbitration than before courts. The mandatory procedural guarantees in international arbitration are set forth in article 182(3) of the PIL. The tribunal and parties are free to choose the arbitral procedure (article 182(1) and (2) PIL), but they must be treated equally, and their right to be heard in adversary proceedings must be ensured.[48]

In Swiss arbitration, one needs to protest immediately, clearly, and with a sufficient degree of insistence at any perceived violation of one's procedural guarantees or one will be deemed, by operation of the principle of good faith, to have waived that basis of the objection.[49] In decision 4A_40/2018 the Swiss Supreme Court considered the interesting legal issue of whether there was a violation of the right to be heard because the arbitrator based his decision on evidence the claimant never had access to. The Supreme Court held, however, that that claim had been validly dismissed by the arbitral tribunal since the claimant failed to protest against this alleged violation before the arbitral tribunal with sufficient alacrity.

In decision 4A_478/2017 the Swiss Supreme Court recalled that it is only entitled to examine the right to be heard but not whether the arbitral tribunal has come to the right legal result.[50] The challenge was, however, partially successful as the Swiss Supreme Court concluded that it was not possible to infer from the award that the arbitrator had implicitly rejected arguments that the claimant presented in its second brief.[51] The court added that these arguments were important for the result of the case and that it was not a simple lack of reasons, which is no basis to set aside an award under article 190(2)(d) PIL. In decision 4A_247/2017 the Swiss Supreme Court rejected a claim of a violation of the right to be heard. The court

---

[46] J. Knoll, *Chapter 2, Part II: Commentary on Chapter 12 PILS, Article 182 [Procedure: Principle]*, in ARBITRATION IN SWITZERLAND: THE PRACTITIONER'S GUIDE 141, N 26 (M. Arroyo ed., 2d ed. 2013).
[47] GEISINGER & VOSER, *supra* note 27, at 214.
[48] Knoll, *supra* note 46.
[49] *Id.* at 145, N 32.
[50] 4A_478/2017 consid. 3.3.2.
[51] *Id.* at 3.3.3 ("*Quoi qu'il en soit, il appert de ces observations que l'arbitre a passé sous silence des éléments que le recourant avait régulièrement avancés à l'appui de l'une de ses conclusions subsidiaires, sans que l'on parvienne à se convaincre qu'il les aurait réfutés de manière implicite*").

recalled that the principle of good faith required the invocation of the procedural irregularity without delay.[52]

The Swiss Supreme Court, in decision 4A_600/2010, also considered that the principle of good faith applied to arbitrators as well. In this case, the arbitral tribunal asked the parties to express their views on costs, which the parties did wish to do but requested an extended deadline. The arbitral tribunal ignored this request and stated that the parties had "voluntarily chosen not to file any brief."[53] The court concluded that the arbitral tribunal violated the principle of good faith and, thus, the right to be heard of the parties. In decision 4A_236/2017 the complainant submitted that the sole arbitrator had treated the parties unequally in comparable situations by allowing the respondent to introduce extensive new evidence into the proceedings only a few hours before an oral hearing. The court concluded that it was obvious that the arbitrator considered the evidence as admissible when he orally declared so during a hearing and that the claimant accepted this fact at the time. In 4A_214/2011 the Supreme Court held that there was no violation of the right to be heard in that the arbitral tribunal did not warn the complaining party that it considered the evidence insufficient.[54]

Equal treatment and rights of the defence have virtually identical content – the right to the "administration of evidence" and to comment on facts relevant to the outcome. The *administration of evidence* will be an unfamiliar term to common law practitioners. It is the functional equivalent of the right to submit evidence but reflects the fact that in Swiss civil procedure (typical of most continental European legal systems) it is the adjudicator who is principally active in deciding what specific evidence will be admitted and taken account of. In the result, parties' evidential rights become generic to the legal issue rather than in respect of specific pieces of evidence.

The right to be heard entails the duty of the arbitral tribunal to treat the parties equally in the administration and weighing of evidence but more generally in all aspects of the procedure.[55] However, small differences of treatment cannot be avoided and are therefore accepted "as long as neither of the parties is substantially disadvantaged by the way the procedure is carried out."[56] The Swiss Supreme Court defines the right to be heard as follows:

> in particular the right of the parties to express themselves on all facts that may be relevant to the outcome of the case, to make legal arguments, to adduce evidence to their relevant factual allegations in the appropriate and timely form.[57]

The right to adversarial proceedings entails in its core the right to comment on the adversary's case, meaning that the arbitral tribunal shall offer to the parties the opportunity to give counter arguments and to have a debate on the other party's evidence and legal reasoning.[58]

In practice, what is most important is the way the arbitral tribunal takes into account the parties' factual and legal submissions. What is decisive is whether a party's argument is relevant to the making of the final decision.[59] The right to be heard is violated when

---

[52] 4A_247/2017 consid. 5.2.2.
[53] 4A_600/2010 consid. 4.4.1.
[54] GEISINGER & VOSER, *supra* note 27, at 245.
[55] Knoll, *supra* note 46, at 143, N 28.
[56] *Id.* at 143, N 29.
[57] *Id.* at 145, N 32; *see also* the Swiss Supreme Court decision 4A_234/2010.
[58] Knoll, *supra* note 46, at 145, N 33.
[59] *Id.* at 147, N 39, 40.

inadvertently or by a misunderstanding, the arbitral tribunal does not take into consideration alleged facts, arguments, evidence and offers of evidence presented by one of the parties and that are important for the decision to be made.[60]

This was the case when, in its legal reasoning, an arbitral tribunal totally ignored a series of arguments presented over twelve pages regarding the legality of a penalty under a potentially applicable law. The court recognized in this particular case that they were *subsidiary* arguments, but it considered that the arbitral tribunal should have *explained* why it did not consider them relevant to make its decision.[61] A violation of the right to be heard was also recognized when an arbitral tribunal did not take into account objections of the appellant that were important and relevant to determine the number of damages.[62] The court considered that it was not possible to conclude that the arbitral tribunal considered those objections or "implicitly rejected them"[63] By consequence, the court found that the arbitral tribunal "did not satisfy its minimal duty to examine relevant issues."[64]

The tribunal is, however, entitled to make a selection of the evidence on which it decides, and the tribunal may make a factual determination as soon as it determines it has heard enough evidence on it and not wait until all evidence is submitted.

There is no right to an oral hearing,[65] but, if one is held, there is a right to active participation in it. The right to be heard in adversarial proceedings includes the duty of the arbitral tribunal to give notice in due time to the parties of the date, time, place, and detailed agenda of the hearings.[66]

The right to be heard in adversarial proceedings does not entail a right to a reasoned arbitral award. The Swiss Supreme Court ruled that it would be contrary to legislative intent to include the right to supporting reasons within the right to be heard in adversarial proceedings.[67] It stated that "article 190(2)(d) PIL only adopts the mandatory procedural provisions of article 182(3) PIL as a ground for appeal, but not the requirement to state reasons prescribed in article 189(2) PIL."[68] This decision has been criticized by some authors alleging that this interpretation of the right to be heard is more restrictive than its application before Swiss courts and according to the Swiss Federal Constitution and the European Convention on Human Rights.[69]

Conclusions manifestly contrary to the evidentiary finding of facts are in themselves not contrary to the right to be heard unless they amount to a formal denial of justice in the sense that party submissions have inadvertently been overlooked or misunderstood.[70] The Swiss Supreme Court stated that "a formal denial of justice exists only if the parties were deprived of their right to participate in the proceedings, to influence them, and to present their case, thus, if the obvious error has in fact negative their right to be heard."[71]

---

[60] ATF 133 III 235 consid. 5.2 (free translation). See also 4A_433/2009. Original text: "*Il [le droit d'être entendu] est violé lorsque, par inadvertance ou malentendu, le tribunal arbitral ne prend pas en considération des allégués, arguments, preuves et offres de preuve présentés par l'une des parties et importants pour la décision à render.*"
[61] ATF 133 III 235 consid. 5.3
[62] 4A_433/2009 of 26 May 2010 consid. 2.4.2
[63] *Id*. (free translation).
[64] *Id*. (free translation).
[65] *See* ATF 117 II 346 consid. E.1b/aa.
[66] Knoll, *supra* note 46, at 145, N 35.
[67] ATF 116 II 373 consid. 7b.
[68] *Id.*
[69] Molina, *supra* note 22, at 257, N 55
[70] ATF 121 III 331 consid. E.3a; also 127 III 576 E.2d. *See also* BERGER & KELLERHALLS, *supra* note 7, at 610, N 1746.
[71] ATF 127 III 576 E.2d and E.2f. For the translation, *see* BERGER & KELLERHALLS, *supra* note 7, at 611, N1747.

6 ANTI-ARBITRATION LAW AND PUBLIC POLICY

By article 177(2) of the PIL, anything of financial value is arbitrable in Swiss international arbitration. "A financial interest of at least one of the parties is fundamental" and

> as a consequence of the wide and liberal approach taken by the Swiss Supreme Court, disputes of financial interest do not only encompass claims based on contract, tort or corporate liability, but also pecuniary claims founded in family, inheritance or property law.[72]

Questions of status, like filiation, for example, are therefore not arbitrable, but very little else is not arbitrable in Swiss international arbitration. Only a "prevailing objective reason"[73] could exclude arbitrability. The Swiss Supreme Court considered that arbitrability could be denied in a case involving an *exclusivity* of jurisdiction of a state court in the context of public policy protection.[74] But Swiss law intervenes to remove certain vulnerable persons from arbitral jurisdiction by application of general contract principles (which may be non-Swiss principles if non-Swiss law applies). Interestingly, domestic arbitration in Switzerland has a different, and one thinks broader, conception[75] of inarbitrability. Article 354 of the CPC provides that the parties may submit to domestic arbitration any claim over which they have free disposition.

There is no proper class action available in Swiss civil procedure, that is, where a claimant or several claimants are certified as representative of a larger number of persons having the same or similar interests to those identified in the claim. Swiss civil procedure does not allow for representative actions (although terminology does vary from legal system to legal system, these may be conceived as a subset of class actions), that is where a person initiates a claim not seeking relief from any wrong caused to him- or herself but to one or usually more persons who allege to have suffered the wrong.

There is no concern about arbitrability and no prospect of an offence against public policy, as far as Swiss law is concerned, if arbitration results in parties being deprived of class and, in particular, representative action rights before foreign courts such as in the United States. Article 71 CPC does provide for joinder of parties whether as claimants or respondents where their interests arise from circumstances or legal grounds that are sufficiently similar. This test differs from the analysis under Swiss arbitration law for including such persons within the same arbitration proceeding since the latter focuses on the similarity of the arbitration clause and for institution arbitration provisions for joinder in the arbitration rules. In the result, joinder in an arbitration will frequently be more restrictive. Where joinder in an arbitration deprives a party of participation in an arbitration with others, this is nonetheless no ground for interfering with the arbitration on the basis of inarbitrability or with the award on the basis of public policy. Arbitrability in the arbitration law system of the state of the seat is of course not the only relevant source of arbitrability restrictions. A lack of arbitrability in the legal system of the state of enforcement is by article V(2)(a) of the NY Convention a ground for refusal of enforcement, and this will be raised sua sponte by the enforcing court.

---

[72] M. Orelli, *Chapter 2, Part II: Commentary on Chapter 12 PILS, Article 177 [Arbitrability]*, in ARBITRATION IN SWITZERLAND: THE PRACTITIONER'S GUIDE 62, N 4 (M. Arroyo ed., 2d ed. 2013)
[73] *Id.*
[74] ATF 118 II 353 consid. 3c, *see also* Orelli, *supra* note 72, at 62, N 5.
[75] BERGER & KELLERHALLS, *supra* note 7, at 735, N 2092; the Swiss Supreme Court has not yet commented on the relative scopes of arbitrability in Swiss international and domestic arbitration.

If an arbitration procedure is incompatible with public policy, arbitrability is equally excluded.[76] A violation of public policy is a basis upon which to set aside an award in Swiss international arbitration (article 190(2)(e) PIL), and by article V(2)(e) of the NY Convention it is a ground to refuse to enforce an award. (Substantive) Public policy is violated when "the material findings ... are against fundamental principles of law and are therefore totally incompatible with the legal order and the system of values."[77] Such fundamental legal principles are for example pacta sunt servanda, good faith, the prohibition of abuse or rights, the prohibition of discriminatory measures or the protection of civilly disabled persons.[78] Public policy remains, however, a fluid concept.[79] The notion of public policy is interpreted extremely restrictively. Very few awards are interfered with on this basis (article 190(2)(e) of the PIL).[80]

Public policy can be either procedural or substantive.[81] Effectively, any setting aside of or refusal to enforce an international arbitration award in Switzerland for a violation of procedural public policy requires a violation of the fundamental procedural guarantees under article 182(2) of the PIL discussed in earlier and if the *result* (not the reasons) of the award itself is contrary to public policy.[82] There is an effective overlap between procedural public policy and the right to be heard.

In a 2010 decision setting aside an award for violation of procedural public policy, the Swiss Supreme Court ruled that the arbitral tribunal wrongly rejected a res judicata objection (procedural public policy).[83] The dispute involved a football player who terminated his contract with a football club (Benfica) to join another club (Atlético). Benfica requested compensation from Atlético according to the 1997 FIFA Regulations for the Status and Transfer of Players. In 2002, the FIFA special committee awarded Benfica compensation of US$2.5 million. Atlético appealed against this decision before the Commercial Court of the Canton of Zurich, which decided in 2004 that the FIFA Regulation was in violation of European and Swiss competition law. It then declared the previous decision as null and void. Later in 2004, Benfica once again claimed compensation for the same dispute before the FIFA Special Committee, which rejected the claim in 2008. In 2009, Benfica appealed against this decision before the Court of Arbitration for Sport (CAS). Atlético invoked especially the res judicata effect of the decision of the Court of Zurich dated 2004. In 2009, the CAS tribunal decided to award compensation of €400,000 to Benfica. This decision was challenged before the Swiss Supreme Court by Atlético, which requested the court set the CAS award aside, arguing that the CAS violated the res judicata effect and thus violated public policy as provided by article 190(2)(e) of the PIL. In its decision the Swiss Supreme Court held that a violation of public policy is effective if a court "disregards in its award the final and binding force of a previous decision."[84] In awarding compensation for Benfica, the CAS tribunal ignored the binding force of the decision made by the Zurich Court in 2004, which led to two contradictory decisions on the same matter. The Swiss Supreme Court concluded that such disregard of the res judicata principle was against procedural public policy.

---

[76] Orelli, *supra* note 72, at 66, N 20.
[77] ATF 120 II 155 consid. 6a; ATF 116 II 634 consid. 4, *see also* Orelli, *supra* note 72, at 66, N 21.
[78] ATF 120 II 155 consid. 6a.
[79] *Id.* at 2.1.
[80] 4A_248/2019 consid. 2.
[81] BERGER & KELLERHALLS, *supra* note 7, at 737, N 2098.
[82] M. Arroyo, *Chapter 2, Part II: Commentary on Chapter 12 PILS, Article 190 [Finality, Challenge]*, in ARBITRATION IN SWITZERLAND: THE PRACTITIONER'S GUIDE 325, N 168 (M. Arroyo ed., 2d ed. 2013).
[83] ATF 136 III 345 consid. 2.2. *See also* Arroyo, *supra* note 82, at 340–342, NN 209–218.
[84] ATF 136 III 345 consid. 2.1.

The violation of substantive public policy is often invoked in appeals but is very rarely accepted by Swiss courts. There has only ever been one award invalidated in Switzerland on this basis. This case involved a football player who terminated his contract with a Ukrainian football club before the agreed duration and without "just cause" or "sporting just cause" in 2007.[85] Later the same year, the player signed a new contract with a Spanish football club. In 2009, the player was transferred definitively to an Italian Football club. But on November 2, 2007, the FIFA Dispute Resolution Chamber awarded compensation of €6.8 million to the Ukrainian football club. A CAS tribunal in 2009 partly invalidated this decision and awarded compensation of 11.8 million euros. The challenge by the player and the Spanish football club was rejected by the Swiss Supreme Court in 2010. Later in the same year, the FIFA Disciplinary Committee informed the player and the Spanish club that they would open a disciplinary proceeding against them for not complying with the CAS tribunal's decision of 2009.[86] The punishment in the 2009 FIFA Disciplinary Code was a ban on taking part in football activities (articles 22 and 64) at the sole request of his former employer (the Ukrainian football club). The committee imposed a final deadline for the payment, and, if no payment was made, a ban on all football activities would be issued against him. Although the Spanish club paid the amount partially (because of serious financial difficulties), a CAS tribunal, on appeal, rejected said appeal and confirmed the ban.[87] The player and the Spanish club appealed against this decision before the Swiss Supreme Court. In this decision dated 2012, the court emphasized that the list of principles constituting substantive public policy was not exhaustive.[88] On this basis, the court ruled that an unlimited ban on a player according to the FIFA Disciplinary Code violated the personality rights of the appellant (article 27(2) CC).[89] The court explained that personality rights are fundamental in the Swiss legal system, are of a constitutional nature and that, in this case, personality rights of the player took precedence over the principle of pacta sunt servanda.[90] This violation was so serious, threatening the player's economic freedom and putting him under the control of his former employer, concluded the court, that it was contrary to substantive public policy.[91]

It should be noted that no violation of public policy has ever been recognized by the Swiss Supreme Court in an international *commercial* arbitration case, and that some authors emphasize that the facts of some of these cases involved rather serious shortcomings and that there is no reason to think that the court will be less restrictive in the future.[92] The Swiss Supreme Court ruled in several decisions that procedural rules established by the parties are not mandatory and that their breach does not necessarily imply a violation of public policy under 190(2)(e) PIL.[93] In decision ATF 130 III 125, the Swiss Supreme Court decided that the "lack of reasons" in an arbitral award is not a violation of procedural public policy nor a violation of the right to be heard.[94]

In decision ATF 4A_150/2012, the Swiss Supreme Court ruled that an intrinsic contradiction within the award's reasons is not a violation.[95] Similarly, the court ruled in decisions ATF 128 III

---

[85] ATF 136 III 345 consid. A.b.
[86] *Id.* at. B.a.
[87] *Id.* at B.b.
[88] *Id.* at 4.1; *see also* Arroyo, *supra* note 82, at 344, N 225.
[89] ATF 136 III 345 consid. 4.3.5. *See* Arroyo, *supra* note 82, at 346, N 232.
[90] ATF 136 III 345 consid. 4.3.1 and 4.3.4.
[91] *Id.* at 4.3.5.
[92] Arroyo, *supra* note 82, at 343, N 233.
[93] 4P.196/2003 consid. 4.2.2.2 ; 126 III 249 consid. 3b.
[94] Arroyo, *supra* note 82, at 330–331, N 184.
[95] *Id.* at 331, N 185.

191 and 4A_386/2010 that an intrinsic contradiction within the operative part of the award is not a violation.[96]

Arroyo summarizes the situation by saying that

> even a manifestly erroneous finding of fact or one which is in contradiction with the case record – and purportedly led to an obviously incorrect or unjust award – does not, as such, justify the setting aside of an international arbitral award.[97]

Neither an arbitrary assessment of evidence nor an arbitrary finding of facts constitutes a violation of public policy.[98] According to the Swiss Supreme Court, there is no breach of public policy in any of the following circumstances: the award incorrectly applied foreign or EU competition law,[99] the lawyers' fees were fixed on a contingency fee basis (pactum de quota litis) amounting to 30 percent of the amount of dispute,[100] compound interest has been awarded,[101] one arbitrator did not sign the award or the wrong law was applied,[102] the solution adopted is different from that under Swiss law or even unknown in Switzerland,[103] or the award failed to state the reasons on which it is based.[104] As Arroyo emphasizes, the principle of compatibility with public policy represents a *minimal* guarantee: "public policy simply seeks to ensure a minimum quality of awards rendered in international arbitrations having their seat in Switzerland."[105] The Swiss Supreme Court has held that an arbitration award ordering the payment of a success fee in respect of the winning party's Swiss lawyers' representation in an arbitration was no basis to set aside the award on public policy grounds even where the structure of that success fee[106] was contrary to Swiss bar rules and would be unenforceable before the Swiss courts.[107]

7 CONCLUSION

Although Switzerland is not a UNCITRAL Model Law country, its international arbitration law is decidedly pro-arbitration. It provides, on the whole, for the broad recognition and scope of international arbitration agreements and only in particularly grievous cases will the Swiss courts disturb an international arbitration award.

---

[96] Id. at 331, N 185. See also BERGER & KELLERHALLS, *supra* note 7, at 628, N 1788.
[97] Arroyo, *supra* note 82, at 332–334, N 189.
[98] Respectively, 4A_360/2001 consid. 4.1; ATF 116 II 634 consid. 4.b.
[99] ATF 132 III 389.
[100] *Decision of the Swiss Supreme Court*, Jan. 9, 1995, 19 ASA BULL. 294 (2001); *see also* 5A_409/2014.
[101] Id.
[102] Basel Country Court of Appeal, June 9, 1971 (1973) Basler Juristische Mitteilungen 193.
[103] 5A_409/2014.
[104] ATF 101 Ia 521, 525.
[105] Arroyo, *supra* note 82, at 330, N 183; *see also* 4A_612/2009 consid. 6.2.2.
[106] A percentage of the party's success in the arbitration, a so-called pactum de quota litis.
[107] 4A_125/2018.

22

Judicial Control of Arbitral Awards in Ukraine

Galyna Mykhailiuk and Nina Mykhailiuk

1 INTRODUCTION

Upon the dissolution of the Soviet Union in 1991, Ukraine as a young independent state faced many challenges including the proper administration of trade disputes with foreign parties. For a certain period there were no such institutions that could resolve these disputes. To prevent the creation of a legal vacuum, the Parliament of Ukraine, along with the establishing of the foreign trade legal framework for Ukrainian nationals and adopting the Law on Foreign Economic Activity,[1] recommended that the Ukrainian Chamber of Commerce and Industry (UCCI) establish a permanent arbitration body for prompt and efficient consideration of "foreign economic disputes." For this purpose, on August 11, 1992, the International Commercial Arbitration Court (ICAC) and the Maritime Arbitration Commission (MAC)[2] were created. However, almost from the very inception both institutions could hardly operate because of lack of legal basis for their functioning. To improve this complicated situation, the Law on International Commercial Arbitration[3] (the International Arbitration Statute; ICA Law) was adopted on February 24, 1994 (effective April 20, 1994).[4]

Up until the reform, the ICA Law reflects the approach of the UNCITRAL Model Law 1985 with minor deviations. In particular, the ICA Law stipulates that the parties may have recourse to international commercial arbitration in the case of cross-border disputes resulting from contractual or other civil law relationships arising in the course of foreign trade and other forms of international economic relations, as well as in the case of disputes involving Ukrainian enterprises with foreign investment or international associations and organizations established in the territory of Ukraine.[5] In order to reconcile the ICA Law with the new editions of the codes of procedure and to implement certain new provisions of the UNCITRAL Model Law 2006, the ICA Law has been updated.

---

[1] No. 959-XII, Vidomosti Verkhovna Rada of Ukraine (VVR), 1991, No. 29, st. 377.
[2] The ICAC and MAC are the only Ukrainian institutions which are authorized to administer international commercial arbitrations seated in Ukraine. However, ICAC's arbitration "monopoly" does not prevent foreign arbitral institutions like the International Arbitration Court of the International Chamber of Commerce or the London Court of International Arbitration from administering arbitrations with their seat in Ukraine.
[3] No. 4004-XII, Vidomosti Verkhovna Rada of Ukraine (VVR), 1994, No. 25, st. 198.
[4] Partially quoted, Sergiy Gryshko, *Ukrainian International Arbitration Law Reform: What Fate Is My Tomorrow Brewing?*, REDCLIFFE PARTNERS (July 2016), redcliffe-partners.com/assets/YAR_Young%20Arbitration% 20Review_Ed %2022_Ukraine.pdf.
[5] OLEG ALYOSHIN & YURIY DOBOSH, UKRAINE IN ARBITRATION WORLD. INTERNATIONAL SERIES 997–1016, 999 (5th ed. 2015).

After years of discussions and active work of various working groups and the Ukrainian Parliament, at the end of 2017 Ukraine finally managed to reform its arbitration-related procedural legislation. Nowadays parties, contemplating the commencement of arbitration, may seek Ukrainian courts' assistance in obtaining interim measures and preserving and collecting evidence necessary for arbitral proceedings, which was practically impossible prior to the reform.[6] The improved rules on judicial control over arbitration make setting aside and enforcement proceedings more efficient while the new arbitrability rules curtail uncertainty regarding many categories of disputes.

Arbitration reform constituted a part of larger judicial reform in Ukraine introduced by the Law No. 2147-VIII amending the Commercial Procedure Code, the Civil Procedure Code, the Code for Administrative Court Proceedings of Ukraine,[7] and other laws[8] (the Law on Procedural Reform), an 800-page document aimed at solving the problems of Ukrainian justice by replacing the three existing procedural codes, adopted by the Ukrainian Parliament on October 3, 2017. Published officially on November 28, 2017, the Law on Procedural Reform entered into force on December 15, 2017, the same day that the new Supreme Court of Ukraine started its functioning. The Law on Procedural Reform is a part of the ongoing judicial reform in Ukraine. It introduced certain important changes to the court procedures in arbitration-related matters aiming to improve the legislative framework for international arbitration. The Law of Ukraine on International Commercial Arbitration is considered the most notable one.

The fundamental objective of the changes was to improve the efficiency of the judiciary control over arbitration by filling in major gaps in procedural legislation.[9] In particular, it pursues three goals: (1) the introduction of a well-functioning procedural framework for judicial assistance in collecting of evidence and providing conservatory measures, (2) the improvement of enforcement and annulment proceedings, and (3) the elimination of onerous arbitrability restrictions and the improvement of the arbitration environment.

The Law on Procedural Reform provides that only two court instances have jurisdiction over international arbitration-related matters – the competent civil Appellate Court (designated depending on the type of proceedings) and the Supreme Court. By contrast to the Model Law, the International Arbitration Statute provides that domestic disputes involving Ukrainian legal entities "with foreign investment" (with at least 10 percent foreign shareholding as defined by the Commercial Code of Ukraine) can also be submitted to international arbitration.[10] Additionally, among the advantages relevant to arbitrating or bringing to arbitration-related proceedings in Ukraine are the following: the domestic courts are relatively arbitration friendly with adverse court interventions occurring only very rarely; the costs of both arbitration fees at permanent arbitral institutions and court fees in matters related to arbitration are comparatively low; under the ICA Law, Ukrainian companies with foreign investment, including the subsidiaries of international companies, can refer to international arbitration with their claims against both Ukrainian legal entities and individuals. In particular, the Law on Procedural Reform changes the Rules of Article 7 of the ICA Law about the form of an arbitration agreement. Now it expressly allows entering into arbitration agreement by way of exchange of

---

[6] Olena Perepelynska, *Arbitration Reform in Ukraine: New Possibilities for Arbitration Users*, CIS ARBITRATION FORUM (2018), www.cisarbitration.com/2018/02/08/arbitration-reform-in-ukraine-new-possibilities-for-arbitration-users/.
[7] Vidomosti Verkhovna Rada of Ukraine (VVR), 2005, No. 40-41, 42, st. 492.
[8] No. 2147-VIII, Vidomosti Verkhovna Rada of Ukraine (VVR), 2017, No. 48, st. 436.
[9] Perepelynska, *supra* note 6.
[10] Gryshko, *supra* note 4.

electronic communications if the information contained therein is accessible and usable for subsequent reference.[11]

Currently these issues are partially regulated by the provisions of Chapter VIII (Proceedings in Cases on Challenges against Awards of [Domestic] Arbitration Courts, Challenges against Awards of Internal Arbitration Courts) and Chapter IX (Recognition and Enforcement of Foreign Court Decisions in Ukraine and Issuance of Execution Writs for Enforcement of Awards of [Domestic] Arbitration Courts) of the Civil Procedure Code of Ukraine,[12] which previously (before the judicial reform) did not take into account the particularities of international commercial arbitration and were obviously insufficient and imperfect.

Domestic arbitration is governed by the Ukrainian law On Domestic Courts of Arbitration[13] adopted on May 11, 2004 and provides for the possibility of institutional or ad hoc arbitration proceedings. It regulates commercial and civil disputes between Ukrainian entities and/or individuals only. The parties are expressly precluded from arbitrating disputes domestically: (1) where at least one of the parties is a foreign company or an individual; (2) where at least one of the parties is a state or local governmental authority, state institution, or organization or fiscal enterprise; (3) on invalidation of legislative acts; (4) issues arising from conclusion, amendment, termination, and performance of state procurement contracts; (5) in bankruptcy cases; (6) in cases related to state secrets; (7) under family law, except in cases arising from prenuptial contracts; and (8) in those cases which by law must be exclusively resolved by the courts of general jurisdiction or by the Constitutional Court of Ukraine.[14]

Under the ICA Law adopted on February 24, 1994, the following disputes may be referred to international commercial arbitration upon agreement of the parties: (1) disputes arising from contractual and other civil relationships related to foreign trade and other types of international economic relations if at least one party is located abroad and (2) disputes between companies with foreign investment and international organizations and associations established in Ukraine, between each other, between their participants, and their disputes with other Ukrainian legal subjects.

2 GROUNDS FOR VACATING ARBITRAL AWARDS DUE TO ARBITRATOR BIAS

Nowadays people's trust in foreign independent arbitration institutions is undisputedly high in Ukraine. Consequently, a number of disputes, encompassing various fields of law, follow the trend of being arbitrated instead of being litigated. This part examines the procedure for challenging an arbitrator and the consequences when the challenged arbitrator withdraws from his or her office.

Article 19 of the DCA Law names grounds for withdrawal or recusal of an arbitrator. The arbitrator cannot take part in the consideration of a case, and after an appointment or election the arbitrator is subject to withdrawal or recusal if he or she has a direct or indirect interest in the matter at stake. At the same time, Article 12 of the ICA Law lists the following among the grounds for challenge of an arbitrator: (1) When a person is approached in connection with possible appointment as an arbitrator, he or she shall without delay disclose any such circumstances

---

[11] Olena Perepelynska, *Arbitration Reform in Ukraine: Enhancing Efficiency of Judicial Control over and Support to Arbitration*, 12 MEALEY'S INTERNATIONAL ARBITRATION REPORT 6 (2017).
[12] Vidomosti Verkhovna Rada of Ukraine (VVR), 2004, No. 40-41, 42, st. 492.
[13] No. 1701-IV, Vidomosti Verkhovna Rada of Ukraine (VVR), 2004, No. 35, st. 412.
[14] Svitlana Romanova, *Dispute Resolution around the World. Ukraine* BAKER MCKENZIE (2011), 15, www.bakermckenzie.com/-/media/files/insight/publications/2016/10/dratw/dratw_ukraine_2011. pdf?la=en.

likely to give rise to justifiable doubts as to his or her neutrality or independence. Any arbitrator may be challenged if circumstances exist that give rise to justifiable doubts as to the arbitrator's impartiality or independence since the start of arbitration and during the proceedings. An arbitrator shall without delay disclose any such circumstances to the parties, unless they have already been informed of them by him or her. (2) An arbitrator can be challenged only if circumstances exist that give rise to justifiable doubts as to his or her impartiality or independence, or if none possess qualifications required by the agreement of the parties. A party may only challenge an arbitrator whom it has appointed or in whose appointment it has participated on the grounds of which it became aware after such appointment.

Regarding the challenge procedure, Article 13 of the ICA Law states that: (1) The parties are free to agree on a procedure for challenging an arbitrator. (2) Failing such agreement, a party who intends to challenge an arbitrator should, within fifteen days after having knowledge of the constitution of the arbitral tribunal, explain in writing the reasons for the challenge to the arbitral tribunal. Unless the challenged arbitrator withdraws from his or her office or the other party agrees to the challenge, the arbitral tribunal shall decide on the challenge. According to the ICAC and MAC Rules, unless a party makes a challenge within the period of time referred to, the party shall be deemed to have waived his or her right to challenge. (3) If a challenge under any procedure agreed upon by the parties is not successful, the challenging party may request, within thirty days from receipt by that party of the notification of the decision to reject the challenge, the president of the UCCI to decide on the challenge; his or her decision shall be final. While such a request is pending, the arbitral tribunal, including the challenged arbitrator, shall continue the arbitration and make an award.

The Authority (Mandate) of Arbitrator can be terminated if an arbitrator is prevented de jure or de facto from fulfilling the arbitrator's functions or for other reasons fails to act without undue delay. His or her mandate terminates if he or she withdraws from the office or upon request of all the parties. Otherwise, if a controversy remains concerning any of these grounds, any party may request the President of the UCCI to decide on the termination of the mandate; his or her decision shall be final, and the reasons for such decisions shall not be communicated.[15]

A party may challenge an arbitrator it has appointed, should any issues or information arise subsequent to the appointment. Under the ICA Law, the parties are free to agree on the procedure for challenges, but after the constitution of the arbitral tribunal any challenge shall be submitted in writing to the arbitral tribunal within fifteen days from the date when relevant facts that have given rise to the challenge become known. Unless the challenged arbitrator withdraws from his or her office, or the other party agrees to the challenge, the arbitral tribunal itself is to decide on the challenge. If the challenge is dismissed, the challenging party may request the UCCI president to make a final decision on the challenge. While such a request is pending, the arbitral tribunal, including the challenged arbitrator, shall continue the arbitration and make an award.

Under the ICAC Rules, the ICAC Presidium is empowered to decide on the challenge if the challenged arbitrator does not withdraw from office or if the other party does not agree to the challenge. The ICAC Presidium can also decide the challenge on its own if any facts or circumstances exist that may give rise to justifiable doubts as to arbitrator's impartiality or independence. In any case, the UCCI president makes the final decision, and the reasons for such a decision of the ICAC Presidium shall not be communicated. The ICAC Rules

---

[15] *See* Art. 14 of the ICA Law.

consider the matter of a challenge as an official function pertaining to the ICAC itself and do not provide for any possibility for the parties to agree on a procedure for challenging an arbitrator. The ICAC Rules state that the ICAC secretariat must give the other party an opportunity to comment in writing on the challenge within a suitable period of time. While the challenged arbitrator and all other persons involved in the arbitration will be given a chance to comment on the challenge, neither the arbitrator nor the challenging party will appear before the ICAC Presidium in defense of their position.

Challenging a member of the tribunal disrupts an ongoing arbitration because it shifts the focus away from the object in dispute onto the tribunal itself. Any action or judgment by a judge in the aforementioned cases shall be void, even if the parties agreed to the same. The awards of the ICAC at the UCCI are successfully executed in more than 110 countries of the world. On average, about 4 percent of the awards of the ICAC at the UCCI are challenged, of which no more than 1 percent is set aside. Such a small number of challenged awards indicate the level effectiveness of the court, as well as the fair and impartial consideration of cases where even the defeated party is morally satisfied with the arbitral proceedings.[16]

3 IMPARTIALITY AND CONFLICT OF INTEREST

In Ukraine, there are no specific rules on disclosure of conflict of interest in arbitration. The ICA Law reiterates the UNCITRAL Model Law provision that, before appointment or confirmation, a prospective arbitrator shall disclose any facts or circumstances that may give rise to justifiable doubts as to his or her impartiality or independence. The ICAC Rules do not contain the list of such circumstances, but it is understood that these situations include any professional relationship with either party, such as any past relationship if the arbitrator was a legal representative of a legal entity in arbitration, has financial or private interests in the matter at stake, or has any kind of a blood or kinship relationship/interest between a party and the arbitrator. According to the ICAC Rules, the arbitrator must complete and sign a special statement of acceptance to act as an arbitrator.

Additionally, the ICA Law reiterates the provisions of UNCITRAL Model Law regarding the independence and impartiality of the arbitrators. The arbitrator shall be independent and impartial in fulfilling his or her functions, and none shall be a representative of either party to the dispute. When a person is approached in relation to his or her possible appointment as an arbitrator, he or she shall disclose any circumstances likely to give rise to justifiable doubts as to his or her neutrality or independence. The arbitrator shall without delay disclose any such circumstances to the ICAC and to the parties once the relevant facts become known to him or her from the time of the appointment and throughout the entire arbitral proceedings.

There are no specific rules or codes of conduct concerning conflicts of interest for arbitrators. The International Bar Association (IBA) Guidelines on Conflicts of Interest in International Arbitration are followed on an individual basis. Ukrainian arbitrators being mostly scholars, former judges, or state officials rarely apply the IBA Guidelines directly; however, they are guided by similar principles established by the IBA.

---

[16] See Mykola Selivon, *International Commercial Arbitration Court at the Ukrainian Chamber of Commerce and Industry Activities*, INTERNATIONAL COMMERCIAL ARBITRATION COURT (2017), https://icac.org.ua/wp-content/uploads/Report-2017.pdf.

4 PROCEDURAL IRREGULARITIES AND MISCONDUCT DURING PROCEEDINGS

This section examines numerous changes introduced by the Law on Procedural Reform that filled many gaps in the Ukrainian procedural legislation governing arbitration-related matters. First, it scrutinizes a lack of procedural rules regulating judicial assistance to arbitration. Prior to the reform, it was impossible to obtain court-ordered interim measures in support of arbitration or to obtain court assistance in taking evidence for arbitral proceedings. The rules on judicial control were not perfect either. They allowed rather lengthy post-award proceedings with respect to setting aside or enforcement of an arbitral award in Ukraine. Sometimes, up to four court instances could have considered a case on setting aside or enforcement of an arbitral award while such a case could have been remanded for reconsideration.[17] Finally, it then discusses the newly introduced opportunity to collect and preserve evidence that is necessary for the arbitral proceedings.

Ukraine is a civil law jurisdiction with an inquisitorial procedure. This background may have some influence on the arbitration proceedings and the way the evidence is dealt with. It means that, although the parties shall provide the arbitrators with the evidence and facts they rely on, the arbitral tribunal is also likely to require the production of further evidence. Furthermore, the arbitral tribunal, either on its own or upon the request of either party, may request that experts or witnesses become involved.[18]

The amendments to the Civil Procedure Code and the ICA Law provide parties with further opportunities available after the commencement of arbitral proceedings, such as the ability to obtain interim measures in support of international arbitration and to obtain a court order on the preservation of evidence necessary for arbitral proceedings.[19] It also allows obtaining judicial assistance in the examination of a witness, evidence production or evidence inspection at its location. The procedure itself and all applicable standards to witnesses and evidence are the same as those established in civil litigation.[20] Such procedural tools are generally available for litigants if there are grounds to believe that the respective evidence could be lost, or their gathering and protection could become impossible or complicated. The judicial assistance in granting interim measures and preserving evidence does not depend on the seat of the arbitral tribunal, while the judicial assistance in the taking of evidence is available only for arbitrations seated in Ukraine. The formal requirements in the ICA Law for arbitral proceedings to be recognizable and enforceable are as follows: (1) the party to the arbitration agreement shall have full capacity and the arbitration agreement must be valid under the relevant law; (2) the parties shall receive proper notice and shall be able to present their case; (3) the arbitral tribunal shall comply with all the requirements set forth in the arbitration clause, in particular, with the time limits and the scope of the submissions to the arbitration; and (4) the arbitral tribunal shall be properly controlled. The representatives of the parties shall be duly granted valid powers of attorney.[21]

Articles 116–118 of the amended Civil Procedure Code of Ukraine now offer this tool for arbitral tribunals and parties to arbitration. At the same time, the abovementioned provisions do not expressly restrict the availability of this tool for arbitrations seated in Ukraine. The procedure itself and all applicable standards are the same as those established in civil litigation. However, for applications in aid of arbitration, it is necessary to provide the state court with a copy of the

---

[17] Perepelynska, *supra* note 11, at 1.
[18] ALYOSHIN & DOBOSH, *supra* note 5, at 1005.
[19] Perepelynska, *supra* note 6.
[20] Perepelynska, *supra* note 11, at 5.
[21] *See* ALYOSHIN & DOBOSH, *supra* note 5, at 1004.

statement of the claim filed in arbitral proceedings in accordance with applicable arbitration rules and a copy of the respective arbitration agreement. The state court shall send protocols and other materials related to the preservation of evidence to the applicant for further submission to the arbitral tribunal.[22]

Principles of organization and activity of the arbitral tribunal are listed in Article 4 of the DCA Law (legality, independence of arbitrators and their loyalty to the law only, equality of all participants in the arbitration before the law and arbitral tribunal, adversarial parties, i.e., the burden of proof that there are facts causing reasonable doubts as to an arbitrator's independence, or impartiality lies with the party making the challenge). Meanwhile, Article 19 of the DCA Law names grounds for withdrawal or recusal of an arbitrator. Thus, an arbitrator cannot take part in the consideration of a case; after the acceptance of an appointment the arbitrator is subject to withdrawal or recusal for the following reasons: if he or she is directly or indirectly interested in the outcome of the arbitration; if he or she is a relative or in-law of one of the parties or other persons involved in the lawsuit or is in contact with these persons or parties in a blood or kinship relationship; at his or her request or if the parties agreed to the same; if the party establishes circumstances which give rise to justifiable doubts as to the arbitrator's impartiality or independence, which became known after the arbitrator accepted the election or appointment; in the case of a prolonged (more than one month from the date of the appointment or election) failure to perform his or her duties as arbitrator in a particular case; in case of a discrepancy of the arbitrator with the requirements established by Article 18 of the DCA Law;[23] or if the arbitrator is involved in resolving a dispute that is directly or indirectly related to the performance of his or her official duties provided by the state.

No person may be an arbitrator in a case in which he or she previously participated as the arbitrator but has been withdrawn or has voluntarily declared to withdraw (to recuse) as a party, a party representative, or in any other capacity. In neither case does this imply acceptance of the validity of the grounds for the challenge. In the arbitral tribunal, for the purpose of resolving a particular dispute, challenging parties can establish additional grounds for replacement or removal of the arbitrator.

Article 38 of the DCA Law determines *evidence* as any actual data, based on which the arbitral tribunal establishes the presence or absence of the circumstances justifying the claims and objections of the parties and other circumstances of a similar nature relevant to the proper resolution of the dispute. At the same time, taking into account the requirements of the DCA Law and in order to resolve a particular dispute in the arbitral tribunal, the means of proof are determined by an arbitration agreement.

The powers conferred upon the arbitral tribunal and provided in Article 19 of the ICA Law on the determination of Rules of Procedure include the power to establish relevance, materiality

---

[22] *Id.*

[23] Article 18 of the DCA Law:

> Arbitrators are not party representatives. An arbitrator may be an appointed or elected person who does not have direct or indirect interest in resolving a dispute and has been recognized by the parties as having the knowledge, experience, business and moral qualities required to conduct the proceedings properly. The following are ineligible to be arbitrators: juveniles and those who are under custody or care, persons who do not possess the qualifications required by the parties directly or specified in the rules of the arbitral tribunal, persons who have a criminal record, persons recognized by the court incapacitated, judges of general jurisdiction courts or the Constitutional Court of Ukraine. In the case of an individual dispute resolution, the arbitrator of a permanent arbitral tribunal must have a higher legal education. In the case of a collegial dispute resolution, the requirements for the availability of higher legal education shall be applied only to the presiding judge of the arbitral tribunal.

and weight of any evidence. The arbitral tribunal is mainly expected to deliver justice and to treat the parties equally, having ensured that each party is given a full opportunity to present their case. Furthermore, the arbitral tribunal shall comply with the arbitral procedure the parties have agreed upon as well as the respective procedural rules laid down in the ICA Law and the rules of the respective arbitral institution, if applicable.[24]

As neither the ICA Law nor the ICAC/MAC Rules provide for separate provisions governing the production of evidence upon the parties' request in arbitration hearings, the involvement of witnesses and the appointment of experts is upon the parties' request; such practice is not established, and those questions are considered on a case-by-case basis. As a rule, the principal evidence is submitted in conjunction with the submission of written records. The submission of further written evidence is also possible. The IBA Rules on the Taking of Evidence in International Arbitration are rarely used. The ICA Law does not contain any provisions regarding disclosure or discovery as part of the procedure. Still, not only the ICA Law but also the arbitration rules of ICAC and MAC directly prohibit the disclosure of documents requested by the parties. The arbitral tribunal shall decide upon such a request in accordance with the parties' agreement and the rules applicable to the proceedings. The arbitrators are likely to dismiss the disclosure requests in proceedings held under the ICAC/MAC Rules, insofar as both disclosure and discovery are not generally inherent to Ukrainian litigation and arbitration.[25]

The Law on Procedural Reform provides parties with an opportunity that never existed before: to obtain judicial support[26] in matters relating to international arbitration, to secure enforcement of a future arbitral award in Ukraine, and to collect and preserve the evidence they need in arbitral proceedings. The reform introduces the long-awaited amendment allowing parties to obtain interim measures in support of international arbitration. The party to arbitration may seek such measures after the commencement of arbitral proceedings according to general rules governing the interim measures in civil litigation. In addition to a standard package of documents, the applicant should enclose a copy of the statement of the claim or a similar document triggering commencement of arbitral proceedings altogether with the proof that such document has been submitted in arbitration and a copy of the respective arbitration agreement. The court shall consider such application within two days without giving notice to the parties to arbitral proceedings.

According to the amended Civil Procedure Code, any application of the above measures is subject to the same standard set forth in civil litigation: an application for interim measures shall not be granted unless the non-application of such measures would complicate or make impossible the enforcement of a future judgment (an arbitral award) or the effective protection of disputed or violated rights or interests of the claimant, protection of which is sought before the court. The tentative list of possible interim measures is set out in Article 150 of the Civil Procedure Code of Ukraine. However, the court is not entitled to grant interim measures, which are in substance tantamount to the subject matter of the claim.[27] Furthermore, interim measures are available at a competent court at the stage of recognition and enforcement of the arbitral awards in Ukraine, according to Article 394(1) of the Civil Procedure Code of Ukraine.[28] The amended Civil Procedure Code of Ukraine provides that the court can change or cancel the interim measures in support of international arbitration following the general

---

[24] Partially quoted ALYOSHIN & DOBOSH, *supra* note 5, at 1004–1005.
[25] *Id.* at 1005.
[26] Partially quoted Perepelynska, *supra* note 11, at 4.
[27] *Id.*
[28] ALYOSHIN & DOBOSH, *supra* note 5, at 1012.

procedure. The grounds for canceling interim measures in aid of arbitration include the situations when the arbitral tribunal denied jurisdiction, terminated the arbitral proceedings, or declined the claim; when the applicant abandoned the arbitral proceedings or failed to participate in the arbitral proceedings; or any other grounds when the interim measures became unnecessary.

The applicant remains liable for any damages suffered by the respondent in connection with granted interim measures. To ensure the respondent's right to compensation for such damages, the amended Civil Procedure Code of Ukraine sets forth the concept of "cross-undertaking/security" that the court may order an applicant as a prerequisite for obtaining interim measures. The court is obliged to order a cross-undertaking if (1) the applicant neither has a registered place of residence nor business in the territory of Ukraine nor has enough assets in Ukraine to compensate for respective damages or if (2) the court obtains evidence that the financial standing of the applicant, actions aimed at dissipating assets or other actions may complicate or make impossible the enforcement of the future court decision on compensation for the respondent's damages resulting from the interim measures, in case the claim is declined.[29] A party can file an application for interim measures in support of arbitration before a Ukrainian court irrespective of whether the seat of arbitration is in Ukraine or abroad.

According to Article 84 of the Civil Procedure Code of Ukraine, if the court grants an application for evidence production in aid of pending international arbitration, it can oblige the person possessing the evidence to produce it directly to the arbitral tribunal or to a party, which has applied to the court, for its further transfer to the arbitral tribunal. The court, in issuing its verdict, shall decide on evidence production and how the related costs are to be covered or advanced. Pursuant to Article 85 of the Civil Procedure Code of Ukraine, if the court grants an application for evidence inspection at the place of its location, the court shall send the protocol of the inspection directly to the arbitral tribunal or to a party that has applied to the court for its further transfer to the arbitral tribunal. The court shall make the appropriate ruling on evidence inspection and how the related costs are to be covered or advanced. Article 94 of the Civil Procedure Code of Ukraine sets out the rules for the examination of witnesses upon an application of the arbitral tribunal or, upon its consent, of the party to the arbitral proceedings. If the court grants such application, it will examine the witness, following the list of questions provided by the arbitral tribunal. The parties to the arbitral proceedings may take part in the witness examination and pose questions to the witness to clarify his or her responses. The court shall decide in its ruling on summoning the witness how the witness's costs are to be covered or advanced.[30]

There are no mandatory provisions requiring hearings to be held in the arbitration proceedings. Because Ukraine is a civil law country, arbitration hearings have a rather formalistic approach, which means that witness testimony does not constitute an essential part of the evidentiary procedure in commercial disputes and is not as important as the documentary evidence. As a rule, every time witness statements are submitted and witnesses are summoned, the arbitrators, unless otherwise agreed by the parties, determine the way in which the witnesses are to be examined. Nonetheless, cross-examination of witnesses is not widely used as during the hearings arbitrators usually prefer to question witnesses directly.[31]

---

[29] Perepelynska, *supra* note 11, at 5.
[30] *Id.* at 6.
[31] ALYOSHIN & DOBOSH, *supra* note 5, at 1005–1006.

Article 17 of the ICA Law (interim measures of the arbitral tribunal) is supplemented by the new provisions on the appropriate security that the tribunal may require from the party requesting an interim measure upon respective application of the opposing party. If so, the arbitral tribunal may order any party to place the respective amount into a deposit account ("security for arbitration costs"). Moreover, the Law on Procedural Reform has added a new paragraph to Article 25 of the ICA Law, which expressly allows an arbitral tribunal to draw an adverse inference in case any party fails to produce (documentary) evidence upon the tribunal's order. In the enforcement context, the reform has changed the requirement of the language rule in Article 35 of the ICA Law. Earlier, this rule allowed an applicant to submit the arbitral award and arbitration agreement in either Ukrainian or Russian.[32] This was particularly important for arbitral awards of the local institutions rendered in Russian.[33] After the amendment has been made, this rule prescribes submission of any documents only in Ukrainian.

Officially, there are no specific limits on arbitrators' powers to fashion any remedies (punitive or exemplary damages, specific performance, rectification, injunctions, interest and costs). However, depending on the substantive law applicable in a particular dispute, there may be different scopes for such remedies. If the arbitral tribunal applies Ukrainian law, not all of the remedies mentioned, for example, punitive or exemplary damages, can be effectively granted. Moreover, if the arbitral tribunal applies foreign law prescribing a particular remedy that is not set out in Ukrainian law, there is a risk that the Ukrainian national court will set aside the award or refuse to recognize and enforce it as being inconsistent with the Ukrainian legal order and public policy.[34]

5 ANTI-ARBITRATION LAW AND PUBLIC POLICY

There is no presumption of arbitrability or policy in support of arbitration in Ukraine. In practice, however, the national courts are now generally reluctant to interfere in matters expressly referred to arbitration.[35] The arbitrability of disputes, i.e. the ability of disputes to be submitted to arbitral tribunals (to bodies of private justice rather than state courts), is a factor of paramount importance both at the stage when disputes are accepted for consideration and, ultimately, at their final stage when the respective awards are enforced. If disputes are non-arbitrable, the related arbitration agreements are also invalid, and the tribunals have no jurisdiction to decide the disputes even if the parties want this. At this point, the autonomy of the parties will come into collision with public interest and public order considerations.[36]

Ukrainian legislation does not provide an exhaustive list of arbitrable or non-arbitrable disputes. Therefore, each particular case should be a carefully studied subject to the applicable provisions of the Ukrainian law. The arbitrability of disputes is even more complicated in Ukraine because the arbitration law is insufficient, and there are a number of shortcomings

---

[32] Perepelynska, *supra* note 11, 6–7.
[33] The total number of cases considered in 2017, the year when the discussed amendments were adopted, was 295. Among them 57 arbitral proceedings (19.3 percent) were conducted in Ukrainian, 9 (3 percent) in English, 1 (0.3 percent) in German, and the remaining 228 (77.28 percent) in Russian.
[34] Partially quoted ALYOSHIN & DOBOSH, *supra* note 5, at 1007.
[35] *Id.* at 1003.
[36] Tatyana Slipachuk, *What Law Is Applicable to Arbitration Agreements: Who Is to Decide and How? Or Yet Again about the Things That Truly Matter*, 2010 LEGAL JOURNAL JUSTINIAN 3 (2010), www.sk.ua/sites/ default/files/article_slipachuk_intl_arbitration_yurzhurnal _eng_2_0.pdf.

in the existing case law.[37] For instance, the last amendments to the Commercial Procedure Code of Ukraine made the issue of arbitrability even more unclear than earlier existing ones. Article 22 of the aforementioned Code contains restrictions and prohibits submitting to the third party of arbitration (the term used for domestic arbitration courts). The following disputes fall within the jurisdiction of the commercial courts of Ukraine: (1) on invalidation of acts; (2) arising out of the conclusion, amendment, termination, and performance of public procurement contracts; and (3) arising out of corporate relations between a company and its participants (founders, shareholders), including former participants, and between the participants (founders, shareholders) related to the establishment, activity, management, and termination of the company.

Hence, non-arbitrable disputes should be considered only in commercial courts: disputes involving strategic companies, disputes regarding calling of the shareholders' meeting and other disputes specified in the Commercial Procedure Code of Ukraine. The legislator chose to oust disputes that might affect the rights of all shareholders from the competence of the arbitral tribunals. The previous list can also be supplemented by the following categories of disputes, which may not be referred to arbitration under Ukrainian law: (1) insolvency cases if the debtor was established under Ukrainian legislation, (2) disputes concerning unfair competition, (3) disputes concerning intellectual property (IP) that require registration of IP rights or issuance of a certificate (patent) in Ukraine, (4) disputes involving the issuance or redemption of securities registered (issued) in Ukraine, and (5) disputes concerning incorporation or liquidation of foreign legal entities in Ukraine.[38]

The general rule is that the parties may refer a dispute to domestic or international commercial arbitration, which falls under the jurisdiction of civil or commercial courts and in respect of which the parties may enter into a settlement agreement unless otherwise provided by law. Currently, such special rules for international commercial arbitration are established in the ICA Law and for domestic arbitration in the DCA Law. Article 1(2) of the ICA Law provided that by agreement parties can submit certain disputes to arbitration if no exception is provided in Ukrainian law, thereby determining that corporate disputes could be the subject of arbitration. In 2004, Ukraine introduced the DCA Law.[39] Therefore, Article 1 provides that the DCA Law should not apply to foreign arbitration disputes as well as the then applicable Code of Commercial Procedure of Ukraine.

Numerous Ukrainian laws governing national and international arbitration distinguish between domestic/national arbitration tribunals – *tretejskie sudy* – and the corresponding provisions of the DCA Law and international arbitration – *meždunarodnyj kommerčeskij arbitraž*, resp. *mižnarodnyj kommercijnyj arbitraž*, as regulated in the ICA Law. The ICA Law makes use of two terms, namely *arbitraž* and *tretejskij sud*, indicating two different dispute resolution mechanisms. The amendments introduced in the Code of Commercial Procedure of Ukraine[40] relate to domestic arbitration proceedings only, leaving disputes with an "international element" to be arbitrable.[41] While there are views that the ICA Law limits the parties to international commercial arbitration in the territory of Ukraine only, in the absence of any direct prohibition,

---

[37] Partially quoting Leonid Shmatenko & Svitlana Bevz, *Arbitrability of Corporate Disputes in Ukraine*, 36 ISA BULLETIN 53–76 (2018), www.kluwerlawonline.com/abstract.php?area=Journals&id=ASAB2018005.
[38] ALYOSHIN & DOBOSH, *supra* note 5, at 1011.
[39] Partially quoting Leonid Shmatenko & Svitlana Bevz, *Arbitrability of Corporate Disputes in Ukraine*, UKRAINIAN JOURNAL OF BUSINESS LAW (Nov. 2017), 32–34, www.ujbl.info/ article.php?id=1028.
[40] Vidomosti Verkhovna Rada of Ukraine (VVR), 1992, No. 6, st. 56.
[41] Shmatenko & Bevz, *supra* note 39.

its reasonable interpretation allows one to conclude that eligible parties may refer their disputes to foreign international commercial arbitration. In any case, this law clearly does not limit the parties in choosing the arbitration rules, which are to be applicable to their dispute.

In essence, Ukrainian legislation does not contain an integrated list of non-arbitrable disputes or a clear mechanism for the determination of a dispute's arbitrability. In 2005, the Ukrainian International Private Law[42] was adopted which regulates the choice of law rules and jurisdiction over disputes with a foreign element. However, even now the adoption of this legal action has not solved the problem of the scope and the extent of the arbitrability of international commercial disputes completely. Indeed, the adoption of the aforementioned law has caused more confusion in determining the arbitrability of immovable property, intellectual property, and securities disputes, having introduced Article 77 on the exclusive jurisdiction of national courts of Ukraine that limits the arbitrability by providing an exhaustive list.[43]

Recent legal practice demonstrates that there is a tendency to apply the provision on the exclusive jurisdiction of courts as a bar to the arbitrability of such disputes; although, it can be argued that international practice demonstrates a provision, establishing exclusive jurisdiction over certain disputes does not render them non-arbitrable per se. Moreover, through relevant amendments of the Code of Commercial Procedure of Ukraine, the Law on Procedural Reform straightens out existing arbitrability rules enshrined therein.

In the eastern European states (Ukraine and Russia), corporate disputes are either non-arbitrable or their arbitrability still remains disputable. In particular, the Ukrainian legal basis is insufficient as well as the existing case law is flawed. Finally, the Law on Procedural Reform has amended and clarified the existing arbitrability rules contained in the Code of Commercial Procedure of Ukraine. After many years of prohibition and uncertainty in regard to the arbitrability of corporate disputes, the new rules allow one to arbitrate corporate disputes arising out of contracts based on the arbitration agreement concluded by a respective legal entity and all of its shareholders.[44]

Furthermore, new arbitrability rules expressly allow references to civil law aspects of competition disputes; likewise, disputes arising out of public procurement or privatization contracts are declared arbitrable.[45] All other aspects of such disputes along with disputes regarding records in real estate registers, IP rights and bankruptcy disputes, as well as disputes against debtors being in bankruptcy proceedings, are now recognized non-arbitrable.[46] Finally, the Law on Procedural Reform purports to channel the courts to take a pro-arbitration approach in regard to the enforcement of arbitration agreements.

The point put forward in Article 4 of ICA Law on the waiver of the right to object is that one shall be deemed to have waived his or her right to object (1) if a party is aware of any provision of the ICA Law from which the parties may derogate, (2) if a requirement under the arbitration agreement has not been complied with and yet the party continues to participate in arbitration without stating his or her objection to such non-compliance without undue delay, or (3) if a time limit is provided, the party fails to object within such period of time. If a party is not satisfied with the decision, he or she can apply to the state courts to decide the issue. The reform is also aimed at improving the established court's approach with regard to the enforcement of arbitration agreements.

---

[42] No. 2709-IV, Vidomosti Verkhovna Rada of Ukraine (VVR), 2005, No. 32, st. 422.
[43] Partially quoting, Romanova, *supra* note 14, at 16.
[44] Perepelynska, *supra* note 11, at 6.
[45] Perepelynska, *supra* note 6.
[46] Perepelynska, *supra* note 11, at 6.

In the meantime, the perspective presented in Article 8 of ICA Law on the arbitration agreement and substantive claim before the court brings the Ukrainian legislation in line with Article II(3) of UN Convention on Recognition and Enforcement of Foreign Arbitral Awards 1958,[47] also known as the New York Convention. It deals with a situation where an action in a matter, which is the subject of an arbitration agreement, is brought to the court and provides that the court must leave the claim without any consideration if the defendant raises a plea that the court does not have jurisdiction any later than the submission of the first statement of defence on the substance of the dispute unless the court finds that the arbitration agreement is null and void, inoperative, or incapable of being performed.

Besides, the Law on Procedural Reform eliminates discrepancies in the current procedural legislation of Ukraine and the ICA Law in situations when a party commences litigation in Ukraine in breach of an arbitration agreement. According to the amendments, the court must leave the claim without consideration if the defendant raises a plea that the court does not have jurisdiction any later than when he or she submits his or her first statement on the substance of the dispute unless the court finds that the arbitration agreement is null and void, inoperative, or incapable of being performed. One may note that provisions of ICA Law and the Code of Commercial Procedure of Ukraine on the arbitrability of disputes between the participants of Ukrainian companies (with foreign investment) are opposite. When evaluating the risks of referring such a dispute to international arbitration, one should bear in mind that even if the arbitral tribunal finds such disputes arbitrable and renders an award thereon, the award will probably be submitted to a local Ukrainian court for obtaining an enforcement permit and writ of execution, and therefore, the existing Ukrainian court practice should also be taken into account. In essence, Ukrainian courts have taken a definite non-arbitrable approach in corporate disputes. Thus, the ability to arbitrate corporate disputes in Ukraine still remains difficult to assess.

To summarize, the amendments to the Code of Commercial Procedure of Ukraine introduced by the Law on Procedural Reform are a significant step forward in the right direction, and it is also a step toward the final clarification of the question of the arbitrability of corporate disputes. The transfer of any disputes under company law to a domestic arbitral tribunal is prohibited, so that they are not arbitrable nationally, which is quite understandable due to widespread corporate raiding.[48]

6 REQUIREMENTS FOR ENFORCING FOREIGN ARBITRAL AWARDS

Ukraine has earned a reputation for not being a particularly arbitration-friendly jurisdiction, but, despite such prevailing opinions and perceptions, Ukraine's legal system and judicial attitudes nowadays are quite favorable to international arbitration. In practice, the average rate of successful applications for leave to enforce foreign arbitral awards normally ranges from 80 to 90 percent.[49] For instance, according to a recent survey, refusals to grant the leave for enforcement of arbitral awards in Ukraine are comparatively low – 10 percent and 18 percent of all considered requests.

Recognition and enforcement of foreign arbitral awards in Ukraine, as well as enforcement of international arbitral awards rendered in Ukraine, are governed by Chapter IX of the Civil

---

[47] 21 U.S.T. (U.S. Treaties) 2517 (June 10, 1958).
[48] Shmatenko & Bevz, *supra* note 39, at 32–34.
[49] See Gryshko, *supra* note 4.

Procedure Code of Ukraine, the ICA Law, and respective bilateral or multilateral international treaties. Ukraine, inter alia, is a signatory to all major international instruments in this field and has implemented:

- the 1954 Hague Civil Procedure Convention, entered into force for Ukraine on September 17, 1966;[50]
- the 1958 New York Convention, entered into force for Ukraine on August 10, 1960;[51]
- the 1961 European Convention on International Commercial Arbitration, (Geneva Convention), entered into force for Ukraine on January 25, 1964;[52]
- the 1965 Washington Convention on the Settlement of Investment Disputes between States and Nationals of Other States (the ICSID Convention), entered into force for Ukraine on July 7, 2000;[53]
- the 1994 Lisbon Energy Charter Treaty, entered into force for Ukraine on January 27, 1999;[54]
- the Commonwealth of Independent States (CIS) Treaty on Settling of Disputes Related to Commercial Activity 1992 (Kyiv Convention), entered into force for Ukraine on March 20, 1992;[55]
- the 1993 CIS Convention on Legal Assistance and Legal Relations in Civil, Family and Criminal Cases[56] (the Minsk Convention), entered into force for Ukraine on November 10, 1994.[57]

Furthermore, agreements on mutual encouragement of investments which provide for mutual recognition and enforcement of court/arbitration judgments were concluded with Denmark (1992), Egypt (1992), Poland (1993), Germany (1993), the United Kingdom (1993), Vietnam (1994), Armenia (1994), Lithuania (1994), the United States (1994), Slovak Republic (1994), the Netherlands (1994), Argentina (1995), Bulgaria (1995), Estonia (1995), France (1995), Georgia (1995), Canada (1995), Kazakhstan (1995), Korea (1995), Czech Republic (1995), Sweden (1995), Austria (1996), Belarus (1996), Lebanon (1996), Chile (1996), Cuba (1996), Greece (1996), Hungary (1996), Israel (1996), Italy (1996), Moldova (1996), Switzerland (1996), Turkey (1996), Azerbaijan (1997), Croatia (1997), Latvia (1997), Indonesia (1997), Iran (1997), Spain (1998), Macedonia (1998), etc. As regards the countries with which Ukraine does not have either multilateral or bilateral agreements providing for recognition and enforcement of foreign arbitral awards, such recognition and enforcement of arbitral awards rendered therein is quite problematic.[58]

Foreign arbitration awards are generally easier to enforce in Ukraine than foreign court decisions as the state is a signatory to the New York Convention; therefore, the grounds for refusing the recognition of an award are clearly stated, and in practice such refusals are relatively

---

[50] See Convention No. 995_083, zakon.rada.gov.ua/laws/show/995_083.
[51] 21 U.S.T. (U.S. Treaties) 2517 (June 10, 1958).
[52] See Convention No. 995_069, zakon.rada.gov.ua/laws/show/995_069.
[53] See Convention No. 995_060, zakon.rada.gov.ua/laws/show/995_060.
[54] See Convention No. 995_056, zakon.rada.gov.ua/laws/show/995_056.
[55] See Convention No. 997_076, zakon.rada.gov.ua/laws/show/997_076.
[56] See Convention No. 997_009, zakon.rada.gov.ua/laws/show/997_009.
[57] The last two documents provide the enforcement procedure of foreign judgments and arbitral awards between the CIS member states that are parties to the Minsk Convention.
[58] Partially quoting Pavlo Byelousov & Sergiy Uvarov, *Enforcement of Foreign Arbitral Awards in Ukraine: Mind the Gaps!*, UKRAINIAN JOURNAL OF BUSINESS LAW (Feb. 2, 2010), www.ujbl.info/article.php?id=12.

rare (less than 20 percent according to recent data[59]). As regards the awards made in non-contracting states, Ukraine will apply the New York Convention only under the reciprocity principle, the existence of which is presumed unless. No reservations have been made. At the same time, it should be noted that important guidelines on recognition and enforcement of foreign arbitral awards can be found in the dated, yet still effective, Resolution of the Plenum of the Supreme Court of Ukraine titled On the Court Practice of Entertaining Applications for the Recognition and Enforcement of the Judgments of Foreign Courts and Foreign Arbitral Awards Rendered in the Course of International Commercial Arbitration in Ukraine, of December 24, 1999, No. 12.[60]

In the volatile and rapidly changing Ukrainian legal environment the International Arbitration Statute has proved to be a testament of stability because it was seriously amended only once within the last twenty years when, in the context of the general civil procedure reform, supervisory and enforcement powers were shifted from courts of appeal down to district courts. As a result, the procedure for annulment and enforcement of arbitral awards has provided parties with more tools for appellate review. However, the introduced new procedural guarantees have come at a cost as the procedure has appeared to be a more complicated and time-consuming one. On the contrary, the International Arbitration Statute has been a remarkably stable piece of legislation which has established and maintained an arbitration-friendly environment.

In accordance with the recently adopted Article 474 of the Civil Procedure Code of Ukraine, national courts shall grant enforcement of foreign arbitral awards provided that recognition and enforcement are permitted under an international treaty ratified by the Ukrainian Parliament or on the basis of the reciprocity principle. The Civil Procedure Code expressly states that where the recognition and enforcement of foreign arbitral awards depend on the reciprocity principle, it shall be presumed that reciprocity exists unless it is proved otherwise.[61]

A foreign arbitral award can be recognized as binding and be enforced provided that the appropriate motion is filed with the competent Ukrainian court unless the losing party proves that (1) the agreement to arbitrate is invalid under the chosen law, (2) one of the parties was legally incapable of entering into the arbitration agreement, (3) the losing party was not duly notified of the appointment of the arbitrator or the commencement of the arbitration proceedings, (4) the losing party could not submit its explanations for valid reasons, (5) the rendered arbitration award was outside the scope of the arbitration agreement, (6) the arbitration panel or procedure did not comply with the arbitration agreement or with the rules of place of arbitration, or (6) the arbitration award did not enter into force or was annulled or its execution was suspended by the court of the country under which laws the arbitration award was rendered.[62] Similarly, the arbitration award may be unenforceable in Ukraine if the Ukrainian court determines that either the object of the dispute cannot be the subject to arbitration under the

---

[59] Ioana Knoll-Tudor & Oleksiy Soloviov, *Recognition and Enforcement of Foreign Arbitral Awards in Ukraine: The Impact of the New Procedural Codes*, KLUWER ARBITRATION BLOG (Jan. 15, 2018), arbitrationblog.kluwerarbitration.com /2018/01/15/recognition-enforcement-foreign-arbitral-awards-ukraine-impact-new-procedural-codes/.

[60] Resolution of the Plenum of the Supreme Court of Ukraine On the Court Practice of Entertaining Applications for the Recognition and Enforcement of the Judgments of Foreign Courts and Foreign Arbitral Awards Rendered in the Course of International Commercial Arbitration in Ukraine of Dec. 24, 1999, No. 12, zakon.rada.gov.ua/laws/show/v0012700-99.

[61] Tatyana Slipachuk, *Arbitration Guide IBA Arbitration Committee Ukraine*, INTERNATIONAL BAR ASSOCIATION (Feb. 2012), 20, www.ibanet.org/LPD/Dispute_Resolution_Section/Arbitration/ Arbcountryguides.aspx.

[62] Romanova, *supra* note 14, at 17.

Ukrainian legislation or that the recognition and enforcement of such arbitral awards contradict public policy.[63]

Prior to the judicial reform introduced in 2016, voluntary compliance with foreign arbitral awards was not possible because of the strict foreign currency regulation. The rules governing the enforcement of arbitration agreements and arbitrability were contradictory, and the respective court practice was not always arbitration-friendly.[64] The amended Civil Procedure Code of Ukraine establishes new specific procedures for recognition and enforcement of arbitral awards in Ukraine irrespective of the place of arbitration, setting aside of arbitral awards and rulings on jurisdiction if the place of arbitration is in Ukraine. It also lists the grounds for setting aside and refusal to enforce an arbitral award replicating, with minor deviations, the grounds referred to in Articles 34 and 36 of the ICA Law (and UNCITRAL Model Law).

The procedure for recognition and enforcement of foreign arbitral awards (and domestic court judgments) is uniform and quite straightforward for all types of awards. An application for leave to enforce a foreign arbitral award in Ukraine can be led only within three years from the date it became effective. A prevailing claimant must file an application for leave to enforce the award with a domestic court in the area where the respondents have their registered office or where they have assets. The court then gives a notice to the respondent and sets a time limit of thirty calendar days for the respondent to submit its defence, if any. Upon the expiry date of the submitting, the court fixes the date of the hearing and summons the parties to appear before it.[65]

The Civil Procedure Code of Ukraine grants jurisdiction over the enforcement of foreign arbitral awards to the local general courts at the place of the debtor's residence or location, or, if the debtor does not have a place of residence or location in Ukraine, to the court at the location of the debtor's property. The local court's ruling can be appealed. The Law on Procedural Reform sets out a specific procedure for recognition and enforcement of arbitral awards in Ukraine irrespective of the place of arbitration (Chapter 3 of Section IX of the Civil Procedure Code of Ukraine) and a procedure for setting aside rulings or awards of arbitral tribunals if the place of arbitration is Ukraine (Section VIII of the Civil Procedure Code of Ukraine). Prior to the reform, these matters were considered under the procedures provided for enforcement of foreign court judgments and setting aside of domestic arbitral awards respectively. The amended Civil Procedure Code of Ukraine sets out a list of grounds for setting aside (Article 459) and refusal to enforce the arbitral award (Article 478) in Ukraine, which replicates (with minor deviations) the wording of Articles 34 and 36 of the ICA Law (and UNCITRAL Model Law), respectively.

The court recognizes the following grounds for refusing recognition or enforcement of an arbitral award: the subject matter of the dispute is not capable of settlement by arbitration under the law of Ukraine or the recognition or enforcement of the award would be contrary to the public policy of Ukraine.[66] Moreover, as proceeds from the text of Article 36(2) of the ICA Law, granting interim injunctions is a power rather than an obligation of the court.[67] Both Article 36 of the ICA Law and Article V of the New York Convention provide almost identical grounds for refusal of recognition or enforcement of an arbitral award. This list of grounds is exhaustive, and thus the court may not invoke any other provision of the Ukrainian legislation to refuse

---

[63] *Id.* at 18.
[64] Perepelynska, *supra* note 11, at 1.
[65] Gryshko, *supra* note 4.
[66] *See* Art. 36 of the ICA Law.
[67] Byelousov & Uvarov, *supra* note 58.

enforcement. However, the ability to interpret the arbitrability of the dispute and the notion of public order still give Ukrainian courts rather wide discretion to deny enforcement.[68] Further, the Law on Procedural Reform creates a number of new possibilities for arbitration-users within judicial control proceedings in Ukraine. It establishes a procedure by which the courts take decisions concerning rulings of arbitral tribunals on their jurisdiction,[69] which was previously not regulated.

First, new procedural rules now govern remittance procedures envisaged in Article 34 of the ICA Law. Under these rules, the court may suspend the setting aside proceedings and remit the award to the arbitral tribunal in order to eliminate the grounds for setting aside of the award.[70] The court may, where it finds it appropriate, suspend the setting aside proceedings for a period of time determined by it in order to give the arbitral tribunal an opportunity to resume the arbitral proceedings or to take such other action that, in the arbitral tribunal's opinion, will eliminate the grounds for setting aside.[71]

Second, the Law on Procedural Reform solves several practical problems and provides users with additional possibilities; to avoid parallel proceedings on setting aside and enforcement of the same arbitral award rendered in Ukraine, the amended Civil Procedure Code now allows considering applications for setting aside an arbitral award as well as for recognition and enforcement of the same award in a single court proceeding. This will ensure procedural efficiency for resolving issues that are the same in essence since the grounds for setting an award aside and refusing to recognize and enforce it are the same, and since – according to the new jurisdictional rules – both cases shall be resolved by the same appellate court at the place of arbitration. The Law on Procedural Reform provides for a thirty-day time limit for setting aside proceedings and a two-month time limit for enforcement proceedings in the appellate court that may be suspended in case of a need to serve subpoenas and procedural documents abroad under the international treaties ratified by Ukraine.[72] The maximum term for recognition and enforcement of an international arbitral award is now limited to two months from the date of registration of the application by the court. Under the previous procedural law, the maximum duration of such procedure was not clearly defined, leaving room for delays.[73] In the cases where the debtor requests the recognition, the updated Procedure Codes provide for an accelerated procedure, which has to be completed within ten days. Furthermore, with the obligor duly notified about the hearing, the failure to appear in court will not prevent the court from recognizing the award and initiating the enforcement measures. Indeed, requests for postponement of a hearing due to mere unwillingness to appear in court and without any valid excuse were often used by Ukrainian obligors as a way to delay the proceeding, at least for several months.[74]

Third, the procedural reform partially solved a problem of voluntary compliance with the arbitral award, which was practically impossible due to a strict foreign currency regulation[75] and was a serious obstacle for Ukraine on its way to becoming a pro-arbitration jurisdiction. In view of applicable currency restrictions, previously it was impossible to comply voluntarily with an arbitral award if the amount in it was fixed in a foreign currency since the designated payer had

---

[68] Slipachuk, *supra* note 61, at 20.
[69] *See* Art. 16(3) of the ICA Law.
[70] Perepelynska, *supra* note 6.
[71] Perepelynska, *supra* note 11, at 3.
[72] *Id.*
[73] Knoll-Tudor & Soloviov, *supra* note 59.
[74] *Id.*
[75] Perepelynska, *supra* note 6.

to provide to his or her servicing bank an execution writ in addition to the arbitral award itself. Prior to the reform, in order to receive such execution writ both parties had to go through the complete recognition and enforcement proceedings before a state court. The Law on Procedural Reform has canceled the currency restrictions but, as a compromise, has provided for a simplified procedure of issuance of execution writs upon the debtor's application. The court shall consider the debtor's application within the ten-day terms in camera. In such a situation, judicial control is limited to arbitrability and public policy issues[76] only.

Fourth, the old rule obliging the court to convert the awarded amount into a national currency of Ukraine has been changed, and now the court may do this only upon the creditor's application.[77] The Law on Procedural Reform solved the problem of the currency of payment pursuant to an arbitral award. Under the previous provision of the Civil Procedure Code of Ukraine, the court was supposed to determine in its ruling on granting permission for enforcement of an arbitral award the amount of payment in national currency of Ukraine (the hryvnia, sometimes hryvnya; sign: ₴; code: UAH), calculated in accordance with the National Bank of Ukraine's exchange rate as of the date of the ruling. This means that the same amount being indicated in UAH was also stipulated in the execution writ, and the Execution (bailiff) Service was entitled to recover the debtor's funds in UAH only.[78] However, in the majority of cases foreign creditors did not have accounts in UAH in Ukrainian banks, so this rendered it impossible to get the awarded money from the Execution Service whenever the money was collected. In addition, this shifted all currency risks associated with conversion of debts into UAH upon foreign creditors.[79] Consequently, the Law on Procedural Reform provides that conversion of the amount to be paid under the arbitral award into UAH or a freely converted currency may be made only pursuant to the creditor's relevant application.

Finally, the Law on Procedural Reform has filled a gap regarding recovery of interest/penalties on payments due under an arbitral award when the latter provides their accrual until a full payment of the awarded amounts.[80] Any interest payments granted in the arbitral award must be calculated as of the day the enforcement measures take place. This provision is expected to minimize the financial risks for foreign applicants in case the enforcement against a Ukrainian obligor is substantially delayed. Provisions of Article 479 (4-5) of the Civil Procedure Code governing this issue entered into force on January 1, 2019.

7 INTERPRETATION OF ARBITRATION CLAUSES BY COURTS

This section studies Ukrainian legislative provisions on correction and interpretation of the awards. Finally, it reviews the contradicting practice regarding the interpretation of arbitration clauses by the new Ukrainian Supreme Court. In particular, different panels of judges in the Court of Commercial Cassation within the Supreme Court have opposite views relating to the mandatory recognition and enforcement of an arbitration clause in dispute resolutions within international commercial arbitration.

Article 33 of the ICA Law repeats the provisions of the UNCITRAL Model Law as to the correction, interpretation and rendering of the award and any additional award. A party, with notice to the other party, may request the arbitral tribunal to correct any errors in the

---

[76] Perepelynska, *supra* note 11, at 3.
[77] *Id.*
[78] Paragraph 8 Article 467, paragraph 6 Article 479 of the Civil Procedure Code of Ukraine.
[79] Perepelynska, *supra* note 11, at 4.
[80] Perepelynska, *supra* note 6.

computation of the award, to remove any clerical error or mistake arising from an accidental slip or omission, or to clarify or remove any ambiguity in the award.

In order to adopt a general approach of the courts to enforcement and interpretation of arbitration agreements, the law on procedural reform provides that any defects in the arbitration agreement and/or doubts as to its validity, operability and capability of being performed shall be interpreted by the court in favor of its validity, operability, and capability of being performed.[81] This promotes a pro-arbitration court practice in cases when, for example, the arbitration agreement has certain defects which may be remedied by interpretation (e.g., mistakes in the names of arbitration institutions).[82] The application of the in favorem validitatis principle of interpretation is part of the pro-arbitration approach. In particular, it is used during the process of determining the law applicable to an arbitration agreement when there are several national laws involved.[83] In Ukraine arbitral tribunals conservatively interpret the arbitration clause and prefer to listen to the party that is bound by the arbitration clause/agreement. Whereas the ICA Law in Article 16 on the competence of arbitral tribunal to rule on its jurisdiction states that the arbitral tribunal may rule on its own jurisdiction, including any objections with respect to the existence or validity of the arbitration agreement. For that purpose, an arbitration clause, which forms a part of a contract, should be treated as an agreement independent of the other terms of the contract. A decision by the arbitral tribunal that the contract is null and void should not entail ipso jure the invalidity of the arbitration clause.

All in all, Article 33 of the ICA Law on the correction and interpretation of awards and additional awards concludes that within thirty days of the receipt of the award, unless another period of time has been agreed upon by the parties, a party, with notice to the other party, may request the arbitral tribunal to give an interpretation of a specific point or part of the award. If the arbitral tribunal considers the request to be justified, it shall make the correction or give the interpretation within thirty days of receipt of the request. The interpretation shall form part of the award. This term may be prolonged by the arbitral tribunal, if necessary.[84] Unless otherwise agreed by the parties, any of the parties, with notice to the other party, may request, within thirty days of receipt of the award, that the arbitral tribunal make an additional award as to claims presented in the arbitral proceedings but omitted from the award. If the arbitral tribunal considers the request to be justified, it shall make the additional award within sixty days.

On August 28, 2018, the Grand Chamber of the new Supreme Court in Ukraine upheld the view on the mandatory recognition and enforcement of an arbitration clause in dispute resolutions within international commercial arbitration.[85] Hence, on February 5, 2019, the panel of judges of the Court of Commercial Cassation Court within the Supreme Court[86] annulled the decisions of the commercial courts of two instances, which, in violation of the law, considered the dispute between the parties despite the fact that the parties had already concluded the agreement on a dispute resolution in the domestic arbitration. It seems that all other similar cases should be settled in the same way; however, on March 4, 2019, the new Supreme Court[87] again adopted a contradictory decision. In that case, the Supreme Court did not agree

---

[81] Paragraph 2 Article 462 of the Civil Procedure Code of Ukraine.

[82] Olena Perepelynska, UAA Working Group Has Elaborated a Draft Law UKRAINIAN ARBITRATION ASSOCIATION (Oct. 10, 2014), arbitration.kiev.ua/en-US/UAA-News/UAA-Working-Group-has-elaborated-a-draft-law-regarding-exercise-of-judicial-control-over-internatio.aspx?ID=193.

[83] Slipachuk, *supra* note 36, at 4.

[84] Partially quoting ALYOSHIN & DOBOSH, *supra* note 5, at 1013–1014.

[85] Resolution of the Supreme Court No. 906/493/16, Grand Chamber, Aug. 28, 2018.

[86] Resolution of the Supreme Court No. 913/783/17, Cassation Commercial Court, Feb. 5, 2019.

[87] Resolution of the Supreme Court No. 910/13366/18, Cassation Commercial Court, Mar. 4, 2019.

to recognize the arbitration clause and, accordingly, the jurisdiction of the international arbitration tribunal to dispute the relationship between the parties. Thus, the Supreme Court opined that the dispute still had to be considered by the commercial court. The issue was about the invalidation of the agreement that the parties had agreed to consider in international arbitration.[88] The commercial courts of two instances refused to consider the claim as it was subordinated to international arbitration. Hence, the International Commercial Arbitration Court ruled in favor of its jurisdiction, considered it, and rendered the arbitral award, whose validity has just been challenged by the Supreme Court. Unfortunately, such a ruling of the Supreme Court may become a precedent for those who wish to avoid the execution of any international or domestic arbitration award in the territory of Ukraine. This is a red line that cannot be crossed, but which, in fact, in the given case has been grossly violated. In this context, one must also bear in mind that around the globe most of commercial disputes are usually resolved in arbitration proceedings.

The right of arbitration tribunals to resolve disputes concerning the invalidity of arbitration agreements, as well as their right to determine independently the extent of their own competence in a particular dispute, is an important safeguard against possible arbitrary interference by the domestic courts into arbitration proceedings. The functioning of arbitration tribunals is highly important not only for the creation of a favorable investment climate in Ukraine but also because it serves as an instrument for the protection of the interests of both the state and private business in foreign economic activity.[89] The incoherent judicial practice of the old Supreme Court of Ukraine was one of the main issues that led to its liquidation and thereafter creation of a completely new one, with new judges, formed from experienced and highly qualified lawyers and academics.

8 CONCLUSION

This chapter has revealed that nowadays it is widely recognized that the law of the place of arbitration governs the following matters before the arbitration proceedings take place and the arbitral award is rendered: (1) the substantive validity of the arbitration agreement, if the parties did not agree otherwise; (2) the formal validity of the arbitration agreement, if it is to be determined by the arbitrators; (3) the arbitrability of the subject matter of the dispute; and (4) the rules of arbitration procedure. It should be noted that, in terms of theory, today there is more consensus than confusion with respect to the law applicable to the arbitration agreement, and the international arbitration practice witnesses a certain commonality of approaches, which makes international arbitration procedures quite predictable. Nonetheless, it is questionable whether such a conclusion may be made with respect to the practices of domestic courts in the place where the award is enforced. Ukraine has made significant steps toward developing and harmonizing its arbitration institutions and processes with international practice. In 2018 as part of the judicial reform, new editions of the Civil Procedure Code of Ukraine and Commercial Procedure Code of Ukraine entered into force. Additionally, on January 1, 2018, the new ICAC Rules came into effect. The amendments to these codes, namely the strengthening of supervising and enforcing arbitration decisions by courts as well as expanding

---

[88] Partially quoting Taras Shepel, *Anti-arbitration Court Practice or When a New Supreme Court takes Old Approach*, UKRAINIAN PRAVDA (Mar. 21, 2103), www.pravda.com.ua/columns/2019/03/21/ 7209814/.

[89] *Id.*

the ICAC jurisdictional possibilities, have brought Ukraine up to the same level as advanced, pro-arbitration countries of the world.

The revised rules introduced by the updated Procedural Codes have the potential of rendering the procedure of recognition and enforcement of international arbitral awards more efficient, fair, and user-friendly. In 2017, a number of other central and eastern European (CEE) countries have also revised their arbitration acts or the procedure applicable to arbitration-related issues, among them Hungary and Bulgaria. In any case, they have experienced significant positive results from the implemented reforms. Most of them are aimed at the modernization of national legislation to become more supportive of international arbitration but also to increase the recourse to domestic arbitration (for example, with the creation of new local arbitration institutions). Although each country maintains its own specificities, the timing of these reforms demonstrates that arbitration in CEE countries is a reality and that local companies are slowly starting to perceive arbitration as a common mechanism of resolving their disputes.

Ukraine has taken great strides in reforming its arbitration legislation, striving to make its rules more transparent while both time and cost efficient for the parties involved. However, although Ukraine has seen much progress in this arena, foreign jurisdictions constantly update, elaborate and propose new, more efficient tools and mechanisms that, if taken into account, can enrich sufficiently the legislation and practice of Ukrainian arbitration centers. Hence, there is no doubt that such amendments to the Commercial Procedure Code of Ukraine would contribute to Ukraine's attractiveness and strong policy favoring arbitration. The introduced novelties of procedural legislation have been developed, having taken into account the latest global arbitration tendencies. They are expected to increase the effectiveness of arbitration in order to make its proceedings faster, more cost efficient and comfortable for the parties. The law on procedural reform has solved a number of striking problems and provided a solid basis for making Ukraine a more arbitration-friendly jurisdiction and an attractive seat for international arbitration.

23

Judicial Control of Arbitral Awards in the United Kingdom

Andrew Tetley*

1 INTRODUCTION

This book provides a forum for discussion of current issues and debates in international arbitration, covering the independence and impartiality of arbitrators; how conflicting interests may affect the conduct of arbitrators; the enforcement of arbitral awards, principally under grounds of procedural irregularity; how to resolve issues of misconduct by arbitrators during proceedings; and the current judicial interpretation of arbitration clauses. In England, the key legislation which governs these issues is contained in the Arbitration Act 1996 (the Arbitration Act). Also influential in shaping these issues are the procedural rules of specific arbitral institutions, and the guidance published by organisations such as the International Bar Association (the IBA).

2 VACATING COMMERCIAL ARBITRATION AWARDS

2.1 *Independence and Impartiality of International Arbitrators*

It is of fundamental importance that international arbitrators are both independent and impartial. It is a human right that 'everyone is entitled to a fair and public hearing within a reasonable time by an independent and impartial tribunal established by law'.[1] Arbitration, although not entirely compatible with such description, is a consensual process which has been held to fall within this right.[2] All arbitral tribunals have a duty to act fairly and impartially between the parties[3] while conducting the arbitration proceedings and while exercising any of its powers including in relation to procedure and evidence.[4]

Independence is easier to demonstrate than impartiality.[5] There are typically objective indicators of proximity or reliance by an arbitrator on a particular party or group. For example,

---

* The author wishes to acknowledge the contribution of Charlotte Simpson, Associate at Reed Smith LLP, for her help in drafting the chapter.
[1] Article 6(1) Convention for the Protection of Human Rights and Fundamental Freedoms, Nov. 4, 1950 (European Convention on Human Rights) and incorporated into English Law under Schedule 1 Article (6)(1) Human Rights Act 1998.
[2] Paul Stretford v. The Football Association Ltd and another [2007] EWCA Civ 238.
[3] Section 33(1)(a) Arbitration Act 1996.
[4] Section 33(2) Arbitration Act 1996.
[5] Bruno Manzanares Bastida, *The Independence and Impartiality of Arbitrators in International Commercial Arbitration*, 6 REV. E-MERCATORIA 4–5 (2007).

the International Chamber of Commerce (the ICC) rules of arbitration specifically require each arbitrator to declare any preexisting relationship of any kind, past or present, direct or indirect, with any party or legal counsel in order to establish their independence.[6] If any pecuniary or proprietary interest is held in one of the parties by an arbitrator, who also demonstrates partiality, this will automatically result in the disqualification of such arbitrator.[7] This can, however, become a fraught issue where an arbitrator is a lawyer operating within a large international law firm, in respect of a dispute where one of the parties is represented by another lawyer from the same firm but in a different office or jurisdiction.

Impartiality is a more abstract concept, requiring the arbitrator to reach a decision with an absence of preference for one party or another. This is ultimately the crucial criterion for an arbitrator, as Bishop succinctly notes: 'an arbitrator who is impartial but not wholly independent may be qualified, while an independent arbitrator who is not impartial must be disqualified'.[8] This need for impartiality is also one of the key reasons for having an odd number of arbitrators within the tribunal, particularly where each party is entitled to appoint its own arbitrator.

One of the reasons that parties choose arbitration is that it is an opportunity to select a commercial arbitrator with knowledge of the market or technical issues in dispute, and who may be better placed to determine the issues than a judge in a traditional court process. However, in selecting a 'commercial' dispute resolution mechanism, the parties are potentially voluntarily submitting to the fact that the arbitrator may have an interest in the outcome of the arbitration through his or her experience. However, it is worth noting that it is almost invariably counter-productive for a party to nominate an arbitrator-advocate. This is because, as one arbitrator noted, '[t]he moment you start advocating for your side your voice is lost',[9] as the rest of the tribunal will disregard that arbitrator's arguments. Therefore, from a practical perspective, the ideal selection of an arbitrator is 'someone with the maximum predisposition towards my client, but with the minimum appearance of bias'.[10]

Often appealing to parties from different jurisdictions is the opportunity for neutrality that international arbitration provides. The parties can decide the law, the venue, the procedure and the tribunal to be applied for the resolution of a dispute. For example, the tribunal members will frequently be of different nationalities to the parties to the dispute. This is not necessarily a requirement, but helps to establish the principles of independence and impartiality, given that the tribunal members are physically removed from the experiences and cultural knowledge of the disputing parties.

2.2 Parameters of Conflict of Interest

Unlike a judge, whose principal authority, duty and accountability is to the state and to the court, an arbitrator's responsibilities are determined primarily by private entities, whether that is an arbitral institution, the appointing parties themselves or another appointing body. One of the key issues in international commercial arbitration is that there is no supranational authority

---

[6] Articles 11(2) and 11(3) International Chamber of Commerce Arbitration Rules 2017.
[7] Locabail v. Bayfield [1999] EWCA Civ 3004.
[8] Doak Bishop & Lucy Reed, *Practical Guidelines for Interviewing, Selecting and Challenging Party Appointed Arbitrators in International Commercial Arbitration*, 14 ARBITRATION INTERNATIONAL 345 (1998), https://academic.oup.com/arbitration/article-abstract/14/4/395/216629 (cited in Bastida).
[9] Richard Woolley, *Is Arbitrator Impartiality a Myth?* GLOBAL ARBITRATION REVIEW (June 9, 2015), https://globalarbitrationreview.com/print_article/gar/article/1034514/is-arbitrator-impartiality-a-myth?print=true.
[10] Martin Hunter, *Ethics of the International Arbitrator*, 4 ASA BULLETIN, ASSOCIATION SUISSE DE L'ARBITRAGE KLUWER LAW INTERNATIONAL 173–196 (1986).

which controls arbitrators.[11] For this reason, the boundaries for what behaviour and actions are acceptable for an arbitrator would not necessarily be acceptable for a judge. Also, given the generally pro-arbitration approach of the English courts, there is limited accountability and oversight of arbitral practices, other than that imposed by arbitral institutions, which of course apply only where their rules are adopted. No such accountability and oversight exists in ad hoc arbitrations. This also means there is no overarching body to determine whether an arbitrator has a conflict of interest disqualifying him from acting. This absence of oversight therefore relies upon the effective use of chosen arbitral rules and the integrity and moral code of individual arbitrators to ensure that decisions are reached following a fair consideration of each party's case.

One instance where the independence and impartiality of an arbitrator may sometimes be questioned is where there is third party funding of the arbitration proceedings. If a member of the tribunal has a relationship of some kind with the funder, that arbitrator may not be deemed to be fully independent. Given the relatively small number of arbitration funders currently, in specific areas of international commercial arbitration, it may be that arbitrators do not infrequently encounter situations where they have a connection of some sort with arbitration funders.

Another point sometimes made is that there is a contractual relationship between the parties and the arbitrator which does not exist in traditional court proceedings.[12] However, referencing *Jivraj v. Hashwani*,[13] Judge Dominique Hascher makes the point that the role of an arbitrator as adjudicator does not fit the traditional conception of a contract for services. The provision of services of the arbitrator is contingent on payment by the parties, but the conduct of those services by the arbitrator should not be.[14]

Statistically, it is fairly unusual for there to be a position where an arbitrator is in a clear and damaging position of conflict. Conflicts of interest relate primarily to the concept of independence[15] and can often be resolved at the outset of proceedings through disclosure by each arbitrator to the parties of any interest or previous connection to any of the parties to the dispute or proceedings which may have a bearing on the decision making that that arbitrator would conduct. However, if this is not done properly, then problems can and do arise. Issues of apparent bias may come into play.

In one recent illustrative case in this area, the English Court of Appeal agreed with the lower court's overall conclusion that 'the fair-minded and informed observer, having considered the facts, would not conclude that there was a real possibility' that the arbitrator had been biased. This was in circumstances where the arbitrator in question had been appointed in respect of multiple overlapping references and where there was a common party, and in circumstances also where the court found that the arbitrator had wrongfully failed to make certain disclosures to the parties at the time of his appointment.[16]

Disclosure by an arbitrator of what may be considered a conflict of interest must be a transparent process in order to be an effective safeguard.[17] This requires honesty and disclosure

---

[11] Sheila Block, *Ethics in International Proceedings*, INTERNATIONAL LITIGATION NEWS – NEWSLETTER OF THE INTERNATIONAL LITIGATION COMMITTEE OF THE SECTION ON BUSINESS LAW, INTERNATIONAL BAR ASSOCIATION Oct. 2004, at 15–22.
[12] Dominique Hascher, *Independence and Impartiality of Arbitrators – Three Issues*, 27 AMERICAN UNIVERSITY INTERNATIONAL LAW REVIEW 789–806 (2012).
[13] Jivraj v. Hashwani [2011] UKSC 40 at 23.
[14] Hascher, *supra* note 12, at 789–806.
[15] See discussion on independence in *id.* at chapter 2.1, 2.
[16] Halliburton Company v. Chubb Bermuda Insurance Ltd. [2018] EWCA Civ 817 at 100.
[17] Cofely v. Bingham and Knowles [2016] EWHC 240 (Comm).

of sufficient detail to enable the parties to adequately assess the potential conflict of an arbitrator. However, if an arbitrator makes an erroneous or incomplete statement,[18] this should not automatically lead to their recusal or to the annulment of the award.[19]

2.3 Procedural Irregularity and Misconduct of Arbitrators during Proceedings

Where an arbitration is seated in England and Wales, an award can be challenged (1) on a point of law,[20] (2) lack of jurisdiction[21] and (3) serious irregularity.[22] We look at each of these in turn. The first two are addressed for completeness. The third type of challenge is the most germane to the subject matter of this chapter. The party challenging the award must make their application or appeal within twenty-eight days of the final award or other arbitral appeal process.[23] Furthermore, certain affected third parties have rights to challenge an award.[24]

2.3.1 Appeal on a Point of Law

An award may be appealed on a point of law arising from such award.[25] Parties can waive their rights to challenge or appeal an award,[26] commonly by agreeing to use a set of arbitral rules which expressly waive such rights. By way of example, this is the case under the ICC, London Court of International Arbitration (LCIA) and Singapore International Arbitration Centre (SIAC) rules. Where parties have a right of appeal against an arbitral award, the court has jurisdiction to confirm, vary, set aside or remit the award. Such a right of appeal is limited to points of English law only, and requires either the leave of the court, or the agreement of the parties pre- or post-dispute to allow appeals.

Successful appeals on a point of law are rare. The recent decision of *Dakshu Patel v. Kesha Patel*[27] was one such case. The court concluded that it was 'clear' that the tribunal had wrongly overlooked the relevant test under Section 19 of the Partnership Act 1890, which requires clear and unambiguous conduct indicating the parties' intention to vary contractual terms. The court concluded that the tribunal made an error of law in finding that there had been a variation to the profit-sharing provisions of two partnership agreements. The court also confirmed that a related Section 68 challenge would have succeeded, had it been necessary to base its decision on this point. The court varied the award and held that the parties were entitled to share the profits and losses equally.

In practice, appeals are rarely pursued by parties, being mostly limited to shipping cases. In the recent case of *J v. K*,[28] it was held that a tribunal had jurisdiction to review the determination of an expert, and to substitute its own determination following a rehearing of the disputed issues. It is clear from these cases that an appeal on a point of law places a high bar on applicants.

---

[18] Halliburton Company, *supra* note 16 offers an example of this.
[19] Hascher, *supra* note 12, at 789–806.
[20] Section 69 Arbitration Act 1996.
[21] *Id.* at Section 67.
[22] *Id.* at Section 68.
[23] *Id.* at Section 70(3).
[24] *Id.* at Section 72
[25] *Id.* at Section 69(1).
[26] *Id.* at Section 73.
[27] Dakshu Patel v. Kesha Patel [2019] EWHC 298 (Ch) at 18.
[28] J v. K [2019] EWHC 273 (Comm).

2.3.2 Substantive Jurisdiction

Where it is found that a tribunal did not have jurisdiction to hear the dispute, the court can confirm, vary or set aside an award made by such tribunal in whole or in part.[29] In order for a court to review the jurisdiction of the tribunal in such cases, an award has to be made. An order will not be sufficient.

A challenge to an arbitral award may be made where the tribunal has no 'substantive jurisdiction'[30] to hear the dispute. This may be done as part of the substantive award on the merits of the claims or, more commonly, in a separate preliminary hearing where the tribunal rules on its own jurisdiction. Section 67 of the Arbitration Act is mandatory – parties cannot contract out of the right to challenge an award on this basis. Grounds for challenging the jurisdiction of the tribunal include (1) existence or validity of the arbitration agreement, (2) scope of the arbitration agreement and (3) constitution of the tribunal.

Generally, the invalidity of a contract will not affect the validity of the agreement to resolve disputes through arbitration, unless the invalidity would effectively make both the contract and the arbitration agreement invalid. This might be the case, for example, if one of the parties did not have capacity to enter into the contract.[31] Furthermore, it will generally be presumed that the parties intended all disputes to be covered by the arbitration agreement, unless the language makes clear that certain matters are expressly excluded from the tribunal's jurisdiction.[32] For example, in *Sonact Group Limited v. Premuda SPA*[33] a settlement agreement (without a jurisdiction clause) was signed in relation to several disputes under a charter party (which contained an arbitration clause). Males J held that the arbitration clause in the charter party ('any and all differences and disputes of whatsoever nature') was wide enough to cover a claim under the settlement agreement. Males J found that it was 'inconceivable' that the parties could have intended that the owner would be unable to pursue a claim under the settlement agreement in arbitration. Males J stated that there was 'no bright line rule' that once parties enter into a new legal relationship, 'an arbitration clause in the underlying contract necessarily can no longer apply'.

Where the tribunal is found to have no substantive jurisdiction, a full retrial of the arbitration will be held. However, it has been reemphasised in several recent decisions that, in general, English courts will take a restrictive approach to such challenges to jurisdiction. For example, in *State A v. Party B*,[34] the court considered an application for an extension of time for a party to bring a Section 67 jurisdictional challenge. The court (per Sir Michael Burton), applied a high threshold and held that an extension of time will be granted only where a delay occurs in making a challenge (and/or applying for an extension of time), where the application is based on new evidence, and such new evidence is 'transformational', 'seismic' or 'a game-changer'. The extension of time was refused because the delay was a 'colossal' 959 days from the deadline to make the Section 67 challenge and the new evidence was not sufficiently 'transformational' to justify the extension of time anyway.

---

[29] Section 67(3) Arbitration Act 1996.
[30] *Id.* at Sections 30(1) and 82(1).
[31] David Wolfson & Susanna Charlwood, *Chapter 25: Challenges to Arbitration Awards*, in ARBITRATION IN ENGLAND 527–562 (Julian D. M. Lew, Harris Bor, et al. eds., 2013).
[32] See further in Section 4 on the scope and interpretation of commercial arbitration clauses. One recent illustrative example of this approach is included in this section, with further recent examples being considered in Section 4.
[33] Sonact Group Limited v. Premuda SPA [2018] EWHC 3820 (Comm) per Males J at 15–17 and 20.
[34] State A v. Party B [2019] EWHC 799 (Comm) per Sir Michael Burton at 53–54 and 56.

In another decision, *Filatona Trading Ltd* v. *Navigator Equities Ltd*,[35] the English court held that an unnamed but disclosed principal of a party to a shareholders' agreement could sue under an arbitration agreement. A and B were named as parties to the agreement, which also provided for all disputes to be referred to arbitration. C was not a named party to the SHA but was the disclosed principal of A, who entered into the contract with B as C's agent. C commenced arbitration proceedings against B. Teare J applied *Aspen Underwriting Ltd* v. *Credit Europe Bank NV*[36] and *Kaefer Aislamientos* v. *AMS Drilling*[37] and held that an undisclosed principal can sue and be sued on a contract on condition that (1) the contractual terms did not confine the application of the contract to the named parties; (2) at the time the relevant contract was entered into, the agent intended to contract on the principal's behalf; and (c) it was within the actual authority of the agent to enter into the contract. The judge held that the evidence satisfied the second and third points. On the first point, he held that, despite an entire agreement clause, the terms of the shareholders agreement did not act to prevent a disclosed principal from having rights under the contract: 'very clear words' were required to show that only the named party, rather than its principal, was intended to have such rights.

2.3.3 Serious Irregularity

It is under the concept of 'serious irregularity' that matters of procedural irregularity and misconduct of arbitrators will typically arise. Under Section 68 of the Arbitration Act, the court has jurisdiction to remit or set aside an award or to declare it to be of no effect where an applicant can show substantial injustice to itself as a result of a 'serious irregularity'. This jurisdiction is limited to listed examples of 'serious irregularity', which affect the tribunal, the proceedings or the award itself.[38] Section 68 of the Arbitration Act is, like Section 67, mandatory. Parties cannot contract out of the right to challenge an award for serious irregularity.

Although of mandatory application, a high threshold must be met before the court will interfere with the arbitral process based on Section 68. As a result, most applications fail. In one case, Morrison J described Section 68 as a 'long stop',[39] to be used in 'extreme cases where ... something ... went seriously wrong with the arbitral process'.[40] In *Vee Networks Ltd* v. *Econet Wireless Special Ltd*,[41] the court stated that the requirement for substantial injustice to a party will be satisfied if that party shows the irregularity caused the tribunal to reach a conclusion which was unfavourable to the applicant and which it might not have reached without the irregularity, provided that it was reasonably arguable that the tribunal could have reached a decision in the applicant's favour.

In order for a party's application for an arbitral award to be set aside under Section 68 of the Arbitration Act, the applicant needs to demonstrate the following:

1. a serious irregularity;
2. which falls within the exhaustive list, described in Section 68 (see later in the chapter); and
3. which has caused or will cause substantial injustice to the applicant.[42]

Section 68 sets out an exhaustive list of qualifying irregularities:[43]

---

[35] Filatona Trading Ltd v. Navigator Equities Ltd. [2019] EWHC 173 (Comm).
[36] Aspen Underwriting Ltd v. Credit Europe Bank NV [2018] EWCA Civ 2590.
[37] Kaefer Aislamientos SA de CV v. AMS Drilling Mexico SA de CV and others [2019] EWCA Civ 10 at 114.
[38] Section 68 Arbitration Act 1996.
[39] Fidelity Management SA v. Myriad International Holdings BV [2005] EWHC 1193 (Comm) at 5.
[40] See also commentary in Wolfson & Charlwood, *supra* note 31, at 527–562.
[41] Vee Networks Ltd v. Econet Wireless Special Ltd [2004] EWHC 2909.
[42] Primera Maritime v. Jiangsu [2013] EWHC 3066 (Comm) at 6.
[43] Section 68(2) Arbitration Act 1996.

1. failure by the tribunal to comply with Section 33 of the Arbitration Act (containing the general duties of the tribunal, e.g., to give each party a reasonable opportunity to present its case);
2. the tribunal exceeding its powers (not including issues of substantive jurisdiction, covered by Section 67);
3. failure by the tribunal to conduct the proceedings in accordance with the procedure agreed by the parties;
4. failure by the tribunal to deal with all of the issues that were put to it;
5. any arbitral or other institution or person vested by the parties with powers in relation to the proceedings or the award exceeding its powers;
6. uncertainty or ambiguity as to the effect of the award;
7. the award being obtained by fraud or the award or the way in which it was procured being contrary to public policy;
8. failure to comply with the requirements as to the form of the award; or
9. any irregularity in the conduct of the proceedings or in the award, which is admitted by the tribunal or by any arbitral or other institution or person vested by the parties with powers in relation to the proceedings or the award.

There have been many cases where disgruntled parties have sought to challenge the arbitral process or an award through use of a Section 68 challenge. Few have succeeded.

In the recent case of A v. B,[44] the applicant applied for the award to be set aside on the basis that the tribunal's decision to exclude factual evidence given in examination-in-chief was a serious irregularity. The court found that the application was based on the applicant's criticism of the tribunal's exercise of a discretion and refused the application. Given that the tribunal had a wide discretion as to how it exercised its powers, the decision made by the tribunal would have to be beyond the bounds of what could be considered an exercise of its discretion under the Arbitration Act and its own procedure. The evidential process that had been adopted provided for the principal evidence to be in writing, with a very short timetable for any oral evidence to be provided. The court held that the tribunal had been entitled to make the ruling it did, that the tribunal had considered the issues and had carried out a balancing exercise to reach its decision and that the tribunal had acted within the bounds of its wide discretion. Finally, the applicant's evidence did not address the relevant clause relating to invoice disputes, and so, even if it was an irregularity it could not be an irregularity affecting the invoice claims.[45]

One relatively recent case in which the court did grant the setting aside of an arbitral award on the basis of procedural irregularity is the case of the M.V. *Ocean Glory*.[46] This was a shipping case. Under a charter party, the owners referred a claim for demurrage to arbitration and, in ambiguously worded claim submissions, requested that the tribunal reserve its jurisdiction in relation to further non-particularised and unquantified claims. The charterers asked the tribunal to dismiss all of these claims on their merits. The tribunal issued a final award in which the tribunal stated:

> 30. Given the length of time since the cargo was discharged and that the Owners' provided no evidence that the cargo receivers / interests had or indeed intended to bring a claim against them under the Bill of Lading, we refuse their application.

---

[44] A v. B [2018] EWHC 3366 (TCC).
[45] *Id.* at 34–40, 42–44.
[46] Lorand Shipping v. Davof Trading (Africa) BV (M.V. *Ocean Glory*) [2014] EWHC 3521 (Comm).

31. In the event that the cargo receivers / interests do make a claim, doubtless the Owners will consider whether it is possible to start new arbitration proceedings against the Charterers. It follows that this award is not made on an interim basis, but is final in respect of the issues decided herein.

The effect of the award was to exhaust the tribunal's jurisdiction over any claims arising under the charter party without any regard to any contractual time bar, and to force any other claims to be brought in a new arbitration. The court found that the tribunal's approach (1) adopted a course of action not advocated by either party, (2) did not give the parties an opportunity to comment on the proposal of the tribunal to make such an award and (3) relied upon considerations not raised by the parties and which the parties had no opportunity to address before the award was made.

For these reasons, it was held, the tribunal's award constituted a serious irregularity. The tribunal neither found that the owner's claims should be rejected on the merits (as sought by the charterers), nor did it reserve the claims for further consideration (as sought by the owners). The court held that, given that neither party had advocated this course of action, the parties should have been given opportunity to address the course of action in fact adopted by the tribunal. In determining whether this failure caused substantial injustice to the owners, it was held to be sufficient that the tribunal 'might realistically' have reached a different conclusion. The court accepted that the threshold of Section 68 of the Arbitration Act is very high. It nevertheless issued a declaration that paragraphs 30 and 31 of the tribunal's award were of no effect and remitted that part of the award back to the tribunal. The fact that the owner's claims were barred constituted a substantial injustice even if starting a new arbitration, the course suggested by the tribunal, might objectively have been a practical solution.

In another recent case, the English court held that an arbitrator had committed a serious irregularity by making enquiries and eliciting information about a matter which proved determinative in the award, without notifying the parties about those enquiries or giving them an opportunity to make representations on the matter in light of those enquiries.[47]

Misconduct by arbitrators is not necessarily procedural and can include a wide range of misdemeanours, including influencing witnesses, failure to disclose an interest, and other grounds.[48] Misconduct is also something that may need to be addressed during the arbitral process, not simply after the award has been issued. Under the Arbitration Act, it is possible to apply to the court for removal of an arbitrator, inter alia, where (1) circumstances exist that give rise to justifiable doubts as to his or her impartiality or (2) where he or she has refused or failed properly to conduct the proceedings and substantial injustice has been caused or will be caused to the applicant.[49]

An example of such an application can be seen in the recent case of *P* v. *Q*.[50] Multiple grounds of misconduct were alleged by the claimant in an LCIA arbitration: (1) tribunal improperly delegated its role to the tribunal secretary by systematically entrusting the secretary with responsibilities going beyond what was permissible under the LCIA Rules and LCIA Policy; (2) chairman breached his mandate as an arbitrator and his duty not to delegate by seeking the views of the tribunal secretary, who was not party to the arbitration or a member of the tribunal, entitled to make decisions on substantial procedural issues; (3) other arbitrators

---

[47] Fleetwood Wanderers Ltd v. AFC Fylde LTD [Nov. 30, 2018] 11 WLUK 540.
[48] See discussion in Section 2.
[49] Section 24 Arbitration Act 1996.
[50] P v. Q [2017] EWHC 194 (Comm) at 14.

forming the tribunal also breached their mandate as arbitrators and their duty not to delegate by failing to participate sufficiently in the arbitration proceedings and the decision making process; (4) circumstances existed which gave rise to justifiable doubts about the chairman's independence and impartiality, following comments that the chairman had made at an international conference; and (5) chairman breached his duty to maintain the confidentiality of the arbitral proceedings. The court had little difficulty in rejecting all the grounds advanced and dismissed the claimant's application in its entirety.

In a similar way, as for serious irregularity under Section 68 of the Arbitration Act, the court will not lightly interfere with the conduct of the arbitral process. If that were not the case, it would serve to encourage frivolous claims intended not to facilitate conduct of the arbitral process but to frustrate it, to the detriment of all stakeholders in that process. In certain sectors of the arbitral community, there is increasing demand for arbitral tribunals to be more prescriptive in their approach. For this to succeed, it will require that the supervising courts continue holding a clear deferential line to procedural decisions of arbitral tribunals, as is presently the case in the English courts.

3 ENFORCING COMMERCIAL ARBITRATION AWARDS

3.1 Anti-arbitration Law and Public Policy

One of the standout features of English courts' approach to arbitration is their acceptance of anti-suit injunctions to prevent foreign proceedings commenced in disregard of any applicable arbitration agreement. An anti-suit injunction is designed to protect a negative obligation which arises under an arbitration (or jurisdiction) agreement: the negative obligation not to commence or continue foreign court proceedings in any other forum.[51] The legal basis for such injunctions is that the foreign proceedings amount to a breach of contract. As Lord Millett explained in the *Angelic Grace*:

> There is no good reason for diffidence in granting an injunction to restrain foreign proceedings on the clear and simple ground that the defendant has promised not to bring them.[52]

The powers of the English court to grant anti-suit injunctions differ depending on whether the court proceedings in breach of the arbitration agreement are brought in a member state court of the European Union (EU) (or Lugano Convention country) or in a court of a country outside the EU (or Lugano Convention country). Following the decision of the European Court of Justice (ECJ) in *West Tankers*,[53] EU member state courts are effectively precluded from granting anti-suit injunctions restraining the pursuit of court proceedings commenced in another member state in breach of an arbitration clause. In *West Tankers*, the ECJ held that the grant of anti-suit injunctions restraining proceedings in an EU member state was inconsistent with the principles of trust that underlie the Brussels Regulation and that such injunctions should not be available to restrain proceedings in the court of another member state. The correlative expectation is that the member state courts will themselves recognise and give

---

[51] David St. John Sutton, Judith Gill, & Matthew Gearing, Russell on Arbitration 384, para. 7-043 (24th ed. 2015).
[52] Aggeliki Charis Compania Maritima S.A. v. Pagnan S.p.A. (the *Angelic Grace*) [1995] 1 Lloyd's Rep 87 per Millett LJ at 96.
[53] Allianz SpA, formerly Riunione Adriatica di Sicurtà SpA and Generali Assicurazioni Generali SpA v. West Tankers Inc. Case C-185/07, interpreting Council Regulation (EC) No 44/2001 of Dec. 22, 2000 (Brussels Regulation).

deference to the arbitration agreement. However, the way in which EU member states approach such matters is not uniform, particularly where the agreement in question may be less than clear in its application and scope.

The recast Brussels Regulation, which came into force in January 2015,[54] has reinforced the position and clarified matters of potential overlap within the EU framework. The regulation retains and clarifies the arbitration exception,[55] such as incorporating new recitals,[56] which include (1) expressly preserving the right of member states' courts to rule on the validity of arbitration agreements; (2) stating that a ruling of a member state court on the validity of an arbitration agreement should not be subject to the rules on recognition and enforcement of the regulation; (3) confirming that the 1958 New York Convention on the Recognition and Enforcement of Foreign Arbitral Awards (NY Convention) takes precedence over the regulation, so member states' courts can recognise and enforce arbitral awards even where these are inconsistent with another member state court's judgment (for example, where a member state court has given judgment that the arbitration agreement is not valid); (4) clarifying that the regulation does not apply to any action or ancillary proceedings relating to the tribunal's establishment, arbitrators' powers, the conduct of the arbitration or any action or judgment relating to the annulment, review, appeal, recognition or enforcement of the award; and (5) expressly stating that the regulation shall not affect the application of the NY Convention.[57]

Where proceedings are brought outside the EU, the objections based on the Brussels Regulation or Recast Brussels Regulation do not arise. Therefore, in the English courts, anti-suit injunctions are permissible where the proceedings in question have been commenced in the courts of a non-Brussels Regulation or non-Lugano Convention country. This position was confirmed in *Shashoua and others v. Sharma*.[58] The Commercial Court confirmed that *West Tankers* did not apply to proceedings commenced in a court outside of the EU member states, including between countries that were party to the NY Convention. Furthermore, in a later judgment, Flaux J confirmed that the *West Tankers* judgment did not require an arbitral tribunal to refuse to grant relief which might be inconsistent with the judgment of another member state's courts.[59] It was within the tribunal's powers to award damages or an indemnity where the court proceedings had been brought in a member state court in breach of the arbitration agreement.

In practice, the English courts are generally receptive to granting injunctions (interim and final) to prevent parties to an arbitration agreement commencing or continuing proceedings in the courts of other jurisdictions outside of the EU.[60] However, this has not always been the case. Until the 1990s, the byword had been that injunctive relief in the face of foreign proceedings was to be exercised with caution, as it was seen as involving interference by the English courts in the proceedings of the foreign court. Matters of comity were sometimes foremost in the minds of the judges. However, this approach changed so that by the turn of the last century, England's

---

[54] SUTTON, GILL, and GEARING, *supra* note 51, 385–389, paras. 7-045–7-047.
[55] Article 1(2)(d) Regulation (EU) No 1215/2012 of the European Parliament and of the Council of Dec. 12, 2012 (Recast Brussels Regulation).
[56] Recital 12 Recast Brussels Regulation.
[57] Article 73(2) Recast Brussels Regulation.
[58] Shashoua and others v. Sharma [2009] EWHC 957 (Comm).
[59] West Tankers Inc. v. Allianz SpA and another [2012] EWHC 854 (Comm).
[60] This article does not contemplate the position that might arise following any exit from the EU by the UK. But, the prospect is clearly on the horizon that the English courts may soon be unshackled from the *West Tankers* decision, allowing them to broaden their injunctive reach to include proceedings commenced in EU members in breach of arbitration agreements.

highest court recognised that strong reasons were required to outweigh the prima facie entitlement to an injunction in such circumstances.[61] The matter was put in the following terms by Lord Hobhouse in a 2001 decision:[62]

> The applicant for a restraining order must have a legitimate interest in making his application and the protection of that interest must make it necessary to make the order. Where the applicant is relying upon a contractual right not to be sued in the foreign country (say because of an exclusive jurisdiction clause or an arbitration clause), then, absent some special circumstance, he has by reason of his contract a legitimate interest in enforcing that right against the other party to the contract.

Perhaps the most extreme example of an English court's readiness to act in this area is provided by the case of *Ust-Kamenogorsk*.[63] The case involved a twenty-five-year concession agreement governed by Kazakh law, containing an ICC London arbitration clause. The appellant was a Kazakh entity while the respondent was a UK entity. Both were parties to the agreement in question. The UK entity sought a declaration that certain claims under the agreement could be brought only in arbitration and/or an injunction against continuation or commencement of foreign proceedings. There was no dispute threatened at the time of events, but there was a history showing prior disregard of the arbitration agreement by the appellant, and indeed court findings obtained by the appellant in Kazakhstan that the arbitration agreement was invalid. At first instance both the declaration and injunctive relief were granted by way of final orders. The injunctive relief was granted in reliance on the court's broad injunctive powers contained in the Senior Courts Act.[64] The orders were upheld on appeal. On final appeal, the Supreme Court upheld the lower courts' decisions. Lord Mance said:[65]

> An injunction [to restrain foreign proceedings in breach of an arbitration agreement] is not "for the purposes of and in relation to arbitral proceedings," but for the purposes of and in relation to the negative promise contained in the arbitration agreement not to bring foreign proceedings.

The decision of the Supreme Court in the *Ust-Kamenogorsk* case cited the further rationale behind such an approach, as articulated by Millett LJ in the *Angelic Grace*:[66]

> The justification for the grant of [an] injunction . . . is that without it the plaintiff will be deprived of its contractual rights in a situation in which damages are manifestly an inadequate remedy. The jurisdiction, is, of course, discretionary and is not exercised as a matter of course, but good reason needs to be shown why it should not be exercised in any given case.

---

[61] Donohue v. Armco Inc [2001] UKHL 64; [2002] 1 All ER 749. This case addressed an exclusive choice of court clause, but the principle applies equally to an arbitration clause.
[62] Turner v. Grovit [2001] UKHL 65; [2002] 1 WLR 107 at p27. The citation is strictly obiter as the case involved claims brought in competing EU member state jurisdictions absent an exclusive jurisdiction clause or an arbitration clause. However, it has been cited with approval in Ust-Kamenogorsk Hydropower Plant JSC v. AES Ust-Kamenogorsk Hydropower Plant LLP [2013] UKSC 35 at p26, which involved an application for an anti-suit injunction in reliance on an arbitration agreement in relation to court proceedings threatened outside the EU, and summarised in the paragraphs that follow.
[63] Ust-Kamenogorsk Hydropower Plant JSC v. AES Ust-Kamenogorsk Hydropower Plant LLP [2013] UKSC 35.
[64] Section 37 Senior Courts Act 1981, which provides 'The High Court may by order (whether interlocutory or final) grant an injunction or appoint a receiver in all cases in which it appears to the court to be just and convenient to do so'.
[65] Ust-Kamenogorsk Hydropower Plant JSC v. AES Ust-Kamenogorsk Hydropower Plant LLP [2013] UKSC 35, per Mance LJ at 48.
[66] *Supra* note 52.

In short, the issue in hand involves a substantive right, enforceable independently of the existence or imminence of any arbitral proceedings. A respondent will thus have to provide good reasons why the court should not exercise its discretion to grant an anti-suit injunction, where the claimant has demonstrated the existence of a binding arbitration clause. If the claimant can show that the respondent will breach the terms of the agreement if it commences proceedings, then an injunction to prevent court proceedings is likely to issue. The claimant does not need to establish that the foreign proceedings are vexatious or oppressive.[67] It is nevertheless strongly advisable to apply for an injunction at the earliest opportunity.

It should be noted too that an anti-suit injunction can have serious consequences if ignored or flouted by continuance of the foreign proceedings in question. Breach of an anti-suit injunction may result in the respondent being found guilty of contempt of court, and subject to a fine and/ or imprisonment. In the recent case of *Mobile Telecommunications Co KSC v. HRH Prince Hussam bin Abdulaziz au Saud*,[68] the English Commercial Court sentenced a Saudi prince to twelve months' imprisonment. This was deemed appropriate to safeguard the function of anti-suit injunctions to preserve a party's rights, which in the case flowed from a valid arbitration award. In the case of a corporate entity, it may be fined, its directors may be sent to prison or fined, or its assets seized. Although it is arguable that it would be contrary to public policy to allow enforcement where the anti-suit injunction has been breached, this will not be the case where, for the purposes of the Civil Jurisdiction and Judgments Act,[69] the parties have submitted to the foreign court's jurisdiction.

Anti-suit injunctions are generally sought prior to the foreign court making its judgment. Apart from anti-suit injunctions, the English courts generally will usually only intervene in arbitral proceedings at the point of enforcement. Section 101 of the Arbitration Act sets out that awards will be enforceable either summarily under Section 66 of the Arbitration Act, or by action on the award:

> (1) A New York Convention award shall be recognised as binding on the persons as between whom it was made, and may accordingly be relied on by those persons by way of defence, set-off or otherwise in any legal proceedings in England and Wales or Northern Ireland.
>
> (2) A New York Convention award may, by leave of the court, be enforced in the same manner as a judgment or order of the court to the same effect.

Whereas an international NY Convention arbitration award made in any other jurisdiction is enforceable anywhere that is party to the NY Convention, once the award is registered as a judgment under English common law under Part I of the Foreign Judgments (Reciprocal Enforcement) Act 1933, an action on the award is pursuant to domestic law. The award is no longer an internationally recognised award, but is merged into a local law judgment and ceases to have independent status. The English law judgment is what is enforced. This is different to where the judgment is entered in terms of the award.[70]

However, the English court may also be called upon to intervene post-judgment to prevent enforcement of a foreign judgment in circumstances where it is alleged that an arbitration

---

[67] *Id.*; Toepfer International v. Societe Cargill France [1998] 1 Lloyd's Rep 379; Navigation Maritime Bulgare v. Rustal Trading Ltd (the *Ivan Zagubanski*) [2000] EWHC 222 (Comm) and Bannai v. Erez (Trustee in Bankruptcy of Eli Reifman) [2013] EWHC 3689 (Comm).

[68] Mobile Telecommunications Co KSC v. HRH Prince Hussam bin Abdulaziz au Saud [2018] EWHC 3749 (Comm).

[69] Section 32(1)(c) Civil Jurisdiction and Judgments Act 1982; Spliethoff's Bevrachtingskantoor BV v. Bank of China Ltd [2015] EWHC 999 (Comm).

[70] SUTTON, GILL, & GEARING, *supra* note 51, at 493, para. 8-059.

agreement has been breached. In these circumstances, the English law concept of comity becomes more preponderant, such that the English court will regard the grant of injunctive relief as a particularly serious matter.[71] An example of this approach can be found in the *Tanoh* case,[72] where the Court of Appeal upheld the first instance judge's refusal to grant injunctive relief. The Court of Appeal confirmed that the threshold requirement on the applicant to show a high probability that there was an arbitration agreement governing the dispute is applicable in respect of both an anti-suit (prejudgment) injunction and an anti-enforcement (postjudgment) injunction.[73] Reasons of comity and delay will often weigh more heavily against an applicant for an anti-enforcement injunction than will be the case in an anti-suit injunction.

3.2 Public Policy

By submitting to arbitration, and especially where the parties have expressly waived all rights to appeal an award, the parties' expectations are that state intervention in arbitration should be minimalist. In general,

> the courts strive to uphold arbitration awards. They do not approach them with a meticulous legal eye endeavouring to pick holes, inconsistencies and faults in awards and with the objective of upsetting or frustrating the process of arbitration. Far from it. The approach is to read an arbitration award in a reasonable and commercial way, expecting, as is usually the case, that there will be no substantial fault that can be found in it.[74]

However, 'participation by the Court, however unwelcome in theory, is in certain situations inevitable'.[75] This is mainly because '[f]ew nations are prepared to lend the power of the state to enforce arbitration awards, without retaining some right to review the awards themselves. This is reflected in [Article V of] the NY Convention'.[76]

The English courts thus retain limited powers over the parties' autonomy in relation to due process and the principles of fairness, independence and impartiality, to ensure that domestic law is being interpreted and applied correctly, and to resolve issues where matters of public policy or the public interest arise. Where the awards are issued by tribunals seated in England and Wales, key modes of court intervention are the review mechanisms of challenge and appeal, as described earlier.

Enforcement may be opposed in respect of a matter which is not capable of settlement by arbitration, or if it would be contrary to public policy to recognise or enforce the award[77] – for example, where there has been a serious irregularity in procedure resulting in substantial injustice to the applicant or where the award was obtained by fraud. The Arbitration Act confines court intervention to situations which risk undermining the integrity of the arbitral

---

[71] Masri v. Consolidated Contractors International (UK) Ltd and others (No 3) [2008] EWCA Civ 625 at 16.
[72] Ecobank Transnational Incorporated v. Tanoh [2015] EWCA Civ 1309.
[73] *Id.* at 91.
[74] Zermalt Holdings SA v. NuLife Upholstery Repairs Ltd [1985] EGLR 14, per Bingham J, cited in Fidelity Management v. Myriad International Holdings [2005] EWHC 1193 (Comm.) at 2, a case directed to a Section 68 challenge for serious irregularity.
[75] Coppee-Lavalin S.A. /N.V. v. Ken-Ren Chemicals and Fertilisers Ltd (In Liquidation in Kenya) and Voest Alpine Aktiengesellschaft v. Ken-Ren Chemicals and Fertilisers Ltd (In Liquidation in Kenya) [1994] 2 Lloyd's Rep 109 at 10.
[76] Mutual Shipping Corporation v. Bayshore Shipping Co. (the *Montan*) [1985] 1 Lloyd's Rep at 192, citing Intermare Transport G.m.b.H. v. International Copra Export Corporation (the *Ross Isle and Ariel*" [1985] 2 Lloyd's Rep at 589.
[77] Section 103(3) Arbitration Act 1996.

process. A key aspect of public policy is to minimise court intervention, on the basis that the parties have chosen to resolve their dispute under arbitral proceedings.

In matters of public policy, the focus of English law is upon domestic public policy. Given that enforcement of arbitral awards is by necessity a local procedure, international public policy is considered to have a more limited role than local public policy. However, it can affect the reasons why the English courts may step in. The starting position for the current English public policy position on enforcement of arbitration awards is that any arbitration has a territorial link to the seat in which such arbitration took place. The award does not exist in a lawless vacuum. In principle, this means that the challenged or unchallenged state of the award in the place of its seat will be an important consideration on any question of challenge in the English courts.

In order for the English courts to enforce an award that has been set aside by a court in the seat of the arbitration, positive and cogent evidence that the decision offended basic principles of honesty, natural justice and domestic concept of public policy will be needed. This approach can be seen in, for example, *Yukos Capital Sarl v. OJSC Oil Co Rosneft*.[78] In that case, the judge held that it was open to the applicant to argue that no effect should be given to the set-aside decision handed down by the Russian courts, 'based on conventional English conflict of law principles, for example that the judgments had been obtained by fraud, that it would be contrary to public policy to enforce the judgements, or that the judgments were obtained in breach of the rules of natural justice'. This case is discussed in more detail in Section 3.4. The approach of the English courts in matters of enforcement of a foreign award can be contrasted with that of the French courts, where the foreign law of the seat is not treated in the same way in matters of enforcement.[79]

One of the key current debates affecting public policy is the question of transparency, and the potentially adverse effect that private arbitration awards have on the development of a body of case law and binding precedent. For example, the ICC has recently published its revised note to parties and arbitral tribunals on the conduct of arbitration,[80] so that unless the parties opt out, ICC arbitral awards may be published in their entirety no less than two years after they have been notified to the parties. This is perhaps the boldest initiative from across a spectrum of transparency initiatives latterly being pursued by some of the world's leading arbitral institutions. In the past, it has not been uncommon to see publication of anonymised excerpts of procedural decisions issued by tribunals under the auspices of an arbitral institution, with the consent of the parties. However, it will be interesting to see how the recent ICC changes will in practice operate, both as to whether parties opt out, and as to how frequently the ICC chooses to publish awards. The new provisions apply to awards made as from January 1, 2019.

3.3 Statistics

As can be seen from the discussion, parties to an arbitration have a number of potential avenues to test the limits of the arbitral process in the English courts. One may legitimately wonder

---

[78] Yukos Capital Sarl v. OJSC Oil Co Rosneft [2014] EWHC 2188.
[79] Société Hilmarton v. Société OTV, Cour de cassation chambre civile 1 Audience publique du mercredi Mar. 23, 1994 N° de pourvoi: 92-15137 (1994) *Bulletin* I No. 104 at 79 (Paris Court of Appeal, Dec. 19, 1991); Société Pt Putrabali Adyamulia v. Rena Holding and others, Cour de Cassation, First Civil Chamber, June 29, 2007 (Petition No Y-06-13.293).
[80] *Note to Parties and Arbitral Tribunals on the Conduct of the Arbitration under the ICC Rules of Arbitration*, INTERNATIONAL CHAMBER OF COMMERCE (Jan. 1, 2019), https://iccwbo.org/publication/note-parties-arbitral-tribunals-conduct-arbitration/.

whether the existence of these potential avenues of challenge might hinder or weaken the arbitral process as a dispute resolution solution. The existence in England of limited appeal rights to court from arbitral awards, for example, might seem counterintuitive where parties have specifically chosen to resolve their disputes in private. Statistics provide some relevant insight as to the courts' practical impact in England on arbitral process:

Claims under Section 68 (Serious Irregularity)

Year	No. of claims	Successful challenges
2015	34	1
2016	31	0
2017–March 2018	47	0

Claims under Section 69 (Appeal on a Point of Law)

Year	No. of claims	Permission for appeal granted	Successful appeals
2015	60	20	4
2016	46	0	0
2017–March 2018	56	10	1

As can be seen from the tables, between 2015 and March 2018, of 274 claims brought under Sections 68 and 69 of the Arbitration Act, only 6 of these reported claims were ultimately successful.[81] By way of limited update, from January 2019 to mid-August 2019, Lloyd's Law Reports published 53 cases of challenge to awards. Of those, 5 considered challenges under Section 67 of the Arbitration Act (of which 1 was successful), 12 considered challenges under Section 68 of the Arbitration Act (of which 3 were successful) and 6 considered challenges under Section 69 of the Arbitration Act (of which 1 was successful).[82] It is clear from these figures that although challenging awards in the English courts may be a regular occurrence, they remain relatively rare set against the total volume of arbitral activity in the UK. And even more rarely do such challenges succeed.

3.4 Requirements for Enforceability of Awards

One of the key advantages of arbitral proceedings over court proceedings is that the award will be recognised and enforced in many more countries than an English court judgment. This is most notably because of the NY Convention.[83] In order to be enforceable, an arbitration award must be a valid award. An order or direction made by the arbitral tribunal will be insufficient to commence enforcement proceedings in the English courts.[84] The award has to form a clear, unambiguous decision by the tribunal on some or all of the issues raised during the proceedings.

---

[81] Statistics obtained from *Commercial Court Users' Group Meeting Report – March 2018*, COURTS AND TRIBUNALS JUDICIARY (Apr. 29, 2018), https://www.judiciary.uk/publications/commercial-court-users-group-meeting-report-march-2018/.
[82] Statistics obtained from analysis of Lloyd's Law Reports cases on I-LAW, https://www.i-law.com/ilaw/doc/view.htm?id=400380.
[83] The 1927 Geneva Convention on the Execution of Foreign Arbitral Awards may also assist.
[84] Michael Wilson & Partners Ltd v. John Forster Emmott [2008] EWHC 2684 (Comm) at 14.

Unless the parties have agreed the award or have agreed that reasons are not necessary, the award must set out the reasoning behind the tribunal's decision.[85]

The award must not leave any matters to be delegated to a third party. The tribunal may consult experts in connection with the issues to be decided upon (for example by appointing an expert or accepting counsel's opinion on certain points of law[86]), but the tribunal must come to its conclusions independently, and not delegate decision making. Where the tribunal has expert knowledge in a relevant field, the parties are deemed to have agreed that such expert knowledge would be used in reaching a decision. However, the tribunal should be careful to ensure that this knowledge is of general application in evaluating the current case, rather than the supply of new or specific comparable evidence.[87]

The award must be 'final', i.e., it must be a complete decision in relation to the issues requiring a decision to be made. Therefore, an interim or a partial award, i.e., one which makes a finding on some but not all of the issues in the dispute or which leave certain aspects of the dispute undecided may not be sufficient to be enforced. The award made must be one in which the tribunal has not exceeded its powers either during proceedings or in making the award, must not have been obtained by fraud, and must not be contrary to public policy.[88]

In England and Wales, an award (including a foreign award) may be enforced by (1) seeking leave to enforce the award as a judgment under Section 66 of the Arbitration Act,[89] (2) an action on the award (common law) or (3) for qualifying awards, under the NY Convention. Further procedure for enforcement is set out in the Civil Procedure Rules.[90] The NY Convention limits a party's grounds to challenge such an enforcement application. This limited approach is also reflected in Section 66 of the Arbitration Act. A resisting party's grounds for challenge may include (1) a lack of substantive jurisdiction,[91] (2) domestic public policy and (3) ambiguity or defect in the form of the award.

The NY Convention is incorporated into English law in the Arbitration Act, which includes provisions relating to the recognition and enforcement of arbitral awards.[92] In order to enforce an NY Convention award, the party seeking enforcement or recognition must produce a duly authenticated original award, or a certified copy of such award and a duly authenticated original arbitration agreement or a certified copy of such agreement, and a certified translation into English, if the award or agreement is written in another language. The NY Convention grounds upon which the English courts may refuse to recognise or enforce an arbitral award are set out in the Arbitration Act:

1. party to the agreement (under the law applicable to him) was under some incapacity;
2. agreement was not valid under the law to which the parties subjected it or, failing any indication thereon, under the law of the country where the award was made;
3. party was not given proper notice of the appointment or of the proceedings, or was otherwise unable to present his case;

---

[85] Section 52(4) Arbitration Act 1996.
[86] *Id.* at Section 37(1)(a); Gladesmore Investments Ltd v. Caradon Heating Ltd [1994] EG.
[87] Checkpoint Ltd v. Strathclyde Pension Fund [2003] EWCA Civ 84; Annie Fox v. PG Wellfair Ltd [1981] 2 Lloyd's Rep 514; JD Wetherspoon plc v. Jay Mar Estates [2007] EWHC 856.
[88] Arab National Bank v. The Registrar of Companies [2005] EWHC 3047 at 8-112.
[89] Section 66(1) Arbitration Act 1996.
[90] Rules 62.17–62.21, Part 62 Civil Procedure Rules as of Dec. 21, 2017, https://www.justice.gov.uk/courts/procedure-rules/civil/rules/part62.
[91] Section 66(3) Arbitration Act 1996.
[92] *Id.* at 101–103.

4. award deals with a difference not contemplated by or not falling within the terms of the submission to arbitration or contains decisions on matters beyond the scope of the submission;
5. composition of the arbitral tribunal or the arbitral procedure was not in accordance with the agreement of the parties or, failing such agreement with the law of the country in which the arbitration took place; or
6. award has not yet become binding on the parties, or has been set aside or suspended by a competent authority of the country in which, or under the law of which, it was made.[93]

As discussed, English courts will generally give recognition to court decisions of the seat setting aside an award, or refusing to set aside an award and may also order the party resisting enforcement to give suitable security for the award.

An illustration of this approach can be found in the relatively recent case of *Yukos Capital Sarl v. OJSC Oil Co Rosneft*, albeit that the judgment was addressed to a series of preliminary issues and did not decide the final issue as to whether the awards in question were enforceable.[94] Yukos was a part of a group of companies involved in oil production in Russia. The group was broken up and Russian government-owned Rosneft acquired the majority of its assets. Yukos had made various intragroup loans to its subsidiary Yugansknefregaz, which was later acquired by Rosneft. Based on the terms of the loans, Yukos made a claim against Rosneft for over $160 million interest for the period between 2006 and 2010 during which Rosneft refused to satisfy four arbitral awards for a total of US $425 million made under the rules of the International Commercial Arbitration Court at the Russian Chamber of Commerce and Industry in Moscow in favour of Yukos. Yukos then commenced enforcement proceedings in The Netherlands. However, on Rosneft's application, the awards were then set aside by the Russian courts. In a judgment of April 28, 2009, the Amsterdam Court of Appeal refused leave to enforce the Russian judgments on the grounds that the annulment decisions made by the Russian courts were not impartial or independent. The English Court of Appeal had earlier held that the Dutch court decision was guided by considerations of Dutch public order rather than English public policy and therefore did not create an issue estoppel on Rosneft in the English court proceedings.[95]

It was left open to the applicant to argue that no effect should be given to the Russian court set-aside decisions. It was thus argued that the set-aside decisions were (1) tainted by bias; (2) contrary to natural justice, in that the Russian courts deliberately misapplied the law; (3) procured in circumstances violating Article 6 of the European Convention on Human Rights; and (4) formed part of an illegitimate campaign of commercial harassment waged against the claimant by the Russian Federation for political reasons. The court's response was to articulate a test: whether the court in considering whether to give effect to an award can (in particular and identifiable circumstances) treat it as having legal effect notwithstanding a later order of a court annulling the award. In applying this test, it was held that it would be both unsatisfactory and contrary to principle if the court were bound to recognise a decision of a foreign court which offended against basic principles of honesty, natural justice and domestic concepts of public policy.[96]

However, an English court will not lightly ignore the decision of a foreign court at the seat of arbitration. In order for English courts to enforce an award that has been set aside in the

---

[93] Section 103 Arbitration Act 1996.
[94] Yukos Capital Sarl v. OJSC Oil Co Rosneft [2014] EWHC 2188.
[95] Yukos Capital Sarl v. OJSC Rosneft Oil Co (No. 2) [2014] QB 438.
[96] *Supra* note 94, at 20.

seat of the arbitration, cogent evidence of the foreign court acting deliberately wrongfully will need to be shown. Parties accordingly face high barriers to enforce awards which have been annulled by the court of the seat of the arbitral proceedings. This approach can be clearly seen in a recent post *Yukos* decision, again involving the Russian courts.[97] In the case, the English court dismissed an attempt to enforce a Russian award which had been annulled by a court in Moscow. The English court held that it was insufficient for the party seeking enforcement to show that the Russian court's decision was 'manifestly wrong or is perverse'. It was necessary that:

(1) The decision must be so wrong as to be evidence of bias, or be such that no court acting in good faith could have arrived at it.
(2) The evidence or grounds must be 'cogent'.
(3) The decision of the foreign court must be deliberately wrong, not simply wrong by incompetence.[98]

Short of refusing enforcement, where an award is being challenged in the courts of the seat, the English court has power to 'suspend' enforcement of an arbitration award in the England, pending an application to challenge it.[99] An example of this is to be found in *APIS AS v. Fantazia Kereskedelmi KFT*.[100] In that case, a company sought a stay of enforcement of an arbitration award, alleging a serious irregularity in the conduct of the proceedings. The court held that it possessed an inherent jurisdiction to stay the enforcement of the award. However, the outcome of a challenge to enforcement of a foreign award in England may not necessarily follow the same path as the enforcement courts in the country of the seat. This issue arises most acutely where there has been no application at the seat to set aside the award. In a seminal case, *Dallah*,[101] the English court refused to enforce an arbitration award made in France against the government of Pakistan. The English court considered that the government of Pakistan had not been a party to the agreement containing the arbitration clause.

In the case, Dallah entered into a Memorandum of Understanding with the government of Pakistan to provide housing in Saudi Arabia for Pakistani pilgrims to Mecca. The president of Pakistan issued an ordinance creating the Awami Hajj Trust. The trust then entered into an agreement with Dallah, reiterating the terms negotiated by the government. The agreement contained an ICC arbitration clause but no choice of law clause. Pakistan was not a signatory to the agreement. The agreement lasted only about four months and disputes arose. The trust first brought claim against Dallah for breach of the agreement in Pakistani courts. The Pakistani courts dismissed the trust's claims on the basis that the trust no longer existed. Dallah then commenced an ICC arbitration against Pakistan, which Pakistan resisted on a number of grounds, including lack of jurisdiction.[102]

In June 2001, an arbitral tribunal made a jurisdictional award, declaring that Pakistan was bound by the arbitration clause in the agreement. Seated in Paris, the tribunal applied principles of French international arbitration law and decided jurisdiction based on 'those transnational general principles and usages reflecting the fundamental requirements of justice in international

---

[97] Maximov v. OJSC Novolipetsky Mettalurgichesky Kombinat [2017] EWHC 1911 (Comm).
[98] *Id.* per Sir Michael Burton at 15. The judge records that there was no issue between the parties on this approach.
[99] See Section 103(5) Arbitration Act 1996 in the case of an NY Convention award. In the case of an English award, the court has an inherent power – *see* APIS AS v. Fantazia Kereskedelmi KFT [2001] 1 All ER (Comm) 348.
[100] APIS AS, *supra* note 99.
[101] Dallah Real Estate & Tourism Holding Co v. Pakistan [2010] UKSC 46.
[102] *See* Gary Born, *Dallah and the New York Convention*, KLUWER ARBITRATION BLOG (Apr. 7, 2011), http://arbitrationblog.kluwerarbitration.com/2011/04/07/dallah-and-the-new-york-convention/.

trade and the concept of good faith in international business'.[103] The tribunal held that the Trust was the 'alter ego' of the Pakistan government, making the government a 'true party' to the agreement and its arbitration clause.[104] The tribunal subsequently made a final award in favour of Dallah in the amount of $20,588,040. Dallah sought to enforce this award in England under the NY Convention and the Arbitration Act and also sought exequatur of the award in France. Pakistan resisted enforcement of the award in England. Pakistan relied on Article V(1)(a) of the NY Convention to argue that that there was no valid arbitration agreement. In August 2009, the French courts granted exequatur of the award for enforcement purposes. However, in its later decision, the UK Supreme Court denied enforcement of the award.

Before the UK Supreme Court, Dallah did not pursue the alter ego theory that had underpinned the tribunal's award. Argument focused instead on the common intention of the parties, applying French law principles. The court read the agreement narrowly and held that there had been no 'common intention'[105] for the government of Pakistan to be a party to the arbitration agreement, commenting that 'there was no material sufficient to justify the tribunal's conclusion'.[106] For one leading commentator, the Supreme Court did not '[apply] the real substance of the French standards when evaluating the parties' actual conduct and agreements'.[107] These would have been the appropriate standards to use, given that the tribunal was seated in France. And there was no choice of law specified in the agreement.

Turning to matters of fraud, alleged fraudulent conduct in arbitral proceedings has led to some recent interesting decisions. In *RBRG Trading (UK) Limited v. Sinocore International Co Limited*,[108] Hamblen LJ, held that a Chinese CIETAC award could be enforced in England even though the arbitrators found that the enforcing party, Sinocore, had behaved fraudulently by using forged bills of lading to demand payment from RBRG. In reaching this conclusion, it was relevant that Sinocore had been caught attempting to defraud RBRG's bank, which had refused to pay against the forged bills of lading, and that Sinocore's actions only constituted 'attempted fraud'.

In *Stati v. Kazakhstan*,[109] the English Court of Appeal allowed an appeal against the first instance decision granting an application to set aside a notice of discontinuance. Stati had obtained an award in a Swedish seated arbitration against Kazakhstan and successfully applied for an order to enforce the award in England. Kazakhstan sought to have the order set aside, alleging that the award had been obtained by fraud. The court gave Kazakhstan permission to add the fraud allegations to its application to set aside the enforcement order, and directed that it should proceed to trial 'as if commenced under CPR Part 7'. Stati then served notice of discontinuance of the enforcement proceedings and offered undertakings not to enforce the award. However, Kazakhstan argued for a final determination on the merits, due to its independent claims for declaratory remedies which would be unaffected by the notice of discontinuance or, alternatively, that the notice of discontinuance should be set aside. Knowles J set aside the notice of discontinuance. While the judge held that the fraud claim was not an independent claim, he considered that Kazakhstan had a legitimate interest in seeking to have the enforcement order set aside on the merits and that it would be useful to have a concluded answer on the

---

[103] Dallah Real Estate, *supra* note 101, at 33.
[104] *Id.* at 39.
[105] *Id.* at 132.
[106] *Id.* at 145.
[107] Born, *supra* note 102, at 4.
[108] RBRG Trading (UK) Limited v. Sinocore International Co Limited [2018] EWCA Civ 838 at 36.
[109] Stati v. Kazakhstan [2017] EWHC 1348 (Comm).

fraud issue. He directed that the fraud allegations should proceed to trial. The Court of Appeal agreed with Knowles J that the fraud claim was a defence to the enforcement action, and not an independent claim. However, for the Court of Appeal, once Stati discontinued the enforcement proceedings, Kazakhstan ceased to have a legitimate purpose in pursuing its defence in the English courts. The appeal was therefore allowed so as to give effect to the notice of discontinuance and bring the English proceedings to an end.[110]

In *Carpatsky Petroleum Corporation v. PJSC Urkrnafta*,[111] upon an application by Urkrnafta to set aside an order granting permission to enforce an award under the NY Convention, the court held that allegations of fraud which came to light only after the arbitral hearing had been concluded and after the award had been issued, would not be permitted to go to trial. In its application, Urkrnafta sought to rely upon documents obtained in March 2011, in circumstances when the award had been made in October 2010. It was urged by Urkrnafta that the new documents showed that the chairman of Carpatsky Petroleum Corporation had lied in his evidence on an issue central to the arbitral award.

Urkrnafta had previously mounted an unsuccessful challenge to the award in the Svea Court of Appeal, in Sweden, which was the competent authority of the seat of the arbitration for such matters. It had previously unsuccessfully contested enforcement in both the United States and The Netherlands. It had successfully resisted enforcement in the Ukraine based on a procedural argument and on an argument that there was no valid arbitration agreement in writing. Fraud had not been alleged in any of these other proceedings.

The court set out the principles to be taken into account when considering the public policy exceptions for enforcing arbitral Awards:[112]

(a) Section 103 of the Arbitration Act reflects and embodies the predisposition in favour of enforcing
New York Convention awards. Grounds for refusing recognition and enforcement of arbitral awards are to be construed narrowly;
(b) Public policy is the public policy of England and Wales;
(c) Public policy exceptions are a safety valve that should only be invoked in a clear case and which must be approached with extreme caution; and
(d) When considering whether an award has been obtained by fraud, nothing short of reprehensible or unconscionable conduct will suffice to invest the court with a discretion to consider denying recognition or enforcement of the award.

The court also set out the evidential threshold facing an applicant seeking to resist enforcement of an award based on allegations of fraud, made up of two conditions: (1) that the evidence to establish the fraud was not available to the party alleging the fraud at the time of the hearing before the arbitrators and could not with reasonable diligence have been discovered before the award and (2) where perjury is the fraud alleged, the evidence must be so strong that it would reasonably be expected to be decisive at a hearing and if unanswered must have that result.[113]

In light of these principles and the evidential threshold facing the applicant, the court had no difficulty in finding that Urkrnafta fell short. For the English judge, Urkrnafta was making

---

[110] Stati and others v. Republic of Kazakhstan [2018] EWCA Civ 1896, Lloyd's Law Reports 2 Lloyd's Rep. 263. The appeal was allowed on terms that the enforcement order be set aside and that the claimants give to the court undertakings, offered by them at first instance, not to enforce the award in England.
[111] Carpatsky Petroleum Corporation v. PJSC Urkrnafta [2018] EWHC 2516 (Comm). The *Stati* case was relied upon by the judge in this case.
[112] *Id.* at 39–42.
[113] The '*Westacre* test': Westacre Investments Inc v. Jugoimport-SDPR Holding Co Ltd [2000] QB 288, per Waller LJ.

essentially the same arguments on matters that had already been before the arbitral tribunal.[114] The new documents were not decisive. There were no abnormal circumstances which would justify the continuance of the fraud allegations. The court considered Urkrnafta's failure to raise fraud in the Swedish proceedings as a relevant factor (although not a bar in itself). Finally, the size of the award – US $145 million compared to the initial investment of US $6 million was not a sufficiently compelling reason to allow the fraud allegations to go to trial.[115]

Where enforcement of awards is concerned, another issue which can sometimes arise is around the claimed sovereign immunity of one of the parties. In a very recent case, *General Dynamics United Kingdom Ltd v. State of Libya*,[116] the principal issue to be considered was whether an arbitration award could be enforced against a state by court proceedings in the English courts, without formal service on that state. Section 12 of the State Immunity Act 1978 governs the service of court proceedings on states, and provides that:

> Any writ or other document required to be served for instituting proceedings against a State shall be served by being transmitted through the Foreign and Commonwealth Office to the Ministry of Foreign Affairs of the State and service shall be deemed to have been effected when the writ or document is received at the Ministry.

An NY Convention award rendered against the state of Libya was not honoured and the claimant sought to enforce the award in England under Section 101 of the Arbitration Act. Application for enforcement was made to the English court. Teare J entered judgment on the award and made an order dispensing with the usual requirements of service on Libya, as he considered he had power to do under the court rules. The judge ordered that:

> Pursuant to Civil Procedure Rules 6.16 and 6.28, the Claimant has permission to dispense with service of the Arbitration Claim Form dated 21 June 2018, any Order made by the Court and other associated documents.

To ensure that the claim form nevertheless came to the attention of the state of Libya, Teare J made orders that the claim form and related documents be couriered to various addressees at various addresses in Tripoli and Paris. The state of Libya applied to set aside Teare J's orders. The court found that service under Section 12 of the State Immunity Act 1978 was mandatory where the English court sought to exercise jurisdiction over a foreign state. No other method of service was permitted. The court considered that the purpose of serving proceedings correctly was especially important in this case, not only to ensure that the content of the document served was communicated to the defendant but also to ensure that the jurisdiction of the English court was invoked against the state of Libya in a proper manner. It was held that the court's general power to dispense with service of a claim form in exceptional circumstances under CPR 6.16 did not apply where service was required to commence proceedings against a state, as this would be contrary to the mandatory terms of Section 12 of the State Immunity Act 1978.[117]

---

[114] Carpatsky Petroleum Corporation v. PJSC Urkrnafta [2018] EWHC 2516 (Comm) at p97: 'The overwhelming impression, in particular from the lengthy evidence of Mr Mascarenhas, is that Urkrnafta cannot accept its defeat before the tribunal on the merits. It wishes to re-run the same arguments on the same material that was before the tribunal', per Carr J.
[115] *Id.* at 89, 93 and 95.
[116] General Dynamics United Kingdom Ltd v. State of Libya [2019] EWHC 64 (Comm).
[117] General Dynamics United Kingdom Ltd v. State of Libya [2019] EWHC 64 (Comm) at 79.

4 JUDICIAL INTERPRETATION OF COMMERCIAL ARBITRATION CLAUSES

Since the Arbitration Act 1996 came into force, and following a Court of Appeal decision,[118] subsequently approved by the House of Lords,[119] the contemporary approach of the English courts is that any jurisdiction or arbitration clause in an international commercial contract should be construed to 'encompass the widest range of potential disputes that its terms will reasonably permit, including non-contractual claims and claims involving an admission of a criminal purpose'.[120] The value of previous authorities when construing arbitration clauses has been diminished considerably following the decision made in *Fiona Trust*, where the Court of Appeal indicated that parties who enter into arbitration agreements do not expect that, in the event of a dispute, there will be detailed argument, by reference to authorities, as to the precise meaning of the particular phrases that they have adopted. Instead, the court should adopt a presumption of 'one-stop adjudication',[121] reviewing the clause or agreement afresh. In the leading judgment in the House of Lords, Lord Hoffman stated the matter in the following terms:[122]

> In my opinion the construction of an arbitration clause should start from the assumption that the parties, as rational businessmen, are likely to have intended any dispute arising out of the relationship into which they have entered or purported to enter to be decided by the same tribunal. The clause should be construed in accordance with this presumption unless the language makes it clear that certain questions were intended to be excluded from the arbitrator's jurisdiction.

Clear words would be necessary to exclude from an arbitration agreement any allegations of criminal conduct linked to the parties' contractual obligations.[123] Where the words 'arising out of or in connection with' (or similar) appear in an arbitration clause, this should generally be sufficient to capture any conceivable dispute linked to the contract, except for disputes where there is a question as to whether the contract in question ever existed.

Generally, claims based on alternative causes of action will be treated as falling within the tribunal's jurisdiction, especially where the facts of the dispute are related to other contractual claims falling within the arbitration agreement. In *JSC BTA Bank* v. *Ablyazov*, the phrase '[a]ny disputes, differences or claims arising from this contract (agreement) or in connection therewith' was held to cover noncontractual claims in connection with the underlying agreement.[124]

There may exceptionally be a question mark over the extent to which tort claims will fall within an arbitration agreement contained in a contract, and whether particular wording is sufficient to include tort claims that are advanced. In *Injazat Technology Capital Ltd* v. *Dr. Hamid Najafi*,[125] on an application for an injunction to restrain the defendant from pursuing a number of arbitrations, Flaux J had to consider whether a noncontractual claim for false imprisonment relating to an order obtained to prevent the defendant from leaving Dubai as part of the steps to enforce the final award in Dubai, fell within the scope of the arbitration

---

[118] Fiona Trust & Holding Corp v. Yuri Privalov [2007] EWCA Civ 20.
[119] Fiona Trust & Holding Corporation v. Privalov [2007] UKHL 40.
[120] SUTTON, GILL, & GEARING, *supra* note 51, at 26, para. 2-004.
[121] Practical Law Arbitration, *Interpreting Arbitration Agreements under English Law*, THOMSON REUTERS PRACTICAL LAW, https://uk.practicallaw.thomsonreuters.com/Document/Id249cb971c9611e38578f7ccc38dcbee/View/FullText.html?navigationPath=Search%2fv1%2f&transitionType=Default&contextData=(sc.Default)&firstPage=true.
[122] Fiona Trust, *supra* note 119, per Lord Hoffmann at 13.
[123] Interprods v. De La Rue International [2014] EWHC 68 per Teare J at 7 and 8.
[124] JSC BTA Bank v. Ablyazov [2011] EWHC 587 (Comm) at p64.
[125] Injazat Technology Capital Ltd v. Dr. Hamid Najafi [2012] EWHC 4171.

agreements in question. As part of his reasoning, he considered that such a claim did not fall within the scope of the arbitration agreements.[126]

The English courts generally strive to give effect to parties' intention to refer disputes to arbitration 'except in cases of hopeless confusion'.[127] In *Paul Smith Ltd* v. *H&S International Holding Inc.*,[128] the court found a binding arbitration agreement to exist in the following provisions:

> 13. Settlement of disputes – ... any disputes or difference ... shall be adjudicated upon under the Rules of Conciliation and Arbitration of the International Chamber of Commerce by one or more Arbitrators appointed in accordance with those Rules.
>
> 14. Language and law – This Agreement is written in the English language and shall be interpreted according to English law. The Courts of England shall have exclusive jurisdiction over it to which jurisdiction the parties hereby submit.

Steyn J interpreted clause 13 as a self-contained arbitration agreement, with clause 14 specifying the lex arbitri, the curial law or the law governing the arbitration. There was no inconsistency between clauses 13 and 14, and both clauses were valid and binding. The reference to the English courts in clause 14 did not affect the validity of the arbitration agreement.

While it can be seen that a broadly expressed arbitration agreement will be given the fullest effect possible by the English courts, it is important to note that the court cannot rewrite the parties' agreement where the arbitration agreement is expressed in more limited terms. In the *Petros Hadjikyriakos*,[129] the arbitration agreement was clearly limited to freight and demurrage claims. The arbitrators had no jurisdiction to hear similar claims relating to losses suffered for overtime for the elevator used to load and discharge cargo, and they could not construe the agreement to cover such claims.

In cases where parties have elected to carve out only certain disputes for arbitration, leaving others for resolution by other means, the English courts have at times been left with a difficult task. Where parties wish to adopt such hybrid or tiered dispute resolution procedures, it is important that the agreement be clearly expressed. In *Lovelock* v. *Exportles*,[130] the arbitration clause purported to submit '[a]ny dispute and/or claim' to arbitration in England and '[a]ny other dispute' to arbitration at the USSR Chamber of Commerce Foreign Trade Arbitration Commission in Moscow. Lord Denning found these clauses 'impossible to reconcile', and 'beyond the wit of man – or at any rate beyond my wit – to say which dispute comes within which part of the clause'.[131] The judge refused to give effect to the clause, with the result that the dispute was left to be decided by the court.

However, it is sometimes possible to 'modify' detailed provisions of an arbitration agreement where necessary to give effect to the parties' intentions. In *Film Finance Inc.* v. *The Royal Bank of Scotland*,[132] the court modified the detailed provisions of the arbitration clause in order to give

---

[126] Id. at 9. The decision does not record the terms of the arbitration agreement in question, which limits the usefulness of this case for the reader. The judge was also clearly unimpressed with the claim: 'the claim for false imprisonment, even if it were not wholly unmeritorious, is not a claim which falls within the scope of the arbitration clause in either contract'.
[127] SUTTON, GILL, & GEARING, *supra* note 51, at 69, para. 2-077.
[128] Paul Smith Ltd v. H&S International Holding Inc. [1991] 2 Lloyd's Rep 127 QBD (Comm) per Steyn J at 129.
[129] Food Corp of India v. Achilles Halcoussis (the *Petros Hadjukyriakos*) [1988] 2 Lloyd's Rep 56.
[130] ERJ Lovelock v. Exportles [1968] 1 Lloyd's Rep 163.
[131] Id. at 164.
[132] Film Finance Inc. v. The Royal Bank of Scotland [2007] EWHC 195 (Comm).

effect to the true intention of the parties. The court justified its approach in the following terms:[133]

> It is a well-established principle of interpretation that in these circumstances provisions may be read subject to necessary modifications, and disregarding what is inapplicable or 'insensible' (to use the word of Lord Esher MR in Hamilton & Co v Mackie & Sons, (1889) 5 TLR 677). This, in my judgment, will lead to an interpretation that was intended by the parties.

In *Mangistaumunaigaz Oil Production Association* v. *United World Trade Inc.*,[134] the court did not accept the argument that the words *if any* were inconsistent with an unconditional agreement to arbitrate. The court upheld the clause which provided for '[a]rbitration, if any, by ICC Rules in London', finding that the words *if any* were either *surplusage* which could be ignored, or an abbreviation for *if any dispute arises*.

By way of contrast, in *Kruppa* v. *Benedetti*,[135] the relevant clause provided that 'the parties will endeavour to first resolve the matter through Swiss arbitration. Should a resolution not be forthcoming the courts of England shall have non-exclusive jurisdiction'. The court found that the clause did not give rise to a binding agreement to arbitrate. Cooke J considered the clause inadequate to form an arbitration agreement on the basis that it was logically not possible to have an effective multitier dispute resolution clause with two binding tiers requiring arbitration and court litigation.[136] Cooke J held that the clause did not require the parties to refer any dispute to arbitration in the sense required by the Arbitration Act but merely envisaged the parties attempting to refer the matter to arbitration by agreement between them, failing which the English courts were to have jurisdiction on a nonexclusive basis.

In a very recent case, *Backos* v. *WFW Global LLP*,[137] and taking a pragmatic and commercial approach to matters, the English court held that disputes which arose out of the operation of an LLP agreement between the parties were to be determined by arbitration, despite the fact that one of the parties to the arbitration had ceased to be a member of the LLP when the dispute arose. After an award was rendered that was adverse to Mr Backos, he made application challenging the award for want of jurisdiction under Section 67 of the Arbitration Act. The arbitration clause on its face appeared to apply only to current 'Members' and not to 'Outgoing Members', with the contractual definition of *Member* excluding an 'Outgoing Member'. However, the court proceeded to construe the word *Member* to include someone who was a member when the relevant events occurred, which was enough to hold that the arbitration agreement applied and the award could stand.[138]

---

[133] *Id.* at 36.
[134] Mangistaumunaigaz Oil Production Association v. United World Trade Inc. [1995] 1 Lloyd's Rep 617 QBD (Comm) at 617.
[135] Kruppa v. Benedetti and another [2014] EWHC 1887 (Comm).
[136] *Id.* per Cooke J at 12.
[137] Backos v. WFW Global LLP [2019] EWHC 243 (Ch).
[138] *Id.* at p34.

24

Judicial Control of Arbitral Awards in the United States

Larry A. DiMatteo

1 INTRODUCTION

The popular image of the American legal system is that it is run amok with litigation-happy disputants. Whether this is true from an empirical perspective is debatable, but in fact American federal law and policy favors arbitration as the country's preferred means of dispute resolution. This is a longstanding position dating back to the enactment of the 1925 Federal Arbitration Act (FAA). However, the history of this Act and its implementation has been inconsistent. It was forgotten at one point as individual American states enacted statutes to limit the use of mandatory arbitration in consumer contracts. Eventually, the US Supreme Court recognized the FAA as prevailing law and voided state laws limiting the use of arbitration under the federal preemption doctrine.[1] In more recent times, the US Supreme Court expanded the scope of private arbitration clauses to include statutory claims, such as in the areas of antitrust, collective bargaining, and civil rights. Even more recently, it has begun to limit the availability of arbitration by placing restrictions on class action arbitration.

Under a number of judicially recognized principles judicial control over arbitration proceedings is limited. The concepts of separability and kompetenz–kompetenz[2] are among the most significant in the field of international arbitration. These principles are the basis for arbitral jurisdiction – how it is defined and how it works on a practical level. The separability principle allows for the very existence of the arbitral proceeding, preserving the autonomy of the arbitration clause as an agreement within an agreement.[3] The separability principle is based on the fiction that an arbitration clause is a standalone contract even in cases where the contract is embedded with is determined to be invalid. Kompetenz–kompetenz cedes the authority of deciding the scope of the arbitration clause to arbitrators.[4] The rationale being that the arbitrators are experts in defining the scope of arbitration clauses and, thereby, determining the scope of their jurisdiction. It can also be said that kompetenz–kompetenz reflects the exercise of private autonomy of the contracting parties, since it was the parties that intended ex ante that disputes would be resolved through extra-judicial means. However, these principles do on have

---

[1] The preemption doctrine found in the US Constitution recognizes federal law as superior to any conflicting state laws.
[2] *See* Adriana Dulic, *First Options of Chicago, Inc. v. Kaplan and the Kompetenz-Kompetenz Principle*, 2 PEPPERDINE DISPUTE RESOLUTION LAW JOURNAL 77 (2002).
[3] *See* GARY BORN, INTERNATIONAL ARBITRATION: LAW AND PRACTICE 56 (2012).
[4] *See* Art. 16(1) of the UNCITRAL Model Law.

unitary meanings. The principle of separability is widely recognized throughout the world, while the kompetenz–kompetenz principle differs in meaning across jurisdictions.

There are two aspects of the kompetenz–kompetenz principle: the first one is related to the ability of the arbitrators to rule on their own jurisdiction, and the second, and more problematic, is related to the fact that national courts can rule on the arbitral tribunal's jurisdiction only after the arbitrators have done so. This second characteristic of the principle, however, is less accepted in national systems, and, as will be illustrated in details later, has given rise to several problems, especially in the United States.

2 PRINCIPLES OF SEPARABILITY AND KOMPETENZ–KOMPETENZ IN AMERICAN LAW

Whereas the English and French approaches are quite straightforward in recognizing the rule of kompetenz–kompetenz, at both the legislative and judicial levels, the United States has been more reluctant in the acknowledgment of this rule; there is no mention of it in the FAA and the initial American case law appears to limit its application, but the trend has been to embrace the concept that arbitrators are best suited to determine their own jurisdiction.

In the United States, the 1978 case *Pollux Marine Agencies Inc.* v. *Louis Dreyfus Corp.*[5] held that "something can be severed only from something else that exists," thus rejecting the ability of the arbitral tribunal to rule on its own jurisdiction. By the same token, it was later held, that even if the issue of the validity of the contract was arbitrable, it is not for the arbitral tribunal to decide issues related to the existence of an underlying agreement. The landmark decision on this topic is represented by the 1995 case *First Option* v. *Kaplan*.[6] The Supreme Court held that the decision related to arbitrability (in this case linked to the scope ratione personae of the arbitration agreement) represents an issue that has to be decided in courts "unless the parties clearly and unmistakably provide otherwise." The so-called arbitrability dicta in *First Option* v. *Kaplan*, however, proves troublesome, since it could be interpreted either in a restrictive or in an excessively broad way. In fact, the Supreme Court held: "Did the parties agree to submit the arbitrability question itself to arbitration? If so, then the court's standard for reviewing the arbitrator's decision about that matter should not differ from the standard courts apply when they review any other matter that parties have agreed to arbitrate." As was noted, after this decision, it became more problematic for judges to determine not only if the arbitrators exceeded their jurisdiction but also if a court should review the arbitrator's decision on its own jurisdiction.

In the United States, the 1925 FAA[7] makes no reference to the separability principle. However, it has been increasingly recognized in American case law, culminating in the landmark decision of *Prima Paint Corp.* v. *Flood & Conklin Mfg. Co.*[8] in which the doctrine of separability was recognized for the first time. In that decision it was held that "arbitration clauses are *separable* form the contract in which they are embedded, and that were no claim is made that fraud was directed to the arbitration clause itself, a broad arbitration clause will be held to encompass arbitration of the claim that the contract itself was induced by fraud."[9]

---

[5] 455 F. Supp. 211 (S.D.N.Y. 1978).
[6] First Options of Chicago, Inc. v. Kaplan, 514 US 938 (1975).
[7] Title 9 (Arbitration), 9 U.S.C. (United States Code) §§1–16 (2012) (hereinafter 9 U.S.C.).
[8] 388 US 395 (1967).
[9] *Id.* at 402.

The *Prima Paint*[10] decision was slightly narrowed in *Three Valleys Municipal Water District v. E.F. Hutton & Co.*,[11] which held that the applicability of the separability doctrine was limited to "challenges seeking to avoid or rescind a contract [and] not to challenges going to the very existence of a contract that a party claims never to have agreed." Therefore, "a party who contests the making of a contract containing an arbitration provision cannot be compelled to arbitrate this threshold issue of the existence of an agreement to arbitrate," which "only a court can make that decision."[12] This decision is limited to its facts as to whether the signatory to the contract had the power to bind other parties to the agreement to arbitrate. In essence, a party cannot be forced to arbitrate where they contest the existence of the very contract in which the arbitration clause is found: "To require [parties] to arbitrate where they deny that they entered into the contracts would be inconsistent with the *first principle* of arbitration that 'a party cannot be required to submit [to arbitration] any dispute which he has not agreed so to submit.'"[13]

In the 2017 case of *Kindred Nursing Centers, L. P. v. Clark*,[14] the Supreme Court again ruled in the areas of the enforceability of arbitration clauses signed by surrogates and the separation between the validity of contract and the validity of the arbitration clause. In this case, the children, possessing a power of attorney, signed an agreement with a nursing home for the benefit of a parent. That agreement included an arbitration clause, which was challenged under the claim that the power of attorney did not empower the children to waive the parent's right to a jury trial. The Kentucky Supreme Court held that the arbitration agreements were invalid because the powers of attorney did not *specifically* entitle the representatives to enter into an arbitration agreement. Section 2 of the FAA provides an equal-treatment principle in which courts may invalidate arbitration clauses or agreements based on "generally applicable contract defenses."[15] However, state laws may not develop specific rules that regulate the enforceability of arbitration agreements. The Supreme Court held that the lower court's argument that the waiver of constitutional rights is so important that it requires an express and specific authority to do so in the power of attorney was incorrect. It notes that other constitutional rights can be waived under a general power of attorney without abiding by any clear-statement rule. The argument that due process concerns relating to a "right" to a trial is a ground for a challenge has been rejected because the courts have held that a proper arbitration process is a fair method of dispute resolution. Justice Kagan states that a state law might avoid referring to arbitration by name; but still would "'rely on the uniqueness of an agreement to arbitrate as [its] basis' – and thereby violate the FAA."[16]

But, more recently the Supreme Court disregarded the distinction between void and voidable contracts in relation to the autonomy of the arbitration agreement. In *Buckeye Check Cashing Inc. v, John Cardegna*,[17] a case involving the alleged illegality of the main contract, it was held that "unless the challenge is to the arbitration clause itself, the issue of the contract's validity is considered by the arbitrator in the first instance." In that case, a loan agreement fixed an illegal

---

[10] See *supra* note 8 and accompanying text.
[11] 925 F.2d 1136 (1991).
[12] *Id.* at para. 23.
[13] *Id.* at para. 33, partially quoting, AT & T Technologies, Inc. v. Communications Workers, 475 US 643, 648 (1986).
[14] 137 S. Ct. 1421 (2017).
[15] Citing AT&T Mobility LLC v. Concepcion, 563 US 333, 339 (2011). This comment that arbitration clauses are subject to invalidation just like any other contract term is in reference to the following phrase in Section 2 of the FAA: "save upon such grounds as exist at law or in equity for the revocation of any contract." Examples would be arbitration agreements that are a product of duress or that are deemed to be unconscionable.
[16] Partially quoting Perry v. Thomas, 482 US 483, n. 9 (1987).
[17] 546 US 440 (2006).

usurious rate. The Florida Supreme Court held that a court rather than an arbitrator should resolve a claim that the contract is illegal and void ab initio. Furthermore, it reasoned that enforcing an arbitration agreement in a contract challenged as unlawful would violate state public policy (against charging usurious interest rates) and contract law. In an opinion written by Anton Scalia, the US Supreme court reversed in a 7 to 1 decision, stating that whether a contract dispute is brought in federal or state court, a challenge to the validity of a contract as a whole, and not specifically to the arbitration clause within it, must go to the arbitrator, not the court.[18] It reinforced the *Prima Paint* decision on the separability or severability of arbitration clauses. The court upheld three core propositions – as a matter of substantive federal arbitration law, an arbitration provision is severable from the remainder of the contract; unless the challenge is to the arbitration clause itself, the issue of the contract's validity is considered by the arbitrator; and the first two propositions apply in state as well as federal courts.

3 STRUCTURE OF ARBITRATION LAW IN THE UNITED STATES

This section examines the substance of American arbitration law as embodied in the FAA and as it has been interpreted by the US Supreme Court and in other case law. It then discusses the grounds for judicial vacation and modification of arbitral awards. In the area of vacatur, American law is briefly compared to French and Italian arbitration laws.

3.1 *Federal Arbitration Act*

The FAA governs almost all types of arbitrations in the United States, regardless of the subject matter of the dispute. It is by no means comprehensive, however, regulating arbitrations only at the beginning and end of their life cycles. Under the FAA, all arbitration agreements "shall be valid, irrevocable, and enforceable, save upon such grounds as exist at law or in equity for the revocation of any contract."[19] The FAA, as stated above, makes arbitration the preferred means of dispute resolution as a matter of federal government policy.[20] Importantly that means that federal law preempts state law on issues of arbitrability.[21] But, it should be noted that the common law resides in state law. Thus, the interpretation of an arbitration agreement is generally a matter of state law.

Upon the application of any party, judicial proceedings are stayed as to any issues determined to be referable to arbitration.[22] As long as an arbitration agreement is deemed enforceable and a dispute arbitrable, the FAA leaves it to the parties and the arbitrators to determine how arbitrations should be conducted. While the FAA allows for some judicial review of arbitral awards, the grounds upon which to vacate awards are limited and exclusive and, in general, are designed

---

[18] The court cited Prima Paint, *supra* note 8 and Southland Corp. v. Keating, 465 US 1 (1984).
[19] *See* 9 U.S.C. §2.
[20] A written provision in any maritime transaction or a contract evidencing a transaction involving commerce to settle by arbitration a controversy thereafter arising out of such contract or transaction, or the refusal to perform the whole or any part thereof, or an agreement in writing to submit to arbitration an existing controversy arising out of such a contract, transaction, or refusal, shall be valid, irrevocable, and enforceable, save upon such grounds as exist at law or in equity for the revocation of any contract.

9 US Code, Chapter 1, §2.
[21] *See* Moses H. Cone Memorial Hosp. v. Mercury Constr. Corp., 460 US 1 (1983).
[22] *See* 9 U.S.C. §3.

to prevent fraud, excess of jurisdiction, or procedural unfairness, rather than to second-guess the merits of the arbitral panel's decision.[23]

The FAA's largely hands-off approach reflects US federal policy strongly favoring arbitration as an alternative to inefficient and congested courts. It was this pro-arbitration policy that led the Supreme Court to interpret an arbitration clause expansively to include statutory antitrust claims in *Mitsubishi Motors Corp. v. Soler Chrysler-Plymouth*,[24] allowing arbitrators to enforce federal antitrust law alongside judges. The Supreme Court held that because of the FAA there is a presumption in favor of arbitration: "as with any contract, the parties' intentions control, but those intentions are generously construed as to issues of arbitrability."[25]

In the international context, this pro-arbitration policy is further evidenced by the implementation of the UN Convention on the Recognition and Enforcement of Foreign Arbitral Awards[26] (New York Convention) and the Inter-American Convention on International Commercial Arbitration (Panama Convention),[27] found respectively in Chapters 2 and 3 of the FAA.[28] The FAA also mandates that arbitral awards are enforceable against actions of a foreign country as an exception to the Act of State Doctrine.[29]

3.2 Grounds for Vacating Arbitral Awards: A Comparative Analysis

In comparing the stated reasons for vacating an arbitral award, American arbitration law differs from some civil law countries, such as French and Italian laws. French and Italian laws focus more on process than the malfeasance of arbitrators. For example, French law allows for vacation were an arbitral tribunal wrongfully accepted or declined jurisdiction. American law provides a limited number of reasons to seek vacation of an arbitration award, including (1) corruption, fraud, or undue means; (2) evident partiality or corruption in the arbitrators; (3) arbitrators were guilty of misconduct in refusing to postpone the hearing, upon sufficient cause shown, or in refusing to hear evidence pertinent and material to the controversy, or of any other misbehavior by which the rights of any party have been prejudiced; and (4) arbitrators exceeded their powers, or so imperfectly executed them that a mutual, final, and definite award upon the subject matter submitted was not made.[30]

In contrast, the French Civil Procedure Code provides that arbitral awards may also be vacated when due process is violated and when the award is contrary to "international public policy" as well as when the arbitral tribunal wrongly upholds or declines jurisdiction, the arbitral panel was wrongly constituted, or when the tribunal rules proceed outside of the mandate conferred upon it.[31] It also should be noted that the French Civil Procedure Code has different

---

[23] An arbitral award may be vacated under the FAA where, for example, the parties or arbitrators behaved fraudulently or where the arbitrators "exceeded their powers" as defined in the arbitration agreement. For a complete list of grounds of vacatur, see the FAA at §10.
[24] 473 US 614 (1985).
[25] *Id.* at 626.
[26] 21 U.S.T. (US Treaties) 2517 (June 10, 1958), 9 U.S.C. §§201–208.
[27] 9 U.S.C. Chapter 3, §§301–307. See note, *Inter-American Convention on International Commercial Arbitration*, 9 UNIVERSITY OF MIAMI INTER-AMERICAN LAW REVIEW 43 (1997).
[28] FAA, 9 U.S.C. §§201–208, 301–307.
[29] 9 U.S.C. §15:"Enforcement of arbitral agreements, confirmation of arbitral awards, and execution upon judgments based on orders confirming such awards shall not be refused on the basis of the Act of State doctrine." The Act of State Doctrine, and subsequently the Foreign Sovereign Immunity Act (FSIA), provides defenses to foreign countries and foreign agencies against private litigation.
[30] 9 U.S.C. §10 (a) (1-4).
[31] French Civil Procedure Code, Article 1520 (1)-(5).

provisions for domestic and international arbitration.[32] Under Italian law, there is no distinction between national and international arbitration, but there is a distinction between formal and informal arbitration. The former is a fully recognized arbitration, while the latter is a sort of contractual mediation, whose enforceability as an arbitral award is disputed, both nationally and internationally.

In Italian law, the rules for vacating formal arbitral awards are set by Article 829 of the Italian Civil Procedure Code.[33] The grounds for vacating arbitral awards is much more expansive than is found in US or French law. It provides that a party may challenge the validity of the award, including in cases were the party had formally waived the right to challenge under the following grounds: (1) arbitration agreement is invalid; (2) arbitrators have not been appointed in the form provided by the code; (3) award has been rendered by a person who could not be appointed as arbitrator; (4) award goes beyond the limits of the arbitration agreement; (5) award does not contain a brief statement of the reasons, decision of the issues, and signature of the arbitrators or of the majority of the arbitrators stating that the award was deliberated with the participation of all the arbitrators;[34] (6) award has been issued after the expiry of the prescribed time limit; (7) formalities prescribed by the parties under express sanction of nullity have not been observed during the proceedings; (8) award is contrary to a previous award which is no longer subject to recourse or to a previous judicial decision which is res judicata between the parties, provided such an award or judicial decision has been submitted in the proceedings; (9) principle of contradictory proceedings has not been respected in the arbitration proceedings; (10) the award does not rule on the merit of the case; (11) award contains contradictory provisions; and (12) award has not settled some of the issues and objections raised by the parties in accordance with the arbitration agreement.[35]

Thus, the four grounds for vacating an arbitral under US law are much narrower than under French or Italian law (twelve grounds). US law focuses almost entirely on the conduct of the arbitrators – partiality or corruption in the arbitrators, arbitrators were guilty of misconduct, and arbitrators exceeded their powers. The other grounds relate to the overall corruption of the arbitral process (fraud or undue means), refusal to postpone hearing due to cause, and the barring of admission of pertinent evidence. French law modestly expands the list of grounds for vacation to include vacating awards contrary to international public policy. As noted, Italian law provides a broad list that allows judicial intervention to vacate arbitral awards. For example, it requires that arbitrators be constituted according to the requirements of the code, seemingly allowing judicial scrutiny of the selection of arbitral rules. Article 829 places an unusual emphasis on form including the form of the selection or arbitrators and the form of the award itself. It is required that the arbitrators provide a reasoned award including a statement of reasons, specific decisions on each issue that was the subject of the arbitration, and formal signature criteria. It also provides grounds for vacation based upon res judicata and contradictory proceedings. Most importantly, Article 829 allows for a judicial review of the merits of the award – when the award does not rule on the merit of the case, award contains contradictory provisions; and award

---

[32] The French rules on vacating domestic arbitral awards are found in Article 1492.
[33] This provision was heavily reformed in 2006.
[34] This provision is a bit controversial because in general arbitrators are not required to give a reasoned decision unless required to do so by the arbitration agreement or in the submission to arbitrate. Further, it is unsettled as to what constitutes a reasoned award. *See* S. I. Strong, *Reasoned Awards in International Commercial Arbitration: Embracing and Exceeding the Common Law and Civil Law Dichotomy*, 37 MICHIGAN JOURNAL OF INTERNATIONAL LAW 1 (2016).
[35] Italian Civil Procedure Code, Article 829 (1)-(12).

has not settled some of the issues and objections raised by the parties in accordance with the arbitration agreement.

The laundry list of judicially reviewable grounds for vacating under Italian law challenges the independent nature of arbitration as an extra-judicial means of dispute resolution. It allows for challenges simply based upon form, as well as the substance of the arbitrator's award. US law has a greater affinity for the principle of the finality and the binding nature of arbitral awards, limiting grounds for appeal to cases of corruption, misconduct, and when arbitrators exceed their powers. French law is somewhere between US and Italian law on the narrowness of appeal, but much more aligned to US law, which makes it difficult to appeal arbitral awards. French law's narrowness of appeal depends on the interpretation of the vague terms of due process and international public policy.

3.3 Grounds for Judicial Modification of Arbitral Awards

The FAA gives judicial power to appoint arbitrators in cases of impasse.[36] In addition federal district courts have the power to modify an arbitral award upon the application of any party to the arbitration. It provides that a court may correct or modify "in order to effect the intent [of the parties] and promote justice between the parties."[37] It provides three narrow grounds for a judicial order to correct or modify: (1) evident material miscalculation of figures or an evident material mistake in the description of any person, thing, or property referred to in the award; (2) arbitrators have awarded upon a matter not submitted to them, unless it is a matter not affecting the merits of the decision; and (3) the award is imperfect in matter of form not affecting the merits of the controversy.[38] The parties have a maximum of three months from the filing or delivering of the award to make a motion to modify, vacate, or correct.[39] On the whole, the FAA provides very narrow grounds for the judicial modification of an arbitral award, mostly focused on technical errors and formalities.

4 RECENT NARROWING IN STANDING IN ARBITRATION

The Supreme Court in the past decade or two has published a series of decisions that have expanded and narrowed the scope of arbitration. On one hand, it has held that statutory rights or protections, including claims for sexual harassment and violations of antitrust law, may be required to be arbitrated.[40] On the other hand, it has moved to limit the ability of collective parties to bring class action arbitration claims. The latter limits arbitration because the nature of the claims do not permit individuals to bring a claim in arbitration because it would be cost prohibitive.

---

[36] 9 U.S.C. §5 (Appointment of Arbitrators): "If for any other reason there shall be a lapse in the naming of an arbitrator or arbitrators, or in filling a vacancy, then upon the application of either party to the controversy the court shall designate and appoint an arbitrator or arbitrators, as the case may require."
[37] 9 U.S.C. §11
[38] 9 U.S.C. §11 (a)-(c).
[39] 9 U.S.C. §12.
[40] See, e.g., Rodriguez de Quijas v. Shearson/Am. Express, Inc., 490 US 477, 485 (1989) (Supreme Court overturned precedent that held private actions under the securities laws could not be arbitrated as decided in the 1953 case of Wilko v. Swan, 346 US 427). See also Am. Express Co. v. Italian Colors Rest., 133 Sup. Ct. 2304 (2013); Gilmer v. Interstate Johnson Lane, Corp., 500 US 20 (1991).

4.1 Class Action Arbitration

There are two types of arbitration – bilateral and class action arbitration. In July 2017, the US government's Consumer Financial Protection Bureau (CFPB)[41] issued a final rule, which (1) prohibited financial products and services providers from using (new) predispute arbitration agreements entered into after March 19, 2018, to block consumer class actions in court and (2) required financial products and services providers to submit to the CFPB certain records of arbitral and court proceedings, regardless of whether there are any class action proceedings involved. The CFPB intended to publish these records on its website, to provide greater transparency into the arbitration of consumer disputes. Unfortunately, the US Congress (Republican controlled) and President Trump voided the new Arbitration Rule under the Congressional Review Act.[42] This pro-waiver (waiver of right to bring class action arbitration) enforceability stance has been replicated in the case law.

The issues relating to class action or class arbitration include whether an individual can be forced to join class action arbitration and what type of language authorizes class arbitration. In 2010, the Supreme Court held in *Stolt-Nielsen SA v. Animal Feeds Int'l Corp*[43] that specific language in the agreement must make clear that an individual will be compelled to submit to class arbitration. Alternatively stated, an agreement that is silent on the issue of class arbitration does not constitute consent to class arbitration because of the major differences between bilateral and class action arbitration.

More importantly, is the issue of whether a party may include a class action waiver in its arbitration clause. The Supreme Court has in a line of precedents supported the enforceability of such waivers. This line of precedent began with *A & T Mobility LLC v. Conception*[44] in 2011, which held that the FAA preempted a California state rule that prohibited the enforcement of class action waivers. The Supreme Court in the 2013 case of *American Express Company v. Italian Colors*[45] rejected another challenge to class action waivers. It recognized such waivers even though acknowledging that class action waivers would discourage plaintiffs from bringing claims under antitrust law since pursuing antitrust claims on an individual basis may be too costly. In 2015, again the Supreme Court rejected a California state court rule that invalidated all arbitration agreements as unenforceable when they contained a class action waiver.[46]

Finally, in 2017, in *Epic Systems Corp. v. Lewis*,[47] the Supreme Court held that nothing in the National Labor Relations Act (NLRA)[48] prohibits employers from entering into collective bargaining or employment agreements barring collective or class action arbitration. The court reasoned that arbitration as envisioned in the FAA is generally a bilateral undertaking between two parties and, therefore, class action exclusion clauses were enforceable. It should be noted that this decision is limited in scope to legal actions taken subject to the NLRA. Nonetheless, it is symbolic of the court's stance against collective rights and the declining power of the American union movement. Although, it must be noted that arbitration clauses with class action

---

[41] *See* Consumer Financial Protection Bureau at https://www.consumerfinance.gov. This bureau was established following the 2008 financial crisis under the Dodd–Frank Act. The bureau's rule-making power is found in §1028 (b) of the Dodd–Frank Wall Street Reform and Consumer Protection Act (Public Law 111-203).
[42] Nonetheless, the rule is likely to resurface if Democrats return to power.
[43] 559 US 662 (2009) (slip opinion).
[44] 563 US 333 (2011).
[45] 133 S. Ct. 2304 (2013).
[46] DIRECTV, Inc. v. Imburgia, 136 S. Ct. 463 (2015).
[47] 138 Sup. Ct. 1612 (2018).
[48] 29 U.S.C. §§151–169 (2012).

waivers may still be challenged under state contract law under the doctrines of fraud, duress, and unconscionability. The Supreme Court simply removed the argument that class action waivers are void because they contradict the FAA.

The New York district court issued a decision in January 2018, vacating an arbitral award and holding that the arbitrator had no authority to certify a class of claimants that included absent class members.[49] The plaintiff had argued that because the arbitrator had authority to decide whether the named plaintiffs' arbitration agreements permitted class procedures, that also meant that the arbitrator had authority to decide whether the absent class members' arbitration agreements permitted class procedures that would bind those absent class members unless they opted out. The court rejected that argument, relying on Supreme Court Justice Alito's concurrence in the *Oxford Health Plans LLC v. Sutter*, in which he had noted that "absent members of the plaintiff's class have not submitted themselves to the arbitrator's authority in any way."[50] The New York court reasoned that although absent class members may have signed contracts with arbitration clauses that were materially identical to those signed by the plaintiff, that did not mean that they were bound by an arbitrator's erroneous interpretation of a contract that did not authorize class arbitration.

5 SCOPE OF ARBITRATION'S JURISDICTION

This section examines the forum for deciding the arbitrability of an issue in dispute – whether arbitrability is determined by arbitrators or judges. The US Supreme Court has largely been supportive of the position that the scope of arbitration clauses or the determination of the arbitrability of various claims is within the domain of the arbitral tribunal or panel.

In 2019, the Supreme Court rejected an exception to arbitrator competence to decide arbitrability in which a lower court held that it was up to the courts to decide if a claim is "wholly groundless." In the case of *Henry Schein v. Archer and White*,[51] the claim was based upon antitrust violations and the respondent asserted that the proper forum was the court since claimant sought injunctive relief. The parties' arbitration agreement incorporated the American Arbitration Association Rules, whereby arbitrability questions are to be decided by arbitrators. The Supreme Court unanimously held that the FAA allows the parties to entrust arbitrators with solving "threshold arbitrability questions."

The court reasoned further that "arbitration is a matter of contract," therefore, the arbitration clause should be construed so that questions of arbitrability, including the evaluation of the merits of the case (frivolousness of the claims), are solely within the province of arbitrators. This case is indicative of a longstanding position of the Supreme Court in support of arbitration. In Europe, the reasoning would be slightly different, but the outcome would be the same. The issue would not be one of arbitrability since that term is used in determining the scope of the arbitration clause. Instead, the issue would be decided under the principle of kompetenz–kompetenz, which would recognize the power of the arbitrators to decide on the reach of their jurisdiction.

A recent case dealt with the issue of arbitrability under a standard arbitration clause ("any dispute or claim arising out of").[52] An employer brought a lawsuit against former employees

---

[49] Jock v. Sterling Jewelers, Inc., 284 F Supp 3d 566 (S.D.N.Y. 2018).
[50] *Id.* at 570–571, quoting Oxford Health Plans LLC v. Sutter, 569 US 564 (2013).
[51] 138 S. Ct. 2678 (2019).
[52] Sikel, LLC v. Penning, Case No. 6:17-cv-01846-AA (Ore. D.C. 2018).

claiming that they misappropriated trade secrets; breached their duty of confidentiality and covenants not-to-compete, their duty of good faith, and their fiduciary duty of loyalty; and intentionally interfered with prospective economic advantage. The former employees filed a petition to compel arbitration pursuant to the terms of the employment agreement. The employment agreements provided that "any dispute, claim or controversy concerning employment or any dispute, claim or controversy arising out of, or relating to, any interpretation, construction, performance or breach of this Agreement, shall be settled by arbitration." The court held that the standard of arbitrability requires a determination that a valid agreement to arbitrate existed and the agreement encompasses the dispute at issue.[53] The court quickly decided that an agreement to arbitrate existed due to the arbitration clause in the employment agreement, leaving the sole issue of whether the employer's claims were within the scope of the arbitration clause. The employer argued that a "carve-out" provision[54] in the arbitration clause, which allowed it to seek injunctive relief from a court in cases such as breach of confidentiality allowed it to pursue the underlying causes of action in court. In making a decision a court is expected to analyze the text and context of the arbitration clause. The court held that, despite the carve-out to obtain remedies in court, the clause was unambiguous in not barring arbitration for specific causes of action.

The employer also contended that its statutory claims as well as those based on tort principles are not arbitrable because that arbitration clause was limited to claims related to "employment or the termination of employment." It argues that claims under the state's Trade Secrets Act, as well as its tort claims for interference with business relationships and breach of duties owed from the employment relationships are not directly related to employment and, therefore, outside the scope of the arbitration clause. The court held that American legal precedent existed that the "incorporation of the AAA rules (in the agreement) constitutes clear and unmistakable evidence that contracting parties agreed to arbitrate arbitrability."[55]

As to the general judicial approach to arbitrability (scope of arbitration clause), courts "broadly favor arbitration even when claims arise *in toto* or from statute." The fact that the employer's claims included those based upon intellectual property law and other statutorily based claims was of no consequence. The key factors being that all of the claims arise from the same set of facts and the arbitration clause was broadly worded.

6 ENFORCEMENT AND VACATION OF ARBITRAL AWARDS

This section examines current developments in the enforcement of arbitral awards in the United States. First, it examines arbitrator misinterpretation of law as a ground to vacate arbitral awards. The threshold for vacating an award on such a ground is high. The reviewing court only has to see that there was a "colorable justification" for the arbitrators' decision in order to enforce the award. The "manifest disregard" of the law doctrine, as a ground for vacating awards, is explored in Section 6.2. Finally, Section 6.3 examines the effect of a subsequent annulment on an American court's power to enforce an arbitral award. In one case, the court elected to enforce the award despite an annulment since not to do so violated the public policy of fundamental

---

[53] The court cited Cox v. Ocean View Hotel Corp., 533 F.3d 1114, 1119 (9th Cir. 2008); United Steelworkers of America v. Warrior & Gulf Navigation Co., 363 US 574, 582–583 (1960).
[54] Larry A. DiMatteo, *Questioning the Ubiquitousness but Not the Value of Arbitration Carve-Outs*, 66 FLORIDA LAW REVIEW FORUM 11–15 (2015).
[55] *See* Brennan v. Opus Bank, 796 F.3d 1125, 1130 (9th Cir. 2015).

fairness. Another court, and the mainstream view, held that a court should honor the annulment of a foreign court, especially when that court is in the place of the arbitration.

6.1 Enforceability of Arbitral Awards

The threshold for vacating an arbitral award is a very high standard. Arbitral awards have been enforced where the arbitrator's findings are suspect and in cases where arbitrators misinterpreted the applicable law: "[An arbitration] award should be enforced ... if there is a *barely colorable justification* for the outcome reached."[56] In 2009, this standard was reaffirmed in *Macromex S.r.l. v. Globex International Inc.*[57] when a federal circuit court upheld the enforcement of an arbitral award since there was at least a barely colorable justification for the arbitrator's finding. Previously, the court held that: "In the context of contract interpretation, we are required to confirm arbitration awards [even though there are] serious reservations about the soundness of the arbitrator's reading of the contract."[58] In the case of arbitrator's application of law, there is an equally high standard to reach in order to vacate an award. The arbitrator must "manifestly disregard the law'" The courts have interpreted this standard to mean more than an error or misunderstanding of the law.[59] The court in *Wallace v. Buttar* reinforced the narrowness of this ground for vacating an arbitral award: "Our cases demonstrate that we have used the manifest disregard of law doctrine to vacate arbitral awards only in the most egregious instances of misapplication of legal principles."[60] This case confirms that arbitrators need not be experts in the applicable law of the case and are given substantial leeway in their application of the law unlike judges. The manifest disregard doctrine will be discussed in more detail in the next section.

The enforcement of foreign arbitral awards continued to be an important topic in American arbitration jurisprudence in recent years, especially with respect to awards issued against foreign sovereigns. The issue being contested is the courts prerogative to enforce a foreign arbitration award that was subsequently annulled in that foreign country. In the 2016 case of *Corporación Mexicana de Mantenimiento Integral v. Pemex-Exploración y Producción*[61] a federal circuit court decided to enforce a foreign arbitral award that had been annulled. The court reasoned that the New York Convention allowed, but did not require, the enforcement of an annulled award. The court acknowledged that the principle of comity[62] suggests that the court should recognize the judicial annulment of a foreign court, but that deference should not be given if the recognition of the annulment would conflict with a public policy of the United States. The court enforced the arbitral award since not to do so would violate "fundamental notions of what is decent and just" – namely, the claimants would be left without a forum to pursue their grievance.

A 2017 case involved a federal district court confirming a foreign arbitral award that was subsequently annulled by a foreign court at the place of arbitration.[63] The court then vacated the

---

[56] *See* Wallace v. Buttar, 378 F.3d 182, 190 (2d Cir. 2004).
[57] Docket No. 08-2255-cv (2d Cir. 2009).
[58] *See* Stolt-Nielsen SA v. Animal Feeds Int'l Corp., 548 F.3d 85, 92 (2d Cir. 2008).
[59] *See* Merrill Lynch, Pierce, Fenner & Smith, Inc. v. Bobker, 808 F.2d 930, 933 (2d Cir. 1986) ("Manifest disregard of the law ... clearly means more than error or misunderstanding with respect to the law").
[60] Wallace, *supra* note 56, at 190.
[61] 832 F.3d 92 (2d Cir. 2016).
[62] The principle of comity is a public policy that one country should respect the acts and rulings of foreign courts in order to maintain good relations. *See* Joel R. Paul, *Transformation of International Comity*, 71 LAW & CONTEMPORARY PROBLEMS 19 (2008); Hessel E. Yntema, *The Comity Doctrine*, 65 MICHIGAN LAW REVIEW 9 (1966).
[63] The court in CBF Indústria De Gusa SA v. AMCI Holdings, Inc., 850 F.3d 58 (2d Cir. 2017), clarified the terms *confirmation*, *enforcement*, and *recognition* as used in the FAA and New York Convention. It noted that the term

enforcing order once evidence of the annulment was provided. The case was appealed to the Third Circuit Court of Appeals.[64] The court held that "prudential concerns for international comity and the high standard for overcoming the presumptive effect of a primary jurisdiction's annulment" should be given serious consideration.[65] As to the propriety of the foreign court annulment, the court stressed that the power and authority of the local courts of primary jurisdiction are of paramount importance under the New York Convention. It further affirmed the lower court's reasoning that the annulment was sought within a reasonable period of time and that the claimants knew of the impending annulment at the time they sought to enforce the award. Finally, it was within the lower court's discretion in weighing the principle of respecting the acts of a foreign court at the place or arbitration as being greater than the policy favoring the finality of arbitral awards. In the end, the two decisions show that the threshold for enforcing an arbitral award is high in cases where it has been or subsequently is annulled by the foreign court of the country of arbitration.

In *Sharpe Corp. v. Hisense USA Corp.*,[66] the District Court of the District of Columbia decided two interesting and important questions related to the enforcement of arbitral awards. The first was whether it had subject matter jurisdiction to declare a foreign arbitral award unenforceable where the prevailing party had not sought enforcement in the court's jurisdiction. In this case the losing party sought to have the award vacated in a US court. The second question was whether tribunal-ordered preliminary measures restraining a party's speech (barring a party from making comments about the other party, also known as a gag order) were enforceable or violated US public policy. The court noted that the arbitrator-issued gag order was potentially contrary to US public policy in favor of freedom of speech.

As to the issue of jurisdiction, the court noted that the New York Convention refers to the secondary jurisdiction as that relating to the enforcement of an award but does not expressly state that a secondary court could not be used to vacate the award or render it unenforceable. In the end, the court determined that it did not have personal jurisdiction over the winning party and that the gag order was not in conflict with US public policy since the interim measure authorization was based upon a private agreement to arbitrate.

6.2 Nonstatutory Grounds for Vacation of Awards: "Manifest Disregard Doctrine"

The New York Convention requires US courts to enforce international arbitration awards but allows for the vacation or nonenforcement of awards in cases where the arbitral proceedings violate the public policy in favor of fair adjudication or due process. Both the FAA and the New York Convention that the former strictly implements limit the grounds upon which a court can vacate an arbitral award. Their intent is to avoid merits-based judicial review of arbitral awards except in very narrow circumstances. Over the past half century, a judicially created doctrine called "manifest disregard" has developed in the United States, and it has allowed parties to seek an expanded review of the merits of arbitrators' decisions, at least in theory. The doctrine was created in the 1953 Supreme Court case of *Wilko v. Swan*.[67] The Court stated that: "The interpretations of the law by the arbitrators in contrast to manifest disregard [of the law], are not

---

confirmation as used in the FAA is equivalent to the terms *recognition* and *enforcement* in the New York Convention and thus held that no separate action is necessary to confirm a foreign arbitral award before seeking to enforce it.

[64] Thai-Lao Lignite (Thailand) Co. v. Gov't of the Lao People's Democratic Republic, 864 F.3d 172 (2d Cir. 2017).
[65] 864 F.3d at 186.
[66] No. 17-1648, 2017 WL 5449805 (DDC Nov. 13, 2017), appeal filed, No. 17-7158 (DC Cir. Nov. 16, 2017).
[67] Wilko v. Swan, 346 US 427, 436–437 (1953).

subject, in the federal courts, to judicial review for error in interpretation."[68] Thus, the court distinguished manifest disregard of law from errors of interpretation as a ground for vacation. Even though the manifest disregard doctrine is recognized as an additional ground for vacating arbitral awards, successful use of the doctrine is rare.[69] In 2008, the US Supreme Court questioned the validity of the manifest disregard ground for vacating arbitral awards, but did not formally overturn it:

> Maybe the term "manifest disregard" was meant to name a new ground for review, but maybe it merely referred to the FAA Section 10 grounds collectively, rather than adding to them. Or, as some courts have thought, "manifest disregard" may have been shorthand for [Section] 10(a)(3) or [Section] 10(a)(4), the paragraphs authorizing vacatur when the arbitrators were "guilty of misconduct' or 'exceeded their powers." We, when speaking as a Court, have merely taken the *Wilko* language as we found it, without embellishment and now that its meaning is implicated, we see no reason to accord it the significance that [petitioner] urges.[70]

The court indicated that manifest disregard is a dangerously amorphous ground for vacation because it poses a direct threat to the finality of arbitral awards. It leads down the costly and time-consuming path where an arbitral panel makes a decision on the merits in issuing an arbitral award, followed by a judicial review on the merits in determining whether to vacate the award. The Supreme Court's criticism of the manifest disregard doctrine, without eliminating it as a ground for vacation of awards, has created confusion as to its use by lower courts. The confusion over the validity of the manifest disregard doctrine was demonstrated in the 2017 case of *Mesa Power Group LLC v. Canada*,[71] where the District of Columbia District Court assumed that that "manifest disregard of the law" was a proper ground for vacating an arbitral award under the FAA, but then rejected its application to the case at bar. The case involved an interpretation of a provision in the North American Free Trade Agreement. The claimant argued that the arbitral tribunal misinterpreted the provision in favor of the respondent. The court held that the interpretation was within the discretion of the tribunal and did not rise to the level of reckless disregard of the law. Other claims relating to arbitrator misconduct – that the alleged misinterpretation amounted to arbitrator misconduct and the deference given to the Canadian government constituted bias – were also rejected by the court. On the later claim the court held that since the case involved public procurement of goods the Canadian government's policy choices affecting procurement should be given deference.

However, in another 2017 case the ground of "manifest disregard of the law" was used successfully in vacating an arbitral award based on a finding that a commercial contract had violated the antitrust laws. In *Daesang Corp. v. NutraSweet Co.*,[72] a New York state court vacated an ICC tribunal award. First the court correctly summarized the state of the law in this area:

> An award may be vacated under federal law only if it violates a ground set forth in Section 10 of the Federal Arbitration Act (FAA) and a court may vacate an arbitration award if it was rendered

---

[68] *Id.* at 436–437.
[69] *See, e.g.*, Stolt-Nielsen SA v. Animal Feeds Int'l Corp., 548 F3d 85, 91–93 (2d Cir. 2008).
[70] Hall Street Associates, LLC v. Mattel, Inc., 552 US 576 (2008). As noted earlier, Section 10 lists grounds for vacating an award, including where the award was procured by "corruption," "fraud," or "undue means," and where the arbitrators were "guilty of misconduct" or "exceeded their powers." Furthermore, under §11, the grounds for modifying or correcting an award include "evident material miscalculation," "evident material mistake," and "imperfections in a matter of form not affecting the merits."
[71] 255 F. Supp. 3d 175 (DDC 2017).
[72] 55 Misc.3d 1218(A), 2017 WL 2126684 (NY Sup Ct May 15, 2017).

in manifest disregard of the law. A court may determine whether the arbitrators knew of a governing legal principle yet refused to apply it or ignored it altogether, and whether the governing law ignored was well defined, explicit, and clearly applicable to the case. Merely an error or misunderstanding of the applicable law does not constitute manifest disregard. Judicial review of arbitration awards is extremely limited. An arbitration award must be upheld when the arbitrator offers even a barely colorable justification for the outcome reached.[73]

The losing party moved to vacate the award on grounds that the arbitrators engaged in a manifest disregard of the law by failing to apply US Supreme Court precedent.[74] It also claimed that the tribunal manifestly disregarded the law by misapplying New York law on fraudulent misrepresentation. The court rejected the manifest disregard claim relating to legal precedent by distinguishing a disregard of law directly applicable to the dispute between the parties and a disregard of law that serve more generally as guidance to the interpretation of contract terms. It found that the precedent went to the latter type of disregard and amounted to a misinterpretation of the contract, which is not a ground for vacating an award. But the court did vacate the award since "the Tribunal manifestly disregarded New York law in dismissing the claim for fraudulent inducement seeking the remedy of equitable rescission. Notwithstanding the presumption in favor of upholding arbitration awards, deference to arbitrators is not without its limits."[75] The court also held that the tribunal refusal to hear on the merits the claimant's breach of contract claim went "beyond a mere error in law or facts, and amounts to an egregious dereliction of duty on the party of the Tribunal."

It is important to note that disregard of contract provisions is a more solid ground in vacating an award than disregard of law. The strongest case for vacation is when the arbitral panel disregards or modifies unambiguous contract provisions. This would amount in a finding that the arbitrators had exceeded the authority granted to them under the contract. However, the New York court, in *Daesang Corp.*, correctly stated that arbitrators should be given discretion in their interpretation of contracts.

6.3 Public Policy Exception

The "public policy exception" is one of the few exceptions open to domestic courts for refusing the recognition or enforcement of a foreign arbitral award under the New York Convention.[76] Since the convention fails to define the term *public policy*, the scope of the public policy exception varies from country to country.[77] That said, the New York Convention's almost universal recognition suggests that the public policy exception should be narrowly construed and the public policy in favor of the finality of arbitral awards should be protected. The US case law on the issue supports the view that the public policy exception should be used only when the

---

[73] Partially quoting, Schwarz v. Merrill Lynch & Co., 665 F. 3d 444, 451 (2d Cir. 2011); Matter of Roffler v. Spears, Leeds & Kellogg, 13 A.D. 3d 308, 310 (1st Dept. 2004); Wien & Malkin LLP v. Helmsley-Spear, Inc., 6 NY 3d 471, 479–480 (2006).
[74] American Pipe & Constr. Co. v. Utah, 414 US 538, 551 (1974).
[75] Sharpe Corp. v. Hisense USA Corp., above fn 66, partially quoting Jock v. Sterling Jewelers, Inc., 142 F. Supp. 3d 127, 133 (S.D.N.Y. 2015).
[76] Article V (2)(b) of the New York Convention.
[77] See ANTON G. MAURER, THE PUBLIC POLICY EXCEPTION UNDER THE NEW YORK CONVENTION: HISTORY, INTERPRETATION AND APPLICATION (2012); Bernard Hanotiau & Olivier Caprasse, *Public Policy in International Commercial Arbitration*, in ENFORCEMENT OF ARBITRATION AGREEMENTS AND INTERNATIONAL ARBITRAL AWARDS: THE NEW YORK CONVENTION IN PRACTICE 787 (Emmanuel Gaillard & Domenico di Pietro eds., 2008).

"enforcement of foreign arbitral awards would violate the forum state's most basic notions of morality and justice."[78]

It is a generic view that public policy considerations may allow a court to preclude a dispute from being settled by arbitration or as a reason for vacating an arbitral award. In the case of *Eastern Associated Coal Corp. v. United Mine Workers of America, District 7*[79] the US Supreme Court dealt with the public policy exception. In that case, a company terminated an employee who twice tested positive for marijuana use. The labor arbitrator ordered the employee's reinstatement. The company filed suit to vacate the order, arguing that reinstatement violated the public policy in favor of workplace safety. In this case, the use of drugs was incompatible to the operation of heavy equipment. The Court upheld the arbitrator's right to order reinstatement since the collective bargaining agreement provided that the employer had the burden of proving just cause termination. Since the agreement mandated arbitration, it is the jurisdiction of the arbitrator to determine what amounted to "just cause." The arbitration provision granted the arbitrator the authority to interpret the meaning of the contract. Thus, the authority of the arbitrator is beyond reproach. Nonetheless, the issue that remains is whether the reinstatement order was contrary to public policy. The cited precedent that the public policy exception only applied to policies that were "explicit, well defined, and dominant," and they must be "ascertained by reference to the laws and legal precedents, not from general considerations of supposed public interests."[80] The court concluded that "the public policy exception is narrow" in that it can only be used when the policy is clearly stated in existing laws or precedents and not in reference to some general public policy concern, thus, affirming the arbitrator's order of reinstatement.

7 ARBITRATOR DISQUALIFICATION

This section reviews a 2018 case on the potential conflict posed by an arbitrator's relationship with one of the parties to the arbitration. It found that something more than a mere relationship suffices to disqualify an arbitrator on grounds of partiality and conflict of interest. Another case deals with the relationship between evidentiary decisions made by arbitrators and the fairness of the hearing. Finally, the section examines the issue of malfeasance by an arbitral association or institution as a ground for vacating an award.

7.1 Impartiality and Conflict of Interest

In 2018, the US District of Columbia Circuit Court denied a petition to set aside an arbitral award being challenged on the ground that that one of the arbitrators was not impartial.[81] The arbitrator was a director of an international financial services company, which held shares in companies doing business with one of the parties. The court explained that an investment of 0.06 percent of its assets was not enough to create a substantial conflict of interest under the FAA in order to set aside the award for evident partiality. Arbitrators are not disqualified by a business relationship with one of the parties if that fact is fully disclosed or the relationship is of a

---

[78] *See* Parsons & Whittemore Overseas v. Société Générale de l'Industrie du Papier, 508 F.2d 769, 974 (1974).
[79] 531 US 57 (2010).
[80] Citing W R. Grace & Co. v. Rubber Workers, 461 US 757, 766 (1993).
[81] Republic of Argentina v. AWG Group LTD (D.C. Cir. 2018) (note that this was an investment dispute being resolved under a Bilateral Investment Treaty).

trivial degree. The decision follows the well-established rule that arbitrators are not automatically disqualified by a business relationship with the parties before them.

A party seeking a vacation of an arbitral award often attempts to broadly construe arbitrator misconduct as described in Section 10 of the FAA. In order to do this, it will often seek discovery from a court to uncover previously nondisclosed information about an arbitrator. In one case, the challenging party found that the arbitrator had arbitrated two previous cases in which the lawyer representing the other party was a participant.[82] The court held that the arbitrator's failure to disclose the previous arbitrations did not constitute "clear evidence of impropriety" justifying post-award discovery of the arbitrator. The factors weighed in denying the motion for discovery included (1) the previous relationship was "strictly professional," (2) the arbitration decision being enforced was based on a unanimous vote (3 to 0), and (3) the arbitrator disclosed the interactions six months before petitioners began alleging that the conduct constituted impropriety.[83] In setting a high threshold for granting discovery on an arbitrator's background in seeking an order or vacation, the court reasoned that to liberally grant such a motion "would encourage the losing party to every arbitration to conduct a background investigation" post-ward and thus, undermine the finality of arbitration awards.[84] The finality of arbitral awards is the core rationale of the FAA as shown by its restrictive view of grounds to challenge awards.

7.2 *Fair Hearing Requirement*

In *Attia v. Audionamix, Inc.*,[85] the Southern District Court of New York vacated an arbitration award holding that the inadmissibility of certain evidence denied one of the parties a "fundamentally fair hearing." In that case, the arbitrator had stricken an affidavit of the petitioner, leaving the respondent's expert testimony completely unchallenged. The court held that the excluded evidence "was pertinent and material to the controversy" and, therefore, denying the petitioner a fair hearing under the FAA.[86] It reasoned that arbitrators should side on the admission of evidence and against the exclusion of evidence – "while arbitrators may set a low threshold to admit evidence and thus hear some irrelevant evidence, in doing so they may avoid excluding relevant evidence."

7.3 *Claims against Arbitral Institutions*

Generally, arbitrators and arbitration associations are provided general immunity under US law. Recently, however, there have been a number of cases in which the immunity of arbitral institutions was challenged, albeit unsuccessfully. In *Al Azzawi v. International Center for Dispute Resolution Organization*,[87] a party argued that a proceeding conducted through the American Arbitration Association (AAA) and the International Center for Dispute Resolution (ICDR) was tainted by misconduct. The court held that the party had no standing to sue since the previous arbitration was in the name of the party's construction company and the current proceeding was under his personal name.

---

[82] Shepherd v. LPL Financial LLC, No. 5:17-CV-00150-D (E.D.N.C. 2017).
[83] Order 9–10, Shepherd v. LPL Financial LLC, No. 5:17-CV-00150-D (E.D.N.C. Nov. 1, 2017), ECF No 45.
[84] *Id.* at 10, quoting Merit Insurance Co. v. Leatherby Insurance Co., 714 F2d 673, 683 (7th Cir. 1983).
[85] 2015 WL 5580501 (S.D.N.Y. 2015).
[86] 9 U.S.C. §10 (a)(3).
[87] Al Azzawi v. Kellogg Brown & Root, No. 2:15-cv-1468 (ED Cal. 2016).

Salsas Castillo v. *Sicana*[88] involved a losing respondent involved in a dispute relating to an arbitration administered by SICANA, the North American provider of ICC arbitration services. A Mexican court placed a stay on the ICC arbitration pending resolution of a lawsuit that respondent had filed in Mexico disputing the validity of the arbitration clause. The ICC ignored the stay and proceeded with the arbitration. The New York court held that respondent's motion to suspend the arbitration was moot because of the issuance of a ruling in the arbitration. Thus in both cases, attempts to challenge the authority and conduct of an arbitration institution were denied.

An associated issue is should a court appoint a substitute arbitrator when the arbitrator or arbitral association specified in the arbitration clause is no longer available? There is a difference in opinion across the courts on the answer to this question. The Federal Second Circuit Court of Appeals found that since the parties had designated an exclusive arbitral forum, the lower court could not appoint a substitute arbitrator because that would be contrary to party intent as expressed in the arbitration clause.[89] The court cited Supreme Court precedent:

> This text reflects the overarching principle that arbitration is a matter of contract. And consistent with that text, courts must rigorously enforce arbitration agreements according to their terms, including terms that specify with whom the parties choose to arbitrate their disputes and the rules under which that arbitration will be conducted.[90]

The court conceded that in the case at bar adherence to the dictates of the arbitration clause was contrary to the general policy of favoring arbitration:

> Although the federal policy favoring arbitration obliges us to resolve any doubts in favor of arbitration, we cannot compel a party to arbitrate a dispute before someone other than the [designated arbitrator] when that party had agreed to arbitrate disputes only before the [arbitrator] and the [arbitrator], in turn, exercising its discretion ... has refused ... to arbitrate the dispute in question.[91]

In such cases, where the designated arbitral forum is not available a court cannot compel arbitration, leaving the claimant free to pursue the dispute in a court of law.

8 CONCLUSION

The arbitration law of the United States is very supportive of arbitration as a preferred means of dispute resolution as a matter of government policy. The US Supreme Court has mostly deferred to arbitral tribunals to determine the scope of their jurisdiction, both in the interpretation of arbitration clauses and in deciding the types of claims that the arbitrators may hear. In fact, the Supreme Court has expanded the scope of private arbitration jurisdiction to include claims brought based upon statutory and constitutional law. However, more recently, it has limited the scope of class action arbitration by upholding the legality of class action waivers. This change of policy will have detrimental effects on consumer protection and collective bargaining claims.

In the area of arbitrator misconduct, the law has also been protective of the arbitrator as ultimate decision maker, whether relating to claims of conflict of interest, evidentiary issues, or

---

[88] Salsas Castillo SAPI de CV v. SICANA, Inc., No. 0656384/2017 (NY Sup. Ct. 2017).
[89] Moss v. First National Bank, 15-2513 (2d Cir. 2016).
[90] Am. Exp. Co. v. Italian Colors Rest., 570 US 228, 133 S. Ct. 2304, 2309 (2013).
[91] Moss, *supra* note 89, quoting In re Salomon Inc. Shareholders' Derivative Litigation, 68 F.3d 554, 557–558 (2d Cir. 1995).

misapplication of applicable law. American courts deference to arbitral tribunals is based upon the public policy in favor of the finality of arbitral awards. The ability to vacate an arbitral award is limited under American law in order to prevent the escalation of costs in dispute resolution and to avoid two reviews of the dispute on its merits (one by the arbitrator and one by the court). The FAA provides only four grounds for vacating awards – for corruption, fraud, or undue means; for evident partiality or corruption of the arbitrators; when arbitrators are guilty of misconduct in refusing to postpone the hearing, upon sufficient cause shown, or in refusing to hear evidence pertinent and material to the controversy; and when arbitrators exceed their powers. Furthermore, the courts have narrowly construed these grounds for vacation of awards.

In the end, US arbitration law strongly advances the core principles of separability (arbitration clause is a standalone agreement within a contract) and kompetenz–kompetenz (competency of arbitral tribunal to determine jurisdiction). Arbitration awards are effectively enforced under the obligations of the New York Convention as adopted by the United States. The scope of arbitral jurisdiction has expanded, as noted, to include claims recognized under statutory and constitutional law that some other countries have viewed as matters of public policy best reserved to the courts.

PART V

Summary and Findings

25

Divergence, Themes, and Trends in National Arbitration Laws

Larry A. DiMatteo, Marta Infantino, and Nathalie M-P Potin

This chapter acts as a capstone to Part IV's presentation of country reports. It presents the findings of a comparative analysis of arbitration laws in the different countries reported. This analysis focuses on the different issues presented in Parts I–III, including scope and interpretation of arbitration clauses, anti-arbitration laws and policies, arbitrator bias and misconduct, the public policy exception, and other limits on arbitrability. Thus, the country reports are reviewed here to determine areas of commonality and divergences across national laws relating to judicial intervention into the arbitration process. It will also assess possible trends in international commercial arbitration.

1 INTRODUCTION

The general areas to be discussed here include grounds for vacating commercial arbitration awards, issues dealing with the enforceability of arbitration awards, and the determination of the scope of arbitration clauses. The first area focuses on arbitrator bias prior to the beginning of an arbitration and misconduct during the arbitration proceeding. The issues discussed include conflict of interest and arbitrator misconduct that result in less than a fair hearing. The requirement of a fair hearing relates to due process elements such as admission or lack thereof of probative evidence and procedural irregularities. The second area focuses on limitations that result in the unenforceability of arbitration awards. The general basis for appeal of an arbitration awards is found in the New York Convention, which, for example, allows for a public policy exception to the enforcement of arbitration awards. If the court of enforcement deems an award to be in conflict with foundational law or public policy, then it can refuse to enforce an award. The variability of enforcement in this area is due to the fact that countries may differ as to what they deem to be within the public policy exception. Countries have different views as to what types of issues preclude arbitrability. The final area deals with the arbitrability of issues based on the interpretation of the scope of the arbitration clause. Of course, interpretation and drafting of arbitration clauses are different sides of a coin. Clearly worded arbitration clauses are less subject to misinterpretation than ones that are vaguely written. Of course, there is much law on the interpretation of generic or boilerplate arbitration that states that "any and all claims related to the contract" are subject to arbitration. This does not mean that such generic wording

Larry DiMatteo is the author of Sections 1, 5–7; Marta Infantino is the author of Section 2; Nathalie Potin is the author of Sections 3–4.

is interpreted in the same way in all countries. Finally, interpretation issues arise in the use of industry-specific arbitration clauses, including how they diverge from generic or institutional clauses.

2 SETTING ASIDE AND ENFORCEABILITY OF ARBITRAL AWARDS

As far as the judicial control over arbitral awards is concerned, the comparative picture from a review of the national reports collected in this book shows that there are multiple overlapping trends of convergence and divergence across the jurisdictions under examination. These trends include the numerous hard and soft law transnational sources aiming at harmonizing arbitration law and easing the global circulation of arbitral awards,[1] the widespread idea, supported by global institutions, that arbitration is the preferable means for handling commercial disputes,[2] the internal cohesion within the arbitration epistemic and professional community,[3] which account for the increasing convergence of national patterns in arbitration law.

Yet the national reports also give evidence of continued diversity and divergence on a multiple set of issues. The place of arbitration in any country still depends on a myriad of factors that are grounded in the country's history, culture, and law, such as the geographical location of a state and the presence of strong competitors in the regional market for arbitration,[4] the presence (or not) of renowned arbitration centers with consistent international caseloads,[5] the unitary or federal structure of the legal system,[6] and the country's recent political and economic developments.[7] Further, judicial approaches to arbitration are obviously influenced by features concerning the jurisdiction itself, such as the type of court which is competent to decide upon

---

[1] As we will see in the next section, the majority of the countries herein studied took inspiration from the UNCITRAL Model Law on Commercial Arbitration (either in its 1985 or 2006 version). Further, all the countries under examination adhere to the 1985 New York Convention on the Recognition and Enforcement of Foreign Arbitral Awards (hereinafter NY Convention). Many countries also adhere to other global or regional international treaties on the subject matter, such as the 1927 Geneva Protocol on the Enforcement of Arbitral Awards, the 1961 European Convention on International Commercial Arbitration, the 1975 Panama Inter-American Convention on International Commercial Arbitration, and the 1979 Inter-American Convention on Extraterritorial Validity of Foreign Judgments and Arbitral Awards.

[2] For instance, since the publication of the first edition in 2003 of its "Doing Business Reports," the World Bank has vigorously held that one of the indicia for a legal system's business friendliness lies in the efficacy of arbitration in commercial disputes: see https://www.doingbusiness.org/en/methodology/enforcing-contracts.

[3] From a variety of perspectives, cf. WON L. KIDANE, THE CULTURE OF INTERNATIONAL ARBITRATION 63–89, 283–289 (2017); Emmanuel Gaillard, Sociology of International Arbitration, in PRACTISING VIRTUE: INSIDE INTERNATIONAL ARBITRATION 187–203 (David D. Caron, Stephan W. Schill, Abby Cohen Smutny, & Epaminontas E. Triantafilou eds., 2015); Tom Ginsburg, The Culture of Arbitration, 36 VANDERBILT JOURNAL OF INTERNATIONAL LAW 1335, 1336 (2003).

[4] The Australian reporters for instance emphasize the country's geographical remoteness on the one hand and its closeness to strong competitors in the region (such as Singapore, Hong Kong, and Malaysia) on the other hand: see Chapter 11 (Australia).

[5] At one extreme, some of the countries herein surveyed (e.g., the United Kingdom, France, Switzerland) have internationally renowned arbitration institutions managing a substantial caseload of international arbitration (respectively, the London Court of International Arbitration, the Paris-based International Chamber of Commerce, the Swiss Chamber of Commerce). At the other extreme, there are countries (e.g., Argentina, Australia, Italy, Spain, Ukraine) with a substantial domestic market of arbitral services that however are not (yet) particularly attractive for handling international arbitration disputes.

[6] See Chapter 11 (Australia), Chapter 17 (Nigeria), and Chapter 24 (United States).

[7] Think, for instance, of the influence that a country's socialist past or present has on arbitration law (e.g., in Bulgaria, China, Poland, Russia, Ukraine) or of the impact that an economic crisis might have on judicial approaches to arbitral awards (as it happened in Argentina and Spain).

arbitration issues,[8] the structure of the appeals system,[9] the more or less global-mindedness of judges, their degree of comity toward arbitrators, and the size of their caseloads[10] as well as judges' understanding of their own role in the system (including as the gatekeepers of the constitutional right of access to justice and of the country's sovereignty[11]). Needless to say, equally important is the role played by other, less visible actors, such as arbitrators and lawyers, even though the impact that the latter might have on the system is particularly hard to trace.

All of this suggests that, in spite of the increasing convergence trend, a comparative approach to the subject matter is still highly needed. Ideally, such a comparative analysis should be fed with statistical data coming from a large sample of jurisdictions. Yet, as many of our national rapporteurs note, in almost every country no official and general statistics about how many cases are arbitrated each year, where and by whom are available.[12] The lack of official data comparable with one another makes it very hard to measure with precision courts' activism vis-à-vis arbitration. Moreover, editorial and organizational constraints obliged us not to cover every country in the world, leaving out some jurisdictions that in recent years have vigorously promoted international arbitration, such as Hong Kong, Singapore, and the United Arab Emirates.

Notwithstanding these limitations, the following overview offers a snapshot of the coexistence in the field of many convergent and divergent pressures. We will first analyze some general features of national approaches to arbitration law and then focus in particular on rules and practices on setting aside of non-foreign arbitral awards and enforcement of foreign arbitral awards.[13]

2.1 *General Features*

In all the jurisdictions examined, there is a distinguishable trend towards favoring arbitration, no matter how arbitration is historically rooted in the legal tradition.[14] All countries, including common law ones, regulate arbitration by statutory law and keep it constantly updated, as it is

---

[8] What might matter, for instance, is whether the court is a first instance, appellate, or apical court; whether it has specialized or general jurisdiction; whether it is a state or federal court; or whether it seats in the capital of the country or not.

[9] It might be the case that judicial decisions on arbitration are not subject to appeal; if they are, the appeal might be a right or might be subject to a leave by the court.

[10] *See* Chapter 10 (Argentina), Chapter 12 (Bulgaria), and Chapter 16 (Italy).

[11] On the impact that constitutional interpretation might have on judicial approaches to arbitration, *see* Chapter 10 (Argentina), Chapter 17 (Nigeria), and Chapter 20 (Spain). On the way in which arguments about national sovereignty might affect the judicial control over arbitration, *see* Chapter 10 (Argentina), Chapter 13 (China), Chapter 23 (United Kingdom), Chapter 14 (France), Chapter 16 (Italy), Chapter 19 (Russia), and Chapter 24 (United States).

[12] *Cf.* Chapter 12 (Bulgaria), Chapter 13 (China), Chapter 14 (France), Chapter 16 (Italy), and Chapter 20 (Spain). Often, arbitral institutions publish their own statistics, which however refer only to arbitral proceedings celebrated before them. Many of the reports (see for instance the Chinese, English, French, Italian, Spanish, Swiss, and Ukrainian ones) offer judicial statistics about courts' decisions on arbitral cases. However, these numbers per se tell very little about the state of arbitration in a given country, because they often report fragmentary information that anyway relate only to arbitral awards that were challenged before courts, which arguably are only a minority of the total number of awards issued in the country.

[13] The following review is based on the national reports collected in Part IV of this book, as well as on the many comparative review of arbitration law available online, such as globalarbitrationreview.com, globallegalinsights.com/practice-areas/international-arbitration-laws-and-regulations, iclg.com/practice-areas/international-arbitration-laws-and-regulations, uk.practicallaw.thomsonreuters.com/Browse/Home/International/EnforcementofJudgmentsGlobalGuide, and thelawreviews.co.uk/edition/1001364/the-international-arbitration-review-edition-10.

[14] In many countries (e.g., Bulgaria, Italy, and Spain) arbitration has deep historical roots, while in others (such as China and Poland) it was only recently introduced in the legal system.

shown by the number of reforms undergone, almost everywhere, in the last decades.[15] In a large majority of countries (the exception being China, Switzerland, and the United States), the current legislative framework, especially as far as international arbitration is concerned, is more or less in line with the UNCITRAL Model Law (either in its 1985 or 2006 version).[16]

At a closer look, however, one discovers that the form, scope, and interpretation of such laws are much more different from one another than one might at first sight think. First of all, sources of arbitration law differ from country to country. In some cases, regulation over arbitration is included in the domestic codes of procedure;[17] more often, it is contained in special acts;[18] sometimes, it is both.[19] In socialist and post-socialist countries,[20] such legislation is complemented by the general guidelines issued by apex courts in their quasi-legislative competence. Further complications arise from the federal structure of some legal systems (namely, Argentina, Australia, Germany, Nigeria, Russia, Switzerland, and the United States plus the "quasi-federal" Spanish system). In all federal systems, arbitration is regulated by the central state,[21] but there are diverging relationships between such federal legislation and state/local ones. In Germany, Russia, and Switzerland (plus in quasi-federal Spain), arbitration is regulated only at the federal level. In Argentina, federal and local laws are applicable to domestic arbitration, while international arbitration is regulated by federal law. In Australia, local law governs domestic arbitration, while federal law applies to international arbitration. In Nigeria, federal and local laws apply to both domestic and international arbitration. In the United States, the Federal Arbitration Act preempts state law, but arbitration remains a matter of state law.

An additional divide concerns the scope of national arbitration laws, and in particular whether they provide or not a unified regime for domestic and international arbitration. Half of the countries surveyed (i.e., Bulgaria, the United Kingdom, Germany, Italy, Poland, Spain, the United States) embrace a monist approach, with general arbitration rules applying both to domestic and international arbitration. The other half (Argentina, Australia, China, France, Nigeria, Switzerland, Ukraine) adopt a dualist approach, with different tracks for domestic and international arbitration. The divide is further complicated by the circumstances that monist countries often have special rules applying to domestic or international arbitration only and that in dualist countries the domestic and international tracks might overlap more or less extensively.

---

[15] Cf. the date of last reforms of arbitration laws: Argentina (2015 and 2018; Chile, 2004), Australia (2010), Bulgaria (2017), China (Chinese law on arbitration was enacted in 1994 and the latest interpretation by the Supreme People's Court on arbitration was issued in 2017), France (2011), Germany (1998, the Arbitration Rules of the German Arbitration Institute were reformed in 2018), Italy (2006 and 2014), Nigeria (the federal statute on arbitration was enacted in 1988, but many local statutes are much more recent: see, for instance, the Lagos State Arbitration Law, enacted in 2009), Poland (2005 and 2019), Russia (2015 and 2018), Spain (2003, 2011, and 2015), Switzerland (1989), Ukraine (2017; Hungary, 2017); the United Kingdom (1996), the United States (whose 1925 Federal Arbitration Act was last amended in 1990). Further, in many states further reforms are under way: this is the case for Argentina, Australia, Germany, and Switzerland.

[16] This is the case of the Argentina (as well as Chile), Australia, Bulgaria, the United Kingdom, France, Germany, Italy, Nigeria, Poland, Russia, Spain, and Ukraine.

[17] See Chapter 14 (France), Chapter 15 (Germany), Chapter 16 (Italy), and Chapter 18 (Poland).

[18] See Chapter 11 (Australia), Chapter 13 (China), Chapter 23 (United Kingdom), Chapter 17 (Nigeria), Chapter 20 (Spain), and Chapter 24 (United States).

[19] This is for instance the case of Argentina, Bulgaria, Russia, Switzerland, and Ukraine.

[20] E.g., China, Russia, and Ukraine.

[21] This is the case in Argentina, Australia, Germany, Nigeria, Russia, Switzerland, and the United States. Similarly, in the "quasi-federal" Spanish system, arbitration is regulated by the central state.

On the top of this, national arbitration laws are interpreted and applied across countries by arbitral tribunals and, most importantly, by courts in dissimilar ways.[22] This holds particularly true for national rules governing the courts' power to intervene in arbitral proceedings and scrutinize arbitral awards, such as rules about judicial power to order the stay of arbitral proceedings, to check whether a dispute is arbitrable and whether the arbitral tribunal has jurisdiction, to decide on a challenge of an arbitrator, to grant interim measures and to assist the arbitral tribunal in the collection of evidence, to set aside the award and to grant or deny its enforcement.

Apart from the cases of setting aside and enforcement, which will be dealt with later, one of the best illustrations of the divergent interpretations and applications of apparently similar rules comes from judicial approaches to the principle of competence–competence. All jurisdictions herein examined recognize the principle that the arbitral tribunal is competent to rule on its own jurisdiction. Yet the interpretation and application of the principle vary from one place to another. Courts in some countries (e.g., France) strictly adhere to the principle and therefore refuse to interfere with an arbitral tribunal's proceedings until the tribunal has made its final determination on the matter.[23] By contrast, courts in other countries interpret competence–competence in a rather loose way. For instance, under Australian and English law, in case of challenges of an arbitration agreement brought to courts after the commencement of an arbitration, courts have to stay judicial proceedings until the arbitral tribunal first resolves any challenge as to the existence and scope of the alleged arbitration agreement; yet, in order to decide on stay applications, courts undertake a full review of the arbitration agreement and of the arbitral tribunal's jurisdiction – a practice that often hollows out the competence–competence principle of its practical effect.[24] In a Nigerian case, the court of appeal restrained the respondent from continuing an ICC Arbitration that was ongoing between the parties before the arbitral tribunal had the opportunity to decide the question alone.[25] In Poland, the final judgment of a court, finding that the arbitral tribunal lacks jurisdiction, is binding for the arbitral tribunal,[26] while the Ukrainian Supreme Court has overriden an arbitral tribunal's ruling affirming its own jurisdiction.[27] In the United States, the Supreme Court's leading decision on the matter held that the decisions related to the arbitrability of the dispute represents an issue that has to be decided in courts unless the parties clearly and unmistakably provide otherwise.[28]

---

[22] One should further consider the local peculiarities that may affect the scope and power of arbitral tribunals in a given jurisdiction: for instance, domestic ad hoc arbitration is not permitted under Chinese law and arbitral tribunals are not allowed to issue intermediary measures under Italian law.

[23] Further, when the challenge of the tribunal's jurisdiction is raised before the constitution of the tribunal, according to art. 1448 of the French Civil Procedure Code, the French judge must decline jurisdiction unless he finds that the arbitration agreement relied upon is "manifestly void" or manifestly inapplicable. In deciding whether an arbitration agreement is manifestly void or inapplicable, the judge does not carry out a substantive, in-depth examination of the agreement, but only reviews its prima facie validity.

[24] Cf. Samsung C&T Corporation v. Duro Felbuera Australia Pty Ltd [2016] WASC 193 and Joint Stock Co "Aeroflot Russian Airlines" v. Berezovsky [2013] EWCA Civ 784.

[25] Shell Petroleum Development Company of Nigeria v. Crestar Integrated Natural Resources Limited (Appeal No. CA/L/331M/2015).

[26] See §1165 of the Polish Code of Civil Procedure.

[27] Resolution of the Supreme Court No. 910/13366/18, Cassation Commercial Court, Mar. 4, 2019.

[28] First Option v. Kaplan, 455 F. Supp. 211 (S.D.N.Y. 1978). Further, in spite of the recognition of the competence–competence principle, courts in some countries (e.g. Argentina and the United Kingdom) are prone to order the parties to refrain from arbitration or arbitral tribunals to stay arbitral proceedings until the court decides about the arbitrability of the disputes and the competence of the tribunal.

In light of this discussion, it comes at no surprise that, in spite of the noticeable convergence trend in rules on setting aside domestic and international arbitral awards and on recognition and enforcement of foreign arbitral awards, national differences still remain. As we will see, differences are more marked as far as vacating domestic and international arbitral awards is concerned, but they are also present in the field of recognition and enforcement of foreign arbitral awards.

2.2 Setting Aside of Domestic and International Awards

All countries herein examined provide that domestic and international arbitral awards stemming from arbitral proceedings (whether purely domestic or international) whose seat is within the country can, within a certain period from the issuance of the decision,[29] be challenged before the courts.[30] Foreign arbitral awards cannot be challenged directly and can only be aggrieved when their enforcement is sought. Yet, as we are going to see in more detail, rules and practices on setting aside arbitral awards differ widely. In some countries, there are two separate tracks for vacating domestic and international awards; in others requirements and procedures for domestic and international awards coincide. Some countries strictly follow the model set forth by Article 34 of the UNCITRAL Model Law on Commercial Arbitration, and others consistently deviate from it. Differences also concern the grounds of challenge, the parties' right to waive them, the courts that are competent to hear the challenge, the appealability of the decision, and the effects of a successful challenge.

Ten out of the fifteen countries surveyed (Australia, Bulgaria, the United Kingdom, Germany, Italy, Poland, Russia, Spain, Ukraine, United States) adopt the same standard of review for both domestic and international arbitral awards. The remaining five (Argentina, China, France, Nigeria, Switzerland) provide for different tracks of setting aside domestic and international awards, typically allowing a larger set of grounds for vacation of domestic awards.[31]

Many of these rules are directly inspired by Article 34 of the UNCITRAL Model Law,[32] sometimes with minor deviations: this is the case in Argentina, Australia, Bulgaria, China (for international awards only), France, Germany, Nigeria (for international awards only), Poland,

---

[29] The period varies from country to country but on average it is around three months, as prescribed by Art. 34(3) UNCITRAL Model Law.

[30] A few countries (e.g., Italy, Poland, Spain, and the United States) also provide for some additional remedies against arbitral awards. We will not deal with them because there remedies either are limited to correction of minor mistakes in the awards or are conditioned upon special circumstances that rarely occur in practice.

[31] All these countries have a dualist system for domestic and international arbitration; what is interesting to note is that some countries which have a dualist system, like Australia and Ukraine, still embrace overall unitary grounds and procedures for setting aside both domestic and international arbitral awards.

[32] It is useful to recall here the text of Art. 34(2) of the UNCITRAL Model Law (2006):

(2) An arbitral award may be set aside by the court specified in article 6 only if:

   (a) the party making the application furnishes proof that:
      (i) a party to the arbitration agreement referred to in article 7 was under some incapacity; or the said agreement is not valid under the law to which the parties have subjected it or, failing any indication thereon, under the law of this State; or
      (ii) the party making the application was not given proper notice of the appointment of an arbitrator or of the arbitral proceedings or was otherwise unable to present his case; or
      (iii) the award deals with a dispute not contemplated by or not falling within the terms of the submission to arbitration, or contains decisions on matters beyond the scope of the submission to arbitration, provided that, if the decisions on matters submitted to arbitration can be separated from those not so submitted, only that part of the award which contains decisions on matters not submitted to arbitration may be set aside; or

Russia, Spain, and Ukraine. As provided in Article 34 of the UNCITRAL Model Law, the focus of rules on setting aside in these countries is on procedural irregularities as well as on lack of arbitrability and public policy. Of the remaining countries, Italian grounds for setting aside and Swiss grounds for vacating international arbitral awards, while not literally coinciding with the ones provided by the UNCITRAL Model Law, also focus on procedural irregularities, lack of arbitrability, and public policy and therefore largely correspond to the Model Law's contents. Quite different from the UNCITRAL Model Law are the Chinese, Nigeria, and Swiss grounds for vacating domestic arbitral awards, as well as the English and US ones for vacating both domestic and international arbitral awards. Chinese rules put a particular emphasis on the right to challenge domestic awards when evidence has been fabricated or arbitrators accepted bribes, misbehaved, or perverted the law.[33] Nigerian domestic awards can be challenged not only if they contain decisions on matters that are beyond the arbitral agreement but also upon proof that "the arbitrator has misconduct himself, of where the arbitral proceedings, or award, has been improperly procured."[34] Swiss domestic awards can be challenged, inter alia, if "the award is arbitrary ... because it constitutes an obvious violation of law or equity" and if "the costs and compensation fixed by the arbitral tribunal are obviously excessive."[35] In England, domestic and international awards under Sections 67–69 of the 1996 Arbitration Act can be challenged on three possible grounds: lack of jurisdiction, serious irregularity (including awards being obtained by fraud), and on a question of law (for cases in which either "the decision of the tribunal on the question is obviously wrong or the question is one of general public importance and the decision of the tribunal is at least open to serious doubt"[36]). Finally, in the United States, awards can be challenged on the basis of the Federal Arbitration Act on four grounds, all revolving around the arbitrators' corruption, fraud, and misconduct plus, according to a much debated doctrine of the US Supreme Court,[37] in cases in which the arbitrators manifestly disregarded the law.

This overview makes it clear that there is a divide (partially, but not entirely, corresponding to a civil–common law divide) between countries in which the courts' focus in setting aside proceedings is on the regularity of the arbitral procedure and countries where that focus lies on arbitrators' misconduct. Yet, it should also be noted that the divide does not necessarily affect the substance of the review. Arbitrators' misconduct actually matters also in countries following Article 34(3) of the UNCITRAL Model Law, as a species of improper constitution of the tribunal or as a violation of due process; conversely, many of the procedural irregularities mentioned by Article 34 of the UNCITRAL Model Law might be seen as a sign of arbitrators' misconduct in jurisdictions in which the challenge of awards is predominantly based on arbitrators' misbehavior. It should be further noted that, no matter what approach is adopted, courts in both type of

      (iv) the composition of the arbitral tribunal or the arbitral procedure was not in accordance with the agreement of the parties, unless such agreement was in conflict with a provision of this Law from which the parties cannot derogate, or, failing such agreement, was not in accordance with this Law; or
  (b) the court finds that:
      (i) the subject-matter of the dispute is not capable of settlement by arbitration under the law of this State; or
      (ii) the award is in conflict with the public policy of this State.

[33] Art. 58, numbers 4–6, of 1994 Chinese arbitration law.
[34] Art. 30(1) of the Nigerian Arbitration and Conciliation Act.
[35] Art. 393 of the Swiss Code of Civil Procedure, letter (e) and (f).
[36] Art. 69(2), letter (c), of the 1996 Arbitration Act.
[37] Wilko v. Swan, 346 US 427 (1953).

systems often attempt to open up the grounds for challenge, typically, in UNCITRAL-like countries, by stretching the notion of public policy includes procedural public policy[38] or, in non-UNCITRAL-like jurisdictions, by adopting a wide standard for evaluating arbitrators' misconduct.[39]

Almost everywhere, a party's failure to promptly react, during the arbitral proceedings, to a potential reason for setting aside that is known to him or her might result in an implicit waiver of the party's right to lodge a request for setting aside when the decision is entered.[40] But countries again take different positions as to whether the parties can preliminarily waive their right to challenge arbitral awards in the arbitration agreement. Such waivers are not allowed in Argentina, Australia, Bulgaria, China, Italy, Nigeria, Poland, Spain, Ukraine, and the United States, while they are allowed on limited (and diverging) grounds in England, France, Germany, Russia, and Switzerland. In England, parties cannot contract out their right to challenge an award on the basis of lack of jurisdiction and serious irregularity, but they might waive their right to lodge an appeal "on a question of law" under Article 69 of the 1996 Arbitration Act. In France, Germany, and Russia, parties might agree upon a waiver, but the waiver does not limit their right to challenge the award for reasons of public policy. Waivers under Swiss law are admissible only in international arbitration and only if "neither party has a domicile, a place of habitual residence or a place of business in Switzerland."[41]

Countries also differ as to the courts competent to hear challenges against arbitral awards. In the majority of countries requests for setting aside awards should be lodged before first-level courts.[42] In Argentina, Australia, China (whose peculiarity is highlighted later), England, Nigeria, Ukraine (for domestic awards) and the United States, first-level decisions are further subject to appeal and then to recourse at the Supreme Court level,[43] while in Poland and Russia the first-level decision may be challenged only through a cassation appeal to the Supreme Court. As mentioned, a special regime is in place in China, where the decisions of Intermediary People's Courts to set aside arbitral awards are subject to the so-called Prior Reporting System (PRS). The PRS implies that the court, when setting an award aside, is obliged to report its intended decision to the higher court, which, if it agrees on the setting aside, will in turn send the decision to the Supreme People's Court.[44] By contrast, in other countries – most notably, France, Germany, Italy, and Spain as well as in Switzerland (for domestic awards) and Ukraine (for international awards) – the competence to hear challenges of arbitral awards lies within appellate courts, whose decisions can be further challenged only once, at the supreme court level.[45] Finally, in Bulgaria and in Switzerland (for international awards), the only court that is competent to hear challenges is the Supreme Court, whose decision is subject to no further review.

---

[38] A common trend is, for instance, that of holding that public policy includes procedural public policy: *see* Chapter 12 (Bulgaria), Chapter 14 (France), Chapter 18 (Poland), and Chapter 20 (Spain).

[39] See Chapter 17 (Nigeria) and Chapter 24 (United States).

[40] The rule is stressed, in particular, by Chapter 14 (France), Chapter 16 (Italy), and Chapter 21 (Switzerland).

[41] Art. 192 Swiss Private International Law Act.

[42] First-level here does not actually mean that these courts are first instance courts; rather, it only means that their decisions are subject to two levels of appeal.

[43] In Argentina, Australia, England, Nigeria, and the United States recourse to the highest courts is premised upon a leave; in China, there is no leave, but the number of challenges is limited by the so-called Prior Reporting System, on which see the following text.

[44] See Chapter 13 (China).

[45] Technically, the competent court in Spain is the High Court of Justice, whose decisions can only be challenged to the Tribunal Supremo.

When a court recognizes that a challenge should be upheld, the general rule is that the court sets the award aside without deciding the merits.[46] Yet such a general rule should be coordinated with the principle provided by Article 34(4) of the UNCITRAL Model Law and adopted by Argentina (for international awards), Australia, China, England, Germany, Nigeria, Poland, Russia, Spain, Switzerland (for domestic cases), and Ukraine. According to Article 34(4) of the Model Law, in such cases, the court may, instead of setting aside the award, "suspend the setting aside proceedings for a period of time determined by it in order to give the arbitral tribunal an opportunity to resume the arbitral proceedings or to take such other action as in the arbitral tribunal's opinion will eliminate the grounds for setting aside." Further, one should take into account that in a not irrelevant minority of countries (Argentina and France for domestic arbitration only, plus England, Italy, and Switzerland), courts under certain circumstances can also, when setting an award aside, rule on the merits of the dispute.

Needless to say, courts in different jurisdictions are more or less prone to hear certain arguments and to set aside arbitral awards for one reason or another. However, undertaking a serious comparative review of such trends is hard, due to the lack of comprehensive statistics about the number of arbitral awards issued every year, the number and grounds of challenges, and the number of successful requests for vacation. Only a few reports contain statistical data, most of which are too fragmentary and concern too many diverse situations to allow a meaningful comparison.[47]

2.3 Enforcement and Recognition of Foreign Arbitral Awards

Once an award becomes final, courts might need to intervene whenever one party refuses to comply with it. In all countries examined, enforcing arbitral awards requires the intervention of courts. The enforcement of (domestic and international) arbitral awards rendered by arbitral tribunals having their seat in the country is everywhere a rather straightforward procedure, no matter whether awards are automatically equated to judgments or whether they have to be recognized by a court before they obtain the same status as judgments. Differences here mostly lie in procedural technicalities grounded in each country's civil procedure.[48]

Less simple is the recognition and enforcement of foreign arbitral awards. The field is deemed to be widely harmonized thanks to the widespread ratification of the 1958 New York Convention on the Recognition and Enforcement of Foreign Arbitral Awards, signed by 164 states. All the jurisdictions under examination are signatories of the Convention. Therefore, the procedure for recognition and enforcement of foreign awards and the grounds on which recognition and enforcement can be challenged are everywhere aligned with the prescriptions of the

---

[46] Argentina (for international awards), Australia, Bulgaria, China, France (for international awards), Germany, Italy (although in certain cases a decision on the merit is possible), Nigeria, Poland, Russia, Spain, Ukraine, and the United States.

[47] The most comprehensive set of information is provided by Chapter 13 (China); the English, Italian, and Swiss reports contain information on the number and rate of successful challenges against arbitral awards, while the Spanish and Ukrainian reports offer data referring to the setting aside of awards issued by the most important national arbitration centers.

[48] See also Leon Trakman, *Domestic Courts Declining to Recognize and Enforce Foreign Arbitral Awards: A Comparative Reflection*, 6 THE CHINESE JOURNAL OF COMPARATIVE LAW 174–227 (2018); George A. Bermann, *Recognition and Enforcement of Foreign Arbitral Awards: The Interpretation and Application of the New York Convention by National Courts*, in RECOGNITION AND ENFORCEMENT OF FOREIGN ARBITRAL AWARDS 1–78 (George A. Bermann ed., 2017); ZHENG SOPHIA TANG, JURISDICTION AND ARBITRATION AGREEMENTS IN INTERNATIONAL COMMERCIAL LAW 223–235 (2014).

Convention.[49] In particular, in all jurisdictions surveyed, recognition and enforcement of foreign arbitral awards may be refused at the request of the party against whom they are invoked in the cases provided by Article IV of the Convention, that is, in cases of incapacity of the parties, invalidity of the arbitration agreement, due process, scope of the arbitration agreement, jurisdiction of the arbitral tribunal, setting aside or suspension of an award in the country in which, or under the law of which, that award was made. Further, following Article IV of the Convention, in all countries a court may, on its own motion, refuse recognition and enforcement of an award for lack of arbitrability and reasons of public policy.

Against such a quite uniform background, there is still room for some divergence. First of all, differences lie in the type and number of courts involved in the procedure for recognition/enforcement. In a minority of countries (Germany, Italy, Poland, Spain), such claims are brought before appellate courts, whose decisions can be challenged only before apex courts. In the majority of jurisdictions (Argentina, Australia, Bulgaria, China, England, France, Nigeria, Russia, Switzerland, Ukraine, the United States), requests for recognition/enforcement are lodged before first-level courts,[50] whose decisions can be appealed to the higher court and then to the apex court. In this regard, it should be noted again the Chinese exceptionalism. It is actually in the context of enforcement of foreign arbitral awards that the PRS (described earlier)[51] was originally conceived. The system implies that any decision by Intermediate People's Court refusing recognition or enforcement of a foreign arbitral award should be preliminary reviewed by the Higher People's Court and by the Supreme Court. The system ensures that recognition/enforcement of a foreign arbitral award is not refused lightly; a side effect of the PRS, however, is that it also lengthens judicial proceedings: according to the Chinese reporters, the average time to obtain a final order on enforcement from time of application is 331 days.

Second, courts differ in the narrowness or openness with which they interpret the grounds for denying recognition/enforcement. There are jurisdictions – e.g., England, France, Germany, and Switzerland – in which historically courts have embraced a rather narrow view of the requirements for denying recognition/enforcement of foreign arbitral awards. By contrast, in others countries, such as Argentina, Australia (especially in the past[52]), Poland, Russia, Ukraine, at least a part of the judiciary embraces an expansive interpretation of the Convention and in particular of its public policy exception. Few reports, however, provide statistical data about courts' overall enforcing rates.[53] In absence of legible and comparable data, it is hard to fully appreciate whether, and to what extent, such diverging interpretation has practical implications.

---

[49] See all the national reports. A caveat is however needed. While all countries herein examined have transplanted the NY Convention criteria in their own law, nothing prevents a country from providing different rules for the enforcement of foreign awards issued by arbitral tribunals having their seats in NY Convention and non–NY Convention signatory states. For reasons of simplicity, and given the widespread ratification of the NY Convention, we will deal only with enforcement of NY Convention awards.

[50] See the caveats expressed *supra* note 42.

[51] See Section 1.2.

[52] It should be noted that Section 8 (7A) of the International Arbitration Act 1974 provides that: "To avoid doubt and without limiting paragraph (7)(b), the enforcement of a foreign award would be contrary to public policy if: (a) the making of the award was induced or affected by fraud or corruption; or (b) a breach of the rules of natural justice occurred in connection with the making of the award."

[53] See Chapter 13 (China) (during the period of 1990 to 2019 there was an overall enforcing rate of 67 percent) and Chapter 22 (Ukraine) (according to which the enforcing rate of foreign arbitral awards is 80–90 percent).

3 ARBITRATOR BIAS AND CONFLICT OF INTEREST

3.1 Arbitrator Bias

When conflicts of interest arise, the most glaring consequence is the perception that an arbitrator is compromised. It means that he or she is biased toward one party or another. That perception will lead to one of three actions taken against the individual and the award rendered by the individual. His or her nomination can be objected to, he or she can be challenged if the arbitral tribunal has already been constituted, and finally if he or she has rendered an award that award can be challenged.

In the context of this book, we have to look at what happens when a tribunal is alleged to have a conflict. Once the application or allegation is made indicating that a tribunal (or a member of that tribunal) has a conflict of interest, then whatever award is rendered by that tribunal might be subject to an enforcement challenge. The courts in all jurisdictions have to take the application seriously as a matter of public policy. The allegation obliges the courts in any jurisdiction to assess whether or not the tribunal was biased in anyway and to review whether the allegation has led to a perceived partiality on the part of the tribunal or one of its member.

The legislation usually determines how far the courts will go to review (1) what the arbitrator should have disclosed and (2) the level of scrutiny afforded to the action or inaction of the arbitrator in disclosing his or her conflict of interest. The actions of tribunals (or individual arbitrators) during the conduct of the arbitration may be reviewed as to whether the tribunal exhibited a level of conscious or unconscious favoritism toward a party. This is generally described as bias or partiality. The levels of scrutiny vary in various jurisdictions. What the courts will consider is dependent on the legislation in place and its wording. In the United States, Section 10 (a) 2 of the Federal Arbitration Act (FAA) allows courts to vacate an award if there is "evident partiality." The phrase *evident partiality* appears to be a higher evidential threshold than "merely the appearance" of partiality.[54] However, the courts do not require proof of actual bias.[55]

Even if countries refer to "justifiable doubts" when dealing with allegations of arbitrators bias, their reference is quite diverse.[56] Australia mentions justifiable doubts in light of impartiality and independence.[57] The United Kingdom and Switzerland suggest "justifiable doubts" in context of independence only, whereas justifiable doubts in Ukraine is dealt with in the context of neutrality or independence.[58] Nigerian courts will review justifiable doubts through the prism of impartiality or independence[59] pursuant to Section 8(1) of the Arbitration & Conciliation Act 1988.

Some arbitration laws narrowly fix the grounds for setting aside arbitral awards, suggesting that the action or inaction of the tribunal will be subject to a stringent test before the award will be compromised. In Australia, the courts refer to the "real danger of bias" test pursuant to Article 18A of the International Arbitration Act 1974. Australian courts appear to be

---

[54] John Buckley Jr & Jonathan M. Landy, *USA: International Arbitration 2019*, INTERNATIONAL COMPARATIVE LEGAL GUIDES (Aug. 22, 2019), iclg.com/practice-areas/international-arbitration-laws-and-regulations/usa.
[55] *Id.*
[56] See Chapter 11 (Australia), Chapter 23 (United Kingdom), Chapter 22 (Switzerland), Chapter 23 (Ukraine), and Chapter 24 (United States).
[57] Chapter 11, Section 2 (Australia).
[58] Chapter 23, Section 2 (United Kingdom) and Chapter 22, Section 4 (Switzerland).
[59] Chapter 17, Section 3.2 (Nigeria).

interpreting the arbitration legislation in a way inimical to arbitration or in a parochial way.[60] The Australia report highlights the similarity in approach with the English courts. In the recent case of *Hui v. Esposito Holdings Pty Ltd*,[61] the Federal Court of Australia explained that "real danger of bias" test shall be done from the perspective of a "reasonable bystander." Beach J confirmed that the applicable legal test is "whether a reasonable person would no longer have confidence in the arbitrator's ability to come to a fair and balanced conclusion on the issues if remitted."[62]

In England, conflict of interest relates primarily to the concept of independence.[63] English courts apply the real danger test developed in the *Regina v. Gough* case,[64] relying on three principles when considering bias (1) actual bias always disqualifies, (2) the importance of public confidence is such that even the appearance of bias will disqualify, and (3) disqualification follows if there is real danger of bias.[65] English courts removed arbitrators for apparent bias[66] instead of actual bias. The recent case of *Halliburton Company v. Chubb Bermuda Insurance Ltd and others*[67] clarified that arbitrators can accept multiple overlapping appointments without necessarily giving rise to doubts. The English Court of Appeal confirmed the lower court decision's conclusion that "the fair-minded and informed observer, having considered the facts, would not conclude that there was a real possibility" that the arbitrator had been biased.[68] The UK report explained that the arbitrator's disclosure of conflict of interest must be "a transparent process in order to be an effective safeguard"[69] and requires "honesty" and "sufficient detail to enable the parties to adequately assess the potential conflict of an arbitrator."[70] The rapporteur adds that if an arbitrator makes an erroneous or incomplete statement, this should not automatically lead to his or her removal, or to the annulment of the award. Both the English and the Australians have taken a cautious and conservative attitude.

For those relying on the independence principle, the Swiss approach has been less conservative. In Switzerland, an arbitrator is considered to be biased and may be challenged if there exist justifiable doubts as to his or her independence pursuant to Article 180(1)(c) of the Private International Law Act (PIL). The Swiss Supreme Court specified that the test for bias is "an objective one (and not merely bias in the subjective eyes of a party)" and requires a "cogent proof" of bias.[71] The Swiss Supreme Court often refers to the IBA Guidelines on Conflicts of Interest in International Arbitration (IBA Guidelines) and described them as being "useful" and

---

[60] *See* Chapter 11, Section 2 (Australia).
[61] [2017] FCA 648.
[62] [2017] FCA 648 at [242].
[63] Chapter 23, Section 2 (United Kingdom).
[64] Regina v. Gough [1993] UKHL 1, 17, which reaffirmed by subsequent cases. *See* Chapter 3.
[65] Peter J. Rees QC, Judicial Decisions on Arbitrator Independence, Speech presented at the ICC Arbitration Day: Arbitrator Independence, Pari (June 4, 2010), 5.
[66] In Cofely Ltd v. Anthony Bingham and Knowles [2016] EWHC 240 (Comm), the court removed the arbitrator following repeat appointment by Knowles. The arbitrator derived 25 percent of his income from these appointments. In W. Ltd v. M. Sdn Bhd [2016] 1 CLC 437, 445, Knowles J held that "the fair minded and informed observer would not conclude that there was a real possibility that the Mr Haigh QC was biased or lack independence or impartiality. *See* Chapter 3.
[67] Halliburton Company v. Chubb Bermuda Insurance Ltd and others [2018] EWCA Civ. 817. In December 2016, the court refused to remove M as arbitrator. Halliburton appealed and the Supreme Court heard the appeal in November 2019.
[68] Chapter 23, Section 2.2 (United Kingdom).
[69] Cofely Ltd v. Anthony Bingham and Knowles [2016] EWHC 240 (Comm).
[70] *Supra* note 68.
[71] Chapter 22, Section 4 (Switzerland).

"'susceptible of contributing to the harmonization and unification of standards governing conflicts of interest."[72] Swiss courts are apparently of the view that the concept of independence should incorporate impartiality when considering bias.[73]

At the other end of the spectrum, French courts have a strict interpretation of the arbitrators' conflict of interest.[74] Article 1456, Paragraph 2 of the Code of Civil Procedure (CPC) requires arbitrators to disclose all circumstances that may give rise to reasonable doubt regarding their independence or impartiality.[75] Arbitrators do not have to disclose a known fact, or a fact, which may not influence the arbitrator's judgment but an arbitrator must disclose an ongoing business relationship with a party deriving from the frequency, or the regularity of appointments and a relationship between an arbitrator and a party's counsel.[76] The judicial saga of *Avax v. Tecnimont*[77] is a seminal case in which French courts examined whether an award should be set aside following the arbitrator's conflict of interest arising out of a gradual and incomplete disclosure.[78] The French report confirmed that French judges check if the information at issue "was publically known or not" and "whether the facts at issue would have affected the arbitrator's judgment."[79]

3.2 Conflict of Interest

Arbitration is now practiced in a global village. Concepts that were local are now global. What was permissible in small villages is now scrutinized through the lens of a larger world, which is intricately connected by technology. Firms have gone global with clients spanning the globe. The obligations for disclosure on individuals are no longer constrained to local offices but must ensure arduous searches in places that these individuals may never have been. Individuals often find that they have conflicts resulting with individuals and entities they did not know existed, that they have never met or are unlikely to ever meet. Conflict of interest has a wide definition in international arbitration.

---

[72] *Id.*
[73] Id.
[74] *See* Chapter 14 (France) and Chapter 3.
[75] For some interesting French cases, *see* Cass. Civ. 1st, Mar. 16, 1999, Etat du Qatar v. Société Creighton, 96-12748, (1999) Revue de l'Arbitrage, 308; CA Paris, Sept. 9, 2010, Consorts Allaire v. SAS SGS Holding France, (2011) Revue de l'Arbitrage, 686; CA Paris, Mar. 10, 2011, Société Nykcool AB v. Société Dole France et al, 09/21413, (2011) Revue de l'Arbitrage, 732; and Cass. Civ., 1st, Oct. 10, 2012, Société Tesco v. Société Neoelectra Group, 11-20299.
[76] *See* Chapter 14, Section 3 (France).
[77] *See* various French courts decisions and comments published in French: CA Paris, Feb. 12, 2009, no. 07/22164 (the Paris Court of Appeal decision), Thomas Clay, (2009) Recueil Dalloz 2959; Thomas Clay, (2009) Revue de l'Arbitrage 186; Philippe Schweizer (2009) ASA Bulletin 520; Cass. Civ., 1st, Nov. 4, 2010, no. 09-12.716 (the first decision of the Cour de Cassation on the matter), Thomas Clay, (2010) Dalloz 2933; Thomas Clay, (2010) Cahiers de l'Arbitrage 1147; CA Reims, Nov. 2, 2011, no. 10/02888 (the Reims Court of Appeal decision setting aside the award again), Thomas Clay, (2011) Dalloz 3023; Eric Loquin (2012) Revue Trimestrielle Droit Commercial 518; Thomas Clay, (2011) Cahiers de l'Arbitrage 1109; Denis Bensaude, (2012) Gazette du Palais no. 22-24, 15; Cass. Civ., 1st, June 25, 2014, no. 11-26.529 (the second decision of the Cour de Cassation), Thomas Clay, (2014) Cahiers de l'Arbitrage 547; Jean-Jacques Arnaldez et Ali Mezghani, (2015) Revue de l'Arbitrage 85; CA Paris, Apr. 12, 2016, no. 14/14884 (another decision of the Paris Court of Appeal), Thomas Clay, (2016) Dalloz 2589; Eric Loquin, (2017) Revue de l'Arbitrage, 234 ; Cass. Civ., 1st, Dec. 19, 2018, no. 16-18.349 (the third decision of the Cour de Cassation), Jérémy Jourdan-Marques, *Chronique d'arbitrage: La fin de la saga Tecnimont*, DALLOZ ACTUALITÉ, Jan. 19, 2019; Claire Debourg, *Obligation de révélation de l'arbitre et obligation de s'informer à la charge des parties: un équilibre encore perfectible*, DALLOZ ACTUALITÉ, Feb. 1, 2019.
[78] See Chapter 14, Section 3 (France) and Chapter 3.
[79] See Chapter 14, Section 3 (France).

In an attempt to narrow the meaning of this wide encompassing obligation, conflict of interest is defined as "a real or seeming incompatibility between the interests of two of a lawyer's clients such that the lawyer is disqualified from representing both clients if the dual representation adversely affects either client or if the clients do not consent."[80] The absence of an independent and impartial tribunal (along with procedural irregularities) poses threats to the enforceability of awards. Countries have different standards of conflict of interest. Soft laws such as the IBA Guidelines provide useful guidance. However, they do not override any applicable national law or arbitral rules chosen by the parties.[81]

A majority of jurisdictions discussed in the various country reports have adopted or incorporated Article 12 of the UNCITRAL Model Law. Their analysis have revealed different approaches on how the UNCITRAL Model Law has been amended and interpreted to compensate for the perceived inadequacies. What is particularly interesting in the reviewed jurisdictions are the rationales behind the various modifications.

Upon initial review, it is apparent that the overall understanding of what constitutes conflict of interest in the various jurisdictions is a reaction to perceived relationships between nominated and/or confirmed arbitrators and their relation to parties and/or their selected counsel. In addition, the reaction by parties and counsel to selected arbitrators appears to vary from jurisdictions to jurisdictions. Several factors come into play depending on the size and sophistication of the jurisdiction. National law, the size of the qualified arbitrators pool, the interrelationship of the law practices in those jurisdictions, and the jurisprudence of what constitutes bias and misconduct all have an impact on how conflict of interest is perceived. The equation ultimately being (but not exclusively) the larger the case is, the more complex the scrutiny is on the nominated or sitting arbitrators based on their relationships in those jurisdictions that the case touches and beyond.

The modifications of the basic principles of the UNCITRAL Model Law have been introduced in the various jurisdictions for the ostensible reasons of protecting the parties and ensuring the integrity of the arbitral systems, which are seen as beyond the constitutional protections afforded by the traditional institutions that offer protection. It is assumed that if the principles are widened and the scope of obligations narrowed, the interest of all concerned are preserved. The result of this has been somewhat mixed and in certain jurisdictions has produced unintended consequences. Those consequences can be seen when we look at the approach taken by various jurisdictions described in this book. The codification of conflicts though legislation, case law precedent and custom have been deemed necessary.[82] It is necessary to tackle perceived deficiencies in the system. However, to varying degrees the outcomes have appeared to be less than optimal.

In Argentina, the notion of conflict of interest has been widened. The legislation enacted has created extra obligations on arbitrators to disclose information that would not be considered as pertinent in other jurisdictions. Article 19 of the Argentinean Federal Law on International Arbitration adds two grounds for the challenge of arbitrators that are not included in the generic definition of the UNCITRAL Model Law.[83] In Argentina, a party can challenge an arbitrator if he or she, or members of his or her law firm, consulting firm,

---

[80] GARNER BLACK'S LAW DICTIONARY 363 (Bryan A. Garner ed., 10th ed. 2014).
[81] See Chapter 3, Section 2.2.
[82] For instance, Chapter 10 (Argentina) and Chapter 21 (Switzerland).
[83] See Chapter 10, Section 4.2 (Argentina). The Argentinean report indicates that an arbitrator's challenge as to his or her independence or impartiality "must be admitted without the possibility of proof to the contrary."

or an entity of that kind, (1) acts as counsel or representative(s) to one of the parties to the arbitration where the arbitrator is being challenged, in another arbitration, or litigation, regardless of the issue under discussion, or (2) if such other arbitration or legal proceeding have the same cause or purpose as the arbitration in which the arbitrator in question is acting, and the arbitrator or the other persons mentioned act as counsel or representative(s) to a third party. The consequences resulting from the modifications have been to widen the scope of the principles beyond interpretation and has led to additional parameters to challenge awards in the courts. The modifications in themselves are not to be criticized given the particularities of the given jurisdiction, but it has been suggested that the grounds codified were meant to achieve another purpose. The execution was misaligned as a result. The Argentinean report views both grounds as "bad legislative technique" and the resulting consequences are "unnecessary and excessive."[84]

Other countries have a very limited reference to the concept of conflict of interest.[85] The approach taken is not to expand the concept or obligations but to redefine them. These obligations have become bespoke. At the end of the spectrum, some countries do not refer to conflict of interest.[86] Poland provides another example of the limited reference to conflict of interest. The Polish Code of Civil Procedure does not indicate any specific examples of situations, which may raise doubts as to an arbitrator's impartiality or independence. As a result, arbitrators usually take into consideration the IBA Guidelines, unless the rules of a permanent arbitration court or the arbitration agreement provide provisions in this respect.[87] This approach is somewhat akin to the approach in Nigeria where there are no separate rules on conflict of interest aside from IBA Guidelines.[88] The approach in both jurisdictions must be contrasted with the Italian approach, which has sought to redefine the international guidelines by employing its own guidelines, which do not align with the internationally recognized IBA Guidelines.[89]

4 ARBITRATOR MISCONDUCT

At a basic level, misconduct is an unacceptable or improper behavior by a professional person. While conducting the proceedings in an international arbitration, an arbitral tribunal has an inherent duty to preserve the fairness and integrity of the arbitral proceedings and the enforceability of the award. This duty stems from public policy. In other words, any kind of misconduct on the part of an arbitral tribunal will be used to set aside that arbitral tribunal's award. The misconduct of an arbitrator when crystallized can lead national courts to set aside any award.

Most national laws do not contain any definition of the term *misconduct*. It is interesting to note that certain country reports do not refer to the concept of misconduct or mention the word of misconduct.[90] Other country reports refer to it in passing but it appears that misconduct is not an issue in itself although the concept seems to be a factor when arbitrators are challenged or

---

[84] *Id.*
[85] *See* Chapter 16 (Italy), Chapter 18 (Poland), Chapter 15 (Germany), and Chapter 17 (Nigeria).
[86] *See* Chapter 13 (China), Chapter 19 (Russia), and Chapter 14 (France).
[87] *See* Chapter 18 (Poland).
[88] *See* Chapter 17 (Nigeria).
[89] *See* Chapter 16 (Italy).
[90] *See* Chapter 15 (Germany), Chapter 13 (China), Chapter 10 (Argentina), Chapter 18 (Poland), Chapter 12 (Bulgaria), Chapter 19 (Russia), and Chapter 23 (Ukraine).

parties are seeking to set aside an award.[91] Other country reports highlight the importance given to the concept of misconduct.[92]

It is this very lack of uniform definition that could lead domestic courts into considering various arbitral misbehaviors or irregularities as fitting the definition. Domestic courts in the various jurisdictions have instead resorted to defining *misconduct* as various acts and procedural irregularities that would constitute either a breach of the rule of natural justice or the arbitrator acting outside his powers or in excess of her jurisdiction. Procedural misconduct raises due process concerns that can support a challenge against the arbitrator.[93]

The UNCITRAL Model law, which influenced many national arbitration legislations, provides in its Article 12(2) that "[a]n arbitrator may be challenged only if circumstances exist that give rise to justifiable doubts as to his impartiality or independence."[94] What constitutes arbitrator or tribunal misconduct has not been dealt with in some of the various chapters, but it is worth looking at a few individual jurisdictions to see how this concept is treated. Procedural misconduct raises due process concerns and challenging an arbitrator on a procedural irregularity can only be successful when the irregularity is of such a severe nature that it does not fall within the discretion that is granted arbitrators.[95]

In England, this lacuna has been minimized as the concept of arbitrator misconduct as a ground for setting aside an arbitral award was replaced in the English Arbitration Act 1996 (the 1996 Act) with the term *serious irregularity*.[96] Parties can also rely on the concept of arbitrator misconduct to apply for the arbitrator removal, inter alia, where (1) circumstances exist that give rise to justifiable doubts as to his impartiality or (2) where she has refused or failed properly to

---

[91] *See* Chapter 14 (France) and Chapter 16 (Italy).
[92] *See* Chapter 11 (Australia), Chapter 22 (Switzerland), Chapter 23 (United Kingdom), Chapter 24 (United States), and Chapter 17 (Nigeria).
[93] *See* Chapter 4.
[94] UNCITRAL Model Law on International Commercial Arbitration (1985), with amendments as adopted in 2006.
[95] See Chapter 4.
[96] What constitutes "serious irregularity" is defined in Section 68(2) and what constitutes "substantial jurisdiction" is also defined in Section 82 (1) of the English Arbitration Act 1996. English courts will apply a high threshold before it will interfere into the arbitration process. The test is onerous since the applicant needs to demonstrate that the serious irregularity falls within the exhaustive list described in section 68 of the 1996 Arbitration Act and caused or will have caused substantial injustice to the applicant. They include (1) failure by the tribunal to comply with Section 33 of the Arbitration Act (containing the general duties of the tribunal, e.g., to give each party a reasonable opportunity to present its case); (2) the tribunal exceeding its powers (not including issues of substantive jurisdiction, covered by Section 67); (3) failure by the tribunal to conduct the proceedings in accordance with the procedure agreed by the parties; (4) failure by the tribunal to deal with all of the issues that were put to it; (5) any arbitral or other institution or person vested by the parties with powers in relation to the proceedings or the award exceeding its powers; (6) uncertainty or ambiguity as to the effect of the award; (7) the award being obtained by fraud or the award or the way in which it was procured being contrary to public policy; (8) failure to comply with the requirements as to the form of the award; or (9) any irregularity in the conduct of the proceedings or in the award, which is admitted by the tribunal or by any arbitral or other institution or person vested by the parties with powers in relation to the proceedings or the award. Although the appeals on serious irregularity are rarely successful, the English Commercial Court recently set aside part of a final award for serious irregularities and remitted the matter to the tribunal in the M.V. Ocean Glory case. The court took the view that the arbitral tribunal had followed a course of action not advocated by either party, did not give the parties an opportunity to comment on the tribunal's proposal to make such an award, and relied upon considerations not raised by the parties and which the parties had no opportunity to address before the award was made. See Lorand Shipping v. Davof Trading (Africa) BV (MV "Ocean Glory") [2014] EWHC 3521 (Comm), as well as Chapter 23 (United Kingdom).

conduct the proceedings and substantial injustice has been caused or will be caused to the applicant pursuant to Section 24 of the 1996 Act.[97]

In Nigeria, the courts have resorted to the definition of misconduct under the common law.[98] In the case of *Kano State Urban Development Board* v. *Fanz Construction Company Limited*,[99] the Supreme Court examined English law and distilled aspects of behavior that could fall into this category. In Italy, Article 829(1) of the Italian Civil Procedure Code makes clear that arbitrators' lack of independence and neutrality or misconduct during the arbitral proceedings is not per se grounds for setting the award aside. However, no definition of misconduct is proffered. In Australia, a party may invoke a lack of due process (or violation of procedural public policy) during arbitral proceedings[100] as a ground to annul the arbitral award. Again, various parties have attempted to vacate arbitral award on such grounds but have usually failed because Australian courts have "construed those grounds narrowly, particularly over the last decade."[101]

In the US, Section 10 of the FAA enumerates four specific grounds on which courts may vacate arbitral awards: corruption, fraud, impartiality, and misconduct or incompetence. However, there has been an intense debate over the existence of an additional ground known as the arbitrator's manifest disregard of the law.[102] Again, misconduct is not specifically defined but the

---

[97] In the recent case of P v. Q, the claimant alleged that the tribunal committed multiple grounds of misconduct were alleged by the claimant in an LCIA arbitration: (1) the tribunal improperly delegated its role to the tribunal secretary, by systematically entrusting the secretary with responsibilities going beyond what was permissible under the LCIA Rules and LCIA Policy; (2) the chairman breached his mandate as an arbitrator and his duty not to delegate by seeking the views of the tribunal secretary, who was not party to the arbitration or a member of the tribunal, entitled to make decisions on substantial procedural issues; (3) the other arbitrators forming the tribunal also breached their mandate as arbitrators and their duty not to delegate by failing to participate sufficiently in the arbitration proceedings, and the decision making process; (4) circumstances existed that gave rise to justifiable doubts about the chairman's independence and impartiality, following comments that the chairman had made at an international conference; and (5) the chairman breached his duty to maintain the confidentiality of the arbitral proceedings. However, the court rejected all the grounds advanced and dismissed the claimant's application in its entirety. P v. Q [2017] EWHC 194 (Comm), 14. *See* Chapter 23 (United Kingdom).

[98] Uzoma H. Azikiwe & Festus Onvia, *Nigeria*, GLOBAL ARBITRATION REVIEW (Oct. 19, 2015), https://globalarbitrationreview.com/insight/the-european-middle-eastern-and-african-arbitration-review-2016/1036953/nigeria.

[99] (1986) 5 NWLR (Pt. 39) 74 at 89–90. The Supreme Court provided a list of situations that may constitute misconduct as follows: (1) where there is irregularity in the proceedings, as, for example where the arbitrator failed to give the parties notice of the time and place of the meeting; or (2) where the agreement required the evidence to be taken orally and the arbitrator received affidavits; or (3) where the arbitrator refused to hear the evidence of a material witness; or (4) where the examination of witnesses was taken out of the parties' hands; or (6) where the arbitrator failed to have foreign documents translated; or (7) where the reference being to two or more arbitrators they did not act together; or (8) where the arbitrator after hearing evidence from both arbitrators, received further evidence from one without informing or hearing the other; or (9) where the arbitrator attended the deliberations of the appeal board reviewing his award; or (10) where the arbitrator failed to act fairly toward both parties. In A. Savoia Ltd v. A.O. Sonubi (2000) 12 NWLR (Part 682) 53, the Supreme Court held that misconduct arises in the following circumstances: (1) where the arbitrator fails to comply with the terms, express or implied, of the arbitration agreement; (2) where, even if the arbitrator complied with the terms of the arbitration agreement, the arbitrator makes an award which on grounds of public policy ought not to be enforced; (3) where the arbitrator has been bribed or corrupted; (4) technical misconduct, such as where the arbitrator makes a mistake as to the scope of the authority conferred by the agreement of reference; this, however, does not mean that every irregularity of procedure amounts to misconduct; (5) where the arbitrator or umpire fails to decide all the matters that were referred to him or her; (6) where the arbitrator or umpire has breached the rules of natural justice; and (7) if the arbitrator or umpire has failed to act fairly toward both parties as, for example, by hearing one party but refusing to hear the other or by deciding the case on a point not put by the parties.

[100] Art. 34(2)(a)(ii) and Art. 34(2)(b)(ii) or the award being beyond the terms of the submission to arbitration (Art. 34(2)(a)(iii)). *See* Chapter 11, Section 4 (Australia).

[101] Chapter 11, Section 4 (Australia).

[102] *See* Chapter 24, Section 7.1 (United States). The Supreme Court enounced the standard in dicta in its 1953 decision in Wilko v. Swan (346 US 427, 436–437 (1953)). For decades, every federal circuit court slowly adopted the standard as binding law. In 2008, the US Supreme Court cast doubt on the standard's universal acceptance when it issued its

US report suggests that in the area of arbitrator misconduct US courts consider the arbitrator as the "ultimate decision-maker, whether relating to claims of conflicts of interest, evidentiary issues, or misapplication of applicable law."[103]

In France, Article 1464 (3) CPC provides that arbitrators shall act with celerity and loyalty in the conduct of the proceedings. But, these obligations will not be considered or construed as misconduct. Instead, the consequences that follows from this are of a more personal nature to the arbitral tribunal.[104] In Switzerland, the interpretation of misconduct is more in line with procedural misconduct.[105] This usually encompasses procedural irregularities that are expressed as the violation of due process pursuant to Article 190(2) of PIL.[106]

Without a proper definition, the concept of misconduct will continue to plague arbitration and awards rendered by arbitrators. This has best been illustrated in the work by Park and Paulson where they indicate that "[t]he power to set aside awards on the vague grounds of arbitrator misconduct should be replaced by a provision allowing awards to be challenged only for clearly enumerated procedural deficiencies, or for fundamental discord between what or how the arbitrator decided and what or how the parties authorized him to decide."[107]

5 ARBITRATION CLAUSES: INTERPRETATION AND SCOPE

The "who" and "how" of the interpretation of arbitration clauses varies among countries. The "who" question refers to the body entrusted in determining the scope of the arbitration clauses – arbitral panel or a court. Under the kompetenz–kompetenz principle courts generally defer to the arbitration panel the jurisdiction to interpret and to determine the scope of an arbitration clause. However, some courts will intervene when the validity of the arbitration clause is at issue. The "how" question relates to the approach of the courts when called upon to interpret a clause – liberally or narrowly. The answer to this question relates to the view of government policy or courts of the value of arbitration. For example, in Argentina, despite a 2018 reform of its arbitration law along the lines of the UNCITRAL Model Law, courts have traditionally disfavored the reach of arbitration and have "favoured a *restrictive* interpretation of arbitration agreements, based on their view of arbitration as the result of the parties' waiver of their constitutional right to

---

decision in Hall Street Associates, L.L.C. v. Mattel, Inc. (552 US 576 (2008)). The majority in Hall Street questioned whether Wilko's use of the term "manifest disregard" merely referred to the aggregate effect of the enumerated section 10 grounds rather than a new standard of review. *See* Stuart M. Boyarsky, *The Uncertain Status of the Manifest Disregard Standard One Decade after Hall Street*, 123 DICKINSON LAW REVIEW 167 (2018), ideas.dickinsonlaw.psu.edu/dlr/vol123/iss1/5.

[103] Chapter 24, Section 8 (United States).
[104] For example, the breach of the deadline to render an award may give rise to the liability of arbitrators, subject to evidence being filed that a damage resulted from the personal misconduct of the arbitrator. Thus, a party can take action before French courts against an arbitrator if he or she committed a "personal fault," which the French report explained as being a fault that is incompatible with his judicial functions.
[105] *See* Chapter 4.
[106] The Swiss Supreme Court recently considered a string of cases (for instance decision 4A_478/2017, decision 4A_247/2017, decision 4A_600/2010 and 4A_214/2011) in which it dismissed the parties' allegation of the parties for violation of due process and particularly the violation of the right to be heard. The Swiss report highlights that a party needs to protest "immediately, clearly and with a sufficient degree of insistence at any perceived violation of one's procedural guarantees, or one will be deemed, by operation of the principle of good faith, to have waived that basis of objection." *See* Chapter 22, Section 5 (Switzerland).
[107] *See* William P. Park & Jan Paulson, *The Binding Force of International Arbitral Awards*, 23 VIRGINIA JOURNAL OF INTERNATIONAL LAW ASSOCIATION 284–285 (1983).

submit their disputes to national courts."[108] In one Argentinean case, parties agreed upon an arbitration clause with a "carve out" provision, according to which claims for price adjustment were to be litigated before a court and all other claims to be arbitrated. However, a court intervened and did not allow the arbitral panel to determine jurisdiction as required in law and claimed jurisdiction over all the different types of claims by simply ignoring the arbitration clause.[109] In sum, Argentina is an arbitration-unfriendly country because of courts restrictive interpretation of the scope of arbitration clauses, failure to fully comply with the principle of kompetenz–kompetenz, and intervening when it determines a basic right or law is involved by asserting that the courts may only judge such matters. In contrast to Argentina, German courts generally apply a broad interpretation to standard arbitration agreements, holding that multiple claims are arbitrable.

The current trend in Australia is to broadly construe generic arbitration clauses ("arising out of," "in connection with," or "relating to" the contract). In contrast, English courts have applied and even more liberal approach by recognizing a presumption that the parties intended all types of disputes to be arbitrated.[110] In sum, the English approach accepts a broad view of the scope of standard arbitration clauses, while Australian law uses a totality of the circumstances providing greater discretion to the courts in determining the scope of such clauses.

Switzerland is clearly a pro-arbitration country where arbitration clauses are broadly construed supported by the rationales of the efficacy of arbitration and the efficiency of having all claims being based on the same facts argued in a single venue. By including an arbitration clause in their contract, the parties are presumed to have waived their constitutional rights to a trial and that the scope of the clause is comprehensive, with the burden on the challenging party to show that the clause should be interpreted more narrowly. Most significantly, unlike English law and many other laws, Swiss courts allow the arbitration clause to extend to third parties. Thus, noncontracting parties who are beneficiaries may seek arbitration under the arbitration clause. One area where Swiss courts have been more restrictive is in areas where a party has failed to meet pre-arbitration conditions or the award is belated. Thus, the parties' failure to fulfill an obligation to first seek mediation or conciliation or the issuance of an award after the time limitation set by the country would invalidate the award.

Current UK law aligns with Swiss on the interpretation of the scope of arbitration clauses. The contemporary approach of the English courts is that any jurisdiction or arbitration clause in an international commercial contract should be construed to "encompass the widest range of potential disputes that its terms will reasonably permit, including non-contractual claims and claims involving an admission of a criminal purpose."[111] Lord Hoffman following the Swiss approach asserts that there should be a presumption that the parties who agree to arbitration intend that all disputes would be satisfied in a "one-stop" dispute resolution.[112] With few exceptions, tort claims are generally, but not always held to be within the scope of a general arbitration clause.

Ukrainian law, under its International Arbitration Statute (IAS), has recognized a number of presumptions favoring the enforceability of arbitration clauses in international contracts even when they prove to be defective. When in doubt, courts are expected to rule in favor of the

---

[108] *See* Chapter 10, Section 4 (Argentina).
[109] Supermarkets Norte v. Carrefour et al., Court of Appeal on commercial matters, Branch F, Nov. 27, 2014, available at Abeledo Perrot No.: AR/JUR/90086/2014.
[110] Fiona Trust & Holding Corp v. Privalov [2007] UKHL 40 (Lord Hoffman).
[111] *See* Chapter 23 (United Kingdom), citing DAVID S. J. SUTTON, JUDITH GILL, & MATTHEW GEARING, RUSSELL ON ARBITRATION 26, para. 2-004 (24th ed. 2015).
[112] Fiona Trust & Holding Corporation v. Privalov [2007] UKHL 40 per Lord Hoffmann at 13.

validity, operability, and capability of arbitration clauses. The courts, if possible, are encouraged to repair defects in the arbitration clause through interpretation (construction) under the principle of in favorem validitatis. In domestic arbitration, the courts are much more conservative in their interpretation of arbitration clauses, including a narrower view of the scope of the clause and less likely to repair defects in the clause.[113]

Article 808 of the Italian Civil Procedure Code states that "in case of doubt, the arbitration clause should be interpreted as applying to all disputes arising out from the contract or from the relationship to which it refers." However, in practice, this is not the case, and there is a reverse presumption that arbitration clauses should be narrowly construed since arbitration is viewed as a less favorable means of dispute resolution and resolution through the court system is preferred. For example, when an arbitration clause in a service contract states only disputes "arising out from the interpretation of the contract," the clause does not apply to claims for breach against the nonperforming party.[114] Similarly, the clause providing for arbitration of "all disputes arising out from the contract" is presumed not to cover tort claims brought by a customer against a contractor,[115] claims of unfair competition and claims for precontractual liability.[116]

In international arbitration is concerned, French courts may be considered to be very liberal in finding a "common intent of the parties" to arbitrate.[117] In fact, the use of the word *arbitration* coupled with a place of arbitration in a contracting is all that is needed to enter into a binding arbitration agreement. Also, there is a long tradition in French law that arbitration clauses may extend to third parties in which they can bring a claim in arbitration and be bound by arbitration agreements. This includes third-party beneficiaries and third parties involved in the performance of the contract.

The question of interpretation of an arbitration agreement has been subject to several Supreme Court judgments in Poland. In the leading case, the court held that an arbitration agreement should be interpreted neither restrictively nor extensively with a view to upholding the jurisdiction of the arbitration tribunal. The interpretation of an arbitration agreement should ensure that the common intention of the parties is established and respected.[118] Some scholarly commentators emphasize that the jurisprudence of the Supreme Court continues to perceive an arbitration agreement as a divergence from a constitutionally guaranteed right to the courts, which has led to restrictive interpretations of the scope of arbitration agreements.[119] Thus, in practice, Poland does not adhere to the pro-arbitration presumption, which is considered international best practice.

The United States has adhered to a pro-arbitration policy, with the US Supreme Court expanding the scope of arbitration. Regarding the interpretation of arbitration clauses, the court has held that questions of arbitrability, including the evaluation of the merits of the case (frivolousness of the claims), are solely within the province of arbitrators.[120] The American courts

---

[113] *See* Chapter 22, Section 7 (Ukraine).
[114] Court of Cassation, Jan. 18, 2017, no. 1213 (2017) 17 Guida al diritto 62. Yet, an arbitration clause referring to "disputes arising out from the interpretation, conclusion, and termination of the contract" also covers disputes about contractual breaches: Court of Cassation, Sept. 10, 2012, no. 15068 (2012) Giustizia civile massimario 1101.
[115] Court of Cassation, Feb. 15, 2017, no. 4035 (2017) Foro Italiano – Repertorio, entry "Arbitrato," no. 39; similarly, *see* Court of Cassation, Feb. 3, 2012, no. 1674 (2014) Rivista dell'Arbitrato 589.
[116] Court of Cassation, Oct. 13, 2016, no. 20673 (2017) Rivista dell'Arbitrato 87.
[117] Chapter 14, Section 2 (France).
[118] Supreme Court of Nov. 16, 2016, case I CSK 780/15, Lex no. 2195669.
[119] Grzegorz Żmij, *Zapis na sąd polubowny*, in DIAGNOZA ARBITRAŻU 82, 152 (Beata Gessel-Kalinowska vel Kalisz ed., 2014). Recently, a more liberal position was taken by Supreme Court, *supra* note 118 .
[120] *See* Henry Schein v. Archer and White, 138 Sup. Ct. 2678 (2019).

have broadened the scope of the standard arbitration clause ("any dispute or claim arising out of") to include issues related to statutory law, employee rights, and intellectual property, as well as tort claims. The court in *Brennan v. Opus Bank*[121] held that claims under the Trade Secrets Act, as well as its tort claims for interference with business relationships and breach of duties owed from employment relationships are within the scope of the standard arbitration clause.

6 ANTI-ARBITRATION POLICY

Australia not only has a pro-arbitration policy, the government is aggressively marketing Australia as a major venue for international commercial policy. Also, the Australian judiciary has advanced a pro-arbitration stance, especially in judicial decisions over the past ten years. The arbitrability of issues depends on whether they are outside the scope of public interests "not capable of settlement by arbitration."[122] For example, disputes that involve the applicability of antitrust or competition law have been considered to involve "wider public interests – being non-arbitrable – due to their impact on third parties."[123] Although, the courts have made it clear that a commercial dispute must have more than a tangential connection to the underlying rationales of public interest or policy behind statutory laws to be non-arbitral. In competition law, the impact on third parties is greatest in the areas of "regulating exclusive dealing, resale price maintenance, horizontal conduct or cartel conduct."[124]

A key area of debate is whether the policy in favor of arbitration extends to consumer transactions. As with competition law, there is no direct statutory law that deals with the issue of the arbitrability of consumer disputes (B2C). So again, the question becomes whether the general public policy relating to the greater public interest is sufficient element in consumer disputes.[125] Under Australian Consumer Law (ACL), three explicit provisions meet the threshold of non-arbitrability – misleading and deceptive conduct, consumer guarantees, and unfair contract terms. But there remains a structural problem relating to international commercial arbitration under Australian law. Oddly, the ACL also applies to various types of commercial transactions.[126] Thus, arbitration clauses can technically be voided in commercial contracts if the dispute involves one of these protected areas in the ACL. More generally, Australian law has developed a principle of unconscionability that applies to consumer and commercial transactions. This is also the case in the United States,[127] but in reality courts almost never use the unconscionability doctrine in commercial contract disputes. There is general agreement that the public policy in favor of arbitration is stronger than the public policy behind the protections given in the ACL, at least in commercial contract disputes. Specific laws in Australia preclude the use of arbitration. This is the case under the Insurance Contracts Act and the Carriage of Goods by Sea Act (ocean transport).

In 2017, Bulgaria amended its Civil Procedure Code and its International Commercial Arbitration Act to void arbitration clauses in consumer contracts. It further states that arbitrators

---

[121] 796 F.3d 1125, 1130 (9th Cir. 2015).
[122] Comandate Marine Corp v. Pan Australia Shipping Pty Ltd. [2006] FCAFC 192 at [200] (Dec. 20, 2006).
[123] Chapter 11 (Australia). *See also* Nicola v. Ideal Image Development Corporation Incorporated [2009] FCA 1177, at 56 (cases involving "competition law have frequently been cited as examples of claims unsuitable, by reason of public policy, for arbitration").
[124] Chapter 11 (Australia).
[125] (2006) 157 FCR 45 at 98.
[126] *See* Luke Nottage & Justin Malbon, *Introduction*, in CONSUMER LAW AND POLICY IN AUSTRALIA AND NEW ZEALAND 3–38 (Justin Malbon & Luke Nottage eds., 2013).
[127] Uniform Commercial Code §2-302; Restatement (Second) of Contracts §208.

that issue an award in a case involving a consumer are subject to fines. Unfortunately, the courts have given the new restriction retroactive effect by refusing to enforce awards issued prior to the enactment of the amendment even in cases where the limitation period has lapsed. In another area, the Bulgarian Supreme Court has placed a restriction on the power of arbitrators to adapt contracts due to change of circumstances. It is no longer an automatic power because it can be used only when the arbitration clause expressly specifies that adaptation is an authorized power or remedy. Further, if an arbitral panel did adapt the contract to a change of circumstances, under Bulgarian law this would not have a res judicata effect and would likely be unenforceable under the New York Convention.[128] Oddly, the grounds for not enforcing an award were reduced in the 2017 Amendments – violation of public policy was removed as a ground for terminating an award. This unusual deletion of a traditional ground for award nullification was due to the over use of this rationale by the Bulgarian Courts.[129]

Russian law broadly recognizes the jurisdiction of arbitration courts to hear any dispute arising from civil law relationships including civil rights claims.[130] In fact, the right to arbitrate is considered a constitutional right.[131] The one exception is that claims made under bankruptcy law cannot be referred to arbitration. A more unique limitation on arbitrability relates to exclusive jurisdiction given to the robust Russian commercial court system. Russian law grants exclusive jurisdiction over certain matters, such as transfer of immovable property and stocks, intellectual property disputes, and corporate disputes, to commercial courts as opposed to courts of general jurisdiction. The issue is whether the exclusivity of commercial courts over these areas of law also applies to arbitrability? A number of awards have been vacated based on the exclusivity argument, but recent amendments have recognized that most of these disputes can be captured within the scope of an arbitration clause. Finally, another vague limitation on arbitrability is that disputes with public aspects can be referred to the court system. The main area of exclusion from arbitration is government procurement contracts. However, the exclusion has also been applied in cases of seizure of public property, foreclosure of a mortgage and in privatization contracts. Interestingly, the rationale given by the Russian High Court was that the confidential nature of arbitration is not appropriate in disputes involving public property. Under French law, arbitrators may not declare a company bankrupt or annul a patent or a trademark. However, disputes relating to the use of patents and trademarks are arbitrable.

In China, some issues are simply the capability of arbitral tribunals to resolve. In solvency, real, and intellectual property issues involving registration, family law, criminal law, succession, and right in rem are generally considered beyond the realm of arbitration. As provided for in the New York Convention, and as recognized by most countries a court may vacate or refuse to enforce an award that is contrary to public policy. The Supreme People's Court reversed a lower court decision that an award was unenforceable because it was unconscionable and noted that "public policy should be applied rigidly and cautiously."[132] One curious exception was a Chinese court decision involving an ICC arbitration clause in a joint venture contract. The court held that one of the disputants was not a party to the joint venture and, therefore, the arbitration clause did not preclude the court from taking jurisdiction. Whether that was a correct decision, a later attempt to enforce an ICC arbitration award was refused on the ground that "the tribunal ignored the

---

[128] Chapter 12, Section 3.2 (Bulgaria).
[129] Id. at Section 4.
[130] Federal Law No. 102, Article 1(2).
[131] Chapter 12, Section 3 (Bulgaria).
[132] Chapter 13, Section 4.8 (China).

effective judgment made previously by the Chinese court, which violated China's judicial sovereignty and therefore is against China's public policy."[133] The key to enforceability of an arbitration award is the timing. A major factor in cases of parallel proceedings is whether the court decision or award happened first. If the award is issued before the court decision, than the claim of unenforceability due to the public policy exception is greatly weakened.

Argentina's view of arbitration is toward the unfriendly side. It not only follows a restrictive approach to interpreting the scope of arbitration clauses, as noted previously, it has adopted an expansive view of judicial intervention based upon public policy and other concerns. First, public policy captures issues of a political, economic, moral or religious nature. Second and more problematic is the Supreme Court's recognition of the appeal of judicial decisions due to arbitrariness as applicable to arbitral awards. The Supreme Court has held that arbitral awards may be reviewed under the principle of arbitrariness when the award may be "unconstitutional, illegal or unreasonable," even if the parties have waived their right of appeal.[134] Thus, an arbitration award may be annulled, at least in domestic commercial arbitration simply because it is deemed to be unreasonable. At its broadest form the arbitrariness principle includes judgments that are "unfounded or because they ignored the law that was undoubtedly applicable to the case, be it because they departed from the proven facts of the case."[135] This disregards the generally accepted view that arbitral awards cannot not be overturned if the arbitrators misapplied or misinterpreted the law or that arbitral panels' finding of facts is not reviewable. Fortunately, the Supreme Court in a subsequent case clarified that arbitral awards are not subject to a de novo review of the facts unless an issue of public policy is at stake. However, the court did not expressly prohibit a judicial review based upon the arbitrariness principles.

German arbitration law merely requires a "proprietary" claim. One noted exception is the non-arbitrability of corporate disputes, such as shareholder claims, if they have binding effect on other shareholders. Over the years, however, the German courts have adopted a more liberal approach. They now allow for arbitrability of shareholder disputes under certain conditions, namely when arbitration clauses meet specific standards that safeguard the procedural participation rights of the other shareholders. One of the most pro-arbitration countries is Switzerland where arbitration clauses are broadly construed and third party arbitration is permitted. Oddly, there is one major exception to Switzerland's pro-arbitration policy (broad construction of arbitration clauses and third party rights to arbitrate). The courts do not automatically defer to the arbitral tribunal's legal treatment of its jurisdiction but rather freely assesses legal questions on jurisdiction and preliminary questions. The courts are bound by the facts as determined by an arbitral panel but not by its reasoning on jurisdictional issues.

English law has traditionally looked favorably on anti-lawsuit injunctions when a party begins litigation in another country despite the existence of an arbitration clause. However, when the disputing parties are from European Union or Lugano Convention countries, the European Court of Justice has held that a member state may not issue anti-lawsuit injunctions. But in cases involving other types of parties, the English courts are generally receptive to granting injunctions (interim and final) to prevent parties to an arbitration agreement commencing or continuing proceedings in the courts of other jurisdictions outside of the EU. Finally, English courts have a narrow view of the public policy exception under the "one-stop" rationale, which holds that

---

[133] *Id.*
[134] José Cartellone Construcciones Civiles S.A. v. Hidroeléctrica Norpatagónica S.A. o Hidronor S.A., Supreme Court, June 1, 2004, Jurisprudencia Argentina (JA) 2004-III-48.
[135] *See* Chapter 10, Section 5.1.3.2 (Argentina).

arbitration clauses should be broadly construed and that courts should refrain from intervening in matters of arbitration. This noninterventionist approach focuses on the state of the arbitration award in the country it was awarded. If there is no challenge being made to the award in the foreign country, then it is unlikely that an English court to allow a challenge in the United Kingdom. If an arbitration award is vacated by a foreign court, English courts require the party attempting to block the enforcement of the award to prove that the annulment decision "offended basic principles of honesty, natural justice and domestic concept of public policy."[136]

Ukrainian arbitration law remains noncomprehensive in context and unclear in meaning. The list of disputes that are not arbitrable include: corporate disputes involving shareholders, disputes related to government procurement contracts, claims related to the insolvency of a Ukrainian company, unfair competition claims, certain issues relating to the ownership of intellectual property, and issues relating to the establishment or liquidation of foreign companies in Ukraine. Most importantly, the law is unclear whether commercial disputes, other than those relating to shareholder rights, are not subject to arbitration.

Italian arbitration law, mostly found in the Civil Procedure Code prohibits the use of arbitration in certain areas of private disputes involving entitlements and in specific legal areas. Non-arbitrable private disputes include issues of citizenship, marriage, parenthood, nationality, and fundamental rights. Areas of law where arbitration are prohibited include public contracts disputes in which the issue at stake concerns the tendering procedure, company disputes in which participation of state prosecutors is mandatory, and disputes concerning debts from bankruptcy.[137] Also, very stringent requirements have made class action arbitration a rarity. Further, class action arbitration has been limited due to the fact that arbitration clauses in consumer contracts are presumed to be unconscionable and invalid.

Areas of French law that bars arbitration include bankruptcy and intellectual property law. For example, arbitrators do not have jurisdiction to declare a patent to be invalid. More importantly, the French Code of Civil Procedure Articles 1448 and 1465 fully embraces the principle of competence–competence, whereby arbitral tribunals have sole authority to determine their own jurisdiction under the arbitration clause. However, French courts may review issues of arbitral jurisdiction after an award is issued.

Under Polish law the public policy exception is used to render awards unenforceable in cases where the damages awarded are punitive in nature or where the damages are considered speculative in nature. In addition, awards most comply with principles (rights) found in the constitution, as well as the core principles of each area of law. More specifically, arbitral awards not conforming to Civil Code provisions dealing with prescription of claims.[138] Another ground for invalidating an award is when there is an incorrect interpretation of provisions on tenders subject to public procurement law.

Surprisingly, the United States, often categorized as a litigation happy country, has pro-arbitration law and policy. The American 1925 Federal Arbitration Act stated that arbitration is the preferred means of dispute resolution as a matter federal policy. In recent times, the US Supreme Court expanded the scope of private arbitration clauses to include statutory claims, such as in the areas of antitrust, collective bargaining, and civil rights. Thus, rights or protections, including claims for sexual harassment in employment may be arbitrated. However, in

---

[136] See Chapter 23, Section 3.1 (United Kingdom).
[137] *See* Chapter 16, Section 4 (Italy).
[138] This position was adopted as early as 1973, and confirmed more recently: see Supreme Court of Dec. 21, 1973, case I CR 663/73, Orzecznictwo Sądów Polskich (OSP) (Jurisprudence of Polish Courts) 1975, no. 1, item. 4; Court of Appeals in Katowice of Oct. 18, 2004, case I ACa 565/04, Lex no. 147145.

one area it has limited the availability of arbitration by placing restrictions on class action arbitration. The Federal Arbitration Act limits merits-based judicial review of arbitral awards, except in very narrow circumstances. The two main anti-arbitration doctrines are the "manifest disregard doctrine" and the public policy exception. Manifest disregard is a judicially created doctrine that allows for a review of a judicial award on its merits. Note that there is no ground for vacating an award where arbitrators merely misinterpret the law. More recently, the Supreme Court has criticized the use of the doctrine to vacate arbitral awards. Unfortunately, the court failed to eliminate the doctrine causing confusion in the lower courts as when it is appropriate to use the doctrine. A more solid ground for vacation is when an arbitral panel disregards clear and unambiguous contract terms.

Since the New York Convention fails to define the term public policy, the scope of the public policy exception varies from country to country.[139] That said, the New York Convention's almost universal recognition suggests that the public policy exception should be narrowly construed and the public policy in favor of the finality of arbitral awards should be protected. The US case law on the issue supports the view that the public policy exception should be used only when the "enforcement of foreign arbitral awards would violate the forum state's most basic notions of morality and justice."[140]

The case of *Eastern Associated Coal Corp. v. United Mine Workers of America, District 7*[141] dealt with the public policy exception. In one case, a company terminated an employee who twice tested positive for marijuana use. The labor arbitrator ordered the employee's reinstatement. The issue in question was whether the reinstatement order was contrary to public policy (safety in the workplace). The US Supreme Court held that the public policy exception applied only to policies that were "explicit, well defined, and dominant," and they must be "ascertained by reference to the laws and legal precedents, not from general considerations of supposed public interests."[142] The court concluded that "the public policy exception is narrow" in that it can be used only when the policy is clearly stated in existing laws or precedents and not to reference to some general public policy concern, thus, affirming the arbitrator's order of reinstatement.

7 CONCLUSION

The country reports showed that countries, as members of the New York Convention, discuss the issues of international commercial arbitration in much the same way through the use of terminology taken from the Convention such as the public policy exception. However, many of the concepts found in the Convention, in national arbitration laws, and in contract practice are empty vessels of meaning. Therefore, despite the great deal of commonality among national arbitration laws the meaning of the concepts used often varies across countries. Examples of key concepts that are generally undefined under black letter law include "agreement in writing,"[143]

---

[139] See Anton G. Maurer, The Public Policy Exception under the New York Convention: History, Interpretation and Application (2012); Bernard Hanotiau & Olivier Caprasse, *Public Policy in International Commercial Arbitration*, in Enforcement of Arbitration Agreements and International Arbitral Awards: The New York Convention in Practice 787 (Emmanuel Gaillard & Domenico di Pietro eds., 2008).
[140] See Parsons & Whittemore Overseas v. Société Générale de l'Industrie du Papier, 508 F.2d 769, 974 (1974).
[141] 531 US 57 (2010).
[142] Citing W R. Grace & Co. v. Rubber Workers, 461 US 757, 766 (1993).
[143] New York Convention, Article II (2).

"under some incapacity,"[144] and "contrary to public policy,"[145] "disputes arising from the contract or related to the contract" (generic arbitration clause); and arbitrator misconduct, such as, (1) "corruption, fraud and undue means,"[146] (2) evident partiality of the arbitrators,[147] (3) "refusing to hear evidence pertinent and material to the controversy or of any other misbehavior by which the rights of any party have been prejudiced,"[148] and where "arbitrators exceeded their powers."[149]

The comparative analyses of the country reports have shown a good deal of variance among countries as to the meaning of these terms. For example, in the area of the public policy exception, what is considered the type of public policy that warrants the vacating of an arbitral award varies significantly. The status of arbitration relative to national courts also diverges across countries from those that can be labeled as pro-arbitration states, arbitration unfriendly states, and those that are somewhere between the two extremes. Thus, it is imperative for the practitioner to consider these variations when drafting an arbitration clause.

In sum, the growth of international arbitration has been accelerating, most recently, the number of cases being heard in Southeast Asian arbitration venues has skyrocketed in recent years. However, this universal recognition of international commercial arbitration as the preferred means of dispute resolution should not be conflated to mean consistency and commonality across national arbitration laws. It is important that the practitioner, academic, and student perform their due diligence in order to understand the nuances of international commercial arbitration.

---

[144] *Id.* at Article V (1)(a).
[145] NY Convention, Article V (2)(b).
[146] American Federal Arbitration Act (FAA), 9 US Code §10 (a)(1).
[147] *Id.* at §10 (a)(2).
[148] *Id.* at §10 (a)(3).
[149] *Id.* at §10 (a)(4).

26

The Shared Control of Arbitral Awards

Friedrich Rosenfeld

1 INTRODUCTION

It is trite law that international arbitration is subject to control. When two parties agree to arbitrate a dispute, the resulting arbitral award will be recognized as producing legal effects only if it fulfills the conditions set forth in the applicable arbitration framework. This is due to the dual foundation of arbitration in party autonomy on the one hand and the applicable arbitration framework on the other.[1] If one turns to the question of who is tasked to exercise this control, the answer is not straightforward. At first glance, it appears as if national courts are the sole guardians to watch over arbitral awards. This view reflects a public–private divide between arbitral tribunals who as private actors render an arbitral award, which is then subject to control by a national court as a public actor.

A closer examination, however, reveals that this impression is inaccurate. The responsibility to control arbitral awards is shared among multiple actors of private and public origin. They include the parties (Section 2), arbitral tribunals (Section 3), arbitral institutions (Section 4), courts at the seat (Section 5), and courts at the place of recognition and enforcement (Section 6). This chapter provides a taxonomy of these five different layers of control.

2 PARTIES

The first actors exercising control over arbitral awards are the parties. While parties neither render arbitral awards nor decide on their vacatur or enforcement, they are able to determine the degree of scrutiny by courts at the post-award stage. Parties thereby exercise a substantial degree of control.

2.1 *Limitations of Post-award Review*

One manifestation of party control is limiting the scope of post-award review.[2] Parties may do so by waiving the right to seek a set-aside of an arbitral award or to oppose its recognition and

---

[1] G. A. Bermann, *International Arbitration and Private International Law*, 381 RECEUIL DES COURS 41, 57 (2015).
[2] *See* M. Scherer, *The Fate of Parties' Agreements on Judicial Review of Awards: A Comparative and Normative Analysis of Party-Autonomy at the Post-award Stage*, 32 ARB. INT'L. 437 (2016); M. Scherer & L. Silberman, *Limits to Party Autonomy at the Post-award Stage*, in LIMITS TO PARTY AUTONOMY IN INTERNATIONAL COMMERCIAL ARBITRATION 443 et seq. (F. Ferrari ed., 2016); Bermann, *supra* note 1, at 398 et seq.

enforcement. A number of jurisdictions acknowledge self-imposed limitations on the scope of review at the post-award stage.[3] Under French law, for example, parties may at any time expressly waive their right to initiate set-aside proceedings.[4] This reflects a liberal approach that emphasizes party autonomy.

Other jurisdictions reject full waivers of recourse against an arbitral award.[5] For example, the Supreme Court of India ruled that parties may not exclude all recourse against an arbitral award.[6] In a similar spirit, the Auckland High Court ruled that any contractual exclusion of a right to review a breach of natural justice will be ineffective.[7] These decisions reflect a more paternalistic approach, which entails limiting parties' autonomy to prohibit post-award institutional or judicial intervention.

In an attempt to strike a balance between these two positions, various jurisdictions have developed more nuanced, intermediary approaches.[8] Some jurisdictions allow parties to waive certain grounds for set-aside that are not directed at protecting the public at large, but exist in the interest of the parties themselves.[9] A California court, for example, ruled that a party can waive only those rights that are conferred under a law created in the parties' benefit.[10] By contrast, a party would be prevented from waiving benefits that are conferred under a law established for a public reason. Other jurisdictions allow waivers from parties that have no link with the place of arbitration.[11] Under Swiss law, for instance, parties may exclude all setting aside proceedings or limit their scope where none of the parties has its domicile, habitual residence or place of business in Switzerland.[12] Beyond this, factors such as the timing of a waiver may also

---

[3] For the approach in Russia, see A. Asoskov, *Admissibility of Agreements on Exclusion of Set-Aside Proceedings with Respect to International Commercial Arbitration Awards Rendered on the Territory of Russia, in* LIBER AMICORUM IN HONOR OF THE 50TH ANNIVERSARY OF ALEXEY ZHILTSOV 15 (A. Muranov et al. eds., 2013).

[4] Article 1522 Code Civil ("By way of a specific agreement the parties may, at any time, expressly waive their right to bring an action to set aside"). Only full waivers are enforceable under French law and parties are not allowed to declare a partial waiver of review; see Scherer & Silberman, *supra* note 2, at 449, with reference to E. Gaillard & P. de Lapasse, *Commentaires Analytiques du Décret du 13 Janvier 2011 Portant Réforme du Droit francais de l' Arbitrage*2011 PARIS J. INT'L ARB. 263 (2011).

[5] See Scherer & Silberman, *supra* note 2, at 448.

[6] Shin Satellite Public Co. Ltd. v. Jain Studios Ltd, Supreme Court of India, Jan. 31, 2006 [2006] 2 628.

[7] Methanex Motunui Ltd v. Spellman [2004] 1 NZLR 95.

[8] For a more detailed overview, see Scherer & Silberman, *supra* note 2, at 446 et seq.

[9] Noble China Inc. v. Lei Kat Cheong, Ontario Court of Justice, Nov. 13, 1998 [1998] Can LII 147908 (ON SC), published in (1998) 42 O.R. (3d) 69; Methanex Motunui Ltd. v. Spellman, Court of Appeal, Wellington, New Zealand, June 17, 2004, [2004] 3 NZLR 454.

[10] Azteca Construction, Inc., v. ADR Consulting, Inc, Court of Appeal, Third District, California, C045316, Aug. 25, 2004.

[11] See, e.g., Article 1718 Belgian Judicial Code ("By an explicit declaration in the arbitration agreement or by a later agreement, the parties may exclude any application for the setting aside of an arbitral award, where none of them is a natural person of Belgian nationality or a natural person having his domicile or normal residence in Belgium or a legal person having its registered office, its main place of business or a branch office in Belgium."). See also Article 51 Swedish Arbitration Act ("If none of the parties is domiciled or has its place of business in Sweden, such parties may in a commercial relationship through an express written agreement exclude or limit the application of the grounds for setting aside an award as are set forth in Section 34. An award which is subject to such an agreement shall be recognized and enforced in Sweden in accordance with the rules applicable to a foreign award.")

[12] See Article 192 (2) Swiss Private International Law Act ("Where none of the parties has its domicile, its habitual residence, or a place of business in Switzerland, they may, by an express statement in the arbitration agreement or in a subsequent agreement in writing, exclude all setting aside proceedings, or they may limit such proceedings to one or several of the grounds listed in Article 190, paragraph 2."). See also, Tunisian Supreme Court, Jan. 18, 2007, Case No. 4674, quoted in UNCITRAL Digest of Case Law on the Model Law on International Commercial Arbitration (United Nations, 2012) 135.

determine its validity.[13] Unlike ex ante waivers, which are declared before a relevant procedural decision has been taken, waivers made on an ex post basis are often viewed less critically.[14] Courts have referred to the prohibition of contradictory behavior,[15] the principle of good faith,[16] principles of reasonableness and fairness,[17] or to the purpose of arbitration to facilitate the efficient resolution of disputes in determining the enforceability of ex post waivers.[18]

---

[13] Likewise, jurisdictions differ as to what constitutes a waiver. Perfunctory arguments without support by pertinent authorities are deemed waived in some jurisdictions. Johnson v. Panetta, 953 F.Supp.2d 244, 250 (D.D.C. 2013); *see also* Nikijuluw v. Gonzales, 427 F.3d 115, 120 n. 3 (1st Cir. 2005) Dillery v. City of Sandusky, 398 F.3d 562, 569 (6th Cir.2005); Bridas S.A.P.I.C. v. Gov't of Turkmenistan, 345 F.3d 347, 356 n. 7 (5th Cir. 2003).

[14] Russian Federation No. 16, Dana Feed A/S v. OOO Arctic Salmon, Federal Arbitrazh Court, Northwestern District, A42-4747/04-13, Dec. 9, 2004 (2008) Yearbook Commercial Arbitration 2008 – Volume XXXIII, 658–665; OLG Karlsruhe [Court of Appeal] (2012) SchiedsVZ, 104. Germany No. 117 / E19, Manufacturer v. Supplier, in liquidation, Oberlandesgericht [Court of Appeal] Munich, 34 Sch 06/05, Mar. 15, 2006 (2009) Yearbook Commercial Arbitration 2009 – Volume XXXIV, 499–503, para. 5; Spain No. 22, Mondial Grain Distributors Company Inc. v. Atlántica Canarias SA, Tribunal Supremo [Supreme Court], Not Indicated, Apr. 26, 1984, (1991) Yearbook Commercial Arbitration 1991 – Volume XVI, 599 – 600, para. 4; Spain No. 72, MK2 S.A. v. Wide Pictures, S.L., Superior Court of Justice of Catalonia, 127/11, Nov. 17, 2011 (2012) Yearbook Commercial Arbitration 2012 – Volume XXXVII, 297–299, para. 35. Spain No. 52, Precious Stones Shipping Ltd v. Querqus Alimentaria, SL, Tribunal Supremo [Supreme Court], Civil Chamber, 2658 of 1999, Nov. 28, 2000 (2007) Yearbook Commercial Arbitration 2007 – Volume XXXII, 540–549, para. 17; Switzerland No. 42, X AG v. Y AS, Bundesgerichtshof, Oct. 4, 2010 (2011) Yearbook Commercial Arbitration 2011 – Volume XXXVI, 340–342, para. 50; Hebei Import & Export Corp v. Polyteck Engineering Co Ltd (1992) 2 HKCFAR 111; China Nanhai Oil Joint Service Corporation Shenzhen Branch v Gee Tai Holdings Co Ltd [1994] 3 HKC 375; Gao Haiyan v. Keeneye Holdings [2012] 1 HKLRD 627, paras. 53 et seq.; Hong Kong No. 26, Astro Nusantara International BV et al. v. PT Ayunda Prima Mitra et al., High Court of the Hong Kong Special Administrative Region, Court of First Instance, Construction and Arbitration Proceedings No. 45 of 2010, Feb. 17, 2015 (2015) Yearbook Commercial Arbitration 2015 – Volume XL, 433–439; Hong Kong No. 8, China Nanhai Oil Joint Service Corporation Shenzhen Branch v. Gee Tai Holdings Co. Ltd., Supreme Court of Hong Kong, High Court, MP 24118, July 13, 1994 (1995) Yearbook Commercial Arbitration 1995 – Volume XX, 671–680, para. 18; Hong Kong No. 10, Jiangxi Provincial Metal and Minerals Import and Export Corp. v. Sulanser Company Ltd, Supreme Court of Hong Kong, High Court, MP 887, Apr. 6, 1995 (1996) Yearbook Commercial Arbitration 1996 – Volume XXI, 546–551, para. 13 (concerning issues pertaining to the arbitration agreement); Hong Kong No. 30, Astro v. Lippo, Court of Appeal, Dec. 5, 2016 (2017) Yearbook Commercial Arbitration 2017 – Volume XLII, 389–395; S Co v. B Co [2014] HKEC 1345, para. 76 China No. 13, Siemens International Trade Co. Ltd v. Shanghai Golden Landmark Co. Ltd, First Intermediate People's Court of Shanghai Municipality (2013) Min Ren (Wai Zhong) Zi No. 2, Nov. 27, 201', (2016) Yearbook Commercial Arbitration 2016 – Volume XLI, 450–453, para. 28. Europcar Italia, S.p.A. v. Maiellano Tours, Inc., 156 F.3d 310, 315 (2d Cir. 1998) (citing National Wrecking Co., 990 F.2d at 960); see AAOT Foreign Econ. Ass'n (VO) Technostroyexport v. Int'l Dev. & Trade Servs., Inc., 139 F.3d 980, 982 (2d Cir. 1998) [hereinafter AAOT Foreign Econ. Assn]; Four Seasons Hotels & Resorts B.V. v. Consorcio Barr, S.A., 613 F.Supp.2d 1362, 1370 (S.D. Fla. 2009); US No. 553, Oh Young Industrial Co., Ltd. v. E & J Textile Group, Inc., Court of Appeal of California, Second Appellate District, Division Four, Not Indicated, Oct. 7, 2005 (2006), Yearbook Commercial Arbitration 2006 – Volume XXXI, 1285–1293; US No. 553, US No. 896, Sural (Barbados) Ltd. v. The Government of the Republic of Trinidad and Tobago, United States District Court, Southern District of Florida, Aug. 12, 2016 (2017) Yearbook Commercial Arbitration 2017 – Volume XLII, 625–627; AO Techsabexport v. Globe Nuclear Services, No. 09-2064 (4th Cir. 2010); Kreiter v. Lufthansa German Airlines, Inc., 558 F.2d 966, 968 (9th Cir. 1977).

[15] Germany No. 147 / E27, Werner Schneider as liquidator of Walter Bau A.G. v. The Kingdom of Thailand, Higher Regional Court of Berlin, Case No. 20 Sch 10/11, June 4, 2012 and Federal Court of Justice of Germany, Case No. III ZB 40/12, Jan. 30, 2013 (2013) Yearbook Commercial Arbitration 2013 – Volume XXXVIII, 384–391.

[16] Switzerland No. 42, X AG v. Y AS, Bundesgerichtshof, Oct. 4, 2010 (2011) Yearbook Commercial Arbitration 2011 – Volume XXXVI, 340–342, para. 50.

[17] China No. 13, Siemens International Trade Co. Ltd v. Shanghai Golden Landmark Co. Ltd, First Intermediate People's Court of Shanghai Municipality (2013) Min Ren (Wai Zhong) Zi No. 2, Nov. 27, 2015 (2016) Yearbook Commercial Arbitration 2016 – Volume XLI, 450–453.

[18] US No. 519, Chemical Overseas Holdings, Inc., et al. v. Republica Oriental del Uruguay, United States District Court, Southern District of New York, Mar. 25, 2005, and May 10, 2005 (2005) Yearbook Commercial Arbitration 2005 – Volume XXX, 1130–1135. *See also*, S Co v. B Co [2014] HKEC 1345, para. 76. Parties may even be required to raise an objection if this risks triggering a conflict with the tribunal. *See* OLG Karlsruhe [Court of Appeal] (2012) SchiedsVZ, 104.

2.2 Expansions of Post-award Review

The parties' ability to limit the control by national courts has remained controversial; similar observations hold true for expansions of post-award review. The German Supreme Court endorsed such an expansion of post-award review.[19] The court enforced an arbitration agreement allowing any party unsatisfied with the award to bring a claim in national courts within one month from the award being rendered. In support of its decision, the German Supreme Court held that: "[b]ecause the binding nature of the award is based on the parties' consent, the parties are also free to restrict the award's binding nature and tie it to certain conditions," including "an expanded review of the award by national courts."[20]

Other courts have taken different positions on parties' control of post-award review. Most prominently, the US Supreme Court ruled in *Hall Street Associates* v. *Mattel* that parties were not at liberty to add to the grounds for vacatur of domestic arbitral awards[21] under the Federal Arbitration Act.[22] In support of its decision, the US Supreme Court referred to a systemic necessity of maintaining arbitration as a system with limited review.[23] It indicated that parties do not have discretion to alter the legal system in which arbitral proceedings take place. French courts have expounded similar views.[24] The conclusion to be drawn from this analysis is that parties exercise different degrees of control over post-award reviews by limiting or expanding the grounds for set-aside in their arbitration agreements. However, the parties' control, such as the use of waiver clauses, may be limited under the law of the jurisdiction of enforcement. Diverging approaches toward these limitations and expansions of review reflect variations in jurisdictions' policies as to where they draw the line between the two pillars of arbitration – party autonomy and the applicable arbitration framework.

3 ARBITRAL TRIBUNAL

The next actor who exercises control over arbitral awards is the arbitral tribunal. Arbitrators perform their services mindful of the fact that their award will be recognized as producing legal effects only if it fulfills the conditions set forth in the applicable arbitration framework. The

---

[19] German Supreme Court, Mar. 1, 2007 (2008) 25 ASA Bulletin, 810; this decision has been criticized; *see*, *e.g.*, R Wolff, *Party Autonomy to Agree on a Non-final Arbitration*, 26 ASA BULL. 626–640 (2008).

[20] Scherer, *supra* note 2, at 437, 446.

[21] Although Hall Street concerns a domestic award rather than a New York Convention award, it has been argued that Hall Street also applies to Convention cases; *see* Scherer & Silberman, *supra* note 2, at 453 et seq.; T. Tyler & A. A. Parasharami, *Finality over Choice: Hall Street Associates, L.L.C. v. Mattel, Inc. (US Supreme Court)*, 25 J. INT'L ARB. 613 at 614 *et seq.* (2008).

[22] Hall Street Associates v. Mattel, Inc., 552 US 576 (2008); *See* C. Drahozal, *Contracting around Hall Street*, 14 LEWIS CLARK L. REV. 905 (2010); S. A. Leisure, Arbitration after Hall Street v. Mattel: What Happens Next, 31 U. ARK. LITTLE ROCK R. L. REV. 273 (2009); *for an assessment of the pre-Hall Street situation*, see, e.g., L. Goldmand, Contractually Expanded Review of Arbitration Awards, 8 HARV. NEGOT. L. REV. 171 (2003); D. C. Hulea, Contracting to Expand the Scope of Review of Foreign Arbitral Awards: An American Perspective, 29 BROOKLYN J. INT'L L. 313 (2003); C. Murray, Contractual Expansion of the Scope of Judicial Review of Arbitration Awards under the Federal Arbitration Act, 76 ST. JOHN'S L. REV. 663(2002).

[23] Hall Street Associates v. Mattel, Inc., 552 US 576 (2008).

[24] French courts originally found that this would entail the invalidity of the arbitration clause. *See* Société Binaate Maghreb v. Société Screg Routes, Cour d'appel de Paris (1 Ch. suppl.), Dec. 12, 1989 (1990) 4 Revue de l'Arbitrage (Comité Français de l'Arbitrage), 863–866 ("Considérant que cette clause est en conséquence frappé d'une nullité qui affecte dans son ensemble la convention d'arbitrage dont elle constitue un élément essential, déterminant du consentement des parties qui ont ainsi affirmé leur volonté de soumettre leur litige à deux degrés de juridiction.") This position has been given up. See 'Société Chefaro International v. Barrère et autres, Cour de cassation (1re Ch. civ.), Not Indicated, Mar. 13, 2007 (2007) 3 Revue de l'Arbitrage (Comité Français de l'Arbitrage), 498–500.

control that national courts exercise at the post-award stage has spillover effects upon arbitrators' conduct at the pre-award stage. Arbitrators are strongly incentivized to exercise self-control and carefully fulfill their mandate in order to reduce the risk of the vacation or nonenforcement of their awards. Not only do they want to avoid the negative reputational costs that attach when a court sets aside an arbitral award due to irregularities in the arbitration process. Arbitral tribunals are also obliged to render enforceable arbitral awards.[25] In order to fulfill this duty arbitrators tend to issue a robust set of procedural rules to reduce the risk of set-aside or refusal of recognition and enforcement. For example, arbitral tribunals may direct parties to make specific reference to relevant passages of documentary exhibits provided in support of their briefs. Cross-references help arbitral tribunals to process relevant passages and consider them in their arbitral award. If a party fails to provide the requested references in their documents, then it will be difficult for that party to challenge the award on the ground that the arbitral tribunal breached the party's right to be heard by failing to address the relevant material in its documents.[26]

In a similar vein, arbitral tribunals may establish a procedural timetable with conclusive deadlines and cut-off dates. Where a party makes unsolicited submissions after a cut-off date, the tribunal may disregard them without breaching the party's right to be heard.[27] Various other procedural techniques help arbitrators to fulfill their duty to render an enforceable award. And yet, the most sophisticated procedural rules that are carefully applied do not insulate an award from being challenged. This gives rise to the question of whether national courts should exhibit a degree of deference to arbitral determinations when exercising their control at the post-award stage.

3.1 No Deference to Arbitral Determinations

Several courts have denied the existence of a general deference principle. According to the Singapore High Court, the judicial review of arbitral awards calls for "an independent determination" without being "constrained in any way by the findings or the reasoning of the arbitral tribunal."[28] The court emphasized that by reviewing an award it is exercising "original jurisdiction and not an appellate one."[29] Cases from other jurisdictions, including Hong Kong,[30] England,[31] Germany,[32] Sweden,[33] and France[34] reflect similar approaches.

---

[25] Such a duty may be stated in the applicable arbitration rules or inferred from the arbitrator contract. See, e.g., Article 42 ICC Rules of Arbitration (2017); Federal Court of Justice, decision of May 5, 1986, (1986) NJW 3077.
[26] On the duty of tribunals to take note of and consider the parties' submissions, see Germany No. 80, Trading company v. Buyer, Oberlandesgericht [Court of Appeal] Cologne, 9 Sch 01-03, Apr. 23, 2004 (2005) Yearbook Commercial Arbitration 2005 – Volume XXX, 557–562; Germany No. 148, German seller v. German guarantor, Oberlandesgericht, Munich, 34 Sch 21/11, Apr. 11, 2012 (2014) Yearbook Commercial Arbitration 2014 – Volume XXXIX, 389–391; Germany No. 145, Joint Stock Company A v. Joint Stock Company B, Higher Regional Court of Munich, 34 Sch 10/11, Nov. 14, 2011 (2012) Yearbook Commercial Arbitration 2012 – Volume XXXVII 231–233, paras. 10 et seq.
[27] On preclusive deadlines, see, e.g., Court of Appeals Naumburg, (2003) NJW-RR, 71, decision of Feb. 21, 2002.
[28] PT Tugu Pratama Indonesia v. Magma Nusantara Ltd [2003] SGHC 204, para. 18.
[29] Insigma Technology Co Ltd. v. Alstom Technology Ltd [2008] SGHC 134, para. 21.
[30] S Co v. B Co [2014] HKEC 1345, para. 36.
[31] Dallah Real Estate and Tourism Holding Company v. The Ministry of Religious Affairs [2010] UKSC 46, paras. 96 and 160; People's Insurance Co of China (Hebei Branch) v. Vysanthi Shipping CO Ltd, 'The Joanna V' [2003] EWHC 1655, decision of July 10, 2003.
[32] Germany No. 126 / E21, Clothing manufacturer v. Textiles manufacturer, Oberlandesgericht [Court of Appeal], Munich, 34 Sch 04/08, Jan. 19, 2009 (2010) Yearbook Commercial Arbitration 2010 – Volume XXXV, 362–364, para. 4.
[33] 'Sweden No. 8, RosInvest Co UK Ltd v. Russian Federation, Högsta Domstolen, Nov. 12, 2010 (2011) Yearbook Commercial Arbitration 2011 – Volume XXXVI, 334–336.
[34] Southern Pacific Properties Ltd. & Southern Pacific Ltd v. République arabe d'Egypte, Cour de Cassation (1Ch. civile), Jan. 6, 1987 (1987) 4 Revue de l'Arbitrage 469–470.

3.2 Deference to Arbitral Determinations

Other cases reflect a more deferential approach to arbitral tribunals and awards. A Hong Kong court described its role as that of an "overseer," which should not "second-guess an arbitration award."[35] Likewise, a Canadian court justified a deferential approach towards foreign arbitral awards by stating the importance of showing "respect for the capacities of foreign and transnational tribunals and sensitivity to the need of the international commercial system for predictability in the resolution of disputes."[36] These courts demonstrated a desire to give credit to the institutional capacities of arbitral tribunals.

A different justification for paying deference can be found in US law. US law accepts that parties can delegate competence–competence to arbitral tribunals where they have "clearly and unmistakenly agreed to arbitrate issues of arbitrability."[37] If such a clear and unmistakable delegation of competence–competence can be established, US courts will give substantial deference to the arbitral tribunal's assessment and refrain from second-guessing the tribunal's decision.[38] The rationale for exercising such deference differs from the one addressed above; it is primarily justified by legal considerations – respect for the autonomous choice of a forum – rather than respect for the institutional capacities of arbitral tribunals. In sum, the belief is that national courts should pay deference in situations where parties have validly delegated competence–competence to an arbitral tribunal. This approach is firmly embedded in American contract law's stance in favor of private autonomy.

3.3 Intermediary Positions

Between the two extremes (deference to arbitral tribunals versus independent assessments), there are various intermediary approaches. Specifically, there is a strong argument that there are rationales for not completely deferring to the decisions of arbitral tribunals. One rationale is that judicial intervention may be necessary to protect the parties. This interest justifies applying less deference when reviewing the existence of consent to arbitrate, while providing greater deference on determining the scope of the arbitration agreement. In the latter case, an error in assessing the scope of the arbitration agreement does not overcome the fact that the parties demonstrated a general willingness to accept arbitration as a legitimate form of dispute resolution.[39] Arguably, these parties deserve less protection than parties who never agreed to arbitrate in the first place.

A second factor relates to the interests of the public at large. Certain grounds of the post-award regime such as restrictions of arbitrability or the assessment of whether enforcement of an arbitral award breaches public policy concern the public interest. Here, the case for deference to the assessment of the arbitral tribunal is substantially lower.

---

[35] 'Hong Kong No. 21, Applicant [Xiamen Xinjingdi Group Ltd] v. Eton Properties Ltd, et al., Court of First Instance, June 24, 2008, and Court of Appeal, May 22, 2009 (2009), Yearbook Commercial Arbitration 2009 – Volume XXXIV, 548–576.

[36] Canada No. 16, Grow Biz International Inc. (US) v. D.L.T. Holdings Inc., Debbie Tanton, Supreme Court, Province of Prince Edward Island, Trial Division, Docket no. GSC-17431, Mar. 23, 2001, 2005 Yearbook of Commercial Arbitration 2005 – Volume XXX, 450. See also, Ace Bermuda Ins. Ltd v. Allianz Ins. Co. of Canada, [2005] ABQB 975.

[37] First Options of Chicago, Inc. v. Kaplan, 514 US 938, 943, 115 S. Ct. 1920, 131 L.Ed.2d 985 (1995).

[38] Parsons & Whittemore Overseas Co., Inc. v. Societe Generale De L'Industrie Du Papier (RAKTA), 508 F.2d 969, 977 (2d Cir. 1974).

[39] Cf., e.g., US No. 598, Sphere Drake Insurance Ltd v. The Lincoln National Life Insurance Company, Fort Wayne Health and Casualty Insurance Company, United States District Court, Northern District of Illinois, Eastern Division, 05 C 6411, Sept. 13, 2006 (2007) Yearbook Commercial Arbitration 2007 – Volume XXXII, 857–870, para. 4.

A third factor concerns the institutional capacities of the decision makers. Some arbitral tribunals may have greater resources, expertise, and access to the relevant facts than a national court reviewing the award. This gap in knowledge justifies deference to the factual assessments made by arbitral tribunals.[40] The Swiss Federal Tribunal noted that the efficiency of the arbitral process "would be seriously compromised if the Federal Tribunal's full power to examine claims [for annulment] were interpreted as entitling it freely to review the findings of fact made by the arbitral tribunal in the same way as an appeal court."[41] Alternatively, the case for deference is lower where there is an error in the composition of the arbitral tribunal, which places the integrity and legitimacy of its decision into question. Other factors influence the degree of deference shown by courts, but the point to be made is that national courts pay different degrees of deference and control over prior arbitral determinations.

4 ARBITRAL INSTITUTIONS

Arbitral institutions also exercise control over arbitral awards. One finds a large number of arbitral institutions around the world, which offer their dispute resolution services to the parties. In their quest to expand market shares, many arbitral institutions strive to enhance their services and offer better dispute resolution services to the parties. As part of this endeavor, arbitral institutions seek to ensure the enforceability of arbitral awards rendered under their auspices. Arbitral institutions use various instruments to attain this goal. A prominent example is the scrutiny of arbitral awards by the ICC Court. This process is geared at identifying issues that may increase the risk of nonenforceability of arbitral awards.[42] Arbitral institutions also exercise control over the constitution of the arbitral tribunal and decide on challenges of arbitrators.[43] They thereby exercise control over issues that arise in the arbitration proceedings.[44] And again, the safeguards and best practices implemented by arbitral institutions impact the degree of deference that courts apply to arbitral awards.

4.1 Deference to Determinations Made by Arbitral Institutions

The English Court of Appeals ruled that it would pay "the closest attention to any interpretation of the ICC Rules adopted by the ICC Court" when examining whether there had been arbitrator misconduct or breach of the arbitration agreement.[45] Likewise, a US federal court

---

[40] US No. 896, Sural Ltd. v. The Government of the Republic of Trinidad and Tobago through its Minister of Finance as Corporation Sole, United States District Court, Southern District of Florida, Aug. 12, 2016 (2017) Yearbook Commercial Arbitration 2017 – Volume XLII, 625–627. See also, A v B [2018] EWHC 3366 (TCC) [34] (paying deference to the tribunal's discretion to manage the proceedings).

[41] Swiss Supreme Court, BGE 119 II 380, p. 381, Sept. 2, 1993. See also, Gao Haiyan v. Keeney Holdings Ltd [2012] 1 HKLRD 627, para. 64. See, however, People's Insurance Co of China (Hebei Branch) v. Vysanthi Shipping Co. Ltd. (The Joanna V) [2003] EWHC 1655, July 10, 2003 ruling that "the Court is not in any way bound or limited to the findings made in the award or to the evidence adduced before the arbitrator; it does not review the decision of the arbitrator but makes its own decision on the evidence before it."

[42] J. FRY ET AL., THE SECRETARIAT'S GUIDE TO ICC ARBITRATION 327 et seq. (2012).

[43] See, e.g., Art. 13 & 14 ICC Rules.

[44] On the separate question of whether rules of arbitral institutions are mandatory, see A. Carlevaris, *Limits to Party Autonomy and Institutional Rules*, in, LIMITS TO PARTY AUTONOMY IN INTERNATIONAL COMMERCIAL ARBITRATION 1 et seq. (F. Ferrari ed., 2016); H. Smith, *Mandatory ICC Arbitration Rules*, in GLOBAL REFLECTIONS ON INTERNATIONAL LAW, COMMERCE AND DISPUTE RESOLUTION, LIBER AMICORUM IN HONOUR OF ROBERT BRINER 845 et seq. (G. Aksen et al. eds., 2005).

[45] AT & T Corporation v. Saudi Cable Co, [2000] APP. L.R. 05/15, May 15, 2000, para. 49.

paid considerable deference to decisions of the ICC. It noted that the ICC Court "is the best judge of whether its procedural rules have been satisfied."[46] By approving the arbitral award, the ICC Court had "certified that the procedural rules had been complied with to its satisfaction."[47]

Other US courts have expressed their sympathy and trust in arbitration proceedings administered by the ICC. For example, a federal court was asked to decide on whether an ICC arbitration clause was unconscionable on the ground that two officers of one of the disputing parties were linked to the International Chamber of Commerce as a business organization. The court found the clause to be enforceable, noting that "there are sufficient mechanisms within and without the ICC Rules to ensure that the arbitration is fair and justice is done."[48] Another federal court reached the same conclusion in a case in which the applicant had challenged the validity of an arbitration clause because one of the participants was the chairman of ICC Indonesia. The court noted that ICC Indonesia, unlike the ICC Court, had no actual involvement in the arbitration proceedings. According to the court, "it would be the height of arrogance ... to assume that the rules and procedures of the ICC governing arbitration are incapable of giving ... a fair shake." The court reached this conclusion in view of the "multiplicity of procedural safeguards built into the ICC rules designed to avoid the possibility of such rank bias and unfair procedures."[49]

4.2 No Deference to Determinations Made by Arbitral Institutions

And yet, courts do not always pay deference to determinations of arbitral institutions. Courts across jurisdictions have hesitated to pay deference to decisions made by arbitral institutions in cases involving challenges of arbitrators.[50] Swiss courts, for instance, have emphasized that they will not defer to arbitral institutions as far as challenges are concerned. They ruled that it would be incompatible with the Swiss legal order to entrust private bodies with the task of ensuring the independence and impartiality of the members of an arbitral tribunal.[51] For this reason, Swiss courts would remain competent to "review freely" whether or not there was an irregularity in the composition of the arbitral tribunal.[52]

US courts have propounded similar views. A federal court of appeals was not willing to pay deference to a challenge relating to a decision of the American Arbitration Association. Considering the crucial role of arbitrator neutrality, the court found that the law does not allow it to delegate such challenges "to the unfettered discretion of private business."[53] Likewise, the Chancery Court of Delaware ruled in *Beebe Med. Center* v. *Insight Health Servs*, that acceptance of arbitration under the rules of the American Arbitration Association does not amount to a waiver

---

[46] Carte Blanche (Singapore) Pte. Ltd. v. Carte Blanche Intern., Ltd., Apr. 8, 1988, 683 F.Supp. 945 (1988).
[47] Id.
[48] Tierra Right of Way Services, Ltd. v. Abengoa Solar Inc., June 9, 2011, US District Court (D. Arizona, 2011) 2011 WL 2292007.
[49] Enviro Petroleum, Inc. v. Kondur Petroleum, SA, 91 F. Supp. 2d 1031 (S.D. Tex. 2000), Mar. 29, 2000.
[50] For an exception, see Germany No. 58, Manufacturer v. Exclusive distributor, Oberlandesgericht [Court of Appeal], Schleswig, 16 SchH 01/99, June 24, 1999 (2004) Yearbook Commercial Arbitration 2004 – Volume XXIX, 687–696. The German court noted that the ICC Court's dismissal of the challenge constituted "the end of the matter" as it did not appear to be "clearly defective, e.g., for evident bias."
[51] First Civil Law Court, Judgment of May 2, 2012, 4A_14/2012; SA v. Y. SA, Tribunal Fédéral, Ière Cour de droit civil, 4A_348/2009, Jan. 6, 2010 (2010) 28(4) ASA Bulletin, 772–777.
[52] Judgment of June 27, 2012, DFT 4A_54/2012, para. 2.1.
[53] Azteca Construction, Inc., v. ADR Consulting, Inc, Court of Appeal, Third District, California, C045316, Aug. 25, 2004.

of independent judicial review at the post-award stage.[54] That said, the court did not exclude that parties can agree to accept a challenge decision of an arbitral institution as final and binding by explicitly stating so in their arbitration agreement. This bears similarities with the decision in *First Options*,[55] in which the court held that parties can delegate competence–competence to an arbitral tribunal. Overall, it appears that national courts' willingness to pay deference to determinations made by arbitral institutions is dependent on the issues in question. The degree of deference is comparable to the one paid to determinations made by arbitral tribunals – even though arbitral institutions differ from arbitral tribunals in that they exercise a second layer of control: they often have the authority to review arbitral awards and the process in which they were rendered.

5 COURTS AT THE SEAT

Further actors exercising control over arbitration proceeding are the courts at the seat. These courts have "primary supervisory jurisdiction," because they may either annul or uphold arbitral awards, as opposed to courts having secondary jurisdiction, which may only decide on the recognition and enforcement of awards.[56] The decision to uphold or annul an arbitral award is an act of control that has significant effects beyond the jurisdiction of the seat.[57]

5.1 Deference to Negative Decisions of Courts at the Seat

As far as decisions annulling an arbitral award are concerned, Article V (1) lit. e of the New York Convention permits courts to refuse recognition and enforcement of arbitral awards if the award was annulled by a competent court at the seat or under the procedural law designated by the parties.[58] While the discretionary character of the language (*may*) in Article V (1) is not similarly reflected in all authoritative versions of the convention, it is widely accepted that courts are at liberty to enforce an arbitral award despite it having been set-aside or annulled. This is due to Article VII of the Convention, which allows states to apply a more favorable enforcement regime.[59] If Article V (1) lit. e is read as imposing an obligation to refuse recognition and enforcement, Article VII of the Convention would nevertheless allow states to recognize and enforce previously annulled arbitral awards.

The relevant case law shows that courts have developed a number of different approaches in exercising their discretion to recognize and enforce annulled awards. At one end of the spectrum, some courts simply refuse recognition and enforcement where an award has been

---

[54] Beebe Med. Center v. Insight Health Servs, 751 A.2d 426 (1999).
[55] First Options of Chicago, Inc. v. Kaplan, 514 US 938, 943, 115 S. Ct. 1920, 131 L.Ed.2d 985 (1995).
[56] TermoRio SAESP & Lease Co Group LLC v. Elecranta SP, 487 F.3d 928 (D.C. Cir., 2007).
[57] See D. F. Donovan, *Chapter 14: Preclusion and the New York Convention: Article V (1) (e) and Converse-Article V (1) (e)*, in THE EVOLUTION AND FUTURE OF INTERNATIONAL ARBITRATION 231–250 (Stavros L. Brekoulakis, Julian D. M. Lew, et al. eds., 2016).
[58] US No. 482, Karaha Bodas Co., L.L.C. v. Perusahaan Pertambangan Minyak Dan Gas Bumi Negara, et al., United States Court of Appeals, Fifth Circuit, 02-20042; 03-20602, Mar. 23, 2004 (2004) Yearbook Commercial Arbitration 2004 – Volume XXIX, 1262–1297, para. 9.
[59] Société Pablak Ticaret Ltd. Sirketi v. Norsolor S.A., Cour de cassation [Cass.] [Supreme court for judicial matters], Oct. 9, 1984, 83-11.355, arret no. 730 (Fr.). More generally on Article VII, see Switzerland, No. 37, Bezirksgericht, Zurich, Feb. 14, 2003 and Obergericht, Zurich, July 17, 2003, Italian party v. Swiss company (2004) Yearbook Commercial Arbitration 2004 – Volume XXIX, 819 – 833.

set-aside. Case law from Chile,[60] Brazil,[61] China,[62] Germany,[63] and Luxemburg[64] is a testament to this territorial approach towards arbitration. It reflects an understanding of arbitration as being anchored in the jurisdiction of the seat of arbitration (or the jurisdiction to which the parties have submitted if they chose a different procedural law).[65] Such a conceptualization results in a control system, in which courts at the place of arbitration enjoy far-reaching nullification power at the pre-enforcement stage, whereas courts in other jurisdictions may only decide on the enforcement of arbitral awards that have not been set-aside.[66]

At the other end of the spectrum, courts in France recognize and enforce arbitral awards irrespective of whether they have been set aside at the place of arbitration. A number of cases reflect this internationalized approach,[67] which conceptualizes arbitration as being delocalized and, hence, not rooted in one particular jurisdiction. This results in a control system in which courts at the seat and courts at the place of enforcement make independent assessments. Between these two positions are various intermediary positions, pursuant to which courts recognize and enforce annulled awards only in exceptional situations.

A distinct approach developed, for example, in the United States. In 2006, a federal court in the case of *Chromalloy Aeroservices v. Arab Republic of Egypt*[68] recognized and enforced an annulled arbitral award. The right to enforce annulled awards was confirmed in the 2016 case of *Commisa v. Pemex*,[69] when a federal court of appeals ruled that the discretion to recognize and enforce annulled awards is constrained by considerations of international comity. Accordingly, US courts would need to pay deference to the foreign set-aside judgment, unless recognition of the annulment would offend public policy on the grounds that it is "repugnant to fundamental notions of what is decent and just in the State where enforcement is sought."[70] In the majority of cases, US courts have paid deference to foreign set-aside decisions.[71] English courts have taken a

---

[60] EDFI Internacional Sociedad Energética Francesa S.A., Corte Suprema, Sept. 8,2011, case reference MJCH_MJJ29225.

[61] Brazil No. 44, EDF International S/A v. Endesa Latinoamérica S/A, Superior Court of Justice of Brazil, Case No. SEC no. 5.782 – EX, Dec. 2, 2015, (2016) Yearbook Commercial Arbitration 2016 – Volume XLI, 415–417.

[62] N. Darwazeh, *Article V(1)(e)*, in RECOGNITION AND ENFORCEMENT OF FOREIGN ARBITRAL AWARDS: A GLOBAL COMMENTARY ON THE NEW YORK CONVENTION 329 (H. Kronke et al. eds., 2010).

[63] Germany No. 51, Not indicated v. Not indicated, Oberlandesgericht [Court of Appeal], Rostock, Oct. 28, 1999 (2000) Yearbook Commercial Arbitration 2000 – Volume XXV, 641–1164.

[64] Luxembourg No. 5, Bolivian Republic of Venezuela v. Company 1 INC., Cour d'Appel, Luxembourg, June 25, 2015, (2017), Yearbook Commercial Arbitration 2017 – Volume XLII, 425–427.

[65] See also F. A. Mann, *The UNCITRAL Model Law – Lex Facit Arbitrum*, 2 ARB. INT'L. 241 (2014) [reprint].

[66] V. M. Reisman & H. Iravani, *The Changing Relation of National Courts and International Commercial Arbitration*, 21 AM. REV. INT'L ARB. 5, 12 et seq. (2010).

[67] Cour de Cassation, Pabalk Ticaret v. Norsolor, Oct. 9, 1984, (1985) 24 I.L.M 360; Bargues Agro Industrie, S.A. v. La Société Young Pecan Company, Cour d'Appel de Paris, June 10, 2004; Cour de Cassation, Société Ryanair Ltd v. Syndicat Mixte des Aéroports de Charente, Arrêt no. 797, July 8, 2015, 13-25.846; Cour de Cassation, Société Hilmarton Ltd. v. Société Omnium de traitement et de valorisation (OTV), 92-15.137, Mar. 23, 1994, Bulletin 1994 I No. 104, p. 79 ; Cour de Cassation, Société PT Putrabali Adyamulia v. Société Rena Holding et Société Moguntia Est Epices, 05-18.053, June 29, 2007, Bulletin 2007, I, No. 250; Cour d'Appel de Paris, La Société S.A. Lesbat et Fils v. Monsieur Volker Le Docteur Grub, Arrêt du Jan. 18, 2007, numéro 05/10887.

[68] In the matter of the arbitration of Certain Controversies between Chromalloy Aeroservices v. The Arab Republic of Egypt, 939 F. Supp. 907 (1996) (D.D.C. 1996), July 31, 1996.

[69] Id., confirming Corporación Mexicana De Mantenimiento Integral, S. De R.L. De C.V. v. Pemex-Exploración y Producción, 962 F. Supp. 2d 642, 659–660 (S.D.N.Y. 2013).

[70] Corporación Mexicana De Mantenimiento Integral, S. De R.L. De C.V. v. Pemex Exploración y Producción, No. 13-4022 (2d Cir. 2016). The case concerned the equivalent provision in the Panama Convention.

[71] Spier v. Calzaturificio Tecnica, SpA, 71 F.Supp. 2d 279 (S.D.N.Y. 1999); US No. 917, Getma International v. Republic of Guinea, United States Court of Appeals, District of Columbia Circuit, July 7, 2017 (2017) Yearbook Commercial Arbitration 2017 – Volume XLII, 706–709; Termorio S.a. E.s.P. and Leaseco Group LLC v. Electranta S.p., et al., 487

similar approach in paying deference to foreign set-aside decisions, unless such recognition would be contrary to the "basic principles of honesty, natural justice and domestic concepts of public policy."[72]

Other jurisdictions like the Netherlands[73] and Hong Kong[74] have combined such a judgment-based approach with an analysis of the grounds on which the arbitral award was set-aside. According to this approach, it matters whether an arbitral award was set-aside based on internationally accepted standards or based on domestic standards. This approach finds precedence in the European Convention on International Commercial Arbitration, which provides that the setting aside of an arbitral award shall constitute a ground for refusal of recognition and enforcement only if the award was set-aside based certain reasons.[75] This case law presents a mixed picture as far as deference to decisions cancelling the effects of an arbitral award. Generally, a great deal of deference is given to the authority of the courts at the seat based on considerations of comity.

5.2 Deference to Positive Decisions of Courts at the Seat

Deference to decisions of courts at the seat confirming an award is to some extent determined by a choice of law analysis. A court at the seat may apply a different concept of public policy than the court at the place of recognition and enforcement.[76] Likewise, the notion of arbitrability may differ and some grounds for setting aside may not even correspond to the grounds for refusal of recognition and enforcement under the New York Convention altogether. In these situations, the question of whether deference should be paid does not arise. Things look different if the grounds for setting aside and the grounds for refusal of recognition and enforcement are the same or if the New York Convention refers to the law of the seat as it does in Article V (1) lit. a or d.

F.3d 928 (D.C. Cir. 2007); United States Court of Appeals, Second Circuit, Baker Marine Ltd. v. Chevron Ltd. and Chevron Inc., Baker Marine (Nig.) Ltd. v. Danos and Curole Marine Contractors, Docket Nos. 97-9615, 97-0617, Aug. 12, 1999; Thai-Lao Lignite Co. Ltd., Hongsa Lignite Co., Ltd. v. Government of the Lao People's Democratic Republic, Nos. 14-597 (United States Court of Appeals, Second Circuit, July 20, 2017).

[72] Malicorp Ltd v. Government of the Arab Republic of Egypt, Egyptian Holding Company for Aviation, Egyptian Airports Company, [2015] EWHC 361 (Comm), Feb. 19, 2015, para. 22. *See also*, UK No. 109, Nikolay Viktorovich Maximov v. Open Joint Stock Company Novolipetsky Metallurgichesky Kombinat, High Court of Justice, July 27, 2017 (2017) Yearbook Commercial Arbitration 2017 – Volume XLII, 558–564, para. 16 (finding that a decision "must be so wrong as to be evidence of bias or be such that no court acting in good faith could have arrived at it" for an English court to recognize an annulled award). *See also*, Yukos Capital S.a.r.L. v. OJSC Rosneft Oil Company [2014] EWHC 2188 (Comm) (July 3, 2014), para. 12.

[73] Netherlands No. 2018-2, Not indicated v. OJSC Novolipetsky Metallurgichesky Kombinat, Hoge Raad, Case No. 16/05686, Nov. 24, 2017 (2018) Yearbook Commercial Arbitration 2018 – Volume XLIII, 1–10.

[74] Hong Kong No. 29, Dana Shipping and Trading SA v. Sino Channel Asia Ltd, High Court of Hong Kong, Court of First Instance, Case No. 47 of 2015 and No. 1676 of 2016, July 28, 2016 (2017) Yearbook Commercial Arbitration 2017 – Volume XLII, 385–388. The High Court of Hong Kong refused recognition and enforcement of an award that had been annulled in England. According to the High Court of Hong Kong, there was no proof that the setting aside proceedings were "in any way procedurally unfair, or irregular, or that the decision maker was not impartial, or that it would in any way be contrary to the court's sense of justice or public policy to recognize the English Judgment." In reaching this conclusion, the High Court of Hong Kong considered that the English court had applied internationally accepted grounds for set-aside.

[75] European Convention on International Commercial Arbitration, Geneva, Apr. 21, 1961, U.N.T.S. vol. 484, p. 364, Article IX.

[76] Spain No. 33/E16, Actival Internacional SA v. Conservas El Pilar SA, Tribunal Supremo [Supreme Court], 3868/1992, Apr. 16 1996 (2002) Yearbook Commercial Arbitration 2002 – Volume XXVII, 528–532.

US courts have shown a willingness to pay deference to the assessment made by the courts at the seat in such situations.[77] It appears that this approach was driven by their trust in the ability of courts at the seat to examine questions governed by the law of that jurisdiction. English courts have even gone a step further. To put it in the words of the English Commercial Court in the *Minmetals* case:

> In a case where a remedy for an alleged defect is applied for from the supervisory court, but is refused, leaving a final award undisturbed, it will therefore normally be a very strong policy consideration before the English courts that it has been conclusively determined by the courts of the agreed supervisory jurisdiction that the award should stand. Just as great weight must be attached to the policy of sustaining the finality of international awards so also must great weight be attached to the policy of sustaining the finality of the determination of properly referred procedural issues by the courts of the supervisory jurisdiction.[78]

The court ruled that different considerations may apply in exceptional cases, such as cases of "obvious and serious disregard for basic principles of justice" or where courts at the place of arbitration decline to exercise their supervisory powers "for unjust reasons, such as corruption."[79] Thus, the legal authority of the courts at the seat is a key consideration in deferring to their decisions, nonetheless, lack of institutional capacity or absence of due process guarantees are reasons not to defer. Hong Kong courts have followed this case law with approval.[80] Likewise, the High Court of Singapore ruled that the principle of comity of nations requires courts at the place of enforcement not to undermine the orders made by courts at the seat absent exceptional circumstances.[81]

5.3 Deference and the Need to Initiate Set-Aside Proceedings at the Seat

This case law gives rise to the question of whether parties are actually even required to initiate set-aside proceedings at the seat prior to invoking grounds for refusal of recognition and enforcement at the place of enforcement. Germany is one of the few jurisdictions that has endorsed such an approach. Under German law, there is support for the proposition that a party is precluded from invoking a particular ground for refusal of recognition and enforcement if it failed to initiate set-aside proceedings at the seat on that ground.[82] An exception applies to issues

---

[77] US No. 280, Europcar Italia, S.p.A. v. Maiellano Tours, Inc., United States Court of Appeals, Second Circuit, 97-7224, Sept. 2, 1998 (1999), Yearbook Commercial Arbitration 1999 – Volume XXIVa, 860–870. Ottley v. Schwartzberg, 819 F.2d 373, 377 (2d Cir. 1987); Florasynth, Inc. v. Pickholz, 750 F.2d 171, 176 (2d Cir. 1984). Compare, India No. 54, Cruz City 1, Mauritius Holdings v. Unitech Ltd, High Court of Delhi, New Delhi, Apr. 11, 2017 (2017) Yearbook Commercial Arbitration 2017 – Volume XLII, 407–411.
[78] Minmetals Germany GmbH v. Ferco Steel Ltd [1999] CLC 647 at 661.
[79] Id. See also Eastern European Engineering (Proprietary) Ltd v. Vijay Construction (Proprietary) Ltd [2018] EWHC 2713 (Comm) [43].
[80] Gao Haiyan v. Keeneye Holdings [2012] 1 HKLRD 627 at paras. 65 to 69 and Hong Kong No. 30, Astro v. Lippo, Court of Appeal, Dec. 5, 2016 (2017) Yearbook Commercial Arbitration 2017 – Volume XLII, 389–395. See also, Hebei Import & Export Corporation v. Polytek Engineering Co. Ltd., FACV10/1998. The Hong Kong courts emphasized that the assessment may differ where the grounds for set-aside and the grounds for refusal of recognition and enforcement are not the same. See Hong Kong No. 15, Hebei Import & Export Corporation v. Polytek Engineering Company Ltd, Court of Final Appeal of the Hong Kong Special Administrative Region, 10 of 1998, Feb. 9. 1999 (1999) Yearbook Commercial Arbitration 1999 – Volume XXIVa, 652–677 (concerning different notions of public policy).
[81] Singapore No. 11, Galsworthy Ltd v. Glory Wealth Shipping Pte Ltd, High Court, Oct. 14, 2010 (2011) Yearbook Commercial Arbitration 2011 – Volume XXXVI, 329–331, para. 7.
[82] OLG Karlsruhe [Court of Appeal], (2012) SchiedsVZ, 101. See also, OLG Frankfurt [Court of Appeal], decision of Oct. 18, 2007, BeckRS 2011, 25398; BGH [German Supreme Court] (2001) NJW-RR, 1059; Voit, in: Musielak/Voit, 15th ed. 2018, Section 1061 ZPO para. 20.

of jurisdiction. In this respect, parties are not estopped from invoking a ground of refusal of recognition and enforcement if they have failed to initiate set-aside proceedings. This is justified by the need to respect their right of access to justice.[83]

Courts in other jurisdictions have taken different views on this subject. Hong Kong courts, for example, have ruled that the failure to apply for setting aside an award at the seat does not estop parties from invoking grounds for refusal of recognition and enforcement. This jurisprudential approach rests on the distinction between the active remedy of applying for setting aside an award and the passive remedy of resisting its recognition and enforcement. Under this approach, the two remedies are conceptualized as being independent of each other.[84] The various jurisdictions that have followed this approach include Switzerland,[85] South Africa,[86] and the United Kingdom.[87] The reluctance of many courts to attribute weight to the mere prospect of obtaining a decision from courts at the seat should not detract from the general conclusion that the control exercised by courts at the seat is influential in deciding on the enforcement of an award or annulment in other jurisdictions.

6 COURTS AT THE PLACE OF ENFORCEMENT

Things look different as far as the degree of control of courts at the place of enforcement over the assessment made by courts at another place of enforcement is concerned. The denial of enforcement in one jurisdiction does not have the same consequences as the set-aside at the seat.[88] A court's ruling not to enforce an award within its own jurisdiction does not work as a nullification but is simply a statement by the court that it will not lend its aid to the enforcement of the award in its jurisdiction.[89] There is no equivalent of Article V (1) lit. e of the New York Convention for decisions refusing recognition and enforcement,[90] and it would be incorrect to conclude that courts at a different place of enforcement are institutionally better equipped to decide on recognition and enforcement.

For similar reasons, a decision allowing recognition and enforcement in one jurisdiction is not a basis to seek recognition and enforcement at a different place of enforcement. While one

---

[83] BGH [German Supreme Court] (2011) NJW, 1290, decision of Dec. 16, 2010.
[84] Paklito Investment Ltd v. Klockner Ltd [1993] 2 HKLR 39. Hong Kong No. 26, Astro Nusantara International BV et al. v. PT Ayunda Prima Mitra et al., High Court of the Hong Kong Special Administrative Region, Court of First Instance, Construction and Arbitration Proceedings No. 45 of 2010, Feb. 17, 2015 (2015) Yearbook Commercial Arbitration 2015 – Volume XL, 433–439, para. 85.
[85] Switzerland No. 42, X AG v. Y AS, Bundesgerichtshof, Oct. 4, 2010 (2011) Yearbook Commercial Arbitration 2011 – Volume XXXVI, 340–342, para. 50; Switzerland No. 48, Club A v. B, Tribunal Fédéral, First Civil Chamber, Feb. 26, 2015 (2016) Yearbook Commercial Arbitration 2016 – Volume XLI, 567–572, para. 10.
[86] South Africa No. 5, Phoenix Shipping Corporation v. DHL Global Forwarding SA (Pty) Ltd et al., High Court of South Africa, Western Cape Division, AC70/2011, Feb. 24, 2012 (2012) Yearbook Commercial Arbitration 2012 – Volume XXXVII, 290–294, para. 42.
[87] UK No. 76, Svenska Petroleum Exploration AB v. Government of the Republic of Lithuania, AB Geonafta (Lithuania), Court of Appeal, Civil Division, B6/2005/2737, Nov. 13, 2006 (2007) Yearbook Commercial Arbitration 2007 – Volume XXXII, 629–653, para. 44; Dallah Real Estate and Tourism Holding Company v. The Ministry of Religious Affairs [2010] UKSC 46.
[88] See Hong Kong No. 26, Astro Nusantara International BV et al. v. PT Ayunda Prima Mitra et al., High Court of the Hong Kong Special Administrative Region, Court of First Instance, Construction and Arbitration Proceedings No. 45 of 2010, Feb. 17, 2015 (2015) Yearbook Commercial Arbitration 2015 – Volume XL, 43339.
[89] Hong Kong No. 30, Astro v. Lippo, Court of Appeal, Dec. 5, 2016 (2017) Yearbook Commercial Arbitration 2017 – Volume XLII, 389–395 (quoting Toby Landau's submission before the Singapore Court of Appeal at paragraph 40 of First Media's case dated Mar. 1, 2013).
[90] Germany No. 73, Buyer v. Seller, Hanseatisches Oberlandesgericht [Court of Appeal], Hamburg, 11 Sch 06/01, Jan. 24, 2003 (2005) Yearbook Commercial Arbitration 2005 – Volume XXX, 509–523.

could be tempted to argue that the decision on recognition and enforcement – the so-called exequatur judgment – could itself be subject to recognition in other countries, such a *double exequatur* is no longer accepted in various jurisdictions.[91] This is primarily due to the fact that the exequatur judgment merely contains a procedural decision as to the requirements for recognition and enforcement in a particular jurisdiction. If the exequatur judgment were declared enforceable merely based on the standards governing the recognition and enforcement of judgments it would circumvent the procedure for recognition and enforcement of arbitral awards under the New York Convention. The overall observation to be made is that courts at the place of recognition and enforcement exercise a form of control whose effects are mainly limited to the laws of its country. However, their assessment may have persuasive authority in other jurisdictions.

7 CONCLUSION

At this juncture, it is time to take a step back and to draw some general conclusions on the state of control exercised over arbitral awards. The main observation is that national courts are not the sole guardians exercising control over arbitral awards. Instead, the responsibility for control is shared among at least five different actors, including the parties, arbitral tribunals, arbitral institutions, courts at the seat, and courts at the (foreign) place of recognition and enforcement. The two principles that regulate the interactions between these five actors of control are party autonomy and deference. Party autonomy determines the scope of control that disputing parties can exercise. It is limited by the legal framework that must recognize arbitration proceedings as producing legal effects. The parties' ability to limit or expand the grounds for review of the award depends on the jurisdiction of enforcement.

Deference regulates the interplay between determinations made by the arbitral tribunal, arbitral institutions, courts at the seat and courts at the (foreign) place of enforcement. Deference is the recognition by one of the actors that a determination made by another actor should be followed even though the reviewing actor might have reached a different decision.[92] The justifications for paying such deference differ significantly. On the one hand, deference is made to the legal authority entrusted with making binding decisions.[93] Where parties delegate competence–competence to an arbitral tribunal, this is a legal act, which, under US law, allocates decision-making power to the arbitral tribunal and justifies judicial deference to the award. Likewise, the deference paid under Article V (1) lit. e of the New York Convention is to the legal authority of national courts at the seat of the arbitration.

On the other hand, there is a form of deference that is commonly labeled as *epistemic deference*.[94] Here, the degree of deference is justified by the institutional competence of the decision maker. This competence may be tied to the information, expertise or skills of the decision maker to whom deference is paid.[95] Representative examples of epistemic deference include a national court paying deference to the factual assessment made by an arbitral tribunal,

---

[91] BGH [German Supreme Court] (2009) NJW, 2826.
[92] R. Schapiro, *Judicial Deference and Interpretive Coordinacy in State and Federal Constitutional Law*, 85 CORNELL L. REV.,656, 665 (2000).
[93] P. DALY, A THEORY OF DEFERENCE IN ADMINISTRATIVE LAW 7 (2012); P. Horwitz, *Three Faces of Deference*, 83 NOTRE DAME L. REV. 1061, 1079 (2008).
[94] Horwitz, *supra* note 93, at 1085.
[95] Cf. G. Lawson & C. D. More, *The Executive Power of Constitutional Interpretation*, 81 IOWA LAW REVIEW 1300 (1996); B. Lipton, *Accountability, Deference and the Skidmore Doctrine*, 119 YALE L.J. 2096, 2121 (2010); P. Horwitz, *supra* note 93, at 1085.

to the interpretation of the arbitration rules by an arbitral institution that issued them, or to a particular interpretation of the law of the seat of arbitration.

Both forms of deference improve the efficiency of the dispute resolution process. From a law and economics perspective, it makes sense for courts to defer to arbitral tribunals and arbitral institutions, especially if there has been no breach of the arbitration rules.[96] After all, considerable resources are spent in devising fair and equitable arbitration rules, which are threatened by inconsistent decisions made by national courts. Yet, deference also comes at a cost if courts blindly defer to arbitral tribunals and allow the perpetuation of errors in the arbitration process. The pivotal challenge for international arbitration is finding the right equilibrium between the five different control mechanisms.

---

[96] *See* P. KRISHNA RAO, THE ECONOMICS OF TRANSACTION COSTS-THEORY, METHODS AND APPLICATIONS (2003); ROBERT COOTER & THOMAS ULEN, LAW AND ECONOMICS (6 vols., 2011).

Printed by Printforce, United Kingdom